T0181842

Communications
in Computer and Information Science 1998

Rationale

The CCIS series is devoted to the publication of proceedings of computer science conferences. Its aim is to efficiently disseminate original research results in informatics in printed and electronic form. While the focus is on publication of peer-reviewed full papers presenting mature work, inclusion of reviewed short papers reporting on work in progress is welcome, too. Besides globally relevant meetings with internationally representative program committees guaranteeing a strict peer-reviewing and paper selection process, conferences run by societies or of high regional or national relevance are also considered for publication.

Topics

The topical scope of CCIS spans the entire spectrum of informatics ranging from foundational topics in the theory of computing to information and communications science and technology and a broad variety of interdisciplinary application fields.

Information for Volume Editors and Authors

Publication in CCIS is free of charge. No royalties are paid, however, we offer registered conference participants temporary free access to the online version of the conference proceedings on SpringerLink (http://link.springer.com) by means of an http referrer from the conference website and/or a number of complimentary printed copies, as specified in the official acceptance email of the event.

CCIS proceedings can be published in time for distribution at conferences or as post-proceedings, and delivered in the form of printed books and/or electronically as USBs and/or e-content licenses for accessing proceedings at SpringerLink. Furthermore, CCIS proceedings are included in the CCIS electronic book series hosted in the SpringerLink digital library at http://link.springer.com/bookseries/7899. Conferences publishing in CCIS are allowed to use Online Conference Service (OCS) for managing the whole proceedings lifecycle (from submission and reviewing to preparing for publication) free of charge.

Publication process

The language of publication is exclusively English. Authors publishing in CCIS have to sign the Springer CCIS copyright transfer form, however, they are free to use their material published in CCIS for substantially changed, more elaborate subsequent publications elsewhere. For the preparation of the camera-ready papers/files, authors have to strictly adhere to the Springer CCIS Authors' Instructions and are strongly encouraged to use the CCIS LaTeX style files or templates.

Abstracting/Indexing

CCIS is abstracted/indexed in DBLP, Google Scholar, EI-Compendex, Mathematical Reviews, SCImago, Scopus. CCIS volumes are also submitted for the inclusion in ISI Proceedings.

How to start

To start the evaluation of your proposal for inclusion in the CCIS series, please send an e-mail to ccis@springer.com.

Huimin Lu · Jintong Cai

Editors

Artificial Intelligence and Robotics

8th International Symposium, ISAIR 2023
Beijing, China, October 21–23, 2023
Revised Selected Papers

 Springer

Editors
Huimin Lu
Kyushu Institute of Technology
Fukuoka, Japan

Jintong Cai
Southeast University
Nanjing, China

ISSN 1865-0929   ISSN 1865-0937 (electronic)
Communications in Computer and Information Science
ISBN 978-981-99-9108-2   ISBN 978-981-99-9109-9 (eBook)
https://doi.org/10.1007/978-981-99-9109-9

This Springer imprint is published by the registered company Springer Nature Singapore Pte Ltd.
The registered company address is: 152 Beach Road, #21-01/04 Gateway East, Singapore 189721, Singapore

Paper in this product is recyclable.

Preface

The integration of artificial intelligence and robotic technologies has become a topic of increasing interest for both researchers and developers from academic fields and industries worldwide. It is foreseeable that artificial intelligence will be the main approach of the next generation of robotics research. These proceedings include high-quality original research papers presented at the 8th International Symposium on Artificial Intelligence and Robotics (ISAIR 2023), which was successfully held in Beijing, China from October 21 to October 23, 2023. The conference was planned to welcome participants from around the world to meet physically in beautiful Beijing to exchange ideas, as we did in our past ISAIR series of conferences. The conference was held in a hybrid format allowing for both on-site and virtual participation. With all your participation and contributions, we believe ISAIR 2023 will be a special and memorable conference in history!

ISAIR 2023 was the 8th conference of its series since it was first held in Wuhan, China in 2016, followed by ISAIR 2017 in Kitakyushu, Japan, ISAIR 2018 in Nanjing, China, ISAIR 2019 in Daegu, South Korea, ISAIR 2020 in Kitakyushu, Japan, ISAIR 2021 in Fukuoka, Japan, and ISAIR 2022 in Shanghai, China. As we know, ISAIR was initiated to promote artificial intelligence and robotic technologies in the world. Over the years, it has welcomed authors from all over the world.

ISAIR 2023 focused on the important areas of pattern recognition, artificial intelligence, robotics, and Internet of Things, covering various technical aspects.

ISAIR 2023 received 212 submissions from 13 countries. The program chairs invited 40 program committee members and more additional reviewers. Each paper was single-blindly reviewed by at least two reviewers, and most papers received three reviews each. Finally, 103 papers were accepted for presentation in the program, resulting in an acceptance rate of 48.58%.

The technical program of ISAIR was scheduled over three days (21-23 October 2023) including 8 keynote speeches, 4 oral sessions, and 1 Online Presentation Session.

Organizing a large event is a challenging task, requiring intensive teamwork. We would like to thank all members from the organizing committee for their hard work, with guidance from the steering committee. The general chairs, program chairs, publicity chairs, award chairs, and area chairs all led their respective committees and worked together closely to make ISAIR 2023 successful. Our special thanks go to the many reviewers, who we could not name one by one, for constructive comments to improve the papers. We thank all the authors who submitted their papers, which is the most important part of a scientific conference. Finally, we would like to acknowledge our volunteers, students from our local organizers.

Tohru Kamiya
Zongyuan Ge
Ruijun Liu
Rushi Lan
Xin Jin
Yuchao Zheng

Organization

Steering Committee

M. Malek (Editor-in-Chief)	Cognitive Robotics Journal, USA
S. Serikawa	Kyushu Institute of Technology, Japan
H. Luk	Southeast University, China

General Chairs

Tohru Kamiya	Kyushu Institute of Technology, Japan
Zongyuan Ge	Monash University, Australia
Ruijun Liu	Beijing Technology and Business University, China

Program Chairs

Rushi Lan	Guilin University of Electronic Technology, China
Xin Jin	Beijing Electronic Science and Technology Institute, China
Yuchao Zheng	Kyushu Institute of Technology, Japan

Publicity Chairs

Jože Guna	University of Ljubljana, Slovenia
Guangwei Gao	Nanjing University of Posts and Telecommunications, China
Shota Nakashima	Yamaguchi University, Japan

Award Chairs

Quan Zhou	Nanjing University of Posts and Telecommunications, China
Jihua Zhu	Xi'an Jiaotong University, China
Zhibin Yu	Ocean University of China, China
Dong Wang	Dalian University of Technology, China

Area Chairs

Csaba Beleznai	Austrian Institute of Technology, Austria
Hao Gao	Nanjing University of Posts and Telecommunications, China
Ainul Akmar Mokhtar	Universiti Teknologi Petronas, Malaysia
Ting Wang	Nanjing University of Technology, China
Weihua Ou	Guizhou Normal University, China
Wenpeng Lu	Qilu University of Technology, China
Xing Xu	University of Electronic Science and Technology of China, China
Shenglin Mu	Ehime University, Japan
Amit Kumar Singh	National Institute of Technology Patna, India
Zhe Chen	Hohai University, China

Program Committee Members

Chiew-Foong Kwong	University of Nottingham, UK
Dario Lodi Rizzini	University of Parma, Italy
Danijel Skocaj	University of Ljubljana, Slovenia
Donald Dansereau	Sydney University, Australia
Guangxu Li	Tianjin Polytechnic University, China
Giancarlo Fortino	Università della Calabria, Italy
Hossein Olya	University of Sheffield, UK
Iztok Humar	University of Ljubljana, Slovenia
Jianru Li	Tongji University, China
Jinjia Zhou	Hosei University, Japan
Keshav Seshadri	Carnegie Mellon University, USA
Levis Mei	Agilent California Research Center, USA
Limei Peng	Kyungpook National University, Korea
Liao Wu	University of New South Wales, Australia
Li He	Qualcomm Inc., USA
Mario G.C.A. Cimino	University of Pisa, Italy
M. Shamim Hossain	King Saud University, UAE
Matjaz Perc	University of Maribor, Slovenia
Oleg Sergiyenko	Baja California Autonomous University, Mexico
Sangeen Khan	COMSATS University, Pakistan
Shuai Chen	Chinese Academy of Sciences, China
Wendy Flores-Fuentes	Universidad Autónoma de Baja California, Mexico
Xin Li	Shanghai Jiao Tong University, China

Xinliang Liu	Beijing Technology and Business University, China
Yin Zhang	Zhongnan University of Economics and Law, China
Yichuan Wang	University of Sheffield, UK
Haitao Cheng	Nanjing University of Posts and Telecommunications, China
Fang Hu	Hubei University of Chinese Medicine, China
Xipeng Pan	Guilin University of Electronic Technology, China
Yun Liu	Southwest University, China
Huadeng Wang	Guilin University of Electronic Technology, China
Haigang Zhang	Shenzhen Polytechnic, China
Xianfeng Wu	Jianghan University, China
Zhihao Xu	Qingdao University, China
Junfei Wang	Jianghan University, China
Zhongyuan Lai	Jianghan University, China
Jianming Zhang	Changsha University of Science and Technology, China
Xiwang Xie	Dalian Maritime University, China
Heng Liu	Anhui University of Technology, China
Fenglian Li	Taiyuan University of Technology, China

Contents

T-spline Surface Fairing Based on Centripetal Re-parameterization

Lin Yu[1], Chuan He[2], Weixiao Tan[2], Yutong Xue[2], Gang Zhao[2], and Aizeng Wang[2(✉)]

[1] Beijing Institute of Astronautical System Engineering, Beijing, People's Republic of China
[2] School of Mechanical Engineering and Automation, Beihang University, Beijing 100191, People's Republic of China
azwang@buaa.edu.cn

Abstract. Compared with non-uniform rational B-splines, T-splines have advantages in data compression, surface merging, and complex surface representation. This paper puts forward a novel T-spline surface fairing algorithm based on centripetal re-parameterization which can improve the knot distribution of T-mesh. Some numerical examples are given to verify the effectiveness and practicability of the algorithm. The Gaussian and Mean curvature graphs show that the proposed method has a good surface fairing effect.

Keywords: T-spline · T-mesh · Re-parameterization · Surface fairing

1 Introduction

Parametric surfaces, especially spline surfaces, have been widely used in nowadays CAD (Computer-Aided Design) and CAGD (Computer-Aided Geometric Design) due to their flexible shape representation and excellent continuity. Among them, NURBS (Non-Uniform Rational B-spline) becomes the only standard for defining the geometry of industrial products because of its rich and complete theory and supporting algorithms. However, NURBS is a kind of tensor product surface and the control mesh must be a rectangular grid in topology, which leads to redundant control points and lacks the ability of local refinement. To get rid of the limitation of rectangular topology, Sederberg et al. [1] introduced a generalization of NURBS called T-splines in 2003, which allows the existence of T-junctions. While retaining many excellent properties of NURBS, the flexible topology makes T-splines also keep some unique properties, such as local refinement [2–5], watertight trimming[6], and data compression [1, 7]. With the above advantages, T-splines are widely used in geometric modeling [6, 8], surface reconstruction [9–12], and isogeometric analysis [13–18].

For free-form surface modeling, how to optimize the geometric shape such that the model meets fairing requirements is an important issue. The methods to improve surface fairness mainly include modifying control points and re-parameterization. For the former, the usual method is to use the optimization process based on the principle of minimum energy, while the latter one is to improve the parameter distribution to obtain

H. Lu and J. Cai (Eds.): ISAIR 2023, CCIS 1998, pp. 1–8, 2024.
https://doi.org/10.1007/978-981-99-9109-9_1

better surface quality. At present, the research on surface fairing mainly focuses on B-spline surfaces and NURBS surfaces. For T-splines, there is some research focusing on obtaining high-quality T-spline fitting surfaces. Ce Shang and Jianzhong Fu et al. proposed an algorithm that can solve the limitation of T-spline surface fitting [12]; Lai et al. introduced an adaptive sampling strategy in the process of T-spline surface fitting [19]; Zheng and Wang introduced a tubular surface fitting algorithm by T-splines [20]; AI Ginnis, KV Kostas, and PD Kaklis used a single piece of cubic T-spline surface based on the previous research of filling holes with contour curves, which effectively solved the smoothing problem of "one-to-many" and "many-to-many" local re-construction [21]. Unfortunately, there is no research on the detail of parameterization of T-spline modeling yet, and most T-Splines use a pre-set uniform parameterization which is regardless of the control grid in three-dimensional space.

Based on the chord length distribution of the control grid in 3D space, this paper uses centripetal re-parameterization [22] of the knot distribution of T-mesh to improve the fairness of T-spline surfaces. The rest of this paper is organized as follows. Section 2 is a brief review of T-splines. Section 3 introduces the centripetal parameterization method with non-uniform knot distribution. In Sect. 4, several examples are given to demonstrate the effectiveness and practicability of the proposed algorithm. Finally, Sect. 5 is the conclusion.

2   Review of T-splines

2.1   T-meshes

A T-mesh is a control grid with T-junctions of a T-spline surface in the parameter domain. If a T mesh is coincidentally a rectangular grid, it degenerates to a NURBS control grid (see Fig. 1).

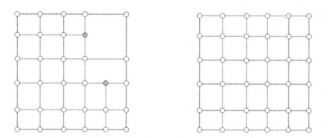

Fig. 1. A T-mesh with two T-junctions (left) and its corresponding NURBS mesh (right).

Each grid point in T-mesh is called a vertex. Regardless of multiple vertices, a vertex corresponds to a control point in the physically 3D space (see Fig. 2), and the distribution of the vertices in the T-mesh determines the corresponding blending functions (see Subsect. 2.2) of the control point. A T-mesh stores the topology information and parameterization of the T-spline surface.

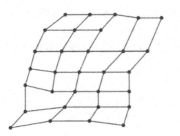 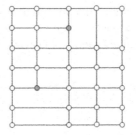

Fig. 2. The control grid of a T-spline surface in 3D space (left) and its corresponding T-mesh in parametric space (right).

2.2 Supporting Region of Blending Functions

The length of each edge is called knot interval and defines the parameterization of a T-mesh, which determines the blending function of each vertex. A blending function is defined over a local region formed by independent knot vectors in different parameter directions. In this paper, we only discuss the blending functions of bi-cubic T-splines. For example in Fig. 3, the horizontal and vertical green lines construct the supporting region of the blending function for the black vertex.

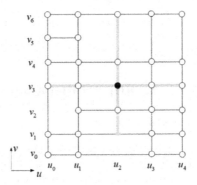

Fig. 3. The supporting region of the blending function for the black vertex, and the knot vectors in u and v direction are $[u_0, u_1, u_2, u_3, u_4]$, $[v_1, v_2, v_3, v_4, v_6]$ respectively.

If all the knot intervals and the control points are determined, then the T-spline surface is determined.

2.3 T-spline Surfaces

The expression of a T-spline surface is defined as:

$$S_T(u, v) = \frac{\sum\limits_{i=1}^{n} w_i P_i B_i(u, v)}{\sum\limits_{i=1}^{n} w_i B_i(u, v)} \tag{1}$$

where P_i is the i-th control point, n is the number of control points, w_i is the corresponding weight of P_i and its value can be adjusted by the designer, $B_i(u, v)$ is the blending function of P_i. Figure 4 shows a Mad Hand Model with the corresponding control grid.

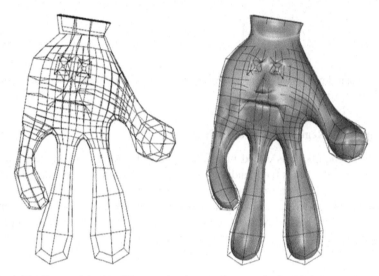

Fig. 4. A T-spline model with 622 control points. Left: control grid. Right: rendering surface.

3   T-splines Fairing with Centripetal Re-parameterization

3.1   Centripetal Re-parameterization

Since the number of control points in different rows or columns of T-mesh is different, the parameterization of the T-spline surface will greatly cost a lot of time. The widely used parameterization method is uniform parameterization, in which the knots are uniformly distributed in the parameter domain, i.e., the knot intervals of T-mesh are equaled. This parameterization is easy to implement and performs well when the distribution of the control points is relatively uniform and the chord length is approximately equal. However, for most T-spline surfaces, the chord lengths differ greatly in different rows or columns and uniform parameterization may lead to a poor surface shape.

Therefore, this paper proposed a centripetal re-parameterization method for the T-spline surface based on the distribution of control points. Different from uniform parameterization or chord length parameterization, this method assumes that the centripetal acceleration on a curve arc is proportional to the rotation angle of the tangent vector from the beginning to the end of the curve. For row j in either parameter direction, such as u direction, the centripetal re-parameterized formula is given as

$$\begin{cases} u_0^j = 0 \\ u_i^j = u_{i-1}^j + \sqrt{\left| t_{i-1}^j \right|} \end{cases} \tag{2}$$

where u_i^j is the knot value and $\left| l_{i-1}^j \right|$ is the absolute value of chord length. After the parameter transformation in both parameter directions, the re-parameterization is established.

3.2 T-spline Surface Fairing Algorithm

This subsection summarizes the fairing algorithm based on the parameter optimization mentioned above. The specific process of the algorithm is as follows:

Step 1: Obtain the 3D coordinate information and topology information of the control points in T-mesh;

Step 2: For each topological edge in T-mesh, calculate all the chord lengths of corresponding control edges by Eq. (2);

Step 3: Update the knot values of each vertex in T-mesh.

Although the implementation of re-parameterization is more complex than uniform parameterization, it can obtain better fairness for most T-spline surfaces, especially with non-uniform distribution of control points. Therefore, this method has certain research significance. To verify the effectiveness of the theory, several typical T-spline surface models were faired by re-parameterization, and the Gaussian-Mean curvature is used to help analyze the fairness of the T-spline surface before and after re-parameterization in the next section.

4 Examples

The example is a Trivalent Point T-spline Surface Model which contains 19 control points (Fig. 5). From Fig. 5(b) and Fig. 5(c), the transition of Gaussian curvature and Mean curvature are getting more even, which means the Trivalent Point T-spline Surface Model is more fairing after parameter optimization. Furthermore, the maximum position error of control points is 0.031615.

Furthermore, the local maximum of Gaussian curvature and average curvature both decrease to a large extent, and the minimum value of Gaussian curvature also tends to zero, which also reflects that the transition of the curvature graph is smoother. The curvatures are shown in Table 1.

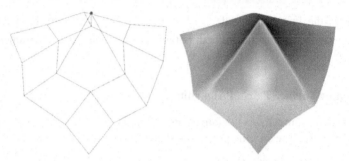

(a) The control mesh and corresponding rendering graph.

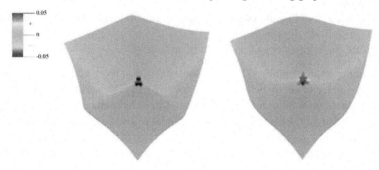

(b) Gaussian curvature of the model before and after re-parameterization.

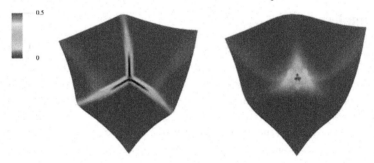

(c) Mean curvature of the model before and after re-parameterization.

Fig. 5. T-spline Trivalent Point T-spline Surface Model and its Gaussian/Mean curvature

Table 1. The curvature of the Trivalent Point T-spline Surface Model before and after fairing.

	Gaussian Curvature (MAX, MIN)	Mean Curvature (MAX, 0)
Before fairing	10.308873226, −0.014568257	3.2263928654
After fairing	0.5163470824, −0.0040315312	0.7189192796

5 Conclusions

This paper proposes an approach to T-mesh re-parameterization, which benefits in improving the fairness of T-spline surfaces. Different from uniform parameterization, this new parameterization method considers the chord length and the vary rate of the parameter. The Gaussian and Mean curvature graphs of the testing models verify the effectiveness of the new fairing algorithm. However, the non-uniform re-parameterization fairing method performs poorly at complex corners and cannot improve the continuity of models, which are the main topics of our future work.

References

1. Sederberg, T.W., Zheng, J., Bakenov, A., et al.: T-splines and T-NURCCs. ACM Trans. Graph. (TOG) **22**(3), 477–484 (2003)
2. Sederberg, T.W., Cardon, D.L., Finnigan, G.T., et al.: T-spline simplification and local refinement. ACM Trans. Graph. (TOG) **23**(3), 276–283 (2004)
3. Wang, A., Zhao, G., Li, Y.D.: An influence-knot set based new local refinement algorithm for T-spline surfaces. Expert Syst. Appl. **41**(8), 3915–3921 (2014)
4. Scott, M.A., Li, X., Sederberg, T.W., et al.: Local refinement of analysis-suitable T-splines. Comput. Methods Appl. Mech. Eng. **213**, 206–222 (2012)
5. Zhang, J., Li, X.: Local refinement for analysis-suitable++ T-splines. Comput. Methods Appl. Mech. Eng. **342**, 32–45 (2018)
6. Sederberg, T.W., Finnigan, G.T., Li, X., et al.: Watertight trimmed NURBS. ACM Trans. Graph. (TOG) **27**(3), 1–8 (2008)
7. Wang, Y, Zheng, J.: Control point removal algorithm for T-spline surfaces. In: International Conference on Geometric Modeling and Processing, pp. 385–396. Springer, Berlin, Heidelberg (2006)
8. Campen, M., Zorin, D.: Similarity maps and field-guided T-splines: a perfect couple. ACM Trans. Graph. (TOG) **36**(4), 1–16 (2017)
9. Wang, Y., Zheng, J.: Adaptive T-spline surface approximation of triangular meshes. In: 2007 6th International Conference on Information, Communications & Signal Processing, pp. 1–5. IEEE (2007)
10. Yang, X., Zheng, J.: Approximate T-spline surface skinning. Comput. Aided Des. **44**(12), 1269–1276 (2012)
11. Wang, Y., Zheng, J.: Curvature-guided adaptive T-spline surface fitting. Comput. Aided Des. **45**(8–9), 1095–1107 (2013)
12. Shang, C., Fu, J., Feng, J., et al.: Effective re-parameterization and GA based knot structure optimization for high quality T-spline surface fitting. Comput. Methods Appl. Mech. Eng. **351**, 836–859 (2019)
13. Bazilevs, Y., Calo, V.M., Cottrell, J.A., et al.: Isogeometric analysis using T-splines. Comput. Methods Appl. Mech. Eng. **199**(5–8), 229–263 (2010)
14. Dörfel, M.R., Jüttler, B., Simeon, B.: Adaptive isogeometric analysis by local h-refinement with T-splines. Comput. Methods Appl. Mech. Eng. **199**(5–8), 264–275 (2010)
15. Da Veiga, L.B., Buffa, A., Cho, D., et al.: IsoGeometric analysis using T-splines on two-patch geometries. Comput. Methods Appl. Mech. Eng. **200**(21–22), 1787–1803 (2011)
16. Scott, M.A., Borden, M.J., Verhoosel, C.V., et al.: Isogeometric finite element data structures based on Bézier extraction of T-splines. Int. J. Numer. Meth. Eng. **88**(2), 126–156 (2011)
17. Li, X., Zheng, J., Sederberg, T.W., et al.: On linear independence of T-spline blending functions. Comput. Aided Geom. Des. **29**(1), 63–76 (2012)

18. Li, X., Zhang, J.: AS++ T-splines: linear independence and approximation. Comput. Methods Appl. Mech. Eng. **333**, 462–474 (2018)
19. Lai, J., Fu, J., Shen, H., et al.: Machining error inspection of T-spline surface by on-machine measurement. Int. J. Precis. Eng. Manuf. **16**(3), 433–439 (2015)
20. Zheng, J., Wang, Y.: Periodic T-splines and tubular surface fitting. In: Boissonnat, J.-D., Chenin, P., Cohen, A., Gout, C., Lyche, T., Mazure, M.-L., Schumaker, L. (eds.) Curves and Surfaces 2010. LNCS, vol. 6920, pp. 731–746. Springer, Heidelberg (2012). https://doi.org/10.1007/978-3-642-27413-8_48
21. Ginnis, A.I., Kostas, K.V., Kaklis, P.D.: Construction of smooth branching surfaces using T-splines. Comput. Aided Des. **92**, 22–32 (2017)
22. Lee, E.T.Y.: Choosing nodes in parametric curve interpolation. Comput. Aided Des. **21**(6), 363–370 (1989)

Enhanced Object Detection of Abnormal Light Based on Multi-scale Retinex with Chromacity Preservation

Zhuyun Yin[1]([⊠])(ID) and Lingyue Guo[2,3](ID)

[1] Shanghaitech University, Shanghai, China
zhuyunyin413@outlook.com
[2] School of Artificial Intelligence,
University of Chinese Academy of Sciences, Beijing, China
[3] Zhongke Wyse (Beijing) Technology Co. Ltd., Beijing, China

Abstract. In autonomous driving scenarios, the lighting conditions can often change rapidly and dramatically, leading to overly bright or dark environments. These abnormal light conditions can negatively impact the accuracy of object detection, potentially causing accidents and posing a threat to pedestrian and driver safety. To address this issue, this paper presents a method to mitigate the effect of abnormal light intensity on object detection in autonomous driving scenarios. We apply Multi-scale Retinex with Chromacity Preservation (MSRCP) processing to abnormal light images based on the YOLO model in order to recover lost information. Our method was evaluated on the publicly available BDD 100k dataset, and the results showed a significant improvement in performance under abnormal lighting conditions, Compared to images without any processing, Yolo-v3 model improve 9.59% total mAP@[.5, .95], and Yolo-v4 model improves 10.86%.

Keywords: object detection · automatic driving · abnormal light · image enhancement

1 Introduction

As an emerging field, automatic drive has vast potential for future development, so one of the important component in autonomous driving, image identification, get people's attention. Compared to other methods, the identification based on visible light camera is a cheaper and more deployable way.

Other the other hand, this method also comes with its issue. For example, the result will heavily affected by lighting conditions. If there is a hash condition, which can cause blurry object shape or inaccurate color, the detection accuracy will significantly drop. We test some common object recognition algorithms, faster-RCNN [11] and Yolo [8]. They are designed for general scenario, and not are optimized for the light condition. So, when the system is operated under

H. Lu and J. Cai (Eds.): ISAIR 2023, CCIS 1998, pp. 9–18, 2024.
https://doi.org/10.1007/978-981-99-9109-9_2

undesired lighting conditions, In the actual usage scenario, at noon or in the late night, these influence may result accidents.

One of the most discerning autonomous driving systems in the industry, Tesla's Autopilot system [9] is a vision-based Autopilot system, which mainly relies on camera sensors to obtain surrounding information. But this system still experiences accidents under poor lighting conditions. In 2016, a Tesla didn't identify a front lorry, eventually cause a rear-end collision. Other Autopilot system, like Google's Waymo [10], Baidu's Apollo Go [3], and so on, they all have same problem.

To address the problem of accuracy faced by autopilot in complex lighting conditions, and does not affect the recognition ability under normal brightness, we develop a algorithm. In this paper, after introducing the related works, we will present our function into two parts, Firstly, we will introduce light-selection. We use the gray processing of the image, and the anomaly image is recognized and classified. Second we will present an image restoration technique based on MSRCP [7] and how it's applied in the autonomous driving scenario. It can enhance the performance of target detection under abnormal lighting conditions by considering the lighting conditions and preserving the color information of the image. This method adjusts the brightness and color distribution of the image to enhance the edges and contours of the target, making it easier to detect under abnormal lighting conditions. Next, in the Experiment and Result section, we test the algorithm, 3000 images with abnormal brightness were selected from bdd-100k [13] as the data set of this project. During the test, we use the same model to identify image to find out the progress of our algorithm. The results showed that our method improves the total mAP@[.5, .95] from 15.22% to 19.57%, this algorithm can also used on yolov3 or other version. It can improve the recognition results of abnormal brightness images.

2   Related Work

2.1   Image Enhancement Algorithm Based on Retinex

The image enhancement algorithm is based on Retinex theory [5,6]. The term "Retinex" stands for "Retina with Cortex" it simulates the biological processes of human's retina and brain cortex, and it suggests that the image I observed by human eyes is the product of light image L and object reflection image R.

$$I(x,y) = L(x,y)^* R(x,y) \tag{1}$$

Take log for both side:

$$\log[R(x,y)] = \log[I(x,y)] - \log[L(x,y)] \tag{2}$$

We can get a reflection property image that preserves the essence of the object from the received image I and the light image L. This method is called "Single Scale Retinex (SSR)" [7,14], and its workflow is shown as follows:

1 Take log for I(x,y)
2 Use Gaussian blur for l(x,y), the result is $\log[L(x,y)]$
3 Calculate $\log[R(x,y)]$ by $\log[I(x,y)]$ and $\log[L(x,y)]$
4 Transfer the $\log[R(x,y)]$ to RGB image, and this is the result.

Further improved can be achieved by, for example, Muti-Scale Retinex(MSR). When calculating the value of $\log[R(x,y)]$, the algorithm performed multiple SSR operations and weighted the calculation. So compare with SSR, this algorithm has better performance on color.

The aforementioned will still face some issues, such as, color cast, which can be mitigated by applying Muti-Scale Retinex with Color Restoration(MSRCR). It takes into account multiple scales or spatial frequencies of the image for more comprehensive enhancement. The algorithm adds multiple parameters to produce color recovery factor C, adjusts the ratio of the 3 channels of the image, reduces the color cast.

At the same time, the MSRCP [1] algorithm was proposed, which carries out an MSR processing on the light intensity image of the original color image to map to each channel in the same proportion as the original image RGB channel. This algorithm can preserve the color distribution of the original image well.

2.2   Object Detection Algorithm Based on YOLOv4 Model

In this paper, YOLO-V4 [2,12] is used as the object detection network. The YOLO network is a single-stage algorithm. Be careful about the comparison between YOLO and two-stage algorithms, such as Fast RCNN [4]. YOLO has been improved a lot over the past a few years. But Fast RCNN and some other algorithms haven't changed since they were published. Various methods are also used to improve accuracy.

The yolo-v4 used in this paper has been optimized in many aspects, making the accuracy significantly improved. The data processing aspect includes mainly Mosaic data enhancement, which can enrich the background of the image and increase the batch size in a different way. Backbone includes the new CSPDarknet53, which replaced ReLu by Mish as the activation function, and the CSP structure prevents different layers from learning the same gradient information. In addition, the loss function has been updated, and the prediction box filtering has been improved. Through this series of optimization, it finally makes the real-time target detection algorithm in the highest accuracy.

3   Method

In this paper, brightness selection algorithm and image restoration algorithm based on MSRCP are used, and then object detection algorithm based on Yolo-v4 is adopted to identify the target. The algorithm flow in this paper is shown in the Fig. 1.

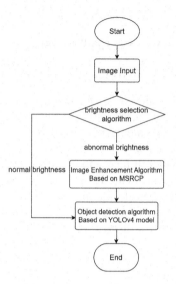

Fig. 1. The Algorithm Worklow

After the input image goes through the brightness selection algorithm, the color information of the image with abnormal brightness will be restored by the image recovery algorithm. Finally, the image recognition will be carried out in the model trained by yolo-v4 and the results will be obtained.

3.1 Brightness Selection Algorithm

Firstly, the brightness selection algorithm is introduced. Through this algorithm, we screen out the images with abnormal brightness. Since brightness equals gray level in gray level image, we can judge brightness by converting the image into gray level image. We first calculate the difference between the gray value pg and 128 of each pixel point:

$$ga = \sum (pg - 128)/N \qquad (3)$$

Then the gray-scale histogram is used to obtain the number of pixels of each gray value between 0 and 255, and the weighted average deviation is calculated with the number of pixels as the weight.

$$Ma = \sum |(pg - 128) - ga|^*\mathrm{G[i]}/ \sum \mathrm{G[i]} \qquad (4)$$

Finally, we calculated according to the average deviation to judge whether the image brightness is unusual, through access to online data, we set threshold is $|ga|$.

3.2 Image Enhancement Algorithm Based on MSRCP

After brightness selection, we need to process the abnormal brightness image. Here we compare several algorithms and finally choose MSRCP. Compared with MSRCR and MSR, MSRCP can increase the highest recognition rate (Fig. 2).

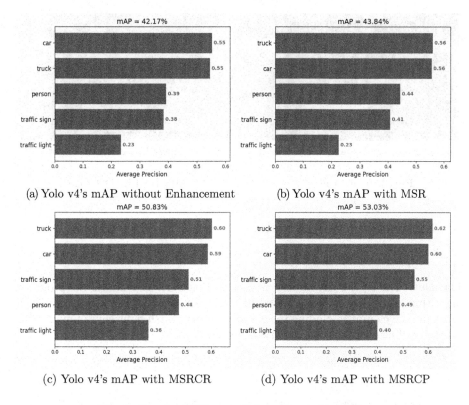

Fig. 2. Result of Different Enhancement Algorithm

In the process of brightness selection, we evaluate the gray image, and then we can compute the intensity image I according to the image component of the RGB three-channel of the original image.

$$I = (I_R + I_G + I_B) \tag{5}$$

In order to make the color of the enhanced image consistent with that of the original image, the amplification factor A is obtained through the intensity image of the single channel:

$$B = \text{Max}\,(I_R + I_G + I_B) \tag{6}$$

$$A = \text{Min}\left(\frac{255}{B}, \frac{I_{nt}}{I_{nti}}\right) \tag{7}$$

In the equation, I is the pixel of the image. Color enhancement is carried out on RGB channels respectively, and the final result is obtained (Fig. 3):

$$I_E = A * I(R, G, B)(x, y) \tag{8}$$

(a) Before Image Enhancement Algorithm (b) After Image Enhancement Algorithm

Fig. 3. Image Enhancement Algorithm for Abnormal Light Image

4   Experiment and Result

4.1   Experimental Setting

Dataset. The BDD100K dataset is used in this work to evaluate the proposed algorithm. This dataset was created by Berkeley AI Laboratory, we select 3875 random images in it, including images of different Harsh light environment. The label distribution of the data set is shown in Fig. 4:

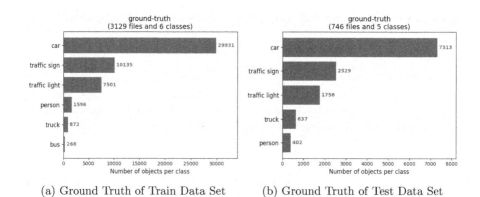

(a) Ground Truth of Train Data Set   (b) Ground Truth of Test Data Set

Fig. 4. Image Enhancement Algorithm for Abnormal Light Image

Evaluation Step. Experiment Setup

* Operating system: Ubuntu 18.04
* Python version: Python3.8
* PyTorch version: Pytorch 1.10
* GPU model: NVIDIA GeForce RTX 2080Ti

4.2   Experiment Result

After producing the data set, we trained it for 1000 generations by yolo-v4 and yolo-v3. The learning rate was adjusted by cosine annealing with the interval of 0.01–0.0001, and SGD was used for optimization. In terms of data enhancement, mosaic enhancement is used in the first 70% generation of training, and the probability of using it in each training step is 50%. After Mosaic is used, mixup data enhancement will continue to be used, and the probability of using is also 50%. The final training results are as follows (Fig. 5):

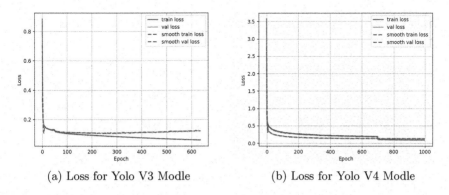

(a) Loss for Yolo V3 Modle   (b) Loss for Yolo V4 Modle

Fig. 5. Loss for Train Process

After training, we test for the MSRCP image recovery algorithm. We selected 746 pictures containing different elements as the test set of the experiment. And we tested them with and without the algorithm. The results are shown in the below (Fig. 6):

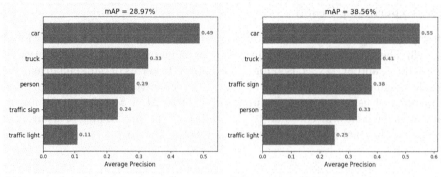

(a)Yolo V3's mAP Without Enhancement   (b)Yolo V3's mAP With Enhancement

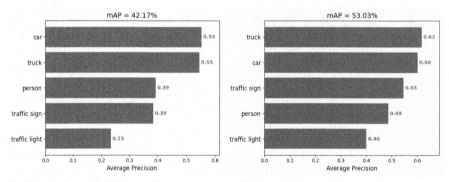

(c)Yolo V4's mAP Without Enhancement   (d) Yolo V4's mAP With Enhancement

Fig. 6. Image Enhancement Algorithm for Abnormal Light Image

As the result, the recognition ability after the processed image has been significantly improved. The overall mAP increased about 10%, and traffic lights in particular have improved by 14% and 17%, respectively. Less improved object categories include people and car. We believe that the unidentified car targets are mainly distant targets and obscured targets. When these objects appear in under dark conditions, more color blocks will be generated after our algorithm is restored, which will cause greater interference, and the same is true for person. And traffic lights themselves emit light, so they're friendly to our algorithm. Totally, the whole recognition rate of image has been improved obviously.

5   Conclusion

In this paper, to mitigate the problem of abnormal image brightness in automatic driving, brightness selection algorithm and image restoration algorithm based on

MSRCP are used to classify images and carry out color restoration. Combined with yolo-v4 target recognition, common targets in automatic driving scenes are identified, which ultimately effectively improves the image recognition rate and provides guarantee for safe driving. On the other hand, there are still issues need further investigation. First, images recovered using MSRCP will blur the image and in some cases even render the object that could have been recognized unrecognizable. Second, in the test of this paper, there are still some kinds of targets that cannot be confirm to improve by the insufficient number of the test set. Later, we will increase the size of the test set and conduct further tests on trucks, bus. We will also increase the recognition of different types of objects to make it closer to real driving scenarios. In the future, we will optimize the algorithm and integrate more advanced image recognition methods, such as YOLOv7, to attempt real-time recognition in low-light conditions.

Acknowledgements. Thanks for the support by open research fund of The State Key Laboratory for Management and Control of Complex Systems (20210110), without these reference material, the study cannot be so propitious.

References

1. Barnard, K., Funt, B.: Investigations into multi-scale retinex. In: Proceedings of the Colour Imaging in Multimedia'98, pp. 9–17 (1998)
2. Bochkovskiy, A., Wang, C.Y., Liao, H.Y.M.: YOLOv4: optimal speed and accuracy of object detection. arXiv preprint arXiv:2004.10934 (2020)
3. Fan, H., et al.: Baidu apollo em motion planner. arXiv preprint arXiv:1807.08048 (2018)
4. Girshick, R.: Fast R-CNN. In: Proceedings of the IEEE International Conference on Computer Vision, pp. 1440–1448 (2015)
5. Land, E.H., McCann, J.J.: Lightness and retinex theory. Josa **61**(1), 1–11 (1971)
6. Li, Y., Yang, S., Zheng, Y., Lu, H.: Improved point-voxel region convolutional neural network: 3D object detectors for autonomous driving. IEEE Trans. Intell. Transp. Syst. **23**(7), 9311–9317 (2021)
7. Rahman, Z.U., Jobson, D.J., Woodell, G.A.: Multi-scale retinex for color image enhancement. In: Proceedings of 3rd IEEE International Conference on Image Processing, vol. 3, pp. 1003–1006. IEEE (1996)
8. Redmon, J., Divvala, S., Girshick, R., Farhadi, A.: You only look once: unified, real-time object detection. In: Proceedings of the IEEE Conference on Computer Vision and Pattern Recognition, pp. 779–788 (2016)
9. Rzadca, K., et al.: Autopilot: workload autoscaling at google. In: Proceedings of the Fifteenth European Conference on Computer Systems, pp. 1–16 (2020)
10. Sun, P., et al.: Scalability in perception for autonomous driving: Waymo open dataset. In: Proceedings of the IEEE/CVF Conference on Computer Vision and Pattern Recognition, pp. 2446–2454 (2020)
11. Sun, X., Wu, P., Hoi, S.C.: Face detection using deep learning: an improved faster R-CNN approach. Neurocomputing **299**, 42–50 (2018)
12. Xu, F., Xu, F., Xie, J., Pun, C.M., Lu, H., Gao, H.: Action recognition framework in traffic scene for autonomous driving system. IEEE Trans. Intell. Transp. Syst. **23**(11), 22301–22311 (2021)

13. Yu, F., et al.: BDD100K: a diverse driving dataset for heterogeneous multitask learning. In: Proceedings of the IEEE/CVF Conference on Computer Vision and Pattern Recognition, pp. 2636–2645 (2020)
14. Zheng, Y., Li, Y., Yang, S., Lu, H.: Global-PBNet: a novel point cloud registration for autonomous driving. IEEE Trans. Intell. Transp. Syst. **23**(11), 22312–22319 (2022)

CS-Net: A Stain Style Transfer Network for Histology Images with CS-Gate Attention

Zhengze Gong[1,2,3], Xipeng Pan[2,3,4], Chu Han[2,3], Bingjiang Qiu[2,3], Bingchao Zhao[2,3], Yu Liu[2,3], Xinyi Chen[2], Cheng Lu[2,3], Zaiyi Liu[2,3], and Gang Fang[1(✉)]

[1] Institute of Computing Science and Technology, Guangzhou University, Guangzhou 510006, China
gangf@gzhu.edu.cn
[2] Department of Radiology, Guangdong Provincial People's Hospital (Guangdong Academy of Medical Sciences), Southern Medical University, Guangzhou 510080, China
[3] Guangdong Provincial Key Laboratory of Artificial Intelligence in Medical Image Analysis and Application, Guangzhou 510080, China
[4] School of Computer Science and Information Security, Guilin University of Electronic Technology, Guilin 541004, China

Abstract. Accurate segmentation of epithelium in Hematoxylin-Eosin (HE)-stained oropharyngeal cancer (OPC) pathological images is the premise for quantitative diagnosis. However, the pathological features of OPC are highly heterogeneous in morphology, while the appearance may be similar between epithelium and other tissues (such as stroma), which increases the difficulty of the segmentation task. To solve the above problem, we propose a two-step framework for epithelium tissue segmentation, including a stain-transfer step and an image-processing step. In the first step, we propose a stain-style transfer network called CS-Net, together with our proposed attention module called CS-Gate, to transform HE-stained images into Immunohistochemistry (IHC)-stained images, with the aim of enhancing the contrast among epithelium and other tissues. In the second step, we perform a series of image processing methods on the synthesized IHC-stained images to obtain the final binary mask of the OPC epithelium. The experimental results show that CS-Net can synthesize more stable images with a higher degree of restoration than the GAN-like networks, and the accuracy of the final obtained mask is also better than the current mainstream segmentation networks, reaching 92.48%. An external validation experiment shows that CS-Net has a stronger generalization capability.

Keywords: Stain style transfer · Convolutional neural network · Attention mechanism · Oropharyngeal cancer · Tissue segmentation

1 Introduction

Oropharyngeal cancer (OPC) is the sixth most common cancer in the world, accounting for 10–15% of cancers of the head and neck [1]. Of the 5000 new cases of OPC diagnosed each year in the United States, 85–90% originated from malignancies of the epithelium

H. Lu and J. Cai (Eds.): ISAIR 2023, CCIS 1998, pp. 19–32, 2024.
https://doi.org/10.1007/978-981-99-9109-9_3

[2]. Although OPC is predominantly diagnosed in individuals over 45 years old, studies in Western Europe and the United States have shown an increasing incidence in people under 45 years old over the past 20–30 years [3]. Therefore, the precise assessment of patients with OPC can help to develop individualized treatment. Pathological examination is the gold standard for the diagnosis of OPC, while the cellular composition and spatial structure of epithelium can reflect tumor heterogeneity. Hence, accurate segmentation of cancer epithelium in OPC pathological images is significant for quantitative diagnosis and subsequent image analysis [4].

Hematoxylin-Eosin (HE) staining is a routine staining method in pathology [5]. Earlier epithelium segmentation tasks were performed by manual annotation of HE-stained pathology images by pathologists, but this process is time-consuming and inefficient [6]. In addition, since the epithelium of OPC often has similar morphological and color characteristics with other tissues (such as stroma), it is difficult to distinguish epithelium from stroma only by HE staining [7]. Using immunohistochemistry (IHC) staining for cytokeratin could specifically detect the epithelium in the OPC samples based on the principle of antigen-antibody-specific binding [8]. As shown in Fig. 1, the epithelium is not evident in the HE-stained image in Fig. 1-a, but is clearly stained brown in the section stained for cytokeratin in Fig. 1-b, while other tissues are stained light blue.

a : HE-Stained Image   b : IHC-Stained Image   c : Mask of Epithelium

Fig. 1. A sample of the OPC dataset.

However, there are some limitations in IHC staining. Firstly, IHC staining is time-consuming and rather not a routine clinical workflow, which requires additional costs. Secondly, the quality of IHC staining is easily affected by staining kits and conditions, which can lead to under/over-staining [6].

With the development of deep learning and the exponential growth of digitalized medical image data, the use of convolutional neural networks (CNN) for tissue/tumor lesion segmentation of digital pathology images has reached unprecedented popularity [9]. U-Net [10] was a milestone in the semantic segmentation of medical images and has been followed by many excellent segmentation networks [11, 12]. In recent years, many GAN-based methods have also been used to accomplish this task in ways of synthesis. It is worth pointing out that these methods are usually used to segment tumor lesions or necrotic regions, but when it comes to the task of segmenting epithelium regions, these methods show their shortcomings for the following reasons: firstly, the epithelium tissue and stroma are all stained in a similar shade of purple; secondly, in terms of morphology, the epithelium does not have obvious characteristics distinguished from the stroma and lymphoid tissue, etc. [13].

To address the above challenges, inspired by the manual annotation process, we propose a two-step epithelial tissue segmentation framework and a stain-style transfer network named CS-Net. The details will be described in Sect. 3. The main contributions of this paper are as follows:

1. A new two-step framework for epithelial tissue segmentation. Compared with the single-step methods that segment epithelial tissue masks directly from HE-stained images, our two-step method overcomes the challenge of "indistinct epithelial tissue information in the HE-stained image", and achieves higher accuracy. The first step of the framework is to generate pseudo-IHC-stained images from HE-stained images; the second step is to perform threshold segmentation to obtain the binary mask from the synthetic IHC-stained image.
2. A novel stain-style transfer network and attention module. For the characteristics of pathological images, we innovatively incorporate U-Net, VGG16, and CS-Gate into U-Net to become CS-Net. CS-Gate is an integration of CBAM and attention-gate, aiming to extract features from the channel and spatial aspects simultaneously (a fusion of channel attention, spatial attention, and attention gate, hence the name CS-Gate). Compared with the mainstream segmentation networks, CS-Net can achieve higher accuracy with 92.48%; compared with the GAN-based networks, CS-Net can generate pseudo-IHC-stained images with colors and textures closer to Ground Truth, reaching SSIM with 82.02%.
3. Better generalization capability. The external generalization experiment show that CS-Net has the highest generalization performance, achieving an accuracy of 85.83% on the BCSS dataset without training on it.

2 Related Works

2.1 Tissue Segmentation

Epithelium tissue segmentation is the key step in the diagnostic analysis of digital pathology images, and the accuracy of the segmentation is crucial to the subsequent diagnosis. In recent years, due to the development of deep learning, convolutional neural networks (CNN) have shone in the field of medical image analysis, displaying superior capabilities that are not inferior to manual annotation at all. Among them, U-Net [10] is the pioneer of using CNN for medical image segmentation, which is featured by an encoder and a decoder, and the features located in the same layer are connected by skip-connection. However, as the tasks became more complex, U-Net began to show its shortcomings: it could only extract relatively simple and obvious features, while often predicting too many false-positive (FP) and false-negative (FN) regions when distinguishing epithelial tissue from stroma [14] since these regions are highly similar in morphology.

After U-Net, many excellent segmentation networks emerged, which can be divided into two categories based on their characteristics. One category is based on feature engineering, and the other is based on feature learning. For the first category, Swin-UNet [15] integrated information on the color and cellular arrangement of tissues in texture features; SegNet [16, 32] constructed a symmetric encoding-decoding structure for capturing similarities in the overall structure and appearance of stained sections; Van [17] proposed an improved DCAN that integrates the original DCAN and the identity mapping method proposed by He [18] into the ResNet architecture. The other category is data-driven, which is highly dependent on a large number of manually annotated datasets and usually requires large data and computational resources, such as [19, 20] which focus on capturing the morphological patterns inherent within the dataset.

Despite the continuous emergence of new models, only a few have been able to significantly improve the segmentation performance of epithelial tissue in pathological images. The reason is that the staining quality of the slides varies from different labs and operators, which causes the high variability of the dataset, hence requiring stronger feature extraction capabilities.

2.2 Attention Mechanism

One way to tackle the challenge of insufficient extraction capacity is the adoption of the attention mechanism. First proposed in 2014 by Bahdanau [2, 33], the attention mechanism can help the models assign different weights to different features within an image while extracting more crucial information. In this way, networks can make more accurate judgments without imposing an extreme burden on computation and storage. In the field of computer vision, attention mechanisms can be divided into three main categories: channel attention, spatial attention, and hybrid domain attention. Channel attention generates and scores the mask of the channel, such as SE-Net [21] and ECA-Net [22]. Spatial attention can be seen as an adaptive spatial region selection mechanism, such as RAM [23], STN [9], and GE-Net [7] are the typical spatial attention modules with different emphases. The hybrid domain attention mechanism evaluates and scores both channel attention and spatial attention, emphasizing meaningful features on both dimensions, like DA-Net [5], Attention gate (AG) [24], and CBAM [25].

In this paper, we integrate AG and the advantages of channel and spatial attention into a new attention module, in order to better adapt to the high variation between different pathological images and the high similarity of features within a pathological image.

2.3 Stain-Style Transfer

Another effective way to improve the accuracy of epithelium segmentation is to transfer HE-stained images into IHC-stained images, for the variability and heterogeneity would be greatly reduced. Subsequently, the epithelium mask can be obtained by image processing methods. Thus our goal can be shifted from a segmentation task to a stain-style transfer task.

Most of the style transfer models are based on Generative Adversarial Networks (GAN) [26], which consist of a Generator (G) and a Discriminator (D). Pix2pix is the pioneer of applying GAN to the field of image conversion, and Isola proposed cycleGAN [27] based on the idea of pix2pix. StainGAN [28] converted Hamamatsu staining to Aperio staining based on cycleGAN and achieved a high degree of visual similarity with the target domain. However, the GAN-based generation method actually has some drawbacks. Firstly, it is difficult to train, like cycleGAN is training two G and two D at the same time, which requires large running memories and storage. Secondly, the loss curve oscillates substantially because different G and D are constantly passing information to each other, and the predicted output is often unstable.

There are also some methods that try to utilize CNN solely to perform stain-style transformation [29]. For example, Gatys improve the performance of stain-style transformation by adding an artistic style algorithm into CNN[30]; based on Gatys, Chen added the Sobel operator and an improved loss function to the network in order to enhance the edge information of the synthetic images [31, 34]. Compared with GAN-like methods, these single CNN models can improve the transformation accuracy by enhancing the feature extraction ability of the network itself, while effectively avoiding loss oscillation and memory consumption problems. However, there is no single CNN model for the stain-style transfer task of the pathological image so far, hence this paper attempts to propose an improved CNN model specifically for the stain-style transformation.

3   Proposed Method

We propose a two-step epithelium segmentation framework, and the key step is stain-style transfer. The two steps will be described in the following two subsections, and the pipeline of the framework is shown in Fig. 2:

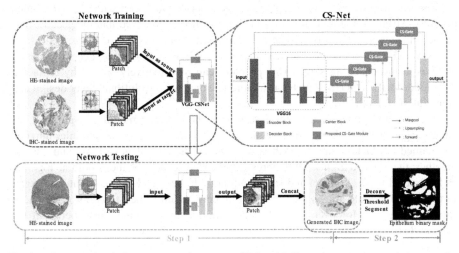

Fig. 2. The Overview of our proposed two-step OPC epithelium tissue segmentation network, and the structure of our proposed CS-Net.

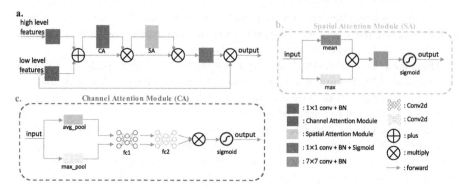

Fig. 3. The details of our proposed CS_Gate module.

3.1 Step 1: Stain-Style Transfer

The first step is stain-style transfer, which is to transfer HE-stained images into IHC-stained images to highlight the epithelium region. We propose a stain-style transfer model named CS-Net (based on U-Net and CS-Gate module, hence the name CS-Net), and the structure is shown in the blue box in Fig. 2. We have made two improvements based on U-Net.

The first improvement is to replace the encoder of the U-Net with VGG16, which possesses stronger feature extraction capabilities. It was observed that the pseudo-IHC stained images generated by U-Net (as a generative network) were blurred and faint with severe FP phenomenon. The reason is that U-Net does not extract deeper, essential features at the encoding stage. This problem can be effectively solved by replacing the encoder with VGG16, which has a more reasonable convolutional layer design and convolutional depth.

The second improvement is the insertion of the attention module. Inspired by the attention gate and CBAM module, we innovatively combine these two modules into one and named CS-Gate. Our approach is to combine the advantages of AG and CBAM together: the low and high-level features are encoded separately, then combine together and extracted by the channel and spatial attention to be encoded into a feature weight. In this way, CS-Gate allows the network to receive multi-dimensional information, as shown in Fig. 3. Moreover, we utilize the smooth L1Loss function to better fit the stain-style transfer task for pathology images, and it can be described as:

$$smooth\ L1\ Loss = \frac{1}{n} \sum_i z_i \qquad (1)$$

where:

$$z_i = \begin{cases} 0.5(x_i - y_i)^2, & |x_i - y_i| < 1 \\ |x_i - y_i| - 0.5, & otherwise \end{cases} \qquad (2)$$

x_i and y_i represent the predicted value and actual value.

3.2 Step 2: Image Processing

The second step is image processing described in Algorithm 1. The corresponding mask would be obtained from the synthesized pseudo-IHC-stained images vis this algorithm.

Algorithm 1 Image Processing Method

Input: Synthesized IHC-stained Image I_{ihc}

Output: Correspond epithelium binary mask I_{bin}

1: Given an input I_{ihc}, select its blue channel as the grayscale map, $I_{gray} = I_{ihc}[:, :, 3]$

2: Set the value of threshold $T_{max} = 210$, to convert I_{gray} into I_{mask}, $I_{mask} = where(0 < I_{gray} < T_{max})$

3: Fill the regions of small holes with area<5000, $I_{bin} = morphology.remove\_small\_holes(I_{mask}, 5000)$

4: Remove the isolated regions with area<800, $I_{bin} = morphology.remove\_small\_object(I_{bin}, 800)$

5: Use the close operation on the I_{bin} with an elliptical structure of size 5×5 as the structural element, $I_{bin} = cv2.morphologyEx(I_{bin}, MORPH\_CLOSE, 5×5)$

6: Fill the small pore regions of area<5000 again to get the Ground Truth mask, $I_{bin} = morphology.remove\_small\_holes(I_{mask}, 5000)$

7: Return I_{bin}

It is worth pointing out that the values of 5000 and 800 in steps 3 and 4 are empirical thresholds obtained from experimental observations on a portion of the dataset. It is observed that the small holes with an area < 5000 inside the tissue and the spots with an area > 800 outside the tissue are generally noisy rather than mistakes due to segmentation, so the epithelial tissue mask obtained by Algorithm 1 is closer to the real label.

4 Experiments

4.1 Dataset Description

The dataset used in this paper is the tissue microarray (TMA) pathology images from the OPC of Guangdong Provincial People's Hospital, with 208 samples of 2048 × 2048 sizes, each with a HE-stained image, a paired IHC-stained image, and an epithelial tissue mask (as shown in Fig. 1). All samples are divided in the ratio of train set: validation set: test set = 6:2:2. We use a sliding window of 256 × 256 sizes from left to right and then from top to bottom with overlap = 50% to take the image patches. All the predicted patches are stitched back together in the order of segmentation, and the maximum value of the overlapping parts is taken as the final pixel value of the region.

In addition, we use BCSS (Breast Cancer Cases) Dataset as external verification to prove the generalization of the proposed method, which contains 151 HE-stained whole-slide images (WSIs), corresponding to 151 tissue classification labels (Fig. 4).

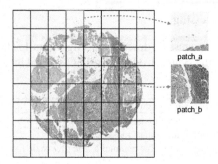

Fig. 4. The method of dividing a 2048 × 2048 image into several 256 × 256 patches.

4.2 Evaluation Metrics

In this paper, Structural Similarity (SSIM) is used to evaluate the similarity between the generated IHC-stained images and Ground Truth (GT):

$$SSIM = \frac{\left(2\mu_x\mu_y + c_1\right)\left(\sigma_{xy} + c_2\right)}{\left(\mu_x^2 + \mu_y^2 + c_1\right)\left(\sigma_x^2 + \sigma_y^2 + c_2\right)} \tag{3}$$

where x stands for the generated IHC-stained image; y stands for the GT; μ_x and μ_y represent the mean value of x and y; σ_x and σ_y represent the standard deviation of x and y; σ_{xy} represents the covariance of x and y; c_1 and c_2 are constants respectively.

In addition, five metrics (Accuracy, Precision, Specificity, Recall, and F1-score) are used to evaluate the results of the final epithelium binary masks obtained via the proposed framework compared with the common segmentation networks:

$$Accuracy = \frac{TP + TN}{TP + TN + FP + FN} \tag{4}$$

$$Precision = \frac{TP}{TP + FP} \tag{5}$$

$$Specificity = \frac{TN}{FP + TN} \tag{6}$$

$$Recall = \frac{TP}{TP + FN} \tag{7}$$

$$F_1 - score = \frac{2 \cdot Precision \cdot Recall}{Precision + Recall} \tag{8}$$

The meanings of TP, TN, FP, and FN are shown in the following Table 1:

Table 1. Confusion Matrix.

Predict\Actual	Positive	Negative
Positive	TP	FP
Negative	FN	TN

4.3 Implementation Details

The device is Dell Precision 3640, with Intel Core i9-10900K CPU@3.70 GHz × 20 and NVIDIA GeForce RTX 3090. Keep the hyper-parameters the same for all experiments, Loss = L1Loss, Batch_size = 16, epoch = 20, Learning_rate = 0.0002, and the Learning_rate decay strategy is to halve every two epochs. To avoid the influence of experimental errors, the results of each network are the average values of training three times ± standard deviation.

Firstly, we conduct experiments on U-Net as the baseline and then combine U-Net with attention gate, CBAM, and our CS-Gate module respectively. Secondly, we replace the encoder of U-Net with VGG16 (which turns into VGG16UNet), then plug the above three attention modules into it. Finally, we compare our method with the two most commonly used generative networks (cycleGAN and pix2pix). The results are shown in Table 2:

Table 2. Comparison of other networks and our CS-Net.

Models	Accuracy	Precision	Recall	Specificity	F1-score	SSIM
U-Net (U1)	0.8486	0.6618	0.8148	0.8383	0.7303	0.7559
AG + U1	0.8622	0.6506	0.8202	0.8569	0.7256	0.7753
CBAM + U1	0.8649	0.6573	0.8307	0.8596	0.7338	0.7712
CS-Gate + U1	0.8371	0.6367	0.8360	0.8511	0.7228	0.7690
VGG16UNet (U2)	0.8833	0.6987	0.8280	0.8982	0.7578	0.7702
AG + U2	0.9082	0.7742	0.8543	0.9054	0.8122	0.8032
CBAM + U2	0.9018	**0.7933**	0.8443	0.9001	0.8180	0.8092
pix2pix	0.7731	0.6888	0.6769	0.8186	0.6827	0.6746
cycleGAN	0.6851	0.6072	0.6851	0.7233	0.6438	0.7397
Ours	**0.9248**	0.7855	**0.8845**	**0.9255**	**0.8320**	**0.8202**

HE   IHC_GT   U-Net   pix2pix   cycleGAN   CS-Net

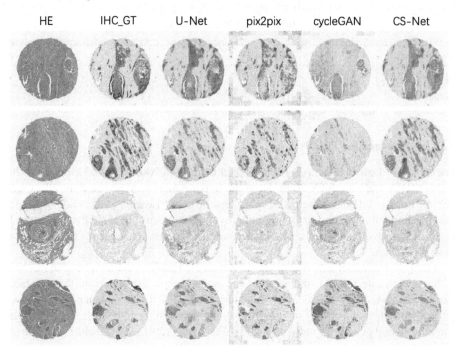

Fig. 5. Pseudo-IHC-stained images generated by different models.

It can be seen that for U-Net, whether it is plugged with AG, CBAM, or CS-Gate, the results have not improved even slightly decreased. However, after replacing the encoder with VGG16 to become VGG16UNet, the results have been greatly improved (from 84.86% to 88.33%). Then three attention modules were plugged into it subsequently, the accuracy and SSIM were improved in different aspects. Among them, our proposed CS-Gate improves the most (from 88.33% to 92.48%). From these results, it is reasonable to deduce that the original encoder of U-Net is not capable of extracting effective features enough from HE-stained images. But once replacing the encoder with VGG16, which has stronger feature extraction capabilities, the accuracy has been significantly improved, and the three attention modules finally work when they are added into VGG16UNet.

4.4   Qualitative Analysis Results

Figure 5 shows the pseudo-IHC-stained images generated by different generative networks. Observing the first and the fourth row, the checkerboard artifact is greatly reduced by CS-Net; in the second row, CS-Net generates the most similar IHC-stained image, while restoring color and texture features as much as possible; in the third row, CS-Net can reduce the FP phenomenon most. It can be seen that CS-Net has synthesized the most similar image to the GT.

Figure 6 shows the mask obtained from the pseudo-IHC-stained images via Algorithm 1. It can be seen that CS-Net can generate the most accurate mask. U-Net has the second-best performance after CS-Net but is still showing a high false positive in the

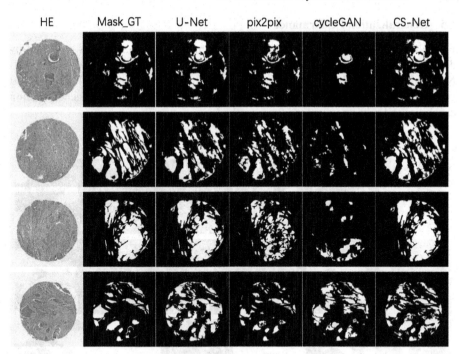

Fig. 6. The epithelium binary masks obtained from the pseudo-IHC-stained images via Algorithm 1.

fourth row. Pix2pix and cycleGAN have the worst performance, showing not only a high chessboard artifact but also high FP and FN phenomena in all samples.

Figure 7 illustrates that CS-Net has higher stability and lower loss than GAN-based generative networks (such as cycleGAN and pix2pix). Table 1 also shows that CS-Net can synthesize more similar images (about 10% higher in SSIM).

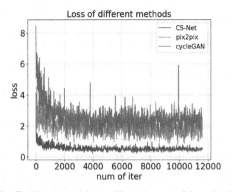

Fig. 7. The comparison of loss curves of 3 methods.

4.5 Generalization Performance

Figure 8 shows the obtained epithelium binary masks of BCSS patches predicted by different methods, aiming to validate their generalization ability. It can be seen that U-Net predicts accurately in some cases, but does not perform well overall. Pix2pix and cycleGAN both exhibit poor generalization ability. CS-Net shows the best generalization capability and robustness among these methods.

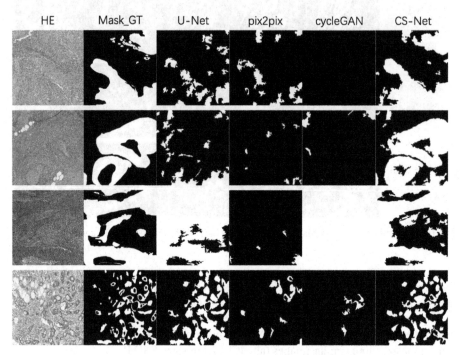

Fig. 8. The epithelium binary masks of BCSS images predicted by different methods.

5 Conclusion

This paper proposes a stain-style transfer network named CS-Net, which has strong feature extraction capability and can synthesize more stable and higher-quality images with better color and texture details. CS-Net outperforms the UNet-based network when performing segmentation task, and outperforms some GAN-based networks when performing style-transfer task, with an outstanding accuracy of 92.48%. CS-Net also shows a higher generalization ability than the U-Net-based and GAN-based networks.

CS-Net is the key step of our presented two-step framework to perform epithelium tissue region segmentation, which is to first generate a psuedo-IHC-stained image and then perform image processing to obtain the mask. Compared with the one-step methods which solely uses HE-stained images to do the segmentation task, our method shows higher superiority.

However, there are also some shortcomings in this work, and more researches could be done in the future. Firstly, we found that the more epochs are trained, the better the results would be, so better results would be obtained theoretically if time allowed. Secondly, a larger batch size would yield better results, but also take up more running memory. If the computing power is increased, such as calling multiple GPUs or providing more running memory to run a larger batch size.

References

1. Amgad, M., et al.: Structured crowdsourcing enables convolutional segmentation of histology images. Bioinformatics **35**(18), 3461–3467 (2019)
2. Bahdanau, D., Kyunghyun, C., Yoshua, B.: Neural machine translation by jointly learning to align and translate. arXiv preprint arXiv:1409.0473 (2014)
3. Chang, H., Alexander, B., Paul, S., Bahram, P.: Classification of tumor histology via morphometric context. In: Proceedings of the IEEE conference on computer vision and pattern Recognition, pp. 2203–2210 (2013)
4. Chen, H., Qi, X., Yu, L., Dou, Q., Qin, J., Heng, P.A.: DCAN: deep contour-aware networks for object instance segmentation from histology images. Med. Image Anal. **36**, 135–146 (2017)
5. Fu, J., Liu, J., Tian, H., Li, Y., Bao, Y., Fang, Z., Lu, H.: Dual attention network for scene segmentation. In: Proceedings of the IEEE/CVF Conference on Computer Vision and Pattern Recognition, pp. 3146–3154 (2019)
6. He, K., Zhang, X., Ren, S., Sun, J.: Deep residual learning for image recognition. In: Proceedings of the IEEE Conference on Computer Vision and Pattern Recognition, pp. 770–778 (2016)
7. Hu, J., Shen, L., Albanie, S., Sun, G., Vedaldi, A.: Gather-excite: Exploiting feature context in convolutional neural networks. In: Advances in neural information processing systems, vol. 31 (2018)
8. Isola, P., Zhu, J.-Y., Zhou, T., Efros, A.A.: Image-to-image translation with conditional adversarial networks. In: Proceedings of the IEEE Conference on Computer Vision and Pattern Recognition, pp.1125–1134 (2017)
9. Jaderberg, M., Karen, S., Andrew, Z., et al.: Spatial transformer networks. In: Advances in Neural Information Processing Systems, vol. 28 (2015)
10. Ronneberger, O., Fischer, P., Brox, T.: U-net: convolutional networks for biomedical image segmentation. In: Navab, N., Hornegger, J., Wells, W.M., Frangi, A.F. (eds.) Medical Image Computing and Computer-Assisted Intervention – MICCAI 2015: 18th International Conference, Munich, Germany, October 5-9, 2015, Proceedings, Part III, pp. 234–241. Springer International Publishing, Cham (2015). https://doi.org/10.1007/978-3-319-24574-4_28
11. Levy, J.J., et al.: A large-scale internal validation study of unsupervised virtual trichrome staining technologies on nonalcoholic steatohepatitis liver biopsies. Mod. Pathol. **34**(4), 808–822 (2021)
12. Xu, R., et al.: Histopathological tissue segmentation of lung cancer with bilinear CNN and soft attention. BioMed. Res. Int. **2022**, 1–10 (2022). https://doi.org/10.1155/2022/7966553
13. Salehi, P., Chalechale, A.: Pix2pix-based stain-to-stain translation: a solution for robust stain normalization in histopathology images analysis. In: 2020 International Conference on Machine Vision and Image Processing (MVIP), pp. 1–7. IEEE (2020)
14. Simonyan, K., Zisserman, A.: Very deep convolutional networks for large-scale image recognition. arXiv preprint arXiv:1409.1556 (2014)
15. Cao, H., et al.: Swin-unet: Unet-like pure transformer for medical image segmentation. arXiv preprint arXiv:2105.05537 (2021)

16. Badrinarayanan, V., Kendall, A., Cipolla, R.: Segnet: a deep convolutional encoder-decoder architecture for image segmentation. IEEE Trans. Pattern Anal. Mach. Intell. **39**(12), 2481–2495 (2017)

17. Van Eycke, Y.R., Balsat, C., Verset, L., Debeir, O., Salmon, I., Decaestecker, C.: Segmentation of glandular epithelium in colorectal tumours to automatically compartmentalise IHC biomarker quantification: A deep learning approach. Med. Image Anal. **49**, 35–45 (2018)

18. He, K., Zhang, X., Ren, S., Sun, J.: Identity mappings in deep residual networks. In: Leibe, B., Matas, J., Sebe, N., Welling, M. (eds.) ECCV 2016. LNCS, vol. 9908, pp. 630–645. Springer, Cham (2016). https://doi.org/10.1007/978-3-319-46493-0_38

19. Sirinukunwattana, K., Ahmed, S.E., Raza, Y.-W.T., Snead, D., Cree, I., Rajpoot, N.: A spatially constrained deep learning framework for detection of epithelial tumor nuclei in cancer histology images. In: Guorong, W., Coupé, P., Zhan, Y., Munsell, B., Rueckert, D. (eds.) Patch-MI 2015. LNCS, vol. 9467, pp. 154–162. Springer, Cham (2015). https://doi.org/10.1007/978-3-319-28194-0_19

20. Zhong, C., Han, J., Borowsky, A., Parvin, B., Wang, Y., Chang, H.: When machine vision meets histology: a comparative evaluation of model architecture for classification of histology sections. Med. Image Anal. **35**, 530–543 (2017)

21. Hu, J., Shen, L., Sun, G.: Squeeze-and-excitation networks. In: Proceedings of the IEEE Conference on Computer Vision and Pattern Recognition, pp. 7132–7141 (2018)

22. Wang, Q., Wu, B., Zhu, P., Li, P., Zuo, W., Hu. Q.: ECA-Net: Efficient Channel Attention for Deep Convolutional Neural Networks (2019)

23. Mnih, V., Heess, N., Graves, A., et al.: Recurrent models of visual attention. In: Advances in neural information processing systems, vol. 27 (2014)

24. Oktay, O., Jo, S., Loic, L.F., Matthew, L., Mattias, H., Kazunari, M., Kensaku, M, et al.: Attention u-net: Learning where to look for the pancreas. arXiv preprint arXiv:1804.03999 (2018)

25. Woo, S., Park, J., Lee, J.-Y., Kweon, I.S.: Cbam: Convolutional block attention module. In: Ferrari, V., Hebert, M., Sminchisescu, C., Weiss, Y. (eds.) ECCV 2018. LNCS, vol. 11211, pp. 3–19. Springer, Cham (2018). https://doi.org/10.1007/978-3-030-01234-2_1

26. Goodfellow, I., et al.: 2020. Generative adversarial networks. *Communications of the ACM* 63. ACM New York, NY, USA: 139–144

27. Mirza, M., Osindero, S.: Conditional generative adversarial nets. arXiv preprint arXiv:1411.1784 (2014)

28. Shaban, M.T., Baur, C., Navab, N., Albarqouni, S.: Staingan: stain style transfer for digital histological images. In: 2019 IEEE 16th International Symposium on Biomedical Imaging (Isbi 2019), pp. 953–956. IEEE (2019)

29. Li, X., Liu, S., Kautz, J., Yang, M.H.: Learning Linear Transformations for Fast Arbitrary Style Transfer (2018)

30. Gatys, L.A., Alexander, S.E., Bethge, M.: Image style transfer using convolutional neural networks. In: Proceedings of the IEEE Conference on Computer Vision and Pattern Recognition, pp. 2414–2423 (2016)

31. 陈志鹏, 郑文秀, and 黄琼丹. 基于Sobel滤波器的图像风格转换算法 (2021)

32. Zheng, Q., Zhu, J., Tang, H., et al.: Generalized label enhancement with sample correlations. IEEE Trans. Knowl. Data Eng. **35**(1), 482–495 (2021)

33. Lu, H., Li, Y., Chen, M., et al.: Brain intelligence: go beyond artificial intelligence. Mobile Netw. Appl. **23**, 368–375 (2018)

34. Li, H., Pun, C.M., Xu, F., et al.: A hybrid feature selection algorithm based on a discrete artificial bee colony for Parkinson's diagnosis. ACM Trans. Internet Technol. **21**(3), 1–22 (2021)

Single-Image 3D Human Pose and Shape Estimation Enhanced by Clothed 3D Human Reconstruction

Leyuan Liu[1,2], Yunqi Gao[1], Jianchi Sun[1], and Jingying Chen[1,2(✉)]

[1] National Engineering Research Center for E-Learning, Central China Normal University, Wuhan, China
{gaoyunqi,sunjc0306}@mails.ccun.edu.cn
[2] National Engineering Laboratory for Educational Big Data, Central China Normal University, Wuhan, China
{lyliu,chenjy}@mail.ccnu.edu.cn

Abstract. 3D human pose and shape estimation and clothed 3D human reconstruction are two hot topics in the community of computer vision. 3D human pose and shape estimation aims to estimate the 3D poses and body shapes of "naked" humans under clothes, while clothed 3D human reconstruction refers to reconstructing the surfaces of humans wearing clothes. These two topics are closely related, but researchers usually study them separately. In this paper, we enhance the accuracy of the 3D human pose and body shape estimation by the reconstructed clothed 3D human models. Our method consists of two main components: the 3D body mesh recovery module and the clothed 3D human reconstruction module. In the 3D body mesh recovery module, an intermediate 3D body mesh is first recovered from the input image by a graph convolutional network (GCN), and then the 3D body pose and shape parameters are estimated by a regressor. In the clothed human reconstruction module, two clothed human surface models are respectively reconstructed under the guidance of the recovered 3D body mesh and the ground-truth 3D body mesh. At the training phase, losses which are described by the residuals among the two reconstructed clothed human models and ground truth are passed back into the 3D body mesh recovery module and used for boosting the body mesh recovery module. The quantitative and qualitative experimental results on THuman2.0, and LSP show that our method outperforms the current state-of-the-art 3D human pose and shape estimation methods.

Keywords: 3D Human Pose and Shape Estimation · Clothed 3D Human Reconstruction · Graph Convolutional Network · SMPL Parameter Regression

This work was supported by the National Natural Science Foundation of China under grant No. 62077026 and the Fundamental Research Funds for the Central Universities under grant No. CCNU22QN012.

H. Lu and J. Cai (Eds.): ISAIR 2023, CCIS 1998, pp. 33–44, 2024.
https://doi.org/10.1007/978-981-99-9109-9_4

1   Introduction

In order to describe 3D human poses and body shapes with a finer granularity while reducing the difficulty of algorithms, the majority of methods [3,8,11,24,25] usually represent human bodies by parametric models such as SMPL [16]. In this way, algorithms only need to output low-dimensional pose and shape parameters, which are then used to recover the corresponding 3D body meshes via the parametric models. Another hot topic is called clothed 3D human reconstruction [15,22,27], which refers to reconstructing 3D surface meshes of humans with clothes. Although 3D human pose and shape estimation and clothed 3D human reconstruction have different goals, representations, methodologies, and outputs, they are two closely related topics.

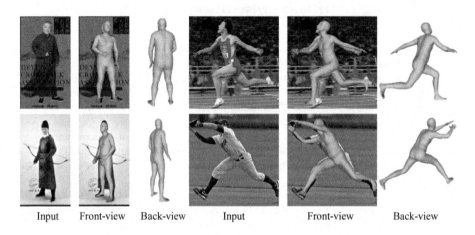

| Input | Front-view | Back-view | Input | Front-view | Back-view |

Fig. 1. Our method can recover accurate 3D poses and body shapes of humans wearing both tight-fitting and loose-fitting clothes.

Estimating 3D human pose and shape from monocular images is quite challenging, not only because it is an inherently ill-posed problem, but also due to complex body kinematic structures, various body shapes, and clothing occlusions. To address these challenges, two different paradigms have been investigated: optimization-based methods and regression-based methods. Optimization-based methods [1,21] usually suffer from local minima due to poor initialization. Thus, the recent mainstream methods [2,3,8,12,18,24,25] have focused on the regression-based paradigm, which usually employs deep learning techniques to regress 3D human poses and shapes directly from the input image information in an end-to-end manner. However, these methods often fail to produce satisfactory results on humans wearing complex and loose-fitting clothing, as the issue caused by clothing occlusions is not given sufficient consideration.

Recently, clothed 3D human reconstruction [15,22,27] has developed rapidly, and most of these methods employ estimated 3D body models as a geometrical prior. Although the estimated 3D body models can help clothed 3D human reconstruction methods recover more plausible global topologies, inaccurate estimation of 3D human poses and shapes usually leads to poor clothed human reconstructions [15,27]. The accuracy of 3D human pose and shape estimation determines the quality of clothed 3D human models reconstructed by these methods. Conversely, the results of clothed 3D human reconstruction effectively indicate the accuracy of 3D human pose and shape estimation. Based on this insight, we argue that clothed 3D human reconstruction can be employed to enhance the accuracy of 3D human pose and shape estimation.

In this paper, we propose a 3D human pose and shape estimation method enhanced by clothed 3D human reconstruction. Our method consists of two main components: the 3D body mesh recovery module and the clothed human reconstruction module. In the 3D body mesh recovery module, an intermediate 3D body mesh is first recovered from an initial SMPL model by a GCN, and then the 3D body pose and shape parameters are estimated by a regressor. In the clothed human reconstruction module, two clothed human surface models are respectively reconstructed under the guidance of the recovered 3D body mesh and the ground-truth 3D body mesh. At the training phase, losses which are described by the residuals among the two reconstructed clothed human models and ground truth are passed back into the 3D body mesh recovery module and used for optimizing the body mesh recovery module. As illustrated in Fig. 1, our method can recover accurate 3D poses and body shapes of humans with both tight-fitting and loose-fitting clothes. Quantitative and qualitative experimental results show that our method achieves state-of-the-art performance on the THuman2.0 and LSP datasets.

In summary, the main contributions of this paper are three-fold:

- We propose a 3D human pose and shape estimation method enhanced by clothed 3D human reconstruction. Our method is the first method that employs reconstructed clothed 3D human models to enhance the accuracy of 3D human pose and shape estimation.
- We propose to use both the absolute and relative clothed 3D human reconstruction errors as losses pass them back into the 3D body mesh recovery module and use them for optimizing the body mesh recovery module.
- Our method recovers accurate 3D poses and body shapes of humans wearing both tight-fitting and loose-fitting clothes.

2   Related Work

In recent years, 3D technology has found extensive applications in various industries, such as transportation [14,26]. In addition, the field of 3D digital human body technology has also made great development and progress.

2.1   3D Human Pose and Shape Estimation

3D human pose and shape estimation methods can be roughly divided into two categories: optimization-based methods and regression-based methods.

Optimization-Based Methods. Optimization-based methods [1,6,13] attempt to fit a 3D body meshes to the image observation in an explicit iterative manner. Although these optimization-based methods have demonstrated high accuracy in many cases, they may be susceptible to local optima due to poor initialization. Additionally, the iterative optimization processes involved in these methods are time-consuming. **Regression-based methods** [2,3,8,12,18,24,25] directly regress the parameters from the input image. With the prosperity of deep learning, many researchers have recently shifted their focus from optimization-based methods to regression-based methods. Kanazawa et al. [8] proposed an end-to-end 3D body mesh recovery framework called HMR, which uses rich and useful mesh representation parameterized by shape and 3D joint angles and utilizes a generative adversary network to constrain body poses. Zeng et al. [24] recovered 3D body meshes by establishing a dense correspondence between the mesh and local image features in UV space. In contrast to most methods that regress SMPL parameters, works proposed by Choi et al. [2] and Kolotouros et al. [12] employ graph convolutional neural networks to estimate 3D locations of vertices on the 3D body models. Despite these regression-based methods yielding promising results on people with tight-fitting clothes, they often fail to produce satisfactory results on humans wearing complex and loose-fitting clothing.

2.2   Clothed 3D Human Reconstruction

In recent years, clothed 3D human reconstruction tends to be guided by the use of parametric human models. Parametric model guided clothed 3D human reconstruction methods [5,15,22,27,28] employ a 3D body model (e.g., SMPL [16]) to guide the reconstruction of the human surface. DeepHuman [28] uses the SMPL model to constrain the degrees of freedom in the output space. HEI-Human [15] and PaMIR [27] also employ the SMPL model as a geometrical prior when using implicit functions to reconstruct surface details of clothed humans. Although the estimated SMPL models can help clothed 3D human reconstruction methods recover more plausible global topology, inaccurate estimation of 3D human poses and shapes often results in poor clothed human reconstructions (Fig. 2).

3   Method

3.1   3D Body Mesh Recovery

Inspired by GCMR [12], we first employ a GCN to predict the vertex coordinates of the intermediate 3D body mesh and then use a regressor to estimate the SMPL model parameters. Given a single input image, visual features are extracted by a CNN-based encoder, e.g., ResNet-50 [4]. The visual features are then embedded in the GCN for predicting an intermediate 3D body mesh. Finally, the vertices of the intermediate 3D body mesh are input into the regressor for estimating the SPML model parameters.

For the GCN, we start from a non-parametric 3D deformable graph, which is initiated by a T-pose SMPL template. As the original SMPL model has as many

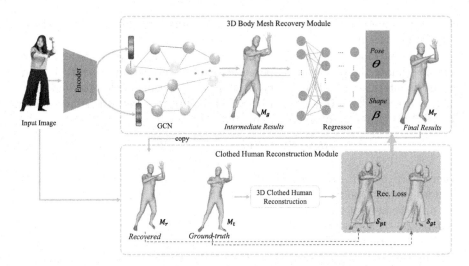

Fig. 2. Overview of our method. Our method consists of two main components: the 3D body mesh recovery module and the clothed human reconstruction module. Given an input image, visual features are first extracted by an image encoder, the image features are then embedded into a GCN for recovering an intermediate 3D body mesh (M_g). The intermediate 3D body mesh is fed into a parameter regressor for regressing the pose and shape parameters of the SMPL model (M_r). Two clothed human models ($\mathcal{S}_{pt}$ and $\mathcal{S}_{gt}$) are respectively reconstructed under the guidance of the recovered 3D body mesh (M_r) and the ground-truth 3D body mesh (M_t). Losses which are described by the residuals among the reconstructed clothed human models $\mathcal{S}_{pt}$ and ground-truth clothed human models $\mathcal{S}_{gt}$ are employed for optimizing the body mesh recovery module.

as 6890 vertices, we use a down-sampling strategy to simplify it to $N(N < 6890)$ vertices. Driven by the visual features embedded in each vertex of the graph, GCN is employed to shift the vertices. Following the work of Kipf et al. [10], our GCN is formulated as:

$$\hat{V} = \tilde{A}(DT \oplus F)W \tag{1}$$

where $T \in \mathbb{R}^{K \times 3}$ and $D \in \mathbb{R}^{N \times K}$ respectively denote the SMPL template and the down-sampling matrix, $\tilde{A} \in \mathbb{R}^{N \times N}$ denotes the row-normalized adjacency matrix of the graph, $F \in \mathbb{R}^{N \times f}$ is the visual feature vector, $W \in \mathbb{R}^{(3+f) \times 3}$ denotes the weight matrix, and $\hat{V} \in \mathbb{R}^{N \times 3}$ is the predicted coordinate vector. To facilitate regressing the SMPL model parameters, we up-sample $\hat{V}$ to 6890 vertices using the bilateral interpolation algorithm and obtain the intermediate 3D body mesh $M_g \in \mathbb{R}^{6890 \times 3}$. Essentially, our GCN is equivalent to performing a full join operation for each vertex with visual features and then performing a neighborhood averaging operation. Neighborhood averaging is essential for generating high-quality shapes since it forces neighboring vertices to have similar features so that the output shape is smooth. In addition to regressing the coordinates of each vertex on the intermediate 3D body mesh, our GCN also estimates camera parameters of the weakly perspective camera model, i.e., the scale and translation parameters $[s, t], t \in \mathbb{R}^2$.

To obtain more smooth and regular 3D body meshes, we employ a regressor to estimate the pose and shape parameters of the parametric SMPL model given the intermediate 3D body mesh as input. A specific 3D human body mesh $(M_r(\beta, \theta) \in \mathbb{R}^{6890 \times 3})$ is described by SMPL [16] using a set of pose parameters $(\theta \in \mathbb{R}^{24 \times 3})$ and a set of shape parameters $(\beta \in \mathbb{R}^{10})$:

$$M_r(\beta, \theta) = W(T_P(\beta, \theta), J(\beta), \theta, \omega) \tag{2}$$

where $T_P(\beta, \theta) = \bar{T} + B_S(\beta) + B_P(\theta)$, $J(\beta; \mathcal{J}, \bar{T}, S) = \mathcal{J}(\bar{T} + B_S(\beta; S))$, $\bar{T}$ is the standard human body model, $W(\cdot)$ is the fusion mask function, $J(\cdot)$ describes the displacement of joint points due to body size change, ω is the fusion weight matrix, $B_P(\cdot)$ is the pose fusion function, $B_S(\cdot)$ is the shape fusion function, $\mathcal{J}$ is a function that transforms rest vertices into rest joints.

Our parameter regressor is simply implemented by a three-layer multi-layer perceptron, which takes the 3D vertex coordinates of the intermediate 3D body mesh as input and outputs the pose (θ) and shape (β) parameters of the SMPL model. The estimated pose and shape parameters are converted to 3D body mesh using the SMPL model described by Eq. 2. So that we can compare whether the 3D body mesh described by the estimated parameters is consistent with the intermediate 3D body mesh.

3.2 Clothed Human Reconstruction

3D body meshes are employed to guide clothed human reconstruction. Similar to PIFu [20], we define the surface of a clothed 3D human model as a level set of an occupancy prediction function $\mathcal{F}(\cdot)$. For each 3D point p in the occupancy field, the occupancy prediction function predicts whether it is on the surface of the clothed 3D human model. To leverage image features and 3D body meshes for predicting the occupancy probability of p, our occupancy probability function $\mathcal{F}$ also takes the input image (I) and the 3D body mesh (M_*) as condition variables and thus is formulated as:

$$S(p|I, M_*) = \mathcal{F}(\ddot{U}(\ddot{f}(I), \pi(p)), \dddot{U}(\dddot{f}(M_*), p)) \tag{3}$$

where $\ddot{f}$ and $\dddot{f}$ are two encoders that respectively extract features from the input image and the 3D body model, $\pi(\cdot)$ denotes the weak perspective transformation that maps the 3D coordinates of point p in the 2D feature plane, and $\ddot{U}(\cdot)$ and $\dddot{U}(\cdot)$ are two sampling functions that respectively take features from the feature maps extracted from the input image and the 3D body mesh. In practice, the two encoders ($\ddot{f}$ and $\dddot{f}$) and the occupancy prediction function ($\mathcal{F}$) are implemented by deep neural networks. In our method, $S(p) < 0.5$ indicates that point p is inside the surface while $S(p) > 0.5$ denotes point p is outside the surface. Hence, the surface of a clothed human model can be denoted as a set of points:

$$S_* = \{p; S(p|I, M_*) := 0.5\} \tag{4}$$

where M_* can be expressed as M_r or M_t, $\mathcal{S}_*$ can be expressed as $\mathcal{S}_{pt}$ or $\mathcal{S}_{gt}$. Specifically, the recovered 3D body model M_r to guide clothed human reconstruction and obtain $\mathcal{S}_{pt}$, and the ground-truth 3D body model M_t to guide clothed human reconstruction and obtain $\mathcal{S}_{gt}$. To facilitate voxelized the reconstructed results, we converted this point set into a mesh using the Marching Cubes algorithm [17].

Then, the residuals among the reconstructed clothed human models $\mathcal{S}_{pt}$, $\mathcal{S}_{gt}$ and ground-truth clothed human model ($\mathcal{S}^*$) can be passed back into the 3D body mesh recovery module for boosting the accuracy of the 3D body pose and shape parameters.

3.3   Loss Functions

We employ a 3-step training scheme. (S1) We train the GCN to recover the intermediate body mesh. (S2) We fix the trained GCN and then train the regressor to estimate the pose and shape parameters of the 3D body. (S3) We unfix the GCN and then retrain the whole network. The loss functions used in these three steps are respectively represented by $\mathcal{L}_{gcn}$, $\mathcal{L}_{reg}$, and $\mathcal{L}_R$.

The GCN used for recovering the intermediate body mesh is trained using two kinds of supervision, that is, the mesh vertices alignment loss ($\mathcal{L}_v$) and the joints alignment loss ($\mathcal{L}_J$). Hence, $\mathcal{L}_{gcn}$ can be formulated as $\mathcal{L}_{gcn} = \lambda_v \mathcal{L}_v + \lambda_j \mathcal{L}_J$.

Besides the losses used to train the GCN, an additional parameter loss ($\mathcal{L}_p$) is also employed to train the regressor. So, $\mathcal{L}_{reg}$ can be formulated as $\mathcal{L}_{reg} = \lambda_v \mathcal{L}_v + \lambda_j \mathcal{L}_J + \lambda_p \mathcal{L}_p$.

As mentioned before, the results of clothed 3D human reconstruction indicate the accuracy of the 3D body pose and shape estimation. Hence, we use the residuals among the reconstructed clothed human models $\mathcal{S}_{pt}$, $\mathcal{S}_{gt}$ and ground-truth clothed human model $\mathcal{S}^*$ to describe the losses and pass them back into the 3D body mesh recovery module and used for optimizing the body mesh recovery module:

$$\mathcal{L}_{R1} = \frac{1}{n_p} \sum_{i=1}^{n_p} |\mathcal{S}_{pt}(p_i) - \mathcal{S}^*(p_i)|^2 \tag{5}$$

$$\mathcal{L}_{R2} = \mathcal{L}_{R1} - \frac{1}{n_p} \sum_{i=1}^{n_p} |\mathcal{S}_{gt}(p_i) - \mathcal{S}^*(p_i)|^2 \tag{6}$$

where n_p is the number of sampled points, and p_i is the sampled point. The $\mathcal{L}_{R1}$ loss represents the absolute reconstruction errors, while $\mathcal{L}_{R2}$ describes the relative reconstruction loss which removes reconstruction errors due to factors other than 3D human pose and shape estimation. Our clothed human reconstruction loss considers both the absolute reconstruction loss and the relative reconstruction loss:

$$\mathcal{L}_R = \lambda_{r1} \mathcal{L}_{R1} + \lambda_{r2} \mathcal{L}_{R2} \tag{7}$$

where λ_r is a weight to balance these two losses. Finally, the total loss for training the whole network is defined as:

$$\mathcal{L}_{tol} = \mathcal{L}_{gcn} + \mathcal{L}_{reg} + \lambda_r \mathcal{L}_R \tag{8}$$

4   Experimental Results

4.1   Datasets

Our method is trained on the training set of THuman2.0 [23] and tested on the testing set of THuman2.0 as well as LSP datasets [7]. The THuman2.0 dataset is composed of 526 high-resolution 3D scans of 526 subjects with various body shapes and poses. The data in THuman2.0 is randomly split into a training set and a testing set at a ratio of 4:1. For each 3D scan, we render it from 360 views and obtain 360 ⟨RGB image, 3D body mesh⟩ pairs. As a result, the training set is extended and contains 151,200 training data in total. The LSP [7] dataset consists of 2,000 in-the-wild images of sportsmen with difficult poses. Since LSP doesn't provide any ground-truth SMPL annotation, it is only used for qualitative evaluation in our experiments.

4.2   Implementation Details

In our implementation, ResNet-50 [4] is employed as the image encoder, the network architecture proposed in [10] is adopted to implement our GCN, the multiple layer perceptron is employed to construct the parameter regressor and the network of PaMIR [27] is adopted to reconstruct the surface of clothed humans. All our networks are implemented based on PyTorch [19]. Adam [9] is employed for optimizing our networks. In the whole training phase, the learning rate is fixed to 3×10^{-4}, and the batch size is set as 16. Our networks are totally trained for 20 epochs, and it takes about 5 days on a computer with a single NVIDIA GeForce RTX 3080 GPU.

4.3   Comparisons

(1)   Quantitative Comparisons

Table 1. Quantitative comparisons on the THuman2.0 dataset.

Method	Publication	MPJPE	PA-MPJPE	MVPE
SPIN [11]	ICCV'2019	64.2	48.9	80.5
GCMR [12]	CVPR'2019	93.7	67.3	111.0
DecoMR [24]	CVPR'2020	112.5	84.5	126.1
PyMAF [25]	ICCV'2021	66.9	49.6	83.8
3DCrowdNet [3]	CVPR'2022	101.3	93.9	118.3
Ours	–	**42.9**	**34.6**	**46.5**

Same as other methods [11,12,25], we use three quantitative metrics (MPJPE, PA-MPJPE, and MPVE) to calculate the experimental results. Table 1 shows the quantitative comparisons on THuman2.0. Our method achieves an MPJPE of 42.9 mm, a PA-MPJPE of 34.6 mm, and an MVPE of 46.5 mm, and outperforms all the other methods involved in the comparison. In terms of pose estimation, our method outperforms the second-best method (i.e., PyMAF [25]) by an MPJPE of 24.0 mm and a PA-MPJPE of 15.0 mm. In terms of shape estimation, our method also achieves the lowest MVPE of 37.3 mm. It can be seen that due to the influence of loose clothing obscuration, most advanced methods are unable to accurately identify not only the human postural motion under the clothing but also the human shape.

(2) Qualitative Comparisons

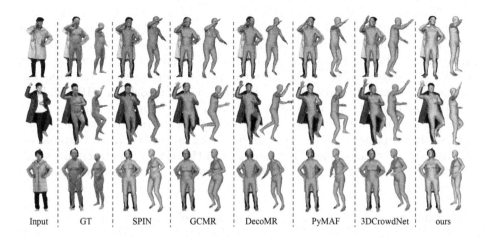

Input   GT   SPIN   GCMR   DecoMR   PyMAF   3DCrowdNet   ours

Fig. 3. Qualitative comparisons on the THuman 2.0 dataset.

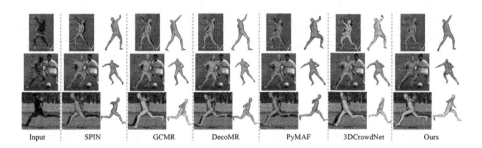

Input   SPIN   GCMR   DecoMR   PyMAF   3DCrowdNet   Ours

Fig. 4. Qualitative comparisons on the LSP dataset.

We compare our method qualitatively with SPIN [11], GCMR [12], DecoMR [24], PyMAF [25] and 3DCrowdNet [3]. We first test these methods on the testing set of THuman2.0 and then test them on LSP for cross-dataset evaluation. Figure 3 shows the results produced by these four methods and our methods on THuman2.0. It can be seen that our method produces the most accurate poses and body shapes that are similar to ground-truth models, whether examined from the visible view or invisible view. Figure 4 illustrates the cross-dataset results on the LSP datasets. Our method still outputs 3D body models with accurate poses and body shapes, while other methods do not estimate the postures of legs and arms precisely in most of their results.

4.4   Ablation Study

To verify that the accuracy of estimated 3D human poses and shapes can be boosted by clothed 3D human reconstruction, we train four different models (m1~m4) of our method using different loss functions and test these models on the Thuman2.0 dataset. The quantitative results achieved by these models are shown in Table 2. Without all the two reconstruction loss functions (i.e., the m1 model), our method only yields an MPJPE of 65.6mm, a PA-MPJPE of 44.2 mm, and an MVPE of 65.1 mm. By adding the $\mathcal{L}_{R1}$ loss (i.e., the m2 model), the MPJPE, PA-MPJPE, and MVPE are respectively decreased by 12.7 mm, 9.2 mm, and 16.5 mm. By adding the $\mathcal{L}_{R2}$ loss (i.e., the m3 model), the MPJPE, PA-MPJPE, and MVPE are respectively decreased by 10.4 mm, 6.5 mm, and 12.7 mm. These results indicate that both the absolute reconstruction errors $\mathcal{L}_{R1}$ and the relative reconstruction loss $\mathcal{L}_{R2}$ are beneficial for the accuracy of estimated 3D human poses and shapes. When using both these two reconstruction losses, the MPJPE, PA-MPJPE, and MVPE respectively drop to 42.9 mm, 34.6 mm, and 46.5 mm.

Table 2. Comparisons of our method trained with different loss functions.

Models	Loss Functions	MPJPE	PA-MPJPE	MVPE
m1	$\mathcal{L}_{reg}$	65.6	44.2	65.1
m2	$\mathcal{L}_{reg} + \mathcal{L}_{R1}$	52.9	35.0	48.6
m3	$\mathcal{L}_{reg} + \mathcal{L}_{R2}$	55.2	37.7	52.4
m4	$\mathcal{L}_{reg} + \mathcal{L}_{R}(\mathcal{L}_{tol})$	**42.9**	**34.6**	**46.5**

5   Conclusion

Estimating 3D human pose and body shape from a single image is challenging. In this paper, we have proposed a 3D human pose and shape estimation method enhanced by clothed 3D human reconstruction. Two clothed 3D human models are respectively reconstructed under the guidance of the recovered 3D body mesh and the ground-truth 3D body mesh. The ablation study has validated that the accuracy of the estimated 3D human poses and shapes is significantly improved by our method. Experimental results show that our method achieves state-of-the-art performance.

References

1. Bogo, F., Kanazawa, A., Lassner, C., Gehler, P., Romero, J., Black, M.J.: Keep it SMPL: automatic estimation of 3D human pose and shape from a single image. In: Leibe, B., Matas, J., Sebe, N., Welling, M. (eds.) ECCV 2016. LNCS, vol. 9909, pp. 561–578. Springer, Cham (2016). https://doi.org/10.1007/978-3-319-46454-1_34
2. Choi, H., Moon, G., Lee, K.M.: Pose2Mesh: graph convolutional network for 3D human pose and mesh recovery from a 2D human pose. In: Vedaldi, A., Bischof, H., Brox, T., Frahm, J.-M. (eds.) ECCV 2020. LNCS, vol. 12352, pp. 769–787. Springer, Cham (2020). https://doi.org/10.1007/978-3-030-58571-6_45
3. Choi, H., Moon, G., Park, J., Lee, K.M.: Learning to estimate robust 3D human mesh from in-the-wild crowded scenes. In: IEEE/CVF Conference on Computer Vision and Pattern Recognition (CVPR) (2022). https://doi.org/10.1109/CVPR52688.2022.00153
4. He, K., Zhang, X., Ren, S., Sun, J.: Identity mappings in deep residual networks. In: Leibe, B., Matas, J., Sebe, N., Welling, M. (eds.) ECCV 2016. LNCS, vol. 9908, pp. 630–645. Springer, Cham (2016). https://doi.org/10.1007/978-3-319-46493-0_38
5. He, T., Xu, Y., Saito, S., Soatto, S., Tung, T.: ARCH++: animation-ready clothed human reconstruction revisited. In: IEEE/CVF International Conference on Computer Vision (ICCV), pp. 11046–11056 (2021). https://doi.org/10.1109/ICCV48922.2021.01086
6. Huang, Y., et al.: Towards accurate marker-less human shape and pose estimation over time. In: International Conference on 3D Vision (3DV), pp. 421–430 (2017). https://doi.org/10.1109/3DV.2017.00055
7. Johnson, S., Everingham, M.: Clustered pose and nonlinear appearance models for human pose estimation. In: British Machine Vision Conference (BMVC), vol. 2, p. 5 (2010). https://doi.org/10.5244/C.24.12
8. Kanazawa, A., Black, M.J., Jacobs, D.W., Malik, J.: End-to-end recovery of human shape and pose. In: IEEE/CVF Conference on Computer Vision and Pattern Recognition (CVPR), pp. 7122–7131 (2018). https://doi.org/10.1109/CVPR.2018.00744
9. Kingma, D., Ba, J.: Adam: a method for stochastic optimization. In: International Conference on Learning Representations (ICLR), pp. 1–15 (2015)
10. Kipf, T.N., Welling, M.: Semi-supervised classification with graph convolutional networks. In: International Conference on Learning Representations (2016)
11. Kolotouros, N., Pavlakos, G., Black, M.J., Daniilidis, K.: Learning to reconstruct 3D human pose and shape via model-fitting in the loop. In: IEEE/CVF International Conference on Computer Vision (ICCV), pp. 2252–2261 (2019). https://doi.org/10.1109/ICCV.2019.00234
12. Kolotouros, N., Pavlakos, G., Daniilidis, K.: Convolutional mesh regression for single-image human shape reconstruction. In: IEEE/CVF Conference on Computer Vision and Pattern Recognition (CVPR), pp. 4501–4510 (2019). https://doi.org/10.1109/CVPR.2019.00463
13. Lassner, C., Romero, J., Kiefel, M., Bogo, F., Black, M.J., Gehler, P.V.: Unite the people: closing the loop between 3D and 2D human representations. In: IEEE/CVF Conference on Computer Vision and Pattern Recognition (CVPR), pp. 6050–6059 (2017). https://doi.org/10.1109/CVPR.2017.500
14. Li, Y., Cai, J., Zhou, Q., Lu, H.: Joint semantic-instance segmentation method for intelligent transportation system. IEEE Trans. Intell. Transp. Syst. 1–8 (2022). https://doi.org/10.1109/TITS.2022.3190369

15. Liu, L., Sun, J., Gao, Y., Chen, J.: HEI-human: a hybrid explicit and implicit method for single-view 3D clothed human reconstruction. In: Ma, H., et al. (eds.) PRCV 2021. LNCS, vol. 13020, pp. 251–262. Springer, Cham (2021). https://doi.org/10.1007/978-3-030-88007-1_21

16. Loper, M., Mahmood, N., Romero, J., Pons-Moll, G., Black, M.J.: SMPL: a skinned multi-person linear model. ACM Trans. Graph. **34**(6), 1–16 (2015). https://doi.org/10.1145/2816795.2818013

17. Lorensen, W.E., Cline, H.E.: Marching cubes: a high resolution 3D surface construction algorithm. In: Conference on Computer Graphics and Interactive Techniques, pp. 163–169 (1987). https://doi.org/10.1145/37401.37422

18. Omran, M., Lassner, C., Pons-Moll, G., Gehler, P., Schiele, B.: Neural body fitting: unifying deep learning and model based human pose and shape estimation. In: International Conference on 3D Vision (3DV), pp. 484–494 (2018). https://doi.org/10.1109/3DV.2018.00062

19. Paszke, A., et al.: PyTorch: an imperative style, high-performance deep learning library. In: International Conference on Neural Information Processing Systems (NIPS) (2019)

20. Saito, S., Huang, Z., Natsume, R., Morishima, S., Kanazawa, A., Li, H.: PIFu: pixel-aligned implicit function for high-resolution clothed human digitization. In: IEEE/CVF International Conference on Computer Vision (ICCV), pp. 2304–2314 (2019). https://doi.org/10.1109/ICCV.2019.00239

21. Xiang, D., Joo, H., Sheikh, Y.: Monocular total capture: posing face, body, and hands in the wild. In: IEEE/CVF Conference on Computer Vision and Pattern Recognition (CVPR), pp. 10965–10974 (2019). https://doi.org/10.1109/CVPR.2019.01122

22. Xiu, Y., Yang, J., Tzionas, D., Black, M.J.: ICON: implicit clothed humans obtained from normals. In: IEEE/CVF Conference on Computer Vision and Pattern Recognition (CVPR), pp. 13296–13306 (2022). https://doi.org/10.1109/TPAMI.2021.3050505

23. Yu, T., Zheng, Z., Guo, K., Liu, P., Dai, Q., Liu, Y.: Function4D: real-time human volumetric capture from very sparse consumer RGBD sensors. In: IEEE/CVF Conference on Computer Vision and Pattern Recognition (CVPR), pp. 5746–5756 (2021). https://doi.org/10.1109/CVPR46437.2021.00569

24. Zeng, W., Ouyang, W., Luo, P., Liu, W., Wang, X.: 3D human mesh regression with dense correspondence. In: IEEE/CVF Conference on Computer Vision and Pattern Recognition (CVPR), pp. 7054–7063 (2020). https://doi.org/10.1109/CVPR42600.2020.00708

25. Zhang, H., et al.: PyMAF: 3D human pose and shape regression with pyramidal mesh alignment feedback loop. In: IEEE/CVF International Conference on Computer Vision (ICCV) (2021). https://doi.org/10.1109/ICCV48922.2021.01125

26. Zheng, Y., Li, Y., Yang, S., Lu, H.: Global-PBNet: a novel point cloud registration for autonomous driving. IEEE Trans. Intell. Transp. Syst. **23**(11), 22312–22319 (2022). https://doi.org/10.1109/TITS.2022.3153133

27. Zheng, Z., Yu, T., Liu, Y., Dai, Q.: PaMIR: parametric model-conditioned implicit representation for image-based human reconstruction. IEEE Tans. Pattern Anal. Mach. Intell. (TPAMI) **44**(6), 3170–3184 (2021)

28. Zheng, Z., Yu, T., Wei, Y., Dai, Q., Liu, Y.: DeepHuman: 3D human reconstruction from a single image. In: IEEE/CVF International Conference on Computer Vision (ICCV), pp. 7739–7749 (2019). https://doi.org/10.1109/ICCV.2019.00783

IoT Botnet Attacks Detection and Classification Based on Ensemble Learning

Yongzhong Cao[1,2]([✉]), Zhihui Wang[1,2], Hongwei Ding[1,2], Jiale Zhang[1,2], and Bin Li[1,2]

[1] College of Information Engineering, Yangzhou University, Yangzhou, China
caoyz@yzu.edu.cn
[2] Jiangsu Province Knowledge Management and Intelligent Services Engineering Research Center, Jiangsu, China

Abstract. With the vigorous development of the IoT, botnet attacks against the IoT have become more frequent and diverse, and the research on attack prevention and detection has become more difficult. This paper proposes an IoT botnet attack detection model based on feature selection and ensemble learning. Specifically, the model first reduces the feature dimension of the data by selecting appropriate feature sets. Then, an optimized LightGBM classifier and Naive Bayes classifier are integrated to improve the robustness of the model and accuracy. Finally, a meta classifier TPE-LightGBM is used to combine the result of the classifiers and make the final classification. The performance of the proposed model is tested on the N-BaIoT dataset. The experimental results show that it has a detection rate of 99.97% and shortens the training time by 63.75% at most, improves 4.95% to the conventional methods.

Keywords: botnet · anomaly detection · feature selection · ensemble learning

1 Introduction

With the vigorous development of IoT technology, IoT devices like smart cameras, smart TV, smart wearables and smart toys have entered people's daily lives in large numbers, and people's smartphones can control these devices. In 2017, the number of devices connected to IoT networks worldwide reached 2.035 billion, which is expected to increase to 7.544 billion by 2025 [1]. With the increasing number of IoT devices connected to the network, the number of safety accidents related to IoT is increasing. Due to the restricted computing and storage capabilities of IoT devices, it is not enough to install complex security defense mechanisms on these devices. Consequently, IoT devices are easily targeted by attackers and they are becoming the target of a botnet infection. In terms of botnet host control, various domestic devices are controlled by a large number of overseas C&C (Command and Control) servers, which are mainly located in the United States, Germany, and other countries, accounting for more than 98% [2]. In the botnet, the controlled host often transmits malicious instructions to the robot through multi-layer forwarding. The communication between the controlled host and the C&C server only consumes a small amount of traffic, which puts the botnet

H. Lu and J. Cai (Eds.): ISAIR 2023, CCIS 1998, pp. 45–55, 2024.
https://doi.org/10.1007/978-981-99-9109-9_5

often in a hidden state. It greatly increases the detection difficulty of botnet attacks. Therefore, for IoT security personnel and developers, establishing an effective botnet attack detection mechanism is important to work to maintain IoT network security.

Due to the heterogeneity of the IoT network and lack of computing and storage capabilities, the traditional network attack detection technology cannot be directly applied to the IoT network [3]. Hence, the present network attack detection scheme for the IoT is unsuitable. This paper proposes an IoT botnet attack detection model based on feature selection and ensemble learning to solve the problems. This model applies traditional network attack detection methods to IoT network attack detection by selecting useful features and integrating different algorithms, which can speed up model training, and improve detection efficiency.

The rest of the paper is organized as follows: Section 2 presents some related works for botnet attack and detection. Section 3 explains the proposed methodology to detect IoT botnet attack. Section 4 discusses the results and conclusions which compare the accuracy rate, training and detection time. Finally, Sect. 5 concludes the paper.

2   Related Works

2.1   Botnet

At present, botnets have emerged for nearly 30 years. Through continuous development, many different types of botnets have been iterated. Mirai is one of the most widely spread and representative botnets. Since its development, it has been used for several large-scale global DDoS attacks, including the large-scale DDoS attack of Mirai botnet encountered by Dyn, the US Internet DNS service provider, on October 21, 2016. Other botnets, such as Gafgyt, Pink, and Mozi, also iterate in a more complex and insidious direction. Despite the constant changes and updates of botnets, there are still certain commonalities among various botnets.

2.2   Methods of Botnet Detection

With the continuous development of botnet and its attack means, researchers are also constantly researching and developing more advanced detection technologies. [4] proposed a cognitive memory-guided autoencoder for effective intrusion detection in IoT. [5] proposed a network intrusion detection system based on Autoencoder and Light-GBM. [6] proposed a dual machine learning method to resist and detect IoT botnet attacks. [7] constructed a hybrid botnet attack detection method by combining supervised and unsupervised learning. [8] proposed a multi-classification detection system using a machine learning algorithm to build botnets. It used Naive Bayes, random forest, and artificial neural network to classify and train network traffic. [9] proposed an algorithm combining graph theory and machine learning to detect abnormal traffic. [10] first collected the benign and botnet traffic data of nine different IoT devices and formed the dataset N-BaIoT, and then realized the detection of the IoT botnet using the deep self-coder. It compressed and reconstructed the benign network traffic image by learning the features of the benign network traffic, thus generating an anomaly detector. When the detector fails to reconstruct the image, it means that the traffic may be abnormal. [11] used CNN classifier based on PSI graph to detect Linux IoT botnet. [4, 12] developed a novel detection model based on a deep Bidirectional Long Short Term Memory based Recurrent Neural Network (BLSTM-RNN). Although the above methods have achieved good results, some things could still be improved. Most of them only focus on the binary detection of abnormal and benign traffic and do not detect specific types of attacks. In addition, they did not analyze the optimal feature number and model robustness required for model training.

3   Methodology

3.1   Fisher Score

The goal of feature selection is to find the most useful feature subset and achieve this goal by eliminating irrelevant or redundant features. Although the more features to be trained, the more category information can be mined, too many features will cause more calculations and may reduce the performance of models. Feature selection can remove noise and improve the classification effect for anomaly detection. The feature selection algorithm used in this paper is a filtered feature selection algorithm called Fisher score. The algorithm is used to calculate and sort the importance of features [13], and the formula is as follows:

$$S_B^k = \sum_{i=1}^{C} \frac{n_i}{n} (m_i^{(k)} - m^{(k)})^2 \tag{1}$$

$$S_\omega^k = \frac{1}{n} \sum_{i=1}^{C} \sum_{x \in \omega_i} (x^{(k)} - m_i^{(k)})^2 \tag{2}$$

$$F_{(k)} = \frac{S_B^k}{S_\omega^k} \tag{3}$$

Define $x^{(k)}$ to denote the value of sample x on the feature k, $m_i^{(k)}$ to denote the mean of the value of the sample of the i th class on the k th feature, and $m^{(k)}$ to denote the mean of the value of the sample of all classes on the k th feature. Define the interclass variance of the feature k on the dataset as S_B^k. Define the intra-class variance of the feature k on the dataset as S_ω^k. Finally, we define the Fisher score of the feature k on the dataset as $F_{(k)}$.

3.2   LightGBM

In 2017, the Microsoft team proposed a new and efficient lightweight GDBT (gradient boosting decision tree) and named it LightGBM [14]. The process of LightGBM is as below:

Firstly, define the training data as $P = \{(x_1, y_1), \ldots, (x_n, y_n)\}$ and let the loss function be $L(y, \gamma)$, the learner is expressed as formula (4).

$$f_0(x) = \arg\min_{\gamma} \sum_{i-1}^{N} L(y_i, \gamma) \tag{4}$$

Then, calculate the negative gradient of each sample $i = 1, 2, \ldots, N$. The formula is as follow.

$$r_{mi} = -\left[\frac{\partial L(y_i, f(x_i))}{\partial f(x_i)}\right]_{f(x)=f_{m-1}(x)} \tag{5}$$

The leaf node area $R_{(jm)}$ of the m-th tree $f_m(x), j = 1, 2, \ldots, J, J$ is the number of leaf nodes of the regression tree, and the regression tree uses (x_i, r_{mi}) as the its training data. The best fit is as formula (6).

$$y_{jm} = arg\ min \sum_{x_i \in R_{jm}} L(y_i, f_{m-1}(x_i) + \gamma) \tag{6}$$

Finally, the strong learner is generated as formula (7).

$$f(x) = f_M(x) = f_0(x) + \sum_{m=1}^{M} \sum_{j=1}^{J} \gamma_{jm} I(x \in R_{jm}) \tag{7}$$

The improvements that LightGBM brings significantly reduce memory consumption and training time. Meanwhile, it improves accuracy compared to the previous classification models, making it very suitable for problems with large data such as attack type classification.

3.3 Naive Bayes Algorithm

The Naive Bayes algorithm is a classification algorithm based on the Bayes formula and probability statistics. Naive Bayes algorithm can be accurately expressed by the mathematical formula [15]. After proper preprocessing, Naive Bayes can compete with more advanced methods in the same field, such as decision tree and support vector machine. The Naive Bayes classifier has strong scalability. It only takes linear time to train maximum likelihood and does not need to spend much time on iterative approximation like other classifiers [16, 22]. The formula of Bayes is expressed as formula (8).

$$P(y|x_1, \ldots, x_n) = \frac{P(y)P(x_1, \ldots, x_n)}{P(x_1, \ldots, x_n)} \tag{8}$$

Define y to denote a category and define x_i to denote an associated feature vector. Then, use the naive assumption that each pair of features is independent of each other, so the formula (8) can be reduced to formula (9).

$$P(y|x_1, \ldots, x_n) = \frac{P(y) \prod_{i=1}^{n} P(x_i|y)}{P(x_1, \ldots, x_n)} \tag{9}$$

3.4 Ensemble Learning

Ensemble learning accomplishes learning tasks by combining multiple learners. This method combines the advantages of every learner to improve the classification accuracy and generalization ability and is one of the leading research directions in machine learning.

For classification tasks, Naive Bayes training and prediction have a high speed. Even the project is large-scale, its training and prediction is only a mathematical operation. LightGBM performs quickly and efficiently in multi-classification tasks and is difficult to overfit. This paper proposes an ensemble learning model by combining Naive Bayes learner and LightGBM learner. The process is shown as Fig. 1.

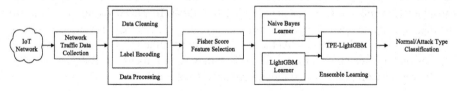

Fig. 1. Scheme of Proposed Model based on Ensemble Learning

Firstly, we use N-BaIoT dataset as the training dataset and the Fisher Score algorithm for feature. The Naive Bayes and LightGBM classifiers are trained in the form of stacking. Finally, we construct a meta classifier TPE-LightGBM (Tree-Structured Parzen Estimator) to process the final input and make the final type classification [17]. The optimization process of TPE is shown as below.

$$x^* = arg \min f(x) \tag{10}$$

In formula (10), $f(x)$ is the objective function, and x^* is the set of hyperparameters in the search space X that minimizes the objective function $f(x)$. [18] proposed a variant of the TPE algorithm for Bayes optimization to optimize the hyperparameters of the model by modeling $p(x|y)$ and $p(y)$ at the same time. $p(y)$ is the distribution of solutions, $p(x|y)$ represents the distribution of the parameter x when the solution is known. In addition, the optimization criterion EI (Expected Improvement) is used to guide the search of the configuration space. $p(x|y)$ is calculated as formula (11):

$$p(x|y) = \begin{cases} l(x) & y < y' \\ g(x) & y \geq y' \end{cases} \tag{11}$$

where y' is the already defined threshold, $l(x)$ denotes the density estimate for which the loss function of the observed value $x(i)$ is smaller than y', and $g(x)$ denotes the density composition for which the loss function of the observed value $x(i)$ is larger than y'.

4   Experiment and Results Analysis

4.1   Experiment Dataset

The N-BaIoT dataset used in this paper contains 117 features. Compared with the dataset used in previous studies, such as NSL-KDD and CICIDS, the number of data features is more, which makes the study more detailed. The dataset is generated by collecting traffic data through the port image of nine IoT devices. There are 555932 benign samples and 6506674 IoT botnet samples.

4.2 Experiment Results and Analysis

The evaluation of the experiment in this section is a multi-classification evaluation. Our work uses the following evaluation methods and indicators: multi-classification confusion matrix [19]. In this paper, the positive label represents the sample with the attack in the data set, while the benign sample is defined as the negative label. On the basis of accuracy, precision, recall, and F1 scores, the balanced accuracy [20] and MCC (Matthews Correlation Coefficient) [21, 23] are added. Balanced Accuracy can avoid making performance estimates that deviate from reality when the dataset has the problem of unbalanced data distribution. At the same time, the Matthews Correlation Coefficient focuses on a few categories that ordinary accuracy cannot focus on. Balance accuracy and Matthews Correlation Coefficient formula are as follows:

$$BalancedAccuracy = \frac{\frac{TP}{(TP+FN)} + \frac{TN}{(FP+TN)}}{2} \tag{12}$$

$$MCC = \frac{TP \times TN - FP \times FN}{\sqrt{(TP + FP)(TP + FN)(TN + FP)(TN + FN)}} \tag{13}$$

Model Performance Analysis on the Number of Features
The detection accuracy changes of the proposed model, Naive Bayes, Random Forest, Decision Tree, and Logistic Regression under different numbers of features are recorded, and the results are shown in Fig. 2.

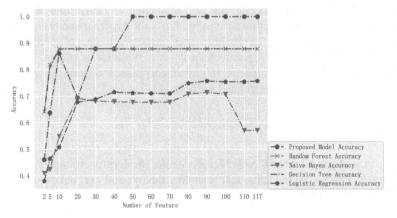

Fig. 2. Prediction accuracy *v.s.* number of features on N-BaIoT

The optimal performance details of the five models are represented in Table 1. In the Table 1, we can see the accuracy rate of our model is much higher than those of the other models, and is at least 12.13% higher than the second one.

Training and Predicting Time Analysis
The time consumption of training and prediction concerning the change in the number of features is shown in Figs. 3 and 4.

Table 1. Optimal Performance Details of Five Models

Model	Minimum Number of Features	Accuracy Rate
Proposed Model	50	99.97%
Random Forest	20	87.84%
Naive Bayes	90	71.45%
Decision Tree	110	87.84%
Logistic Regression	90	75.72%

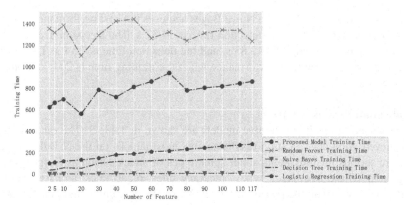

Fig. 3. Training time *v.s.* number of features on N-BaIoT

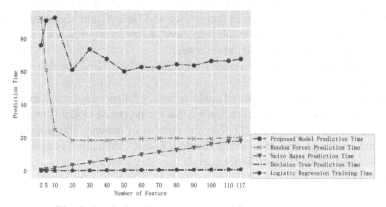

Fig. 4. Prediction time *v.s.* number of features on N-BaIoT

In Table 2, we can see the proposed model is not the least time-consuming in terms of training and prediction time, but it can achieve the highest accuracy rate. The training time of the proposed model 63.75% shorter than its slowest time, and the detection time is 53.11 s. The Random Forest performs best when the training time is 1109.93 s, and

Table 2. Shortest Training and Prediction Time of Five Models Based on Optimal Performance

Model	Training Time(s)	Prediction Time(s)
Proposed Model	538.9	53.11
Random Forest	1109.93	19.68
Naive Bayes	6.65	14.57
Decision Tree	142.85	0.54
Logistic Regression	244.39	0.87

the detection time is 19.68 s. The Naive Bayes achieves the best performance when the training time is 6.65 s, and the detection time is 14.57 s. The Decision Tree performs best when the training time is 142.85 s, and the detection time is 0.54 s. The Logistic Regression achieves the best performance when the training time is 244.39 s, and the detection time is 0.87 s.

Classification Results Analysis
The classification results of the five models are shown in Table 3. The random Forest has achieved good classification results against most attacks on the N-BaIoT dataset. There are serious misjudgments about some types of attacks, such as Gafgyt_tcp and Gafgyt_udp. These two attack types' accuracy rates, recall rates, and F1-scores are significantly lower than the proposed model. Naive Bayes training and prediction time are significantly lower than the other two models, but its classification performance could be better, and many attacks cannot be classified correctly. The proposed model also has advantages over Decision Tree and Logistic Regression, especially in categories where both have poor performance, such as Gafgyt_tcp and Gafgyt_udp. Combined with the distribution of the dataset, all the models are more or less error-prone for a few classes, but the proposed model is generally more robust.

The classification accuracy, balanced accuracy and MCC of the five models are shown in Table 4.

It can be seen that: (1) the proposed model accuracy, balanced accuracy and MCC are better than those of the other four, indicating that the proposed model is more efficient and robust to the minority class; (2) With any number of features, the proposed model training and prediction time is less than Random Forest. Although it is slower than the others, its classification is much better than all the other models.

Table 3. Proposed Model Classification Results

Types of attack	Precision	Recall	F1-score
Proposed Model/Random Forest/Naive Bayes/Decision Tree/Logistic Regression			
Gafgyt_combo	1/0.74/1/1/0.81	1/0.88/1/1/0.75	1/0.81/1/1/0.78
Gafgyt_junk	1/0.52/1/1/0.58	1/0.09/1/1/0.66	1/0.15/1/1/0.62
Gafgyt_scan	1/0.84/1/1/0.97	1/1/1/1/0.98	1/0.91/1/1/0.97
Gafgyt_tcp	1/0.09/0.98/0.97/0.09	1/0/0/0/0	1/0/0/0/0
Gafgyt_udp	1/0.52/0.52/0.52/0.52	1/1/1/1/1	1/0.69/0.69/0.69/0.69
Mirai_ack	1/0.58/1/1/0.77	1/0.29/1/1/0.4	1/0.39/1/1/0.52
Mirai_scan	1/0.99/1/1/0.98	1/1/1/1/0.99	1/0.99/1/1/0.98
Mirai_syn	1/0.86/1/1/1	1/0.99/1/1/0.98	1/0.92/1/1/0.99
Mirai_udp	1/0.62/1/1/0.71	1/0.89/1/1/0.93	1/0.73/1/1/0.81
Mirai_plainudp	1/0.99/1/1/0.87	1/0.61/1/1/0.75	1/0.75/1/1/0.8
Gafgyt_scan	1/1/1/1/0.99	1/0.91/1/1/0.99	1/0.95/1/1/0.99
Benign	1/0.74/1/1/0.81	1/0.88/1/1/0.75	1/0.81/1/1/0.78

Table 4. Classification accuracy, balanced accuracy and Matthews correlation coefficient

Types of Models	Accuracy	Balanced Accuracy	MCC
Proposed Mode	99.97%	99.97%	99.95%
Random Forest	87.84%	90.90%	87.81%
Naive Bayes	71.45%	69.56%	69.25%
Decision Tree	87.84%	90.91%	87.82%
Logistic Regression	75.73%	76.59%	74.09%

5   Conclusion

Aiming at the problem of botnet attack detection and classification in IoT network, this paper proposes an IoT botnet attack detection and classification model based on feature selection and ensemble learning. This model can effectively reduce the training and detection time of the model by using feature selection, which can effectively reduce the workload of detecting botnet attacks for IoT devices with limited hardware. Then, ensemble learning is adopted to enhance the model's robustness and performance. Finally, the proposed model is compared with the Random Forest, Naive Bayes, Decision Tree and Logistic Regression. Experimental results show that the proposed model can achieve a detection rate of 99.97% and shorten the training time by 63.75%. Due to the high heterogeneity and complexity of the real IoT network environment and strict requirements for low power consumption, we should also consider building a general classification model with less training and prediction time and high prediction efficiency.

References

1. Zhou, W., et al.: The effect of IoT new features on security and privacy: new threats, existing solutions, and challenges yet to be solved. IEEE Internet Things J. **6**(2), 1606–1616 (2019)
2. https://www.nsfocus.com.cn/html/2022/136_0524/184.html (2022)
3. Zarpelão, B.B., et al.: A survey of intrusion detection in Internet of Things. J. Netw. Comput. Appl. **84**, 25–37 (2017)
4. Lu, H., Wang, T., Xu, X., Wang, T.: Cognitive memory-guided autoencoder for effective intrusion detection in internet of things. IEEE Trans. Ind. Inf. **18**(5), 3358–3366 (2022)
5. Tang, C., Luktarhan, N., Zhao, Y.: An efficient intrusion detection method based on LightGBM and Autoencoder. Symmetry **12**(9), 1458 (2020)
6. Hussain, F., et al.: A two-fold machine learning approach to prevent and detect IoT botnet attacks. IEEE Access **9**, 163412–163430 (2021)
7. Desai, M.G., Shi, Y., Suo, K.: A hybrid approach for IoT botnet attack detection. In: 2021 IEEE 12th Annual Information Technology, Electronics and Mobile Communication Conference (IEMCON). IEEE (2021)
8. Tran, T.C., Tran, K.D.: Machine Learning for Multi-Classification of Botnets Attacks. In: 2022 16th International Conference on Ubiquitous Information Management and Communication (IMCOM). IEEE (2022)
9. Pranav, P.R.K., et al.: Detection of Botnets in IoT Networks using Graph Theory and Machine Learning. In: 2022 6th International Conference on Trends in Electronics and Informatics (ICOEI). IEEE (2022)
10. Meidan, Y., et al.: N-baiot—network-based detection of iot botnet attacks using deep autoencoders. IEEE Pervasive Comput. **17**(3), 12–22 (2018)
11. Nguyen, H.-T., Ngo, Q.-D., Le, V.-H.: IoT botnet detection approach based on PSI graph and DGCNN classifier. In: 2018 IEEE international conference on information communication and signal processing (ICICSP). IEEE (2018)
12. McDermott, C.D., Majdani, F., Petrovski. A.V.: Botnet detection in the internet of things using deep learning approaches. In: 2018 international joint conference on neural networks (IJCNN). IEEE (2018)
13. Singh, B., Singh Sankhwar, J., Prakash Vyas, O.: Optimization of feature selection method for high dimensional data using fisher score and minimum spanning tree. In: 2014 annual IEEE India conference (INDICON). IEEE (2014)
14. Ke, G., et al. Lightgbm: A highly efficient gradient boosting decision tree. In: Advances in Neural Information Processing Systems, vol. 30 (2017)
15. Zhang, H., et al.: Textual and visual content-based anti-phishing: a Bayesian approach. IEEE Trans. Neural Netw. **22**(10), 1532–1546 (2011)
16. Bootkrajang, J., Chaijaruwanich, J.: Towards an improved label noise proportion estimation in small data: a Bayesian approach. Int. J. Mach. Learn. Cybern. **13**, 851–867 (2021)
17. Bergstra, J., et al.: Algorithms for hyper-parameter optimization. Advances in neural information processing systems, 24 (2011)
18. Bergstra, J., Bengio, Y.: Random search for hyper-parameter optimization. J. Mach. Learn. Res. **13**(2), 281–305d (2012)
19. Tran, T.C., Dang, T.K.: Machine learning for prediction of imbalanced data: Credit fraud detection. In: 2021 15th International Conference on Ubiquitous Information Management and Communication (IMCOM). IEEE (2021)

20. Luque, A., et al.: The impact of class imbalance in classification performance metrics based on the binary confusion matrix. Pattern Recognit. **91**, 216–231 (2019)
21. Chicco, D., Jurman, G.: The advantages of the Matthews correlation coefficient (MCC) over F1 score and accuracy in binary classification evaluation. BMC Genomics **21**, 6 (2020)
22. Chen, Z., Lu, H., Tian, S., et al.: Construction of a hierarchical feature enhancement network and its application in fault recognition. IEEE Trans. Industr. Inf. **17**(7), 4827–4836 (2020)
23. Teng, Y., Lu, H., Li, Y., et al.: Multidimensional deformable object manipulation based on DN-transporter networks. IEEE Trans. Intell. Transp. Syst. **24**(4), 4532–4540 (2022)

STGAN: Sonar Image Despeckling Method Utilizing GAN and Transformer

Xin Zhou, Kun Tian$^{(\boxtimes)}$, and Zihan Zhou

Dalian Maritime University, Dalian 116000, Liaoning, China
30397175@qq.com

Abstract. This study presents an innovative method, denoted as STGAN, aimed at enhancing the quality of sonar images by addressing the pervasive issue of speckle noise. The proposed approach leverages a generative adversarial network framework, wherein Transformer blocks are harnessed to capture global features, while Convolution blocks focus on extracting local features within both the generator and discriminator architectures. Through adversarial training, STGAN acquires a holistic understanding of feature distributions from the training data, resulting in the production of high-fidelity denoised images. A novel loss function is introduced, amalgamating adversarial loss, content preservation, local texture style, and global similarity considerations. This multifaceted loss function effectively mitigates image distortion and information loss inherent in feature extraction. Empirical evaluations, conducted on synthetic speckle noise images and authentic sonar data, substantiate STGAN's remarkable denoising capabilities, showcasing performance enhancements of approximately 10.70%–58.73% and 2.74%–22.97%, respectively, over established baseline methods.

Keywords: Sonar image · Speckle denoising · Generative Adversarial Networks · Transformer

1 Introduction

The rapid advancement of ocean engineering has led to the successful application of underwater sonar imaging systems in deep-sea operations. These systems significantly contribute to enhancing our understanding of the marine environment and facilitating exploration. They play pivotal roles in offshore defense, marine resource investigation, and the development of the marine economy. However, underwater sonar imaging encounters challenges due to the complex and diverse underwater conditions, resulting in issues such as poor visualization, low resolution, weak texture, and blurred edges in the final images. Among these challenges, speckle noise [1] significantly impacts sonar images.

Existing methods aimed at removing speckle noise from sonar images can be categorized into conventional despeckling approaches and deep learning-based despeckling methods. PPB formulates the denoising procedure as a weighted

H. Lu and J. Cai (Eds.): ISAIR 2023, CCIS 1998, pp. 56–67, 2024.
https://doi.org/10.1007/978-981-99-9109-9_6

maximum likelihood estimation problem. It leverages the similarity between noisy patches within the sonar image and the resemblance between patches obtained from prior iterations. The weights used are determined through a data-driven approach and can be iteratively refined based on the comparison between noisy patches and those derived from preceding estimates. This iterative process contributes to enhancing the denoising performance. BM3D [3] is a novel image denoising approach based on transform domain enhanced sparse representation. The decoupling algorithm, derived from the Nash equilibrium point formula, exhibits the most favorable numerical and visual effects. It has also demonstrated promising outcomes when applied to sonar images, showcasing proficient speckle denoising performance. Deep learning-based methods also exhibit promising despeckling performance. Neighbor2Neighbor [4] employs a random neighborhood subsampler for generating training image pairs. A denoising network is trained on the generated subsampled training pairs, utilizing a regularization term as an additional loss for improved performance. SAR-CNN [5] generates clean images via multi-temporal fusion. It employs residual learning strategies and discriminative model learning for speckle denoising. Zhou et al. [6] proposed a self-supervised denoising method for sonar images without requiring high-quality reference images. This method employs a single sonar image for self-supervised denoising. The approach adjusts the denoising model's parameters to address the challenge of obtaining high-quality reference images during the sonar image denoising process. Chen et al. [7] introduced the ANLResNet network for sonar image denoising, which combines SRResNet and non-local blocks of asymmetrical pyramids to tackle speckle noise in sonar images, achieving impressive visual outcomes. A Transformer-based speckle denoising network [8] pioneers the application of the Transformer model to the task of speckle denoising. It introduces a Transformer-based speckle denoising network, attaining effective denoising outcomes.

Traditional image denoising methods [2,3] are computationally complex and not highly tailored to the specific noise characteristics of sonar images. Sonar image denoising approaches [4–8] based on convolutional neural networks (CNN) typically focus solely on modeling the relationship between adjacent pixels, potentially resulting in the loss of global information. To address the limitations of the aforementioned denoising methods and to incorporate both global and local (spatial) features, this paper proposes a novel Transformer-based sonar image enhancement model referred to as STGAN. The primary contributions of this study are outlined below:

(1) A multi-scale local-to-global feature learning is performed on the input image to obtain comprehensive feature information. This is achieved by integrating Transformer and Convolution blocks into both the generator network and the discriminator network of STGAN, rather than solely decomposing the image into local windows.

(2) A new loss function is designed to combine image content, local texture style, and global similarity, aiming to better preserve the relationship mapping

between local and global information, and reduce information loss during
feature transfer.

(3) Comprehensive comparative experiments have been conducted on synthetic
noise images and real sonar images. The results show that STGAN achieves
state-of-the-art denoising performance on both synthetic noise images and
real sonar images.

In this paper, the architecture and loss function of STGAN are introduced in
detail in Sect. 2. Extensive experiments and visualization results are presented
in Sect. 3 to verify the denoising performance of STGAN. Section 4 summarizes
our work in this paper and proposes future directions for research.

2   Proposed Method

2.1   Sonar Image Noise Simulation

This paper considers that sonar images are affected by multiplicative speckle
noise during the imaging process. The observed relationship between a noisy
image Y with multiplicative speckle noise N and a clean image X is as follows:

$$Y = XN \tag{1}$$

where Y is the noisy image, X is the clean image, and N is the corresponding
speckle noise, the goal of this paper is to eliminate the speckle noise N from Y
and restore the clean image X.

2.2   Network Architecture of STGAN

STGAN comprises a generator and a discriminator. Given a noisy image Y, the
generator of STGAN produces a denoised image G. Subsequently, the discriminator of STGAN distinguishes the generated image G from the clean image
X, thereby refining the quality of denoised sonar images through adversarial
training.

Inspired by Restormer [9], the generator network architecture of STGAN is
depicted in Fig. 1. There are three essential steps to generate the denoised image
G from the input noisy image Y:

(1) The noisy image Y acquires low-level shallow features Y_o through a deep convolutional layer with a kernel size of 3×3. Subsequently, Y_o derives high-level
features Y_s through an encoder. The encoder is composed of three layers of
Transformer blocks and three downsampling operations. The initial encoding
layer incorporates 8 Transformer blocks, while the subsequent encoding layers have a decreasing number of Transformer blocks. The spatial dimensions
of the feature maps in each encoder layer progressively decrease through the
downsampling operation, while concurrently enhancing their channel capacity.

(2) The encoder and decoder are connected through a Transformer layer comprising 2 Transformer blocks, alongside a deep convolutional layer with a kernel size of 3 × 3. The Transformer layer further extracts high-level global intricate features, while the convolutional layer captures local intricate features from Y_s.

(3) The decoder, which is utilized to fuse multi-scale features and restore the image, comprises three decoding groups that correspond to the encoder. Each decoding group encompasses an up-sampling layer to reduce channel capacity by half and double the size of the feature map, a skip layer to merge deep and shallow features via channel-wise concatenation operation, a 1 × 1 convolutional layer to reduce the channel count of the feature map outputted by the skip layer, and a Transformer block layer to capture global fine features. The resulting feature map, denoted as Y_d, from the decoder is fed into a convolutional layer, and the output features are combined with the noisy image Y to generate an image G. The Transformer structure is borrowed from Restormer [9]. This structure, depicted in Fig. 2, ensures the network effectively processes high-resolution images and focuses on finer image attributes.

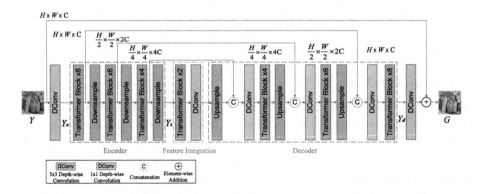

Fig. 1. The Generator Network Architecture of STGAN.

The discriminator of STGAN distinguishes the generated image G from the clean image X, as illustrated in Fig. 3. The discriminator comprises four 3 × 3 deep convolutional layers and two layers of Transformer blocks. The input image initially passes through a layer of Transformer blocks to extract shallow global features. Subsequently, it acquires deep local features through three deep convolutional layers. Finally, another layer of Transformer blocks fuses the feature maps, and the final discrimination result is obtained by applying a sigmoid activation function. Following each convolutional layer, a layer normalization operation [10] is applied to prevent overfitting. Additionally, a non-linear activation function, LeakyReLU [11], is utilized to avoid the vanishing gradient issue and retain some of the negative gradient information to prevent complete loss.

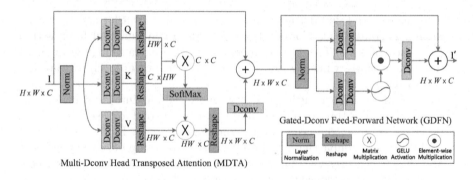

Fig. 2. The internal structure of the Transformer Block [9].

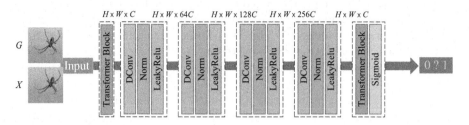

Fig. 3. Discriminator Network Architecture of STGAN.

2.3   Loss Function

In STGAN, three factors are correlated to quantify perceptual image quality within the loss function: Global Similarity, Image Content, and Local Texture and Style.

Global Similarity. Global similarity measures the similarity between two images from a global perspective to detect the degree of image distortion. Since the L1 loss doesn't easily introduce blurriness, and multiplicative speckle noise is more challenging to address than additive noise, we simplify the multiplicative noise model into an additive model through logarithmic transformation. This approach better preserves the original information while removing noise, as demonstrated in Formula 2:

$$L_{\mathrm{GS}}(G) = \mathbb{E}_{X,Y}\left[\|\log(X) - \log(G(Y))\|_1\right] \tag{2}$$

where X represents the clean reference image and G denotes the output of the generator.

Image Content. Image content loss can enhance the ability to describe and distinguish image details and edge information. The loss between the high-level features extracted by the generator is used to measure the content similarity between images, encouraging the generator to produce images that closely resemble the content of the reference image, as shown in Eq. 3:

$$L_{\mathrm{IC}}(G) = \mathbb{E}_{X,Y}[\| X - G(Y) \|_2] \tag{3}$$

Local Texture and Style. Local texture and style describe the surface properties of the scene corresponding to the image or image area and preserve the image's authenticity. As WGAN-GP effectively captures high-frequency information associated with local texture and style [12], we employ a conditional adversarial loss to fine-tune both the generator and discriminator adversarially while ensuring the coherence of local texture and style information in sonar images. The adversarial loss function is expressed as Eq. 4:

$$L_{\mathrm{WGAN\text{-}GP}}(G, D) = \mathbb{E}_{\tilde{x} \sim P_g}[D(\tilde{x})] - \mathbb{E}_{x \sim P_r}[D(x)]$$
$$+ \lambda \mathbb{E}_{\hat{x} \sim P_{\hat{x}}}\left[(\| \nabla_{\hat{x}} D(\hat{x}) \|_2 - 1)^2\right] \tag{4}$$

where the generator G aims to minimize the loss function while the discriminator D aims to maximize it, P_r is the data distribution, P_g is the model distribution implicitly defined by $\tilde{x} = G(Y, N)$, $P_{\hat{x}}$ denotes a uniform sampling along straight lines between pairs of points sampled from the data distribution P_r and the generator distribution P_g, and $\lambda = 10$ is the hyper-parameter. In general, this paper employs Eq. 5 as the loss function for model training:

$$L = L_{\mathrm{WGAN\text{-}GP}} + \lambda_1 L_{\mathrm{GS}} + \lambda_2 L_{\mathrm{IC}} \tag{5}$$

where λ_1 and λ_2 are hyperparameters.

3 Experimental Evaluation

3.1 Setting up

We randomly sampled 5500 different types of natural optical grayscale images with a size of 128×128 from the ImageNet dataset [13] and synthesized speckle noise images by adding speckle noise following a gamma distribution. Among them, 4500 images were randomly selected for the training set, 500 for validation, and 500 for testing. The evaluation metrics included PSNR, SSIM, and MGHC [14]. For denoising real sonar noise images, this paper randomly selected 500 uniform areas of size 20×20 with an average standard deviation of 17.011 from 500 images in the ARIS Explorer 3000 dataset [15] as the test set. The evaluation metrics included ENL, SSI, SMPI [16], and MSD (Mean Standard Deviation of Uniform Area). Additionally, this paper employed the Faster RCNN image target detection model to detect denoised real sonar images. It randomly selected 1457 images from the [15] dataset for training and 411 images for testing. Common object detection standard metrics [17] were used, namely Average Precision (AP), AP at an IOU threshold of 0.5 (AP50), and AP at an IOU

Table 1. Despeckling performance of different methods on optical images.

Method	PSNR (↑)	SSIM (↑)	MGHC (↑)
PPB [2]	16.15	0.302	0.536
BM3D [3]	19.83	0.499	0.525
NBR2NBR [4]	21.12	<u>0.634</u>	0.535
SAR-CNN [5]	22.46	0.493	<u>0.659</u>
SAR-Transformer [8]	<u>23.16</u>	0.612	0.579
SID-TGAN (* this paper)	**25.63**	**0.695**	**0.760**

Table 2. Despeckling performance of different methods on sonar images.

Method	ENL (↑)	SSI (↓)	SMPI (↓)	MSD (↓)
PPB [2]	<u>1036.309</u>	0.233	19.535	6.901
BM3D [3]	432.300	0.237	<u>0.524</u>	4.201
NBR2NBR [4]	410.702	0.246	1.688	3.771
SAR-CNN [5]	630.179	0.192	1.503	3.602
SAR-Transformer [8]	739.520	<u>0.167</u>	1.477	<u>3.051</u>
SID-TGAN (* this paper)	**3454.513**	**0.087**	**0.445**	**1.514**

threshold of 0.75 (AP75). During training, the weights 1 and 2 in Eq. 5 were set to 0.5 and 1, and the number of epochs was set to 150. This paper compares the performance of STGAN with PPB [2], BM3D [3], Neighbor2Neighbor [4], SAR-CNN [5], and SAR-Transformer [8]. All networks utilize the same dataset and experimental environment.

3.2 Comparative Experiment

In the synthetic speckle noise image denoising results presented in Table 1, the best and second-best results are highlighted using bold and underlined text, respectively. It is evident that the proposed method achieves the highest values for the PSNR, SSIM, and MGHC metrics. Figure 4 visually illustrates the outcomes of each method in terms of removing synthetic speckle noise. Figure 5 provides an intuitive comparison of the degree of concurrence between image gray histograms before and after applying each denoising method. The x-axis represents pixel values, while the y-axis represents the count of pixel values. The reference image is depicted by the red line, and the image after denoising with each method is shown using the blue line.

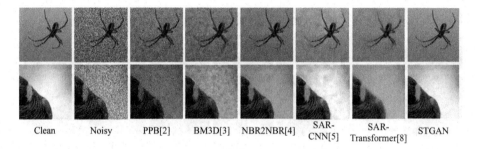

Clean   Noisy   PPB[2]   BM3D[3]   NBR2NBR[4]   SAR-CNN[5]   SAR-Transformer[8]   STGAN

Fig. 4. Visual Comparison of Synthetic Speckle Noise Removal Performance.

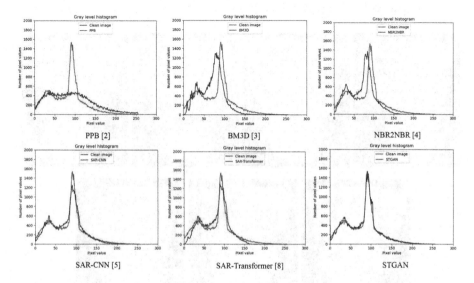

Fig. 5. Comparison of gray histogram coincidence before and after image denoising. (Color figure online)

Regarding the experimental outcomes for real sonar image denoising, as shown in Table 2, this paper's model has demonstrated superior performance in speckle removal and detection accuracy. Figure 6 displays a visual comparison of despeckling results for each method applied to real sonar images. The first row illustrates the overall despeckling effect, while the second row provides detailed denoising results for homogeneous regions outlined by the red box in the first row. The detection outcomes for sonar images containing specific items post-denoising are documented in Table 3. Figure 7 visually represents the detection results from Table 3. The green box indicates the actual item's location, the yellow box represents the model's correct prediction, and the red box indicates an incorrect prediction by the model. It is evident that this paper's model has achieved superior denoising performance both quantitatively and visually.

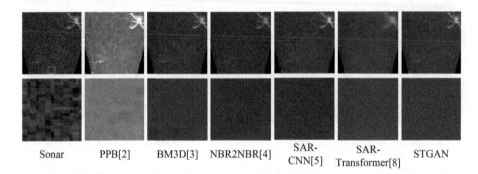

| Sonar | PPB[2] | BM3D[3] | NBR2NBR[4] | SAR-CNN[5] | SAR-Transformer[8] | STGAN |

Fig. 6. Visual comparison of real speckle noise removal performance.

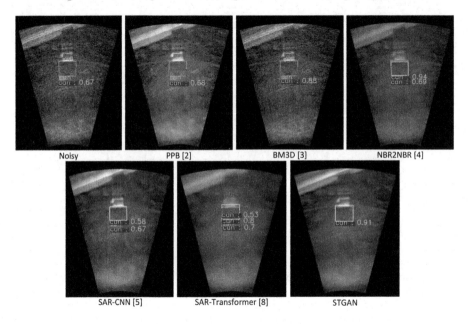

Fig. 7. Visual comparison of target detection results.

3.3   Ablation Experiment Results

Based on the network consisting of solely convolutional operations, we conduct ablation experiments to assess the integration of each network component into the Transformer module and the various components of the loss function. Analyzing the results presented in Table 4, it becomes evident that the incorporation of the Transformer module can compensate for the limitations of the convolutional operation and significantly enhance the denoising capability of the network.

Similarly, we conducted ablation experiments on the composition of the loss functions. The results in Table 5 demonstrate that incorporating the global similarity loss function (L_{GS}) into the loss function not only effectively removes noise

Table 3. Object detection accuracy on sonar images using different despeckling methods.

Method	mAP (↑)	mAP@50 (↑)	mAP@75 (↑)
No-despeckling	0.584	0.937	0.644
PPB [2]	0.588	0.940	0.654
BM3D [3]	0.595	0.941	0.676
NBR2NBR [4]	0.556	0.910	0.596
SAR-CNN [5]	0.605	0.942	0.682
SAR-Transformer [8]	0.619	0.956	0.693
SID-TGAN (* this paper)	**0.622**	**0.958**	**0.712**

Table 4. Despeckling performance of STGAN with or without transformer module, where D and G are the abbreviations for the discriminator and generator of STGAN.

Model	Transformer	PSNR (↑)	SSIM (↑)	SSI (↓)	SMPI(↓)
WGAN [12]	w/o	23.01	0.524	0.397	5.243
STGAN	Dw Gw/o	23.27	0.563	0.346	5.017
	Gw Dw/o	25.26	0.639	0.101	0.591
	Gw & Dw	**25.63**	**0.695**	**0.087**	**0.445**

but also more efficiently preserves global information, significantly enhancing the performance of speckle removal. Simultaneously, by introducing the image content loss function (L_{IC}), we further improve the image quality, retain original details, and effectively prevent information loss. The optimization process of the overall loss function involves adversarial interactions between the generator and discriminator, and this optimization process fully takes into account the impact of image detail content and global similarity during the adversarial process, leading to outstanding achievements in denoising performance.

Table 5. Despeckling performance of STGAN with different loss functions.

Loss Function	PSNR (↑)	SSIM (↑)	SSI (↓)	SMPI (↓)
$L_{WGAN\text{-}GP}$	14.15	0.253	0.976	20.113
$L_{WGAN\text{-}GP} + L_{GS}$	24.48	0.644	0.124	0.563
$L_{WGAN\text{-}GP} + L_{IC}$	25.20	0.665	0.095	0.543
$L_{WGAN\text{-}GP} + L_{IC} + L_{GS}$	**25.63**	**0.695**	**0.087**	**0.445**

4   Conclusion

Overall, the proposed STGAN method effectively eliminates speckle noise in sonar images, offering a feasible solution to enhance the quality of sonar images. This bears great significance for the utilization of sonar images in domains such as ocean exploration and medical imaging. In the future, additional research could explore ways to further optimize the STGAN method for improved performance in a wider range of scenarios, thereby advancing the progress of sonar image denoising technology.

References

1. Huo, G., Yang, S.X., Li, Q., Zhou, Y.: A robust and fast method for side scan sonar image segmentation using nonlocal Despeckling and active contour model. IEEE Trans. Cybern. **47**(4), 855–872 (2017). https://doi.org/10.1109/TCYB.2016. 2530786
2. Deledalle, C.A., Denis, L., Tupin, F.: Iterative weighted maximum likelihood denoising with probabilistic patch-based weights. IEEE Trans. Image Process. **18**(12), 2661–2672 (2009)
3. Danielyan, A., Katkovnik, V., Egiazarian, K.: BM3D frames and variational image deblurring. IEEE Trans. Image Process. **21**(4), 1715–1728 (2011)
4. Huang, T., Zhang, Y., Huang, Y., Wang, L., Huang, T.: Neighbor2neighbor: self-supervised denoising from single noisy images. In: Proceedings of the IEEE/CVF Conference on Computer Vision and Pattern Recognition, pp. 13730–13739 (2021)
5. Chierchia, G., Cozzolino, D., Poggi, G., Verdoliva, L.: SAR image despeckling through convolutional neural networks. In: 2017 IEEE International Geoscience and Remote Sensing Symposium (IGARSS), pp. 5438–5441. IEEE (2017)
6. Zhou, X., Yu, C., Yuan, X., Luo, C: Deep denoising method for side scan sonar images without high-quality reference data. In: 2022 2nd International Conference on Computer, Control and Robotics (ICCCR), pp. 241–245. IEEE (2022)
7. Chen, P., Xu, Z., Zhao, D., Guo, X.: ANLResNet network-based speckle denoising method for forward-looking sonar images. Small Micro Comput. Syst. **43**(02), 355–361 (2022)
8. Perera, M.V., Bandara, W.G.C., Valanarasu, J.M.J., Fernando, C.: Transformer-based SAR image despeckling. arXiv preprint arXiv:2201.09355 (2022)
9. Zamir, S.W., Khan, S., Hanif, M.A., Shah, M.: Restormer: efficient transformer for high-resolution image restoration. In: Proceedings of the IEEE/CVF Conference on Computer Vision and Pattern Recognition, pp. 10017–10026 (2022)
10. Ba, J.L., Kiros, J.R., Hinton, G.E.: Layer normalization. arXiv preprint arXiv:1607.06450 (2016)
11. Zhang, X., Zou, Y., Shi, W.: Dilated convolution neural network with LeakyReLU for environmental sound classification. In: 2017 22nd International Conference on Digital Signal Processing (DSP), pp. 1–5 (2017)
12. Isola, P., Zhu, J.-Y., Zhou, T., Efros, A.A.: Image-to-image translation with conditional adversarial networks. In: Proceedings of the IEEE Conference on Computer Vision and Pattern Recognition, pp. 1125–1134 (2017)
13. Deng, J., Dong, W., Socher, R., Li, L.-J., Li, K., Fei-Fei, L.: ImageNet: a large-scale hierarchical image database. In: 2009 IEEE Conference on Computer Vision and Pattern Recognition, pp. 248–255 (2009)

14. Shuang, Z.: Image similarity computation by using histogram method. Bull. Survey. Mapp. (12), 96–100 (2018)

15. Singh, D., Valdenegro-Toro, M.: The marine debris dataset for forward-looking sonar semantic segmentation. In: Proceedings of the IEEE/CVF International Conference on Computer Vision, pp. 3741–3749 (2021)

16. James, R., Supriya, M.H.: Blind estimation of single look side scan sonar image from the observation model. Procedia Comput. Sci. **93**, 336–343 (2016)

17. Lin, T. Y., Goyal, P., Girshick, R., He, K., Dollár, P.: Focal loss for dense object detection. In: Proceedings of the IEEE International Conference on Computer Vision, pp. 2980–2988 (2017)

Teacher Classroom Behavior Detection Based on a Human Pose Estimation Algorithm

Yong Wang[1], Haidong Hu[1], and Hao Gao[2]([✉])

[1] Beijing Institute of Control Engineering, Beijing, China
[2] Nanjing University of Posts and Communications, Nanjing, China
tsgaohao@gmail.com

Abstract. Teachers' classroom behavior testing can help the understand the learning situation of students, feedback the teaching effect, and formulate corresponding measures to help. Traditional evaluation methods rely on manual testing, which is time-consuming and lacks objectivity. This article suggests a new approach to analyze the behavior of teachers by using the human skeleton posture. This method first uses the popular human posture gesture estimation technology to obtain the skeleton joint node of the teacher in the teaching process, and then remove several of the joint nodes that have a weaker effect on the classification of teachers in class. Finally, a convolutional neural network was designed to classify the teacher's behavior based on the skeleton joint nodes and confidence obtained from processing the input. The experimental results show that the effectiveness of the method helps the dynamic management and evaluation of classroom teachers' behavior.

Keywords: Teacher behavior analysis · pose estimation · deep learning

1 Introduction

In the process of classroom learning, teachers often play a leading role in guiding students to engage in effective learning [1]. However, in previous classroom teaching analyses, the focus has often been placed on the students' classroom performance, while the behavior of teachers has been neglected [2, 3]. In fact, the rationality of the teacher's behavior in classroom teaching plays an important role in the development of the class. Traditional evaluation of teachers' classroom behavior often involves experienced teachers observing new teachers' overall performance during trial teaching and conducting scoring evaluations [4]. Although this method is simple and straightforward, it often involves subjective opinions from the teacher and cannot effectively track the teacher's classroom behavior in the long term. In addition, during the process of observation, it may not be possible to accurately evaluate the teacher's usual performance in the classroom. Based on the analysis, this method is inefficient, time-consuming, subjective, and must be completed by professionals with relevant background knowledge. The use of artificial intelligence to automate and batch real-time detection of teachers' behavior in the classroom can help teachers to discover shortcomings in classroom teaching and make timely improvements. This can also address the lag in optimizing their own teaching models based on evaluations.

H. Lu and J. Cai (Eds.): ISAIR 2023, CCIS 1998, pp. 68–75, 2024.
https://doi.org/10.1007/978-981-99-9109-9_7

With the rapid development of artificial intelligence technology, computer vision has become a widely-used tool in various fields [6–8]. This has resulted in an increase in its business applications and market size. Additionally, the integration of multiple fields has become a prominent feature of artificial intelligence. As a result, combining artificial intelligence with education has become an area of focus for research [5], offering new possibilities for traditional education. The advancement of education technology has led to the installation of multimedia devices such as computers, displays, and cameras in many classrooms. This has resulted in the availability of video data based on classroom live broadcasts and recordings, which provides a large amount of data support in the field of artificial intelligence. This has led to the development of new methods for evaluating teacher behavior, which is constantly evolving with the advancements in the field.

This article conducts behavioral videos of teachers based on the body's gesture estimation technology to detect the classroom videos taught by teachers to achieve automated testing teachers' classroom behavior. It helps teachers to carry out after-school reflection, timely discover the shortcomings in the teaching process, and build an intelligent classroom testing system. The main work is:

1) According to the relevant theories of classroom teacher behavior analysis, establish a set of visual human action behavior detection mode, mainly through human posture estimation algorithms, obtain teachers' skeleton information and eliminate redundant information.
2) For the joint nodes of the teacher's classroom skeleton, remove several joint nodes that have a weak impact on classifying the teacher's classroom behavior. Input the coordinates and confidence of the remaining joint nodes that have a greater impact on the movement into the classification network, and classify the teacher's behavior during class into five common actions.

The rest of this article is as follows. The second section introduces the proposed method. The third section provides experimental results, and conclusions are given.

2 Our Approach

2.1 Classification of Teacher Behavior

In recent years, there has been an increasing amount of research on using machines to replace human labor in recognizing teacher's teaching status. However, there is a lack of research on the theory of new technology action recognition and analysis, and the number of action categories with high recognition rates is very limited. Flanders interaction analysis (FLAS) [9] is the most detailed and mature methods for studying classroom teacher-student interaction, and it is still the most frequently used research tool for empirical research on teacher-student interaction. But FLAC contains a large number of categories that cannot be recognized by images alone. For teacher action recognition, we need a behavior framework based on information expression to describe which information can be recognized and analyzed, and then a classification framework based on specific analysis requirements.

S-T analysis method, which stands for Student-Teacher analysis method, is suitable for the analysis of teacher-student interaction behavior during classroom teaching process, and is currently a more mature teaching analysis method. It records, processes and analyzes the data during teaching process and uses the obtained information to evaluate and improve the teaching process. This method can avoid too many subjective factors in teaching evaluation and provide quantitative and objective guidance for classroom evaluation.

Table 1. S-T teacher behavior classification table

	Teacher behavior
Linguistic activity	Commentary, Questioning, Roll call, Evaluate, Feedback
Nonlinguistic activity	Demonstration, Writing on the blackboard, Media display

The traditional S-T behavior classification table is shown in the Table 1, and the main problem with this classification method is that it is difficult to distinguish language behaviors from images, such as "questioning," "commentary," and "evaluation" in teacher behavior. In order to avoid such problems as much as possible, we have modified some behaviors based on the original classification, and this study starts from the perspective of teachers, hoping to reflect the overall situation of teacher's teaching through teacher behavior and make new behaviors more practical for image recognition.

Finally, the teacher's teaching action classification table is determined as shown in the Table 2 below.

Table 2. Action classification description

Teacher action	Expression of action
Teaching	The eyes are facing forward, and the body posture will show different postures according to the teacher's habits
blackboard-writing	The whole body is facing backwards, and the right hand is raised
Watch podium	Similar to operating a computer, the head looks down, and the body parts are the same as lecturing
Watch blackboard	The head will look to the left and right, and the body posture will be the same as the lecture
Show	Head facing students or presenting content, hands raised outward

According to the existing data, this paper changes the s-t teacher behavior table, and classifies the teacher's actions into the above five categories for nonverbal behaviors.

2.2   Skeleton Joint Point Extraction

There are two methods for estimating human body posture: bottom-up and top-down [10, 15]. The bottom-up method detects all key points in an image and connects them to form a complete posture. The top-down method detects local parts first, then infers the posture through connections. The top-down approach has advantages in accuracy, efficiency, and robustness. It avoids false positives and negatives and requires less computation since it only detects local parts. It is adaptable to different postures and actions and can handle special cases such as occlusion and complex backgrounds more easily.

We use a top-down approach for human pose estimation in the behavior analysis of teachers in a classroom. Our focus is on detecting the teacher's behavior while ignoring other information to improve accuracy. We employed the HRNet [11] algorithm. HRNet is the most classic top-down attitude detection method, which originally used Faster R-CNN [12] for object detection, but we replaced it with YOLOv7 [14] to improve detection accuracy. HRNet is trained on the COCO Human Pose Estimation dataset [13, 16], which includes over 130,000 images annotated with keypoints on the human body. We use 13 keypoints to detect the teacher's upper body movements on the platform (Fig. 1).

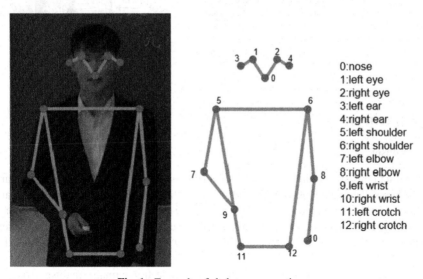

Fig. 1.   Example of skeleton connection.

2.3   Behavior Classification

Build a convolutional neural network model for classifying teacher actions. The input of the model consists of the coordinates and confidence scores of 13 key points obtained from a pose estimation algorithm, and the output is a 5-class classification. The model includes two convolutional layers, two fully connected (FC) layers, and a normalization layer, activation layer, and pooling layer after each convolutional layer. The first FC layer is followed by an activation function and a dropout layer. The last FC layer is followed by a softmax activation function, which is used to calculate the loss function for classification. The cross-entropy loss function is used, which is a commonly used loss function for classification tasks and can effectively solve classification problems.

$$L = -[y \log \bar{y} + (1 - y) \log(1 - \bar{y})] \tag{1}$$

y is the true label value (positive class value is 1, negative class value is 0), $\bar{y}$ is the predicted probability value ($\bar{y} \in (0,1)$). It characterizes the difference between the true sample label and the predicted probability (Fig. 2).

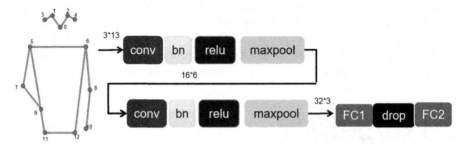

Fig. 2. Classification network structure diagram.

3 Experiment

3.1 Dataset

Our dataset consists of classroom videos from different subject teachers in middle and high schools. The videos were recorded in a real classroom using 1080p cameras, and we have a total of 70 videos, each ranging from 20 to 30 min. The videos are captured from the teacher's perspective and depict various scenarios, including instances where multiple people are present on the stage. However, we have only retained the frames that contain the image of the teacher.

Our action recognition algorithm is based on single-frame image analysis. To avoid excessive variations in action patterns within a short time frame, we captured one frame every 2 s and labeled each frame. Eventually, we obtained a certain number of labeled frames for each type of action. We randomly selected 10% of the frames as the validation set and another 10% as the test set.

3.2   Teacher Behavior Detection In Our Dataset

The Fig. 3 shows the training and validation losses of the dataset, both of which converge effectively, indicating that the model fits well with the training data and has good generalization ability for unseen data.

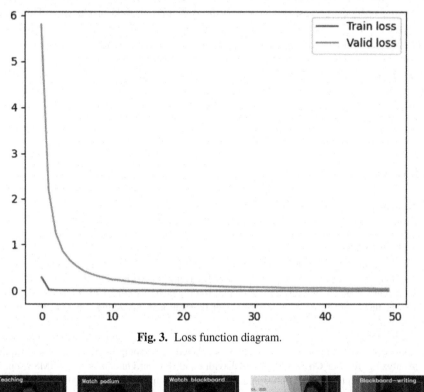

Fig. 3. Loss function diagram.

Fig. 4. Visualization of teacher behavior analysis.

The visual program output is shown as Fig. 4. The green box represents the human target obtained by the object detection algorithm, and the human body, left and right hands skeleton joints are marked with different colors. The obtained skeleton joint coordinates and confidence are input into a classification network to obtain five common teaching states of teachers during the teaching process. The accuracy rate on our dataset is 92.13%.

4 Conclusion

This paper proposes a teacher behavior detection method based on human pose estimation. By inputting each frame of the video of the teacher's class into a popular human pose estimation algorithm, the obtained human skeleton keypoints are processed through a simple classification network to obtain the teacher's classroom behavior. Image-based processing reduces the research cost and the difficulty of data production. This study can judge the teacher's proficiency in teaching content through their classroom behavior and help them improve their teaching methods in a timely manner.

Acknowledgement. This work is supported in part by the National Nature Science Foundation of China (No. 61931012), the Natural Science Foundation of Jiangsu Province of China (Grant No. BK20210594), in part by the Natural Science Foundation for Colleges and Universities in Jiangsu Province (Grant No. 21KJB520016).

References

1. Brophy, J.E.: Teacher behavior and its effects. J. Educ. Psychol. **71**(6), 733 (1979)
2. Lin, J., Jiang, F., Shen, R.: Hand-raising gesture detection in real classroom. In: 2018 IEEE International Conference on Acoustics, Speech and Signal Processing (ICASSP), pp. 6453–6457. IEEE (2018)
3. Shao, B., Jiang, F., Shen, R.: Multi-object detection based on deep learning in real classrooms. In: Geng, X., Kang, B.-H. (eds.) PRICAI 2018: Trends in Artificial Intelligence: 15th Pacific Rim International Conference on Artificial Intelligence, Nanjing, China, 28–31 Aug 2018, Proceedings, Part II, pp. 352–359. Springer International Publishing, Cham (2018). https://doi.org/10.1007/978-3-319-97310-4_40
4. Burroughs, N., Gardner, J., Lee, Y., et al.: A review of the literature on teacher effectiveness and student outcomes. In: Burroughs, N., et al. (eds.) Teaching for Excellence and Equity: Analyzing Teacher Characteristics, Behaviors and Student Outcomes with TIMSS, pp. 7–17. Springer International Publishing, Cham (2019). https://doi.org/10.1007/978-3-030-16151-4_2
5. Agbo, G.C., Agbo, P.A.: The role of computer vision in the development of knowledge-based systems for teaching and learning of English language education. ACCENTS Trans. Image Process. Comput. Vis. **6**(19), 42 (2020)
6. Kaplan, S., Guvensan, M.A., Yavuz, A.G., et al.: Driver behavior analysis for safe driving: a survey. IEEE Trans. Intell. Transp. Syst. **16**(6), 3017–3032 (2015)
7. Shirazi, M.S., Morris, B.T.: Vision-based pedestrian behavior analysis at intersections. J. Electron. Imaging **25**(5), 051203 (2016)
8. Rautaray, S.S., Agrawal, A.: Vision based hand gesture recognition for human computer interaction: a survey. Artif. Intell. Rev. **43**, 1–54 (2015)
9. Flanders N A. Analyzing teaching behavior (1970)
10. Khan, N.U., Wan, W.: A review of human pose estimation from single image. In: 2018 International Conference on Audio, Language and Image Processing (ICALIP), pp. 230–236. IEEE (2018)
11. Sun, K., Xiao, B., Liu, D., et al.: Deep high-resolution representation learning for human pose estimation. In: Proceedings of the IEEE/CVF Conference on Computer Vision and Pattern Recognition, pp. 5693–5703 (2019)

12. Ren, S., He, K., Girshick, R., et al.: Faster r-cnn: Towards real-time object detection with region proposal networks. In: Advances in Neural Information Processing Systems, 28 (2015)
13. Lin, T.Y., Maire, M., Belongie, S., et al.: Microsoft coco: Common objects in context. In: Computer Vision–ECCV 2014: 13th European Conference, Zurich, Switzerland, 6–12 Sept 2014, Proceedings, Part V 13, pp. 740–755. Springer International Publishing (2014). https://doi.org/10.1007/978-3-319-10602-1_48
14. Wang, C.Y., Bochkovskiy, A., Liao, H.Y.M.: YOLOv7: Trainable bag-of-freebies sets new state-of-the-art for real-time object detectors. arXiv preprint arXiv:2207.02696 (2022)
15. Zhao, W., Wang, M., Liu, Y., et al.: Generalizable crowd counting via diverse context style learning. IEEE Trans. Circuits Syst. Video Technol. **32**(8), 5399–5410 (2022)
16. Xu, X., Song, J., Lu, H., et al.: Modal-adversarial semantic learning network for extendable cross-modal retrieval. In: Proceedings of the 2018 ACM on International Conference on Multimedia Retrieval, pp. 46–54 (2018)

Condition Monitoring of Wind Turbine Anemometers Based on Combined Model Deep Learning

Anfeng Zhu, Qiancheng Zhao$^{(\boxtimes)}$, Tianlong Yang, and Ling Zhou

Engineering Research Center of Hunan Province for the Mining and Utilization of Wind Turbines Operation Data, Hunan University of Science and Technology, Xiangtan 411201, China
hnustzaf@mail.hnust.edu.cn

Abstract. The dynamic working environment brings challenges to the condition monitoring of anemometers. To accurately grasp the actual performance status of wind turbines (WTs) and timely detect anemometer faults, a combination of Particle Swarm Optimization (PSO) and the long and short term memory network (LSTM) based anemometer status monitoring method is proposed. Firstly, utilizing the wind speed data collected by the anemometer as an input variable, select the wind turbine (WT) with high similarity through similarity analysis. Then, use the PSO to enhance the structural parameters of the LSTM network to acquire efficient anemometer state estimation. This method can monitor the abnormal state of the anemometer and reconstruct the faulty wind speed data. Finally, to demonstrate the efficiency of the approach, the condition of the WT anemometer is predicted using examples.

Keywords: Wind turbine · Anemometer · Deep learning networks · Condition monitoring

1 Introduction

Due to the growth of industrialization, the dilemma of petrochemical energy is becoming increasingly apparent. As an environmentally friendly and economical green energy, wind energy has great development potential [1]. Over the past few years, WT assembly capacity has continued to grow both onshore and offshore. However, as a large and complex electromechanical equipment, WTs are generally located in remote areas and operate in harsh environments [2]. Most components of WTs, such as generators, bearings, and anemometers, are prone to failures, with electrical system components having the highest frequency of failure, followed by sensors [3]. Therefore, it is necessary to monitor the status of WT sensors, which helps to increase improving the economic benefits of the wind power industry [4, 14].

The monitoring system for WTs includes anemometers, wind vanes, voltage sensors, and current sensors. Over 40% of WT failures are caused by sensor related system failures [3–5]. A sensor failure may result in the control mechanism to issue incorrect

H. Lu and J. Cai (Eds.): ISAIR 2023, CCIS 1998, pp. 76–85, 2024.
https://doi.org/10.1007/978-981-99-9109-9_8

control instructions, which will directly affect the safety of WTs and personnel [6]. As a result, it is crucial to monitor the condition of the anemometer. Domestic and foreign scholars have made many research achievements involving fault detection and status monitoring of WT sensors. In reference [7, 15], a condition monitoring approach of temperature sensor of the main bearing and generator based on deep learning is proposed. In reference [8] used a novel auto associative neural network for fault diagnosis of WT anemometers. In reference [9] condition monitoring of WT gearbox gear based on SCADA data using cascaded and bidirectional deep learning approach is proposed. In reference [10], a condition monitoring method based on classifier fusion is recommended to extract characteristics from the observed dates, which improves the accuracy of fault detection.

However, these methods do not account for the relationship between sensors and how that relationship affects WTs. Therefore, a state monitoring method for WT anemometers based on deep learning is proposed. Aiming at the problem that it is difficult to reasonably select LSTM network parameters, PSO is used to improve the model parameters. This method can monitor the abnormal state of the anemometer and reconstruct the faulty wind speed data. Finally, the examples are used to predict the state of the WT anemometer, verifying the effectiveness of this approach. It can realize the status monitoring of the anemometer.

2 Methodology

2.1 Correlation

Correlation analysis is the analysis of the relevant factors of two or more variables, thereby determining the degree of correlation between variable factors. Highly connected variables are those with a correlation coefficient higher than 0.8. The Pearson correlation coefficient is calculated as follows:

$$r = \frac{\sum\limits_{i=1}^{n} (X_i - \overline{X})(Y_i - \overline{Y})}{\sqrt{\sum\limits_{i=1}^{n} (X_i - \overline{X})^2} \sqrt{\sum\limits_{i=1}^{n} (Y_i - \overline{Y})^2}} \tag{1}$$

where $\overline{X}$ represents X average value, $\overline{Y}$ indicates Y average value, n is the number of samples.

2.2 Particle Swarm Optimization

The PSO is commonly employed to enhance each hyperparameter of a neural network to obtain the parameter combination with the highest accuracy of the neural network. The purpose of this approach is designed to simulate the behavioral characteristics of animal foraging behavior in nature. Compared to random search algorithms such as grid search and genetic algorithm, PSO has better performance [11, 13].

Establish a particle group $X = \{x_1, x_2, \cdots, x_m\}$ with a scale of m, in which a particle can be represented as a coordinate $x_i = (x_{i1}, x_{i2}, \cdots, x_{im})^T$ in the D-dimensional space, the velocity of the particle can be written as $v_i = (v_{i1}, v_{i2}, \cdots, v_{im})^T$, and the fitness function is $f(X_i)$. During the calculation iteration process, the localized best solution of a single particle and the global best solution of the entire society will be saved, and the position and velocity of each particle will always be refreshed during this process. The updated equation is:

$$V_{id}^{k+1} = \omega V_{id}^k + c_1 r_1 \left(P_{id}^k - X_{id}^k \right) + c_2 r_2 \left(P_{gd}^k - X_{id}^k \right) \tag{2}$$

$$X_{id}^{k+1} = X_{id}^k - V_{id}^{k+1} \tag{3}$$

where $d = 1, 2, 3 \cdots, n, \quad i = 1, 2, \cdots, m$, that is, there are m particle elements in the particle swarm, k represents the iteration number of particles, c_1 and c_2 is the acceleration factor, and P_{gd}, P_{id} are the global and self optimal solutions of the particle.

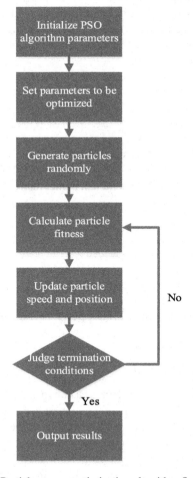

Fig. 1. Particle swarm optimization algorithm flowchart.

Figure 1 shows the workflow of the PSO. The following are the steps to apply the PSO:

(1) Set the PSO algorithm parameters, including inertia weight, acceleration factor, and population size.
(2) The dimension of the population particles is determined based on the parameters to be optimized in the neural network prediction approach. These parameters to be optimized are the optimization objectives of the particle swarm optimization algorithm. At the same time, it is necessary to determine the value range of these parameters, and randomly generate particle positions within the value range.
(3) Set the fitness function, input the parameters to be optimized into the PSO algorithm, and set the initialization value. Input the initialization value as the optimal result into the neural network to calculate the fitness.
(4) Compare the fitness of all particles with their optimal location, and then select the optimal location as the optimal historical location.
(5) Refresh the position and velocity of particles according to formulas (2) and (3).
(6) Set the optimization goal, and stop when the goal requirements are met. If the requirements are not met, rerun Step 3. The optimization goal is usually achieved by setting a fitness threshold and a maximum number of iterations.

2.3   Long and Short Term Memory Network

LSTM is an improved version of RNN. To address the issue that RNN is not suitable for long sequence information, an LSTM additionally sets a forgetting gate to control memory transfer and update in addition to the existing input and output gates of RNN. The forgetting gate prevents the movement of pointless information from the past while

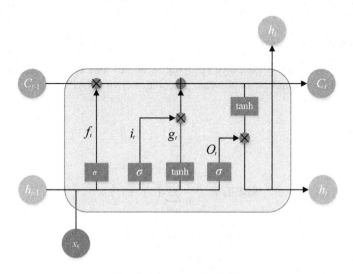

Fig. 2. Structure of LSTM.

preserving useful information. This measure optimizes RNN's performance for long-term memory, Optimized the performance of the algorithm [12]. Figure 2 depicts the construction of the LSTM.

3 Experimental Settings

3.1 Data Preparation

The data employed in this study originated from a wind farm in southern China. To confirm the predictive capability of the proposed approach, the data utilized is from the No. 7 WT in June 2015, with a data sampling time of 10 min. The data includes 2000 samples, the 1–1600 samples for training, and the 1601–2000 samples for testing. Figure 3 displays the time series for wind speed.

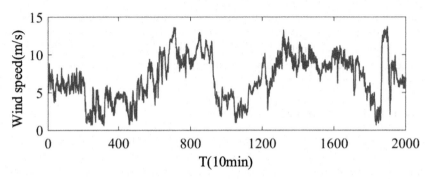

Fig. 3. Wind speed time series.

3.2 Evaluation Indicators

The modelling accuracy is evaluated applying mean absolute error (MAE), root mean square error (RMSE) and mean absolute percentage error (MAPE) indicators, and the calculation formula is:

$$MAE = \frac{1}{n}\sum_{i=1}^{n}\left|\widehat{y}_i - y_i\right| \tag{4}$$

$$RMSE = \sqrt{\frac{1}{n}\sum_{i=1}^{n}\left(\widehat{y}_i - y_i\right)^2} \tag{5}$$

$$MAPE = \frac{1}{n}\sum_{i=1}^{n}\left|\frac{\widehat{y}_i - y_i}{y_i}\right| \tag{6}$$

where y_i is the real value; $\widehat{y}_i$ is the predicted value.

3.3 Model Structure

This study suggests a state monitoring approach for anemometers based on PSO-LSTM. Firstly, the wind speed data collected by the anemometer is employed as an input variable to select WTs with strong similarity by similarity analysis. Then, using the normal historical data of similar WTs as input data, PSO is employed to improve the parameters of the LSTM structure to enhance the state estimation of the anemometer. Finally, the prediction residual analysis is used to monitor whether the anemometer is malfunctioning, and the malfunctioning wind speed data is reconstructed. Accordingly, Fig. 4 presents the flowchart of the main contents of this study.

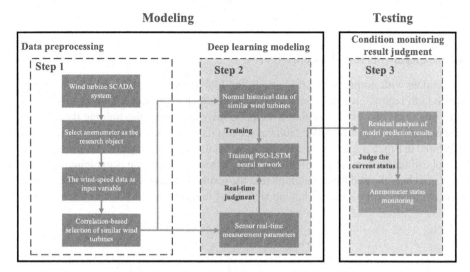

Fig. 4. Flowchart of the main contents in this study.

4 Results and Analysis

4.1 Wind Speed Correlation Analysis

Due to the complex terrain in mountainous areas, the wind speed and direction are variable, and the climate change is complex. Wind speed, as the environmental parameter that has the greatest influence on the operation of WTs, directly determines the operating status of WTs. Therefore, wind speed can be selected as a parameter to measure the similarity of the operating environment. Calculate the Pearson correlation coefficients of the wind speed series of each WT and the target WT No. 7 in the same time period. The correlation coefficients between the target WT and other WTs are shown in Table 1.

From Table 1, it can be inferred that the wind speed of the target WT No. 7 and WTs 6, 8, and 10 have extremely high correlations in wind speed data. Therefore, it is possible to choose the WT No. 7 and the WTs 6, 8, and 10 as a group of WTs with high similarity.

Table 1. Correlation between No. 7 wind turbine and others.

Wind Turbine No	Wind speed data
7	1
3	0.463
6	0.9132
8	0.9058
10	0.8906
14	0.5371
17	0.6247

4.2 Experiments Based on PSO-LSTM

Select data with normal similarity among the four WTs to train the model. According to the fault records, it can be seen that the anemometer has failed. During this period, selecting 1600 pieces of data that were previously normal as the training dataset, and 400 pieces of data that included faults as the test dataset. The final test set outcomes are exhibited in Fig. 5. Figure 5 (a) demonstrates that the model fitting effect is good and the model estimation accuracy is high. The specific residual variation is exhibited in Fig. 5 (b). It can be indicated from the graph that the residual variation is stable for most of the time, with only a few samples having significant jumps.

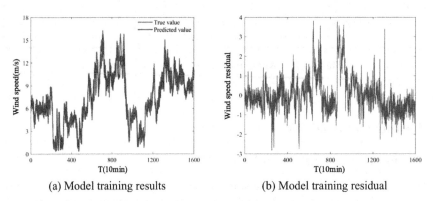

(a) Model training results   (b) Model training residual

Fig. 5. Residual performance of normal data.

The PSO-LSTM model is utilized to estimate the wind speed data of the No. 7 WT that has failed. The estimated outcomes of the model are exhibited in Fig. 6 (a), and some data are abnormal due to the failure of the anemometer. The residual error is used as the basis for anomaly determination, as exhibited in Fig. 6(b). From the graph, it can be indicated that the residual error output from the 290th data point has significantly increased compared to the normal data, so it can be determined that the anemometer of No. 7 WT during this time period is in an abnormal state.

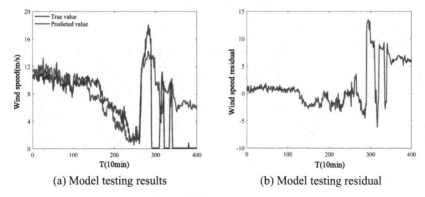

(a) Model testing results   (b) Model testing residual

Fig. 6. Model test residual.

The abnormal data is reconstructed using the PSO-LSTM, as exhibited in Fig. 7. It could be found that the residual variation of the model returns to a normal range at this time. This indicates that when the anemometer is abnormal, the PSO-LSTM model is used to reconstruct the abnormal data using the similarity between WT groups. This experiment proves the effectiveness of state monitoring based on PSO-LSTM model.

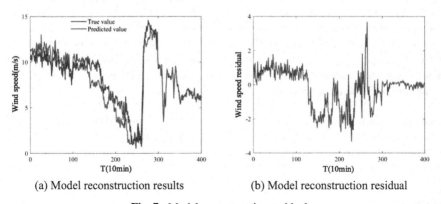

(a) Model reconstruction results   (b) Model reconstruction residual

Fig. 7. Model reconstruction residual.

4.3 Comparative of Models

For further confirming the advantages of this suggested model, the reconstructed data is contrasted with the PSO-LSTM through the evaluation index of the combination Genetic Algorithm (GA) and LSTM model. The prediction results of PSO-LSTM, GA-LSTM, and LSTM are shown in Fig. 8 (a). At the same time, the assessment index of the recommended PSO-LSTM in Fig. 8(b) is greater than other approaches, so the PSO-LSTM is more precise in monitoring the operation status of the anemometer.

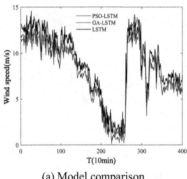

(a) Model comparison

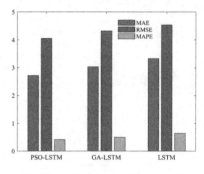

(b) Comparison of model error values

Fig. 8. Comparisons of prediction results.

5   Conclusion

Considering the dynamic working conditions of anemometer, a condition monitoring model named PSO-LSTM is suggested in this study, which is applied for condition assessment of anemometer. Using the wind speed data collected by the anemometer as input variables, select WTs with high similarity through similarity analysis. Then, take the PSO to improve the parameters of the LSTM network structure to obtain model estimates. Finally, four groups of anemometer data were analyzed to find abnormal conditions, and the abnormal wind speed data is reconstructed using the similarity between WT groups. The analysis outcomes demonstrate that the method has good accuracy, can identify abnormal states of the anemometer, and reconstruct abnormal data, improving the reliability of the anemometer.

Acknowledgments. This work is supported by National Key Research and Development Program of People's Republic of China (grant number 2022YFF0608700) and National Natural Science Foundation of China (No. 51875199).

References

1. Liu, H., Chen, C.: Data processing strategies in wind energy forecasting models and applications: a comprehensive review. Appl. Energy **249**, 392–408 (2019)
2. Zhu, A., Zhao, Q., Wang, X., et al.: Ultra-short-term wind power combined prediction based on complementary ensemble empirical mode decomposition, whale optimisation algorithm, and elman network. Energies **15**(9), 3055 (2022)
3. Pieraccini, M., Parrini, F., Fratini, M., et al.: In-service testing of wind turbine towers using a microwave sensor. Renew. Energy **33**(1), 13–21 (2008)
4. Chehouri, A., Younes, R., Ilinca, A., et al.: Review of performance optimization techniques applied to wind turbines. Appl. Energy **142**(15), 361–388 (2015)
5. Kayikci, M., Milanovic, J.V.: Reactive power control strategies for DFIG-based plants. IEEE Trans. Energy Convers. **22**, 389–396 (2007)
6. Zhu, A., Xiao, Z., Zhao, Q.: Power data preprocessing method of mountain wind farm based on POT-DBSCAN. Energy Eng. **118**(3), 549–563 (2021)

7. Fang, L., Liu, P., Zhang, B.: Sensor faults simulation of DFIG control system. Instrum. Technol. **2**, 52–54 (2014)

8. Tao, Z., Zhu, C., He, M., et al.: A physical modeling-based study on the control mechanisms of Negative Poisson's ratio anchor cable on the stratified toppling deformation of anti-inclined slopes. Int. J. Rock Mech. Min. Sci. **138**, 104632 (2021)

9. Zhu, A., Zhao, Q., Yang, T., et al.: Condition monitoring of wind turbine based on deep learning networks and kernel principal component analysis. Comput. Electr. Eng. **105**, 108538 (2023)

10. Zhou, L., Zhao, Q., Wang, X., et al.: Fault diagnosis and reconstruction of wind turbine anemometer based on RWSSA-AANN. Energies **14**(21), 6905 (2021)

11. Xiang, L., Yang, X., Hu, A., et al.: Condition monitoring and anomaly detection of wind turbine based on cascaded and bidirectional deep learning networks. Appl. Energy **305**, 117925 (2022)

12. Pashazadeh, V., Salmasi, F.R., Araabi, B.N.: Data driven sensor and actuator fault detection and isolation in wind turbine using classifier fusion. Renew. Energy **116**, 99–106 (2018)

13. Roy, C., Das, D.K.: A hybrid genetic algorithm (GA)-particle swarm optimization (PSO) algorithm for demand side management in smart grid considering wind power for cost optimization. Sādhanā **46**(2), 101 (2021)

14. Jaseena, K.U., Kovoor, B.C.: A hybrid wind speed forecasting model using stacked autoencoder and LSTM. J. Renew. Sustain. Energ. **12**(2), 023302 (2020)

15. Fu, Y., Zhang, M., Xu, X., et al.: Partial feature selection and alignment for multi-source domain adaptation. In: Proceedings of the IEEE/CVF Conference on Computer Vision and Pattern Recognition, pp. 16654–16663 (2021)

16. Kang, S., Wu, H., Yang, X., et al.: Discrete-time predictive sliding mode control for a constrained parallel micropositioning piezostage. IEEE Trans. Syst., Man Cybern. Syst. **52**(5), 3025–3036 (2021)

17. Yang, X., Wu, H., Li, Y., et al.: Dynamics and isotropic control of parallel mechanisms for vibration isolation. IEEE/ASME Trans. Mechatron. **25**(4), 2027–2034 (2020)

C2FC: Coarse-to-fine Contour-Based Method for Interactive Medical Image Segmentation

Wenrui Luo[1], Yingxuan Zhang[1], Bohua Wang[1], Lei Sun[1], Hua Liu[2], Hui Ma[3], and Zhiqiang Tian[1(✉)]

[1] School of Software Engineering, Xi'an Jiaotong University, Xi'an, Shaanxi, China
zhiqiangtian@xjtu.edu.cn
[2] Shenergy Company Limited, Shanghai, China
[3] Beijing Goldwind Smart Energy Technology Co., Ltd., Beijing, China

Abstract. Existing contour-based methods for interactive segmentation of medical images have achieved great success. However, these methods neglect the large shape error between the initial contour and the ground truth. The details of the contour are focused on too early, which can easily lead to unsatisfactory segmentation quality. To address this problem, we propose a coarse-to-fine contour-based method for interactive medical image segmentation. This method includes automatic segmentation and interactive segmentation. We propose a coarse deformation module (CDM) to generate a coarse contour for automatic segmentation to reduce the shape error. In addition, we propose a fine deformation module (FDM) to refine the coarse contour for automatic segmentation. The FDM is also presented to adjust the local contour for interactive segmentation. Our experimental results show that the proposed method outperforms the state-of-the-art segmentation methods on the PROMISE12 and our in-house nasopharyngeal carcinoma (NPC) datasets.

Keywords: Interactive segmentation · Coarse-to-fine · Medical images

1 Introduction

Manual segmentation of medical images is very time-consuming and requires experienced specialists to perform the segmentation of medical images [1,2]. Many automatic segmentation methods have been proposed that improve the performance of medical image segmentation, such as U-Net [3], MedT [4], and so on. However, medical images often suffer from issues such as blurring and low contrast, resulting in unsatisfactory automatic segmentation results. To enhance the quality of medical image segmentation, researchers have explored interactive segmentation techniques, which enable users to intervene in the segmentation process and improve the model's performance through user interaction.

In recent years, deep neural network architectures have been commonly applied to image segmentation [5]. The main interactive segmentation methods

© The Author(s), under exclusive license to Springer Nature Singapore Pte Ltd. 2024
H. Lu and J. Cai (Eds.): ISAIR 2023, CCIS 1998, pp. 86–93, 2024.
https://doi.org/10.1007/978-981-99-9109-9_9

based on deep learning are contour-based and click-based methods, etc. There have been contour-based methods such as Curve-GCN [6], Tian's [7] methods, etc. In these methods, the user can drag and drop contour points to the correct location, after which the model predicts the location of the contour points around the user-corrected contour points. There have been click-based methods such as DEXTR [8], FocusCut [9], etc. DEXTR guides the model to better segment the image by allowing the user to give the four extreme points of the object being segmented. FocusCut allows the user to click on an undesirable segmented area of the image to optimize the quality of that area.

However, current contour-based interactive segmentation methods don't consider the problem that there is a large shape error between the initial contour and the ground truth, and these methods focus on the details of the contour too early when there is large shape error, which can lead to unsatisfactory segmentation quality. To address this problem, a coarse-to-fine contour-based method for interactive medical image segmentation is proposed in this paper. The main contributions of this paper are summarized as follows:

1. We propose a coarse-to-fine contour-based method for interactive medical image segmentation. Our method considers the problem of unsatisfactory segmentation quality due to the large shape error between the initial contour and the ground truth.
2. We propose a coarse deformation module (CDM) to correct the large shape error between the initial contour and the ground truth. Furthermore, we propose a fine deformation module (FDM) to refine the coarse contour. FDM is also used for interactive segmentation to improve automatic segmentation results.
3. Our experimental results show that our proposed method outperforms the state-of-the-art segmentation methods on the PROMISE12 and NPC datasets.

2   Method

2.1   Overview

The overview of our method is shown in Fig. 1. In our method, we assume that the contour can be accurately represented by N contour points. The neighboring points are connected with spline curves to form the contour. The pipeline is divided into two stages: automatic segmentation and interactive segmentation. In the automatic segmentation stage, the user first gives the region of interest. A circle of contour points is initialized in this region, which are the initial contour points that can form the initial contour. This region is cropped from the image and resized, and fed into the CNN to extract the CNN feature. The CNN is a modified mobilenetv3-large [10]. Specifically, the last two bottlenecks and subsequent structures are removed. The last 14×14 and 28×28 size features are both upsampled to 56×56. The upsampled features are concatenated with the last 56×56 size feature to obtain multi-scale feature. The CDM and FDM can deform the contour by predicting the offset of the contour points. Three CDMs are used to deform the initial contour to reduce the large shape error between the initial contour and the ground truth, generating a coarse contour. After that, three FDMs are used to refine the coarse contour and obtain a high-quality automatic segmentation result. After obtaining the result of the automatic segmentation, the result of automatic segmentation is used as the basis for interactive segmentation. In the interactive segmentation stage, an FDM is used to predict the offset of the surrounding contour points of the user-corrected contour points, thus refining the local contours and improving the segmentation quality. To do this, a local range r is chosen as an effective range for interactive segmentation prediction. The offset prediction will only be effective for the $2r$ neighboring contour points (r neighbors on either side) of the user-corrected contour points, and the offset prediction values of other contour points are set to zero. Here, the r is set to 4. In the training phase of interactive segmentation, user correction of incorrect contour points is simulated by the program.

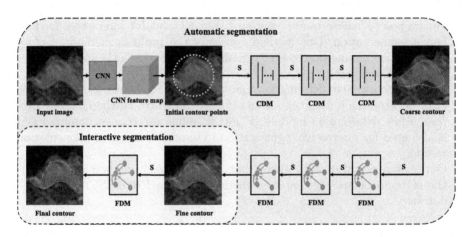

Fig. 1. Overview of the proposed C2FC. CDM is the coarse deformation module, and FDM is the fine deformation module. The symbol S denotes the operation of sampling the CNN feature corresponding to the contour points.

The input to the CDM and FDM are the features of the contour points. The feature of a contour point consists of its corresponding CNN feature and its coordinates. Every time before using the CDM or FDM to deform the contour, the features of the current contour points need to be obtained. Specifically, the position of a contour point on an image is (x, y). The position on the image is mapped to the position on the feature map generated by CNN. Then the corresponding feature is extracted, which is denoted as f_{cnn}. The f_{cnn} is concatenated with (x, y) as the feature of the contour point. The feature f_p of this contour point is shown as follows:

$$f_p = concat\left\{f_{cnn}, (x, y)\right\}. \tag{1}$$

The output of CDM and FDM is the offset of each contour point. The offset of a contour point can be denoted as $(\Delta x, \Delta y)$. The new coordinates (x', y') of a contour point are calculated by the following equation:

$$(x', y') = (x + \Delta x, y + \Delta y). \tag{2}$$

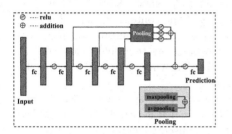

Fig. 2. Overview of the coarse deformation module (CDM).

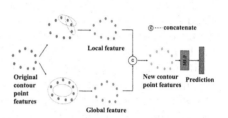

Fig. 3. Overview of the fine deformation module (FDM).

2.2 Coarse Deformation Module

The shape error between the initial contour and the ground truth is often significant. In this case, it is difficult to obtain a high-quality segmentation result directly. Because considering the details of the contour too early, in this case, can lead to large prediction errors that are difficult to correct between the predicted contour and ground truth. Therefore, a coarse deformation module (CDM) is proposed to be aware of the general shape of the contour to be deformed, generating a coarse contour. The shape error between the coarse contour and the ground truth is smaller than the shape error between the initial contour and the ground truth. The CDM focuses only on the global feature and not on the local feature, avoiding the introduction of attention to local details of the contour in case of the large shape error. Therefore, a global receptive field is used in the CDM.

As shown in Fig. 2, this is the overview of the CDM. The fc denotes the fully connected layer. The input of the CDM is a vector concatenated by the features of N contour points. The length of the input vector is $N \times D$, where N denotes the number of contour points and D denotes the length of the feature vector for each contour point. Here, the number of contour points is set to 40. To fully extract the global feature of the contour, the outputs of multiple fully connected layers are pooled and then added together to fuse global features at different depths. The fused global features are fed into a fully connected layer to obtain the prediction. The prediction is the offset of each contour point in the x-axis and y-axis direction, and the length of the output is $N \times 2$.

2.3   Fine Deformation Module

The CDM reduces the shape error between the initial contour and the ground truth, generating a coarse contour. To further refine the coarse contour, we propose a fine deformation module (FDM). Because the shape error between the coarse contour and the ground truth is smaller than the shape error between the initial contour and the ground truth, considering details on the coarse contour is less likely to cause large prediction errors than the initial contour. Therefore, the FDM extracts the local and global features of the contour, which allows the FDM to take into account both the general shape of the contour and the local details of the contour, so that the contour can be accurately deformed. That is, the local feature within the constraints of global features is used to refine the contour, thus avoiding large prediction errors.

Specifically, the FDM uses a two-branch architecture, as shown in Fig. 3. The top branch is the local branch, and the bottom branch is the global branch. For the local branch, a circular convolution [11,12] is used to aggregate the features of a contour point with the features of $2k$ neighboring contour points. Each side has k neighboring contour points. The feature being aggregated is used as the local feature perceived by that contour point. Here, k is set to 4. For the global branch, multi-head attention [13,14] is used for global feature extraction. Each contour point can perceive the features of all contour points. In this way, each contour point can perceive the global feature of the contour. Compared to the CDM, the FDM does not need a very deep global feature. Because the large shape error in the coarse contour have been corrected. The FDM concatenates the global and local features perceived by each contour point as a new feature. The offset of each contour point is predicted by an MLP from the new feature of that contour point.

3   Experiments

3.1   Datasets and Metrics

The PROMISE12 dataset and our in-house NPC dataset are used to evaluate our method. The PROMISE12 [15] dataset contains the prostate in T2-weighted MR images. We randomly selected 626 slices from this dataset for training, 152 slices for validation, and 424 slices for testing. The NPC dataset is our in-house dataset. The NPC dataset contains 1620 MR images of nasopharyngeal carcinoma. The dataset is split into a training set of 970 images, a validation set of 325 images, and a test set of 325 images. Three metrics are used to evaluate the performance of segmentation, namely the Dice similarity coefficient (DSC), the relative volume difference (RVD), and the average symmetric surface distance (ASSD). For a detailed description of these three metrics, refer to [7].

3.2   Comparison Experiments

The above three metrics are used to quantitatively evaluate our method on test sets of the PROMISE12 and NPC datasets, respectively. U-Net [3], MedT [4],

Table 1. Comparison experiments on the PROMISE12 test set.

Methods	DSC (%)	RVD (%)	Assd (mm)
U-Net [3]	83.84	−1.45	5.48
DEXTR [8]	91.68	16.16	2.98
Tian's method [7]	92.47	4.25	2.72
MedT [4]	77.98	−2.42	−
Focuscut-resnet50 [9]	94.64	−1.96	1.88
Focuscut-resnet101 [9]	94.45	−6.01	1.84
C2FC (ours)	**95.45**	**0.07**	**1.55**

Table 2. Comparison experiments on the NPC test set.

Methods	DSC (%)	RVD (%)	ASSD (mm)
U-Net [3]	64.14	9.05	−
DEXTR [8]	78.51	53.97	3.78
Tian's method [7]	85.83	5.65	2.03
MedT [4]	61.72	42.29	7.51
Focuscut-resnet50 [9]	87.78	−7.99	1.62
Focuscut-resnet101 [9]	88.88	−4.13	1.46
C2FC (ours)	**90.73**	**3.31**	**1.34**

DEXTR [8], Tian's method [7], and Focuscut [9] were chosen to compare with our method. DEXTR, Tian's method, Focuscut are interactive segmentation methods. U-Net and MedT are automatic segmentation methods. Table 1 shows that our method achieves the best performance on the PROMISE12 dataset in all metrics compared to other methods. Table 2 shows that our method also achieves the best performance compared to other methods on the NPC dataset with complex boundaries.

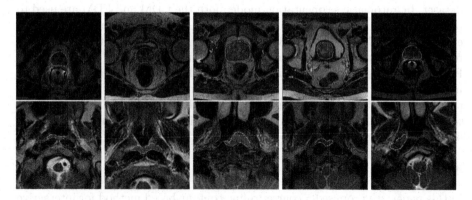

Fig. 4. Qualitative results of ten MR images from the PROMISE12 test set and NPC test set. The red contours are the ground truth, and the yellow contours are the prediction result of our proposed method. The images in the first row are from the PROMISE12 test set, and the images in the second row are from the NPC test set. (Color figure online)

3.3 Qualitative Results

Figure 4 shows the qualitative results of ten MR images using our method from the PROMISE12 test set and the NPC test set. As shown in Fig. 4, our method can accurately segment the prostate region for the PROMISE12 test set. Moreover, our method can also accurately segment the lesion region for the NPC test set with more complex boundaries.

3.4 Evaluation of Interactions

As shown in Fig. 5, as the number of interactions gradually increases, the DSC value increases. This indicates that the segmentation performance of our method becomes better as the number of interactions increases.

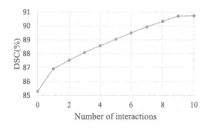

Table 3. Ablation experiments on the PROMISE12 test set in automatic segmentation mode.

Methods	DSC (%)	RVD (%)	ASSD (mm)
without FDM	88.08	−4.62	4.28
without CDM	92.23	−1.19	2.81
C2FC	**92.94**	**−0.42**	**2.48**

Fig. 5. The DSC values vs the number of interactions on the NPC test set.

3.5 Ablation Experiments

Table 3 shows the results of our ablation experiments on the PROMISE12 dataset. In automatic segmentation mode, both the CDM and FDM are used to perform segmentation on the test set of the PROMISE12 dataset. To verify the effectiveness of CDM and FDM, we first removed FDM and kept CDM, and later removed CDM and kept FDM. Compared with the method using both CDM and FDM, it can be seen that the segmentation results show a decrease in DSC values, an increase in ASSD value and the absolute value of RVD. This means that the segmentation performance decreases when CDM or FDM is removed, which proves that both CDM and FDM play an important role in improving the segmentation performance.

4 Conclusion

In this paper, we proposed a coarse-to-fine contour-based method for interactive medical image segmentation. This method consists of two stages: automatic segmentation and interactive segmentation. In the automatic segmentation stage, we present three coarse deformation modules to deform the initial contour to generate a coarse contour. After that, we present three fine deformation modules to refine the coarse contour to generate the automatic segmentation result. In the interactive segmentation stage, we correct the incorrect contour points based on the automatic segmentation results. We use a fine deformation module to correct the contour points surrounding the user-corrected contour points to adjust the local contour. Our experimental results show that the proposed method outperforms the state-of-the-art segmentation methods on the PROMISE12 dataset and our in-house nasopharyngeal carcinoma (NPC) dataset.

Acknowledgements. This work was supported by NSFC under grant No. 62173269, Shaanxi Province Key Research and Development Program (No.: 2022 ZDLSF07-07).

References

1. Zhao, F., Xie, X.: An overview of interactive medical image segmentation. Ann. BMVA **2013**(7), 1–22 (2013)
2. Alzahrani, Y., Boufama, B.: Biomedical image segmentation: a survey. SN Comput. Sci. **2**(4), 1–22 (2021)
3. Ronneberger, O., Fischer, P., Brox, T.: U-Net: convolutional networks for biomedical image segmentation. In: Navab, N., Hornegger, J., Wells, W.M., Frangi, A.F. (eds.) MICCAI 2015. LNCS, vol. 9351, pp. 234–241. Springer, Cham (2015). https://doi.org/10.1007/978-3-319-24574-4_28
4. Valanarasu, J.M.J., Oza, P., Hacihaliloglu, I., Patel, V.M.: Medical transformer: gated axial-attention for medical image segmentation. In: de Bruijne, M., et al. (eds.) MICCAI 2021. LNCS, vol. 12901, pp. 36–46. Springer, Cham (2021). https://doi.org/10.1007/978-3-030-87193-2_4
5. Minaee, S., Boykov, Y.Y., Porikli, F., Plaza, A.J., Kehtarnavaz, N., Terzopoulos, D.: Image segmentation using deep learning: a survey. IEEE Trans. Pattern Anal. Mach. Intell. **44**, 3523–3542 (2021)
6. Ling, H., Gao, J., Kar, A., Chen, W., Fidler, S.: Fast interactive object annotation with curve-GCN. In: Proceedings of the IEEE/CVF Conference on Computer Vision and Pattern Recognition, pp. 5257–5266 (2019)
7. Tian, Z., et al.: Graph-convolutional-network-based interactive prostate segmentation in MR images. Med. Phys. **47**(9), 4164–4176 (2020)
8. Maninis, K.K., Caelles, S., Pont-Tuset, J., Van Gool, L.: Deep extreme cut: from extreme points to object segmentation. In: Proceedings of the IEEE Conference on Computer Vision and Pattern Recognition, pp. 616–625 (2018)
9. Lin, Z., Duan, Z.P., Zhang, Z., Guo, C.L., Cheng, M.M.: FocusCut: diving into a focus view in interactive segmentation. In: Proceedings of the IEEE/CVF Conference on Computer Vision and Pattern Recognition, pp. 2637–2646 (2022)
10. Howard, A., et al.: Searching for MobileNetV3. In: Proceedings of the IEEE/CVF International Conference on Computer Vision, pp. 1314–1324 (2019)
11. Peng, S., Jiang, W., Pi, H., Li, X., Bao, H., Zhou, X.: Deep snake for real-time instance segmentation. In: Proceedings of the IEEE/CVF Conference on Computer Vision and Pattern Recognition, pp. 8533–8542 (2020)
12. Zhao, W., Lu, H., Wang, D.: Multisensor image fusion and enhancement in spectral total variation domain. IEEE Trans. Multimedia **20**(4), 866–879 (2017)
13. Vaswani, A., et al.: Attention is all you need. In: Advances in Neural Information Processing Systems, vol. 30 (2017)
14. Lan, R., Sun, L., Liu, Z., Lu, H., Pang, C., Luo, X.: MADNet: a fast and lightweight network for single-image super resolution. IEEE Trans. Cybernet. **51**(3), 1443–1453 (2020)
15. Litjens, G., et al.: Evaluation of prostate segmentation algorithms for MRI: the PROMISE12 challenge. Med. Image Anal. **18**(2), 359–373 (2014)

DDTM: A Distance-Based Data Transformation Method for Time Series Classification

Huarong Xu[1], Ke Wang[1], Wu Sun[1], Mei Chen[1], Hui Li[1(✉)], and Heng Zhao[2(✉)]

[1] College of Computer Science and Technology, Guizhou University, Guiyang, China
cse.HuiLi@gzu.edu.cn
[2] College of Big Data and Internet, Shenzhen Technology University, Shenzhen, China
15186958102@163.com

Abstract. Time series classification (TSC) relies primarily on similarity or dissimilarity measurements. In numerous scenarios, classification accuracy can be improved by removing interference variables. DDTM is proposed, which investigates the changes in the distance between the category and the subsequence on time series to determine if the subsequence influences the determination of the category. The main idea consists of three steps. First, propose a window division strategy to compare the Dynamic Time Warping (DTW) distances between time series categories at different window positions. Next, capture the influence of class division by calculating the average distance under various windows and measure the efficiency of window position for class division using information gain. Finally, transform the series according to the information gain. The research shows that the proposed DDTM method achieves superior classification results.

Keywords: Time Series Classification · Data Transformation · DTW · Sliding Window

1 Introduction

Time series analysis has been identified as one of the ten most challenging research issues in the field of data mining [1]. TSC is a key time series analysis task. TSC aims to build a machine learning that predicts a discrete target variable from a time series (potentially multivariate) [2–5].

The rapid development of low-cost sensors coupled with IoT devices and cloud infrastructure has facilitated time series data collection in agriculture [24], equipment monitoring [25], health [26], sports, and fitness [27]. Many applications require time series analysis such as human activity recognition [28–30], diagnosis based on electronic health records [31, 32], and systems monitoring problems [6].

Time series data is ubiquitous, making time series analysis methods particularly significant. TSC problems are differentiated from traditional classification problems because the attributes are ordered. The nearest neighbor (NN) algorithm was the most accurate and reliable method over the past decade [7]. Classification problems typically rely on similarity or dissimilarity measures. Major studies on the similarity of time series include the following.

H. Lu and J. Cai (Eds.): ISAIR 2023, CCIS 1998, pp. 94–111, 2024.
https://doi.org/10.1007/978-981-99-9109-9_10

The Similarity in the Time. A typical example is the simple nearest neighbor algorithm based on distance measures. Essential measurements include the Euclidean distance, DTW, Derivative DTW (DDTW), Weighted DTW (WDTW), and Time Warp with Edit (TWE) distance, among others. Keogh [35] devised precise indexing based on DTW for time-series mining. Ensemble-based approaches utilize ensembles of TSC methods. The algorithm elastic ensemble (EE) [38] is one of the most prominent. It is a collection of 11 NN classifiers that have learned various time series measures with their parameters tuned accordingly.

The Similarity in the Shape. Eamonn Keogh [2, 33–37] asserted that Matrix Profile [18] is the most effective technique for time series data mining in the last decade. In time series, shapelets are the most discriminating subsequences. Ye et al. [33] proposed the original classification algorithm based on shapelets. It identified the optimal shapelets through recursion and constructed a decision tree. Mueen et al. [37] constructed a decision tree using logical shapelets due to the lack of interpretability of singular shapelets.

The Similarity in the Change. Two methods can measure the similarity in the change: Hidden Markov Model (HMM) and Auto Regressive Moving Average (ARMAR).

The distanced-base method relies on distance similarity, using all data in the comparison series, but there may be interference variables. It highly affects classification results. Consequently, based on the distance measure, we can perform transformation operations on the subsequences that influence the classification judgment, thereby alleviating the interpretability issue.

The method is named DDTM (Distance-based Data Transformation Method). It can capture changes in categories and subsequences, and measure the impact of subsequences, which can guide us to perform data transformations on sequences.

The remaining sections of the paper are structured as follows. Section 2 introduces the relevant related work of TSC, including research and an evaluation of various methods. Section 3 explains our method DDTM in detail. Section 4 presents and analyze the performance of DDTM, which achieves superior classification result. Section 5 summarizes our findings and discusses the future direction.

2   Related Work

Recent TSC algorithms [8–10] have addressed the problem of ever-increasing data volumes, attaining greater efficiency and scalability than conventional TSC algorithms. Comparing the research on TSC has been the subject of a meticulous investigation [3]. The following are the conclusions: (1) Collective of transformation-based ensembles (COTE) [15], Elastic Ensemble (EE) [38], Shapelet transform (ST) [36], and Bag-of-SFA-Symbol (BOSS) [39] are the leading classifiers at present; (2) COTE is exceptional in that it encompasses two other classifiers; on average, COTE is "clearly superior to other published techniques".

According to the realization principle of the algorithm, we make the following summary of the classification method.

Distance-Based methods. Two series are compared either as a vector (as with traditional classification) or by a distance measure that uses all the data. As described in *"The Similarity in the Time"*.

Shapelet-Based Method. Hills et al. [36] propose a shapelet transformation (ST) that separates the shapelet discovery from the classifier by finding the top k shapelets on a single run (in contrast to the decision tree, which searches for the best shapelet at each node). More detail is described in *"The Similarity in the Shape"*.

Dictionary-Based Methods. Most dictionary (or 'bag of words') methods work in broadly the same way, i.e., by passing a sliding window over each time series, smoothing or approximating the values in each window, and assigning the resulting values to letters from a symbolic alphabet [23]. The counts of the resulting patterns are used as the basis for classification.

The most prominent dictionary methods are BOSS, cBOSS [22], S-BOSS [19], WEASEL [16], and, more recently, TDE [17], MrSQM [18], and Hydra [23].

BOSS is a large ensemble of such classifiers using different hyperparameter configurations. The resulting feature space is typically very large and very sparse, and the resulting patterns represent a high degree of approximation, as the input is both smoothed and quantized to a very small set of discrete values. In addition, for methods using SFA or a variation thereof, the patterns are formed over values in the frequency domain, rather than the original input.

HC2 supersedes earlier variants of HIVE-COTE [11, 14], and is an ensemble comprising TDE, Shapelet Transform. HC2 is currently the most accurate method for time series classification on the datasets in the UCR archive.

Hydra [23] is a dictionary method that uses convolutional kernels, incorporating aspects of both ROCKET [13] and conventional dictionary methods. Dictionary methods and ROCKET represent two seemingly quite different approaches to time series classification. Hydra is faster and more accurate than the most accurate existing dictionary methods and can be combined with ROCKET and its variants to further improve the accuracy of these methods.

Tree-Based Methods. A family of algorithms derives features from intervals of each series. TS-CHIEF [12] is an extension of an earlier method, Proximity forest [8], and is an ensemble of decision trees using distance measures, intervals, and spectral splitting criteria.

Time series forest (TSF) [40] generates summary features from time series by dividing them into intervals and summarizing each interval by its mean, standard deviation, and gradient. Generalized random shapelet forest (gRSF) [41] derives a shapelet from a randomly selected time series and calculates the distance between each pair of time series.

Deep Learning-Based Methods. A highly influential review paper on deep learning-based TSC [20] was published in 2019. InceptionTime [21] is an ensemble of deep convolutional neural networks based on the Inception architecture, and is currently the most accurate convolutional neural network model for time series classification on the UCR archive.

Dictionary-based methods, while highly accurate, are all burdened by high computational complexity [23]. Shapelet-based methods include a data transformation phase where the time series is transformed into a new feature space. We want to make a small change in the origin series. We try to make as few changes as possible to the original sequence to improve the accuracy. Based on the distance measure, we can perform transformation operations on the subsequences that influence the classification judgment, thereby alleviating the interpretability issue.

Shapelet-based methods have a data transformation phase, which transforms time series into a new feature space. Dictionary-based methods, while highly accurate, are all burdened by high computational complexity [23]. To improve accuracy while making minimal changes to the original sequence, we perform transformation operations on the subsequences that impact the classification decision based on the distance measure. This approach helps address the interpretability issue.

3   Method

The TSC problem relies on the measurement of similarity or dissimilarity between the data. Since time series contain interference factors such as noise and phase difference, if these interference factors can be eliminated reasonably, a more accurate classification can be achieved. We propose the DDTM for time series classification primarily for this reason.

In Sect. 3.1, a detailed explanation was provided of the definitions and specifications used in the implementation of the algorithm. Next, a brief description of the algorithm execution is given.

First, calculate the average distance of subsequences under various windows. Next, the DDTM algorithm involves calculating the maximum information gain for each window position and using it to determine the classification of the time series. Specifically, the algorithm measures the average distance between instances under the specified window position and evaluates the discrimination of subsequences in the window using information gain. By applying this method to all windows, we obtain the optimal window position that maximizes the information gain and improves the accuracy of the classification. The final step is data reduction.

The primary procedure of DDTM is divided into three parts: (1) determination of slide window sizes and calculation of average distance, (2) calculation of information gain and ranking of all windows, and (3) data reduction.

3.1   Definitions and Notions

Definition 1: Time Series. A time series $T = \{t_1, \ldots, t_m\}$ is an ordered set of m real-valued variables.

Data points $t_1, \ldots, t_m$ are arranged in temporal sequence and separated by equal intervals of time. Instead of the global characteristics of a time series, we are more interested in the local properties. A subsequence is a discrete division of a time series.

Definition 2: Subsequence. A time series T with length m, a subsequence S of T is a sample with length $1 < = m$ of contiguous positions from T, that is $S = \{t_p, \ldots, t_{p+l-1}\} 1 \leq p \leq m - l + 1$. The sliding window technique must be used by our algorithm to extract the subsequences with a fixed length.

Definition 3: Sliding Window. By swiping a frame of size w across a time series T with length m and a user-defined subsequence length of l, the subsequences can be extracted by taking into account each subsequence, S_p^l of T. Here, the sliding window's starting location in the time series is indicated by the subscript p, and the length of the subsequence is denoted by the superscript l. S_T^l is the collection of all subsequences with length w that are extracted from T. $S_T^l = \left\{ S_p^l of\, T, for\, 1 \leq p \leq m - l + 1 \right\}$. We need to provide a similarity measure between the time series S and R.

Definition 4: Distance between the time series. $Dist(S, R)$ is a distance function to measure the distance of two time series S and R. In the calculation, the subsequences are z-normalized with $mean = 0$ and $std = 1$.

As we'll discuss in Sects. 3.2 and 3.3, our algorithm requires a few metrics to assess how well the subsequences with a sliding time series window can split the combined dataset into its two original classes based on distance measures.

Suppose that dataset D contains n time series from c different classes. The number of time series in class i is n_i and we define class probability as $p_i = n_i/n$. Hence, we define the entropy of the dataset D as follows.

Definition 5: Entropy. The entropy is defined as $E(D) = \sum_{i=1}^{c} p_i \log(p_i)$.

Definition 6: Average Distance in the Window. It defines the average distance (DTW distance) in the window as the average distance between each instance and other instances in the window position subsequence. For one position p of the sliding window, we can get a set of distances AD_m ($AD_m = \{ad_1, \ldots, ad_m\}$), where ad_m is the max distance of instances.

The average distance quantifies the distance between subsequences across all instances, which influences the categorization of groups. Therefore, it is necessary to determine the effect of various apertures. Therefore, we incorporate a split gap to determine the window's significance.

Definition 7: Split Gap. Split Gap divides the sequence's time series into two parts based on the average distance's increase under the specified window position. For an average distance ad_i which can split the AD_p into two parts, $Part_1$ and $Part_2$. We define the information gain of the split gap.

Definition 8: Information Gain of the Split Gap. The information gain of the split gap in distance ad_i is: $I(ad_i) = E(AD_p) - E(Part_1) - E(Part_2)$. For window position p, $E(AD_p) = \sum_{i=1}^{c} p_i \log(p_i)$.

We calculate the average distance of subsequences under various windows and then the utmost value of information gain based on the split gap. Finally, we obtain the rank of all windows, which are ordered according to their information gain.

According to the window's split strategy, the average distance of subsequences under distinct windows is computed, and then the maximum information gain under the window is determined based on the split gap. Then, we rank all window positions according to their information gain. Finally, we eliminate subsequences in data transformation window positions with a reduced information gain.

3.2 Case Study

We show the positions and values of the dataset and visually analyze the relationship between distances and classes. The x-axis displays the item of position, while the y-axis represents the value of the series. And different colors represent different categories.

Figures 1 and 2 depict the alterations of data points and data values for the time series datasets Ham (length 431) and GunPoint (length 150).

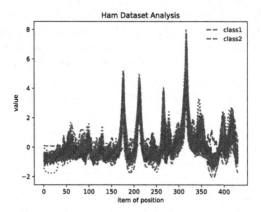

Fig. 1. Changes in data points and class values in Ham.

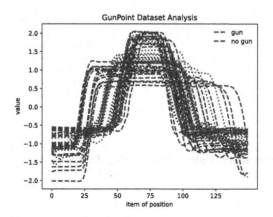

Fig. 2. Classes and the value of data points in GunPoint.

The visualization of the Ham dataset in Fig. 1 shows that when the item points are located at initial positions 160–180, 210–220, 310–330, and 390–400, the curves of the three categories are very close, indicating small inter-class distance at these positions. In contrast, at items 50 to 100 and 230 to 250, there are clear distinctions between the data of various categories. The results of the DTW-based sliding window suggest that the distance between classes is relatively large close to these positions. These positions represent essential data for various categories and are distinct from the rest of the data.

The same conclusion can be drawn from the GunPoint of Fig. 2. According to the similarity between categories and local distances, we evaluate the significance of data segments under various frames as a guideline for data transformation.

We quantified the inner-class and outer-class distances of Fig. 2's subsequences, which can be used to analyze the significance of the divided classes of the time series at various window positions. Figure 3 illustrates the mean distance between classes in window positions (set window size with 12). The x-axis indicates the window positions, while the y-axis represents the average distances of items. The red line represents the same class, while the green one represents the average distance of different classes.

Compared to Figs. 2 and 3, the average differentiation within and between classes within the window is more evident for time series data with large differences (in Fig. 2 such as items 0–24 and items 108–130, in Fig. 3 at window position 0–2 and window position 9–10) between the values of different categories; thus, it can be captured through the window as a prerequisite for classification.

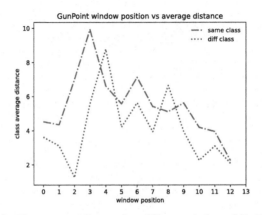

Fig. 3. Class average distance in a different window of GunPoint.

3.3 Window Division and Calculating Average Distance

As the window size changes, there are some changes in the classification accuracy of different datasets. Different windows represent the characteristics of captured data sets at partial resolutions. Strictly speaking, we need to try more window sizes, but exhaustively enumerating all windows will require a lot of calculations, and it is not universal. The sequence is a subset of the larger window, so we choose a smaller window to capture the impact of subsequences in the window on the classification results from a fine-grained level.

Using the time series T of length t, the sliding window size is set to w, the window step is set to s, and the cardinality is set to r = 0.0125.

For the size of the sliding window, we used an even number of coefficients between 2 and 4 based on r. This setting is intended to prevent brute force and can be applied to datasets of varying lengths.

Algorithm 1. Calculate the average distance under each window.

Algorithm 1: Calculate the average distance for each window based on SW
Input: Time series $T = \{T_1,,,T_m\}$, Length L, window size w, window step s
Output: Sets of average distance under all window

```
Sets of average distance AD, ∅ → AD
for j=0 to 1/s do
    window: p begins L * s * j, end L * s * j + L * w
    for k=1 to m do
        Subsequences are z-normalized with mean=0 and
std=1
        Calculating average distance adₖ using DTW
distance
        Add adₖ into ADₚ
    end for
end for
Return AD
```

ad_k, AD_p

In Algorithm 1, for each window split parameter (input), the algorithm implements the split strategy into windows (lines 3 to 4) and calculates the average distance between itself and others (line 6). Subsequences are z-normalized during this procedure (line 5). Finally, insert each ad_k into AD_p and return the AD (line 10).

Algorithm 2. Calculate the average distance under each window.

Algorithm 2: Calculate information gain for each window based on *Split Gap*
Input: All windows size with $floor(L/w)$ as size
Output: Sets of information gained under all window

Sets of information gain I, $\emptyset \rightarrow I$
for j=1 to size do
    window: p with Average Distance AD_p
    for ad_i in AD_p do
        ad_i split the AD_p into two parts, $Part_1$ and
$Part_2$
$$I(ad_i) = E(AD_p) - E(Part_1) - E(Part_2)$$
        Calculating maximum of $I(ad)$ for this window p
as I_p
        Add I_p to I
    end for
end for
Return I

In Algorithm 2, it takes total window positions as the input. For each window position, the algorithm employs a split gap to divide the time series into two parts (line 5) and calculates the information gain for each instance (line 6). The algorithm then returns (lines 7 to 8) the maximum value of information gain for each window position (line 11).

3.4 Data Transformation Method based on Average Distance

We can create data transformation operators based on the metrics mentioned above, such as the average distance and information gain calculated in Sect. 3.3 at different window positions. In Algorithm 3, we propose a data transformation process based on the window position hierarchy.

To reduce data loss, we set the threshold of the lost subsequence to be no more than 2 windows (line 3) of the original sequence and cease deleting the subsequence when the information gain does not change significantly. We remove the window with the least amount of information gain. To prevent excessive information loss, we set a maximum delete length (no more than 20% of the length of the time series).

Algorithm 3. Data transformation based on the rank of the window position.

Algorithm 3: Data transformation of time series based on window position
Input: All windows rank
Output: Time series

---

for j=1 to size do
    window: p with information gain I_p
    If delete window size d <= 20%*size and the
value of I_p not increase rapidly
        Delete window position
    else continue
end for
Return Time series T'

We have analyzed the average sequence distance across several datasets. When the average distance between changes is small, the change in information gain between windows is also small. To avoid eliminating valid information, we must regulate the total number of removed subsequences and the probability of information gain. Therefore, in Algorithm 3, we specify the maximum delete window size (no more than 20 percent of the length of the time series) and information gain increment parameters.

4 Result and Evaluation

Experimental Setup. After the training of the data transformation procedure finishes, the performance of the method is evaluated by calculating the testing dataset's precision. We predict the class designation using a conventional 1-NN algorithm based on DTW distance. We evaluate DDTM (based on DTW) with Euclidean distance (1NN-ED), 1NN-DTW, and Elastic ensemble (EE).

Datasets. In our investigations, we chose specific datasets from the UCR archive [4–6]. In addition, the dataset is divided into two categories: short-length datasets (Short-Dataset) and long-length datasets (Long-Dataset). Tables 1 and 2 present the fundamental characteristics (including dataset name, classes as c, length as l, and train/test number).

Figures 4, 5 and 6 illustrates the classification performance of four algorithms, namely 1NN-ED, 1NN-DTW, EE, and DDTM, on two types of datasets, namely long-length and short-length. The sliding window size increases progressively from r = 0.0125 to 0.05, indicating the results of the algorithm on the respective datasets. The x-axis displays the names of the datasets, while the y-axis represents the classification accuracy.

From the classification results of the long-length datasets in Figures 4, 5 and 6 (left), we find that on the CBF, Coffee, and Traces, the classification accuracy of the original

Table 1. Short time-series datasets.

Short-Dataset	train	test	l	c
CBF	30	900	128	3
Coffee	28	28	286	2
DiatomSizeReduction	16	306	354	4
ECG200	100	100	96	2
FaceFour	24	88	350	4
GunPoint	150	150	150	2
Trace	100	100	275	4

Table 2. Long time-series datasets.

Long-Dataset	train	test	l	c
ACSF1	100	100	1460	10
Beef	30	30	470	5
BeetleFly	20	20	512	2
Earthquake	322	139	512	2
Ham	109	105	431	2
OliveOil	30	30	570	4
Worms	181	77	900	5
WormsTwoClass	181	77	900	2
Yoga	300	300	426	2

algorithm is close to 100%. When we reduce the data of the data set, it will inevitably affect the important data of classification calculation, which will lead to the decline of classification accuracy. But the EE algorithm performs poorly on the CBF.

Under different parameters r, the DDTM algorithm shows a relatively large difference in performance on the FaceFour dataset, and it is more sensitive to the window size. In total, the accuracy of our DDTM has improved on the other datasets.

After comparing Figs. 4 and 5, we observed that using smaller window sizes on short-length datasets can capture more fine-grained changes and filter out noise, leading to improved classification accuracy. As dataset length increases, the window size becomes crucial as it affects not only the resolution in capturing intra-class and inter-class distance changes but also the amount of data reduction achieved through the reduced operation.

For longer datasets, using smaller sliding windows can capture finer-grained features, but at the cost of discarding the length features of larger windows (composed of multiple small-size windows) subsequences. The classification accuracy of the ACSF1 dataset is higher at r = 0.025 compared to r = 0.0125.

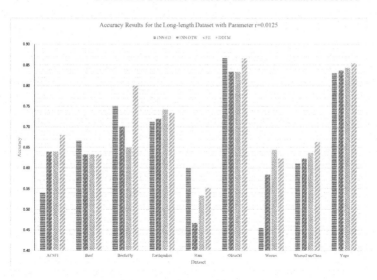

(a) Long time series dataset.

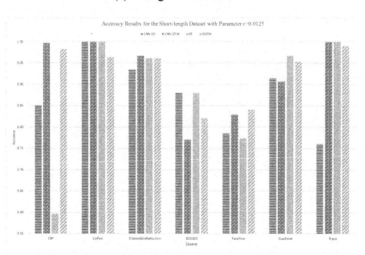

(b) Short time series dataset.

Fig. 4. Accuracy Result for the Dataset with Parameter r = 0.0125.

So, choosing an appropriate window size becomes even more important for longer datasets, as the reduced operation can significantly impact the amount of data retained for analysis.

As the value of parameter r increases, the classification accuracy of long datasets such as ACSF1 and Worms tends to decrease, whereas the accuracy of other datasets remains relatively stable. Furthermore, we observed that increasing the window size can make the classification accuracy of longer datasets more unstable. We also noticed that controlling for the number of deleted windows could cause fluctuations in accuracy. Thus,

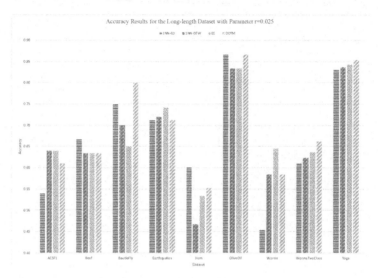

(a) Long time series dataset.

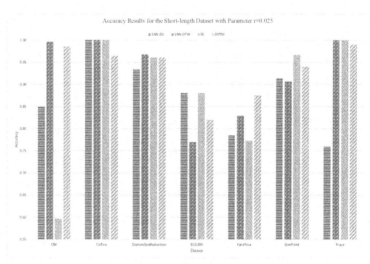

(b) Short time series dataset.

Fig. 5. Accuracy Result for the Dataset with Parameter r = 0.025.

we can conclude that the size of data reduction has a significant impact on classification accuracy.

Furthermore, as the window size increases, the classification accuracy of longer datasets becomes unstable. During our testing, we observed fluctuations in accuracy when controlling for the number of deleted windows. Hence, we conclude that the size of the data reduction significantly impacts the classification accuracy.

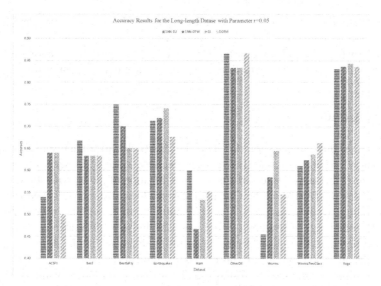

(a) Long time series dataset.

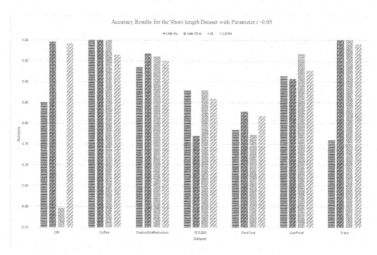

(b) Short time series dataset.

Fig. 6. Accuracy Result for the Dataset with Parameter r = 0.05.

The experimental results show that DDTM is more accurate than the 1-NN algorithm of Euclidean distance and DTW distance, indicating that redundant subsequences in the data influence the distance-based class division. The results confirmed that DDTM can identify the sequences in the data sequence which affect classification results and that removing these sequences improves classification accuracy. On some datasets, DDTM outperformed EE in terms of accuracy, while on others, EE outperformed DDTM. Also problematic is the fact that EE has even longer training periods. If we can effectively transform data for time series that are unfavorable for classification, the classification accuracy will be enhanced. For certain time series, DDTM can identify the window positions at which the influence of the inner class and outer class on class division is most pronounced. After data reduction, classification accuracy was improved.

5 Conclusions

Time series has interference variables, it maybe affects classification results. We investigate the variations in the distance between the category and a subsequence of time series to determine if the subsequence affects the determination of the classification.

We present the DDTM method, which measures local distance and class sensitivity using a sliding window and calculates information gain at various window positions to evaluate the effects of window position on class division. The outcomes are utilized to direct data transformation operations. Our results indicate that the proposed method outperforms other algorithms in terms of classification accuracy.

In the future, by combining distance-based and shapelet-based methods, superior results in both interpretability and accuracy can be achieved. And, the deep learning techniques have a great potential for improving TSC.

Acknowledgement. This work was supported by the Fund of National Natural Science Foundation of China (No. 62162010, G0112), Research Projects of the Science and Technology Plan of Guizhou Province (No. [2021]449, No. [2023]010).

References

1. Yang, Q., Wu, X.: 10 Challenging problems in data mining research. Int. J. Info. Tech. Dec. Mak. **05**(04), 597–604 (2011). https://doi.org/10.1142/S0219622006002258
2. Keogh, E., Kasetty, S.: On the need for time series data mining benchmarks: a survey and empirical demonstration. Data Min. Knowl. Disc. **7**, 349–371 (2003)
3. Bagnall, A., Lines, J., Bostrom, A., et al.: The great time series classification bake off: a review and experimental evaluation of recent algorithmic advances. Data Min. Knowl. Disc. **31**, 606–660 (2017)
4. Chen, Y., Keogh, E., Hu, B., Begum, N., Bagnall, A., Mueen, A., Batista, G.: The UCR time series classification archive (2015). www.cs.ucr.edu/~eamonn/time_series_data/
5. Dau, H.A., Bagnall, A., Kamgar, K., et al.: The UCR time series archive. IEEE/CAA J. Autom. Sinica **6**(6), 1293–1305 (2019)
6. Bagnall, A.J.: The UEA multivariate time series classification archive. CoRR. 2018;abs/1811.00075 (2018). http://arxiv.org/abs/1811.00075. Accessed 14 May 2023
7. Xi, X., Keogh, E., Shelton, C., et al.: Fast time series classification using numerosity reduction. In: Proceedings of the ICML, pp. 1033–1040 (2006)
8. Lucas, B., Shifaz, A., Pelletier, C., et al.: Proximity forest: an effective and scalable distance-based classifier for time series. Data Min. Knowl. Disc. **33**(3), 607–635 (2019)
9. Schäfer, P., Leser, U.: Fast and accurate time series classification with Wease. In: Proceedings of the CIKM, pp. 637–646 (2017)
10. Schäfr, P.: Scalable time series classification. Data Min. Knowl. Disc. **30**(5), 1273–1298 (2016)

11. Lines, J., Taylor, S., Bagnall, A.: Time series classification with HIVE-COTE: The hierarchical vote collective of transformation-based ensembles. ACM Trans. Knowl. Discov. Data **12**(5), 1–35 (2018)
12. Shifaz, A., Pelletier, C., Petitjean, F., et al.: TS-CHIEF: a scalable and accurate forest algorithm for time series classification. Data Min. Knowl. Disc. **34**(3), 742–775 (2020)
13. Dempster, A., Petitjean, F., Webb, G.I.: ROCKET: exceptionally fast and accurate time series classification using random convolutional kernels. Data Min. Knowl. Disc. **34**(5), 1454–1495 (2020)
14. Middlehurst, M., Large, J., Flynn, M., et al.: HIVE-COTE 2.0: a new meta ensemble for time series classification. Mach. Learn. **110**(11–12), 3211–3243 (2021)
15. Bagnall, A., Lines, J., Hills, J., et al.: Time-series classification with COTE: the collective of transformation-based ensembles. IEEE Trans. Knowl. Data Eng. **27**(9), 2522–2535 (2015)
16. Schäfr, P., Leser, U.: Fast and accurate time series classification with WEASEL. In: Proceedings of the 2017 ACM on Conference on Information and Knowledge Management. CIKM'17, pp. 637–646. Association for Computing Machinery (2017). https://doi.org/10.1145/3132847.3132980
17. Middlehurst, M., Large, J., Cawley, G., Bagnall, A.: The temporal dictionary ensemble (TDE) classifier for time series classification. In: Hutter, F., Kersting, K., Lijffijt, J., Valera, I. (eds.) ECML PKDD 2020. LNCS (LNAI), vol. 12457, pp. 660–676. Springer, Cham (2020). https://doi.org/10.1007/978-3-030-67658-2_38
18. Le Nguyen, T., Ifrim, G.: MrSQM: Fast Time Series Classification with Symbolic Representations (2021)
19. Large, J., Bagnall, A., Malinowski, S., Tavenard, R.: On time series classification with dictionary-based classifiers. Intell. Data Anal. **23**(5), 1073–1089 (2019). https://doi.org/10.3233/IDA-184333
20. Ismail Fawaz, H., Forestier, G., Weber, J., Idoumghar, L., Muller, P.A.: Deep learning for time series classification: a review. Data Min Knowl Discov. **33**(4), 917–963 (2019). https://doi.org/10.1007/S10618-019-00619-1/METRICS
21. Ismail Fawaz, H., Lucas, B., Forestier, G., et al.: InceptionTime: finding AlexNet for time series classification. Data Min Knowl Discov. **34**(6), 1936–1962 (2020). https://doi.org/10.1007/S10618-020-00710-Y/METRICS
22. Middlehurst, M., Vickers, W., Bagnall, A.: Scalable dictionary classifiers for time series classification. In: Yin, H., Camacho, D., Tino, P., Tallallesteros, A.J., Menezes, R., Allmendinger, R. (eds.) IDEAL 2019. LNCS, vol. 11871, pp. 11–19. Springer, Cham (2019). https://doi.org/10.1007/978-3-030-33607-3_2
23. Dempster, A., Schmidt, D.F., Webb, G.I.: HYDRA: Competing convolutional kernels for fast and accurate time series classification. ArXiv (2022). https://doi.org/10.48550/ARXIV.2203.13652
24. Riaboff, L., Shalloo, L., Smeaton, A.F., Couvreur, S., Madouasse, A., Keane, M.T.: Predicting livestock behaviour using accelerometers: a systematic review of processing techniques for ruminant behaviour prediction from raw accelerometer data. Comput. Electron. Agric. **192**, 106610 (2022). https://doi.org/10.1016/J.COMPAG.2021.106610
25. Kanawaday, A., Sane, A.: Machine learning for predictive maintenance of industrial machines using IoT sensor data. In: Proceedings of the IEEE International Conference on Software Engineering and Service Sciences, ICSESS, pp. 87–90 (2018). https://doi.org/10.1109/ICSESS.2017.8342870
26. Fabietti, M., Mahmud, M., Lotfi, A.: On-chip machine learning for portable systems: application to electroencephalography-based brain-computer interfaces. In: Proceedings of the International Joint Conference on Neural Networks (2021). https://doi.org/10.1109/IJCNN52387.2021.9533413

27. Singh, A., Le, B.T., Le, N.T., et al.: Interpretable classification of human exercise videos through pose estimation and multivariate time series analysis. Stud. Comput. Intell. **1013**, 181–199 (2022). https://doi.org/10.1007/978-3-030-93080-6_14/COVER

28. Nweke, H.F., Teh, Y.W., Al-garadi, M.A., Alo, U.R.: Deep learning algorithms for human activity recognition using mobile and wearable sensor networks: state of the art and research challenges. Expert Syst. Appl. **105**, 233–261 (2018). https://doi.org/10.1016/J.ESWA.2018. 03.056

29. Wang, J., Chen, Y., Hao, S., Peng, X., Hu, L.: Deep learning for sensor-based activity recognition: a survey. Pattern Recognit Lett. **119**, 3–11 (2019). https://doi.org/10.1016/J.PATREC. 2018.02.010

30. Chen, K., Zhang, D., Yao, L., Guo, B., Yu, Z., Liu, Y.: Deep learning for sensor-based human activity recognition: overview, challenges, and opportunities. ACM Comput. Surv. **54**(4), 1–40 (2021). https://doi.org/10.1145/3447744

31. Schirrmeister, R.T., Springenberg, J.T., Fiederer, L.D.J., et al.: Deep learning with convolutional neural networks for EEG decoding and visualization. Hum. Brain Mapp. **38**(11), 5391–5420 (2017). https://doi.org/10.1002/HBM.23730

32. Rajkomar, A., Oren, E., Chen, K., et al.: Scalable and accurate deep learning with electronic health records. NPJ Digit Med. **1**(1), 18 (2018). https://doi.org/10.1038/S41746-018-0029-1

33. Ye, L., Keogh, E.: Time series shapelets: a new primitive for data mining. In: Proceeding of the KDD, pp. 947–956 (2009)

34. Rakthanmanon, T., Keogh, E.: Fast shapelets: a scalable algorithm for discovering time series shapelets. In: Proceedings of the SDM, pp. 668–676 (2013)

35. Ding, H., Trajcevski, G., Scheuermann, P., et al.: Querying and mining of time series data: experimental comparison of representations and distance measures. Proc. VLDB Endow. **1**(2), 1542–1552 (2008)

36. Hills, J., Lines, J., Baranauskas, E., et al.: Classification of time series by shapelet transformation. Data Min. Knowl. Disc. **28**(4), 851–881 (2014)

37. Mueen, A., Keogh, E., Young, N.: Logical-shapelets: an expressive primitive for time series classification. In: Proceedings of the KDD, pp. 1154–1162 (2011)

38. Lines, J., Bagnall, A.: Time series classification with ensembles of elastic distance measures. Data Min. Knowl. Disc. **29**(3), 565–592 (2015)

39. Schäfr, P.: The BOSS is concerned with time series classification in the presence of noise. Data Min. Knowl. Disc. **29**(6), 1505–1530 (2015)

40. Deng, H., Runger, G., Tuv, E., et al.: A time series forest for classification and feature extraction. Inf. Sci. **239**, 142–153 (2013)

41. Karlsson, I., Papapetrou, P., BostrH.: Generalized random shapelet forests. Data Min. Knowl. Disc. **30**(5), 1053–1085 (2016)

42. Lu, H., Zhang, M., Xu, X., Li, Y., Shen, H.T.: Deep Fuzzy Hashing Network for Efficient Image Retrieval. IEEE Trans. Fuzzy Syst. **29**(1), 166–176 (2021). https://doi.org/10.1109/ TFUZZ.2020.2984991

43. Ma, C., Li, X., Li, Y., et al.: Visual information processing for deep-sea visual monitoring system. Cogn. Robot. **1**, 3–11 (2021). https://doi.org/10.1016/J.COGR.2020.12.002

44. Lu, H., Teng, Y., Li, Y.: Learning latent dynamics for autonomous shape control of deformable object. IEEE Trans. Intell. Transport. Syst. **24**(11), 13133–13140 (2023). https://doi.org/10. 1109/TITS.2022.3225322

45. Li, Y., Cai, J., Zhou, Q., Lu, H.: Joint semantic-instance segmentation method for intelligent transportation system. IEEE Trans. Intell. Transport. Syst. **24**(12), 15540–15547 (2023). https://doi.org/10.1109/TITS.2022.3190369

46. Zheng, Y., Li, Y., Yang, S., Lu, H.: Global-PBNet: a novel point cloud registration for autonomous driving. IEEE Trans. Intell. Transp. Syst. **23**(11), 22312–22319 (2022). https:// doi.org/10.1109/TITS.2022.3153133

47. Yang, S., Lu, H., Li, J.: Multifeature fusion-based object detection for intelligent transportation systems. IEEE Trans. Intell. Transp. Syst. **24**(1), 1126–1133 (2023). https://doi.org/10.1109/TITS.2022.3155488
48. Zhao, F., Zhao, W., Lu, H., Liu, Y., Yao, L., Liu, Y.: Depth-distilled multi-focus image fusion. IEEE Trans. Multimed. (2021). https://doi.org/10.1109/TMM.2021.3134565
49. Lu, H., Tang, Y., Sun, Y.: DRRS-BC: decentralized routing registration system based on blockchain. IEEE/CAA J. Autom. Sinica **8**(12), 1868–1876 (2021). https://doi.org/10.1109/JAS.2021.1004204

Two Stream Multi-Attention Graph Convolutional Network for Skeleton-Based Action Recognition

Huijian Zhou[1], Zhiqiang Tian[1(✉)], and Shaoyi Du[2]

[1] School of Software Engineering, Xi'an Jiaotong University, Xi'an, Shaanxi, China
zhiqiangtian@xjtu.edu.cn
[2] Institute of Artificial Intelligence and Robotics, Xi'an Jiaotong University, Xi'an, Shaanxi, China

Abstract. The skeleton-based action recognition has attracted much attention of researchers. The existing methods mostly introduce motion information into models by using multi-stream architecture, which leads to more parameters and FLOPs. In this paper, to resolve this problem, the proposed 2s-MAGCN (Two-Stream Multi-Attention Graph Convolutional Network) introduces motion information by applying the Motion Excitation attention module, which not only leads to less parameters and FLOPs by merging multi-stream into two-stream, but also improves the performance of the model. By proposing new strategies of pooling operations in attention modules, we get attention modules with better performance. It includes Spatial Excitation and Temporal Excitation, which are proposed to enhance the spatio-temporal expression ability of the model. On cross-subject benchmark and cross-view benchmark of NTU-RGB+D datasets, the proposed model achieves 88.60% and 97.16% accuracy respectively, and 35.62% accuracy on the Kinetics dataset. On both datasets, our method outperforms state-of-the-art methods.

Keywords: Attention mechanism · Skeleton-based action recognition · Spatial temporal graph convolution

1 Introduction

Human action recognition has attracted much attention in recent years, as it can be applied in many applications, such as virtual reality, intelligent monitoring and human-computer interaction. Researchers proposed many different models to solve this task. Human action can be recognized by different modalities, such as RGB [15], optical flow [14], skeleton [16], and so on. In this work, the proposed model is based on skeleton data.

Skeleton data does not contain the information of human appearances or scenes where people do the actions. Therefore, the skeleton-based models do not be influenced by occlusion, illumination changes, which makes models more

H. Lu and J. Cai (Eds.): ISAIR 2023, CCIS 1998, pp. 112–120, 2024.
https://doi.org/10.1007/978-981-99-9109-9_11

robust. Moreover, skeleton-based methods generally need less computation and storage, which is also a huge advantage comparing to other methods.

Yan et al. [16] applied GCNs to model dynamic human skeletons, which leads to higher performance and better expressive power than previous works. However, as a pioneering work of applying GCNs to the task, ST-GCN also has many drawbacks to be improved. In the past few years, researchers improved models by constructing more flexible graph topology [7], applying multi-stream as input [10,13], representing skeletons by heat maps [4]. Among these improvements, we notice that the attention mechanism still has room for improvement. Therefore, we try to improve the model from the perspective of attention mechanism, which consists of three parts: Motion Excitation, Spatial Excitation and Temporal Excitation.

By researches, we find two disadvantages in ST-GCN [16]: 1) skeleton data contains less information comparing to other modalities like RGB videos. To overcome this drawback, multi-stream (including joint-stream, bone-stream and their motion-stream) were introduced in many skeleton-based models [13], which leaded to more parameters and FLOPs. We present Motion Excitation (ME) module to capture motion information instead of motion-stream, which can leads to higher performance and less parameters and FLOPs. 2) The convolution kernels of ST-GCN can only extract local features, which makes the model lack of global information. To solve this problem, Spatial Excitation (SE) and Temporal Excitation (TE) are proposed, which can extract global features. Finally, combining three modules above, we get an MST (Motion Spatial Temporal) attention module.

Moreover, we notice that average pooling is usually used as pooling operation in previous attention modules. However, recent researches [11] prove that average features are suboptimal features. As a result, in order to improve the performance of attention modules, we propose new strategies to combine average pooling with max pooling, which can be introduced in other works that having pooling operations.

Finally, to verify the effectiveness of the proposed MST module, we added it to ST-GCN. The experiments were performed on two large-scale datasets: NTU-RGB+D [12] and Kinetics [5,6].

The major contributions of this paper lie in three points:

1) We propose an MST attention module to capture motion and global information of skeleton data, which not only reduces the FLOPs and parameters of the model comparing to multi-stream methods, but also improves the performance of the model.
2) We propose new strategies to combine average pooling with max pooling in attention modules to improve the performance of attention modules, which can be introduced in other works having pooling operations.
3) On two large-scale datasets, NTU-RGB+D [12] and Kinetics [6], the proposed model outperforms state-of-the-art methods.

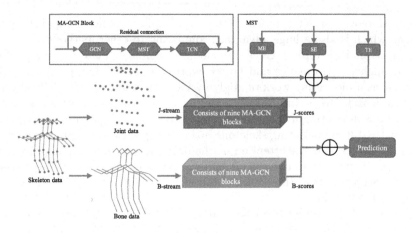

Fig. 1. The framework of 2s-MAGCN. GCN represents Graph Convolutional Networks. TCN represents Temporal Convolutional Networks. MST represents Motion-Spatial-Temporal module. ME represents Motion Excitation. SE represents Spatial Excitation. TE represents Temporal Excitation

2   Method

2.1   Framework

The framework of 2s-MAGCN is shown in Fig. 1. The network consists of joint-stream whose input is joint-data, and bone-stream whose input is bone-data. Two streams have the same structure. Each stream consists of nine MA-GCN blocks. Each stream is followed by a global pooling and a full connection layer to get classification scores. Finally, the classification scores obtained by each stream are added together as the final scores.

2.2   Motion Excitation, Spatial Excitation and Temporal Excitation

The Motion Excitation (ME) is shown in Fig. 2. Given the skeleton features $F_{in} \in \mathbb{R}^{M \times C \times T \times V}$ as input, a squeeze operation is firstly applied to reduce the computation by using a 2D convolutional layer K_1 with kernel size 1×1, which can be represented as

$$F_s = K_1 * F_{in}, \tag{1}$$

where $F_s \in \mathbb{R}^{M \times \frac{C}{r} \times T \times V}$ represents skeleton features squeezed. The parameter r is a scale ratio ($r = 16$ in our work). To capture the motion information, the differences between adjacent frames are calculated, which can be formulated

$$F_m = K_2 * F_s[:, :, t + 1, :] - F_s[:, :, t, :], \tag{2}$$

where K_2 is a 2D convolution layer with kernel size 1×3 and $F_m \in \mathbb{R}^{M \times \frac{C}{r} \times 1 \times V}$ are the motion features of single frame. In this case, the motion features in a

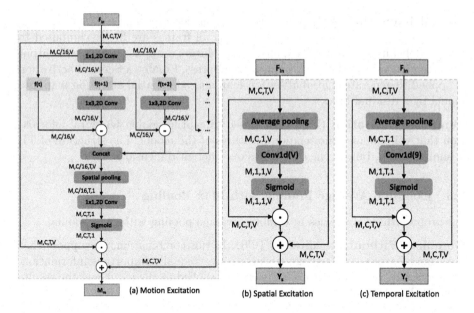

Fig. 2. (a) Motion Excitation. Given the skeleton features $F_{in} \in \mathbb{R}^{M \times C \times T \times V}$ as the input, M is the number of skeletons in one video clip, C is the number of channels, T is the number of frames, V is the number of joints. M_m is the output, representing motion attention map. $\ominus$ represents element-wise reduce, $\odot$ represents element-wise multiply, $\oplus$ represents element-wise add. (b) Spatial Excitation (SE) and (c) Temporal Excitation (TE). The inputs of SE and TE are the same as the input of Motion Excitetion. M_s represents spatial attention map. M_t represents temporal attention map.

single frame are obtained, which will be concatenated to other frames according to temporal dimension and the last frame will be padded with 0. Finally, the total motion features, $F_{tm} \in \mathbb{R}^{M \times \frac{C}{r} \times T \times V}$, are acquired.

The spatial pooling is then adopted to total motion features F_{tm}. Moreover, the unsqueeze operation is done to ensure that the channel number of the feature map is consistent with the input. Finally, the motion attention map M_m is obtained by applying a Sigmoid activation to excite important features and add motion attention map into model by a residual block, which can be represented as

$$M_m = \delta(K_3 * \frac{1}{V} \sum_{i=1}^{V} F_{tm}[:,:,:,i]), \tag{3}$$

$$Y_m = F_{in} + F_{in} \odot M_m, \tag{4}$$

where K_3 is a 2D convolution layer with kernel size 1×1, $M_m \in \mathbb{R}^{M \times C \times T \times 1}$ is motion attention map, $\odot$ represents element-wise multiply, δ represents Sigmoid activation and $Y_m \in \mathbb{R}^{M \times C \times T \times V}$ are the features enhanced by motion information.

Spatial Excitation (SE). Given the skeleton features $F_{in} \in \mathbb{R}^{M \times C \times T \times V}$ as input, the average features of every joint on all frames are firstly computed to obtain global information. Then, an 1D convolution is applied, which will output the attention values where to strength or suppress. Finally, a Sigmoid activation is applied to generate spatial attention map and add spatial attention map into model by a residual block.

Temporal Excitation (TE) is proposed to capture global temporal information that will enhance the temporal features of the model. The structure of TE is similar to SE, but do the operations on different dimensions.

2.3   Combine Average Pooling with Max Pooling

We propose three strategies to combine average pooling with max pooling.

Combine Without Parameters (C0). In this combination, we suppose that both max features and average features convey equally important information. Consequently, two poolings are respectively applied to the input and the results are added together. Formally, we have

$$F_{out} = AvgPool(F_{in}) + MaxPool(F_{in}), \tag{5}$$

where $F_{in} \in \mathbb{R}^{M \times \frac{C}{r} \times T \times V}, F_{out} \in \mathbb{R}^{M \times \frac{C}{r} \times T \times 1}$ in ME, $r = 16$ in this work.

Combine with One Parameter (C1). Based on C0, we think average features and max features may do different contributions to the action recognition. We assume the total contributions to be 1, while set α to be the contributions of average features and $1 - \alpha$ to be the contributions of max features. Formally, we have

$$F_{out} = \alpha * AvgPool(F_{in}) + (1 - \alpha) * MaxPool(F_{in}), \tag{6}$$

where α is a learnable parameter. It is initialized to 0.5.

Combine with Two Parameters (C2). Setting total contributions to be 1 may bind the performance of module. Therefore, two learnable parameters are set. In that case, the enhancement or suppression of pooling features will be determined by two learnable parameters. Formally, we have

$$F_{out} = \alpha * AvgPool(F_{in}) + \beta * MaxPool(F_{in}), \tag{7}$$

where both α and β are learnable parameters that are initialized to 1.

3   Experiments

3.1   Dataset

NTU-RGB+D. NTU-RGB+D [12] is one of biggest skeleton-based daraset, which contains 56,880 action clips in 60 action classes. The actions are performed by 40 volunteers with three cameras to capture joint information at different angles at the same time. There are two benchmark evalution for this dataset: 1) **cross-subject** (CS); 2) **cross-view** (CV).

Kinetics. Kinetics [6] contains over 300,000 action videos in 400 action classes. However, as the dataset only provides raw videos, OpenPose toolbox [2] was adopted to generate skeleton data.

3.2 Ablation Study

Table 1. Ablation Study for three strategies of pooling combination.

Models	Top1/%
baseline ST-GCN [16]	81.5
MotionExcitation	86.2
ME with C0	86.4
ME with C1	86.6
ME with C2	86.7

Table 2. Ablation study for MST modules.

Models	FLOPs	Param	Top1/%
ST-GCN	32.68G	3.1M	81.5
2s-STGCN	65.36G	6.2M	86.18
ME	32.92G	3.13M	86.7
SE	32.68G	3.13M	85.7
TE	32.70G	3.11M	85.3
MA-GCN	32.94G	3.18M	87.3

Table 3. Comparisons of the validation accuracy with skeleton-based action recognition methods, which are also state-of-the-art methods on both NTU-RGB+D and Kinetics.

Models	NTU/%		Kinetics/%	
	CS	CV	Top1	Top5
ST-GCN [16]	81.5	88.3	30.7	52.8
AS-GCN [7]	86.8	94.2	34.8	56.5
PB-GCN [17]	82.7	88.6	30.9	52.8
SS-GCN [3]	83.6	90.3	35.2	57.5
AMV-GCNs [9]	83.8	92.2	–	–
PR-GCN [8]	85.2	91.7	33.7	55.8
ST-AGCN [1]	88.2	94.3	–	–
Js-MAGCN (Ours)	87.3	94.8	34.6	57.2
Bs-MAGCN (Ours)	87.0	95.2	32.6	54.6
2s-MAGCN (Ours)	**88.6**	**96.1**	**35.6**	**58.0**

To evaluate the proposed components, experiments were performed on cross-subject (CS) benchmark of the NTU-RGB+D dataset.

Combine Average Pooling with Max Pooling. To prove the effectiveness of the proposed modules, ST-GCN [16] is set as a baseline. ME is used as an example to adopt three combinations. In addition, to prove the improved performance is due to combinations of pooling operations rather than Motion Excitation, an intermediate model whose pooling operation is only average pooling is set, which referred as "Motion Excitation". Seen from Table 1, the models, applying ME with the proposed combinations, consistently achieve better performance than ST-GCN and "Motion Excitation". Moreover, the results also prove that the model with more learnable parameters achieves better performance. Based on above experiments, the average pooling in SE and TE are also replaced by the C2 combination for the rest of the experiments.

MST Modules. By calculating the displacement of joints between adjacent frames, the joint-motion data is obtained to be as the input of ST-GCN, referred

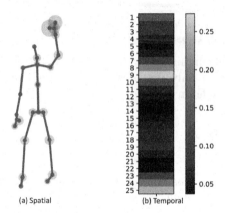

Fig. 3. Visualization of spatial attention map and temporal map for hand waving. In (a), the larger circular area represents the higher attention. In (b), the left is the attention of each frame, and the right is the attention value represented by color. (Color figure online)

as motion-stream. Combining motion-stream with joint-stream that use original joint data as the input, the model "2s-STGCN" is obtained. To compare with "2s-STGCN", we set model "ME", which applies Motion Excitation with C2. We can see from Table 2, the performance of "ME" have improved 0.52% comparing to "2s-STGCN" with less FOLPs and Parameters, which proves the effectiveness of Motion Excitation. Besides of Motion Excitation, there are still Spatial Excitation and Temporal Excitation. As shown in Table 2, by adding few FLOPs and parameters, SE and TE can respectively improve the performance of models by 4.2% and 3.8% comparing to ST-GCN. In Fig. 3, we show the visualization of (a) spatial attention map and (b) temporal attention map of final MA-GCN block. In Fig. 3(a), we pay more attention to the waving hand, which is helpful to recognize the action of hand waving. In Fig. 3(b), with only 25 frames remaining after convolution, we also pay more attention to the key frames. The visualization of two attention maps also prove the effectiveness of SE and TE. Finally, combining three attention modules can get best performance.

3.3 Comparison with State of the Arts

The model using joint data and bone data as the input is respectively referred as "Js-MAGCN" and "Bs-MAGCN". Combining them together, we obtain "2s-MAGCN". 2s-MAGCN is compared with state-of-the-art action recognition methods based on skeleton on the datasets of NTU-RGB+D and Kinetics. For NTU-RGB+D, the model is trained on two benchmarks: CS and CV, then obtain the top-1 validation accuracy on test set. In the Kinetics dataset, top-1 and top-5 validation accuracy are used as metrics. The results are shown in Table 3. On both datasets, our method outperforms state-of-the-art methods.

4 Conclusion

In this work, we propose a 2s-MAGCN for skeleton-based action recognition. By proposing MST attention module, the model improves the performance and reduce the computation. In addition, we propose new strategies of pooling operations to improve the performance of attention modules. We validate 2s-MAGCN in action recognition based on two data sets, NTU-RGB+D and Kinetics. On both datasets, the 2s-MAGCN outperforms state-of-the-art methods.

Acknowledgements. This work was supported by the National Key Research and Development Program of China under Grant No. 2020AAA0108100.

References

1. Cao, Y., Liu, C., Huang, Z., Sheng, Y., Ju, Y.: Skeleton-based action recognition with temporal action graph and temporal adaptive graph convolution structure. Multimed. Tools Appl. **80**(19), 29139–29162 (2021)
2. Cao, Z., Simon, T., Wei, S.E., Sheikh, Y.: Realtime multi-person 2D pose estimation using part affinity fields. In: Proceedings of the IEEE Conference on Computer Vision and Pattern Recognition, pp. 7291–7299 (2017)
3. Chen, S., Xu, K., Jiang, X., Sun, T.: Spatiotemporal-spectral graph convolutional networks for skeleton-based action recognition. In: 2021 IEEE International Conference on Multimedia & Expo Workshops (ICMEW), pp. 1–6. IEEE (2021)
4. Duan, H., Zhao, Y., Chen, K., Lin, D., Dai, B.: Revisiting skeleton-based action recognition. In: Proceedings of the IEEE/CVF Conference on Computer Vision and Pattern Recognition, pp. 2969–2978 (2022)
5. Fu, Y., et al.: Partial feature selection and alignment for multi-source domain adaptation. In: Proceedings of the IEEE/CVF Conference on Computer Vision and Pattern Recognition, pp. 16654–16663 (2021)
6. Kay, W., et al.: The kinetics human action video dataset. arXiv preprint arXiv:1705.06950 (2017)
7. Li, M., Chen, S., Chen, X., Zhang, Y., Wang, Y., Tian, Q.: Actional-structural graph convolutional networks for skeleton-based action recognition. In: Proceedings of the IEEE/CVF Conference on Computer Vision and Pattern Recognition, pp. 3595–3603 (2019)
8. Li, S., Yi, J., Farha, Y.A., Gall, J.: Pose refinement graph convolutional network for skeleton-based action recognition. IEEE Robot. Autom. Lett. **6**(2), 1028–1035 (2021)
9. Liu, X., Li, Y., Xia, R.: Adaptive multi-view graph convolutional networks for skeleton-based action recognition. Neurocomputing **444**, 288–300 (2021)
10. Lu, H., Li, Y., Chen, M., Kim, H., Serikawa, S.: Brain intelligence: go beyond artificial intelligence. Mob. Netw. Appl. **23**, 368–375 (2018)
11. Qin, Z., Zhang, P., Wu, F., Li, X.: FcaNet: frequency channel attention networks. In: Proceedings of the IEEE/CVF International Conference on Computer Vision, pp. 783–792 (2021)
12. Shahroudy, A., Liu, J., Ng, T.T., Wang, G.: NTU RGB+ D: a large scale dataset for 3D human activity analysis. In: Proceedings of the IEEE Conference on Computer Vision and Pattern Recognition, pp. 1010–1019 (2016)

13. Shi, L., Zhang, Y., Cheng, J., Lu, H.: Skeleton-based action recognition with multi-stream adaptive graph convolutional networks. IEEE Trans. Image Process. **29**, 9532–9545 (2020)
14. Simonyan, K., Zisserman, A.: Two-stream convolutional networks for action recognition in videos. In: Advances in Neural Information Processing Systems, vol. 27 (2014)
15. Wang, Z., She, Q., Smolic, A.: Action-net: multipath excitation for action recognition. In: Proceedings of the IEEE/CVF Conference on Computer Vision and Pattern Recognition, pp. 13214–13223 (2021)
16. Yan, S., Xiong, Y., Lin, D.: Spatial temporal graph convolutional networks for skeleton-based action recognition. In: Thirty-Second AAAI Conference on Artificial Intelligence (2018)
17. Zhao, M., et al.: PB-GCN: progressive binary graph convolutional networks for skeleton-based action recognition. Neurocomputing **501**, 640–649 (2022)

Aesthetic Multi-attributes Captioning Network for Photos

Hongtao Yang[1,4], Yuchen Li[2], Xinghui Zhou[3], Xin Jin[2(✉)], Ping Shi[1], and Yehui Liu[4]

[1] School of Information and Communication Engineering, Communication University of China, Beijing 100024, China
[2] Beijing Electronic Science and Technology Institute, Beijing 100070, China
jinxinbesti@foxmail.com
[3] University of Science and Technology, Hefei 230026, China
[4] School of Electrical and Information Engineering, Beijing Polytechnic College, Beijing 100042, China

Abstract. In recent years, image aesthetic quality assessment has become increasingly popular. In addition to numerical assessment, aesthetic captioning has been proposed to capture the overall aesthetic impression of an image. To further advance this field, we address a task of aesthetic attribute assessment, which is the aesthetic multi-attributes captioning. Labeling the comments of aesthetic attributes is a non-trivial task, which limits the size of available datasets. We construct a novel DPChallenge Multi-Attributes Captions Dataset (DPC-MACD) dataset by a semi-automatic way. We propose two novel aesthetic multi-attributes captioning networks, which are the Bottom-Up and Top-Down Attention Network (BUTDAN) and Object-Semantics Aligned Pretrained Network (OSAPN). The experimental results show that our method can predict the comments, which are more closely aligned to aesthetic topics than those produced by the previous models. Through the evaluation criteria of image captioning, the specially designed model outperforms other methods.

Keywords: Aesthetic quality assessment · Image captioning · Aesthetic attributes assessment · Semi-supervised learning

1 Introduction

Text and images are both effective media for conveying information; image language is concise, effective, and rich in artistic expression, but it is difficult to directly extract high-level semantic information from images. Text, on the other hand, is rich in semantic information and can assist in interpreting image content. For an image, not only low-dimensional features such as object edges need to be detected, but also higher-dimensional image features such as fashion matching and photography techniques are important presentation methods. Image comments can also be used to effectively express these features, providing additional context and insight into the aesthetic qualities of an image.

H. Lu and J. Cai (Eds.): ISAIR 2023, CCIS 1998, pp. 121–130, 2024.
https://doi.org/10.1007/978-981-99-9109-9_12

Fig. 1. Aesthetic multi-attributes assessment of images.

In this work, we construct a novel DPC-MACD, which is depicted in Fig. 1. DPC-MACD is constructed by transferring from PCCD, a small-scale image dataset with full annotations to our large-scale dataset with weak annotations. The aesthetic attributes are classified into four main attributes of photography: composition, lighting, color, and subject, providing a data foundation for multi-modal aesthetic prediction. The comment matching algorithm is updated from simple keyword matching in DPC-Captions [1] to Bag of Words (BoW) with a BERT based text classification model, which reduces the bias of BoW to aesthetic comments in PCCD. Using the new matching algorithm, up to 5 comments can be matched for each attribute. One of them is chosen as the ground truth caption and the others are used as reference ones, which makes the output captions more stable and reliable. Compared to DPC-Captions, DPC-MACD provides more extensive aesthetic captions, resulting in an improved quality of the dataset and a better understanding of the aesthetic qualities of an image. We then propose a base image captioning network with bottom-up and top-down attention networks and object-semantics aligned pretrained network. The network uses a two-stage training process on a small-scale full annotated dataset and a large-scale weakly annotated one. The smaller datasets are used to filter the required aesthetic comments from the original data. The model is trained on both small-scale PCCD dataset and our large-scale DPC-MACD, while it is evaluated on DPC-MACD using image captioning criteria. In summary, the contributions of this paper are as follows:

- An aesthetic multi-attributes assessment database, DPC-MACD, is constructed for research on image aesthetic captioning and image aesthetic quality assessment. DPC-MACD is a novel dataset containing large number of multi-attributes aesthetic images and comments.
- We add embedding layers to OSAPN to fuse text information, image features, target tags, and image aesthetic features, all of these information is then output through multi-layer transformers to generate captions.
- Based on DPC-MACD, we have developed the new model capable of producing not only aesthetically relevant but also diverse image captions.

2   Related Work

2.1   Image Aesthetic Quality Assessment

Image Aesthetic Quality Assessment Dataset. One of the main challenges in IAQA is the lack of large scale high quality annotated datasets. Chang et al. [8] issued the first aesthetic captioning dataset called Photo Critique Captioning dataset (PCCD), which is based on a professional photo critique website that provides experienced photographers reviews of photos. It contains 4235 images and more than sixty thousands captions. PCCD is an almost entirely annotated dataset that contains ratings and scores of each of the seven aesthetic attributes. The AVA-Comments [7] and AVA-Reviewers [18] are designed from AVA [16] and adding single sentence comments to describe overall impression. Both AVA-Reviews [18] and PCCD [8] could only provide a single sentence as the comments of the aesthetics of an image and could not give a full review of aesthetic attributes. And the size of PCCD is relatively small compared to the AVA [16] dataset, which does not have ground truth of aesthetic captions and attributes. Ghosal [26] proposed a probabilistic aesthetic caption-filtering method for cleaning internet data to generate the AVA-Captions dataset, which has more higher quality captions than the PCCD dataset. Jin et al. [1] built DPC-Captions dataset, which contains 154,384 images and 2,427,483 comments of up to 5 aesthetic attributes. Nieto et al. [3] proposed the Reddit Photo Critique Dataset (RPCD), which contains tuples of image and photo critiques. Zhong et al. [4] first introduced the concept of Aesthetic Relevance Score (ARS) of a sentence and developed a model to automatically label a sentence with its ARS.

Image Aesthetic Quality Assessment Method. Deep learning methods have already been used in aesthetic quality assessment [2,12,19]. Jin [1] propose aesthetic multi-attribute captioning network, which is composed of multi-attribute feature network, channel and spatial attention network, and language generation network. The core of multi-attribute feature network contains general feature network and attribute feature network, which regress the global score and attribute scores of an image in PCCD using multi-task regression. They share the dense feature map and have separate global and attribute feature maps, respectively. Ke [28] introduced a vision-language aesthetic learning framework (VILA) to provide a comprehensive understanding of image aesthetics through image-comment pairs. To make the model suitable for various image aesthetic assessment (IAA) tasks, a rank-based module was developed, allowing the model to be adapted without perturbing the original pretrained weights. For the specific task, Zou [27] proposed the task of food image aesthetic captioning and decomposed it into two tasks: single aspect captioning and an unsupervised text compression. They also collected a dataset which contains comments related to six aesthetic attributes.

2.2   Image Captioning

Most image captioning work follows the CNN-RNN framework, which has achieved good results in the literature [10,13]. Some works [5,6,9,14,15] have also introduced an attention scheme, which is also incorporated into our network with the addition of an attention model. Recent studies [20–23] have shown that vision-language pretraining (VLP) can effectively learn generic representations from large image-text datasets, and that fine-tuning VLP models on task-specific data can achieve state-of-the-art results on established visual and language tasks. The latest research results in the field of vision-language pretraining are Object-Semantics Aligned Pre-training [24] and Contrastive Language Image Pre-training [25]. MiniGPT-4 [29] is designed to combine visual information from trained ViT [30] with large language models (LLMS) to perform a variety of complex language tasks, ViT supports image parsing, while Vicuna [31] enhances generation with session rounds. The MiniGPT-4 model achieves visual language understanding by utilizing pre-trained models and innovative training strategies.

3   Aesthetic Multi-attributes Assessment Database

In the process of making the datasets, we use the knowledge transfer method from PCCD [8] to DPC-MAC. The aesthetic attributes of PCCD dataset include *Color Lighting, Composition, Depth of Field, Focus, General Impression* and *Use of Camera*. For each aesthetic attribute, the five most frequent keywords are selected from the captions. We omit the adverbs, prepositions and conjunctions. We merge words of similar meaning such as color and colour, color and colors.

Compared with DPC-Captions [1], DPC-MACD has more keywords for the classification of aesthetic captions. The tags of captions we used contain more vocabulary related to aesthetic attributes. After two screening weeks, there are still 92,006 DPC subtitle images. Since the images do not contain any photography attributes or information about *use of camera*, it is difficult for the subtitles to learn relevant features directly from the image. Therefore, we deleted the images related to *use of camera* attributes. We also found that the keywords *composition*, *depth of field* and *focus* are similar, so we merged them. Finally, we obtained the 4 attributes of DPC-MACD.

In subsequent experiments, it was found that the task of image captioning in aesthetics is more difficult to learn and generate than the task of general image captioning. Based on this, we adjust the captions' length in the DPC-MACD to make it shorter than DPC-Captions. At the same time, we require each caption to have at least 3 reference comments, so that the training and validation process can be easier.

4   Aesthetic Multi-attributes Captioning Network

Aesthetic multi-attributes captioning network includes two model solutions, Bottom-Up and Top-Down Attention Network (BUTDN) and Object-Semantics Aligned Pretrained Network (OSAPN). The aesthetic attributes assessment are relatively independent, while the model training process is similar.

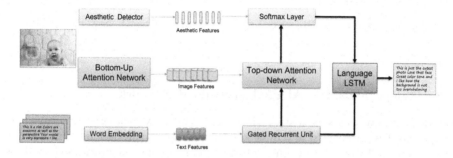

Fig. 2. The framework of Bottom-Up and Top-Down Attention Network.

4.1   Bottom-Up and Top-Down Attention Network

BUTDAN consists of Bottom-Up Attention and Top-Down Attention, which is shown in Fig. 2. The bottom-up attention model is used to extract the region of interest in the image to obtain object features. The top-down attention model is then used to learn the weights corresponding to the features to achieve a deeper understanding of the visual images. Faster R-CNN implements a bottom-up attention model, which is used to extract the image features of the image, and the preprocessing model is used to extract the object features and the position information corresponding to the object in the image. This bottom-Up attention network allows the overlap of interest frames through a set threshold, which could have a more effective understanding of the image content. In bottom-up attention network, not only the object detector but also the attribute classifier are used for each region of interest, so a binary description of the object (attribute, object) can be obtained. Meanwhile, Aesthetic Detector gets the easthetic features, which is evaluated by DenseNet-161 and finetuned in PCCD dataset. After changing the captions related with the image to the word tokens, Word Embedding Module is used to get the text features. Top-down Attention network is used to fuse image features and text features output by GRU units, while Language LSTM is used to implement a language model to generate captions.

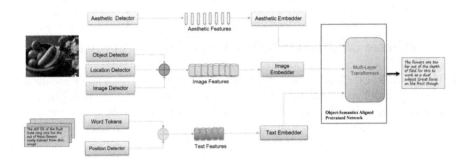

Fig. 3. The framework of Object-Semantics Aligned Pretrained Network (OSAPN).

4.2   Object-Semantics Aligned Pretrained Network

OSAPN mainly includes feature detectors, which extracts text information, image features, target tags and image aesthetic features through different feature extraction modules, then through object-semantics aligned pretrained module to generate the caption, which is depicted in Fig. 3. We take the visual area of the image and the text token of the sentence as input for VLPSA. Aesthetic features are obtained by the aesthetic detector, which is evaluated by DenseNet-161 and finetuned in PCCD Database. Image features are obtained through object, location and image detectors, which are evaluated by ResNeXt-152 and Faster RCNN, and finetuned in Visual Genome database. Text features are extracted through word detector, which includes object tags from MS COCO and Visual Genome. All of this information is then transformed through multi-layer transformers to generate captions. The model uses the semantic information of the image to guide the generation of the word sequence in the decoder stage. This avoids the problem of using the image information only at the beginning of the decoder, which can lead to the image information being gradually lost over time. In order to obtain the high-level semantic information of the image, the model improves the original convolutional neural networks, including the method of multi-task learning, which can extract the high level semantic information of the image and enhance the extraction of image features in the encoder stage.

5   Experiments

5.1   Implementation Details

Our experiments are based on the Pytorch framework. The length of the LSTM units is 1000. The features of images sent to the LSTM unit include ResNet-152 [11] attribute features. The two-stage training of AMACN is our contribution of using bottom-up and top-down attention and visual language pre-training and self-attention. Except for the two-stage training, the baseline methods CNN-LSTM use the same training parameters as follows: The word vector dimensionality is set to 300. The underlying learning rate is 0.01. The dimensions of the force module and channel attention module are 512. The dropout is used in training to prevent overfitting. The network is optimized using a stochastic gradient descent optimization strategy. The batch size is set to 64 for DPC-MACD and 16 for PCCD.

Attribute: Composition

GT: I love the soft focus and sepia tone I think maybe a bit more of her face close less background would've worked a bit better with this angle

Reference Caption 1: Nice perspective angle very good color toning and composition and most all beautiful model congrats

Reference Caption 2: Interesting composition nice contrast and lighting

Reference Caption 3: I love the expression and the overall mood lighting and composition

Reference Caption 4: Nice coloring I like the soft focus and the use of the negative space really pulls her face out with the very dark background

Our: I like the contrast and lighting. A bit more of her face, it will be better in this angle.

Fig. 4. Aesthetic multi-attributes assessment of images. The last sentence with the red color is the caption generated by our proposed model. (Color figure online)

5.2   Attribute Captioning Results

As shown in Table 1, the comparison results reveal that our model outperforms the previous models in the aesthetic image captioning performances. CNN-LSTM is based on Goolge's NIC model [17]. The differences between this baseline and our approach include: (1) no introduction of attention mechanism to enhance feature extraction process; (2) no usage of aesthetic multi-attribute network to extract features of different attributes. Instead, this approach trains a CNN network separately for each attribute. It fails to make full use of aesthetic features while extracting CNN features, and there is no effective knowledge transfer process. AMAN [1] is pre-trained on PCCD and finetuned on DPC-Captions dataset. The performance is measured using SPICE. Both BUTDAN and OSAPN achieve better SPICE on both DPC-Captions and DPC-MACD. Figure 4 is one of the aesthetic attributes image captioning results of AMACN on DPC-MACD, which demonstrate that they are able to accurately capture features and produce a variety of attribute results with high relevance of comments and attributes, whereas the method in PCCD can only produce one sentence. In addition, the results of our methods tend to be objectively evaluated, whereas approach in PCCD favors subjective evaluation.

Table 1. Performance of the proposed models on DPC-Captions and DPC-MACD.

Dataset	Method	SPICE
DPC-Captions	CNN-LSTM (Composition)	0.1670
	AMAN (Composition)	0.1970
DPC-MACD	CNN-LSTM (Composition)	0.1920
	BUTDAN (Composition)	**0.2113**
	OSAPN (Composition)	0.2024
DPC-Captions	CNN-LSTM (Color and Lighting)	0.1660
	AMAN (Color and Lighting)	0.1960
DPC-MACD	CNN-LSTM (Color)	0.1810
	BUTDAN (Color)	**0.2171**
	OSAPN (Color)	0.2129
	CNN-LSTM (Light)	0.1660
	BUTDAN (Light)	**0.1902**
	OSAPN (Light)	0.1883
DPC-Captions	CNN-LSTM (Impression and Subject)	0.1580
	AMAN (Impression and Subject)	0.1810
DPC-MACD	CNN-LSTM (Subject)	0.1840
	BUTDAN (Subject)	**0.2043**
	OSAPN (Subject)	0.2024

6   Conclusions and Future Work

In this paper, image aesthetic attributes assessment is fully investigated. We get help from PCCD and propose a new vision-language dataset called DPC-MACD and two novel multimodal network. Our model can generate diverse captions of individual aesthetic attributes. In the future, we will explore captioning from sentences to paragraphs. We will also explore knowledge transfer methods to build larger datasets for weakly supervised learning, leveraging the relations among attributes for caption learning, and using reinforcement learning for caption generation.

Acknowledgements. We thank the ACs and reviewers. This work is partially supported by the Fundamental Research Funds for the Central Universities, the Natural Science Foundation of China (62072014), the Key Program of Beijing Polytechnic College under Grant No. BGY2023KY-16Z and No. BGY2021KY-13, Innovation Fund for

Chinese Universities-Beichuang Teaching Assistant Project (Phase II) under Grant No. 2021BCE01010.

References

1. Jin, X., et al.: Aesthetic attributes assessment of images. In: Proceedings of the 27th ACM International Conference on Multimedia (2019)
2. Pandit, A., Animesh, Gautam, B.K., Agarwal, R.: Image aesthetic score prediction using image captioning. In: Kumar, A., Mozar, S., Haase, J. (eds.) ICCCE 2023. Cognitive Science and Technology, pp. 413–425. Springer, Singapore (2023). https://doi.org/10.1007/978-981-19-8086-2_41
3. Nieto, D.V., Celona, L., Fernandez-Labrador, C.: Understanding aesthetics with language: a photo critique dataset for aesthetic assessment. In: NeurIPS Track on Datasets and Benchmarks (2022)
4. Zhong, Z., Zhou, F., Qiu, G.: Aesthetically relevant image captioning. arXiv preprint arXiv:2211.15378 (2022)
5. Anderson, P., et al.: Bottom-up and top-down attention for image captioning and visual question answering. In: Proceedings of the IEEE Conference on Computer Vision and Pattern Recognition (2018)
6. Aneja, J., Deshpande, A., Schwing, A.G.: Convolutional image captioning. In: Proceedings of the IEEE Conference on Computer Vision and Pattern Recognition (2018)
7. Zhou, Y., et al.: Joint image and text representation for aesthetics analysis. In: Proceedings of the 24th ACM International Conference on Multimedia (2016)
8. Chang, K.-Y., Lu, K.-H., Chen, C.-S.: Aesthetic critiques generation for photos. In: Proceedings of the IEEE International Conference on Computer Vision (2017)
9. Chen, F., et al.: GroupCap: group-based image captioning with structured relevance and diversity constraints. In: Proceedings of the IEEE Conference on Computer Vision and Pattern Recognition (2018)
10. Donahue, J., et al.: Long-term recurrent convolutional networks for visual recognition and description. In: Proceedings of the IEEE Conference on Computer Vision and Pattern Recognition (2015)
11. He, K., et al.: Deep residual learning for image recognition. In: Proceedings of the IEEE Conference on Computer Vision and Pattern Recognition (2016)
12. Jin, X., et al.: Predicting aesthetic score distribution through cumulative Jensen-Shannon divergence. In: Proceedings of the AAAI Conference on Artificial Intelligence, vol. 32, no. 1 (2018)
13. Karpathy, A., Fei-Fei, L.: Deep visual-semantic alignments for generating image descriptions. In: Proceedings of the IEEE Conference on Computer Vision and Pattern Recognition (2015)
14. Luo, R., et al.: Discriminability objective for training descriptive captions. In: Proceedings of the IEEE Conference on Computer Vision and Pattern Recognition (2018)
15. Mathews, A., Xie, L., He, X.: SemStyle: learning to generate stylised image captions using unaligned text. In: Proceedings of the IEEE Conference on Computer Vision and Pattern Recognition (2018)
16. Murray, N., Marchesotti, L., Perronnin, F.: AVA: a large-scale database for aesthetic visual analysis. In: 2012 IEEE Conference on Computer Vision and Pattern Recognition. IEEE (2012)

17. Vinyals, O., et al.: Show and tell: a neural image caption generator. In: Proceedings of the IEEE Conference on Computer Vision and Pattern Recognition (2015)

18. Wang, W., et al.: Neural aesthetic image reviewer. IET Comput. Vision **13**(8), 749–758 (2019)

19. Pfister, J., Kobs, K., Hotho, A.: Self-supervised multi-task pretraining improves image aesthetic assessment. In: Proceedings of the IEEE/CVF Conference on Computer Vision and Pattern Recognition (2021)

20. Lu, J., et al.: ViLBERT: pretraining task-agnostic visiolinguistic representations for vision-and-language tasks. In: Proceedings of the 33rd International Conference on Neural Information Processing Systems (2019)

21. Tan, H., Bansal, M.: LXMERT: learning cross-modality encoder representations from transformers. In: Proceedings of the 2019 Conference on Empirical Methods in Natural Language Processing and the 9th International Joint Conference on Natural Language Processing (EMNLP-IJCNLP) (2019)

22. Chen, Y.-C., et al.: UNITER: UNiversal image-TExt representation learning. In: Vedaldi, A., Bischof, H., Brox, T., Frahm, J.-M. (eds.) ECCV 2020. LNCS, vol. 12375, pp. 104–120. Springer, Cham (2020). https://doi.org/10.1007/978-3-030-58577-8_7

23. Su, W., et al.: VL-BERT: pre-training of generic visual-linguistic representations. In: International Conference on Learning Representations (2019)

24. Li, X., et al.: OSCAR: object-semantics aligned pre-training for vision-language tasks. In: Vedaldi, A., Bischof, H., Brox, T., Frahm, J.-M. (eds.) ECCV 2020. LNCS, vol. 12375, pp. 121–137. Springer, Cham (2020). https://doi.org/10.1007/978-3-030-58577-8_8

25. Radford, A., et al.: Learning transferable visual models from natural language supervision. arXiv preprint arXiv:2103.00020 (2021)

26. Ghosal, K., Rana, A., Smolic, A.: Aesthetic image captioning from weakly-labelled photographs. In: Proceedings of the IEEE/CVF International Conference on Computer Vision Workshops (2019)

27. Zou, X., et al.: To be an artist: automatic generation on food image aesthetic captioning. In: 2020 IEEE 32nd International Conference on Tools with Artificial Intelligence (ICTAI). IEEE (2020)

28. Ke, J., Ye, K., Yu, J., et al.: VILA: learning image aesthetics from user comments with vision-language pretraining. arXiv preprint arXiv:2303.14302 (2023)

29. Zhu, D., Chen, J., Shen, X., et al.: MiniGPT-4: enhancing vision-language understanding with advanced large language models. arXiv preprint arXiv:2304.10592 (2023)

30. Dosovitskiy, A., Beyer, L., Kolesnikov, A., et al.: An image is worth 16×16 words: transformers for image recognition at scale. arXiv preprint arXiv:2010.11929 (2020)

31. Chiang, W.-L., et al.: Vicuna: an open-source chatbot impressing GPT-4 with 90 (2023)

Improving Road Extraction in Hyperspectral Data with Deep Learning Models

Xuying Zhao⬤, Zhibo Xing⬤, Zexiao Zou⬤, Wu Zhou⬤, Zhonghui Bian⬤, and Xiaodong Li(✉)⬤

Beijing Electronic Science and Technology Institute, Fufeng Road. 7, Fengtai District, Beijing 100070, China
yundingyi@163.com

Abstract. Accurately extracting road networks from hyperspectral data using convolutional neural network models is challenging due to various factors such as occlusion, changing lighting conditions, and blur. To address this issue, this paper proposes a new model that combines the advantages of U-net and Transformer architectures. This hybrid model effectively captures both local and long-range features, thus improving the accuracy and efficiency of road extraction. Evaluation of the method is performed on the AeroRIT hyperspectral dataset using performance metrics such as overall accuracy, average per-class accuracy, and average Jaccard index. Compared with traditional convolutional neural network models such as U-net. The results show that the proposed method improves the average per-class accuracy by more than 18% over the traditional methods, demonstrating its potential to optimize road extraction from hyperspectral data. Further research can focus on improving the accuracy and efficiency of road network extraction from hyperspectral data.

Keywords: Transformer · Hyperspectral Data · Road Extraction · Convolutional Neural Network

1 Introduction

Hyperspectral imaging provides detailed spectral information about materials in a scene, including roads. However, accurate extraction of roads from hyperspectral data is challenging due to their complex structure and similarity to other materials. Road extraction is a specific type of semantic segmentation task, and while deep learning models such as SegNet, U-net, and ResNet have shown promise, they have limitations such as loss of details [1, 2, 22] or high computational requirements [3]. To overcome these limitations, we propose a novel approach that combines Transformer and U-net architectures to capture global and local features, allowing long-range dependencies while maintaining fine-grained details. Few studies have explored this combination for hyperspectral image segmentation, making our proposed method an innovative one.

The structure of this article is as follows:

Introduction: Outline the goals and motivation of the study.

H. Lu and J. Cai (Eds.): ISAIR 2023, CCIS 1998, pp. 131–138, 2024.
https://doi.org/10.1007/978-981-99-9109-9_13

Related work: Discusses existing methods for semantic segmentation of hyperspectral data, road extraction, and deep learning models.

Proposed Approach: Describe methods for enhancing road extraction using deep learning models, including Transformer and U-Net architectures.

Datasets and Experiments: Details the datasets used for evaluation, the experiments performed, and a discussion of the results.

Discussion: The proposed method is compared with existing methods and its advantages and disadvantages are analyzed.

Conclusions and future work: The main findings are summarized and directions for future research are proposed.

Acknowledgement.

2 Related Work

2.1 Overview of Existing Hyperspectral Data Semantic Segmentation Methods

There are four main categories of methods for semantic segmentation of hyperspectral data: traditional machine learning, deep learning, hybrid and other methods.

Traditional machine learning methods, including support vector machines [4], and random forests [5]. They typically involve feature extraction and selection, followed by applying a classifier to the selected features. Deep learning methods, such as Convolutional Neural Networks (CNNs) [6, 23], and fully convolutional networks (FCNs) [7], have shown great promise in hyperspectral image segmentation. In addition, there are hybrid approaches [8] that combine traditional machine learning and deep learning methods. Other methods, such as clustering, graph-based methods [9], and active learning [10], have also been used for hyperspectral image segmentation.

2.2 Literature Review of Existing Approaches for Road Extraction in Hyperspectral Data

Extracting roads from hyperspectral data can be divided into two main methods: traditional methods and deep learning-based methods [11]. Traditional methods utilize spectral features and statistical/mathematical models to extract roads [12], but have limitations in handling complex scenes and illumination changes. Deep learning-based methods, such as U-Net [13] and ResNet [3], have shown great potential for solving such problems, but require large amounts of annotated data and computational resources.

2.3 Overview of Existing Deep Learning Models for Hyperspectral Data Analysis

Deep learning models have shown great potential in hyperspectral data analysis by automatically learning complex features from high-dimensional data.

U-Net and SegNet [14] are popular for hyperspectral image segmentation. U-Net captures both local and global features, but requires more data and computation. SegNet is computationally efficient and preserves spatial information, but may not perform as well on tasks requiring high-level context. ResNet is suitable for high-context tasks, but may not be as effective as U-Net or SegNet for hyperspectral segmentation. Transformers

[15] achieve state-of-the-art results in language processing but may not be efficient for large amounts of hyperspectral data.

In our proposed method, we combine Transformer and U-net architectures to process hyperspectral images to capture global and local features, allowing long-range dependencies to be captured while maintaining fine-grained details (Fig. 1).

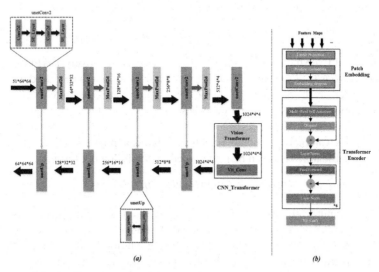

Fig. 1. Flowchart of the proposed method. (a) CNNTrans, (b) ViT.

3 Proposed Method

3.1 Description of the Proposed Approach for Improving Road Extraction with Deep Learning Models

Inspired by the Vision Transformer (ViT) model proposed by Dosovitskiy [16, 21], for image classification, we modify the U-Net architecture by incorporating a CNN-Transformer block at the center of the network. This block utilizes the ViT encoder to extract positional embeddings from the output feature map of U-Net, which is then passed to the Transformer decoder to generate the final segmentation map. The decoder consists of multiple Transformer blocks that can perform nonlinear transformations on input features and capture long-range dependencies in feature maps. This architecture enables us to efficiently extract road features from hyperspectral data while reducing computational cost.

The CNN-Transformer block in the proposed approach can be represented by the following formula:

$$y = Concat(xcontract, CNN - Transformer(xcenter)) \qquad (1)$$

where $x_{contract}$ is the feature map from the contracting path of the U-Net architecture, x_{center} is the feature map from the center of the U-Net architecture, and CNN-Transformer is the modified ViT model followed by a convolutional layer. The output of the CNN-Transformer block is then concatenated with the corresponding features from the contracting path and fed into the expansive path.

The multi-head self-attention mechanism in the Transformer block of the ViT model can be represented by the following formula:

$$MultiHead(Q, K, V) = Concat(head_1, \ldots, head_h)W^o \tag{2}$$

where Q, K, and V are the query, key, and value matrices, respectively. h is the number of heads, and $head_i$ is the i-th head output. W^o is the output weight matrix used to combine the concatenated heads. In this model, using the original query (the content of the query), relative positional embeddings are used as keys, and values refer to the matrix of values obtained from the input sequence.

The feed-forward network in the Transformer block applies a nonlinear transformation to the input features and can be represented by the following formula:

$$FFN(x) = PReLU(xW_1 + b_1)W_2 + b_2 \tag{3}$$

where x is the input feature vector, W_1, b_1, W_2, and b_2 are the weights and biases of the two fully connected layers, and PReLU is the rectified linear unit activation function.

Overall, the proposed approach offers a promising solution to improve road extraction from hyperspectral data by leveraging the strengths of both CNN and Transformer-based networks.

3.2 Details on the Transformer and U-Net Architectures Used

We name the whole work CNNTrans. The input to the model is first normalized by spectral bands and resized to a fixed resolution of 64x64 pixels. The input is then subjected to four rounds of convolution and max pooling before being fed into the central convolutional layer of the U-Net architecture and output to the CNN-Transformer block.

The CNN-Transformer block processes the input image by dividing it into equal blocks, producing tensors of shape (batch_size, num_patches, output_channels). The output tensor is then reshaped to (batch_size, output-put_channels, num_patches_sqrt, num_patches_sqrt) and passed through a single convolutional layer before being used as input to the decoder part of the U-Net architecture. Here, batch_size is the number of samples in a batch, num_patches is the number of patches (or markers) extracted and processed by the transformer in the input image, output_channels is the number of channels in the output feature representation, num_patches_sqrt is the size height and width dimension, and passed upsampling outputs the final segmentation map.

The ViT part in the CNN-Transformer block captures global contextual information, while the convolutional layers extract local features. Since the final output of the ViT model is not the final result, we remove the classification head of the ViT model and add a convolutional layer at the end to reduce the feature dimension and computational cost. The output of the CNN-Transformer block is concatenated with the corresponding features in the contraction path and fed into the expansion path.

The Vit_conv layer performs a single convolution operation before feeding the output of the ViT model to the decoder part of the U-Net architecture. The forward method of the CNNTransformer class processes the input image through the convolutional layers, ViT model, SignleConv layer and U-Net architecture to produce the final segmentation map.

4 Dataset and Experiments

4.1 Description of the Dataset Used for Evaluation

To evaluate the proposed CNN-Transformer based U-Net architecture for road extraction from hyperspectral data, we use the publicly available AeroRIT dataset [17] with a spatial resolution of 1973×3975 pixels covering the spectral range 397 nm–1003 nm, The step size is 1 nm. The dataset contains 12 spectral bands, which provide important information for distinguishing different materials and surfaces in the scene. Furthermore, this dataset includes ground truth labels of road pixels, which are manually annotated and considered accurate. Due to the complexity of the scene and the presence of other objects and materials, the AeroRIT dataset is a challenging benchmark dataset for hyperspectral image analysis, making it suitable for evaluating the performance of our proposed architecture.

4.2 Description of the Experiments Conducted to Evaluate the Proposed Approach

To evaluate the performance of the proposed CNN-Transformer based U-Net architecture on road extraction, we conduct a series of experiments on the AeroRIT dataset. The dataset was randomly split into 80% for training and 20% for testing, ensuring that no overlapping patches were used in the two groups.

To train the model, we used several parameters to ensure the best results. The PreLU [18] activation function is used and the mini-batch size is set to 100. The learning rate is set to 1e−4, and the cross-entropy loss function of the Adam optimizer is applied. The number of spectral bands used in the analysis will depend on the setting, with 5 options ranging from 3 (RGB) to 51 (all). Finally, the model is trained for 60 epochs on a single NVIDIA GTX 3080 GPU with 10 GB of memory.

We evaluated the proposed method using three metrics: Overall Accuracy (OA) [19], Mean PerClass Accuracy (MPCA), and Mean Jaccard Index (MIOU) [20]. OA and MPCA report the percentage of correctly classified pixels, while MIOU is used to mitigate dataset bias when class representations are small. Among these metrics, we adopt MIOU as the main metric for performance evaluation, because it measures the overlap between predicted masks and ground truth masks for all classes, which is a good way to evaluate the same degree of predicted segmentation maps and ground truth labels.

We compare the performance of the proposed CNN-Transformer based U-Net architecture with the baseline U-Net architecture and other state-of-the-art road extraction methods. The experimental results are presented in the next section.

4.3 Discussion of the Experimental Results

Our experimental results show that the proposed CNNTrans model outperforms other models in all aspects, among which MIOU is the most important reference index for this segmentation task. Specifically, CNNTrans has a MIOU of 74.7, which is 16.1 percentage points higher than the second-best model, Resnet, and 21.2 percentage points higher than the worst-performing model, Segnet. We also observe that all models achieve overall accuracy (OA) scores, with CNNTrans achieving the highest score of 90.4%, followed by ResNet (89.1%), U-net (89.3%) and Se-gnet (87.2%) (Table 1).

Table 1. Performance of various models on the AeroRIT test set.

Model	Overall acc.(OA) ↑	MPCA↑	MIOU↑
Segnet	87.2	66.7	53.5
U-net	89.3	69.2	57.4
ResNet	89.1	68.6	58.6
CNNTrans	**90.4**	**87.4**	**74.7**

5 Discussion

5.1 Comparison of the Proposed Approach with Existing Methods

In this study, we compare the proposed method with several existing methods, including Segnet, U-Net, ResNet. Experimental results show that all models are able to correctly classify most of the pixels, but the proposed CNNTrans model achieves the highest overall performance by using CNN-Transformer block to consider global and local information.

Overall, our experimental results demonstrate the effectiveness of the proposed CNNTrans model for the segmentation task on this dataset. However, further research is needed to investigate the robustness and generalization ability of the proposed method to other datasets and spectral ranges.

5.2 Discussion of the Strengths and Weaknesses of the Proposed Approach

Compared with existing methods such as Segnet, U-net, ResNet, etc., the advantage of our proposed method is that it can efficiently process high-dimensional hyperspectral data and capture spatial and spectral information. The combination of Transformer and U-Net architecture enables us to efficiently process input data and capture relevant features for accurate segmentation.

However, our proposed method has some limitations. One of the main limitations is its high computational cost, which may limit its practical use in real-time applications. Furthermore, the proposed method requires a large amount of labeled data for training, which may not always be feasible in some applications.

Overall, our proposed method shows promising results and has potential for further optimization and improvement for more efficient and accurate hyperspectral image segmentation.

6 Conclusion and Future Work

The main contribution of this research is to provide a new solution for hyperspectral image segmentation. The method outperforms existing methods in terms of overall accuracy, MPCA, and MIOU, indicating that it can accurately segment hyperspectral images and has the potential to advance hyperspectral imaging applications. A limitation of this approach is its relatively high computational complexity.

Future work could extend the model to include more spectral bands or higher spatial resolution data and apply it to other types of aerial or satellite imagery for object detection and segmentation tasks.

Acknowledgement. This work was supported by "the Fundamental Research Funds for the Central Universities" (Grant Number: 328202234).

References

1. Yang, R., Yu, J., Yin, J., et al.: An FA-SegNet image segmentation model based on fuzzy attention and its application in cardiac MRI segmentation. Int. J. Comput. Intell. Syst. **15**, 24 (2022)
2. Siddique, N., Paheding, S., Elkin, C.P., Devabhaktuni, V.: U-Net and Its variants for medical image segmentation: a review of theory and applications. IEEE Access **9**, 82031–82057 (2021). https://doi.org/10.1109/ACCESS.2021.3086020
3. He, K., et al.: Deep residual learning for image recognition. In: Proceedings of the IEEE Conference on Computer Vision and Pattern Recognition (2016)
4. Gualtieri, J.A., Robert, F.C.: Support vector machines for hyperspectral remote sensing classification. In: Other Conferences (1999)
5. Ham, J., Chen, Y., Crawford, M.M., Ghosh, J.: Investigation of the random forest framework for classification of hyperspectral data. IEEE Trans. Geosci. Remote Sens. **43**(3), 492–501 (2005)
6. López, J., Torres, D., Santos, S., Atzberger, C.: Spectral imagery tensor decomposition for semantic segmentation of remote sensing data through fully convolutional networks. Remote Sens. **12**(3), 517 (2020)
7. Jiao, L., Liang, M., Chen, H., Yang, S., Liu, H., Cao, X.: Deep fully convolutional network-based spatial distribution prediction for hyperspectral image classification. IEEE Trans. Geosci. Remote Sens. **55**(10), 5585–5599 (2017)
8. Roy, S.K., et al.: HybridSN: exploring 3-D-2-D CNN feature hierarchy for hyperspectral image classification. IEEE Geosci. Remote Sensing Lett. **17**(2), 277–281 (2020). https://doi.org/10.1109/LGRS.2019.2918719
9. Bandyopadhyay, D., Mukherjee, S.: Tree species classification from hyperspectral data using graph-regularized neural networks. ArXiv abs/2208.08675 (2022)
10. Lenczner, G., et al.: DIAL: deep interactive and active learning for semantic segmentation in remote sensing. IEEE J. Sel. Top. Appl. Earth Observations Remote Sens. **15**, 3376–3389 (2022)

11. Chen, Y., Lin, Z., Zhao, X., Wang, G., Gu, Y.: Deep learning-based classification of hyperspectral data. IEEE J. Sel. Top. Appl. Earth Observations Remote Sens 7(6), 2094–2107 (2014). https://doi.org/10.1109/JSTARS.2014.2329330

12. Patil, D., Jadhav, S.: Road extraction techniques from remote sensing images: a review. In: Raj, J.S., Iliyasu, A.M., Bestak, R., Baig, Z. A. (eds.) Innovative Data Communication Technologies and Application: Proceedings of ICIDCA 2020, pp. 663–677. Springer Singapore, Singapore (2021). https://doi.org/10.1007/978-981-15-9651-3_55

13. Ronneberger, O.: Invited Talk: U-Net Convolutional Networks for Biomedical Image Segmentation. Presented at the (2017). https://doi.org/10.1007/978-3-662-54345-0_3

14. Badrinarayanan, V., Kendall, A., Cipolla, R.: SegNet: a deep convolutional encoder-decoder architecture for image segmentation. IEEE Trans. Pattern Anal. Mach. Intell. 39(12), 2481–2495 (2017). https://doi.org/10.1109/TPAMI.2016.2644615

15. Vaswani, A, et al.: Attention is all you need. In: Advances in Neural Information Processing Systems 30 (2017)

16. Dosovitskiy, A., et al.: An Image is Worth 16x16 Words: Transformers for Image Recognition at Scale. ArXiv abs/2010.11929 (2020)

17. Rangnekar, A., Mokashi, N., Ientilucci, E.J., Kanan, C., Hoffman, M.J.: AeroRIT: a new scene for hyperspectral image analysis. IEEE Trans. Geosci. Remote Sens. 58(11), 8116–8124 (2020). https://doi.org/10.1109/TGRS.2020.2987199

18. He, K., et al.: Delving deep into rectifiers: surpassing human-level performance on imagenet classification. In: 2015 IEEE International Conference on Computer Vision (ICCV), pp. 1026–1034 (2015)

19. Wang, Z., Wang, E., Zhu, Y.: Image segmentation evaluation: a survey of methods. Artif. Intell. Rev. 53, 5637–5674 (2020)

20. Costa, L.D.F.: Further generalizations of the Jaccard index. arXiv preprint arXiv:2110.09619 (2021)

21. Zhao, W., Lu, H., Wang, D.: Multisensor image fusion and enhancement in spectral total variation domain. IEEE Trans. Multimedia 20(4), 866–879 (2017)

22. Xu, F., Xu, F., Xie, J., Pun, C.M., Lu, H., Gao, H.: Action recognition framework in traffic scene for autonomous driving system. IEEE Trans. Intell. Transp. Syst. 23(11), 22301–22311 (2021)

23. Zheng, Y., Li, Y., Yang, S., Lu, H.: Global-PBNet: a novel point cloud registration for autonomous driving. IEEE Trans. Intell. Transp. Syst. 23(11), 22312–22319 (2022)

Human Related Information Extraction from Chinese Archive Images

Xin Jin[1] (ID), Hangbing Yin[1], Xiaoyu Chen[2], Huimin Bi[1], Chaoen Xiao[1(✉)],
and Yijian Liu[1]

[1] Beijing Electronic Science and Technology Institute, No. 7, Fufeng Street, Fengtai District,
Beijing 100070, China
xcecd@qq.com

[2] Information Center of China North Industries, Group Corporation Limited, Beijing 100089,
China

Abstract. With the rise of the information age, digitalization and paperless processes have become the norm in managing archive images. However, research on extracting and managing image content from archives is still in its early stages, and is primarily focused on recognizing fixed-format archive images. As a result, there is a lack of technology for extracting key personal information applicable to all types of archive images. To address this, we have identified two main tasks: extracting identity photos and key personal information. To ensure confidentiality of real data, we created a dataset that simulates certificate photo files. We then used a YOLOv5-based object detection network to train a model that can detect document photos in archive images. We also used a combination of PP-OCR text recognition and object detection to extract key information from document images.

Keywords: File image processing · Certificate photo extraction · PP-OCR · YOLOv5 · Key information extraction

1 Introduction

In recent years, with the continuous development of digital archiving, many archival institutions have entered the "post-digitization" stage. A large number of archives are saved in image or PDF formats, but their content has not been fully explored and developed. When document images have intelligent analysis and review functions, key content such as ID photos, names, gender, birthdates, and important dates can be intelligently extracted from digital files through image analysis, thereby reducing the workload of inspection personnel. Regarding the face photos, traditional face detection methods are difficult to extract ID photos: there are various forms of ID photos in archival materials, many photos are severely worn, or become black and white blocks after multiple copies. Face recognition cannot identify the range of ID photos containing information such as hair, shoulders, and background, which does not meet the needs of extracting and cropping ID photos. As for the OCR model extraction method, traditional OCR methods are difficult to extract key information from table images: under the influence of table horizontal and vertical lines, it is easy to recognize the lines as numbers or text, and the recognition efficiency and accuracy are poor, especially for archives with handwritten fonts, the recognition effect is extremely poor. OCR alone cannot realize the need to centrally extract handwritten information images for handwriting comparison.

To solve the above problems, our main research content is as follows: (1) Construction of archival image dataset: based on real archival datasets, relying on image processing and other technologies, a dataset containing various personnel ID photos and a table image dataset containing personnel key information are constructed to meet the needs of subsequent training and optimizing models. (2) Proposed a method for detecting archival certificate photos: automatically extract portraits from archival materials, comprehensively consider the detection and segmentation of facial parts and other parts in certificate photos, recognize and extract certificate photos in the input image, and batch output/save/display the source images. (3) Proposed a key information extraction method: intelligently analyze form files and propose a method that combines table recognition, Chinese OCR, and object detection to extract key personnel information from document images, and output the structured content to CSV for summary storage. This article consists of four chapters: Section 1 is the introduction, which introduces the main problem that the experiment is trying to solve. Section 2 details the design and experiment of extracting archival ID photos. Section 3 details the specific implementation process of extracting key personnel information. Section 4 summarizes the work.

2   Photo Extraction

2.1   Scheme Design

This article proposes a document ID photo extraction technology based on object detection. The document images containing ID photos are labeled using the LabelImg annotation tool to generate YOLO-format annotation files, which constitute the ID photo detection dataset. Then, the YOLOv5 [1, 9] network is used to train the object detection model. In practical applications, the document images to be processed are placed in a specified folder, and the inference detection module is run to display all the ID photos in the document. Finally, based on the detection results, OpenCV is used to crop the ID photos from the document and output them to a specified folder for centralized storage. The design of the document ID photo extraction module is shown in the Fig. 1 below.

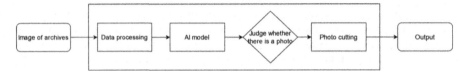

Fig. 1. Extraction technology of certificate photo.

2.2 Construction of Photo Dataset

To solve the problem of scarce real document data and diverse ID photo types, we propose a semi-automatic document image generation method with ID photos based on the real document image effect, which is used to construct a self-made ID photo document dataset. The document images containing ID photos can be divided into three categories: yellowed old documents, color documents, and black and white documents that have been copied. Based on these three categories, ID photos can be divided into five types: low-quality old photos, color photos, yellowed photos, black and white photos, and copied photos. In this section, we first use a web crawler to obtain corresponding color ID photos, and then use OpenCV to process the color space of the ID photos to obtain the effect of yellowing and black-and-white binarization. We also apply noise addition and smoothing to simulate the effect of multiple copies. The specific effects are shown in the Fig. 2 below.

Fig. 2. All kinds of homemade images.

2.3 Photo Extraction Model

Data Preparation and Model Training. In this paper, we utilized the open-source image annotation tool LabelImg to manually label seal images on the archive and obtain pixel information when synthesizing the homemade ID photo and real archive background. Then, when generating the composite archive, we directly generated the txt labels in YOLO [2] format according to the relative position of the ID photo in the archive and saved them. Automated label generation can greatly improve the efficiency of data annotation for creating a dataset, and manual review can be done later with the help of the LabelImg interface. We then chose YOLOv5s to train the model, trained it for 300 epochs, and obtained the ID photos [3, 8].

Image Cropping. During network training, YOLOv5 sets the initial anchor box size and outputs the predicted box based on it, and then updates the parameters of the network structure by propagating the error direction between the predicted box and the real box. During inference, the location of the ID photo is indicated and the type of the ID photo is displayed above the anchor box. Finally, the ID photo is clipped along the edge of the anchor box and the seal image is classified and stored in different folders.

2.4 Experimental Process and Analysis of Results.

The Verification about Validity of Self-made Data. We trained the model using a dataset of 698 real documents containing ID photos. The box_loss and obj_loss of the training set showed a decreasing trend overall, but their performance on the validation set was not stable and fluctuated greatly. Although the Precision and Recall of the model were both at a high level, the mAP@0.5:0.95 value was low and varied greatly, which affected the overall performance of the model. Therefore, the real document model was able to extract ID photos, but its performance needed improvement. On the other hand, the model trained using the self-made document dataset achieved good results, with GIoU and Objectness both at a low level. The Precision and Recall were close to 1, and the mAP@0.5 reached 0.99, while the MAP@0.5:0.95 reached 0.98. Therefore, the ID photo model had a high comprehensive recognition accuracy and was suitable for the document ID photo extraction module. After balancing the number of samples, the model's performance was greatly improved.

Validity Verification. We tested the real document model and self-made document model on real document and self-made document datasets, respectively. The self-made document model performed well on the self-made dataset, recognizing all ID photos with a recognition accuracy of 1. However, due to the richer information in real documents, although the self-made ID photo file model was able to recognize all ID photos during testing on a real dataset, there were still issues with over-detection and false detection. Therefore, we added some elements of misidentified images as negative samples in the self-made dataset to optimize it. By testing, we found that applying object detection to extract ID photos from documents was feasible. The next step would be to expand the dataset, optimize its composition, and improve the model's detection performance.

The Verification about Validity of Fusion Photo. The overall performance of the model fused with the archive data set is relatively stable, and the loss functions of the training set and the test set show an overall downward trend. Both Precision (accuracy rate) and Recall (recall rate) have reached close to 1. And mAP@0.5 reaches 0.99, and MAP@0.5:0.95 reaches 0.98. In summary, the ID card photo model has a high comprehensive recognition accuracy and is suitable for the file ID photo extraction module. The fusion photo model was tested on authentic data and homemade data, producing the corresponding metrics as presented in Table 1.

Table 1. Testing Results of Fused Identification Photo Model.

	Images	Labels	P	R	mAP@.5	mAP@.5:.95
Authentic Data	100	101	0.990	0.986	0.992	0.809
Homemade data	100	100	0.997	0.972	0.991	0.964

3 Character Key Information Extraction

For the content of the form filling, there are two types: printed and handwritten. To clarify, we process the printed and handwritten forms separately to ensure accurate extraction of key information from both types of content filling.

3.1 Printed Information

When processing forms that contains only printed font, the form regions are first detected, and then the table structure of the archive image is recognized based on OpenCV. The image is segmented into sub-images according to the table structure. The outcomes of segmenting archival sub-images are showcased in Fig. 3.

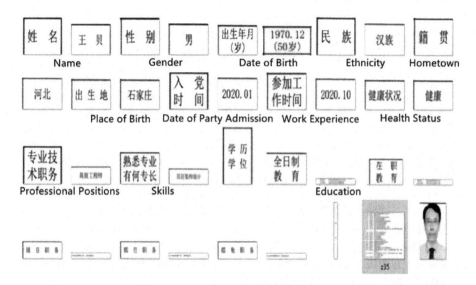

Fig. 3. The outcomes of segmenting archival sub-images.

Then the sub-images are input into a Chinese lightweight OCR model trained in advance to recognize and classify the text in the images using OCR technology [4]. The PP-OCR [5] technique is used to understand the recognized text content. The predicted results for each archive are written into a text file, converted, and finally stored as a CSV file that is easy for statistical analysis, achieving automatic extraction and structured processing of archive content. The structured extraction process is shown in the Fig. 4 below.

Fig. 4. The flow chart of structured extraction.

3.2 Handwritten Information

We propose a method that combines OCR with object detection. Before training the object detection model, OCR text recognition is used for auxiliary positioning and detection. The key printed words of the required fields are recognized to locate the range of the approval form [6, 10]. The entire archive image is then cropped into small images centered around the key information, reducing the feature extraction range during object detection. A personnel key information detection model based on the YOLOv5 network structure is then trained [7]. Through model inference prediction and image cropping functions. The tangible results of extracting pivotal personal information are showcased in Fig. 5.

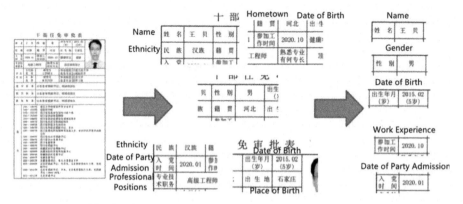

Fig. 5. The results of extracting pivotal personal information

And the name, gender, date of birth, important dates, and work start date in the archive are classified and output to the designated folder, and the information source is displayed. The workflow design is shown below Fig. 6.

Fig. 6. ORC auxiliary detection technique and techniques for extracting key information

3.3 Ablation Experiment

We adopted the extraction strategy from archive ID photos and trained an archive key information extraction model using a lightweight object detection algorithm YOLOv5 to extract text blocks containing key information. To use it, the archive image to be processed is placed in a designated folder, and after model inference and cropping, all key elements in the archive can be obtained. All the key information is marked in the tabular archive, and a single archive image usually contains three or more key pieces of information. The person key information detection and extraction model was trained on a real dataset of 399 complete archive images.

As shown in figure, the overall performance of the model on the real archive dataset is poor. Although the loss function of the training set and the test set shows a general downward trend, the loss function of the test set fluctuates sharply. Precision and recall are both low, the data is highly disparate, and the accuracy is also low. The mAP@0.5 reaches 0.85, and the MAP@0.5:0.95 is only 0.68. In summary, the person key information model has low comprehensive recognition accuracy and is not suitable for the person key information extraction module (Table 2).

Table 2. The detection effect on the real archive images data set.

	Images	Labels	P	R	mAP@.5	mAP@.5:.95
All labels	119	345	0.851	0.802	0.841	0.728
Name	119	132	0.844	0.822	0.894	0.765
Gender	119	93	0.923	0.903	0.955	0.814
Date fo birth	119	24	0.834	0.667	0.693	0.614
Employment date	119	12	0.823	0.833	0.814	0.726

4 Conclusion

In this paper, we discuss the technology of extracting key information from archival images of individuals and its domestic implementation, based on the problem scenarios of an actual project. We propose a method for extracting key content from archival images using deep learning. Specifically, we train a YOLOv5 object detection model to extract identity photos. We then use a combination of PP-OCR and YOLOv5 to extract key information such as names, gender, date of birth, and date of employment for content and handwriting comparison. We also perform structured extraction and recognition of fully printed personnel appointment and removal approval forms, storing the archival content as editable and searchable text in a CSV file. The archival image person information extraction technology can be used to batch identify and extract identity photos and key information from archival images. This method provides a way to digitize archival images, not only facilitating centralized comparison of identification photos of the same person during archival review, but also confirming the three ages and two histories of the archival review, verifying the key information and handwriting anti-counterfeiting, reducing the workload of review, and improving the efficiency of review.

Acknowledgements. We thank the ACs and reviewers. This work is partially supported by the Fundamental Research Funds for the Central Universities (3282023014), and the Project of Information Center of China North Industries Group Corporation Limited (20220100H0113).

References

1. Liao, M., Wan, Z., Yao, C., Chen, K., Bai, X.: Real-time Scene Text Detection with Differentiable Binarization. arXiv preprint arXiv:1911.08947
2. Bochkovskiy, A., Wang, C.Y., Liao, H.Y.M.: Yolov4: Optimal speed and accuracy of object detection. arXiv preprint arXiv:2004.10934 (2020)
3. Nguyen, D.T., Nguyen, T.N., Kim, H., et al.: A high-throughput and power-efficient FPGA implementation of YOLO CNN for object detection. IEEE Trans. VLSI Syst. **27**(8), 1861–1873 (2019)
4. Sun, Y., Liu, J., Liu, W., Han, J., Ding, E., Liu, J.: Chinese street view text: Large-scale chinese text reading with partially supervised learning. In: Proceedings of the ICCV, pp. 9086–9095 (2019)
5. Du, Y., et al.: PP-OCR: A Practical Ultra Lightweight OCR System. arXiv preprint, arXiv: 2009.09941
6. Liao, M., Wan, Z., Yao, C., et al.: Real-time scene text detection with differentiable binarization. Proc. AAAI Conf. Artif. Intell. **34**(07), 11474–11481 (2020)
7. Fischer, P., Smajic, A., Abrami, G., et al.: Multi-type-TD-TSR – extracting tables from document images using a multi-stage pipeline for table detection and table structure recognition: from OCR to structured table representations. In: Edelkamp, S., Möller, R., Rueckert, E. (eds.) KI 2021: Advances in Artificial Intelligence: 44th German Conference on AI, Virtual Event, 27 Sep–1 Oct 2021, Proceedings, pp. 95–108. Springer International Publishing, Cham (2021). https://doi.org/10.1007/978-3-030-87626-5_8
8. Zheng, Q., Zhu, J., Tang, H., et al.: Generalized label enhancement with sample correlations. IEEE Trans. Knowl. Data Eng. **35**(1), 482–495 (2021)
9. Wang, G., Xu, X., Shen, F., et al.: Cross-modal dynamic networks for video moment retrieval with text query. IEEE Trans. Multimedia **24**, 1221–1232 (2022)
10. Xu, X., Lu, H., Song, J., et al.: Ternary adversarial networks with self-supervision for zero-shot cross-modal retrieval. IEEE Trans. Cybern. **50**(6), 2400–2413 (2019)

Multi-virtual View Scoring Network for 3D Hand Pose Estimation from a Single Depth Image

Yimeng Tian, Chen Li[✉], and Lihua Tian

School of Software Engineering, Xi'an Jiaotong University, Xi'an, China
`lynnlc@126.com`

Abstract. 3D hand pose estimation is a crucial subject in the domain of computer vision. Recently researchers transform a single depth image into multiple virtual view depth images. By projecting a single depth image through point cloud transformation and using the depth images of multiple virtual views together for hand pose estimation, these methods can effectively improve the estimation accuracy. However, current methods have issues with distorted generated depth images, insufficient usage of the depth image of each view, and high computational overhead. To overcome these problems, we introduce a multi-virtual view scoring network (MVSN). Our proposed MVSN consists of a single virtual view estimation module, virtual view feature encoding module, and virtual view scoring module. To generate an intermediate feature map suitable for virtual view scoring, the single virtual view estimation module uses a feature map offset loss function and enhance information interaction between channels in the backbone network. The virtual view feature encoding module adopts a two-branch structure to capture information about all joints and single joints from the intermediate feature map, respectively. This structure effectively improves model sensitivity to each view, better integrates information from each virtual view, and obtains a more appropriate scoring feature for each virtual view. The virtual view scoring module scores each view based on the scoring feature, and gives a higher score to the more accurately estimated virtual view. We also propose a dynamic virtual view removal strategy to remove poor quality views in the training process. Our model is tested on the NYU and ICVL datasets, and the mean joint error is 6.21 mm and 4.53 mm, respectively, exhibiting better estimation accuracy than existing methods.

Keywords: Computer vision · 3-D hand pose estimation · Depth image · Hand pose estimation

1 Introduction

Hand pose estimation has become a significant research topic in computer vision due to its potential applications in various human-computer interaction scenarios, such as virtual reality, augmented reality, and robot control tasks. In recent years, with the emergence of deep learning techniques and advanced commercial depth cameras, researchers have

H. Lu and J. Cai (Eds.): ISAIR 2023, CCIS 1998, pp. 147–164, 2024.
https://doi.org/10.1007/978-981-99-9109-9_15

been focusing on the problem of 3D hand pose estimation based on depth images. The depth map provides rich 3D spatial information as each pixel in the depth image represents the linear distance between the object and the camera plane. Moreover, the depth map can be converted into a point cloud, allowing researchers to study problems such as 3D pose estimation and gesture estimation.

The availability of large-scale datasets [1–4] and the increase in hardware computing performance have led to the use of deep neural network models as the mainstream approach to solve 3D hand pose estimation problems. Three primary methods have been proposed in the literature. The first method, such as A2J proposed by Xiong et al. [5], directly feeds the depth map as a two-dimensional image into the network model to estimate the hand joint coordinates. This method uses a complex network structure or a mature pre-trained model for the RGB image domain to extract the depth image features, making it computationally light and achieving good estimation accuracy. However, it does not fully exploit the rich 3D spatial information contained in the depth map. The second method converts the depth image into 3D spatial information data, such as point clouds and 3D voxels, and then uses the converted data as input for the network. This approach makes effective use of the 3D spatial information in the depth map. However, it significantly increases the complexity of data pre-processing and the computational parameters of the neural network model. The third method addresses the limitations of the first two methods by generating multiple virtual views. It combines the advantages of the first two methods by using the properties of depth images in the data pre-processing stage to transform a single depth map of the same hand pose into multiple virtual depth images at different angles through spatial variations. This method makes full use of the spatial semantic information in the depth image while still inputting the 2D depth image into the deep neural network, balancing estimation accuracy and computational effort. Overall, the third method is a promising approach to 3D hand pose estimation that utilizes the rich spatial information in depth maps, providing a balance between estimation accuracy and computational efficiency. However, the method of generating multiple virtual views for 3D hand pose estimation has its own limitations. Firstly, depth images do not provide complete 3D information, and in case of overlapping occlusion of the hand, they cannot fully represent the spatial structure of the hand. During the pre-processing stage, distorted virtual views with poor quality may be generated, and these distorted data can introduce a lot of noise into the dataset, thus affecting the training effectiveness of the model. Secondly, different virtual views of the same hand pose may vary in their utility for estimating joint positions, and the model needs to make trade-offs between the generated virtual view of each hand pose to achieve optimal estimation accuracy. To address these issues, Jian et al. propose VVS [6], which involves independent estimation of joint positions for each view using the A2J method [5], followed by a confident net that evaluates the intermediate feature maps of each view, and finally, a weighted averaging of the results of each view. However, the VVS approach has a major drawback in that it uses the intermediate feature maps of each view directly as input to the scoring net, which was originally designed to estimate joint coordinates and not score the view.

In order to tackle the aforementioned issues, we propose a novel approach for 3D hand pose estimation from a single depth image using a Multi-View Scoring Network, which is comprised of three main components: a single virtual view estimation module, a virtual view feature encoding module, and a virtual view scoring module. Firstly, the single virtual view estimation module integrates an inter-channel attention mechanism into the original feature extraction backbone network and generates an intermediate feature map for each joint to enhance the model's perception of local and global information of each joint. Additionally, an offset loss function is employed to constrain the intermediate feature maps for improved feature extraction and to generate more explicit information. The intermediate feature map can be used for joint estimation of the current view and as shallow features in the virtual view feature encoding module to extract deeper scoring features for view scoring. Secondly, in the virtual view encoding module, a two-branch view encoding method is proposed to extract local feature information of each joint and global feature information between joints, respectively, and encode the intermediate feature maps of each view. This module effectively extracts hidden scoring feature information of each joint and cross-joints in each view. Finally, the scoring features of all the views are sent to the scoring module, which obtains the scores of each view using a self-attention mechanism. By applying a final scoring loss constraint, the scoring module assigns higher scores to views with more accurate estimation. The final estimation results are obtained by weighting the estimation results of each single virtual view according to their scores. To further improve the quality of the dataset, we propose a dynamic virtual view removal strategy during the training process, which eliminates virtual views with low scores that have low-quality depth images with severe distortion, thereby reducing the negative impact of dirty data on the model.

The contributions of our proposed method can be summarized as follows.

1) We introduce an inter-channel attention mechanism into the single virtual view estimation module, along with a feature offset loss constraint to generate intermediate feature maps that can better represent hand contours and focus on each joint's information. These features are subsequently used for joint estimation and provide essential scoring information for the virtual view scoring module.

2) We propose a two-branch view feature encoding module that extracts global features for cross-joint intermediate feature maps and local features for single joint intermediate feature maps. This module can simultaneously consider the estimation accuracy information of a single joint and cross-joint under a specific view, providing scoring features for the subsequent virtual view scoring module.

3) Based on the scores of each view, we dynamically remove virtual views with lower scores during model training. By dynamically adjusting the virtual views used in the model weight updates in each training iteration, the problems of view distortion and image distortion caused by the virtual view can be effectively reduced, improving the accuracy of the model. These contributions demonstrate the effectiveness and practicality of our proposed multi-view scoring network for 3D hand pose estimation from a single depth image.

The second section provides a brief overview of the main methods for 3D hand pose estimation in different directions based on depth images, as well as the related work used in our model. The third section provides a detailed introduction of the single virtual view estimation module, virtual view encoding module, virtual view scoring module, and dynamic virtual view removal strategy proposed in our model. The fourth section demonstrates the effectiveness of the proposed method through ablation experiments and comparison with mainstream methods.

2 Related Works

For 3D hand pose estimation from a single depth image, there are three main types of methods based on the type of data preprocessing and model input data: direct input of a single depth image, input of transformed 3D data information, and input of depth images under multiple virtual views.

Direct input of a single depth image methods typically fall into two categories: regression-based and detection-based. Regression-based methods [7–11] directly input a single depth image and use convolutional neural networks (CNNs) to extract features from the depth image and output direct regression joint coordinates. In contrast, detection-based methods generate dense estimations, such as heatmaps or offset vector fields, to estimate joint coordinates [5, 12–15]. Huang et al.'s adaptive weighting regression (AWR) network [12], for example, uses a dense estimation method that outputs four intermediate feature maps to estimate the 3D spatial position of a single joint. This method has low computational overhead and can extract global and local information directly from the depth map.

In the method of inputting transformed 3D data information [16–19], the depth images are converted into 3D data information as model input. V2V [16, 30] converts depth images to voxels as model input and then uses 3D convolution processing. Hand-FoldingNet [18] and HandPointNet [19] convert the depth images to point cloud as model input. These methods fully exploit the 3D spatial information of depth images. However, the data preprocessing is more complicated, and the research on deep learning models is not as mature in 3D input as in 2D image input, which is a limitation of this method.

The multiple virtual view input method [6, 20] involves preprocessing a single input depth image to generate multiple depth images from virtual views. This is achieved by estimating each view independently and then combining the final results. Ge et al. [20] proposed a method that converts a single depth map into a point cloud, which is then projected in three orthogonal directions to obtain depth image projections. These projections are fed into the network separately, and a fusion network is used to combine the results. VVS [6] converts the single depth image into 3D point cloud information and projects the 3D point cloud at different angles to generate multiple virtual view depth images of the same hand pose. Each virtual view is then fed separately into the backbone network to obtain their own estimation results. A confidence net is used to evaluate all intermediate feature maps from the views and fuse the results.

However, the intermediate feature map used in A2J [5, 31], which is the backbone network of VVS, is only designed for regressing joint positions and not for view scoring, which limits its effectiveness. In this paper, we propose an intermediate feature map suitable for virtual view scoring in the single virtual view estimation module. Additionally, we propose an efficient virtual view encoding module that integrates global and local information in the virtual view scoring module to address the limitations of the previous method. Our proposed method is inspired by the VVS approach, but we address the deficiencies by incorporating novel methods to improve the accuracy of virtual view scoring.

3 Proposed Method

The structure of MVSN consists of three main parts, which are Single Virtual View Estimation Module, Virtual View Encoding Module, and Scoring Module. The backbone network of the Single View Estimation Module consists of ECA-ResNet50 and ECA-DeconvNet, which incorporate the attention mechanism.

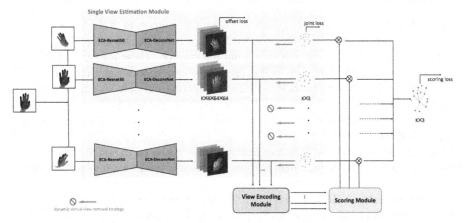

Fig. 1. Multi-virtual view scoring network.

The MVSN process is depicted in Fig. 1, and it involves several steps. Initially, a rough hand depth map is obtained through preprocessing a single depth image. Then, multiple virtual views are generated using the same approach as the VVS method. This process involves converting the single depth image into a point cloud, which is subsequently rotated and projected to generate N virtual view depth images from different perspectives. The depth images of the N virtual views are then processed by the single virtual view estimation module to produce a set of intermediate feature maps for each view. To obtain joint estimation results for the current virtual view depth image, the AWR method [12] is applied to independently regress the intermediate feature maps of each virtual view. Unlike the VVS method, our method employs a backbone network with a channel attention mechanism to generate intermediate feature maps and a loss function constraint on the intermediate feature maps to focus on each joint and retain sufficient semantic information for scoring the virtual view.

In the virtual view scoring module, the intermediate feature maps of each virtual view are passed through the virtual view feature encoding module to obtain the scoring features for each view. This module comprises a self-attention module and a fully connected layer that compares the scoring features of each virtual view and ultimately determines the score of each view. The final estimation result of the depth image is obtained by a weighted sum of the hand joint estimation results of the M virtual views with the highest scores.

During model training, loss function constraints are applied to the intermediate feature map, the estimation result of a single virtual view, and the final estimation result, respectively. Moreover, a dynamic virtual view removal strategy is employed to restrict the learning of certain virtual view data by the single virtual view estimation module during model training. Low-scoring virtual view images are not used as training data to avoid the negative impact of poor-quality views on the model.

Each module of the MVSN is described in detail in the following sections.

3.1 Single Virtual View Estimation Module

The single virtual view estimation module is a critical component of the MVSN, which extracts semantic features from the input virtual view depth images and produces intermediate feature maps that can represent joint information. These intermediate feature maps serve two purposes: they are used to regress the joint coordinates under the current virtual view, and they also provide the basis for scoring multiple virtual views. Prior research methods did not employ virtual views, and thus, the intermediate feature maps were only used for regression estimation of joint coordinate results. However, after the independent estimation of virtual views is used in this method, the scoring module must also select a virtual view with clearer joint positions based on it, which requires generating an intermediate feature map with more semantic information to achieve better scoring results.

To extract features, ResNet-50 is employed, which produces feature maps with high channel counts but low resolution. These feature maps are challenging to integrate and are not conducive to subsequent joint density estimation. To address this, several deconvolution layers are added to improve the resolution of the extracted feature maps.

The number of channels in the intermediate feature map obtained for each virtual view through the backbone network is K $\times$ 4, where K is the number of joints to be estimated. The adaptive weighting regression (AWR) method has been shown to achieve high accuracy in joint estimation for a single view, and its dense estimation method can effectively utilize the rich explicit semantic information contained in the intermediate feature maps, making it well-suited for virtual view scoring. The intermediate feature maps are regressed using the feature map dense estimation method proposed in the AWR for a single virtual view to produce joint estimation results. Each pixel value on different channels represents the horizontal, vertical, and depth offsets of the predicted joint position relative to that pixel point, as well as the probability heatmap. The 3D coordinates of the corresponding joints are obtained by discrete integration of all pixels on the four feature maps corresponding to each joint.

Since different joints of the same hand have strong positional correlation with each other, and this joint structure information is implicit in multiple neighboring channels, the intermediate feature maps between different channels should have strong information correlation and implicit rich semantic information. Thus, several efficient channel attention (ECA) modules have been added to the backbone network for feature extraction to better perceive the joint structural information contained in multi-channel feature maps. The ECA module is an inter-channel attention mechanism that performs a 1D convolution between multiple adjacent channels after averaging pooling of all pixels in each channel of the feature map, and the corresponding weight of each channel is obtained after sigmoid of the results. Adding multiple ECA modules to the ResNet and deconvolution layers can effectively extract implicit structural information of the hand, making the generated intermediate feature map more suitable for adaptive weighting regression and view scoring.

3.2 Virtual View Feature Encoding module

After selecting a virtual view depth image and inputting it into the single virtual view estimation module described in Sect. 3.1, the 4-channel intermediate feature map of a certain hand joint is shown in Fig. 2.

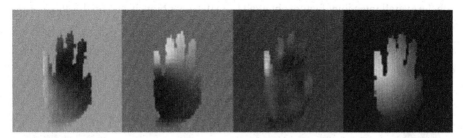

Fig. 2. The 4-channel intermediate feature map of a certain hand joint in the single virtual view estimation module.

It can be observed that the obtained set of intermediate feature map is rich in semantic information. In the single virtual view estimation module, for the feature maps using the AWR method [12], only the pixels of the hand region are used to compute the joint coordinates, so the values of the background regions on the feature maps generated by the model are invariant, so the full contour information of the hand is preserved. Meanwhile, because the geometric meaning of the intermediate feature map itself is the coordinate offset of pixel positions relative to joint points or the probability heat map, a rich set of explicit semantic features can be preserved on the intermediate feature map. For example, Fig. 2 shows a 4-channel intermediate feature map of the estimated second knuckle of the little finger generated by the single virtual view estimation module from a certain virtual view. Then, the adaptive weighting regression method proposed in AWR is used to obtain the three-dimensional result of the joint from this view. It can be seen that the distribution of the larger pixel values is concentrated in all four channels, i.e. the highlighted central part of the figure is approximately at the second knuckle of the little finger, indicating that the model is more certain about the location of this joint. For a virtual view, if all the feature maps corresponding to the joints in this view have similar situations, then it can be considered a good virtual view. The proposed virtual view feature encoding module can be used to encode the view based on these semantic features for subsequent scoring of different virtual views, and then filter out the better quality views based on the scoring results, and synthesize the final joint estimation results based on the estimation results of these virtual views.

The virtual view feature encoding module is used to encode the intermediate feature maps of each virtual view, converting the original multi-channel 2D feature maps into 1D features for scoring in the scoring module. To evaluate a view, it is necessary to focus on whether the estimation of certain key joints is accurate, and also to comprehensively consider the overall estimation of all joints under that view. Therefore, the feature map encoding of the view needs to consider both global multiple joints and local key joints simultaneously. To better extract intra- and inter-joint information of the virtual view from both global and local, a two-branch structured view feature encoding module was used, as shown in Fig. 3. One branch encodes the feature maps of all the joints in the virtual view, and sends all the intermediate feature maps of a virtual view together to a CNNs to obtain the overall inter-joint feature information between the joints of the entire view. Another branch sends the feature map of each joint under this view to a CNNs to encode the features of each joint. Then, the features of multiple joints are concatenated with the overall inter-joint feature obtained from the other branch, and finally, the scoring features of these virtual views are obtained.

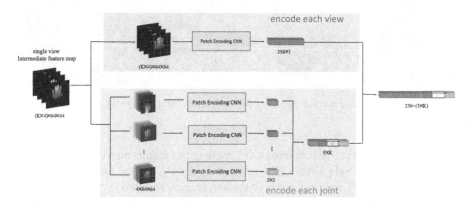

Fig. 3. Virtual view feature encoding module.

At the same time, it is obvious in Fig. 2 that highlighted areas in the feature map tend to be concentrated in some localities, while the rest of the feature map has more useless information. To help the model focus more on the local key features and less on the useless regions when encoding the view feature map, we propose a method of Patch Encoding CNN in the process of view feature encoding. Patch Encoding CNN divides the feature map into several small patches and encodes the features in small patches so that the model can extract only local features in one or more small patches instead of extracting features in the whole space, thus helping the model to focus on some important regions. Patch Encoding CNN is implemented by using multiple successive stacks of convolutional layers and adding a layer of convolutional layers with larger kernels to achieve segmentation of small patches.

3.3 Scoring Module

The virtual view feature encoding module can be used to obtain the 1D scoring features of all views, and then all these scoring features are sent to the scoring module for scoring, and the structure of the scoring module is shown in Fig. 4.

Fig. 4. Scoring module.

Similar to the confidence net in VVS, the scoring module consists of a self-attention module followed by a fully connected layer. After inputting the scoring feature of each virtual view, the self-attention module compares the feature of each view and finally obtains the scores of each virtual view. It selects M hand joint estimation results of the virtual views with the highest score, and then weights them based on the score to obtain the final joint estimation result.

$$\hat{J} = \sum_{i=1}^{M} c_i(R_i\hat{J}_i + t_i) \tag{1}$$

where $\hat{J}_i$ is the estimation result of the virtual view i, and c_i is the score for the virtual view i, and $[R_i, t_i]$ is the camera internal parameters for the virtual view i.

Due to the fact that the dataset itself does not have true labels for scoring from various virtual view, the scoring module indirectly constrains the scoring process of the scoring module through scoring loss (Eq. 4). Constrained scoring modules tend to score higher for those views with more accurate estimation results under a single view, and higher scores will make the estimation results of this view have a higher weight in the process of obtaining the final estimation results, thereby making the final estimation results more accurate.

3.4 Dynamic Local View Removal Strategy

Taking advantage of the property that point clouds and depth images can be transformed into each other, the virtual view method projects point clouds at multiple fixed angles into multiple virtual view depth images, and then estimates the joint coordinates for these depth images independently. However, when generating the virtual views, the point cloud projections will occur with some points occluding each other, which inevitably leads to some information loss in the depth image generated by the virtual views.

Figure 5 shows the result of converting the depth map of a certain hand pose into a depth map under 25 virtual views. It can be found that the views marked by the green box can better represent the position of each joint under some angles, and the whole hand pose structure is clearer. However, there are also many cases where the quality of the generated hand depth image is very poor, as shown in the views marked by the red boxes, where the information of these views is seriously missing and the hand shape is incomplete.

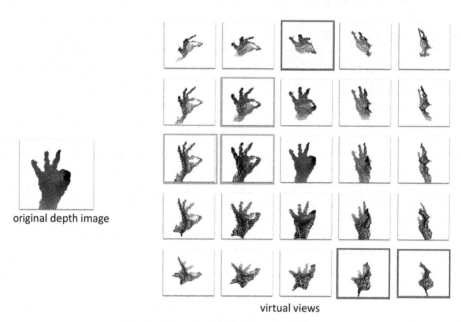

original depth image

virtual views

Fig. 5. Generated virtual view depth images.

Essentially, generating virtual views can also be seen as a data augmentation strategy for existing training data. By utilizing the ability of depth images and point cloud to convert each other, multiple depth images from different virtual views under the same hand pose are generated to expand the training sample. However, it can be seen that using this data augmentation method will inevitably introduce a large amount of low-quality training data, which will actually have an adverse impact on model training.

To solve the above problem, a dynamic virtual view removal strategy is used in the training process. During each iteration, based on the scores of each virtual view by the scoring module, the M views with the highest scores are selected to participate in the final estimation. At the same time, remove the rest of the virtual views, do not calculate the joint loss function of this virtual view branch, and do not use the data of this branch to update the model weight of the single virtual view estimation module to avoid the negative impact of these low-quality virtual views.

3.5 Loss Function

Three loss functions are used for training: single view joint loss, scoring loss, and feature map offset loss. The VVS model only uses the loss function to constrain the estimation results. However, since the intermediate feature map is the key information in the scoring module, it will directly affect the accuracy of the view scoring. Therefore, in order to obtain more accurate intermediate feature maps with richer semantic information, we also add offset losses for the feature map in the single virtual view estimation module during training.

Due to the addition of the dynamic virtual view removal strategy, some view branches with lower scores are removed and do not participate in weight training of the model, as shown in Eq. 2 and 3:

$$
L_{joint,i} = \begin{cases} 0, & if \ i \notin S \\ \sum\limits_{m=1}^{K} L_\tau (\mathbf{J}_{i,m} - \hat{\mathbf{J}}_{i,m}), & if \ \in S \end{cases}
\tag{2}
$$

$$
L_{joint} = \sum\limits_{i=1}^{N} L_{joint,i}
\tag{3}
$$

where S is the m virtual views with the highest score, K is the number of joints. L_τ is the smooth L1 loss. $\mathbf{J}_{i,m}$ is the true coordinate of the joint i in the virtual view m, and $\hat{\mathbf{J}}_{i,m}$ is the predicted coordinate of joint i in the virtual view m.

The scoring loss is used to constrain the effect of the scoring module, and $\mathbf{J}_i$ is the true coordinate of the joint i, and $\hat{\mathbf{J}}_i$ is the predicted coordinate of the joint obtained by weighting all the virtual views.

$$
L_{scoring} = \sum\limits_{m=1}^{K} L_\tau \left(\left\| \mathbf{J}_i - \hat{\mathbf{J}}_i \right\| \right)
\tag{4}
$$

weighting all the virtual views.

In addition, constraints are added to the intermediate feature maps to improve the scoring effect of the scoring module. Since the L1 loss is not as sensitive to outliers as the L2 loss, the smooth L1 loss is also used for densely represented feature maps. The feature map offset loss L_{offset} is shown in Eq. 5:

$$
L_{offset} = \sum\limits_{i=1}^{h} \sum\limits_{j=1}^{w} L_\tau (d_{i,j} - \hat{d}_{i,j})
\tag{5}
$$

where h and w are the height and width of the feature map, and $d_{i,j}$ is the value of each pixel on the feature map generated based on the real hand joint position labels.

In summary, the loss function is shown in Eq. 6:

$$
L = \lambda_1 L_{joint} + \lambda_2 L_{scoring} + L_{offset}
\tag{6}
$$

where λ is the weighting factor for each loss function.

4   Experimental results and analysis

4.1   Dataset

The proposed method is validated on two mainstream 3D gesture estimation depth map datasets, the NYU dataset [1] and the ICVL dataset [2]. The NYU dataset is captured using the Microsoft Kinect sensor and acquired from three different camera positions.

Each camera contains more than 72,000 depth images of the training set and more than 8,000 depth images of the test set. Following the criteria of previous researchers, we used only one of the camera positions and 14 of the 36 annotated joints for training and testing. Images from the ICVL dataset were acquired using Intel's Realsense camera depth camera, containing 330,000 training set depth images and more than 1,500 test set depth images. Sixteen joint positions of the hand were annotated.

4.2 Evaluation Metric

We use two of the most commonly used metrics to evaluate the performance of 3D hand pose estimation models. The first is the average 3D distance error, measured in millimeters. The second is the percentage of success frames. The percentage of success frames is defined as the rate of frames in which all Euclidean errors of joints are below a certain threshold.

4.3 Implementation Details

The experimental equipment used for training and testing comprised an Intel Xeon E5–2690 v3 processor, 128G RAM, and Nvidia RTX3090 GPU. The network model was developed using PyTorch and the Adam optimizer, with an initial learning rate of 0.0005 that decayed by 0.9 per epoch. The training process included random data augmentation by rotating the hand depth image from -37.5 to $37.5°$ around the z-axis and randomly scaling it between 0.9 and 1.1 times, to prevent overfitting. The resolution of the hand depth image was fixed at 128 for the NYU dataset and 192 for the ICVL dataset, while the resolution of the intermediate feature maps obtained from the backbone network of the single virtual view estimation module was set at 64. The input depth map was converted into a point cloud using the VVS method, which was then rotated horizontally and vertically on a sphere with the center of the point cloud as the center, respectively. A total of 25 virtual views were uniformly selected in the range of -60 to 60 degrees, and the point cloud was projected under 25 viewpoints to generate 25 virtual view depth images. The dynamic view removal strategy was used to dynamically remove the 10 lowest scoring views from the 25 views during the training process and keep 15 views. The weights of the loss function were set at $\lambda 1 = 0.5$ and $\lambda 2 = 0.2$.

4.4 Ablation experiments

In order to validate the effectiveness of the proposed MVSN, we conducted two sets of ablation experiments. The first set aimed to examine the effectiveness of each module in the MVSN, while the second set investigated the rationality of setting up the view feature encoding module alone. As the NYU dataset is more challenging, we conducted the ablation experiments on this dataset.

The baseline for the ablation experiments is a ResNet-50 followed by 3 deconvolution layers. The virtual view feature encoding module used single branch convolutional and pooling layer stacked CNNs and did not employ the dynamic virtual view removal strategy. We made the following modifications to the baseline in turn for the ablation experiments: replacing the backbone network with the backbone network of the single virtual view estimation module (SVEM) proposed by us, replacing the feature encoding part with the virtual view feature encoding module (VFEM), and adding the dynamic virtual view removal strategy (DVR) to the training.

Table 1. Results of ablation experiments with each module added in turn.

Component	Mean error (mm)
baseline	6.73
baseline-SVEM	6.50
baseline-SVEM-VFEM	6.29
baseline-SVEM-VFEM-DVR	6.21

The experimental results are presented in Table 1. According to the results of the ablation experiments, the estimation error of the model is significantly reduced after the addition of the single virtual view estimation module (SVEM), and it is concluded that the introduction of the ECA module into the backbone network of the single virtual view estimation module (SVEM) can sufficiently extract the implicit joint information in the cross-channel feature maps and enrich the semantic information of the output intermediate feature maps, which is suitable for the subsequent view scoring module. In addition, the model accuracy is also improved by adding the dynamic virtual view removal (DVR) strategy, which confirms that the distorted depth image data generated by the use of virtual views are detrimental to the model training, and it makes sense for the backbone model not to learn these samples. The dynamic virtual view removal strategy removes the branch data with low scores, which can effectively mitigate the negative impact of this dirty data.

To further investigate the effectiveness of the virtual view feature encoding module (VFEM), an experiment for this module is conducted. A modified feature encoding module is used for both backbone networks. The two-branch structure of the virtual view feature encoding module(VFEM) is tested separately using only one of the individual branches, i.e., encoding only each view as a whole (PV) and encoding only each single joint of the view (PJ). The effect of adding and removing the Patch Encoding layer (PE) from the VFEM is also tested.

Table 2. Ablation experimental results of two-branch structure of VFEM.

Component	Mean error (mm)	Component	Mean error (mm)
PV w/o PE	6.50	PV	6.39
PJ w/o PE	6.51	PJ	6.42
PV + PJ w/o PE	6.34	PVPJ	6.29

The results of the ablation experiments on the two-branch structure of the virtual view feature encoding module (VFEM) are shown in Table 2. First, the model estimation effect was generally improved after the addition of patch encoding, which proves that dividing the feature map into several small patches is useful to help the model focus on the key regions of the feature map. Second, using only a single branch of VFEM for feature extraction cannot achieve the best model estimation effect, which also illustrates that in order to achieve the best feature extraction effect, both a view overall encoding branch for extracting inter-joint information and a single joint encoding branch for local feature extraction of a single joint are needed. The VFEM module needs both branches to work together to extract intra-joint and inter-joint information in the feature map to better score the virtual views in the scoring module (Fig. 6).

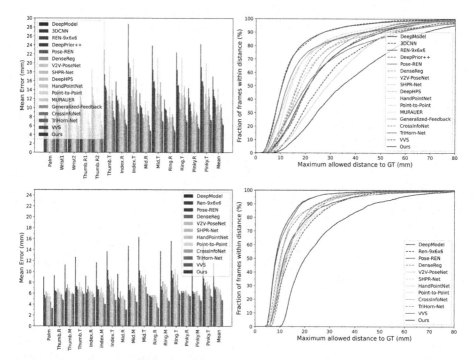

Fig. 6. Comparison of MVSN with state-of-the-art methods. Left: the percentage of success frames over different error thresholds. Right: 3D distance errors per hand keypoints. Top: NYU dataset. Bottom: ICVL dataset.

4.5 Comparison with State-of-the-Art Methods

We compare the MVSN with some of the SoTA approaches, including CrossInfoNet [10], AWR [12], DenseReg [13], TriHorn-Net [15], V2V-PoseNet [16], HandPointNet [19], DeepPrior++ [22], DeepModel [23], 3DCNN [24], REN-9 × 6 × 6 [25], Pose-REN [26], SHPR-Net [27], MURAUER [28], Point-to-Point [29] and VVS [6]. Experiments were conducted on the NYU and ICVL datasets, respectively, and the average 3D estimation error and the percentage of success frames over different error thresholds are shown in

Table 3. Performance comparison on the NYU dataset.

Methods	Year	Mean error (mm)
DeepModel	2016	17.036
3DCNN	2017	14.113
REN-9x6x6	2017	12.694
DeepPrior++	2017	12.238
Pose-REN	2018	11.811
SHPR-Net	2018	10.775
HandPointNet	2018	10.540
DenseReg	2018	10.214
CrossInfoNet	2019	10.078
MURAUER	2019	9.466
Point-to-Point	2018	9.045
V2V-PoseNet	2018	8.419
TriHorn-Net	2022	7.68
AWR	2020	7.37
VVS	2022	6.40
Ours	2023	**6.21**

Table 4. Performance comparison on the ICVL dataset.

Methods	Year	Mean error (mm)
DeepModel	2016	11.561
REN-9x6x6	2017	7.305
DenseReg	2018	7.239
SHPR-Net	2018	7.219
HandPointNet	2018	6.935
Pose-REN	2018	6.791
CrossInfoNet	2019	6.732
Point-to-Point	2018	6.328
V2V-PoseNet	2018	6.284

(continued)

Table 4. (*continued*)

Methods	Year	Mean error (mm)
AWR	2020	5.98
TriHorn-Net	2022	5.73
VVS	2022	4.76
Ours	2023	**4.53**

Table 3 and 4 present the performance comparison of different methods on the NYU and ICVL datasets, respectively. The virtual view generation method generates multiple virtual views by projecting the point cloud transformed from the original single-view depth image. After joint estimation on each virtual view, the final result is obtained, which can effectively utilize the spatial information in the depth image and use mature 2D convolutional networks. Both the VVS and our proposed MVSN, which use the virtual view generation method, show significantly improved accuracy in joint estimation compared to previous methods. Our MVSN also overcomes the problems of insufficient view scoring and distorted images that can affect the model estimation results in the VVS method. We design a single virtual view estimation module with a channel attention mechanism and an intermediate feature map with explicit semantic information to provide richer view features for the view scoring module. Finally, we introduce a dynamic virtual view removal strategy to prevent the model from learning virtual view depth images with poor image quality. The experimental results demonstrate that our proposed MVSN outperforms other methods and achieves state-of-the-art results. However, there is still room for improvement, such as reducing the computational cost of the single virtual view estimation module and optimizing the selection of the best viewpoint for each virtual view score in the scoring module.

5   Conclusion

In this paper, we propose a multi-view scoring network (MVSN) for 3D hand pose estimation from a single depth image. The proposed method addresses some of the shortcomings of current methods, such as insufficient view evaluation and distorted images, which can negatively impact the model estimation results. The single virtual view estimation module is designed to effectively extract key information and implicit semantic information of cross-channel feature maps in the depth image, and generate intermediate feature maps with explicit semantic information, which are more suitable for subsequent processing. The virtual view feature encoding module uses a two-branch structure that can better take into account the influence of single and multiple joints on a view score, leading to more reasonable view scores. Furthermore, we propose a dynamic virtual view removal strategy during training, which effectively reduces the adverse effects of virtual view image distortion on the model.

Experimental results on the NYU and ICVL datasets demonstrate the effectiveness and feasibility of our proposed MVSN method, which can significantly improve the joint estimation accuracy compared to the comparison methods. However, there are still some areas for improvement in our method. For instance, the computational volume of the single virtual view estimation module remains large, and the scoring module has room for optimization in selecting the best virtual view for each virtual view score. In the future, we plan to focus on these areas and continue to improve the performance of our method.

References

1. Tompson, J., Stein, M., Lecun, Y., et al.: Re.-time continuous pose recovery of human hands using convolutional networks. ACM Trans. Graph. **33**(5), 1–10 (2014)
2. Tang, D., Chang, H.J., Tejani, A., et al.: Latent regression forest: structured estimation of 3D articulated hand posture. In: 2014 IEEE Conference on Computer Vision and Pattern Recognition. IEEE (2014)
3. Sun, X., Wei, Y., Liang, S., et al.: Cascaded hand pose regression. In: 2015 IEEE Conference on Computer Vision and Pattern Recognition (CVPR). IEEE (2015)
4. Yuan, S., Ye, Q., Garcia-Hernando, G., et al.: The 2017 Hands in the Million Challenge on 3D Hand Pose Estimation. https://doi.org/10.48550/arXiv.1707.02237 (2017)
5. Xiong, F., Zhang, B., Xiao, Y., et al.: A2J: Anchor-to-Joint Regression Network for 3D Articulated Pose Estimation from a Single Depth Image (2019)
6. Cheng, J., Wan, Y., Zuo, D., et al.: Efficient virtual view selection for 3d hand pose estimation. Proc. AAAI Conf. Artif. Intell. **36**(1), 419–426 (2022). https://doi.org/10.1609/aaai.v36i1.19919
7. Ren, P., Sun, H., Qi, Q., et al.: SRN: stacked regression network for real-time 3D hand pose estimation. In: The British Machine Vision Conference (2019)
8. Zhang, Z., Xie, S., Chen, M., et al.: HandAugmentation: a Simple Data Augmentation Method for Depth-Based 3D Hand Pose Estimation, https://doi.org/10.48550/arXiv.2001.00702 (2020)
9. Ren, P., Sun, H., Huang, W., et al.: Spatial-aware stacked regression network for real-time 3D hand pose estimation – ScienceDirect. Neurocomputing **437**, 42–57 (2021)
10. Du, K., Lin, X., Sun, Y., et al.: Crossinfonet: multi-task information sharing based hand pose estimation. In: Proceedings of the IEEE/CVF Conference on Computer Vision and Pattern Recognition, pp. 9896–9905 (2019)
11. Xu, L., Hu, C., Xue, J., et al.: Improved regression network on depth hand pose estimation with auxiliary variable. IEEE Trans. Circuits Syst. Video Technol. **31**(3), 890–904 (2020)
12. Huang, W., Ren, P., Wang, J., et al.: AWR: adaptive weighting regression for 3D hand pose estimation. Proc. AAAI Conf. Artif. Intell. **34**(7), 11061–11068 (2020)
13. Wan, C., Probst, T., Van Gool, L., et al.: Dense 3d regression for hand pose estimation. In: Proceedings of the IEEE Conference on Computer Vision and Pattern Recognition, pp. 5147–5156 (2018)
14. Fang, L., Liu, X., Liu, L., et al.: Jgr-p2o: Joint graph reasoning based pixel-to-offset prediction network for 3d hand pose estimation from a single depth image. In: Computer Vision-ECCV 2020: 16th European Conference, Glasgow, UK, 23–28 Aug 2020, Proceedings, Part VI 16, pp. 120–137. Springer International Publishing (2020)
15. Rezaei, M., Rastgoo, R., Athitsos, V.: TriHorn-Net: A Model for Accurate Depth-Based 3D Hand Pose Estimation. arXiv preprint arXiv:2206.07117 (2022)
16. Moon, G., Chang, J.Y., Lee, K.M.: V2V-PoseNet: Voxel-to-Voxel Prediction Network for Accurate 3D Hand and Human Pose Estimation from a Single Depth Map. https://doi.org/10.48550/arXiv.1711.07399

17. Cheng, W., Park, J.H., Ko, J.H.: HandFoldingNet: A 3D Hand Pose Estimation Network Using Multiscale-Feature Guided Folding of a 2D Hand Skeleton (2021)
18. Huang, L., Tan, J., Liu, J., et al.: Hand-transformer: non-autoregressive structured modeling for 3d hand pose estimation. In: Computer Vision-ECCV 2020: 16th European Conference, Glasgow, UK, 23–28 Aug 2020, Proceedings, Part XXV 16, pp. 17–33. Springer International Publishing (2020)
19. Ge, L., Cai, Y., Weng, J., et al.: Hand pointnet: 3d hand pose estimation using point sets. In: Proceedings of the IEEE Conference on Computer Vision and Pattern Recognition, pp. 8417–8426 (2018)
20. Ge, L., Liang, H., Yuan, J., et al.: Robust 3D hand pose estimation in single depth images: from single-view CNN to multi-view CNNs. IEEE **27**, 4422–4436 (2016)
21. Wang, Q., Wu, B., Zhu, P., et al.: ECA-Net: Efficient channel attention for deep convolutional neural networks. In: Proceedings of the IEEE/CVF Conference on Computer Vision and Pattern Recognition 11534–11542 (2020)
22. Oberweger, M., Lepetit, V.: DeepPrior++: improving fast and accurate 3D hand pose estimation. IEEE Comput. Soc. (2017)
23. Zhou, X., Wan, Q., Zhang, W, et al.: Model-based Deep Hand Pose Estimation. AAAI Press (2016)
24. Ge, L., Hui, L., Yuan, J., et al.: 3D convolutional neural networks for efficient and robust hand pose estimation from single depth images. In: 2017 IEEE Conference on Computer Vision and Pattern Recognition (CVPR). IEEE (2017)
25. Wang, G., Chen, X., Guo, H., et al.: Region ensemble network: towards good practices for deep 3D hand pose estimation. J. Vis. Commun. Image Represent. **55**, 404–414 (2018)
26. Chen, X., Wang, G., Guo, H., et al.: Pose guided structured region ensemble network for cascaded hand pose estimation. Neurocomputing **395**, 138–149 (2017)
27. Chen, X., Wang, G., Zhang, C., et al.: SHPR-Net: deep semantic hand pose regression from point clouds. IEEE Access **6**, 43425–43439 (2018)
28. Poier, G., Opitz, M., Schinagl, D., et al.: MURAUER: Mapping Unlabeled Real Data for Label AUstERity (2018)
29. Ge, L., Ren, Z., Yuan, J.: Point-to-Point Regression PointNet for 3D Hand Pose Estimation. In: European Conference on Computer Vision (2018)
30. Zhao, F., Lu, H., Zhao, W., et al.: Image-scale-symmetric cooperative network for defocus blur detection. IEEE Trans. Circuits Syst. Video Technol. **32**(5), 2719–2731 (2021)
31. Teng, Y., Lu, H., Li, Y., et al.: Multidimensional deformable object manipulation based on DN-transporter networks. IEEE Trans. Intell. Transp. Syst. **24**(4), 4532–4540 (2022)

Digital Archive Stamp Detection and Extraction

Xin Jin[1] , Qiuyang Mu[1], Xiaoyu Chen[2], Qingyu Liu[1], and Chaoen Xiao[1(✉)]

[1] Beijing Electronic Science and Technology Institute, No. 7, Fufeng Street, Fengtai District, Beijing 100070, China
xcecd@qq.com

[2] Information Center of China North Industries, Group Corporation Limited, Beijing 100089, China

Abstract. Archives contain valuable historical information and must be properly preserved. However, traditional archival materials are vulnerable to damage from water, fire, and mold, making long-term storage difficult. To address this issue, digital archives have been established for management. As a result, effective storage, detection, extraction, and utilization of archive information has become a focus of attention. This paper focuses on the feature extraction of archival stamp images, proposing a network structure of stamp extraction based on generative adversarial network for texture feature extraction of stamp images. This method aims to extract more refined texture features, improving the accuracy of stamp text recognition. An improved stamp text recognition method is proposed using PP-OCR, which can recognize text for multiple shape seals. This method effectively solves the problem of deep learning models being unable to recognize text due to the bending and tilting of the ring-shaped text in the stamp. Overall, this research aims to enhance the preservation and utilization of archival materials by improving feature extraction and text recognition methods.

Keywords: target detection · stamp extraction · image segmentation · stamp text recognition

1 Introduction

Despite in-depth research on image detection and extraction by both domestic and foreign scholars, there has been little focus on the extraction of key information, particularly seal information, from real old archives. To address this gap, we propose a digital archival seal image detection and extraction technique for seals on old archives, which has significant practical value.

This paper includes three main chapters: "Dataset construction", "Image extraction model", and "Seal image text recognition scheme", in addition to "Introduction" and "Conclusions". In "Data set construction", we describe how we constructed the dataset. In "Image extraction model", we explain how we trained the stamp image extraction model on the dataset. Finally, in "Seal image text recognition", we present a scheme for seal image text recognition.

H. Lu and J. Cai (Eds.): ISAIR 2023, CCIS 1998, pp. 165–174, 2024.
https://doi.org/10.1007/978-981-99-9109-9_16

166   X. Jin et al.

Overall, this research provides a novel approach for the detection and extraction of seal information from old archives, with the potential to significantly enhance
preservation and utilization efforts.

Our contributions to the field can be summarized as follows:

- Construction of a new dataset of archival seal images
- Development of an archival seal image extraction model
- Proposal of a lightweight text recognition scheme for archival seal images

2 Dataset Construction

To address the issue of small sample sizes and uneven distribution in seal images, this
paper utilized the seal making software Sedwen combined with OpenCV to manually
create 2,000 seal images. Each shape of seal was represented by 500 images. The seals
were added to the archives with rotation angles ranging from [−45°, 45°], accounting
for 90% of the images; [−30°, 30°], accounting for 70% of the images; and [−10°, 10°],
accounting for 50% of the images. This generated a large number of archival samples
with seals adjacent to each other and overlapping, allowing for more diverse and realistic
training data.

Additionally, the paper collected fingerprint images and added them to the archives
as a background component. The resulting dataset consisted of a mixture of real archive
images and generated archive images, totaling 11,068 mixed archive images. Figure 1
shows examples of the generated archive images.

Overall, this approach allowed for the creation of a larger and more diverse dataset of
digitized archive seal images, providing a more comprehensive foundation for training
machine learning models.

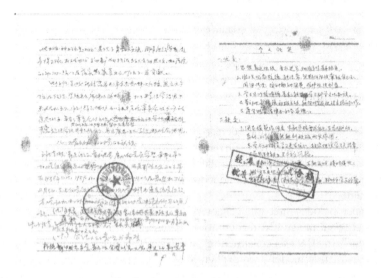

Fig. 1. Generated archive images

2.1 Archival Stamp Image Detection Model

Archival Stamp Image Detection Model Information. To facilitate subsequent deep learning training, this paper used the LabelImg open source tool to manually annotate stamp images on archives. The fully labeled digitized archival stamp image dataset was divided into a training set (7/10) and a validation set (3/10). The training images and labels were input together into the YOLOv5 [1, 7] detection model for training, resulting in a stamp detection model file with the suffix pt after 300 epochs of training. This file saved various parameter information during the model's training.

To detect stamps in new archive images, the image was input into the AI model for inference, and the location of the stamp image was marked and saved. The general framework diagram of stamp detection is shown in Fig. 2. The type of stamp detected and the probability of correctness of this type were displayed at the top of the target detection box. Based on the detection box and coordinate information obtained through inference, the target was cropped, and the stamp images were stored in separate folders.

Using the location information saved by YOLOv5 inference, the stamp area can be easily obtained in subsequent label production, enabling the creation of a large dataset of digitized archival stamp images with simple manual verification.

Overall, this approach provides an efficient and effective method for detecting and extracting stamp images from archives, enabling the creation of a more comprehensive digitized archive dataset for preservation and utilization purposes.

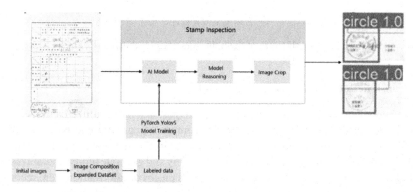

Fig. 2. General framework diagram of stamp detection

Experimental Results and Analysis. Figure 3 shows that the box_loss, obj_loss, and cls_loss for both the training and validation sets are infinitely close to 0, indicating that the stamp detection model can accurately respond to both box and target detection and classification situations. Table 1 shows that the four metrics of AP, AR, mAP_0.5, and mAP_0.5:0.95 all converge to 1 indefinitely, indicating a high level of accuracy.

Overall, the YOLOv5 network model demonstrates a high comprehensive detection rate and accuracy, making it well-suited for the field of detection and classification of stamp images.

Table 1. Combined archive image stamp detection index table

Classification	Training	Validation	Accuracy	Recall	mAP@.5	mAP@.5:.95
Circle	4151	1873	0.997	0.995	0.995	0.87
Rectangle	4062	1353	0.99	0.989	0.994	0.731
Oval	3844	1459	0.997	0.998	0.995	0.933
Rhombus	3302	1561	0.999	0.995	0.995	0.898
Total	15359	6246	0.996	0.994	0.995	0.858

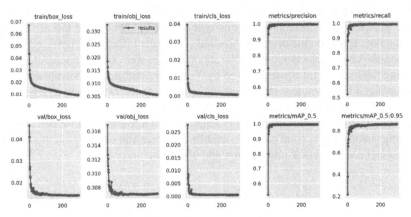

Fig. 3. Consolidation of the indicators of the archival test stamp

2.2 Construction of Stamp Extraction Dataset

To accurately extract the foreground of stamp images, this paper utilized a model based on generative adversarial network to segment image foreground and background. To improve the accuracy and reliability of the model, Ground Truth was produced to help the GAN model learn image features more effectively and generate more accurate results.

To produce a label map of the seal data, several pieces of information were recorded, including the size of the archive image (w_1, h_1, c_1), the rotation angle α of the seal, the size of the seal image (w_2, h_2, c_2), and the coordinates of the upper left corner of the stamped seal (a, b). A blank canvas with the same size as the archive image was generated, and the same seal image was stamped on the canvas at the same position with the same rotation angle, according to the three values of α, (w_2, h_2, c_2), and (a, b).

Using a series of operations such as color space conversion, binarization processing, and mask map inversion, the mask map of the canvas was obtained. The archive image and the canvas mask image were then cropped according to the coordinates of the stamped seal's position, retaining only the smallest rectangular part of the area where the stamp was located. Figure 4 provides a diagram of the label making process.

Finally, the real stamp dataset and the mask label map of the stamp necessary for generating the adversarial network, i.e. Ground Truth, were obtained. This approach allowed for the creation of more accurate and reliable data for training the generative adversarial network.

The stamp extraction dataset was constructed with 4,000 sets of stamp images, consisting of a set of images including stamp images and stamp mask label images. Of these, 2,800 sets were included in the training set, and 1,200 sets were included in the validation set. The stamp extraction dataset contained four types of images, including circle, rectangle, oval, and diamond shapes.

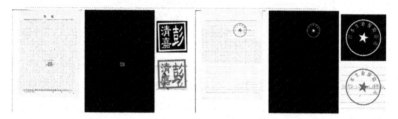

Fig. 4. Diagram of the process of making a stamp label

3 Digital Archival Stamp Image Extraction Model

3.1 Digital Archival Stamp Image Extraction Model Information

Building upon the success of the generative adversarial network, this paper designed the SealNet network structure to implement the extraction function of seal images and ensure accurate segmentation of both foreground and background parts of the seal.

The SealNet network structure diagram, shown in Fig. 5, includes a modified generator network based on U-Net [2, 8], with an attention mechanism-based CBAM module added to focus on image segmentation after the convolution operation of the U-type network downsampling process. The generator's role is to extract the foreground part of the seal image and remove the part of the seal image with the archival background. In addition, a pre-trained external VGG-19 [3] network is used for texture feature extraction of the stamp image.

The stamp image is output as a foreground mask map after extraction by the generator network. The sample mask map output by the generator is then fed into the seal texture extraction module together with the real label mask map of the seal image, allowing the network to extract texture features more finely and guide the generator to generate a mask map more similar to the label map.

The discriminator network determines whether the input data is true or false by comparing the real stamp labels with the generated virtual stamp sample features and classifies them according to the true or false category. If the discriminator judges the input data as false, it helps the generator learn how to generate more realistic samples for the discriminator to judge.

Through alternating training, learning, and parameter optimization, SealNet achieves the best performance when converging and improves the accuracy of seal image segmentation and extraction. Overall, this network structure represents a significant advance in the field of seal image extraction and has the potential to enhance preservation and utilization efforts for archives.

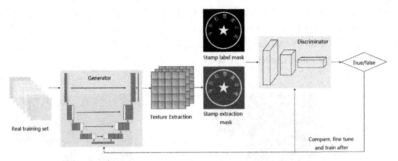

Fig. 5. SealNet network structure diagram

3.2 Experimental Results and Analysis

Figure 6 shows the extraction effect of four shapes of seals using the SealNet model. The first column of the image is the original image of the seal obtained by cropping, the second column of the image is the label mask image obtained by the SealNet model, and the third column of the image is the extracted image of the foreground of the seal obtained by overlaying the original image and the mask image. From Fig. 6, it is clear that the seal extraction model has a better segmentation effect, as the seal foreground image can be separated more completely from the red striped archival background.

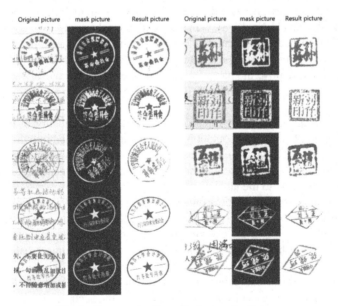

Fig. 6. Stamp extraction effect example diagram

4 Digital Archival Stamp Image Text Recognition

4.1 Digital Archival Stamp Image Text Recognition Information

After stamp detection, cropping, and extraction, the irrelevant background information is removed, and a valid region containing stamp graphics and text is obtained. First, the center point of the segmented instance of the stamp is found based on contour information. Using this center point as the rotation center, the stamp image is rotated in a specific direction and angle each time until it completes one full rotation, resulting in a series of rotated new images.

The new images are input into the PP-OCR model for text recognition in the horizontal direction for each frame in turn. The text content of individual characters and the location information of the smallest outer wrapping rectangle are recorded. The position of each character in the original stamp image is obtained by semantic continuity association calculation, and the association between each character is determined by discriminating the most similar path. Based on the trajectory information and support vector machine algorithm, the two clusters of circular text and linear text are segmented and used as the paragraph semantic output results. The improved stamp text recognition model based on PP-OCR [4–6] is shown in Fig. 7.

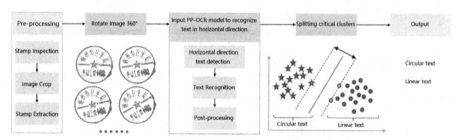

Fig. 7. Structure diagram of the improved stamp text recognition model based on PP-OCR

4.2 Experimental Results and Analysis

Figure 8 shows the stamp text recognition results, displaying the recognition results of ring text and linear text separately, along with the probability of correct text recognition results. While this algorithm can accurately recognize clear text, it struggles with fuzzy text, resulting in a higher false detection rate. For example, the recognition result of linear text 1 in the circular stamp is wrong, as it is mistakenly detected as "labor injury special stamp" instead of "labor wage special stamp". Another example is the recognition result of linear character 1 in the diamond-shaped stamp, which is mistakenly detected as "Paddle Yuzhi" instead of "Liu Yuzhi".

Circular moment transformation can be used to better recognize text in circular seals. This is because the circular seal image in the right-angle coordinate system can be easily mapped to the polar coordinate system. However, this method is only applicable

1: ring text   : 锦州市卫生局   0.878
2: linear text1： 劳动工商专用章   0.657

1: ring text   : 中国共产党内蒙古中城县   0.878
2: linear text1： 二龙乡人民公社   0.899
3: linear text2： 委员会   0.921

1: linear text1： 忠王   0.903
2: linear text2： 印明   0.884

1: linear text1 ： 划玉芝   0.657
2: linear text2 ： 医+用   0.712

Fig. 8. Stamp text recognition result chart

to circular seals and cannot be applied to oval seals. The oval seal image after circular moment transformation is shown in Fig. 9.

The algorithm proposed in this paper requires less accuracy for the center point of the stamp in comparison to the polar coordinate expansion method. As long as the hyperplane solved by the support vector machine is guaranteed to completely separate the two rotated coordinate information points, the algorithm can be adapted to any shape of the stamp image, circumventing the problem of text image bending caused by polar coordinates unfolding the stamp image, which can lead to misrecognition and missed recognition by the detector.

In terms of execution efficiency, polar coordinates need to perform a rotational projection transformation for each point, and then use an interpolation algorithm to find the value of the middle point after the rotation. In contrast, this algorithm only needs to perform a parallelized projection transformation without calculating interpolation, which can theoretically be executed faster and substantially improve accuracy and robustness.

The advantages of this algorithm are verified by comparing the recognition results after polar coordinate expansion. Overall, this approach represents a significant advance in the field of stamp text recognition, providing a more accurate and efficient method for recognizing text in stamped images of various shapes.

Fig. 9. Image of elliptical stamp after circular moment transformation

5   Conclusions

This paper focused on studying the key information of stamps in cadres' personnel files and developed a method for stamp image detection, extraction, and text recognition. The main research results of this paper included:

(1) Construction of a digital archive stamp image dataset.
(2) Design of a stamp image extraction network model, SealNet.
(3) Proposal of an improved stamp text recognition method based on PP-OCR.

Through this research, the key information of seals in archives was extracted and studied, and stamp target detection, stamp foreground extraction, and stamp text recognition were realized.

Moving forward, there is room for further optimization of the stamp extraction model's performance. While the current model is effective in extracting the foreground of stamp images with dark colors, it struggles to extract images with light colors and similar background colors and stamp colors. For example, it is difficult to extract the foreground of black seals in photocopies. In future research, a larger dataset could be used to allow the SealNet network to learn more detailed features and improve the accuracy and reliability of stamp extraction.

Overall, this research represents a significant advance in the field of stamp image extraction and recognition and has the potential to enhance the preservation and utilization of archives for research purposes.

Acknowledgements. We thank the ACs and reviewers. This work is partially supported by the Fundamental Research Funds for the Central Universities (3282023014), and the Project of Information Center of China North Industries Group Corporation Limited (20220100H0113).

References

1. Jiang, P., Ergu, D., Liu, F., et al.: A review of Yolo algorithm developments. Procedia Comput. Sci. **199**, 1066–1073 (2022)
2. Ronneberger, O., Fischer, P., Brox, T.: U-net: Convolutional networks for biomedical image segmentation. In: Medical Image Computing and Computer-Assisted Intervention–MICCAI 2015: 18th International Conference, Munich, Germany, 5–9 Oct 2015, Proceedings, Part III 18. Springer International Publishing, pp. 234-241 (2015)
3. Mateen, M., Wen, J., Song, S., et al.: Fundus image classification using VGG-19 architecture with PCA and SVD. Symmetry **11**(1), 1 (2018)
4. Du, Y., Li, C., Guo, R., et al.: Pp-ocr: A practical ultra lightweight ocr system. arXiv preprint arXiv:2009.09941 (2020)
5. Du, Y., Li, C., Guo, R., et al.: Pp-ocrv2: Bag of tricks for ultra lightweight ocr system. arXiv preprint arXiv:2109.03144 (2021)
6. Lan, R., Sun, L., Liu, Z., et al.: MADNet: A fast and lightweight network for single-image super resolution. IEEE Trans. Cybern. **51**(3), 1443–1453 (2020)
7. Zheng, Q., Zhu, J., Tang, H., et al.: Generalized label enhancement with sample correlations. IEEE Trans. Knowl. Data Eng. **35**(1), 482–495 (2021)
8. Lu, H., Yang, R., Deng, Z., et al.: Chinese image captioning via fuzzy attention-based DenseNet-BiLSTM. ACM Trans. Multimedia Comput. Commun. Appl. **17**(1s), 1–18 (2021). https://doi.org/10.1145/3422668

Underwater Image Enhancement Using Improved Shallow-UWnet

Toyoki Yasukawa[✉], Keisuke Hamamoto, Yuchao Zheng, and Huimin Lu

Kyusyu Institute of Technology, Kitakyushu, Japan
`yasukawa.toyoki296@mail.kyutech.jp`

Abstract. Currently, with the development of industrialization, ocean exploration is actively carried out to investigate energy resources and undersea ecosystems. Remotely Operated Vehicles (ROVs) and Autonomous Underwater Vehicles (AUVs), which are fully automated and not operated by humans, are used for these surveys. However, it is difficult to obtain clear images underwater due to low contrast and blur caused by the unique optical characteristics of the underwater environment. In recent years, many methods have been proposed for underwater image enhancement, with the most common methods using deep learning, such as generative adversarial networks (GANs) and convolutional neural networks (CNNs). Most of these methods are computationally and memory intensive, making real-time underwater image correction difficult. The Shallow-UWnet method is developed to solve this problem, and it enables a significant reduction in computational complexity compared to conventional methods.

In this study, we improve Shallow-UWnet using Deformable Convolution, propose a new method with higher accuracy, compare its accuracy with that of the previous method, and verify its usefulness.

Keywords: Underwater Image Enhancement · Deformable Convolution · Deep Learning

1 Introduction

1.1 Background

The oceans are home to many living organisms and resources that play an important role in sustaining life on Earth. In recent years, the consumption of oil, coal and minor metals, which are energy resources, has increased year by year due to industrialization. In particular, rare metals are essential materials for the production of lithium-ion batteries, semiconductors, motors, and other components that are indispensable in industries [1, 2] such as automobiles, AI-equipped devices, and IoT devices that are powered by electricity. However, Japan imports almost all of its rare metals, making their supply unstable. To solve this problem, Japan is actively exploring and developing mineral resources within its exclusive economic zone (EEZ). In addition, since the mid-20th century, not only Japan but also the world has been actively engaged in ocean exploration

H. Lu and J. Cai (Eds.): ISAIR 2023, CCIS 1998, pp. 175–180, 2024.
https://doi.org/10.1007/978-981-99-9109-9_17

using high technology to develop energy resources. Among these, underwater robots that can explore even in harsh environments inaccessible to humans have attracted much attention. Currently, underwater robots are playing an important role in a variety of fields, including marine geological exploration, resource development, ecosystem research, and fisheries.

Several papers have been published on underwater image enhancement and restoration, and Yan [3] et al. The two types are described below.

- IFM-based: The IFM-based method analyzes the image formation and light propagation in water, constructs an effective underwater degradation model, infers the parameters of the physical model, and finally reconstructs the image through a compensation process.
- IFM-free: IFM-free corrects images mainly based on pixel intensity redistribution, so it does not need to consider underwater-specific optical properties as IFM-based methods do.

Recently, it has been used for image enhancement based on the idea of learning CNN hidden features to improve image quality.

2   Method

2.1   Shallow-UWnet [4]

Shallow-UWnet is an IFM-free CNN-based model with significantly lower computational complexity and memory requirements than conventional CNN-based models and adversarial generative networks. The architecture of Shallow-UWnet is a convolutional network consisting of three densely connected ConvBlocks connected in series, as shown in Fig. 1. The input image is connected to the output of each ConvBlock by skip connections.

Although the shallow-UWnet is a lightweight model, we believe it can improve the quality of image correction.

2.2   Proposed Method

In this research, the proposed method is to change the second convolution layer in each ConvBlock of the Shallow-UWnet to Deformable Convolution, as shown in Fig. 2. The reason for this is that Deformable Convolution can extract features more efficiently than the convolution layer, and thus can provide more accurate image correction than conventional methods.

Deformable Convolution [5]: Convolutional layers are not always able to extract features properly because the shape and scale are fixed at the network design stage, and the scale and shape of objects in an image differ from each other. There are obvious problems in dealing with object viewpoints, distortions, etc. in visual recognition tasks, especially for non-rigid objects. Moreover, convolution has the disadvantage of processing fixed positions, which makes it vulnerable to geometric deformations. Deformable Convolution was introduced to solve this problem. It adds a two-dimensional offset to

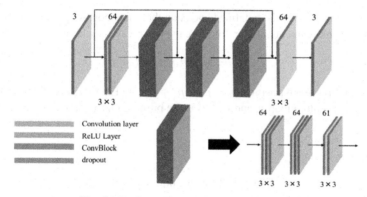

Fig. 1. Shallow-UWnet network architecture

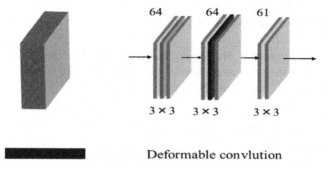

Deformable convlution

Fig. 2. Image of the proposed method

the sampling position of the regular grid in the standard convolution. This allows free deformation of the sampling grid. The offset is learned from the previous feature map via an additional convolution layer. In this way, deformations can be applied to the input features in a localized, dense, and adaptive manner.

Deformable Convolution consists of two steps: (1) Sampling using a regular grid R for the input feature x (2) Summing the sampled values weighted by ω.

$$R = \{(-1, -1), (-1, 0), \ldots, (0, 1), (1, 1)\} \quad (1)$$

defines a kernel of 3×3 with a dilation 1. For each position p_0 on the output feature map y

$$y(p_0) = \sum_{p_n \in R} \omega(p_n) \cdot x(p_0 + p_n) \quad (2)$$

The following is an example of the grid R. where p_n enumerates the positions of the grid R. The regular grid R is extended by the offset $\{\ \Delta p_0 | n = 1, \ldots, N\}$ where $N = |R|$.

$$y(p_0) = \sum_{p_n \in R} \omega(p_n) \cdot x(p_0 + p_n + \Delta p_0) \quad (3)$$

The sampling position is undefined and is on the offset position $p_n + \Delta p_0$. Since the offset Δp_0 is usually not an integer, Eq. (3) can be expressed by bilinear interpolation as

$$x(p) = \sum_q G(q, p) \cdot x(q) \tag{4}$$

where p is any fractional position ($p = p_0 + p_n + \Delta p_n$ in Eq. (3)), q is all integer spatial positions of the feature map x, and $G(\cdot, \cdot)$ is the bilinear interpolation kernel.

2.3 Training

We used 1500 images of UFO-120 [6] as training data. For the test data, we used 120 images from the UFO-120 dataset and 890 images from the UIEB dataset [7]. We also use PSNR, SSIM, and UIQM [8] as our evaluation metrics.

3   Results and Discussion

Experimental environments are Intel® core™ i9-10900X and NVIDIA GeForce RTX3090. Table 1 shows a comparison of the metrics between the original model and the proposed method. The comparison image is also shown in Fig. 3.

Table 1. Comparison of evaluation metrics

	UFO-120			UIEB		
	PSNR	SSIM	UIQM	PSNR	SSIM	UIQM
original	26.211	0.777	2.806	19.319	0.720	**2.785**
proposed	**26.602**	**0.785**	**2.810**	**19.382**	**0.721**	2.764

Figure 1 shows that the proposed method has a higher evaluation index for both UFO-120 and UEIB. Furthermore, from the image in Fig. 3, the proposed method removes slightly more blue and green colors, which is closer to the correct image. However, there are still some green and blue colors in the image, and we believe this is because Shallow-UWnet and the proposed method are not IFM-based methods. The IFM-based method, which considers an optical model, can correct images by taking into account the distance decay of light, so if the distance of the subject from the camera is known, the original color can be approximately identified, and thus more appropriate image correction can be performed. However, it has the disadvantage that it requires the use of images that include depth data in the dataset [9–11], which limits the selection of underwater image datasets, which are already limited.

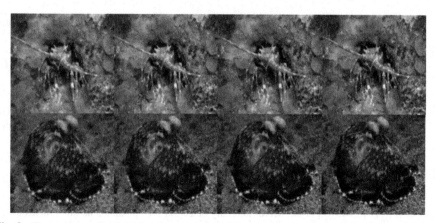

Fig. 3. Comparison of original and proposed underwater image enhancement Input, Original, Proposal, Grand Truth

4 Conclusion

In this paper, we propose an improved method of Shallow-UWnet with Deformable Convolution and compare its accuracy using two datasets UFO-120, UIEB. As a result, we confirmed that the PSNR, SSIM, and UIQM indices increased for almost all datasets. This indicates that offset learning, in which the kernel of the Deformable Convolution is dynamically transformed to match the shape and scale of the object, is enhancing the underwater image correction.

Currently, underwater images are used for processing [12–14]. Future work is to perform real-time processing in an actual underwater environment to compare and verify the results [15, 16].

References

1. Lu, H., Tang, Y., Sun, Y.: DRRS-BC: decentralized routing registration system based on Blockchain. IEEE/CAA J. Autom. Sinica **8**(12), 1868–1876 (2021). https://doi.org/10.1109/JAS.2021.1004204
2. Lu, H., Zhang, M., Xing, Xu., et al.: Deep fuzzy hashing network for efficient image retrieval. IEEE Trans. Fuzzy Syst. **29**(1), 166–176 (2021)
3. Yan, W., Wei, S., Giancarlo, F., et al.: Antonio liotta an experimental-based review of image enhancement and image restoration methods for underwater imaging. IEEE Access 140233–140251
4. Naik, A., Swarnakar, K.: Shallow-UWnet: Compressed models for underwater image enhancement
5. Jifeng, D., Haozhi, Q., Yuwen, X., et al.: Deformable convolutional networks. In: IEEE International Conference on Computer Vision (ICCV), pp. 764–773 (2017)
6. The UFO-120 https://irvlab.cs.umn.edu/resources/ufo-120-dataset. Last accessed 26 Apr 2023
7. UIEB dataset https://li-chongyi.github.io/proj_benchmark.html. Last accessed 26 Apr 2023
8. Panetta, K., Gao, C., Agaian, S.: Human-visual-system-inspired underwater image quality measures. IEEE J. Oceanic Eng. **41**(3), 541–551 (2016)

9. Lu, H., Li, Y., Chen, M., et al.: Brain Intelligence: go beyond artificial intelligence. Mobile Netw. Appl. **23**, 368–375 (2018)

10. Lu, H., Yang, R., Deng, Z., et al.: Chinese image captioning via fuzzy attention-based DenseNet-BiLSTM. ACM Trans. Multimedia Comput. Commun. Appl. **17**(1s), 1–18 (2021). https://doi.org/10.1145/3422668

11. Lu, H., Qin, M., Zhang, F., et al.: RSCNN: A CNN-based method to enhance low-light remote-sensing images. Remote Sens. **13**(1), 62 (2020). https://doi.org/10.3390/rs13010062

12. Lu, H., Wang, D., Li, Y., et al.: CONet: a cognitive ocean network. IEEE Wirel. Commun. **26**(3), 90–96 (2019)

13. Lu, H., Zhang, Y., Li, Y., et al.: User-oriented virtual mobile network resource management for vehicle communications. IEEE Trans. Intell. Transport. Syst. **22**(6), 3521–3532 (2021)

14. Lu, H., Li, Y., Nakashima, S., et al.: Underwater image super-resolution by descattering and fusion. IEEE Access **5**, 670–679 (2017)

15. Lu, H., Li, Y., Mu, S., et al.: Motor anomaly detection for unmanned aerial vehicles using reinforcement learning. IEEE Internet Things J. **5**(4), 2315–2322 (2018)

16. Xu, X., Lu, H., Song, J., et al.: Ternary adversarial networks with self-supervision for zero-shot cross-modal retrieval. IEEE Trans. Cybern. **50**(6), 2400–2413 (2020)

Single Image Reflection Removal Using DeepLabv3+

Keisuke Hamamoto[✉], Naoya Hideshima, Huimin Lu, and Seiichi Serikawa

Kyushu Institute of Technology, Kitakyushu, Fukuoka, Japan
`hamamoto.keisuke806@mail.kyutech.jp`

Abstract. When photographing near transparent objects such as glass, things in the area often appear in the image (reflected light). This reflected light degrades the image information and affects computer vision task such as object detection and segmentation. Separating reflected light in an image is a challenging task in computer vision. In this study, we create synthetic images and increase the number of training data. We proposed a reflection rejection method that used DeepLabv3+ as a deep learning model and measured the accuracy of the proposed method using PSNR and SSIM, commonly used evaluation methods for reflection rejection. The accuracy of the proposed method is improved compared to the conventional method due to the feature of DeepLabv3+ to obtain information in a wide range of contexts efficiently.

Keywords: Deep Learning · SIRR · DeepLabv3

1 Background

When photographing near-transparent objects such as glass, reflected light can appear in the image, as shown in Fig. 1. This loss of image information due to reflected light can frequently occur, making SIRR a challenging problem that has attracted considerable attention in the computer vision community. The image containing reflected light consists mathematically of the image I, a linear combination of a transmitted image layer T and a reflected image layer R, as in Eq. (1).

$$I = T + R \tag{1}$$

Hence, reflected light rejection can achieve its goal by estimating the transmitted image layer T. Many researchers have tackled the technical challenge of reflected light rejection. Many solutions have been proposed. However, many currently have limitations in performance, robustness, and versatility.

In the early statistical models of SIRR, removing the reflective layer from a single image was avoided because it was impossible to separate the transmission layer from the reflective layer. Conversely, multiple images have been used to estimate the transmission layer T [1–3]. The problem has been solved by adding and formulating constraints to the images. And even when only a single image is used, the transmission layer T has been estimated using the formulated equation [4–6].

© The Author(s), under exclusive license to Springer Nature Singapore Pte Ltd. 2024
H. Lu and J. Cai (Eds.): ISAIR 2023, CCIS 1998, pp. 181–188, 2024.
https://doi.org/10.1007/978-981-99-9109-9_18

(a) Images with reflected light   (b) Images without reflected light

Fig. 1. Examples of images containing reflected light

However, it is difficult to construct a versatile light-reflectance removal model by simply adding these simple constraint conditions to image processing since various assumed situations are possible. Against this background, research on constructing deep learning models has been active in recent years [7–9].

There are two problems with SIRR using deep learning models [10, 11]. One is that extracting background images without reflection is illogical, and the other is that the training data is tiny. For the former, the performance of the model is limited. The latter problem arises because of the difficulty in obtaining paired datasets of images with and without reflections. Because of the rare case of reflected light, rather than a simple dataset such as Image Net or MNIST. Therefore, in SIRR, synthetic images obtained by merging images are often used because it is difficult to get true values.

2 Methods

2.1 Proposed Model

The network model proposed in this study is shown in Fig. 1. Six-layer convolution is performed in the encoder part. The bottleneck part employs Deeplabv3+ [12], followed by six-layer convolution in the decoder part to obtain the estimated transmitted image layer $\breve{T}$ and the estimated reflected image layer $\breve{R}$ as outputs.

The bottleneck part, the Deeplabv3+ module, uses MobileNetv2 [13] as the backbone. This is followed by ASPP (Atlas Spatial Pyramid Pooling), which uses Image Pooling with atlas convolution rates of 1, 6, 12, and 18, respectively (Figs. 2 and 3).

2.2 Loss Function

As the basis of many neural networks, in image restoration techniques, the loss function is generally optimized for the network using the mean squared error (MSE) between the output and the true value.

$$L_{MSE} = \|F(I) - T\|_2^2 \tag{2}$$

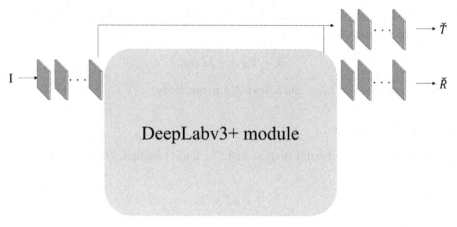

Fig. 2. Proposal Network

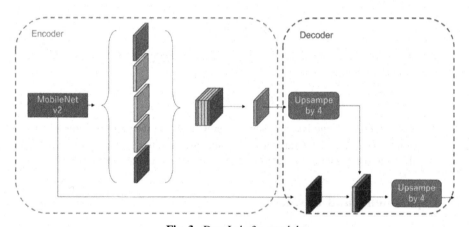

Fig. 3. DeepLabv3+ module

However, F is the data after processing. However, models optimized using only L_{MSE} often fail to retain the high-frequency content. In the case of de-reflection, both the reflective and the transparent layers are natural images with different characteristics. To obtain the best restoration results, the network needs to learn the perceptual properties of the transmission layer. Therefore, we adopt a loss function close to a high-level feature abstraction. The VGG loss is calculated as the difference between the layer representation of the restored transmission and the actual transmission image on the pre-trained 19-layer VGG network proposed by Simonyan and Zisserman [14].

$$L_{VGG} = \tfrac{1}{W_i H_i} \sum_{i=1}^{M} \|\varphi_i(T) - \varphi_i(F(I))\|_2^2 \qquad (3)$$

where φ_i is the feature map obtained by the i-th convolutional layer (after activation) in the VGG19 network, M is the number of convolutional layers used, W_i and H_i are the dimensions of the i-th feature map.

This study uses the loss function consisting of the sum of these two loss functions. The equation is expressed as follows.

$$L = L_{MSE} + \lambda L_{VGG} \tag{4}$$

λ is a parameter of L_{VGG} and is set to 0.1 in this study.

2.3 Dataset Creation

Equation (1) will be used in this study as well. The Eq. (1) multiplied by the transmittance α is given below.

$$I = \alpha T + R \tag{5}$$

In this study, two R patterns in Eq. (5) are set and used.
The first equation is,

$$R = \beta G * R' \tag{6}$$

R' is the reflective image layer, β is the reflectance, and G is the Gaussian kernel. The second equation is,

$$R = G * R' - \gamma \tag{7}$$

R' is the reflective image layer, γ is a constant, and G is the Gaussian kernel.
The values of α, β, γ, and G are varied as there are various patterns of reflected light in the real image. In some cases, gamma correction is used to darken R.

3 Experiments and Results

3.1 Dataset

3890 images from the MIT-67 Dataset [15] and 17000 images from the PASCAL VOC 2012 Dataset [16] were collected to generate images with pseudo-reflected light using Eqs. (5), (6), and (7) as the training dataset. The datasets used for the evaluation were Object, Post, and Wild from the SIR2 Dataset [17] and the Real20 Dataset [18]. These datasets are real images, not pseudo-synthesized images containing reflected light. The number of each type of data used in the evaluation is shown in Table 1.

3.2 Experimental Procedure

In this study, training was carried out using the same learning setup under the same conditions to perform a control experiment. The training was carried out with a batch size of 16, 100 epochs, a learning rate of 0.0003, and Adam as optimizer. PSNR and SSIM were used as evaluation metrics [19–21]. The GPU used for training was an NVIDIA GeForce RTX 3090, the CPU was an Intel Core i9, the RAM was 64GB and the OS was Ubuntu 20.04 [22]. The combinations used in the experiments are listed in Table 2.

Table 1. Number of data used in the evaluation.

Datasets	Number of datasets
Object	20
Post	20
Wild	101
Real20	109

Table 2. Proposed methods

	Proposed method 1	Proposed method 2
Proposed Network	○	○
Conventional reflectance generation model	○	
Proposed reflection generation model		○

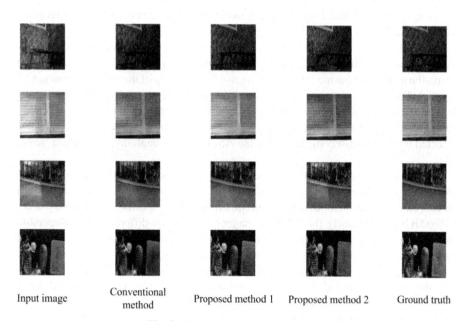

| Input image | Conventional method | Proposed method 1 | Proposed method 2 | Ground truth |

Fig. 4. Comparison of output images

3.3 Experimental Results

The experimental results are shown in Fig. 4. The evaluation indices are given in Table 3. Note that the values shown in the table are average.

Table 3. Results of experiments

Data set	Evaluation metrics	Conventional method	Proposed method 1	Proposed method 2
Object	PSNR	21.57	22.98	23.57
	SSIM	0.82	0.84	0.86
Post	PSNR	15.93	21.54	16.91
	SSIM	0.72	0.79	0.77
Wild	PSNR	23.60	25.23	24.91
	SSIM	0.83	0.86	0.87
Real20	PSNR	17.79	19.30	18.85
	SSIM	0.65	0.70	0.72

4 Discussion

The results in Fig. 4 and Table 3 are discussed. We also discuss each of the proposed methods listed in Table 2.

First, a comparison is made between the conventional and proposed methods 1. These are controlled experiments because the network models are different, and the reflection formation model is the same. Table 3 shows that the accuracy of the proposed method 1 is superior. The resultant images in Fig. 4 show that the reflections are removed. It can also be seen that the pixel values do not drop much. It is considered that the network model (DeepLabv3+) of the proposed method 1 has a significant influence on the removal of reflected light. It is also considered that the ASPP in the DeepLabv3+ structure plays a role.

Next, we compare the proposed method 1 with the proposed method 2. These are contrasting experiments under the condition that the network models are the same and the reflection formation models are different. From Table 3, it is impossible to say which method is better. Similarly, the resultant images in Fig. 4 show different results depending on the image. The reflection formation model influences these. The reflection formation model affects the results by the similarity with the real image.

The proposed method is superior to the conventional methods [23]. However, even with the proposed method, there were some images where the reflection could not be removed. There are two possible reasons for this. The first is the network model. As can be seen from this study, the results vary greatly depending on the network model. Constructing and improving a network model suitable for reflection removal is necessary. The second is the reflection formation model. As the images created by the reflection formation model are used for training, the real data must approximate it.

Moreover, as can be seen from the results, there are various patterns of reflected light in the real data [24], and images must be created for each. In the future, solving these two causes will lead to the removal of reflected light. Furthermore, in this study, learning was carried out using only synthetic data, but learning using real data is also considered one of the measures.

5   Conclusion

DeepLabv3+ is proposed as a deep learning model for single-image reflection removal in this paper. A reflection formation model is also proposed, and a synthetic image is generated.

Experiments are conducted on four datasets commonly used in the SIRR field to compare the proposed methods. The proposed method shows better results through the experiments than the conventional methods. It is also confirmed that the results are affected by the different reflection formation models used in the synthetic data. Although the proposed method in this paper was trained only on the synthetic data, it gave excellent results on the real data.

Future tasks are to study the construction of a model more suitable for removing reflections, to study a reflection formation model similar to real data, and to study learning with real data. Learning using real data is the most effective method, and transfer learning, and meta-learning can be used for this purpose.

References

1. Xue, T., et al.: A computational approach for obstruction-free photography. ACM Trans. Graph. **34**(4), 1–11 (2015)
2. Guo, X., et al.: Robust separation of reflection from multiple images. In: CVPR, pp. 2195–2202 IEEE Computer Society (2014)
3. Lu, H., Li, Y., Nakashima, S., et al.: Underwater image super-resolution by descattering and fusion. IEEE Access **5**, 670–679 (2017)
4. Levin, A., et al.: Separating reflections from a single image using local features. In: CVPR (1). pp. 306–313 (2004)
5. Li, Y., Brown, M.S.: Single image layer separation using relative smoothness. In: CVPR, pp. 2752–2759. IEEE Computer Society (2014)
6. Lu, H., Yang, R., Deng, Z., et al.: Chinese image captioning via fuzzy attention-based DenseNet-BiLSTM. ACM Trans. Multimedia Comput. Commun. Appl. **17**(1s), 1–18 (2021)
7. Chi, Z., et al.: Single Image Reflection Removal Using Deep Encoder-Decoder Network. CoRR. abs/1802.00094 (2018)
8. Wen, Q., et al.: Single Image Reflection Removal Beyond Linearity. In: CVPR, pp. 3771–3779. Computer Vision Foundation/IEEE (2019)
9. Li, T., et al.: Improved multiple-image-based reflection removal algorithm using deep neural networks. IEEE Trans. Image Process. **30**, 68–79 (2021)
10. Lu, H., Li, Y., Chen, M., et al.: Brain Intelligence: go beyond artificial intelligence. Mobile Netw. Appl. **23**, 368–375 (2018)
11. Lu, H., Tang, Y., Sun, Y.: DRRS-BC: decentralized routing registration system based on blockchain. IEEE/CAA J. Autom. Sinica **8**(12), 1868–1876 (2021)
12. Chen, L.C., et al.: Encoder-decoder with atrous separable convolution for semantic image segmentation. In: Ferrari, V., Hebert, M., Sminchisescu, C., Weiss, Y. (eds.) ECCV 2018. LNCS, vol. 11211, pp. 833–851. Springer, Cham (2018). https://doi.org/10.1007/978-3-030-01234-2_49
13. Sandler, M., et al.: MobileNetV2: inverted residuals and linear bottlenecks. In: 2018 IEEE/CVF Conference on Computer Vision and Pattern Recognition. pp. 4510–4520 (2018)
14. Simonyan, K., Zisserman, A.: Very Deep Convolutional Networks for Large-Scale Image Recognition. http://arxiv.org/abs/1409.1556 (2014)

15. Quattoni, A., Torralba, A.: Recognizing indoor scenes. In: CVPR, pp. 413–420 IEEE Computer Society (2009)

16. Everingham, M., et al.: The PASCAL Visual Object Classes Challenge 2012 (VOC2012) Results (2012)

17. Wan, R., et al.: Benchmarking single-image reflection removal algorithms. In: ICCV, pp. 3942–3950. IEEE Computer Society (2017)

18. Zhang, X.C., et al.: Single image reflection separation with perceptual losses. In: CVPR, pp. 4786–4794. IEEE Computer Society (2018)

19. Lu, H., Qin, M., Zhang, F., et al.: RSCNN: a CNN-based method to enhance low-light remote-sensing images. Remote Sens. **13**(1), 62 (2020)

20. Lu, H., Wang, D., Li, Y., et al.: CONet: a cognitive ocean network. IEEE Wirel. Commun. **26**(3), 90–96 (2019)

21. Xu, X., Lu, H., Song, J., et al.: Ternary adversarial networks with self-supervision for zero-shot cross-modal retrieval. IEEE Trans. Cybern. **50**(6), 2400–2413 (2020)

22. Lu, H., Zhang, Y., Li, Y., et al.: User-oriented virtual mobile network resource management for vehicle communications. IEEE Trans. Intell. Transport. Syst. **22**(6), 3521–3532 (2021)

23. Lu, H., Li, Y., Mu, S., et al.: Motor anomaly detection for unmanned aerial vehicles using reinforcement learning. IEEE Internet Things J. **5**(4), 2315–2322 (2018)

24. Lu, H., Zhang, M., Xu, X., et al.: Deep fuzzy hashing network for efficient image retrieval. IEEE Trans. Fuzzy Syst. **29**(1), 166–176 (2021)

Improved GR-Convnet for Antipodal Robotic Grasping

Kyosuke Shibasaki[✉], Keisuke Hamamoto, and Huimin Lu

Kyushu Institute of Technology, 1-1 Sensui-Cho, Tobata-Ku, Kitakyushu-shi, Fukuoka, Japan
shibasaki.kyosuke602@mail.kyutech.jp

Abstract. This paper introduces a robot system designed to address the problem of performing antipodal robot grasping for unknown objects. We focus on the high-level approach of GR-Convnet for the task and propose a neural network with high robustness while maintaining real-time performance. The three improvements include introducing Squeeze and Excitation (SE) blocks, removing Dropout in the final layer, and using Residual Block and Concurrent Spatial and Channel Squeeze and Channel Excitation (scSE) Block. We evaluate the proposed network on the Jacquard dataset containing information on various household objects. As a result, we achieved an approximately 7.2% improvement in accuracy compared to GR-Convnet. Additionally, using a real robot, we demonstrated a grasp success rate of 93.3% and 92.5% for household and adversarial objects, respectively.

Keywords: Antipodal Robotic Grasping · Deep learning · Grasping Point Estimation

1 Intorduction

In recent years, Japan has faced a social problem of a declining working population due to rapid aging and a low birthrate after peaking in 2008. [1] This has led to a reduction in the size of the economy and a decline in international competitiveness. Thus, it is necessary to create more added value with a limited labor force. Industrial robots are an effective solution to this problem since they can perform tasks in place of humans, stabilize production efficiency, operate for long hours, and improve quality by preventing human error [2, 3]. As a result, the demand for industrial robots has been growing and is expected to continue to grow in the future. By 2025, the Japanese domestic robotics market will be worth approximately 5.3 trillion yen and 9.7 trillion yen by 2035 [4, 5]. However, conventional industrial robots require predefined movements, which is an obstacle to their widespread use. To overcome this difficulty, the use of deep learning to make industrial robots intelligent has been attracting attention. Therefore, many network models for grasp position estimation by deep learning have been proposed. In the early studies of grasp position estimation, rule-based methods [6, 7] and object detection-based methods [8, 9] were mainly used. Therefore, a generative convolutional neural network [10, 11] was applied and succeeded in reducing the weight. Furthermore, a suitable grasping posture can be predicted from extracted pixel-by-pixel features, making the

H. Lu and J. Cai (Eds.): ISAIR 2023, CCIS 1998, pp. 189–197, 2024.
https://doi.org/10.1007/978-981-99-9109-9_19

method more suitable for grasping tasks. [12–14] Recently, GR-ConvNet [15] achieved state-of-the-art graspingt detection accuracy by introducing a residual structure [16] into the network model.

2 Method

In this chapter, we use a method to represent the grasping position that is similar to the one used in GR-Convnet. This helps us detect the grasping position accurately. Next, we introduce an even better architecture. In the bottleneck, we merge the ResNet block and the SE block composite module together at the same time, and also bring in the csSE block to the decoder. In the output layer, we create a network that predicts the grip's quality, angle, and width separately, by utilizing the features we have extracted, and without needing to use dropout.

2.1 Formulation of Grasping Position

The position of a gripper in 3D space is expressed as

$$G_r = (P, \theta_r, W_r, Q) \tag{1}$$

where P is the center position of the gripper tip, θ_r is the rotation of the gripper, W_r is the gripper width, and Q is the probability of a successful grasp. The position of the grasp in the image is expressed as

$$G_i = (x, y, \theta_i, W_i, Q) \tag{2}$$

where (x, y) is the center point of the object in the image, θ_i is the rotation angle, W_i is the width of the gripper in the image, and Q is the probability of a successful grasp. The transformation of the grasping position information from the image to the camera space and then to the world coordinates is expressed as

$$G_r = T_{rc}(T_{ic}(G_i)) \tag{3}$$

The grasping positions of multiple objects are expressed as

$$G = (\theta, W, Q) \in \mathbb{R}^{n \times h \times w} \tag{4}$$

in Eq. (4), where θ is a quality map representing the success rate of grasping, W is a width map representing the width of the end-effector, and Q is an angle map representing the angle of the end-effector.

2.2 Proposed Network Model

This is the network architecture proposed in Fig. 1 we constructed a network model with reference to the GR-convnet. The E block and D block have the same conventional structure and are shown at the bottom of Fig. 1. The B block, F block, and output layer will be described in a later section.

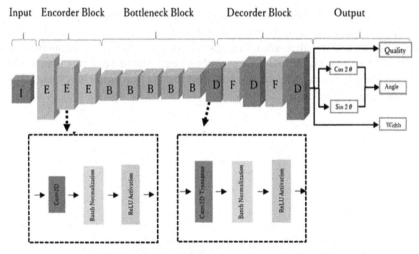

Fig. 1. Network model of the proposed method

Bottlenck Module: The bottleneck module shown in Fig. 1 utilizes the module shown in Fig. 2 and combines SE blocks with ResNet to emphasize pixel-level information by weighting each channel with a sigmoid function. In [17], the optimal placement of the SE block in the Residual Block [16] is investigated. Among the tested patterns, this paper uses the SE-Identity Block [17]. Similarly, it has been applied to ResNet-50 [18] and inception-resnet [19], achieving top scores in the ILSVRC 2017 competition.

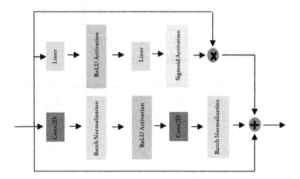

Fig. 2. Improved bottleneck block, combining Resnet with SE block in parallel.

Deletion of Output Layer Dropout: Dropout [20] and Batch Normalization [21] are techniques to prevent overfitting in deep learning models. Dropout randomly selects certain neurons to be unused during each mini-batch, while Batch Normalization normalizes each node's output to prevent bias. Combining these techniques may lead to decreased accuracy [22], so Dropout is not used in the paper according to previous research.

Decoder Module: The decoder module, shown in Fig. 1, also includes the F block (Fig. 3) that combines the Concurrent Spatial and Channel Squeeze and Channel Excitation (scSE) Block [23] with ResNet. The scSE Block was designed for segmentation and emphasizes pixel-level information by convolving each channel and calculating weighting for each pixel. The module aims to reduce noise and information loss when restoring the image to its original size.

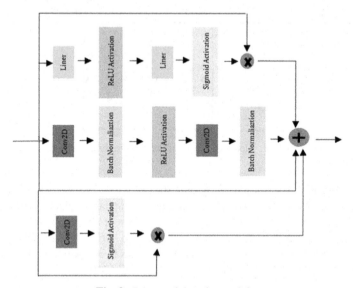

Fig. 3. Improved decoder module.

3   Evaluation of Network Models

In this chapter, we define assumptions and evaluation methods for inference and perform inference. Furthermore, we compare the performance of the proposed method with that of previous research [16], and discuss the results.

3.1   Learning Environment

In this section, we used Nvidia's 32[GB], RTX2080Ti. Each network is trained for 100 epochs with a learning rate of 10^{-3} and a batch size of 8.

3.2   Dataset

The Jacquard dataset [24] is annotated using a simulation environment and CAD model, without human intervention. It was split into training, validation, and test data with an 8:1:1 ratio using two methods: IW (image-wise) for evaluating generalization ability for unknown object postures, and OW (object-wise) for evaluating generalization performance for unknown objects. In GR-ConvNet [15], training and validation were divided 9:1.

3.3 Optimization Function

We used Radam [25] as our optimization function in this study, which was proposed by Liu et al. in 2020. Adam is a commonly used optimization function for deep learning, but Liu et al. found that it has a high variance in the early stages of learning. To address this, they proposed a method that uses SGD [20] with momentum in the initial stages and corrects Adam [26] with a correction term afterwards. This method outperforms Adam on tasks such as ImageNet image classification.

3.4 Loss Function

In this study, we use the Smooth L1 Loss used in Gr-ConvNet [8].

$$loss(G_t - G_p) = \begin{cases} 0.5(G_t - G_p)^2, & if \, |G_t - G_p| < \beta \\ |G_t - G_p| - 0.5, & otherwise \end{cases} \tag{5}$$

Here, G_t represents the true value and G_p the predicted value, where β is the threshold value, and the upper and lower equations are used separately. MAE Loss and MSE Loss are common loss functions in deep learning. MAE Loss is good for outliers because it treats errors as absolute values, but it cannot be differentiated when the true and predicted values are equal. Smooth L1 Loss uses MSE Loss when the absolute error is smaller than the threshold β, and uses MAE Loss when the absolute error is larger than the threshold β to reduce the effect of outliers. In this study, the threshold β is set to 1.0.

3.5 Evaluation Index

This is an evaluation index similar to GR-ConvNet [15]. The condition for considering the grasping position estimated by the network model as correct is when the following two conditions are satisfied:

1. The IOU between the bounding box of the inferred grasping position and the ground truth value is greater than 0.25.
2. The error between the inferred grasp angle and the ground truth value is less than 30°.

The evaluation index is calculated using the following Eq. (6).

$$\text{Accuracy rate}[\%] = \frac{\text{The number of correct answers}}{\text{number of datasets}} \tag{6}$$

3.6 Object to be Grasped

This section describes the grasping object in the grasping experiment using the actual machine.

Household Test Objects: Twelve objects of different shapes and sizes from each other were prepaed. For example, there are objects that are similar to the objects in the dataset, smaller, transparent, reflective, soft, reflective, and black, which are considered to be difficult to visualize. The household test objects are shown on the left in Fig. 4.

Adversarial Test Objects: These are objects in the dataset Dex-Net 2.0 [27] used by Mahler et al. to validate the performance of the Grasping Quality CNN, and are objects that are considered difficult to grasp. In this study, eight objects were prepared. The adversarial test objects are shown on the right in Fig. 4

Fig. 4. Left: Test object for home use, right: Adversarial test object

4   Result

In this chapter, we present the results of inference performed with each network model, as well as experimental results using a physical robot arm, and demonstrate the process of inference during the experiments.

4.1   Inference with Network Models

We made three different versions of the model. Modification (1) improved only one part, the bottleneck. Modification (2) improved two parts, the bottleneck and output layer. The proposed method improved three parts, the bottleneck, output layer, and decoder. We compared the original model with the three improved models to show how effective each improvement was. Results are shown in Table 1.

Table 1. Results for each network model

Method	Accuracy (%)		Inference time (ms)	Parameters
	Object-Wise	Image-Wise		
GR-ConvNet [8]	86.54	85.22	18.1	1,900,900
Modification (1)	90.34	90.89	18.4	1,904,108
Modification (2)	90.40	92.09	18.4	1,904,108
Proposed Method	91.37	92.62	20.3	1,992,862

4.2 Experiments with Robotic Arms

Experiments were conducted on GR-ConvNet [15] and the proposed method, which was the most accurate according to Table 3. The experimental results are shown in Table 2. 86.5% for GR-ConvNet[15] and 93% for the proposed method.

Table 2. Experimental results

Object	Method	
	GR-ConvNet [15]	Proposed Method
Home test objects	104/120	112/120
Adversial test objects	69/80	74/80
total amount	176/200(86.5%)	1 86/200(93%)

4.3 Visualization of Inference

To show the results of grasping position inference, a Quality Map is used as an image to indicate that red has a high probability of grasping. Table. 3 shows the inference results.

5 Discussion and Conclusion

The effectiveness of the proposed method was demonstrated through network evaluation and gras experiments using a robot [28, 29]. As shown in Table 1, each improvement was found to improve the accuracy of the network. Additionally, it is believed that the accuracy was improved without significantly increasing the number of parameters. Furthermore, as shown in Table 2, it was confirmed that improving the accuracy of the network also improves the accuracy of the physical grasp experiment using a robot arm.

According to Table 3, the success rate of grasping difficult-to-recognize black objects has improved. In the case of failure with GR-ConvNet, it was found that the grasping angle was not appropriate for the remote control. In addition, for wristwatches, there were cases where the reflection part was not detected at the appropriate grasping position. However, the proposed method makes it clear where the expected position for high success rate of grasping is located. Moreover, both methods showed low accuracy for small and transparent objects. One of the reasons for grasp failure is that these objects are difficult for humans to visually recognize. Due to their low visibility, the amount of image information obtained is limited, and accurate inference needs to be made from this limited information.

In the future, efforts will be focused on improving the grasp grip of objects that are difficult for humans to visually recognize [30, 31], by improving the network model and changing evaluation criteria. Preprocessing techniques such as removing reflections and enlarging small objects, as well as other approaches, will also be considered to obtain more information.

Table 3. Inference by actual equipment

	Original image	GR-Convnet[15]	Proposed-method
Only the proposed method succeeded			
Both failed			

References

1. Ministry of Internal Affairs and Communications. https://www.soumu.go.jp/johotsusintokei/whitepaper/ja/h30/html/nd101200.html. Last accessed 9 Jan 2022
2. KEYENCE. https://www.keyence.co.jp/ss/products/vision/fa-robot/industrial_robot/merit.jsp. Last accessed 2022
3. Lu, H., Li, Y., Nakashima, S., et al.: Underwater image super-resolution by descattering and fusion. IEEE Access **5**, 670–679 (2017)
4. Ministry of Internal Affairs and Communications. https://www.soumu.go.jp/johotsusintokei/whitepaper/ja/h27/html/nc241330.html. Last accessed 2022
5. Lu, H., Li, Y., Chen, M., et al.: Brain Intelligence: go beyond artificial intelligence. Mobile Netw. Appl. **23**, 368–375 (2018)
6. Pokorny, F.T., Bekiroglu, Y., Kragic, D.: Grasp moduli spaces and spherical harmonics. ICRA (2014)

7. Lu, H., Yang, R., Deng, Z., et al.: Chinese image captioning via fuzzy attention-based DenseNet-BiLSTM. ACM Trans. Multimedia Comput. Commun. Appl. **17**(1s), 1–18 (2021). https://doi.org/10.1145/3422668
8. Redmon, J., Farhadi, A.: YOLO9000: better, faster, stronger. CoRR (2015)
9. Lu, H., Yu, T., Sun, Y.: DRRS-BC: decentralized routing registration system based on blockchain. IEEE/CAA J. Autom. Sinica **8**(12), 1868–1876 (2021)
10. Morrison, D., Corke, P., Leitner, J.: Learning robust, real-time, reactive robotic grasping. The Int. J. Robot. Res. **39**, 183–201 (2020)
11. Lu, H., Wang, D., Li, Y., et al.: CONet: a cognitive ocean network. IEEE Wireless Commun. **26**(3), 90–96 (2019)
12. Wang, S., Jiang, X., Zhao, J., Wang, X., Zhou, W., Liu, Y: Efficient fully convolution neural network for generating pixel wise robotic grasps with high resolution images. CoRR (2019)
13. Lu, H., Qin, M., Zhang, F., et al.: RSCNN: a CNN-based method to enhance low-light remote-sensing images. Remote Sens. **13**(1), 62 (2020)
14. Xu, X., Lu, H., Song, J., et al.: Ternary adversarial networks with self-supervision for zero-shot cross-modal retrieval. IEEE Trans. Cybern. **50**(6), 2400–2413 (2020)
15. Kumra, S., Joshi, S., Sahin, F.: Antipodal robotic grasping using generative residual convolutional neural network (2019)
16. He, K., Zhang, X., Ren, S., Su, J.:. Deep residual learning for image Recognition. In: CVPR770–778 (2016)
17. Hu, J., et al.: Squeeze-and-Excitation Networks. In: CVPR (2018)
18. He, K., Zhang, X., Ren, S., Sun, J.: Deep residual learning for image recognition. In: CVPR (2015.)
19. Szegedy, C., Ioffe, S., Vanhoucke, V., Alemi, A.: Inceptionv4, inception-resnet and the impact of residual connections on learning. In: AAAI Conference on Artificial Intelligence (2015)
20. Hinton, G.E., Srivastava, N., Krizhevsky, A., Sutskever, I., Salakhutdinov, R.R.: Improving neural neworks by preventing co-adaptation of feature detectors (2012)
21. Ioffe, S., Szegedy, C.: Batch normalization: Accelerating deep network training by reducing internal covariate shift. In: International Conference on Learning Representations (2015)
22. Li, X., Chen, S., Hu, X., Yang, J.: Understanding the disharmony between dropout and batch normalization by variance shift (2018)
23. A. G. Roy, N. Navab, and C. Wachinger. Concurrent spatial and channel 'squeeze & excitation' in fully convolutional networks. In: International Conference on Medical Image Computing and Computer Assisted Intervention 2018. https://doi.org/10.1007/978-3-030-00928-1_48
24. Depierre, A., Dellandrea, E., Chen, L.: Jacquard: A large scale dataset for robotic grasp detection. In: IEEE/RSJ International Conference on Intelligent Robots and Systems (2018)
25. Liu, L., He, J., Chen, P., Liu, W., Gao, J., Han, J.: On the variance of the adaptive learning rate and beyond. In: ICLR (2020)
26. Diederik, J.B., Kingma, P.: Adam A method for stochastic optimization. In: International Conference for Learning Representations (2015)
27. Nitanda, A.: Stochastic proximal gradient descent with acceleration techniques. In: Advances in Neural Information Processing Systems (2014)
28. Mahler, J., et al.: Dex-net 2.0: Deep learning to plan robust grasps with synthetic point clouds and analytic grasp metrics (2017)
29. Lu, H., Zhang, Y., Li, Y., et al.: User-oriented virtual mobile network resource management for vehicle communications. IEEE Trans. Intell. Transport. Syst. **22**(6), 3521–3532 (2021)
30. Lu, H., Li, Y., Mu, S., et al.: Motor anomaly detection for unmanned aerial vehicles using reinforcement learning. IEEE Internet Things J. **5**(4), 2315–2322 (2018)
31. Lu, H., Zhang, M., Xu, X., et al.: Deep fuzzy hashing network for efficient image retrieval. IEEE Trans. Fuzzy Syst. **29**(1), 166–176 (2021)

An Indirect State-of-Health Estimation Method for Lithium-Ion Battery Based on Correlation Analysis and Long Short-Term Memory Network

Zhiying Zhang[1(✉)], Gong Meng[2], Shenhang Wang[2], Xiaojun Bai[1], and Yanfang Fu[1]

[1] School of Computer Science and Engineering, Xi'an Technological University, Xi'an, China
zhangzhiying@st.xatu.edu.cn
[2] Beijing Aerospace Automatic Control Institution, Beijing, China

Abstract. State of Health (SOH) is a key indicator to describe battery's health status, which is important in terms of extending battery life, reducing failures and losses. Battery capacity are commonly used indicators for SOH estimation, but it's difficult to monitor capacity online because of battery working conditions. To overcome this challenge, this paper proposes an indirect method for SOH estimation. The study found a correlation between battery capacity and measured voltage during discharge. This correlation was confirmed using correlation analysis methods. The measured voltage sequence of the battery discharge phase is chosen as a health indicator to measure SOH. An LSTM network was used to create a model predicting battery capacity based on the health indicator. Optimization of LSTM model hyperparameters using whale optimization algorithm. The proposed method achieved a mean absolute percentage error of 0.53%, 11.38% higher than the traditional method.

Keywords: state of health · lithium-ion battery · correlation analysis · long short-term memory network · whale optimization algorithm

1 Introduction

Lithium-ion batteries are a vital technology for renewable energy storage due to their high energy density, extended cycle life, minimal self-discharge, and absence of memory effect in contrast to other battery chemistries. [1–4]. Repeated charge and discharge cycles cause chemical and physical changes within the battery, leading to a gradual decrease in capacity and discharge voltage over time. Such performance degradation can damage electrical equipment and even pose a threat to personal safety [5]. SOH of battery estimation could be achieved by deploying sensors on batteries to collect various data such as current and voltage during battery usage. Real-time monitoring of the battery's health condition enables the replacement of problematic batteries, ensuring that the battery pack is always in optimal working condition.

Scholars have devised methods to estimate battery SOH in recent years. There are two main categories of approaches for the task at hand: model-based methods [6] and data-driven methods [7, 20]. Model-based methods leverage expert knowledge and experience to construct models of battery life degradation, from which capacity is analytically computed. Commonly employed models include equivalent circuit models (ECM), electro-chemical models (EM), and empirical models. Ahwiadi [8] developed enhanced mutated PF (EMPF) for predicting lithium-ion battery RUL and improving its performance in solving degeneracy and depletion problems. Shi[9] used an improved unscented particle filter (IUPF) that considers the internal resistance of the battery to estimate its SOH. Experimental data demonstrates that this method consistently achieves SOH estimation errors of under 3%.

However, model-based methods rely on accurate models for their effectiveness. Batteries are difficult to monitor and collect the state parameters needed for modeling during use. Therefore these types of methods are difficult to use and have low prediction accuracy.

Data-driven prediction obviates the need to comprehend intricate chemical changes in lithium-ion batteries, but rather models predictions from a large number of externally measured parameters. By collecting cyclic charge and discharge data from lithium-ion batteries via sensors, algorithms can extract features embedded in the data and derive effective aging characteristics. Consequently, employing machine learning methods to predict battery capacity has emerged as the mainstream approach in recent years. Wu [10] proposed a capacity estimation method for lithium-ion batteries based on principal component analysis (PCA) and a genetic optimization BP neural network (GA-BP).PCA was employed to fuse IC curve peaks and multiple characteristic parameters that reflect battery performance degradation. Capacity prediction using an optimized BP neural network with less than 2% error. Zhang [11, 19] proposed an integrated approach for battery capacity prediction. The battery capacity is decomposed into two components using an optimized variational modal decomposition(VMD): the residual sequence and the aging trend sequence. Then Gaussian process regression (GPR) and particle filtering (PF) models are constructed to predict these sequences. The results of these two models are fused to obtain the capacity prediction results, and the method exhibits strong generality and low error. Cao [12] proposed a prediction model that combines a self-encoder with a deep neural network, using 20-dimensional data from battery charging and discharging as input and battery capacity as output. Results shown that prediction accuracy was improved by automatically fusing features and achieving feature dimension reduction through the self-encoder.

In summary, it can be seen that there are two important parts to using data-driven methods for accurate prediction: effective HI extraction and network model construction. Inspired by the above content, a method based on correlation analysis to extract HI and indirect estimation of SOH by an optimized LSTM model proposed by this paper. Battery's measured voltage in the discharge phase is selected as HI for accurate capacity prediction.

2 Capacity of Lithium-Ion Battery Prediction Framework

Figure 1 shows the framework of the SOH estimation model for lithium-ion batteries proposed in this paper. Initially, correlation analysis is conducted on the raw data to extract health indicator for battery capacity. Subsequently, an LSTM network is trained on the selected HI and capacity data to model their relationship. Then to enhance the LSTM model's effectiveness, WOA optimizes network hyperparameters. Finally, made predictions by the optimized model on the proposed health indicator data that is measurable.

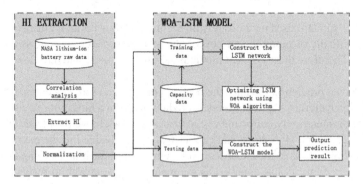

Fig. 1. Prediction framework

3 Data Analysis and Health Indicator Extraction

3.1 Dataset and Visualization

This paper use NASA's lithium-ion battery dataset for research and experimentation. It includes measurement data of cyclic charging and discharging of four battery models, B0005, B0006, B0007 and B0018 at 24 °C. While the discharging /charging cycles increase, the capacity of the battery decreases gradually, and its performance gradually degenerate. And the capacity is considered to fail when it drops to 70% of the original capacity. The degradation curve of capacity with charging /discharging cycles is shown in Fig. 2.

Data collected by sensors during cyclic is extracted and analyzed, with each cycle consists of charging and discharging. From Fig. 3, measured voltage data during the discharge period before and after 50 cycles, with the solid line representing data before 50 cycles and the dashed line representing data after 50 cycles. It can be observed from the figure that data before 50 cycles is chaotic and irregular. In contrast, the measured voltage data after 50 cycles exhibits a certain geometric pattern with the change of cycles, i.e., the curve gradually flattens to the left as the cycles increases. Since there is no significant degradation trend in battery capacity during the first 50 discharge cycles,this study focuses on the measured voltage data after 50 cycles.

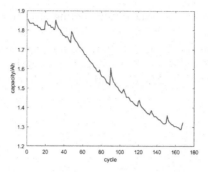

Fig. 2. Capacity degradation curve

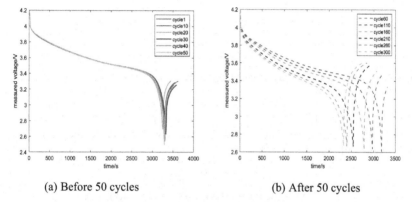

(a) Before 50 cycles   (b) After 50 cycles

Fig. 3. Discharge measured voltage data curve

3.2 Correlation Analysis and Feature Selection

In working environment, it is difficult to measure capacity of batteries online; therefore, we need some measurable data that can be easily obtained as HI to predict battery capacity. The key to selecting a HI is to consider whether the indicator can effectively represent the trend of capacity degradation. From Fig. 2, we can see that the overall trend of battery capacity decreases with increasing charge/discharge cycles. From Fig. 3, we can see that the measured voltage data, depicted by the dashed line in Fig. 3(b), gradually decreases with increasing cycles at the same sampling time point. Within the same cycle, the measured discharge voltage also gradually decreases with time increasing. Thus, it is hypothesized that the measured voltage during discharge period may be correlated with changes in capacity.

To validate the correlation between capacity and measured voltage during discharge period, sampling every 100 s for each cycle and recorded as follows:

$$V_t = \{V_t^1, V_t^2, V_t^3, ..., V_t^i\} \quad t = 100, 200, 300, 400, ..., T \quad i = 1, 2, 3, 4, ..., n \quad (1)$$

$$C = \{C^1, C^2, ..., C^n\} \quad i = 1, 2, 3, 4, ..., n \quad (2)$$

where V_t denotes the measured voltage value during discharge period, C denotes the capacity of battery, t denotes sampling time, i denotes the cycle number, n is the final number of cycles, T is the final sampling time. Trend graphs then plotted based on the above data sequences, as shown in Fig. 4. We can find that the measured voltage curve between 800s and 1500s follows a highly similar trend to the capacity degradation curve.

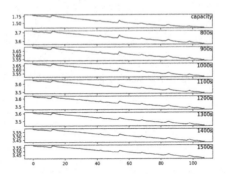

Fig. 4. Capacity degradation curve and measured voltage curve between 800 s and 1500

To further examine the correlation, correlation analysis were made between the sequence data of measured voltage and the capacity of batteries, the data sequences were noted as follows:

$$V_t = \{V_t^1, V_t^2, V_t^3, ..., V_t^i\}$$
$$t = 800, 900, 1000, 1100, 1200, 1300, 1400, 1500 \qquad (3)$$
$$C = \{C^1, C^2, C^3, ..., C^i\}$$

The grey correlation and Pearson correlation coefficients were calculated respectively for the battery capacity and each data sequences of measured voltages.

The grey correlation analysis method [13] measures the degree of association between sequences based on the similarity of their trends. In this paper, battery's capacity is selected as the reference sequence, i.e., $C = \{c(k)|k = 1, 2, 3, ..., n\}$, and that of measured voltages during discharge period V_t ($t = 800, 900, 1000, ..., 1500$) as the comparison sequence, i.e., $V_t = \{v_t(k)|k = 1, 2, 3, .., n\}$, n, n means the length of the sequence, and k corresponds to the k-th value in the sequence. The equation of grey correlation coefficient is (4).

$$\xi_t(k) = \frac{\rho \max\limits_t \max\limits_k |c(k) - v_t(k)| + \min\limits_t \min\limits_k |c(k) - v_t(k)|}{\rho \max\limits_t \max\limits_k |c(k) - v_t(k)| + |c(k) - v_t(k)|} \qquad (4)$$

where s $\rho \in [0, 1]$ [0, 1] denotes resolution factor. The smaller value of ρ, the larger the resolution, usually taken $\rho = 0.5$. Then the grey correlation can be calculated by Eq. (5).

$$r_t = \frac{1}{n} \sum_{k=1}^{n} \xi_t(k) \qquad (5)$$

The correlation coefficient, denoted as r_t, ranges between (0,1]. When r_t approaching to 1 indicates that have a strong positive correlation between reference and comparison sequences.

The Pearson correlation coefficient [14] has a range of -1 to 1, indicating negative linear correlation when close to -1, positive linear correlation when close to 1, and linearly uncorrelated when close to 0. Its formula is given as eq. (6).

$$r_t = \frac{\sum_{i=1}^{n}(V_t^i - \overline{V_t})(C^i - \overline{C})}{\sqrt{(V_t^i - \overline{V_t})^2}\sqrt{\sum_{i=1}^{n}(C^i - \overline{C})^2}} \qquad (6)$$

where r_t denotes Pearson correlation coefficient, and t = 800, 900, 1000, 1100, 1200, 1300, 1400, 1500 represents 8 sampling points in time, ii denotes the i-th cycle, nn denotes final number of cycles. C^i denotes capacity of i-th cycle, $\overline{C}$ means average value of capacity. V_t^i denotes the measured voltage at tt time of the i-th cycle, and $\overline{V_t}$ denotes average of measured voltage at t time of all cycles.

Results of Grey correlation and Pearson correlation coefficients are shown in the Table1 on the batteries data from B0005, B0006 and B0007.As we can see from the above table, the Pearson correlation coefficients of all three batteries' measured voltage data series are above 0.99, almost perfectly positive correlated. Except for some values of 0.89 in gray correlation, most of the grey correlation are above 0.9, indicating that the measured voltage data sequences from 800 s–1500 s have a strong positive correlation with the capacity sequences. Thus we confirmed that the measured voltage sequence during discharge is suitable for use as HI to describe battery's degradation state.

Table 1. Results of correlation analysis

Measured voltage data sequence	No. B0005		No. B0006		No. B0007	
	Grey correlation	Pearson's correlation coefficient	Grey correlation	Pearson's correlation coefficient	Grey correlation	Pearson's correlation coefficient
V_{800}	0.8977	0.9955	0.9176	0.9955	0.9019	0.9944
V_{900}	0.8963	0.9957	0.9157	0.9958	0.8986	0.9943
V_{1000}	0.9062	0.9966	0.9247	0.9960	0.9081	0.9957
V_{1100}	0.9101	0.9968	0.9275	0.9960	0.9091	0.9960
V_{1200}	0.9127	0.9969	0.9266	0.9961	0.9096	0.9961
V_{1300}	0.9077	0.9968	0.9261	0.9960	0.9101	0.9964
V_{1400}	0.9004	0.9962	0.9245	0.9960	0.9111	0.9965
V_{1500}	0.8922	0.9950	0.9224	0.9959	0.9105	0.9961

4   Time Series Prediction Model

In this study, we aim to develop a model of time series prediction that can forecast the battery capacity for the upcoming cycle based on the measured voltage data obtained from the preceding cycle. Commonly used time series prediction models include RNN, LSTM, GRU and so on. In this paper, an optimized LSTM model will be employed for prediction.

4.1   LSTM

LSTM network is a special kind of recurrent neural network. The aim of creating it was to address the issue of vanishing and exploding gradients that arise in traditional neural networks during training on lengthy series, commonly employed for predicting time series. Figure 5 depicts the LSTM architecture.

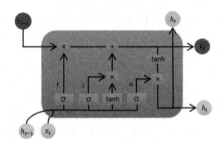

Fig. 5. Architecture of LSTM neural network

In Fig. 6, f denotes forget gate, o denotes output gate and ii denotes input gate. x_t denotes the input state, C_t denotes the unit state, and h_t denotes the hidden state, t denotes current moment; σ denotes the sigmoid activation function and tanh denotes the tanh activation function. A typical LSTM unit is calculated in Eq. (7).

$$\begin{cases} i_t = \sigma(W_i h_{t-1} + U_i x_t + b_i) \\ f_t = \sigma(W_f h_{t-1} + U_f x_t + b_f) \\ o_t = \sigma(W_o h_{t-1} + U_o x_t + b_o) \\ \widetilde{c}_t = tanh(W_g h_{t-1} + U_g x_t + b_g) \\ c_t = c_{t-1} \cdot f_t + \widetilde{c}_t \cdot i_t \\ h_t = tanh(c_t) \cdot o_t \end{cases} \tag{7}$$

where σ represents sigmoid activation function; WW denotes the weight matrix with the hidden state; U denotes weight matrix with the input state, b denotes the bias vector; and $\widetilde{c}_t$ represents the unit candidate state.

On training of LSTM, the 8-dimensional feature vector was extracted from raw data as input of LSTM. The feature vector is shown in Eq. (8), in which, i represents the number of cycle; Battery capacity was used as the label of this sample, shown in Eq. (9).

$$\{V^i_{800}, V^i_{900}, V^i_{1000}, V^i_{1100}, V^i_{1200}, V^i_{1300}, V^i_{1400}, V^i_{1500}\} \tag{8}$$

$$\{Capacity^{i+1}\} \tag{9}$$

The performance of LSTM are highly related to its setting of hyper-parameters [15], traditionally, the hyper-parameters are adjusted by experience and experiments, obviously it is difficult to obtain best solution. To address this problem, this paper introduces the whale optimization algorithm to optimize the LSTM model, which can easily obtain the best hyperparameters and construct a high-performance optimization model, thus significantly improving the prediction accuracy.

4.2 Whale Optimization Algorithm

The main process of the WOA algorithm [16, 21] is as follows:

1) Encircling prey
   When humpback whale engages in encircling its prey, it selects the optimal orientation and direction of encirclement. Assuming that the current prey position is the best position vector, the humpback whales will try to move towards the best position vector to update their position. The calculation formula is as follows:

$$D = |C \cdot X^*(t) - X(t)| \tag{10}$$

$$X(t+1) = X^*(t) - A \cdot D \tag{11}$$

The equation involves vectors A and C, where $X^*(t)$ denotes the prey's position vector and $X(t)$ denotes the remaining whales' position vector. The absolute value is denoted by "| |", and the dot product of vectors is represented by "•".
   A and C are calculated as follows:

$$A = 2a \times r_1 - a \tag{12}$$

$$C = 2 \times r_2 \tag{13}$$

where a as an adjustment vector decreases linearly from 2 to 0; r_1 and r_2 vectors is the [0,1] in the random vectors.

2) Bubble-net attacking method

   ① Shrinking encircling mechanism: To implement the shrinking encircling mechanism, a random vector A with values in $[-a, a]$ is used in Eq. (12), where the value of a is linearly decreased from 2 to 0.
   ② Spiral updating position: This approach computes the distance between a humpback whale at (X, Y) and its prey at (X^*, Y^*), and models the humpback whale's spiral motion towards the prey using an equation. The position update equation is then derived from this model. After then, the humpback whale's spiral hunting mode is simulated to establish the spiral equation as Eqs. (14) and (15).

$$X(t+1) = D'e^{bl}\cos(2\pi l) + X^*(t) \tag{14}$$

$$D' = |X^* - X(t)| \tag{15}$$

where b denotes the spiral parameter, and l is a random number in the range of -1 to 1.

To mimic humpback whales' prey encircling behavior, positional updates will be probabilistically generated between a shrinking encirclement and a spiral pattern. Use the variable pp to represent the probability, ranging from 0 to 1. The equation is as follows:

$$X(t+1) = \begin{cases} X^*(t) - A \cdot D & P \le 0.5 \\ D \times e^{bl} \times \cos(2\pi l) + X^*(t) & P \ge 0.5 \end{cases} \tag{16}$$

3) Search for prey

To ensure that all humpback whales can search adequately in the solution space, humpback whales update their positions based on each other's positions for the purpose of random search. To displace search individuals from the reference point, randomly select a values outside the range of -1 to 1 and adjust the search individual's location accordingly. When $|A| > 1$, the WOA algorithm conducts a global search by moving search agent moves from reference whale. The equation is as follows:

$$D'' = |C \bullet X_{rand}(t) - X(t)| \tag{17}$$

$$X(t+1) = X_{rand}(t) - A \cdot D \tag{18}$$

where $X_{rand}(t)$ represents the present position of the random individual.

LSTM hyperparameters were optimized using the WOA algorithm in this study. The dimensions of the whale positions correspond to the hyperparameters to be optimized, and each whale is considered as a solution. This allows for the optimal combination of parameters for the model to be obtained as the whales continually update their positions.

In the model training, MSE was employed as the loss function. Learning rate (lr) and the quantity of cells in the hidden layers of LSTM (hidden1, hidden2) were then optimized by the Whale Optimization Algorithm for a total of three parameters. The data before and after hyperparameter optimization are shown in Table 2.

Table 2. Parameter optimization results

Parameters	lr	hidden1	hidden2
Initial value	0.006	256	128
After optimization	0.004	216	141

5   Experimental Analysis

5.1   Model Training and Testing

The WOA-LSTM indirect estimation model was employed to select B0005 and B0006 battery data operating at room temperature for training and B0018 battery data operating at room temperature for validation. During testing, we experimented with and verified this prediction model with B0007 battery data operating at room temperature. Figure 6 shows loss variation curves for training and validation. Figure 9 illustrates that loss remains steady from 200 to 1000 epochs. Consequently, 1000 epochs were selected as the training epochs.

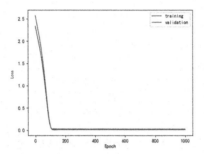

Fig. 6. Loss of network training process

After network training, capacity prediction for batteries using B0007 battery data, and corresponding results are presented in Fig. 7. The plot displays a true value with a blue curve and a predicted value with a red curve. The prediction curve closely agrees with the true value.

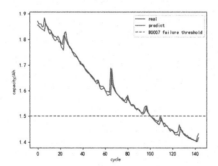

Fig. 7. Capacity predicted results(B0007)

To assess the model's capacity for generalization, Fig. 8 shows the use of B0045, B0046, and B0047 battery data operating at low temperatures as the training set and B0048 battery data as the test set. Compared to the solid blue curve representing the true value, the solid red curve depicting the predicted value better aligns with the values shown in the prediction curves.

According to the *SOH* calculation formula $SOH = \left(\frac{Q_n}{Q_d}\right)$, where SOH indicates battery health status, Q_n indicates rated capacity, and Q_d indicates actual capacity. Figure 9 shows the true and predicted values of SOH for lithium-ion batteries.

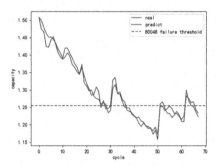

Fig. 8. Capacity predicted results(B0048)

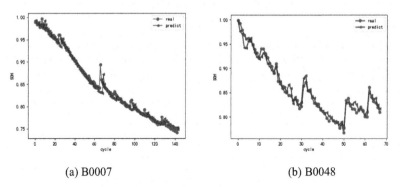

(a) B0007   (b) B0048

Fig. 9. SOH estimation results

5.2 Assessment Indicators

Table 3 displays the chosen evaluation metrics in this study, where $\widehat{y}_i$ denotes the predicted value, y_i denotes the true value, m denotes the predicted sample size.

Table 3. Assessment indicators

Assessment indicators		
Mean Square Error (MSE)	Mean Square Error (RMSE)	Mean Absolute Percentage Error (MAPE)
$\frac{1}{m}\sum_{i=1}^{m}(\widehat{y_i}-y_i)^2$	$\sqrt{\frac{1}{m}\sum_{i=1}^{m}(\widehat{y_i}-y_i)^2}$	$\frac{100\%}{m}\sum_{i=1}^{m}\left|\frac{\widehat{y_i}-y_i}{y_i}\right|$

5.3 Analysis of Results

LSTM and Bilstm models, as well as WOA-LSTM optimization models, were constructed for experiments respectively. The prediction effects were evaluated in terms of three metrics: MSE, RMSE, and MAPE. This paper compared the proposed method with prediction methods from other literature, as shown in Table 4.

Table 4. Prediction performance of different models

Model type	MSE	RMSE	MAPE/%
ELM [17]	/	/	5.25
CNN-LSTM [18]	/	/	0.88
DNN [12]	0.003679	0.060654	11.91
ADNN [12]	0.000473	0.021770	4.09
LSTM	0.000471	0.021717	0.94
Bilstm	0.000371	0.019252	2.04
WOA-LSTM	0.000231	0.015219	0.53

Table 5 presents a comparison results of the proposed model for the B0007 battery operating at 24 °C and the B0048 battery operating at 4 °C.

Table 5. Comparison of results at different temperatures

Battery number	MSE	MAPE/%	RMSE
B0007	0.000231	0.53	0.015219
B0048	0.000298	0.88	0.016102

It is evident that the WOA-LSTM optimization model produces the best results in all three-evaluation metrics. Therefore, the proposed prediction model in this study can precisely and dependably predict capacity of lithium-ion batteries using measured data, subsequently enabling reliable prediction of the SOH of the batteries.

6 Conclusion

Accurately predicting lithium-ion battery capacity is crucial for effective health and condition management. In this study, we extract the HI by correlation analysis and feed the HI into an optimized LSTM network to indirectly predict the lithium ion health state. By analyzing the correlation between measured data sequences and battery capacity data during charging and discharging processes, relevant features that align with the capacity degradation trend are extracted. Subsequently, an LSTM time series prediction model is developed, and its hyper-parameters are optimized using WOA. The final optimized model demonstrates high accuracy in predicting capacity of lithium-ion batteries.

References

1. Zhang, G.A.: The lithium-ion battery characteristics research. Electron. Meas. Technol. **37**(10), 41–45 (2014)
2. Zhao, C., Yin, H., Ma, C.: Quantitative efficiency and temperature analysis of battery-ultracapacitor hybrid energy storage systems. IEEE Trans. Sustain. Energy **7**(4), 1791–1802 (2016)
3. Hu, X.S., Zou, C.F., Zhang, C.P.: Technological developments in batteries: a survey of principal roles, types, and management needs. IEEE Power Energy Mag. **15**(5), 20–31 (2017)
4. Zou, C.F., Manzie, C., Nesic, D.: A framework for simplification of PDE-based lithium-ion battery models. IEEE Trans. Control Syst. Technol. **24**(5), 1594–1609 (2016)
5. Si, X., Li, T., Zhang, Q.: Prognostics for linear stochastic degrading systems with survival measurements. IEEE Trans. Industr. Electron. **67**(4), 3202–3215 (2019)
6. Sun, T., Wu, R., Cui, Y.: Sequent extended Kalman filter capacity estimation method for lithium-ion batteries based on discrete battery aging model and support vector machine. Energy Storage **39**, 102594 (2021)
7. Wei, Z., Zhao, J., Ji, D.: A multi-timescale estimator for battery state of charge and capacity dual estimation based on an online identified model. Appl. Energ. **204**, 1264–1274 (2017)
8. Ahwiadi, M., Wang, W.: An enhanced mutated particle filter technique for system state estimation and battery life prediction. IEEE Trans. Instrum. Meas. **68**(3), 923–935 (2019)
9. Shi, E., Xia, F., Peng, D.: State-of-health estimation for lithium battery in electric vehicles based on improved unscented particle filter. J. Renew. Sustain. Ener. **11**(2), 024101 (2019). https://doi.org/10.1063/1.5065477
10. Wu, Q., Xu, R.L., Yang, Q.X., Xu, L.Y.: Lithium battery capacity estimation method based on PCA and GA-BP neural network. Electron. Meas. Technol. **45**(06), 66–71 (2022)
11. Zhang, C.L., Zhao, S.S., He, Y.G.: An integrated method of the future capacity and RUL prediction for lithium-ion battery pack. IEEE Trans. Veh. Technol. **71**(3), 2601–2613 (2022)
12. Cao, M.D., Zhang, T., Wang, Y., Zhang, Y.J., Liu, Y.J.: Remaining useful life estimation for lithium-ion battery using deep learning method. Radio Eng. **51**(07), 641–648 (2021)
13. Pang, J.Y., Ma, Y.T., Liu, D.T., Peng, Y.: Indirect remaining useful life prognostics for lithium-ion battery. China Sciencepaper **9**(1), 28–36 (2014)
14. Gong, Y.Q., T L., Yu, Z., Zhang, X.: Research on the misalignment fault diagnosis method of rotating machinery based on Pearson correlation coefficient. New Technol. New Product. China (05), 48–50 (2022)
15. Yu, Y.J., Jiang, Y.N., Li, C.Y.: Prediction method of insulation paper remaining life with mechanical-thermal synergy based on WOA-LSTM model. Trans. China Electrotech. Soc. **37**(12), 1–10 (2022)

16. Mirjalili, S., Lewis, A.: The whale optimization algorithm. Adv. Eng. Softw. **95**, 51–67 (2016)
17. Jiang, Y.Y., Liu, Z., Luo, H., Wang, H.: ELM indirect prediction method for remaining life of lithium-ion battery. J. Electron. Meas. Instrument. (02), 179–185 (2016)
18. Chen, C.Y., Chen, D.W.: Research on indirect prediction of lithium battery RUL based on CNN-LSTM. Chin. J. Power Sources **45**(05), 589–594 (2021)
19. Zhu, J., Hu, J., Lu, H., et al.: Robust motion averaging under maximum correntropy criterion. In: 2021 IEEE International Conference on Robotics and Automation (ICRA), pp. 5283–5288. IEEE (2021)
20. Fu, Y., Zhang, M., Xu, X., et al.: Partial feature selection and alignment for multi-source domain adaptation. In: Proceedings of the IEEE/CVF Conference on Computer Vision and Pattern Recognition, pp. 16654–16663 (2021)
21. Xu, X., Lin, K., Lu, H., et al.: Correlated features synthesis and alignment for zero-shot cross-modal retrieva. In: Proceedings of the 43rd International ACM SIGIR Conference on Research and Development in Information Retrieval, pp. 1419–1428 (2020)

A Quantum Behaved Particle Swarm Optimization with a Chaotic Operator

Mingming Li[1], Dandan Cao[1,2], and Hao Gao[3(✉)]

[1] Beijing Institute of Control Engineering, Beijing, China
[2] China Academy of Space Technology Hangzhou Institute, Hangzhou, China
[3] Nanjing University of Posts and Communications, Nanjing, China
tsgaohao@gmail.com

Abstract. As a popular population based Evolutionary Algorithm, quantum behaved particle swarm optimization (QPSO) has applied widely in many real-world problems. In this paper, for further enhancing the performance of QPSO, we proposed a popular chaotic map into it. The new chaotic operator not only accelerate the convergence rate but also strengthen the search ability in the total space of the original QPSO. Furthermore, we verify the revised algorithm on some traditional benchmark functions. The final compared results on the images prove the superior of our algorithm.

Keywords: quantum behaved · particle swarm optimization · chaotic operator

1 Introduction

As a popular branch of Optimization algorithm, Evolutionary Algorithms (EAs) have undertook different role in their application [1, 2]. Due to its easy to implement and less limitation for the solved problems, EAs attract many researchers to make further revision or apply them into real world problems. Furthermore, many new EAs have been proposed in different ways, i.e., Genetic Algorithm [3], Differential Algorithm [4, 14], Artificial Bee Colony algorithm [5, 15] and Particle Swarm Optimization algorithm (PSO) [6, 18].

In 1995, Kennedy and Eberhart first proposed the PSO algorithm by inspiring from the behavior of birds and fishes [7, 16]. Same with other EAs, they hope to find an acceptable result of a real problem in a short time, which could find an optimum efficiently. But different with other EAs, PSO proposed two concepts named as pbest and gbest, which record the historic experience of individuals and population respectively. Compared with other EAs, the proposed concepts not only accelerate the convergence rate of finding an optimum but also make precise search of a local optimum. Furthermore, the total dimensional updating mechanism further accelerate the convergence rate on dimensional level. In general, PSO shows fast rate on finding a local optimum. But each coin shows two sides, the global search ability of PSO is deteriorated by its power local search ability. It is often trapped into a local optimum especially on a multi modal problem, which means the found results are not as good as the other EAs found. For

H. Lu and J. Cai (Eds.): ISAIR 2023, CCIS 1998, pp. 212–218, 2024.
https://doi.org/10.1007/978-981-99-9109-9_21

further enhancing its global search ability, some researchers propose new operators or strategies into it. In 2004, Sun et. al propose a new PSO with quantum behavior (QPSO) [8] which demonstrate more power global search ability. They first propose a quantum operator to strengthen the global search ability of particles. Furthermore, they also suggest a new attractor for particles to efficiently search in a local optimum. The two operators effectively balance the exploration and exploitation abilities. The QPSO has been successfully applied into different real-world problem in recently years [9–11].

For further enhancing the performance of QPSO, we first introduce a chaotic map into it. Then for verifying its effectiveness, we apply the improve QPSO into medical image segmentation to verify its superior. The total paper is arranged as following.

The original PSO and QPSO are described in Sect. 2. Our proposed chaotic based QPSO is introduced in Sect. 3. At last, the verification of the effectiveness of our proposed algorithm is described in Sect. 4. Conclusion and further work are presented in Sect. 5.

2 PSO and QPSO Algorithms

2.1 Particle Swarm Optimization

Aiming to find an acceptable result in a short time, Kennedy and Eberhart propose a population-based optimization algorithm named as particle swarm optimization in 1995, which is inspired by the behavior of birds and fishes. Similar with the other EAs, PSO algorithm utilizes the concept of population and individual to represent the potential solutions and a potential solution respectively. Unlike with the other EAs, PSO introduces two new concept pbest and gbest to represent the historic experiences of individual and population respectively. The updating formulas of PSO are listed as following:

$$v_{id}(t+1) = v_{id}(t) + c_1 rand_1 * (p_{pid}(t) - x_{id}(t)) + c_2 rand_2 * (p_{gd}(t) - x_{id}(t)) \quad (1)$$

$$xidt + 1 = xidt + vidt + 1 \quad (2)$$

in which $v_{id}(t)$ and $x_{id}(t)$ denotes the velocity and position of the ith particle's dth dimension on iteration t respectively. c_1 And c_2 are two constants equals 2. p_p And p_g denote pbest and gbest respectively. $rand_1$ And $rand_2$ are two randomly generated values within [0, 1].

2.2 Quantum Behaved Particle Swarm Optimization

As mentioned in [12], PSO algorithm has the premature problem, which means the global search ability of PSO is weak especially in the last iteration and can't jump out of the current search area. It is not acceptable for optimization algorithm. For conquering this problem, Sun et al. proposed a PSO with quantum behaved to increase the chances of particle to search in a larger space. The updating formulas of QPSO are listed as following:

$$x_{id}(t+1) = p_d(t) + \alpha * v * (\Upsilon_d - x_{id}(t)) \quad (3)$$

$$p_d(t) = rand2 * p_{pid}(t) + (1 - rand2) * p_{gd}(t) \qquad (4)$$

$$v = \ln(\frac{1}{rand1}) \qquad (5)$$

In the two equations, α represent a linear decreasing value from 1 to 0.5 with iterations. Rand1 and rand2 denote two randomly generated values within [0, 1].

3 Quantum Behaved Particle Swarm Optimization with a Chaotic Operator

Although QPSO algorithm strengthen the global search ability of PSO, but it still has the space to further improve the performance of QPSO. Aiming to this, we propose a new QPSO algorithm with chaotic operator.

Chaos theory has shown as a new branch of mathematics which hope to find a theory of dynamical systems [13, 17]. It is very sensitive to its initial conditions. The basic principle of chaos is described as the butterfly effect, which means a very small change in a nonlinear system could lead to a very large differences in the last stage of iteration. Based on this theory, in this paper, we hope to employ the chaos theory to generate dynamic changed values which could simulate the motion of particles. In recently years, many chaos based operators have been suggested. The Gauss map (mouse map) is described as a nonlinear iterated map generated by the Gaussian function.

$$xt + 1 = exp - axt2 + \beta \qquad (6)$$

where α and β denotes two real parameters.

In our paper, we employ another format of Gauss map shown as following:

$$temp = mod\left(\frac{1}{rand3}, 1\right) \qquad (7)$$

in which rand3 represents a randomly generated value within [0, 1].

Based on (7), the updating (3) is modified as following:

$$x_{id}(t + 1) = p_d(t) + \alpha * temp * (\Upsilon_d - x_{id}(t)) \qquad (8)$$

For shown the role of Gauss map, we randomly generated 5000 values to find the distribution of it. The Figs. 1 and 2 show the generated Gauss map values are smaller or bigger than 2 respectively.

4 Experiment

4.1 Set Up

For test our proposed gauss operator, we verify the algorithm Quantum behavior particle swarm optimization with Gaussmap (GQPSO) on some benchmark functions which often utilizes as the test function in many papers. Five benchmark functions are listed

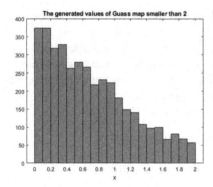
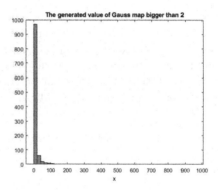

Fig. 1. The generated values of Gauss map.

in Table 1, which includes the formulas, the according range and the global solution. The total functions are verified on 20 and 40 dimensions respectively. We compare our proposed GQPSO with PSO and QPSO. For fair, 30 independent runs are run on a same random seed of MATLAB command. The max iterations are set as 2000 and 4000 on 20 and 40 dimensions of variables respectively. The population size and the max function evaluations are set as 40 and 40000*dimensions respectively. The best results achieved by the compared algorithm are in bold.

4.2   The Compared Results

According to the results shown on Table 2, 3 and Fig. 2, we can easily find that our proposed GQPSO achieves better results than that of QPSO and PSO. The only reason

Table 1. The formula of 12 benchmark functions.

Benchmark Functions	Formula	Initialization Range	Global Optimum
$f1$	$\sum_{i=1}^{n} x_i^2$	$[-100, 100]$	0
$f2$	$f(x) = \sum_{i=1}^{n} [100(x_{i+1} - x_i^2)^2 + (x_i - 1)^2]$	$[-100, 100]$	0
$f3$	$\sum_{i=1}^{n} \sum_{k=1}^{i} x_k^2$	$[-100, 100]$	0
$f4$	$\sum_{i=1}^{n} i * x_i^2$	$[-100, 100]$	0
$f5$	$\sum_{i=1}^{n} \left(x_i^2 - 10\cos(2\pi x_i) + 10 \right)$	$[-10, 10]$	0
$f6$	$\frac{\pi}{n} \left\{ 10\sin^2(\pi y_i) + \sum_{i=1}^{n-1} (y_i - 1)^2 \left[1 + \sin^2(\pi y_{i+1}) \right] + (y_n - 1)^2 \right\}$ $+ \sum_{i=1}^{n} u(x_i, 10, 100, 4)$	$[-50, 50]$	0

is that our proposed Gauss chaos operator could better find a favorable balance on local and global search. The smaller values help our algorithm to make a precise search on local area. This property could help our algorithm to get more favorable results. The bigger values enable our algorithm could jump out of the local area to guarantee the reliability of the results. In general, our algorithm outperforms the compared algorithm not only on the precision but also the global search ability.

Table 2. The comparison results on 20 dimensions.

	F1	F2	F3	F8	F10	
PSO	1.78e−16	102.718	7.8056	3.88e−16	20.7308	94.7319
	5.18e−16	153.23	8.28	1.4e−15	4.399	79.35
QPSO	1.08e−31	74.427	2.142	3.9e−30	11.7902	8.936
	2.27e−31	79.627	1.96	1.43e−29	**4.24**	27.433
GQPSO	**1.59e−56**	**29.048**	**0.0145**	**6.17e−55**	**10.8897**	**1.74e−30**
	4.87e−56	**40.782**	**0.0211**	**1.67e−54**	4.2625	**5.03e−30**

Table 3. The comparison results on 40 dimensions.

	F1	F2	F3	F8	F10	
PSO	**3.43e−11**	**103.122**	**2.26e3**	1.064e−9	71.54	**1.22e3**
	5.39e−11	**81.34**	**1.034e3**	2.716e−9	15.674	**368.54**
QPSO	1.97e−18	129.168	1.65e3	7.19e−16	40.254	433.258
	5.295e−18	152.7543	590.035	3.706e−15	7.8072	289.618
GQPSO	2.68e−36	80.6184	47.298	**2.887e−35**	**34.151**	**12.559**
	7.208e−36	85.619	22.655	**7.171e−34**	**5.0437**	**58.425**

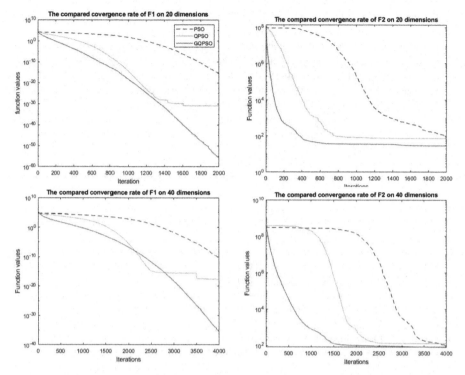

Fig. 2. The compared convergence rate of F1~F2 on 20 and 40 dimensions.

5   Conclusion

In this paper proposes a new quantum behaved particle swarm optimization with a Gauss chaotic map operator. By introducing the Gauss chaos into QPSO, the new operator helps the algorithm to make a good choice on local and thorough searches. This experimental results on some traditional benchmark functions verify the superior of our algorithm. In future, we hope to find the basic theory in EAs. Then more efficient algorithms are proposed.

References

1. Gao, H., Shi, Y.J., Pun, C.M., Kwong, S.: An improved artificial bee colony algorithm with its application. IEEE Trans. Industr. Inf. **15**(4), 1853–1865 (2019)
2. Cheng, W., Li, Z., He, Y.: Strategy and control for robotic detumbling of space debris by using flexible brush. In: 2019 3rd International Conference on Robotics and Automation Sciences, ICRAS, Wuhan, China, pp. 41–47. IEEE (2019)
3. Mirjalili, S.: Genetic algorithm, evolutionary algorithms and neural networks, studies in computational. Intelligence **780**, 43–55 (2019)
4. Li, X., Yin, M.: Hybrid differential evolution with artificial bee colony and its application for design of a reconfigurable antenna array with discrete phase shifters. IET Microwaves Antennas Propag. **6**(14), 1573–1582 (2012)

5. Karaboga, D.: An idea based on honey bee swarm for numerical optimization. Technical report - TR06. Technical report, Erciyes University (2005)
6. Ge, J., Wang, S.Q., Dong, H.B., et al.: Real-time detection of moving magnetic target using distributed scalar sensor based on hybrid algorithm of particle swarm optimization and gauss-newton method. IEEE Sens. J. **20**(18), 10717–10723 (2020)
7. Kennedy, J., Eberhart, R.C.: Particle swarm optimization. In: Proceeding IEEE International Conference Neural Network, Perth, pp. 1942–1948 (1995)
8. Sun, J., Palade, V., Wu, X.J., Fang, W.: Solving the power economic dispatch problem with generator constraints by random drift particle swarm optimization. IEEE Trans. Indus. Inf **10**, 222–232 (2013)
9. Allioui, H., Sadgal, M., Elfazziki, A.: Optimized control for medical image segmentation: improved multi-agent systems agreements using particle swarm optimization. J. Ambient. Intell. Humaniz. Comput. **12**, 8867–8885 (2021)
10. dos Santos Coelho, L.: An efficient particle swarm approach for mixed-integer programming in reliability–redundancy optimization applications. Reliab. Eng. Syst. Saf. **94**(4), 830–837 (2019)
11. Chen, H.X., Fan, D.L., Fang, L., et al.: Particle swarm optimization algorithm with mutation operator for particle filter noise reduction in mechanical fault diagnosis. Int. J. Pattern Recognit. Artif. Intell. **34**(10), 2058012 (2020)
12. Xu, Y.H., Hu, C.H., Wu, Q., et al.: Research on particle swarm optimization in LSTM neural networks for rainfall-runoff simulation. J. Hydrol. **608**(127553) (2022)
13. Lorenz, E.: The Essence of Chaos, pp. 181–206. University of Washington Press (1993)
14. Coelho, L.D.S., Alotto, P.: Gaussian artificial bee colony algorithm approach applied to Loney's solenoid benchmark problem. IEEE Trans. Magn. **47**(5), 1326–1329 (2011)
15. Lu, R., Hu, H.D., Xi, M.L., et al.: An improved artificial bee colony algorithm with fast strategy and its application. Comput. Electr. Eng. **78**, 79–88 (2019)
16. Yang, S., Lu, H., Li, J.: Multifeature fusion-based object detection for intelligent transportation systems. IEEE Trans. Intell. Transp. Syst. **24**(1), 1126–1133 (2022)
17. Lu, H., Zhang, M., Xu, X., et al.: Deep fuzzy hashing network for efficient image retrieval. IEEE Trans. Fuzzy Syst. **29**(1), 166–176 (2020)
18. Zhao, W., Lu, H., Wang, D.: Multisensor image fusion and enhancement in spectral total variation domain. IEEE Trans. Multimed. **20**(4), 866–879 (2017)

A Novel Small Object Detection Method Based on Improved Transformer Model

Zixuan Wei, Guokuan Zan, and Zhibo Wan[✉]

Qingdao University, Qingdao, China
wanzhibo@qdu.edu.cn

Abstract. Detection Transformer (DETR) transforms queries into unique objects and supports end-to-end object detection by using bipartite matching for training. This end-to-end design has greatly improved the generality of DETR and has been widely used in various downstream tasks. However, small objects are frequently missed or falsely detected due to poor features and high noise. To reduce these problems, we improve the encoder and decoder and introduce feature-enhanced auxiliary head. We advance the spatial correlation between adjacent tokens using the Locally-enhancement FeedForward (LeFF) module to enhance the extraction of local features and establish remote dependencies. Additionally, in order to increase positive queries, we change one-to-one matching for IoU assignment. We have addressed the issue of small object false and missed detection, and achieved better detection results. On the MS COCO datasets, our proposed method has 1.8% improved to the conventional methods and achieves 67.4% mAP@0.5 better than the powerful DINO.

Keywords: Object detection · Transformer · Feature Fusion · Locally-enhanced Feed-Forward

1 Introduction

Object detection requires localization and classification of objects which is the fundamental task of computer vision. Numerous other tasks related to object detection such as instance segmentation, image annotation and object tracking.

Object detectors classified detection as region (two-stage) or anchor (one-stage) classification based on their architecture. Representative works in two-stage detectors include Faster-RCNN [1], RetinaNet [2], and R-FCN [3]. He et al. [4] proposed SPP-Net (Spatial Pyramid Pooling Network) is a network structure that can be used without considering the image size and can achieve stable performance under image distortion. Liu et al. [5] proposed the SSD (Single shot multibox detector) network, which greatly improves the detection of small objects. Yang et al. [6] applied multi-feature fusion for object detection in an intelligent traffic system. The DETR series detectors have been continuously new work with improved performance and better applications in engineering, and have been generally accepted.

Compared with other methods, our method detection accuracy is greatly improved and can be well used in engineering applications.

H. Lu and J. Cai (Eds.): ISAIR 2023, CCIS 1998, pp. 219–225, 2024.
https://doi.org/10.1007/978-981-99-9109-9_22

(a)

(b)

(c)

(d)

Original   Ours

Fig. 1. Comparison with the results of vanilla DETR. The left is the original, and the right is ours.

The Detection Transformer [7] was proposed, which introduced a transformer-based encoder-decoder architecture with higher detection performance. Due to the general architecture and high accuracy, it can be well used in engineering applications. However, DETR performs well for large object detection, but is not ideal for small objects and the loss based on bipartite matching makes training is hard to converge.

As Fig. 1 shows that we find that DETR performs well in detecting large objects, but some small objects cannot be detected well through experimental results. In this research, we propose methods to improve the performance of small object detection by addressing the issues of false and missed detection.

On the MS COCO (Microsoft COCO) [8] datasets, our proposed method achieved detection performance of 31.8% mAP for small objects at mAP@[0.5:0.05:0.95], better than the Deformable-DETR [9] by 2.2%. Significantly, our proposed method also better than DINO and H-Deformable-DETR [10] on mAP@[0.5:0.95].

2 Approach

2.1 Model Architecture

Figure 2 illustrates the overall structure of our model. First, the input image size is $3 \times H \times W$. We flattend the backbone output to generate feature map. This feature map was fed to the transformer encoder to generates implicit features. The implicit features was sent to the decoder as input and transformed N embeddings that has box coordinates and class labels into output embeddings. The bipartite matching was calculated between the predictions and the ground truth bounding boxes and labels, associating each ground truth with the prediction that has the minimum matching loss. The final prediction consists of height, width and normalized center coordinates.

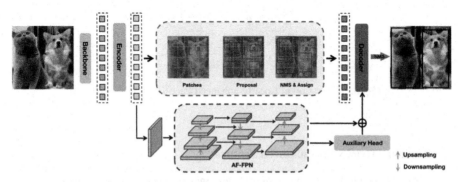

Fig. 2. Overall architecture of our model.

Meanwhile, we combine the auxiliary head with different one-to-many label assignments in order to enrich the output of the encoder. Specifically, we sent the implicit features of the encoder to convert them to AF-FPN by multi-scale permutation, and used the AAM and FEM to reduce information loss and increase the diversity of object detection. The output of the feature pyramid was passed to the auxiliary head to obtain the prediction. Finally, we performed post-processing using NMS to obtain the final output.

2.2 LeFF

The LeFF module [11] combines the advantages of CNN in extracting local information and transformer in establishing remote dependencies, as well as reducing the number of parameters.

Figure 3 illustrates the LeFF module. First, the input $X_t^h \in R^{(N+1) \times C}$ was split into patch tokens $X_p^h \in R^{(N+1) \times C}$ and a class token $X_c^h \in R^C$. The class token was kept. Then, the patch tokens were linearly projected to rectify the spatial dimension to a higher dimension of $X_p^{l_1} \in R^{N \times (e \times C)}$, where e represents the expansion ratio. The output were converted to a 2D image of size $X_p^s \in R^{\sqrt{N} \times \sqrt{N} \times (e \times C)}$. Then, a depth-wise convolution was applied to these restored patch tokens resulting in $X_p^d \in R^{\sqrt{N} \times \sqrt{N} \times (e \times C)}$. Then, the output of previous were flattened to $X_p^f \in R^{N \times (e \times C)}$. Finally, the output was adjusted back to dimension with $X_p^{l2} \in R^{N \times C)}$ after projection and concatenated with the class tokens to obtain $X_p^{h+1} \in R^{(N+1) \times C}$. These procedures can be summarized as follows:

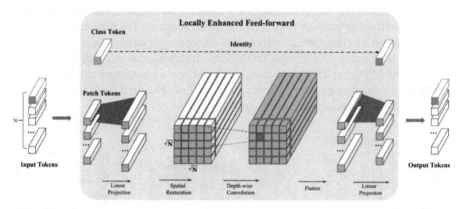

Fig. 3. Illustration of Locally-enhanced Feed-Forward module.

2.3 Auxiliary Head with Enhanced Feature

We combined the auxiliary heads with different one-to-many label assignment to enrich the output of the encoder. The process started with the encoder generating implicit features, converting them to AF-FPN [12] through multi-scale permutation, and increasing the diversity of object detection by using AAM and FEM to make a better representation of the feature pyramid.

The auxiliary heads include FCOS [13], Faster-RCNN [1], and RetinaNet [2]. We followed the original implementation, including anchor point generation, and defined multiple auxiliary heads with corresponding label assignment methods. The output of feature pyramid network was fed to the auxiliary head to obtain the corresponding prediction results.

2.4 IoU Assignment

In the two-stage Deformable-DETR [9], the first N proposal boxes was predicted by the encoder were used as object queries in the second stage. We replaced the Hungarian matching with a fixed overlap-based assignment, which allows for one-to-many assignments.

In the first stage, DETR generated a fixed query feature F. Each query was fixed at a specific position in the W × H image. We generated boxes using a fixed box size of width W and height H, which generated multiple initial box definitions. We utilized these initial boxes for the positional embedding and the overlap-based assignment process, and we assigned each prediction to the ground truth object with the highest overlap.

The Hungarian mathing loss Eq. 1 assigned each network output O to one of the annotated objects G or background. The formula is as follows:

$$\mathcal{L}_{\text{Hungarian}}(O, G) = \sum_{i=1}^{N} \left[\mathcal{L}_{\text{cls}}(\hat{s}_i, c_{\sigma i}) + \mathcal{L}_{\text{box}}(\hat{b}_i, b_{\sigma i}) \right] \tag{1}$$

where O and G are the predicted and baseline objects, is the optimal assignment, $\hat{s}_i$ and $c_{\sigma i}$ are the predicted and category labels of the objects, and $\hat{b}_i$ and $b_{\sigma i}$ are the prediction wrap-around box and baseline wrap-around box. The classification loss L_{cls} is the focal-loss based classification loss, which distinguishes between foreground and background. L_{box} is the boundary loss consisting of GIoU [14] and L1 loss, λ_{iou} and λ_{L1} are hyperparameters to adjust the IoU loss and the L1 loss of the prediction box. L_{iou} is used as the GIOU loss.

3 Experiment

In this study, we evaluate our method on the COCO 2017. COCO contains 118k training and 5k validation images over 80 object categories. We report bounding box mAP as the evaluation metric.

3.1 Experimental Details

We utilized 300 queries, 4 feature scales, and 6 transformer encoder and decoder layers with a ResNet50 backbone. In this study, we used the AdamW optimizer with the learning rate of 0.0002 and set the total batch size to 8.

Table 1. Compared with other methods on the COCO validation datasets with ResNet50 backbone.

Method	Epochs	mAP@0.5	mAP@0.75	mAP@0.5:0.95
Faster-RCNN [1]	12	58.8%	41.0%	37.9%
FCOS [13]	12	57.4%	41.4%	38.6%
Deformable-DETR [9]	50	65.6%	51.0%	46.9%
H-Deformable-DETR [15]	12	66.4%	52.9%	48.7%
DINO [16]	12	66.9%	53.8%	49.4%
Ours	12	67.4%	54.2%	49.5%
Ours	24	67.8%	54.8%	50.1%

3.2 Experimental Details

As shown in Table 1, we compared the performance of our method with different models on the MS COCO datasets. Obviously, our method still better than the novel H-Deformable-DETR. Compared to the second-best performance, our method achieves an increase of 0.8 in mAP@0.5, 0.6 in mAP@0.75, and 0.3 in mAP@[0.5:0.95]. Our method achieves 67.4% mAP@0.5 and 49.5% mAP@[0.5:0.95] in 12 epochs and 50.1% mAP@[0.5:0.95] in 24 epochs.

Compared with Deformable-DETR, we achieved 67.4% mAP@0.5 and 54.2% mAP@0.75. Table 1 shows that our method are better than transformer-based detectors on large-scale mAP@[0.5:0.95] on the MS COCO datasets. This demonstrates that our method is effective in detecting smaller objects.

Table 2. Component ablations of our method.

aux head	IoU settings	mAP@0.5	mAP@0.75
✗	✗	55.2%	40.3%
✓	✗	59.6%	45.7%
✗	✓	59.1%	45.0%
✓	✓	61.0%	46.9%

3.3 Ablation Studies

As shown in Table 2, we conducted initial experiments on both the auxiliary head and IoU settings. The method's effectiveness is demonstrated through the experimental results obtained from different combinations of components. Our method performed best when using both auxiliary head and IoU settings. Compared to the baseline model, our method improved mAP@0.5 by 5.8%.

IoU assignment assigns more positive queries to each ground truth, whereas one-to-one matching guarantees only one positive query per object. Therefore, more positive samples can speed up training and improve performance [17]. By refining and classifying region boundaries, we quantify easier tasks as those with lower model complexity.

4   Conclusion

In this paper, we propose methods for small object detection on transformer model. Our method based on the DETR model, with the following improvements.First, we replace the bipartite matching with simple IoU assignment on the two-stage DETR, which generates more positive queries and helps to improve the object detection ability. Then, we introduce the auxiliary head with the AF-FPN module. The improved model has higher performance and lower loss values than the baseline model. Our approach improves the false and missed detection problems of small objects and achieves better performance.

References

1. Ren, S., He, K., Girshick, R., Sun, J.: Faster R-CNN: towards real-time object detection with region proposal networks. In: Advances in Neural Information Processing Systems, vol. 28 (2015)
2. Lin, T.-Y., Goyal, P., Girshick, R., He, K., Dollár, P.: Focal loss for dense object detection. In: Proceedings of the IEEE International Conference on Computer Vision, pp. 2980–2988 (2017)
3. Dai, J., Li, Y., He, K., Sun, J.: R-FCN: object detection via region-based fully convolutional networks. In: Advances in Neural Information Processing Systems, vol. 29 (2016)
4. He, K., Zhang, X., Ren, S., Sun, J.: Spatial pyramid pooling in deep convolutional networks for visual recognition. IEEE Trans. Pattern Anal. Mach. Intell. **37**(9), 1904–1916 (2015)
5. Liu, W., et al.: SSD: single shot multibox detector. In: Leibe, B., Matas, J., Sebe, N., Welling, M. (eds.) ECCV 2016, Part I. LNCS, vol. 9905, pp. 21–37. Springer, Cham (2016). https://doi.org/10.1007/978-3-319-46448-0_2
6. Yang, S., Lu, H., Li, J.: Multifeature fusion-based object detection for intelligent transportation systems. IEEE Trans. Intell. Transp. Syst. (2022)
7. Carion, N., Massa, F., Synnaeve, G., Usunier, N., Kirillov, A., Zagoruyko, S.: End-to-end object detection with transformers. In: Vedaldi, A., Bischof, H., Brox, T., Frahm, J.M. (eds.) ECCV 2020, Part I. LNCS, vol. 12346, pp. 213–229. Springer, Cham (2020). https://doi.org/10.1007/978-3-030-58452-8_13
8. Lin, T.-Y., et al.: Microsoft COCO: common objects in context. In: Fleet, D., Pajdla, T., Schiele, B., Tuytelaars, T. (eds.) ECCV 2014, Part V. LNCS, vol. 8693, pp. 740–755. Springer, Cham (2014). https://doi.org/10.1007/978-3-319-10602-1_48
9. Zhu, X., Su, W., Lu, L., Li, B., Wang, X., Dai, J.: Deformable DETR: deformable transformers for end-to-end object detection. arXiv preprint arXiv:2010.04159 (2020)
10. Chen, K., et al.: Hybrid task cascade for instance segmentation. In: Proceedings of the IEEE/CVF Conference on Computer Vision and Pattern Recognition, pp. 4974–4983 (2019)
11. Yuan, K., Guo, S., Liu, Z., Zhou, A., Yu, F., Wu, W.: Incorporating convolution designs into visual transformers. In: Proceedings of the IEEE/CVF International Conference on Computer Vision, pp. 579–588 (2021)
12. Wang, J., Chen, Y., Dong, Z., Gao, M.: Improved YOLOv5 network for real-time multi-scale traffic sign detection. Neural Comput. Appl. 1–13 (2022)
13. Tian, Z., Shen, C., Chen, H., He, T.: FCOS: fully convolutional one-stage object detection. In: Proceedings of the IEEE/CVF International Conference on Computer Vision, pp. 9627–9636 (2019)
14. Rezatofighi, H., Tsoi, N., Gwak, J., Sadeghian, A., Reid, I., Savarese, S.: Generalized intersection over union: A metric and a loss for bounding box regression. In: Proceedings of the IEEE/CVF Conference on Computer Vision and Pattern Recognition, pp. 658–666 (2019)
15. Jia, D., et al.: DETRS with hybrid matching. arXiv preprint arXiv:2207.13080 (2022)
16. Zhang, H., et al.: DINO: DETR with improved denoising anchor boxes for end-to-end object detection. In: The Eleventh International Conference on Learning Representations (2022)
17. Ouyang-Zhang, J., Cho, J.H., Zhou, X., Krähenbühl, P.: NMS strikes back. arXiv preprint arXiv:2212.06137 (2022)

A Novel Full-Scale Skip Connections Approach Based on U-Net for COVID-19 Lesion Segmentation in CT Images

Yuchai Wan[1], Yifan Li[1], Shuqin Jia[1], Lili Zhang[1], Murong Wang[2], and Ruijun Liu[1（✉）]

[1] Beijing Key Laboratory of Big Data Technology for Food Safety, Beijing Technology and Business University, Beijing 100048, China
`liuruijun@btbu.edu.cn`
[2] Guangzhou Perception Vision Medical Technologies Co., Ltd., Guangzhou, China

Abstract. In the post-pandemic era, as COVID-19 continues to spread, CT imaging is indispensable for diagnosing COVID-19. Utilizing computer vision techniques to segment the lesion regions in CT scans can assist doctors in efficient and accurate diagnosis. However, traditional CNN-based U-net segmentation models are more adept at extracting local information, lacking overall awareness of the data, and suffering from semantic loss in the upsampling and downsampling process. To tackle these concerns, we present a Transformer-based full-scale skip connections Unet model. By transforming the traditional CNN structure into a SwinTransformer structure, the model can focus more on the global information of the image, making the instance features more robust and informative. Additionally, we incorporate full-scale skip connections to facilitate the upsampling module to simultaneously access the spatial information from each downsampling module, reducing spatial information loss and improving the segmentation accuracy of the model. We trained and tested our model using an independent dataset of COVID-19 from Wuhan. Experimental results demonstrate that our model exhibits good segmentation capability for COVID-19 lesions and outperforms other methods in terms of average precision. Furthermore, we performed ablation experiments for validation. The effectiveness of the full-scale skip connections.

Keywords: COVID-19 · Lesion Segmentation · U-Net · Full-scale Skip Connections · SwinTransformer

1 Introduction

Even though the World Health Organization (WHO) claimed that COVID-19 no longer constitutes a worldwide health crisis, but it is still an ongoing health issue, which threats to health in every outbreak in the future [1]. By the end of May 2023, there had been about 766 million reported cases of COVID-19 globally and over 6.9 million deaths [2, 3]. A common method of detection in the early stages of COVID-19 is diagnosed through reverse transcription polymerase chain reaction (RT-PCR) testing [4]. In addition to the commonly used RT-PCR, studies have shown that CT technology is effective in diagnosing COVID-19 and assessing its severity [5]. Through CT imaging doctors can observe lesion traces of pneumonia, such as ground-glass opaque (GGO) lesions, which can allow doctors to better diagnose and treat patients. However, during the COVID-19 pandemic, hospitals are overwhelmed with a large number of patients, which brings huge workload to doctors who need to diagnostic numerous CT scans. Computer vision technology holds promise in alleviating this issue. In recent times, advancements in deep learning and artificial intelligence technology have good results in various fields [6–8]. The automatic segmentation of lung CT images based on deep learning methods is promising to help doctors make diagnosis more efficiently.

However, the texture, size, and location of lesions vary widely in CT images, making segmentation of diseased areas in COVID-19CT images challenging. Convolutional Neural Networks (CNNs) are frequently employed in the realm of medical image segmentation, including applications like U-net [9], unet++ [10] and Unet3+ [11]. However, the inductive bias strategy used in CNN lacks an overall focus on the input image. They excel at extracting local information but struggle to extract long-distance global features. Therefore, due to the inherent limitations of convolution operations, CNN-based techniques frequently face difficulties in capturing explicit global and long-range semantic interactions [12]. In recent times, transformer-based models have garnered significant attention in the field of computer vision, such as Vision Transformer (ViT) have showcased state-of-the-art performance across a range of benchmarks [13]. Transformer is powerful in modeling global contexts. However, due to the considerable parameter count and the intricacy inherent in the Transformer architecture, training models based on the Transformer structure requires more computational resources.

At present, the mainstream segmentation method of medical images is mainly based on U-shaped networks. But, current U-shaped networks suffer from spatial information loss when using single-scale skip connections. This connection strategy fails to fully explore the spatial information at all scales, potentially leading to inaccurate identification of lesion boundaries in medical images.

In this article, we introduce an innovative approach involving full-scale skip connections U-shaped segmentation architecture based on SwinTransformer [14], called FST-Unet. We have designed a segmentation model with a symmetric structure. The proposed full-scale skip-connections structure integrates global and local features, significantly reducing the loss of spatial information during upsampling and downsampling processes, thereby augmenting the model's resilience. To achieve better capture the spatial information of medical images, we have combined the SwinTransformer structure with the U-Net architecture. Compared to the Transformer, SwinTransformer has significantly reduced computational complexity, making our model more lightweight. The experimental results indicate the model's strong performance on the Wuhan COVID-19 training set, securing the top position during the validation phase and delivering outstanding results in the testing phase.

The subsequent sections of this paper are structured as follows: In the Sect. 2, we delve into the related research in the field. The Sect. 3 outlines the primary methodologies and innovative aspects of this work. Section 4 presents the outcomes of our experiments. We wrap up with concluding remarks in Sect. 5.

2 Related Work

2.1 Covid-19 Segmentation

Recently, many scholars have proposed new COVID-19 lesion segmentation algorithms based on traditional methods. For example, Shen et al. [15] used thresholding and region growing for lesion segmentation, while Oulefki et al. [16] proposed an image contrast enhancement algorithm and a multi-level image thresholding method for pneumonia lesion segmentation. At the same time, Numerous deep learning-based approaches have been extensively explored. Cao et al. [17] and Huang et al. [18] used Unet to segment pneumonia lesion regions for quantitative analysis. Oktay et al. [19] proposed the use of U-Net combined with attention mechanism to obtain fine information in medical images, which is more suitable for COVID-19 lesion segmentation.

2.2 Transformer

ViT [13] applied Transformer technology to image classification tasks successfully. In contrast, TransUNet, proposed by Chen et al. [20], marked the entry of Transformers into medical image segmentation. Unlike TransUNet's U-shaped structure with just encoder and decoder branches, TransClaw (Claw U-NET with Transformers) [21] introduced a three-branch network structure—encoder, up-sampling, and decoder—utilizing skip connections to connect multi-scale feature maps. Swin UNETR [22] developed a self-supervised pre-trained segmentation model based on SwinTransformer, pretraining it on various tasks to acquire Region of Interest (ROI) information, neighboring voxel information, and structural knowledge. In contrast, Cao et al. introduced Swin-Unet [23], a novel Unet-inspired Transformer model for medical image segmentation. It involves image patch division and a U-shaped Encoder-Decoder architecture built on the Transformer framework, featuring skip connections to facilitate the learning of local and global semantic features.

3 Proposed Method

3.1 SwinTransformer

In our model's U-shaped structure, we use SwinTransformer Block instead of traditional convolutional neural networks. SwinTransformer [13] is an improvement on the original Transformer [12] structure, as shown in Fig. 1. The Swin-Transformer employs the innovative concept of Windows Multi-Head Self-Attention (W-MSA). During down-sampling, the feature map undergoes partitioning into distinct non-overlapping regions known as "Windows." Multi-Head Self-Attention is then exclusively applied within each of these windows. This approach contrasts with the strategy in the Vision Transformer, where Multi-Head Self-Attention is directly applied across the entire (Global) feature map. This design choice serves the purpose of computational reduction, particularly when dealing with expansive shallow feature maps. Although this reduces computation, it also isolates information transmission between different windows, to address this, the creators of the ST model introduce the innovative notion of Shifted Windows Multi-Head

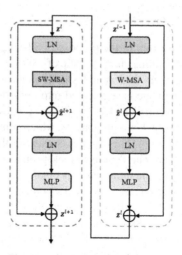

Fig. 1. SwinTransformer structure.

Self-Attention (SW-MSA). This concept aims to streamline computation without compromising the fundamental aspects of convolution. These aspects encompass critical properties such as translation invariance, rotation invariance, and the intricate interplay between receptive field and layer dimensions. Compared to ViT, SwinTransformer greatly reduces the computation complexity and exhibits linear computational complexity in relation to the input image size. SwinTransformer gradually merges image blocks to build hierarchical Transformer as the depth increases. In Fig. 1, the entire process is represented as follows:

$$\hat{z}^l = W - MSA\left(LN\left(z^{l-1}\right)\right) + z^{l-1} \tag{1}$$

$$z^l = MLP\left(LN\left(\hat{z}^l\right)\right) + \hat{z}^l \tag{2}$$

$$zl + 1 = Sw - MSALNzl + zl \tag{3}$$

$$z^{l+1} = MLP\left(LN\left(\hat{z}^{l+1}\right)\right) + \hat{z}^{l+1} \tag{4}$$

In this context, $\hat{z}^l$ and z^l symbolize the outputs from the (S)W-MSA module. MLP denotes a multilayer perceptron comprising two fully connected layers, both utilizing a Gaussian Error Linear Unit (GELU) activation function. The computation of self-attention unfolds as follows:

$$Attention(Q, K, V) = SoftMax(\frac{QK^T}{\sqrt{d}} + B)V \tag{5}$$

In which Q, K, V represent queries, keys, and values, respectively; while "d" signifies the dimension or size of the query and key.

3.2 Network Architecture Overview

Figure 2 illustrates the architecture of the proposed FST-Unet. This model adopts a U-shaped structure, which is a defining characteristic of the U-net architecture. This design encompasses complete symmetry and includes both an encoder and a decoder. In the encoder, the COVID-19 CT image is segmented into non-folding patch of size 4*4 to achieve the feature size of each block as $4 \times 3 \times 48$. The processed patch undergoes three SwinTransformer blocks and patch merging layers, which contribute to feature representation learning and down-sampling. The decoder consists of the SwinTransformer block and the patch expanding layer. The decoder block primarily performs further feature optimization and processing on the input features obtained from the encoder to achieve the goal of semantic segmentation. We propose a symmetric structure in our FST-Unet, and design the full-scale skip connections to connect the extracted context features. The implementation of the full-scale skip connections strategy maximizes the utilization of multi-scale features, combining low-level semantics and high-level semantics from full-scale feature maps, by doing so, the aim is to prevent the degradation of semantic information that often arises from the process of down-sampling. In comparison to the patch merging layer, the patch expanding layer is intricately designed to perform up-sampling, thereby enabling the capture of finer details. This layer facilitates a 2× up-sampling of the feature map, while the last SwinTransformer module further conducts a 4× up-sampling to restore the feature map's resolution to the original input resolution. This sequential process ultimately concludes with pixel-level segmentation prediction.

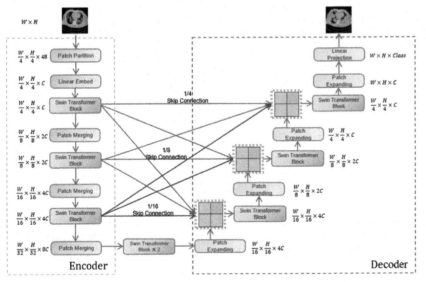

Fig. 2. Network structure, he green box on the left is the Encoder area and the blue box on the right is the Decoder area.

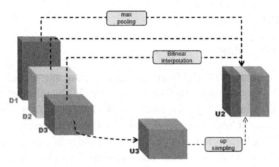

Fig. 3. This diagram depicts the construction process of a complete-scale aggregation feature map for the second decoder layer.

3.3 Full-Scale Skip Connections

Spatial information about lesions is crucial for learning features in medical imaging. In the widely used U-shaped segmentation models, the strategy of skip connections or multi-scale skip connections is used. However, skip connections although effective in preserving and propagating features, may still result in some loss of spatial information during the upsampling and downsampling processes. This loss can impact the precise identification of organ positions and boundaries in medical images. Hence, we devised the full-scale skip connections strategy, aimed at reinforcing interconnections both between the encoder and decoder, and within the decoder subnetwork itself. To better combine the spatial features from the encoder, our model captures shallow and deep features at full-scale and merges them to mitigate the loss of spatial information due to downsampling, we introduced linear layers. These layers maintain the dimension of concatenated features consistent with the dimension of upsampled features. As shown in Fig. 3, full-scale skip connections are constructed by receiving spatial feature maps from encoder layers at different scales directly in each decoder. Unlike traditional skip connections, a set of encoders facilitate the transfer of low-level detailed information from smaller-scale encoder layers to the decoder using skip connections. This information is transmitted to the decoder through non-overlapping max-pooling operations. Conversely, higher-level detailed information is conveyed from larger-scale encoder layers to the decoder by cropping central area information, resulting in feature maps of matching resolution. Within the decoder, patch expanding layers are employed for upsampling, allowing the transmission of high-level semantic information. With four feature maps of identical resolution, we amalgamate shallow and deep semantic information as the input for the subsequent decoder layer.

By using the SwinTransformer structure to capture global information of images, our proposed method can better capture the full-scale information and reduce information loss during downsampling through full-scale skip connections. Furthermore, it enhances the effect of upsampling by obtaining feature information from all scales and improves the model's ability to capture edge features of images for better segmentation results. Experimental results show that full-scale connections can significantly improve image segmentation performance.

4 Experiments

4.1 Experimental Settings

Dataset. Our proposed FST-Unet is an end-to-end trainable model. We verified the effectiveness of the model on the Wuhan dataset. The Wuhan dataset contains CT volumes of 300 patients who tested positive for COVID-19. The images were obtained using a Siemens CT scanner at Wuhan Third Hospital and were segmented into 3 mm, 5 mm, and 10 mm slices. The lesions in the images were manually labeled by seven experienced radiologists, and their annotations were further verified by other radiologists to ensure accuracy. As the experimental model was designed for 2D images, the 3D CT volumes were converted into 2D slices. After preprocessing and threshold screening, a total of 14,743 2D slices were used for training and testing.

Evaluation Criteria. We employed four widely recognized segmentation metrics to assess the quality of the segmentation outcomes: specifically, the Dice similarity coefficient (DSC), Hausdorff Distance (HD), Intersection over Union (IoU), and Average symmetric surface distance (Assd).

Dice and IoU are based on the representation of positive and negative class samples in the confusion matrix, and reflect the area similarity and accuracy of the segmentation results. The closer the values are to 1, the better the results. The formulas for DSC and IoU are shown below.

$$Dice = \frac{2TP}{FP + 2TP + FN} \tag{6}$$

$$IoU = \frac{A \cup B}{A \cap B} \tag{7}$$

The Hausdorff distance quantifies the similarity between two sets of points, offering a formal measurement of their distance. For two distinct point sets, represented as A = {a1,...,ap} and B = {b1,...,bq}, the Hausdorff distance is mathematically defined as in Formula (9). The terms h(A,B) and h(B,A) are accurately delineated by Formulas (10) and (11), respectively.

Assd is a metric that describes the average surface distance between two images, as shown in Formula (11).

$$H(A, B) = max(h(A, B), h(B, A)) \tag{8}$$

$$h(A, B) = max(a \in A)min(b \in B)\|a - b\| \tag{9}$$

$$h(B, A) = max(b \in B)min(a \in A)\|b - a\| \tag{10}$$

$$ASSD = \frac{\sum_{x \in X} min_{y \in Y} d(x, y) + \sum_{y \in Y} min_{x \in X} d(y, x)}{len(X) + len(Y)} \tag{11}$$

Table 1. Values of the four evaluation indicators for the six network models.

Methods	U-net	Unet++	R50 UNet	TransUnet	SwinUnet	FSTUnet
DSC↑	67.96	68.02	67.23	70.81	72.96	**73.87**
HD↓	47.81	44.94	43.11	37.18	**29.68**	31.62
IoU↑	51.47	51.54	50.94	54.81	57.43	**58.57**
Assd↓	14.77	15.06	14.86	9.62	10.28	**8.94**

4.2 Performance Comparison

To assess the segmentation efficacy of our model, we used the Wuhan dataset to train six classical deep network segmentation models, namely U-Net [9], Unet++ [10], R50 U-Net [24], TransUnet [20] SwinUnet [23] and FSTUnet. Similarly, the four metrics in Evaluation Criteria are used to quantify and evaluate the performance of the network model. The assessment metric scores for the six network models are displayed in Table 1. In the Table, larger values for Dice and IoU indicate better segmentation performance, while smaller values for HD and Assd indicate more accurate segmentation. Arrows in the table are used to indicate the trend of the values. An upward arrow suggests that the value should be larger, while a downward arrow suggests that the value should be smaller. From Table 1, we can see that: The model using Transformer as the underlying architecture of the U-shaped network demonstrates superior segmentation performance compared to using CNNs as the underlying architecture. Furthermore, by comparing TransUnet, SwinUnet, and FSTUnet, it can be observed that the combination of SwinTransformer and the U-shaped network achieves better results than using Transformer alone. Among the other five models, FSTUnet outperforms the others in terms of segmentation accuracy, as indicated by higher values in the Dice coefficient, IoU (Intersection over Union), and lower values in the distance metric Assd (Average Symmetric Surface Distance). For the HD (Hausdorff Distance) metric, although FST-Unet did not achieve the best result, it obtained a second-best performance. It was only two points higher than SwinUnet, but both models significantly outperformed the other four segmentation models.

Furthermore, we present some segmentation results of our model in Fig. 4. We conducted a visual analysis of the results using a subset of the test set data. From the figure, it is evident that our model has achieved impressive segmentation results compared to the original labels. It is capable of accurately segmenting small lesion areas, and the boundaries of the segmented lesions appear relatively smooth. This indicates that our model demonstrates strong performance and accuracy in medical image segmentation tasks.

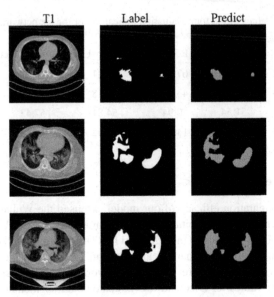

Fig. 4. Visual representations of segmented results from a partial test set are compared with segmentation labels. Within each set of three images, ordered from left to right, are: the original CT image (T1), manual annotations, and the model's predicted segmentations.

4.3 Ablation Study

In order to intuitively and quantitatively demonstrate the effectiveness of full-scale skip connections, we designed comparative experiments using networks trained with conventional skip connections and full-scale skip connections, respectively. In this experiment, the experimental group and the control group were tested on three datasets: Synapse Kidney (L), Synapse Stomach, and the Wuhan COVID-19 dataset, using full-scale skip connections and without full-scale skip connections, respectively. The model results on the test set were evaluated and compared using the Dice similarity coefficient, and the experimental results are shown in Table 2. The models using full-scale skip connections showed better performance on all three datasets.

Table 2. Evaluation results of Dice coefficients using full-scale skip connections and without full-scale skip connections on three datasets.

Methods/Dice	Synapse Kidney(L)	Synapse Stomach	Wuhan Covid-19
Skip Connections	81.31	75.02	71.98
Full Skip Connections	**82.73**	**76.16**	**73.87**

We compared the visual segmentation results using full-scale skip connections and without full-scale skip connections, as shown in Fig. 5. The use of the full-scale skip connections method reduces spatial information loss, resulting in better segmentation performance in small target lesions, and making the segmentation of edges smoother.

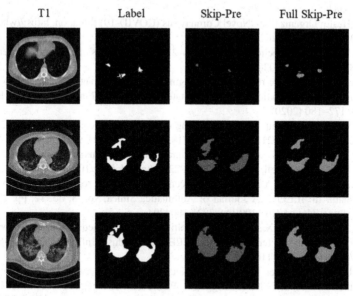

Fig. 5. Some test sets use Full-scale skip connections and do not use Full-scale skip connections to compare the segmentation results with the segmentation label. Each set of four images, arranged from left to right, consists of: the T1 image, manual labels, No Full prediction model results, and Full prediction model results.

5   Conclusions

In this paper, we introduced the FST-Unet, an innovative U-shaped segmentation model grounded in the SwinTransformer architecture and featuring full-scale skip connections. By integrating these connections within the U-Net framework and employing SwinTransformer for both the encoder and decoder, our model exhibited notable enhancements. It effectively captured spatial information within medical images, improved the segmentation of small-scale lesions, and generated smoother edge features for segmented lesions. The experimental findings underscored the competitive performance of our proposed model in the segmentation of COVID-19 CT images. Particularly, it excelled during the testing phase of the Wuhan COVID-19 dataset. However, we also observed limitations in segmenting other body regions using FST-Unet. These shortcomings will be central to our future efforts for refinement and innovation. Our goals include optimizing and expanding the model to enhance segmentation across various body parts. Moreover, we plan to explore alternative approaches to further amplify the model's performance.

Acknowledgments. This work is supported by The Project of Cultivation for Young Top-notch Talents of Beijing Municipal Institutions (BPHR202203046).

References

1. Zhu, N., et al.: A novel coronavirus from patients with pneumonia in China, 2019. New Engl. J. Med. **382**, 727–733 (2020)
2. World Health Organization. Novel Coronavirus (COVID-19) Situation. https://who.sprinklr. com. Accessed 11 Jan 2021
3. Wang, W.L., et al.: Detection of SARS-CoV-2 in different types of clinical specimens. JAMA **323**(18), 1843–1844 (2020)
4. Rubin, G.D., et al.: The role of chest imaging in patient management during the COVID-19 pandemic: a multinational consensus statement from the Fleischner society. Radiology **296**(1), 172–180 (2020)
5. Zhao, W., Jiang, W., Qiu, X.: Deep learning for COVID-19 detection based on CT images. Sci. Rep. **11**, 14353 (2021). https://doi.org/10.1038/s41598-021-93832-2
6. Lu, H., Teng, Y., Li, Y.: Learning latent dynamics for autonomous shape control of deformable object. IEEE Trans. Intell. Transp. Syst. (2022). https://doi.org/10.1109/TITS.2022.3225322
7. Lu, H., Tang, Y., Sun, Y.: DRRS-BC: decentralized routing registration system based on Blockchain. In: IEEE/CAA Journal of Automatica Sinica, vol. 8, no. 12, pp. 1868–1876 (2021). https://doi.org/10.1109/JAS.2021.1004204
8. Lu, H., Wang, T., Xu, X., Wang, T.: Cognitive memory-guided AutoEncoder for effective intrusion detection in internet of things. IEEE Trans. Industr. Inf. **18**(5), 3358–3366 (2022). https://doi.org/10.1109/TII.2021.3102637
9. Ronneberger, O., Fischer, P., Brox, T.: U-Net: convolutional networks for biomedical image segmentation. In: Navab, N., Hornegger, J., Wells, W.M., Frangi, A.F. (eds.) MICCAI 2015. LNCS, vol. 9351, pp. 234–241. Springer, Cham (2015). https://doi.org/10.1007/978-3-319-24574-4_28
10. Zhou, Z., Siddiquee, M.M.R., Tajbakhsh, N., Liang, J.: UNet++: a nested U-Net architecture for medical image segmentation. In: Stoyanov, D., et al. (eds.) Deep Learning in Medical Image Analysis and Multimodal Learning for Clinical Decision Support. DLMIA ML-CDS 2018 2018. Lecture Notes in Computer Science, vol. 11045, pp. 3–11. Springer, Cham (2018). https://doi.org/10.1007/978-3-030-00889-5_1
11. Huang, H., et al.: UNet 3+: a full-scale connected UNet for medical image segmentation. In: IEEE International Conference on Acoustics, Speech and Signal Processing (ICASSP), Barcelona (2020)
12. Fan, D., et al.: Inf-Net: automatic covid-19 lung infection segmentation from CT images. IEEE Trans. Med. Imaging **39**(8), 2626–2637 (2020)
13. Dosovitskiy, A., et al.: An image is worth 16x16 words: transformers for image recognition at scale. arXiv preprint arXiv:2010.11929 (2020)
14. Liu, Z., et al.: Swintransformer: hierarchical vision transformer using shifted windows. CoRR, vol.abs/2103.14030 (2021)
15. Shen, C., et al.: Quantitative computed tomography analysis for stratifying the severity of coronavirus disease 2019. J. Pharm. Anal. **10**(2), 123–129 (2020)
16. Oulefki, A., Agaian, S., Trongtirakul, T., Laouar, A.K.: Automatic COVID-19 lung infected region segmentation and measurement using CT-scans images. Pattern Recogn. **114**, Article No. 107747 (2021)
17. Cao, Y.K., et al.: Longitudinal assessment of COVID-19 using a deep learning-based quantitative CT pipeline: illustration of two cases. Radiol. Cardiothorac. Imaging **2**(2), Article No. e200082 (2020)
18. Huang, L., et al.: Serial quantitative chest CT assessment of COVID-19: deep-learning approach. Radiol. Cardiothorac. Imaging **2**(2), Article No. 200075 (2020)

19. Oktay, O., et al.: Attention U-Net: learning where to look for the pancreas. arXiv preprint arXiv:1804.03999 (2018)
20. Chen, J., et al.: TransUNet: transformers make strong encoders for medical image segmentation. https://arxiv.org/abs/2102.04306.pdf (2021)
21. Yao, C., Hu, M., Li, Q., Zhai, G.: Transclaw U-Net: claw U-Net with transformers for medical image segmentation (2021)
22. Ali, H., Nath, V., Tang, Y., Yang, D., Roth, H., Xu, D.: Swin Unetr: Swin transformers for semantic segmentation of brain tumors in MRI images. arXiv preprint arXiv:2201.01266 (2022)
23. Cao, H. et al.: Swin-Unet: Unet-like pure transformer for medical image segmentation (2021). In: Karlinsky, L., Michaeli, T., Nishino, K. (eds.) Computer Vision – ECCV 2022 Workshops. ECCV 2022. Lecture Notes in Computer Science, vol. 13803, pp. 205–218. Springer, Cham (2023). https://doi.org/10.1007/978-3-031-25066-8_9
24. Jha, D., et al.: ResUNet++: an advanced architecture for medical image segmentation. In: Proceedings of the 2019 IEEE International Symposium on Multimedia (ISM). Piscataway: IEEE, pp. 225–2255 (2019)

Personnel Intrusion Detection in Railway Perimeter with Improved YOLOv7

Zhongda Jin[1], Zhibin Hu[2(✉)], He Wang[1], and Peiyun Li[3]

[1] Sichuan Branch of China Tower, Chengdu 610000, Sichuan, China
`{jinzd,wanghe}@chinatowercom.cn`
[2] University of Electronic Science and Technology of China, Chengdu 611731, Sichuan, China
`zhibinhu920@gmail.com`
[3] Chengdu Koala Uran Technology Company, Chengdu 610000, Sichuan, China
`lipeiyun@yourangroup.com`

Abstract. In the field of intelligent railway security, personnel intrusion within the railway perimeter is a dangerous behavior. However, detection of such personnel intrusion can be unsatisfactory due to various environmental factors and detection distance. Therefore, this article presents a comprehensive analysis of this problem and proposes three strategies to improve the accuracy and robustness of the detection model, which have achieved excellent results in recent times. Firstly, we replace the traditional convolution module in YOLOv7 with the SPD-Conv module, which applies no stride convolution or pooling layers to enhance feature extraction of small objects in the backbone network. Secondly, we introduce the SimAM attention mechanism in the neck network to increase the aggregation network's attention to target features. Thirdly, we create a simple decoupling detection head for this specific single-category detection task. To verify the effectiveness of our proposed method, we created a railway perimeter personnel intrusion detection dataset from both real scenes and simulated events and conducted several comparative experiments. The results demonstrate our method significantly improves detection accuracy, and detects small objects with increased accuracy. Additionally, our method exhibits strong robustness in project field testing.

Keywords: Railway Perimeter · Personnel Intrusion Detection · YOLOv7 · Improvement Strategy

1 Introduction

As an important transportation facility that brings convenience to people's travel and economic development, railway security within its perimeter has received widespread attention. Personnel intrusion within railway perimeter is a common abnormal event in railway security, despite relevant regulations and signage. Such incidents have a great impact on social order and personal safety. Therefore, timely detecting railway perimeter intrusions has significant implications. Due to the extremely long railway route, relying solely on manual monitoring of personnel intrusion is impractical. With the development of intelligent security, some intelligent monitoring systems have been proposed and applied to personnel intrusion tasks in railways [1–3]. As shown in Fig. 1, personnel detection algorithms determine the performance of the entire system in the railway perimeter intrusion detection system process.

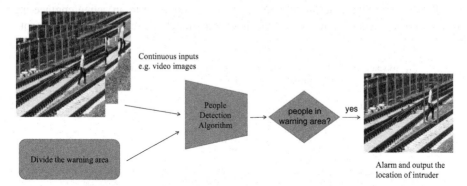

Fig. 1. Schematic diagram of the railway perimeter personnel detection task system process. In continuous monitoring input, warning areas are manually defined, and the personnel detection algorithm is used to determine whether personnel have intruded into the warning areas, thereby triggering an alarm and outputting the location of the intruding personnel.

Most personnel detection algorithms are derived from the field of object detection. With the exploration and analysis of deep learning methods, many model algorithms in the object detection field have been found to be effective and applicable to specific tasks. From the classic RCNN series [4–6] to the recent YOLO series [7, 8], these algorithms have gradually improved in detection accuracy and inference speed, meeting the needs of many specific tasks and even exceeding the detection effect of pure manpower. In the task of personnel detection within railway perimeters, because the task is highly similar to object detection, some methods naturally transfer to this task. However, the personnel detection task within railway perimeters has its own particularities, such as the possibility of small pixel situations in the detection scene and environmental factors caused by weather changes, which will greatly affect the detection accuracy. Therefore, when transferring methods, a design plan should consider these factors and improve the detection accuracy accordingly.

Based on the above observations, we started with the latest YOLOv7 algorithm in object detection, using its current highest detection accuracy and speed as a starting point. We proposed three improvement strategies to enhance the detection accuracy after transfer to personnel detection within railways. As shown in Fig. 2, we used the original YOLOv7 as the basic model and replaced the convolution module in the backbone with the SPD-Conv module [9]. We added the SimAM [10] attention mechanism in the Neck and used a simple decoupled detection head to obtain our railway personnel detection model.

Our contributions are presented as follows:

We transferred the YOLOv7 algorithm model to the task of detecting personnel intrusion within railway perimeters and designed three strategies to improve the model for task-specific characteristics, further enhancing detection accuracy.

We collected data and created a dataset for railway personnel intrusion and conducted experiments on this dataset to demonstrate the effectiveness of our proposed model. We also designed ablation experiments to verify the effectiveness of each improvement strategy.

To further validate the model's robustness, we applied it to an actual engineering project to test the detection effect of the algorithm model in a real-world environment.

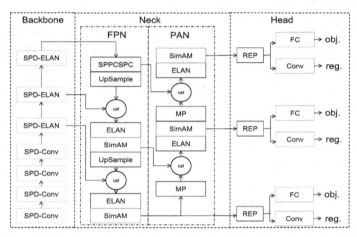

Fig. 2. The overall framework diagram of our railway perimeter personnel intrusion detection model. The overall structure and basic module are based on the YOLOv7 model (the black box in the figure), and three improvement strategies are proposed to adapt to the railway perimeter personnel intrusion task (the colored box in the figure). Specifically, in the backbone network, the SPD-Conv without stride convolution or pooling layer are used instead of the traditional convolution module (the yellow box in the figure); in the neck structure, the attention module SimAM is added after the aggregation network (the red box in the figure); in the head network, the simple decoupling detection head is used for single-category object confidence and localization judgment (the blue box in the figure). (Color figure online)

In the following sections of the paper, we first discuss the classical methods and recent advancements in object detection and railway perimeter personnel intrusion detection in the related work section. Then, in the methods section, we begin by revisiting the latest methods of object detection, which is our baseline method, the YOLOv7 algorithm model. Subsequently, we present three improvement strategies for the task of railway perimeter personnel intrusion detection. In the experimental section, we substantiate the effectiveness of our proposed strategies through a significant number of comparative experiments and ablation experiment results. Finally, in the conclusion section, we provide a summary of our paper and discuss future work.

2 Related Work

2.1 Object Detection

The Object detection is a critical task in computer vision. It involves predicting the bounding box coordinates and classification of each object of interest [11]. Currently, object detection approaches based on deep convolutional networks are divided into one-stage and two-stage methods. In the two-stage methods, a separate framework is used to identify region proposals, and such proposals are usually classified into known categories. The earliest model of this kind was the R-CNN [12], which utilized selective search [13] to choose its region proposals. Nonetheless, the inference speed of this model was slow. To address this issue, the same authors proposed the Fast-RCNN [4], which used a feature mapping strategy to accelerate inference speed. Subsequently, Ren et al. [5] developed the region proposal network (RPN) to identify object regions that are more likely to appear in the image, hence improving the inference speed. They named the resulting model Faster-RCNN. For one-stage methods, each position is classified as a background or target cate-gory. Such methods are usually quicker than the two-stage models, but with poorer prediction performance than their corresponding two-stage models [14]. Among the earliest models to accurately balance accuracy and speed was the You Only Look Once (YOLO) detector [7]. It divides the image into grid cells and predicts whether objects exist in each cell. Several versions of YOLO have been developed and optimized to narrow the mAP performance gap with two-stage models while maintaining real-time performance [15].

2.2 Intrusion Detection for Railway

Recently, many machine learning methods have been applied to intelligent transportation security, multiple approaches have been proposed and implemented to detect intrusions on railways. Li et al. [31] proposed a new feature extraction network for segmentation by adding an encoder-decoder structure, which improves the performance of distinguishing different objects in intelligent transportation system scenes. Li et al. [1] integrated multi-scale images with background subtraction and suggested a dynamic candidate region method based on automatic detection for overseeing foreign objects on railways. Sun et al. [3] used a Gaussian mixture model (GMM) and YOLOv3 detection algorithm to identify images with intrusion targets using GMM and then conducted a secondary detection and recognition of intrusion targets using the YOLOv3 algorithm. Cao et al. [16] proposed a monitoring technique that integrates dynamic intrusion regions and lightweight neural networks to locate intrusions using a dynamic intrusion positioning algorithm, followed by event classification using a classification network. Liu et al. [17] combined support vector machines and radial basis function neural networks to suggest classification for discriminating between various intrusion event types. Cai et al. [18] carried out the detection process based on distributed acoustic sensing, employing support vector machines as classifiers to categorize the three types of trains on railways.

3 Proposed Methodology

3.1 SPD-Conv Structure

In the task of personnel intrusion detection within the railway perimeter, there is often a demand for small object detection due to the distance of the target personnel. However, the detection accuracy of small objects by general-purpose object detection models still needs to be improved. Many studies have been conducted to enhance the detection accuracy of small objects [20–22], but some methods are not applicable to real-time detection due to their large time cost. We use the SPD-Conv [9] method with lower time cost to improve the detection accuracy of intruders at a long distance. The main idea is as follows: since the stride convolution and pooling layers may lose the learnable features of small pixels or low-resolution targets, leading to a decrease in detection accuracy, a structure without a stride convolution or pooling layer is proposed to replace the traditional convolution module. The main process is shown in Fig. 3. For the three-dimensional feature map, it is first decomposed into feature subgraphs alternately according to the two-dimensional spatial position, and then the feature subgraphs are concatenated in the channel dimension, and finally the output dimension number is changed through point-wise convolution to achieve down-sampling and dimension change in the traditional convolution module.

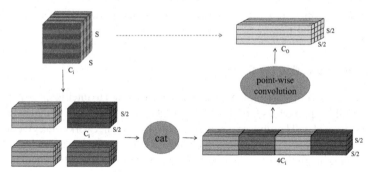

Fig. 3. The schematic diagram of the SPD-Conv method for implementing down-sampling by a factor of 2. The dashed line represents the input-output in a traditional convolution module, while the solid line represents the same structure achieved using the SPD-Conv method.

3.2 Attention Mechanism

Numerous studies have shown that adding attention modules to models can improve the model's ability to focus on the target and its useful contextual information [23–25], thereby integrating more effective features for subsequent specific tasks. YOLOv7 [19] proposes an efficient feature aggregation network for fusing features of different scales, but in the task of railway perimeter intrusion detection, we need to pay more attention to the features of the target personnel. Therefore, we combine the SimAM [10] attention mechanism with ELAN for feature fusion. For the three-dimensional feature map of C * H * W in convolutional networks, unlike the consideration of one-dimensional channel attention or two-dimensional spatial attention alone, SimAM proposes an attention module that directly calculates the three-dimensional weights, allowing the model to learn more discriminative features. SimAM refers to mature neural science theories and designs an energy function to evaluate the importance of each neuron. The energy function is as follows:

$$e_t(w_t, b_t, y, x_i) = \frac{1}{M-1} \sum_{i=1}^{M-1} (-1 - (w_i x_i + b_t))^2 + (1 - (w_t t + b_t))^2 + \lambda w_t^2 \tag{1}$$

where t and x_i denote the target neuron and other neurons, respectively, on a single channel of the input features X. Here, i represents the index of the spatial dimension, and M = H * W represents the total number of neurons on this channel.

By solving the closed-form analytical solution of the energy function, the formula for calculating the neuron with the minimum energy is as follows:

$$e_t^* = \frac{4(\hat{\sigma}^2 + \lambda)}{(t - \hat{\mu})^2 + 2\hat{\sigma}^2 + 2\lambda} \tag{2}$$

where $\hat{u} = \frac{1}{M} \sum_{i=1}^{M} x_i$ and $\hat{\sigma}^2 = \frac{1}{M} \sum_{i=1}^{M} (x_i - \hat{\mu})^2$ are the mean and variance of all neurons.

Finally, use the scaling operator to refine the features, as shown in the following formula:

$$\tilde{X} = sigmoid \left(\frac{1}{E} \right) \odot X \tag{3}$$

where E groups all e_t^* across channel and spatial dimensions, monofonic function sigmoid is added to restrict too large value in E.

3.3 Simple Decoupled Head for Single Class Detection

Object detection requires attention not only on object localization accuracy but also on classification. In addition, recent studies have demonstrated that these two subtasks cannot be generalized. Song et al. [26] noted that the focus of the classification and localization subtasks in object detection varies. Classification is focused on object texture content, whereas localization is concerned with object edge information. Accordingly, it is necessary to separately calculate these two subtasks to avoid spatial displacement and other issues. YOLOX [15] introduced decoupled detection heads to independently analyze classification and detection tasks. Employing the traditional decoupled detection head directly can lead to excessive redundant computations, which is unsuitable for this task that necessitates both accuracy and real-time processing. Based on the preceding analysis, a simple decoupled detection head for detecting a single category is proposed in this study. In contrast to the coupled detection head in YOLOv7, which calculates position, classification, and confidence score simultaneously using a single branch, or to the YOLOX decoupled detection head, which employs two branches of identical sizes for computing the object category and position and confidence scores, two different sized branches were designed in this study, where one calculated position and the other calculated confidence score. Figure 4 illustrates the network architecture. As our objective is focused on detecting a single category, we contend that the confidence score can also classify object categories and backgrounds to some extent.

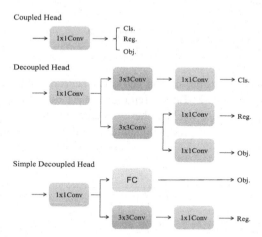

Fig. 4. Schematic diagram of different detection heads. 1×1Conv and 3×3Conv represent convolutional layers with kernel sizes of 1 and 3, respectively. FC represents fully connected layer, and Cls, Reg, and Obj represent classification, localization, and confidence respectively.

3.4 Overall Objective

Based on the above design and analysis, the overall objective is to minimize the sum of confidence loss and localization loss. We use BCELoss and CIoU[27] to calculate these two types of losses, and set hyperparameters to balance their relative importance. The calculation formula is shown as follows:

$$L_{obj} = o * \ln(\hat{c}) - (1 - o) * \ln(1 - \hat{c}) \tag{4}$$

$$L_{reg} = 1 - \left(IoU - \frac{d_c^2}{d_r^2} \right) - \left(\frac{v^2}{(1 - IoU) + v} \right) \tag{5}$$

$$L_{total} = \sum (\lambda L_{obj} + (1 - \lambda) L_{reg}) \tag{6}$$

where L_{obj}, L_{reg}, and L_{total} are the confidence loss, localization loss and total loss of the model, λ is the hyperparameter that balance the importance of confidence and localization. o represents the intersection-over-union (IoU) of the predicted object box and the ground-truth bounding box, $\hat{c}$ is the predicted confidence obtained through the sigmoid function. d_c represents the distance between the center points of the predicted box and the ground-truth box, d_r represents the diagonal length of the minimum bounding rectangle that contains the predicted and ground truth boxes. v is a parameter that measures the consistency of the aspect ratio between predicted boxes and ground-truth boxes.

4 Experiments

4.1 Datasets and Setup

Datasets. We collected and compiled a dataset to test the effectiveness of our proposed approach. The dataset included two methods of collecting images: simulated intrusion events and genuine railway perimeter personnel intrusion. However, due to the limited data available from real-life settings, we relied primarily on simulating intrusion events. In these simulations, we selected five typical railway testing sections, and chose single or multiple people to simulate events under different lighting, weather, and clothing conditions as well as different camera-to-event distances. Our dataset comprised a total of 1000 data samples collected under various scenarios. We standardized our data into the standard input size of 640 × 640 RGB images through data preprocessing. We used the LabelImg annotation tool to label each intrusion personnel in every image, obtaining annotation boxes of 2400 different sizes for intrusion personnel. We incorporated a reasonable proportion of small objects (size < 48*48 pixels), which closely resembled realistic scenarios at 40%. We used 10% of all the images as the test set, selecting them randomly while the remaining images were utilized as the training set. Using the K-fold cross-validation method, we tuned our hyperparameters on the training set.

Implementation Details. Our experiment is implemented under Linux Ubuntu 18.04.3 LTS operating system, and the PyTorch deep learning framework was used to implement the model architecture. During training, four GeForce RTX 2080Ti were used for parallel accelerated computing, and the inference speed and accuracy of a single GeForce RTX 2080Ti were evaluated during inference. The batch size for each round of iteration was set to 64 during model training, resulting in 16 images per GPU. And we refer to previous research and assess model performance using the Average Precision (AP) metric.

4.2 Main Results

The training process was composed of 300 iterations, with the first 50 iterations utilizing a linear warm-up strategy. The training process monitored the changes in model loss and AP_{50}, and the result shows that the model has converged by the 260th iteration, with its AP_{50} surpassing 90%. The improved YOLOv7 network model proposed in this article has demonstrated excellent performance during the training stage. After completing the model training, we performed model inference on test set and assessed its AP metrics. We additionally used frames per second (FPS) to evaluate its inference speed, and compared our model to other models trained using the same methodology in the object detection domain for a comparative analysis. As shown in Table 1, our model achieved the highest accuracy at a relatively high inference speed. And for the task of detecting railway personnel intrusion, we can forsake some inference speed to increase AP metrics, which is more crucial for this unique task. This result highlights the suitability of our model for this task.

Table 1. Comparison results of our method and the compared approaches. FPS is used to evaluate the detection speed, and AP metrics evaluate the detection accuracy under different settings.

Method	FPS	AP_{50}	AP_S	AP_S	AP_M	AP_L
F-RCNN-R101 [28]	20	86.1%	80.4%	83.7%	86.4%	88.2%
YOLOX-S [15]	102	80.2%	76.7%	77.6%	80.6%	82.4%
YOLOv5-M [29]	122	83.4%	79.6%	80.1%	83.7%	86.4%
PPYOLOE-M [30]	123	85.9%	81.2%	82.8%	86.2%	88.7%
YOLOv7 [19]	161	88.6%	83.5%	85.0%	89.6%	91.2%
Ours	146	90.7%	85.2%	88.4%	91.1%	92.6%

4.3 Ablation Studies

Effect of the SPD-Conv Module in Backbone. The backbone network extracts useful features from input images. However, stride convolution and pooling operations in the general convolutional module automatically ignore some fine-grained features, which ultimately impacts the detection accuracy of small objects. Ablation experiments were conducted to evaluate SPD-Convolution module's efficacy in replacing the traditional convolution module of the backbone network. This module has been designed to retain fine-grained features and improve the accuracy of small object detection. We sequentially replaced the traditional convolution modules in the first four convolutional layers of the backbone network, in the Extended and Efficient Layer Aggregation Network (ELAN), and in the entire backbone network. The impact of replacement on the inference speed (FPS) and average precision using the IOU threshold of 0.5 were compared, as shown in Table 2. The replacement of the traditional convolution module with the SPD-Convolution module does not lead to any additional time overhead. Furthermore, it has significantly improved the average precision AP_S, primarily for small objects.

Table 2. Experimental results of different alternatives in the backbone. Conv-only means to replace only the first four convolutional layers, and ELAN-only means to replace only the convolution in the ELAN module.

Model	FPS	AP_{50}	AP_S	AP_M	AP_L
Base (YOLOv7)	161	88.6%	85.0%	89.6%	91.2%
Conv-only	159	89.5%	87.4%	89.8%	91.3%
ELAN-only	159	89.0%	86.1%	89.7%	91.2%
Both	157	89.7%	87.7%	90.1%	91.3%

Effect of the Use and Position of SimAM. As previously mentioned, the incorporation of the SimAM attention module allows the model to focus on the target in the image and include contextual information from the target layer, thereby improving detection accuracy. However, incorporating attention modules leads to increased model complexity and longer inference time. To explore the speed-time balance in this improvement strategy, we designed ablation experiments to explore the impact of the SimAM attention module addition in the neck and backbone network, and in both parts, and evaluated their inference speed, and average precision AP_{50} and AP_{75}. As shown in Table 3, it can be seen that the accuracy gain per time is highest when only the attention module is added to the neck, which may be due to the neck mainly responsible for aggregating and refining the features extracted by the backbone.

Table 3. Experiments under different settings of the attention module SimAM.

Model	FPS	AP_{50}	AP_{75}
Base (YOLOv7)	161	88.6%	83.5%
Neck-only	151	89.7%	84.4%
Backbone-only	153	89.5%	84.3%
Both	145	89.8%	84.4%

4.4 Test in Real-World

The dataset utilized in this article includes daytime and nighttime footage, diverse weather conditions, and intricate background interference, which theoretically greatly enhances the robustness of the model, ensuring that the model can perform stable and reliable detection under various circumstances. However, practice is the only criterion for testing truth, and high-precision detection of railway personnel intrusion in real scenarios is our ultimate goal. We applied the algorithm model proposed in this article to specific project processes and conducted field tests in conjunction with the entire railway perimeter personnel detection system. In most of the field tests, our model can perform real-time monitoring and ensure an accuracy rate of over 90%, further proving the effectiveness of our model. Figure 5 shows some visual detection results in real scenarios.

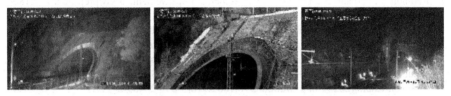

Fig. 5. Visualization detection effect of our model in real application scenarios. Red box is the position of the intruder detected by the model. Irrelevant project information has been masked. (Color figure online)

5 Conclusions

In this study, we are dedicated to addressing the challenging task of detecting intruders around railways. Through comprehensive analysis, we propose three effective strategies to enhance the accuracy and robustness of the YOLOv7 detection model. Extensive experiments demonstrate the effectiveness of our proposed methods in improving precision. It is noteworthy that our approach exhibits significant improvement in detecting small objects, which aligns better with the practical task requirements of railway perimeter personnel detection. Furthermore, our method demonstrates strong robustness in project field tests, further emphasizing its practicality and enormous potential for real-world applications. Future research can focus on balancing detection speed and accuracy, further optimizing and expanding these methods to meet the evolving needs of intelligent railway security, and exploring similar challenges in other domains.

References

1. Li, C., Xie, Z., Qin, Y., Jia, L., Chen, Q.: A multi-scale image and dynamic candidate region-based automatic detection of foreign targets intruding the railway perimeter. Measurement **185**, 109853 (2021)
2. Sun, Y., Xie, Z., Qin, Y., Chuan, L., Wu, Z.: Image detection of foreign body intrusion in railway perimeter based on dual recognition method. In: Rizzo, P., Milazzo, A. (eds.) European Workshop on Structural Health Monitoring. EWSHM 2020. Lecture Notes in Civil Engineering, vol. 128, pp. 645–654. Springer, Cham (2021). https://doi.org/10.1007/978-3-030-64908-1_60
3. Pan, H., Li, Y., Wang, H., Tian, X.: Railway obstacle intrusion detection based on convolution neural network multitask learning. Electronics **11**(17), 2697 (2022)
4. Girshick, R.: Fast R-CNN. In: Proceedings of the IEEE International Conference on Computer Vision (2015)
5. Ren, S., He, K., Girshick, R., Sun, J.: Faster R-CNN: towards real-time object detection with region proposal networks. In: Advances in Neural Information Processing Systems, vol. 28 (2015)
6. He, K., Gkioxari, G., Dollár, P., Girshick, R.: Mask R-CNN. In: Proceedings of the IEEE International Conference on Computer Vision (2017)
7. Redmon, J., Divvala, S., Girshick, R., Farhadi, A.: You only look once: unified, real-time object detection. In: Proceedings of the IEEE Conference on Computer Vision and Pattern Recognition (2016)
8. Redmon, J., Farhadi, A.: YOLOv3: an incremental improvement. arXiv preprint arXiv:1804.02767 (2018)
9. Sunkara, R., Luo, T.: No more strided convolutions or pooling: a new CNN building block for low-resolution images and small objects. In: Amini, MR., Canu, S., Fischer, A., Guns, T., Kralj Novak, P., Tsoumakas, G. (eds.) Machine Learning and Knowledge Discovery in Databases. ECML PKDD 2022. Lecture Notes in Computer Science, vol. 13715, pp. 443–459. Springer, Cham (2023). https://doi.org/10.1007/978-3-031-26409-2_27
10. Yang, L., Zhang, R.Y., Li, L., Xie, X.: SimAM: a simple, parameter-free attention module for convolutional neural networks. In: International Conference on Machine Learning. PMLR (2021)
11. Menezes, A.G., de Moura, G., Alves, C., de Carvalho, A.C.: Continual object detection: a review of definitions, strategies, and challenges. Neural Networks (2023)

12. Girshick, R., Donahue, J., Darrell, T., Malik, J.: Rich feature hierarchies for accurate object detection and semantic segmentation. In: Proceedings of the IEEE Conference on Computer Vision and Pattern Recognition (2014)

13. Uijlings, J.R., Van De Sande, K.E., Gevers, T., Smeulders, A.W.: Selective search for object recognition. Int. J. Comput. Vis. **104**, 154–171 (2013)

14. Javed, K., White, M.: Meta-learning representations for continual learning. In: Advances in Neural Information Processing Systems, vol. 32 (2019)

15. Ge, Z., Liu, S., Wang, F., Li, Z., Sun, J.: YOLOX: exceeding yolo series in 2021. arXiv preprint arXiv:2107.08430 (2021)

16. Cao, Z., et al.: An effective railway intrusion detection method using dynamic intrusion region and lightweight neural network. Measurement **191**, 110564 (2022)

17. Liu, K., et al.: A combined events recognition scheme using hybrid features in distributed optical fiber vibration sensing system. IEEE Access **7**, 105609–105616 (2019)

18. Cai, Y., Xu, T., Ma, J., Yan, W.: Train detection and classification using distributed fiber-optic acoustic sensing. Interpretation **9**(4) SJ13–SJ22 (2021)

19. Wang, C.Y., Bochkovskiy, A., Liao, H.Y.M.: YOLOv7: trainable bag-of-freebies sets new state-of-the-art for real-time object detectors. In: Proceedings of the IEEE/CVF Conference on Computer Vision and Pattern Recognition (2023)

20. Li, J., Liang, X., Wei, Y., Xu, T., Feng, J., Yan, S: Perceptual generative adversarial networks for small object detection. In: Proceedings of the IEEE Conference on Computer Vision and Pattern Recognition (2017)

21. Liu, M., Wang, X., Zhou, A., Fu, X., Ma, Y., Piao, C.: UAV-YOLO: small object detection on unmanned aerial vehicle perspective. Sensors **20**(8), 2238 (2020)

22. Benjumea, A., Teeti, I., Cuzzolin, F., Bradley, A.: YOLO-Z: Improving small object detection in YOLOv5 for autonomous vehicles. arXiv preprint arXiv:2112.11798 (2021)

23. Niu, Z., Zhong, G., Hui, Y.: A review on the attention mechanism of deep learning. Neurocomputing **452**, 48–62 (2021)

24. Guo, M.H., et al.: Attention mechanisms in computer vision: a survey. Comput. Vis. Media **8**(3), 331–368 (2022)

25. Yang, X.: An overview of the attention mechanisms in computer vision. In: Journal of Physics: Conference Series, vol. 1693. no. 1. IOP Publishing (2020)

26. Song, G., Liu, Y., Wang, X.: Revisiting the sibling head in object detector. In: Proceedings of the IEEE/CVF Conference on Computer Vision and Pattern Recognition (2020)

27. Zheng, Z., Wang, P., Liu, W., Li, J., Ye, R., Ren, D.: Distance-IoU loss: faster and better learning for bounding box regression. In: Proceedings of the AAAI Conference on Artificial Intelligence, vol. 34. No. 07 (2020)

28. Carion, N., Massa, F., Synnaeve, G., Usunier, N., Kirillov, A., Zagoruyko, S.: End-to-end object detection with transformers. In: Vedaldi, A., Bischof, H., Brox, T., Frahm, J.-M. (eds.) ECCV 2020. LNCS, vol. 12346, pp. 213–229. Springer, Cham (2020). https://doi.org/10.1007/978-3-030-58452-8_13

29. Jocher, G.: YOLOv5 release v6.1 (2022). https://github.com/ultralytics/yolov5/releases/tag/v6.1

30. Xu, S, et al.: PP-YOLOE: an evolved version of YOLO. arXiv preprint arXiv:2203.16250 (2022)

31. Li, Y., Cai, J., Zhou, Q., Lu, H.: Joint semantic-instance segmentation method for intelligent transportation system. IEEE Trans. Intell. Transp. Syst. (2022)

32. Lu, H., Wang, T., Xu, X., Wang, T.: Cognitive memory-guided autoencoder for effective intrusion detection in internet of things. IEEE Trans. Ind. Inform. **18**(5), 3358–3366 (2021)

Research on Watermark Embedding of Fax Channel Images Based on U-Net Network

Chaoen Xiao$^{(\boxtimes)}$, Ruiling Luo, Xin Jin, Jianxin Wang, Lei Zhang,
and Yu Wang

Beijing Electronic Science and Technology Institute, No. 7, Fufeng Street,
Fengtai District, Beijing, China
xcecd@qq.com

Abstract. This paper introduces a novel watermarking algorithm based on the U-Net Network to manage and trace the source of fax document leaks. The goal is to enable the embedding and extraction of watermark information in fax text images. To adapt the U-Net structure to the unique characteristics of text images transmitted through fax channels and cross-media channels, we have enhanced it. During joint training of the encoder and decoder, we have incorporated several functions, including the introduction of Gaussian noise, JPEG compression, motion and bokeh blur, and shot correction. These enhancements aim to improve both the visual quality of the images and the accuracy and robustness of watermark extraction. The results demonstrate that this approach achieves an image similarity of 0.977 and an image signal-to-noise ratio of 34.96. These outcomes surpass those of three other image watermarking algorithms in terms of image visual quality, watermark embedding capacity, and robustness.

Keywords: Image Watermarking · Cross-media Transmission · U-Net Networks · Deep Learning

1 Introduction

Due to advancements in network technology, the way people communicate and share information has evolved from traditional mail and telephone calls to modern Internet transmission. While information exchange has become increasingly convenient, the government and military still require high levels of confidentiality. In this context, fax remains an indispensable means of data transmission due to its secure nature.

Fax involves the conversion of still images on paper, such as text, diagrams, and photographs, into electrical signals through scanning and photoelectric conversion. These signals are then transmitted to the destination through various channels. At the receiving end, a series of inverse conversion processes recreates a copy of the original document. However, the process of sending and receiving fax text images carries a risk of information leakage, posing a security threat. Therefore, it is essential to control and trace the source of fax text image leaks.

H. Lu and J. Cai (Eds.): ISAIR 2023, CCIS 1998, pp. 250–261, 2024.
https://doi.org/10.1007/978-981-99-9109-9_25

In fax communication, all information must be converted into a format suitable for transmission via paper before it can be sent using a fax machine. To protect fax text images, researchers have explored text image watermarking techniques. Most of these techniques are designed for text images transmitted over digital channels, making it challenging to track and trace printed text images. This paper focuses on scanned and printed text images produced by fax machines, aiming to establish tracking and traceability measures to safeguard text images. Text watermarking algorithms commonly fall into one of four categories.

Text Watermarking Algorithm Based on Document Structure [1]. This method primarily focuses on fine-tuning the character structure of text to embed watermarks. This involves adjusting elements like word spacing, line spacing, or adding spaces in various ways. Watermark information for "1" is encoded by modifying the line or word spacing, while no adjustments are made for "0". When the changes in spacing are subtle, they become difficult for the human eye to discern. However, this approach has limitations such as a small embedding capacity, noticeable visual effects from spacing adjustments, reduced robustness, and suitability mainly for digital channel transmission. It is not effective in resisting changes in spacing caused by variations in shooting angles.

Binary Image-Based Text Image Watermarking Methods [2]. This method is designed for black and white binary text images, or it begins by converting text into binary text images for watermark embedding. It achieves this by altering the black and white pixel points in the image. However, modifying these pixel points results in uneven stroke boundaries, which in turn diminishes the visual quality of the text image. Furthermore, it can cause distortion in the original image when it's printed or displayed on screens using cross-media methods. As a consequence, successful watermark extraction becomes challenging with this approach.

Text Image Watermarking Methods Based on Character Geometric Features [3]. This method primarily accomplishes watermark embedding by altering the geometric characteristics of characters. This includes modifying aspects like stroke positioning, character brightness, and character topology. While this approach offers robustness, it has certain drawbacks when applied to Chinese text. Changes in the geometric features of Chinese characters are more visually apparent, and implementing this method typically requires manual adjustment of character geometry. Given the vast number of Chinese characters, this approach can result in a substantial workload in practical applications.

Text Watermarking Methods Based on Underlining [4]. This method involves incorporating an additional underline layer into the text image, with the watermark information concealed within the underline. It is suitable for scenarios involving printing and scanning and offers a relatively high embedding capacity. However, the effectiveness of this approach varies depending on whether the text image is in color or black and white binary format. In color images, it provides a better hiding effect for the underline, while in black and white binary text, the underline tends to be more noticeable. Additionally, successful watermark extraction using this method demands high-quality printing, increased ink consumption, and elevated printing costs.

This paper addresses the need for traceability in faxed text images. It achieves this by utilizing a fully convolutional neural network known as the U-net Network to add watermarks to text images before transmission. Each department assigns a code name to the watermark, which is then encoded and embedded within the text image. The embedded code watermark can be extracted from either the electronic text or a paper version of the text by capturing an image of the screen on the receiving end, thus enabling traceability of the text image.

The key contributions of this work are as follows:

- A watermarking model specifically designed for single-channel black-and-white text images in the context of faxing is proposed. This model is based on the fully convolutional neural network, U-net. The training dataset comprises single-channel Chinese text images, and the watermark is defined as a predetermined group of watermarks.
- A correlated noise perturbation scheme is developed to replicate the impact of fax transmission on text images. This scheme introduces various functions, including Gaussian noise, JPEG compression, motion and bokeh blur, and shot correction, to enhance the robustness of watermark extraction.
- The paper conducts experimental verification to assess the visual quality and robustness of images after watermark insertion. It also demonstrates the effectiveness of the proposed approach for watermark extraction from text images after they have been printed and photographed using fax machines.

2   Network Architecture

The U-net network [5,6] based watermark traceability scheme for fax single-channel text images consists of three stages. The first stage is the generation of the watermark, the watermark code is generated based on the required watermark information; the second stage is the watermark embedding stage, where the information of the watermark is combined with the text image using the U-net network, and the image and the information of watermark are combined and passed through the encoder to generate the watermarked images [7]; the third stage is the watermark extraction stage, where the image is printed and photographed after cross-media transmission and then enters the decoder, which decodes the noise-added The third stage is the watermark extraction stage, where the image enters the decoder after being printed and photographed after cross-media transmission. The watermark traceability process for text images is shown in Fig. 1.

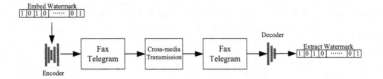

Fig. 1. Text image watermarking traceability process.

2.1 Watermark Embedding and Extraction Network

In the watermark embedding stage [8], the input is a 400×400 black and white binary text image, and the embedded watermark information is represented as an n-bit binary string, which forms a $5 \times 5 \times 512$ tensor through a fully connected layer. The watermark information is added after five downsamples, and the watermark information is upsampled to generate a tensor of the same size as the image downsample, stitched together, and then upsampled back to obtain the watermark information image, as shown in Fig. 2. The watermarked image is obtained by stitching the watermarked information image with the original image, and the loss between the watermarked image and the original input image is minimized using adversarial network learning.

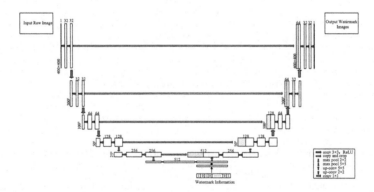

Fig. 2. Improving U-Net watermark embedding Network.

2.2 Watermark Extraction Network

The decoding network is shown in Fig. 3 The image entering the decoder is a $400 \times 400 \times 1$ tensor after noise scrambling, which is convolved three times with a convolution step of 2 to obtain a tensor of size $50 \times 50 \times 128$, which enters the transition layer. The multidimensional tensor is one-dimensionalized at the transition layer, and the transformed image is passed through a series of convolutions and a sigmoid activation function to produce a final output of the same length as the message, using cross-entropy loss supervised training, which requires a loss of information about the gap between the target and the predicted value [9,10].

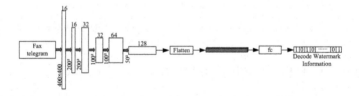

Fig. 3. Decoder Network.

2.3 Cross-Media Channel Transmission Robustness Training

To enable accurate extraction of the watermark after fax transmission against these perturbing changes, a noise layer is added to the network, as shown in Fig. 4.

Fig. 4. Robustness training process.

Noise Disturbance Training. Gaussian noise arises from causes including uneven brightness of the image sensor during capture, the circuit components' noise and interactions, etc., in line with the analog distortion of the channel transmission. Gaussian noise is used to add noise scrambling to text images, adding a noise tensor that conforms to the Gaussian distribution to the target tensor. If the standard deviation of the noise perturbation used is too large, making the image distortion severe, the loss in the model training process can never be minimized and will lead to model training failure. The Gaussian perturbation range used in the model training process is $\sigma \sim U[0,0.02]$.

JPEG Image Compression Training. Images captured by cameras are usually stored in lossy formats such as JPEG, and the effect of this compression on the image is unavoidable, so this paper uses the method in Shin [11] to approximate the quantization step near zero using a segmentation function.

Motion and Bokeh Blur Training. Inaccurate focusing during the photography process may lead to blurred images. To simulate out-of-focus, this paper introduces a Gaussian fuzzy kernel, which divides the image by center and lets the weight value corresponding to each pixel point change as their distance to the center varies, but too large a fuzzy kernel can lead to increased computation, and reduced performance during model training. The standard deviation is chosen to be sampled randomly between 1–3 pixels.

The linear blur kernel is a mathematical representation of the relative motion between the imaging device and the target. The blur kernel for uniform linear motion is a blur kernel of length M at a certain angle to the horizontal. To simulate motion blur, a random angle is sampled during model training and a linear blur kernel of width between 3 and 7 pixels is generated.

Loss Function Settings. To evaluate the difference between the original image and the watermarked image in the image, a loss function is introduced to evaluate the difference between the two images and the difference between the encoded and decoded information. The L_2 parametric loss function minimises the sum of squares S of the difference between the estimated value $f(x_i)$ and the target value Y_i, and regularises the L_2 residuals to obtain L_R as the edge loss function of the image. The LPIPS [9] loss is extracted from features in the image layer and unit-specified in the channel dimension, computed as an average over space, and summed by channel. As this paper uses a single-channel image input, only one channel needs to be computed. The evaluation loss between the added watermarked image and the original image is referred to as the L_C, and the cross-entropy information loss L_M is used to represent the difference between the extracted watermarked information and the original watermarked information. The total loss in the training process is the weighted sum of the four loss components mentioned above, i.e.:

$$L = \lambda_R L_R + \lambda_P L_P + \lambda_C L_C + \lambda_M L_M \qquad (1)$$

When training the network, the loss weights L_R, L_P and L_C are all initially set to zero and then increased linearly to enable decoder training to achieve a high accuracy rate. L_M is set to 1 to allow for a 1-bit loss of information during model training and to prevent overfitting.

3   Results and Analysis

3.1   Experimental Settings

In this paper, the training set of DocImgCN [12,13] was randomly selected to be 25,000 text images, and 100 each from the validation and test sets. In the experiments, the input image size is 400 × 400 pixels, and the watermark is an 8-group 100-bit binary string randomly generated in advance, with one group of watermarks randomly selected in each training round. In this paper, a computer network-based fax software was used to test the effect of watermark extraction, and the experimental communication process is shown in Fig. 5 [14].

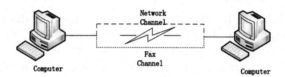

Fig. 5. Experimental communication process.

3.2 Experimental Results

Image Visual Quality Assessment. The means in this paper are compared with several image watermarking methods to evaluate visual quality of images, including literature [15], literature [9] and literature [16], where literature [17] and literature [9] are deep learning network based image watermarking algorithms and literature [16] is a feature point based image watermark embedding algorithm, both embedded with 100 bits of watermark information. The original image without watermark embedding shows in Fig. 6.

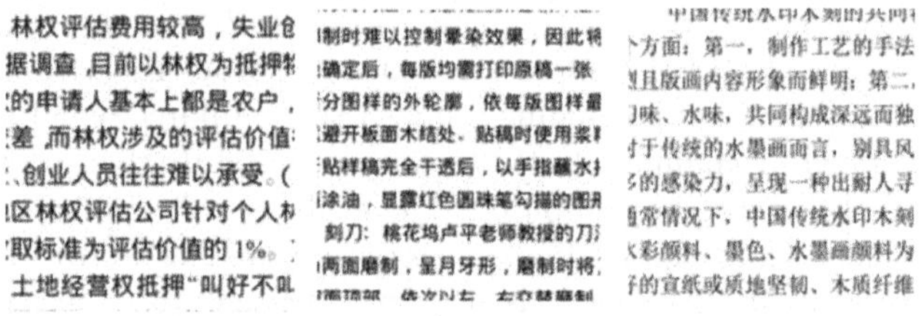

Fig. 6. Original image.

The method proposed in the literature [12] generates a watermarked image, which is based on SIFT key points and DCT coefficients to embed the watermark, and the generated watermark information is difficult to see without careful identification by the naked eye. However, the watermark robustness will be more fragile and not robust to the noise generated after faxing (Fig. 7).

Fig. 7. Watermarked images generated by Tancik.

The method proposed in the literature [16] generates a watermarked image with a random 100 bits of embedded watermark information. The method is mainly for adding image watermarks to colour images. When the same watermark is added to colour images and black and white text images, the colour images produce less visual distortion effect due to the abundance of pixel points, so the network trains out a model that is more obvious when the watermark is added to black and white text images (Fig. 8).

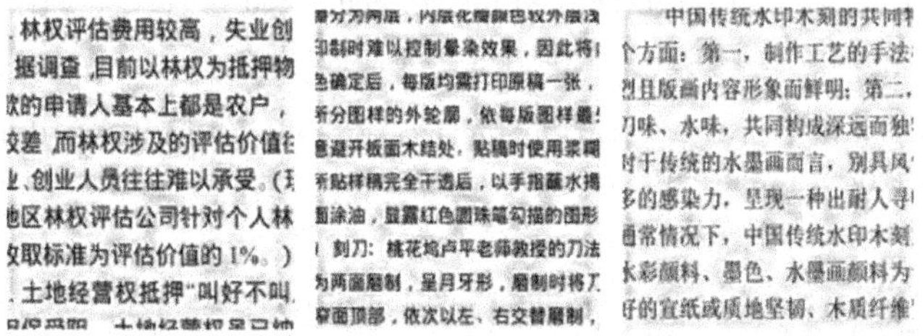

Fig. 8. Watermarked images generated by Fang.

The method proposed in the literature [9] generates a watermarked image with the embedded watermark information as binary random 100 bits. The method is trained with a large number of black and white text images, but the network is learning the image features from three channels, generating a more vibrant yellow underlined watermark with a strong visual impact. The image needs to be binarised when faxing, so watermarked information with colour cannot be used in some special needs communications (Fig. 9).

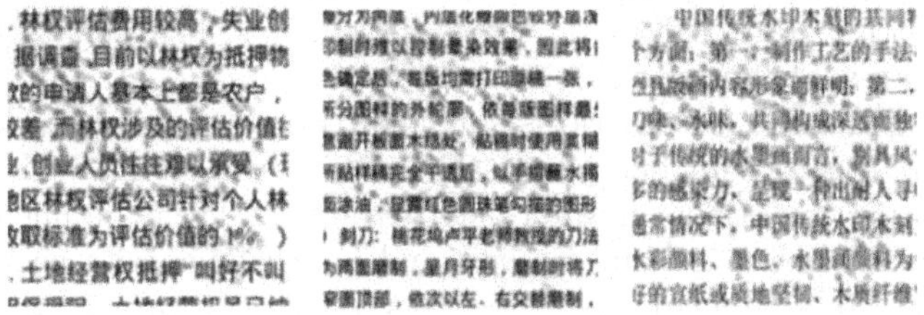

Fig. 9. Watermarked images generated by Ge.

In this paper, black and white text images are used for training, besides, in the network the images are single-channel, so the network can learn to generate watermarks suitable for black and white text images based on the binary of the input single-channel image, which is visually better compared to Tancik [9] and Ge [17] watermarks (Fig. 10).

We estimate the difference between the generated watermarked text image and original text image by using the objective image rating metrics peak-signal-to-noise ratio (PSNR) [18] and structural similarity index measure (SSIM) [15,

Fig. 10. The watermarked images generated in this paper.

19], and the quantitative evaluation metrics are shown in Table 1, Fig. 3.3 and Fig. 3.4 show the quantitative comparison histograms of the 2 metrics.

Table 1. Comparative quantification of image visual quality.

Methodology	SSIM	PSNR
Tancik	0.992	28.30
Fang	0.977	35.50
Ge	0.928	33.20
This paper	**0.977**	**34.96**

Robustness Evaluation. Watermark robustness, in this context, pertains to the accuracy of image extraction after the addition of a watermark, as measured by the Bit Error Rate (BER). It serves as a metric to evaluate how well a watermark can withstand perturbations.

In this experiment, a scenario is simulated where an image is leaked after being captured using a mobile phone. The aim is to investigate the impact of different capture conditions on watermark extraction. The experiment considers both color and black-and-white images, and it encompasses a shooting range spanning from 20 to 60 cm. The iPhone 13 serves as the capturing device for this study. Form Table 2, the accuracy of extracting watermark information from colour images at different distances sends changes, and the visual quality of the text watermark generated by literature [9] performs worse among several methods, but the robustness of the watermark extraction after shooting at different distances is stronger due to the obvious underlining of the watermark generated in the text image; literature [16] has good visual quality of the image after watermarking, but the robustness is poor; literature [17] added a function based on anti-disturbance in the photographic environment, and the robustness was improved. The results obtained from the training model of the watermarking algorithm proposed are very robust in the range of 20–60 cm shots, and the extraction accuracy can all reach 100.

Table 2. Accuracy of different methods for extracting watermark information from colour images at a different distance.

Methodology	20	30	40	50	60
Tancik	97.2	96.8	99.6	98.5	99.1
Fang	66.1	68.7	67.9	65.3	63.2
Ge	98.4	99.9	99.8	99.8	99.7
This paper	**100**	**100**	**100**	**100**	**100**

From Table 3, the accuracy of extracting watermark information from black and white images at different distances also sends variations. In scenarios involving black and white fax conditions, the accuracy of extracted black and white watermarks tends to be lower. This is primarily attributed to the distortion of the watermark in Tancik and Ge color due to changes in color, which adversely affect the extraction process.

Table 3. Accuracy of different methods for extracting watermark information from black and white images at different distance.

Methodology	20	30	40	50	60
Tancik	95.6	95.2	96.9	95.3	97.2
Fang	50.1	47.3	49.6	48.2	51.2
Ge	57.3	55.6	53.2	54.5	52.8
This paper	**100**	**100**	**100**	**100**	**100**

According to the results, the 8 groups of 100-bit watermark groups that were randomly generated and embedded into the text images can be accurately extracted. This successful extraction occurs whether it is done through screen capture after transmission, scanning, or printing photos. The model effectively embeds all 100 bits of the watermark, which not only ensures precise watermark extraction but also enhances the amount of useful information carried by the watermark.

For text traceability, different individuals' identity information can be predefined as needed. This identity information can be embedded within the text image before sending it. Subsequently, when traceability is required, the captured text image can be input into the U-net network, which will extract the identity information, thus ensuring the accuracy of the traceability process.

4   Conclusion

The paper introduces a digital watermarking scheme designed to enable traceability of faxed text image files after they have been sent. Given the potential quality degradation of text during transmission across different media, the paper employs the fully convolutional neural network U-net for embedding digital watermarks. The evaluation considers both color and black-and-white images, taking into account the unique characteristics of text images and the potential distortions that may arise during file transmission.

The experimental results demonstrate the effectiveness of the proposed method in comparison to several other image watermarking algorithms. It excels in terms of image quality and watermarking capacity for both color and black-and-white images. Furthermore, the accuracy and efficiency of watermark extraction after training are notably improved, thanks to a reduced random rate of watermarking during embedding. This is achieved by generating the necessary watermark group codes in advance.

The paper also assesses the method's effectiveness under cross-media channels, showing its capability to successfully add watermarks to text images. This holds true for both electronic text after transmission and text images printed on physical media and captured through photographic means.

Acknowledgement. This work was supported in part by the Fundamental Research Funds for the Central Universities under Grant 328202205, Grant 328202278, Grant 3282023005, Grant 328202261, and Grant 3282023054; in part by the National Key Research and Development Program under Grant 2017YFB0 801803; in part by the Undergraduate Teaching Reform and Innovation Project of Beijing Higher Education under Grant 202110018002; and in part by the First-Class Discipline Construction Project under Grant 20210036Z0401.

References

1. Brassil, J.T., Low, S., Maxemchuk, N.F., O'Gorman, L.: Electronic marking and identification techniques to discourage document copying. IEEE J. Sel. Areas Commun. **13**(8), 1495–1504 (1995)
2. Barouqa, H., Al-Haj, A.: Watermarking E-government document images using the discrete wavelets transform and Schur decomposition. In: 2021 7th International Conference on Information Management (ICIM), pp. 102–106. IEEE (2021)
3. Qi, W., Guo, W., Zhang, T., Liu, Y., Guo, Z., Fang, X.: Robust authentication for paper-based text documents based on text watermarking technology. Math. Biosci. Eng. **16**(4), 2233–2249 (2019)
4. Briffa, J.A., Culnane, C., Treharne, H.: Imperceptible printer dot watermarking for binary documents. In: Optics, Photonics, and Digital Technologies for Multimedia Applications, vol. 7723, pp. 166–174. SPIE (2010)
5. Ronneberger, O., Fischer, P., Brox, T.: U-Net: convolutional networks for biomedical image segmentation. In: Navab, N., Hornegger, J., Wells, W.M., Frangi, A.F. (eds.) MICCAI 2015. LNCS, vol. 9351, pp. 234–241. Springer, Cham (2015). https://doi.org/10.1007/978-3-319-24574-4_28
6. Zhao, W., Huimin, L., Wang, D.: Multisensor image fusion and enhancement in spectral total variation domain. IEEE Trans. Multimedia **20**(4), 866–879 (2017)
7. Boujerfaoui, S., Riad, R., Douzi, H., Ros, F., Harba, R.: Image watermarking between conventional and learning-based techniques: a literature review. Electronics **12**(1), 74 (2022)

8. Duan, X., Jia, K., Li, B., Guo, D., Zhang, E., Qin, C.: Reversible image steganography scheme based on a u-net structure. IEEE Access **7**, 9314–9323 (2019)
9. Tancik, M., Mildenhall, B., Ng, R.: Stegastamp: invisible hyperlinks in physical photographs. In: Proceedings of the IEEE/CVF Conference on Computer Vision and Pattern Recognition, pp. 2117–2126 (2020)
10. Fu, Y., et al.: Partial feature selection and alignment for multi-source domain adaptation. In: Proceedings of the IEEE/CVF Conference on Computer Vision and Pattern Recognition, pp. 16654–16663 (2021)
11. Talebi, H., Milanfar, P.: Learned perceptual image enhancement. In: 2018 IEEE International Conference on Computational Photography (ICCP), pp. 1–13. IEEE (2018)
12. Ge, S., Xia, Z., Fei, J., Tong, Y., Weng, J., Li, M.: A robust document image watermarking scheme using deep neural network. Multimedia Tools Appl. 1–24 (2023)
13. Xu, X., Lu, H., Song, J., Yang, Y., Shen, H.T., Li, X.: Ternary adversarial networks with self-supervision for zero-shot cross-modal retrieval. IEEE Trans. Cybern. **50**(6), 2400–2413 (2019)
14. Sun, X., Zhang, X., Xia, Z., Bertino, E.: Advances in Artificial Intelligence and Security, vol. 1424. Springer, Cham (2021). https://doi.org/10.1007/978-3-030-78621-2
15. Hore, A., Ziou, D.: Image quality metrics: PSNR vs. SSIM. In: 2010 20th International Conference on Pattern Recognition, pp. 2366–2369. IEEE (2010)
16. Fang, H., Zhang, W., Zhou, H., Cui, H., Nenghai, Yu.: Screen-shooting resilient watermarking. IEEE Trans. Inf. Forensics Secur. **14**(6), 1403–1418 (2018)
17. Ge, S., Fei, J., Xia, Z., Tong, Y., Weng, J., Liu, J.: A screen-shooting resilient document image watermarking scheme using deep neural network. IET Image Proc. **17**(2), 323–336 (2023)
18. Shin, R., Song, D.: JPEG-resistant adversarial images. In: NIPS 2017 Workshop on Machine Learning and Computer Security, vol. 1, p. 8 (2017)
19. Xudong, Z.: Research on absolute group time delay measurement of systems. In: Modern Radar, vol. 11, pp. 75–80 (2006)

An Enhanced Downsampling Transformer Network for Point Cloud Semantic Segmentation

Yang Wang, Zixuan Wei, and Zhibo Wan[✉]

Qingdao University, Qingdao, China
wanzhibo@qdu.edu.cn

Abstract. In outdoor environments, point cloud collection is often affected by external factors, leading to noisy and outlier points. Despite various pre-processing methods, noise is difficult to completely remove from training data. In addition, due to the disorderly nature of point clouds, traditional models have difficulty in extracting local information from point clouds, resulting in low accuracy. Therefore, we propose an enhanced down-sampling Transformer network for point cloud processing. Firstly, to tackle the influence of noise on feature extraction, we propose an enhanced down-sampling method, which constructs a graph by connecting the central point and its neighbors after down-sampling, and trains the weight between points to eliminate the effect of noise on feature aggregation. Secondly, after down-sampling, we use a novel Transformer module to train and update point cloud features, which includes residual modules and MLP to adapt to our down-sampling module and prevent model overfitting. Finally, extensive experiments are conducted on the S3DIS dataset, and the Mean Intersection over Union reaches 64.5%, indicating that our model is highly competitive in point cloud processing.

Keywords: Point cloud segmentation · Down-sampling · Noise points · Transformer · Residual

1 Introduction

As a highly representative storage format for 3D data, point clouds can not only save auxiliary information such as color and intensity but also contain the spatial and geometric information inherent in the data. Point cloud processing has been widely applied in fields like VR/AR, robotics [1], autonomous driving, and 3D scene analysis [2]. However, during the point cloud acquisition process, it is inevitable that external environmental factors. Therefore, most of the point clouds used for training undergo rich preprocessing steps such as point cloud filtering and cropping. Even after these preprocessing steps, it is hard to guarantee that the training data does not contain noise. Moreover, the disorderliness of point cloud data poses a challenge for extracting information and features from them.

In order to address these issues, many researchers have made significant efforts. Among them, the most classic one is the PointNet network proposed by Qi et al. [3]. It

H. Lu and J. Cai (Eds.): ISAIR 2023, CCIS 1998, pp. 262–269, 2024.
https://doi.org/10.1007/978-981-99-9109-9_26

directly processes point cloud data, which saves a lot of resources required for data conversion operations and achieved significant success. In our work, in order to eliminate the noise impact on point cloud processing and extract point cloud features more fully, we propose an enhanced down-sampling point cloud Transformer network. Specifically, in our work, first at the down-sampling stage, we construct a graph by grouping a set of central and neighbor points sampled through KNN sampling, and train the weight between different points and the central point to reduce the impact of noise on feature aggregation as much as possible. Then, we improved the Transformer module by introducing residual connections to prevent overfitting caused by the complexity of the down-sampling stage and increase the model's generalization performance.

To sum up, our work makes the following main contributions:

We design an enhanced down-sampling module to address noisy points and other outliers in point cloud data that affect processing.

To adapt to our down-sampling module, we designed an improved Transformer module, and based on this, we designed a point cloud processing network.

We conducted extensive experiments on challenging public datasets and the results show that our method has strong competitiveness for point cloud processing.

2 Related Work

In 3D tasks, existing research is not the same. The following are the main methods in the field of semantic segmentation.

2.1 Point Cloud Based Methods

The method is the most widely used and effective point cloud processing method today. The PointNet is groundbreaking in that it takes points as input data for their model [3]. They independently learn the features of point clouds through multiple MLPs, and then obtain global features through max-pooling to finally obtain segmentation results after down-sampling. However, Point- Net ignores the connections between points, resulting in the inability to learn features. On this basis, PointNet ++ is organized hierarchically, which effectively extracts structural information between points [4]. Subsequent research has mostly adopted this hierarchical structure as the overall framework of the model. PointNext [5] focuses on training strategies and optimization techniques such as data augmentation, and proposes many effective training strategies that can significantly enhance the performance of the original network. In addition, PointMLP [6] abandons the use of increasingly complex feature processing methods, and only uses residual MLPs to achieve relatively good results, providing a new idea for subsequent research.

2.2 Transformer Based Method

With the significant achievements of Transformers in 2D tasks, many researchers have started to apply Transformers to 3D point cloud processing tasks. Point Transformer (PT) developed a Point Transformer layer that exhibits a remarkably high level of expressiveness for the purpose of processing point clouds [7]. Point-MAE [8] designs a mask auto-encoder for point cloud self-supervised learning and achieves significant success. Similarly, Point Cloud Transformer (PCT) proposes a new transformer-based point cloud learning framework [9]. It employs a self-attention mechanism with positional offsets for training.

3   Method

3.1   Enhanced Down-Sampling

Although it is more and more convenient to acquire 3D point clouds, external factors such as illumination and weather will significantly affect the final accuracy of the acquisition during the acquisition process. Even after preprocessing, there is no guarantee that there will be no noise point data in the end. In addition, farthest point sampling is the most widely used method in point cloud processing, but this method is very sensitive to noisy points. The selection of the center point is very important. To solve this problem, we design an enhanced down-sampling module, as shown in the Fig. 1.

To begin, the input point cloud is first subjected to farthest point sampling, ensuring that the selected center points cover the entire point cloud as much as possible. Then, based on the sampled center points, the KNN algorithm is used to obtain the neighbor points around each center point. For each pair of center point and neighbor point $x_{i,1}, \ldots, x_{i,k}$, $i \in N$ and their respective features $f_{i,1}, \ldots, f_{i,k}$. A simple graph is constructed with the K points as the center and their neighbor points. The attention mechanism is then used to update their features and reduce the impact of noisy points on the results, according to (1)–(3).

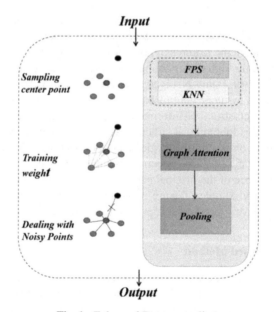

Fig. 1. Enhanced Down-sampling.

$$Attention = \rho(\theta(f_{1,k})^T \gamma(f_{1,k}) \odot \vartheta(f_{1,k})) \qquad (1)$$

$$F = \sum_{k=0}^{k=K} Attention(f_{1,k}) \qquad (2)$$

$$W = Softmax(\mu(F))F_{final} = W^T F \qquad (3)$$

In the equations, ρ is the aggregation function, which is often implemented using softmax. θ, γ, ϑ is a linear function that transforms the features, increasing their dimensionality from the original dimension D to a more suitable dimension. After these steps, the attention weights are obtained. The normalized weight is then used to update the features, reducing the impact of noisy points.

3.2   Residual Transformer

The core self-attention mechanism in Transformers is permutation-invariant in nature, making it well suited for 3D point cloud analysis tasks. In addition, to prevent feature training from being too complex and overfitting, we specially design a residual Transformer for our model to improve its generalization ability. The specific structure is shown in Fig. 2.

Similarly in our Transformer, we use linear functions to obtain the corresponding Query, Key, and Value matrices by the original feature matrix X. First, we perform a matrix multiplication of Q and K to obtain the Attention- Map, which is then multiplied by the corresponding Value matrix to obtain the final Attention Feature. Based on this, we design a residual structure that uses an MLP to process and align the input matrix and then applies an offset operation to the corresponding Attention Feature to reduce the complexity of the model and prevent overfitting. This is shown specifically in (4)–(6).

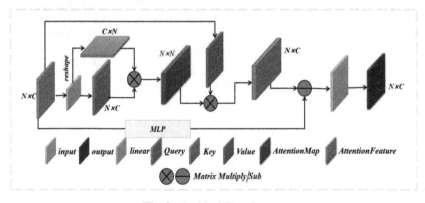

Fig. 2. Residual Transformer.

$$Q = Linear_q(X), K = Linear_k(X), V = Linear_v(X) \qquad (4)$$

$$f = Linear(softmax(Q \cdot K/\sqrt{D}) \cdot V) \tag{5}$$

$$F = Linear(f - MLP(X)) \tag{6}$$

By utilizing the feature processing module described above to learn and update the features, we are able to provide a strong foundation for the final point cloud processing task.

3.3 Model Architecture

By combining the two modules we have proposed, we have developed a neural network model that is specifically designed for performing point cloud segmentation tasks, as shown in Fig. 3.

Our model adopts the U-net structure, consisting of encoders and decoders. The encoder is composed of the down-sampling module and feature processing module we designed, and consists of four layers in total. Similarly, in the decoder stage, we use nearest-neighbor interpolation to perform up-sampling. The transfer of features between different layers is facilitated through intermediate connections.

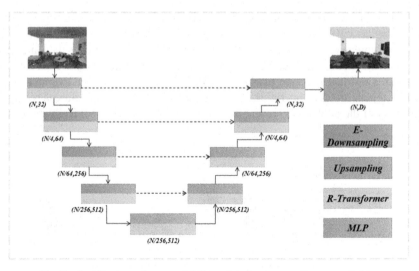

Fig. 3. Architecture of our model for point cloud semantic segmentation.

4 Experiments

To appraise the efficacy of our point cloud analysis network, we carried out comprehensive experiments on the S3DIS benchmark dataset that is publicly accessible and compared it with state-of-the-art model.

Unlike the classification task on artificially synthesized datasets, segmenting indoor 3D scenes is an arduous undertaking, primarily because of the real- world point cloud data used, which contains a significant number of outliers and noise.

Experiments are performed using the PyTorch framework and trained on NVIDIA RTX 2060. In the experiment, a total of 100 epochs were trained, the initial learning rate was 0.5, the learning rate was reduced after 60 epochs, and the batch size was 4. Below are the details of the entire experiment.

The S3DIS dataset comprises six large indoor areas and 271 rooms extracted from three distinct buildings. It contains point-level annotations with 13 semantic categories. We compared the Mean Intersection over Union (miou) and accuracy of each class on the difficult Area 5. The comparison results are shown in Tables 1 and 2.

In Table 1, we compared our method on Area 5 of the S3DIS dataset with other advanced models under the same training strategy for the segmentation task. We analyzed and compared the results from three dimensions: Overall Accuracy (OA), Mean Accuracy (mAcc), and Mean Intersection over Union (mIoU). As shown in the table, our method achieved a 23.4% increase in mIoU compared to the original PointNet method, reaching 64.5%. We also observed improvements compared to other methods, which indicates the effectiveness of our approach. Additionally, we presented the results of each class in Table 2, where we analyzed the classification abilities of our model on each class, providing insights for further research improvements.

Table 1. Results of Indoor Scene Segmentation on S3DIStested on Area 5.

Method	mIoU	mAcc	OA
PointNet [3]	41.1	49.0	–
PointCNN [10]	57.3	63.9	85.9
PAT [11]	60.1	70.8	–
DGCNN [12]	56.1	–	–
PointWeb [13]	60.3	66.6	87.0
PointNext-S [5]	63.4	–	87.9
SCF-Net [14]	63.7	71.8	87.2
PCT [9]	61.3	67.7	–
Ours	**64.50**	**72.04**	**87.06**

Table 2. Results for each category on S3DIStested on Area 5.

Method	ceiling	floor	wall	beam	column	window	door	chair	table	sofa	bookcase	board	clutter
PointNet [3]	88.8	97.3	69.8	0.1	3.9	46.3	10.8	59.0	52.6	5.9	40.3	26.4	33.2
PointCNN [10]	92.3	98.2	79.4	0.0	17.6	22.8	62.1	74.4	80.6	31.7	66.7	62.1	56.7
PAT [11]	93.0	98.5	72.3	1.0	41.5	85.1	38.2	57.7	83.6	48.1	67.0	61.3	33.6
PointWeb [13]	92.0	98.5	79.4	0.0	21.1	59.7	34.8	76.3	88.3	46.9	69.3	64.9	52.5
HPEIN [15]	91.5	98.2	81.4	0.0	23.3	65.3	40.0	75.5	87.7	58.5	67.8	65.6	49.4
Ours	**94.8**	**97.9**	**94.3**	**0.0**	**34.8**	**51.3**	**76.9**	**84.1**	**94.8**	**87.0**	**77.9**	**68.8**	**67.2**

5 Discussion

In this paper, we proposed an enhanced down-sampling Transformer network for point cloud semantic segmentation. This network consists of our designed enhanced down-sampling module and residual Transformer module, which can effectively extract point cloud features and reduce the impact of noise points on the final accuracy, greatly improving the traditional methods. Through a large number of experiments on the S3DIS dataset, the mIoU reached 64.5%, which is 23.4% higher than the traditional PointNet, which proves the effectiveness and competitiveness of our model. We hope that our work can inspire further research on Transformer and noise point related issues.

References

1. Zheng, Y., Li, Y., Yang, S., Lu, H.: Global-PBNet: a novel point cloud registration for autonomous driving. IEEE Trans. Intell. Transp. Syst. **23**(11), 22312–22319 (2022)
2. Li, Y., Cai, J., Zhou, Q., Lu, H.: Joint semantic-instance segmentation method for intelligent transportation system. IEEE Trans. Intell. Transp. Syst. (2022)
3. Qi, C.R., Su, H., Mo, K., Guibas, L.J.: PointNet: deep learning on point sets for 3d classification and segmentation. In: Proceedings of the IEEE Conference on Computer Vision and Pattern Recognition, pp. 652–660 (2017)
4. Qi, C.R., Yi, L., Su, H., Guibas, L.J.: PointNet++: deep hierarchical feature learning on point sets in a metric space. In: Advances in Neural Information Processing Systems, vol. 30 (2017)
5. Qian, G., et al.: PointNeXt: revisiting pointNet++ with improved training and scaling strategies. In: Advances in Neural Information Processing Systems vol. 35, pp. 23192–23204 (2022)
6. Ma, X., Qin, C., You, H., Ran, H., Fu, Y.: Rethinking network design and local geometry in point cloud: a simple residual MLP framework. arXiv preprint arXiv:2202.07123 (2022)
7. Zhao, H., Jiang, L., Jia, J., Torr, P.H., Koltun, V.: Point Transformer. In: Proceedings of the IEEE/CVF International Conference on Computer Vision, pp. 16259–16268 (2021)
8. Pang, Y., Wang, W., Tay, F.E., Liu, W., Tian, Y., Yuan, L.: Masked autoencoders for point cloud self-supervised learning. In: Avidan, S., Brostow, G., Cissé, M., Farinella, G.M., Hassner, T. (eds.) Computer Vision – ECCV 2022. ECCV 2022. Lecture Notes in Computer Science, vol. 13662, pp. 604–621. Springer, Cham (2022). https://doi.org/10.1007/978-3-031-20086-1_35

9. Guo, M.-H., Cai, J.-X., Liu, Z.-N., Mu, T.-J., Martin, R.R., Hu, S.-M.: PCT: Point cloud transformer. Comput. Vis. Media **7**, 187–199 (2021)
10. Li, Y., Bu, R., Sun, M., Wu, W., Di, X., Chen, B.: PointCNN: convolution on x-transformed points. In: Advances in Neural Information Processing Systems, vol. 31 (2018)
11. Yang, J., et al.: Modeling point clouds with self-attention and Gumbel subset sampling. In: Proceedings of the IEEE/CVF Conference on Computer Vision and Pattern Recognition, pp. 3323–3332 (2019)
12. Phan, A.V., Le Nguyen, M., Nguyen, Y.L.H., Bui, L.T.: DGCNN: a convolutional neural network over large-scale labeled graphs. Neural Netw. **108**, 533–543 (2018)
13. Zhao, H., Jiang, L., Fu, C.-W., Jia, J.: PointWeb: Enhancing local neighborhood features for point cloud processing. In: Proceedings of the IEEE/CVF Conference on Computer Vision and Pattern Recognition, pp. 5565–5573 (2019)
14. Fan, S., Dong, Q., Zhu, F., Lv, Y., Ye, P., Wang, F.-Y.: SCF-Net: Learning spatial contextual features for large-scale point cloud segmentation. In: Proceedings of the IEEE/CVF Conference on Computer Vision and Pattern Recognition, pp. 14504–14513 (2021)
15. Jiang, L., Zhao, H., Liu, S., Shen, X., Fu, C.-W., Jia, J.: Hierarchical point-edge interaction network for point cloud semantic segmentation. In: Proceedings of the IEEE/CVF International Conference on Computer Vision, pp. 10433–10441 (2019)

Improved DGCNN Based on Transformer for Point Cloud Segmentation

Guokuan Zan, Yang Wang, and Pengxiang Gao[(✉)]

Qingdao University, Qingdao, China
gaopengxiang@qdu.edu.cn

Abstract. Semantic segmentation task is an important branch of computer vision field. We propose a new model based on DGCNN [3] and Transfromer [6]. DGCNN is an excellent model that has achieved good results in semantic segmentation tasks. However, there are still some shortcomings, so we propose two blocks feature reinforcement block (FRB) and transformer feature block (TFB). The global feature is very important to the model, but in DGCNN it is only obtained through symmetric functions. Therefore, we use both FRB and TFB based on Transformer to improve the original model, because the self-attention block in Transformer has a natural advantage for global feature extraction. In the FRB block, we use the local features extracted by the Edgeconv block and the address coding information to extract the global features. In the TFB block, we integrate the output features of the first three stages to enrich the semantic information of the features. The model was tested on the Dataset Stanford Large-Scale 3D Indoor Spaces Dataset (S3DIS) [5]. The three metrics improved, Mean Intersection over Union (mIoU), overall accuracy (OA) and mean accuracy (mAcc). The mIoU increased by 2%, OA increased by 3%, and mAcc increased by 1.3% compared to the original model.

Keywords: DGCNN · Point Clouds · Edgeconv · Transformer

1 Introduction

In recent years, with the development of deep learning technology, the efficiency of point cloud processing has superior advances. Point cloud is used in more fields, such as autonomous driving, unmanned aircraft, robots and so on. The reason for using them is inseparable from the nature of three-dimensional point clouds. Unlike pictures, point clouds have location information that can meet the needs of many industries. However, point clouds also have some disadvantages compared to images, which makes them unusable for convolution operations. The image data is regularly arranged in a grid, conforming to the format of convolution operations. Convolution cannot be directly applied to three-dimensional point clouds due to their disorderliness, sparsity, and irregularity.

In order to apply deep learning to 3D point clouds, new methods emerged to deal with point clouds, such as voxelization [12]. However, these methods have certain limitations, and it is easy to lose some details in the three-dimensional point cloud.

H. Lu and J. Cai (Eds.): ISAIR 2023, CCIS 1998, pp. 270–277, 2024.
https://doi.org/10.1007/978-981-99-9109-9_27

Until Charles came up with PointNet [1] that directly dealt with point clouds, further improving the performance of point cloud processing and avoiding the loss of point cloud details. PointNet operates directly with the point cloud, gathering information from adjacent points and then extracting information from adjacent points using multi-layer perceptron (mlp) operations. Most models accomplish various recognition tasks to extract local features through collecting adjacent points, while ignoring global features. Global features including global context information, play an important role in semantic segmentation. With the emergence of Transformer, many have applied them to the visual field, which has greatly improved the model performance. Transformer [6] fits the point cloud structure well. Self-attention mechanism can extract the overall semantic information and supply the deficiency of local features. It has been applied to many models [11, 13]. Point Transformer [11] uses Transformer model to extract features and produce good results.

Based on DGCNN model, an improved model is proposed in this paper. In this model, the feature reinforcement block is proposed to extract the global features of point cloud according to self-attention. The transformer feature block is also proposed, which is an improved feature fusion block based on Transformer. Both blocks strengthen the point cloud extraction capability of the model and improve the accuracy of the model. To sum up, the contribution of this paper is as follows:

- We propose a new model based on DGCNN.
- We propose the feature reinforcement block and transformer feature block based on Transformer, and strengthen the feature extraction.

2 Related Work

In recent years, Transformer model has been increasingly used in other fields, including 2D image applications such as DETR [7], and SETR [14]. For DETR models, Transformer is used to extract features, and get good results. Having other models use Transformer to extract both local and global features. Cswin transformer [9] and Twins [8], which contain two branches at the same time, capture local features and global features.

Transformer has long been used in the 2D space, but has rarely been used in the 3D space. Inspired by these methods, feature reinforcement block and transformer feature block are added to the model to extract global features.

Segmentation of point clouds is an important task in computer vision, and many methods are used for this purpose. There are two approaches to handle point clouds, one is to use voxelization, and the other is to deal with point clouds directly. The model based on voxelization [10, 12, 15, 16] has many limitations, the most important of which is the loss of some cloud details, which affects the accuracy of models. The pioneering model that directly processes point clouds is PointNet [17, 18]. From then on, many models have begun to take this way to process point clouds. Directly processing the point cloud can retain the original characteristics of the point cloud without losing the details of the point cloud.

Our model leverages Transformer to extract robust features, thereby augmenting the accuracy of our model.

3 Methodology

DGCNN is a competent model, however, it neglects the significance of global features and relying solely on symmetric functions for extracting them is evidently inadequate. Therefore, we propose a feature enhancement block to enhance the global features of the point cloud. Global features play an important role in executing point cloud tasks. After the first Edgeconv block, we use FRB to extract the global features from the output of Edgeconv, and then combine them with local features. The processed features optimize the precision of the model. We noticed that DGCNN used symmetric functions to generate global features after three Edgeconv blocks, which could not fully extract features. Therefore, we based on Transformer model and proposed a Transfromer feature block. The model structure has three Edgeconv blocks (see Fig. 1). The feature reinforcement block is added after the first Edgeconv. The transformer feature block is used to make full use of the features and improve the accuracy of the model.

3.1 Feature Reinforcement Block

Global features are important for computer vision tasks and can improve the accuracy of models. Global features are not only used in 2D models, but also in 3D and other fields. In many models, extracting global feature blocks is an integral part, such as Point Transformer, enriching higher-level semantic information and contextual comprehension.

Adding global features to the model can improve the accuracy of the model. The feature reinforcement block (FRB) is incorporated to the original model DGCNN for extracting the global features, which are then combined with the upper-level features as input of the lower layer (see Fig. 2).

The first Edgeconv generates features of size (n, 64). These features are then fed into FRB to produce a global feature of size (1, 64), which is combined with the input features. Finally, an MLP is used to generate new features of size (n, 64).

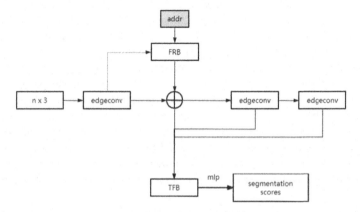

Fig. 1. The model structure.

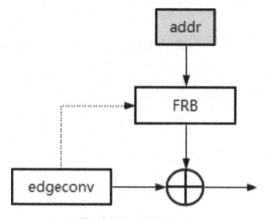

Fig. 2. The FRB using.

Since the address information is also very important for visual tasks, we encode them to enhance the spatial semantic information, so that the features of each point are more distinguished. We utilize a multilayer perceptron to encode (x, y, z) addresses and generate spatial semantic information. Meanwhile, the self-attention block is employed by FRB to extract features. The characteristics of Transformer model enable point clouds to be directly processed, and self-attention block is a suitable choice to extract the global features of point clouds. The output S produced by Edgeconv is fed into the FRB block, and we improve its feature extraction capability by concatenating the address code A = (n, 64) with V. The K, Q, and V are generated through linear operations with S serving as the input data (see Fig. 3).

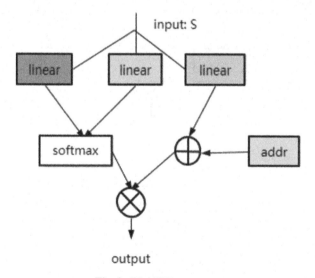

Fig. 3. The FRB structure.

$$K = Linear\_k(S) \tag{1}$$

$$Q = Linear\_q(S) \tag{2}$$

$$V = Linear\_v(S) \tag{3}$$

$$G = softmax(QK^T/\sqrt{d}) * (V + A) \tag{4}$$

The concatenated G and S are fed into an MLP to generate features.

$$F = mlp(concat(G, S)) \tag{5}$$

3.2 Transformer Feature Block

To enhance the capabilities to extract features, we propose the Transformer Feature Block (TFB). TFB leverages the benefits of Transformer to extract global features. In contrast, the original DGCNN model solely employs symmetric functions for global feature extraction, leading to suboptimal results. Therefore, we proposed TFB to make full use of semantic information and strengthen contextual comprehension.

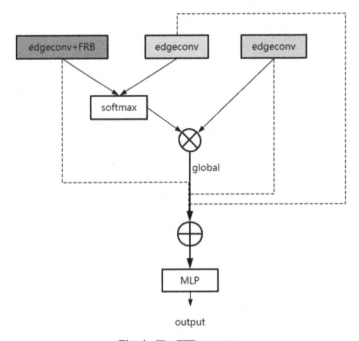

Fig. 4. The TFB structure.

We consider the feature produced by the FRB block and Edgeconv block as Q, the features generated by the second Edgeconv block produced as K, and the features generated by the third Edgeconv block as V (see Fig. 4). We propose a modification by replacing Q times k transpose with KQ, because K has richer semantic information than Q after the second feature extraction, and Q also has richer spatial information. Through sub operation, spatial information and semantic information can be obtained. Then operate on V to generate global features.

$$K = edgeconv\_one() \tag{6}$$

$$Q = FRB() \tag{7}$$

$$V = edgeconv\_two() \tag{8}$$

$$G = solf\ tmax((K - Q)/(\sqrt{d})) * V \tag{9}$$

We concatenate the matrices of Q, K, V, and G and apply an MLP to generate the resulting features.

$$F = mlp(concat(Q, K, V, G)) \tag{10}$$

4 Experiment

In the experiment, the Dataset we used in the semantic segmentation task was Stanford Large-Scale 3D Indoor Spaces Dataset (S3DIS) [5]. The data set contains a total of 272 rooms in six indoor areas. Each point belongs to one of 13 semantic categories-e.g. board, ceiling, bookcase. Each room is divided into 1mx1m blocks, in which 4096 points are selected. The dimension of each point is 9, including 3D coordinates, colors and normalized spatial coordinates. We used a fifth area for testing and the rest for training the model.

Table 1. Results on S3DIS Area5 for semantic segmentation.

Model	OA	mAcc	mIoU
PointNet [1]	–	49.0	41.1
SegCloud [4]	–	57.4	48.9
DGCNN [3]	80.0	57.9	48.5
Ours	82.3	59.2	50.5

In this paper, we predict the category of each point in the S3DiS dataset. The evaluation metrics used include Mean Intersection-over Union (mIoU), Overall Accuracy

(OA), and Mean Accuracy (mAcc). We compared some models and the results are shown in Table 1. The table shows the differences between the models in terms of mIoU, mAcc, and OA. It is evident that our model has achieved a 2% increase in mIoU and a 1.3% increase in mAcc compared to DGCNN.

And, our model outperformed other models in terms of the mIoU metric, with a 9.4% improvement over PointNet and a 1.6% improvement over SegCloud.

5   Conclusion

In this paper, we propose novel approaches for semantic segmentation tasks. The feature reinforcement block and transformer feature block are both adaptations of the transformer model, which offers significant advantages in point cloud processing. Our model achieved a 2% improvement in mIoU, a 1.3% increase in mAcc, and a 2.3% enhancement in OA compared to the original model. However, there is still ample room for further advancement, and we will continue our research efforts in this field. The Transformer has gained widespread attention across various domains, and we will persistently explore its potential.

References

1. Qi, C.R., Su, H., Mo, K., Guibas, L.J.: PointNet: deep learning on point sets for 3d classification and segmentation. In: Proceedings of the IEEE Conference on Computer Vision and Pattern Recognition (2017)
2. Qi, C.R., Yi, L., Su, H., Guibas, L.J.: PointNet++: deep hierarchical feature learning on point sets in a metric space. In: Advances in Neural Information Processing Systems (2017)
3. Wang, Y., Sun, Y., Liu, Z., Sarma, S.E., Bronstein, M.M., Solomon, J.M.: Dynamic graph CNN for learning on point clouds. ACM Trans. Graph. (tog) **38**, 1–12 (2019)
4. Tchapmi, L., Choy, C., Armeni, I., Gwak, J., Savarese, S.: SEGCloud: semantic segmentation of 3D point clouds. In: 2017 international conference on 3D vision (3DV), IEEE (2017)
5. Armeni, I., et al.: 3D semantic parsing of large-scale indoor spaces. In: Proceedings of the IEEE Conference on Computer Vision and Pattern Recognition, IEEE (2016)
6. Vaswani, A et al.: Attention is all you need. In: Advances in Neural Information Processing Systems (2017)
7. Carion, N., Massa, F., Synnaeve, G., Usunier, N., Kirillov, A., Zagoruyko, S.: End-to-end object detection with transformers. In: Vedaldi, A., Bischof, H., Brox, T., Frahm, J.-M. (eds.) ECCV 2020. LNCS, vol. 12346, pp. 213–229. Springer, Cham (2020). https://doi.org/10.1007/978-3-030-58452-8_13
8. Chu, X., et al.: Twins: revisiting the design of spatial attention in vision transformers. arXiv: 2104.13840 (2021)
9. Dong, X., et al.: CSWin transformer: a general vision transformer backbone with cross-shaped windows. arXiv:2107.00652 (2021)
10. Choy, C., Gwak, J.Y., Savarese, S.: 4D spatiotemporal ConvNets: Minkowski convolutional neural networks. In: Proceedings of the IEEE/CVF Conference on Computer Vision and Pattern Recognition (2019)
11. Zhao, H., Jiang, L., Jia, J., Torr, P.H., Koltun, V.: Point transformer. In: Proceedings of the IEEE/CVF International Conference on Computer Vision (2021)

12. Mao, J., et al.: Voxel transformer for 3D object detection. In: Proceedings of the IEEE/CVF International Conference on Computer Vision (2021)
13. Touvron, H., et al.: Training data-efficient image transformers, distillation through attention. In: International Conference on Machine Learning, PMLR (2021)
14. Strudel, R., Garcia Pinel, R., Laptev, I., Schmid, C.: Segmenter: transformer for Semantic Segmentation. In: Proceedings of the IEEE/CVF International Conference on Computer Vision (2021)
15. Graham, B., Van der Maaten, L.: Submanifold sparse convolutional networks. arXiv:1706.01307 (2017)
16. Graham, B., Engelcke, M., Van Der Maaten, L.: 3D semantic segmentation with submanifold sparse convolutional networks. In: Proceedings of the IEEE Conference on Computer Vision and Pattern Recognition (2018)
17. Zheng, Y., Li, Y., Yang, S., Lu, H.: Global-PBNet: a novel point cloud registration for autonomous driving. IEEE Trans. Intell. Transp. Syst. 23(11), 22312–22319 (2022)
18. Li, Y., Yang, S., Zheng, Y., Lu, H.: Improved point-voxel region convolutional neural network: 3D object detectors for autonomous driving. IEEE Trans. Intell. Transp. Syst. (2021)

Symmetry Analysis of Face from a Video Image of 3D Point Cloud

Narumi Kihara[1]($\boxtimes$), Namiko Kimura-Nomoto[2], Takako Okawachi[3], Guangxu Li[4], Norifumi Nakamura[2], and Tohru Kamiya[1]

[1] Kyushu Institute of Technology, 1-1, Sensui, Tobata, Kitakyushu, Japan
`kihara.narumi101@mail.kyutech.jp`
[2] Kagoshima University, 8-35-1, Sakuragaoka, Kagoshima, Japan
[3] National Hospital Organization Kagoshima Medical Center, 8-1, Shiroyama, Kagoshima, Japan
[4] Tiangong University, 399, BinShuiXi Road, XiQing District, Tianjin, China

Abstract. Cleft lip surgery is performed several times. The problem is that the criteria for facial symmetry are unclear. We propose a method for the facial symmetry analysis using the 3D point cloud which is obtained as a video image. Pseudo video images are created by making multiple point cloud data with slightly different deformations. If we see the data in chronological order, the face appears to be gradually deforming. The symmetry is evaluated using the movement of the face landmarks. We detect face landmarks from an initial frame and perform matching technique on successive frames. After the matching process, we calculate a shift vector that describes the temporal change between the frames. Finally, we evaluate the symmetry by comparing its components on the left and right sides of the face. As an experimental result, the matching is performed with small error, and the symmetry is evaluated in a quantitative way.

Keywords: Cleft Lip · Point Cloud · Symmetry Analysis · Video Image

1 Introduction

Cleft lip is a congenital anomaly that occurs when one or both sides of the upper lip are not completely formed. The incidence of cleft lip is known to be high, and particularly in Japan, it accounts for over twenty percent of all birth defects [1]. It causes functional and aesthetic disorders. For example, a functional disorder is a delay in the development of the ability to speak, and an aesthetic disorder is a deformation of the nose and lip. In particular, it is known that the facial asymmetry has a profound psychological impact on cleft lip patients [2]. Therefore, surgical repair of the lip is of great importance to them.

The surgery for cleft lip is usually performed around three months of age to improve the lip function and aesthetic. However, surgical correction does not eliminate facial asymmetry and additional surgery is required to improve the facial symmetry [3]. The problem with additional surgery is that the criteria for the facial symmetry are unclear and depend on the subjective judgement of the surgeon. In fact, it has been shown

H. Lu and J. Cai (Eds.): ISAIR 2023, CCIS 1998, pp. 278–287, 2024.
https://doi.org/10.1007/978-981-99-9109-9_28

that surgeons often disagree about the outcomes of surgery [4]. An indicator for the quantitative assessment of the facial symmetry is needed to solve the problem.

Facial symmetry is analyzed using 3D images in conventional methods. For example, Hosoki et al. [5] proposed a method for facial symmetry analysis using 3D point cloud data. In this method, a symmetric plane of the face is detected by aligning an original point cloud and its mirror-inverted point cloud, and the symmetry is analyzed by comparing the left and right sides of the face using a detected plane. Although this method enables the quantitative analysis to some extent, there is still a problem to be solved. When it is applied to cleft lip patients and healthy controls around the age of five, no significant differences have been found. One of the reasons for this is thought to be that an assessment based on a single image is not sufficient, as it only captures a moment of the face.

Recently, deep learning has been applied to some tasks in 3D point clouds, such as object detection, object classification and semantic segmentation. Qi et al. proposed PointNet [6] and PointNet++ [7] for classification and segmentation tasks. This study is a pioneer in deep learning applications to the 3D point cloud, therefore many of the networks proposed after PointNet are based on it. For example, PointPillars [8] is proposed to detect objects from a 3D point cloud mainly for autonomous driving, and MT-PNet [9] is proposed to segment real scenes. On the other hand, it is difficult to use deep learning techniques in our study due to data and memory constraints. There is no open data set of cleft lip patients and healthy controls of 3D video data, and the data requires extremely large amounts of memory for the learning process.

We propose a method for symmetry analysis of the face using the 3D point cloud of video image without deep learning. The 3D point cloud data can hold rich information about the facial structure, and a video image enables more accurate analysis. A 3D point cloud of video image is considered to be effective for the facial analysis by these two characteristics.

We create video images for the experiment and evaluate the facial symmetry based on the temporal changes of facial landmarks (Sect. 2). Finally, we show that our proposed method detects the temporal changes with small error and evaluates the facial symmetry in a quantitative way (Sect. 3).

2   Method

2.1   Creating Video Image

We create the video image with a still 3D point cloud because it is difficult to get real data. A video image is a series of still images in chronological order. Based on this idea, we artificially add time-series changes to a still 3D point cloud by creating several point cloud files with slightly different deformations. This process can be divided into three steps: symmetric plane detection, face landmark detection and point cloud deformation.

Symmetric Plane Detection. The first step is to detect a symmetric plane of the face using a method proposed by Hosoki [5]. Although the outline of the method has already been mentioned above, we explain it in more detail because it plays an important role in our method. The two point clouds are aligned by global registration and local registration. First, in global registration, FPFH (Fast Point Feature Histograms) [10] is introduced. It is a feature that describes the local geometry around a point in 3D point cloud data. Therefore, points in an original point cloud can be corresponded to those in its mirror-inverted cloud by comparing FPFH values. However, the result contains false correspondences. Therefore, RANSAC (Random Sample Consensus) [11] is used to eliminate false correspondences. After that, a rotation matrix is found using SVD (Singular Value Decomposition) [12] to superimpose these two point clouds. Next, in local registration, ICP (Iterative Closest Point) [13] is used to improve the alignment. The ICP algorithm repeats the estimation of a rotation matrix based on the correspondence of two point clouds until the converge condition is satisfied, and finds the rotation matrix that minimizes the squared error of the distance between the point cloud after the transformation and that of the alignment target. Finally, the coordinates of the point cloud are transformed by finding a rotation matrix such that the face faces forward. This transformation simplifies subsequent processes.

Face Landmark Detection. The second step is to detect face landmarks using a method proposed by Kazemi [14]. In this method, face landmark positions are detected using an ensemble model that has learned features by comparing the estimated landmark positions with the ground truth. The training process is expressed in (1), where $\hat{S}$ is the estimated shape, I is the input image, t is the estimation times, and r_t is the difference between the ground truth and the estimated shape.

$$\hat{S}^{(t+1)} = \hat{S}^{(t)} + r_t\left(I, \hat{S}^{(t)}\right) \tag{1}$$

This model requires a 2D image as an input, and hence a 3D point cloud should be projected to the 2D plane. Each point in a 3D point cloud has xyz coordinates and rgb values and is assigned to neighboring pixels in the xy plane. At the same time, the value of z-coordinate of the assigned point is held in that pixel as depth information. When more than two points are assigned to the same pixel, the average value is calculated. After detecting face landmarks on the 2D image, they are re-projected to the 3D point cloud using depth information of their pixels to perform the analysis in 3D space.

Point Cloud Deformation. The third step is to deform the point cloud using FFD (Free-Form Deformation) [15]. In FFD, a local coordinate system and 3D grids are defined. The deformation is performed by moving points that are in grids with the same rule for moving the control points. The position x_{ffd} after applying FFD is calculated in (2), where P_{ijk} is the control point, s, t and u are the coefficients in the local coordinate system, l, m, and n are the numbers of control points set on each axis of the local coordinate system, and $B_{p,q}(r)$ is the Bernstein polynomial defined in (3). The position x_{ffd} is calculated as the weighted sum of control points, therefore x_{ffd} will change if the control points are moved to the new positions. We set control points around the lip based on the detected face landmarks, and add the deformation to the lip part.

$$x_{ffd} = \sum_{i=0}^{l} \sum_{j=0}^{m} \sum_{k=0}^{n} B_{i,l}(s)B_{j,m}(t)B_{k,n}(u)P_{ijk} \tag{2}$$

$$B_{p,q}(r) = {}_qC_r r^p(1-r)^{q-p} \tag{3}$$

We have prepared video images by creating several point cloud files with slightly different deformations. In this paper, these 3D point clouds containing artificial time-series changes are referred to as pseudo video image, and each point cloud file is referred to as frame. The deformation is added around the nose and lip considering the aesthetic disorder of cleft lip. A pseudo video image has sixty point clouds. The initial frame is an original point cloud, and the bigger frame number is, the bigger deformation is added (see Fig. 1).

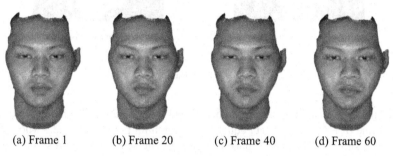

(a) Frame 1   (b) Frame 20   (c) Frame 40   (d) Frame 60

Fig. 1. Example of the Video Image.

A 3D point cloud to create video images was taken with VECTRA® H1 manufactured by Canfield Scientific. In this paper, we create two types of pseudo video images. One is called "asym-data" (asymmetrically deformed data), and it has a deformation added to the right side of the face. The other is called "sym-data" (symmetrically deformed) data, and it has the same amount of deformation added to both sides of the face.

2.2 Symmetry Analysis Based on the Movement of Landmarks

A video image can capture changes in the face, which is more realistic than the expression on a 2D image because the human expression is always changing. In order to take advantage of the video image, we propose a method of the symmetry analysis based on the movement of landmarks, which cannot be realized by a still 2D image. This process can be divided into three steps: face landmark detection, face landmark matching and symmetry analysis.

Face Landmark Detection. The first step is to detect face landmarks from the initial frame using a method proposed by Kazemi [14]. Although this method detects sixty-eight landmarks, two of them that correspond both corners of mouth are used for the symmetry analysis to reduce computation time and focus on the deformed part (see Fig. 2).

Face Landmark Matching. The second step is to match the same landmarks in different frames. The reason to perform matching is to minimize the dependency on the face landmark detection method. In the matching process, FPFH [10] values are calculated for the face landmarks and candidate match points. It is estimated that the same landmarks in different frames have the similar geometric feature, and hence their FPFH values are

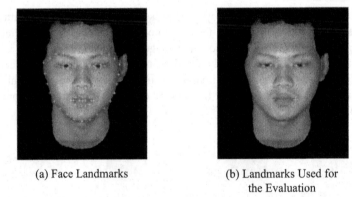

(a) Face Landmarks   (b) Landmarks Used for
                                       the Evaluation

Fig. 2. Example of Face Landmark Detection.

also similar. The matching process is performed by comparing FPFH in frame t with that in frame $(t + 1)$. At first, let t equal 1 and search for points in frame 2 whose FPFH is the most similar to each landmark in frame 1. The search area is restricted around the landmark position in frame 1 to reduce computation time and false matches. The landmark positions in all frames are determined by repeating this search inductively. A pseudo video image has sixty point clouds, and hence fifty-nine points are obtained for each landmark as a result of matching. These points express the temporal changes in landmarks.

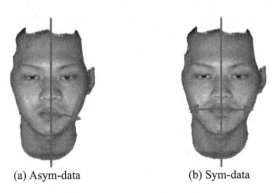

(a) Asym-data   (b) Sym-data

Fig. 3. Conceptual Diagram of Shift Vector.

Symmetry Analysis. The third step is to analyze the symmetry of the face using the result of the matching. As a descriptor of the changes, a shift vector is calculated in (4), where $p^{(t)}$ is the position of a certain face landmark in frame t. All the shift vectors are obtained for each landmark and each frame by repeating the calculation.

$$ShiftVector = \begin{pmatrix} p_x^{(t+1)} - p_x^{(t)} \\ p_y^{(t+1)} - p_y^{(t)} \\ p_z^{(t+1)} - p_z^{(t)} \end{pmatrix} \tag{4}$$

The shift vector expresses the direction in which each landmark moves between the frames. The conceptual diagram of the shift vector is shown in Fig. 3. A red arrow is an example of the shift vector. In Fig. 3(a), the left corner of the mouth does not move at all, and the right corner of it moves to the lower right. Therefore, this data is highly asymmetric. On the other hand, in Fig. 3(b), both corners of the mouth move to "the same direction" by the same amount, where the word "the same direction" means that two shift vectors are identified when one of the vectors is mirror-inverted with respect to the symmetric plane. Therefore, this data is highly symmetric.

The method to compare two shift vectors in a quantitative way is expressed in (5), where e_M is a vector that describes the left-right difference of the shift vectors, v is a shift vector of a landmark on the left side of the face and v' is that on the right side. (5) presupposes that the face faces forward, which simplifies the calculation: we can find e_M just by addition and subtraction. The reason for adding the x-coordinates is that the x-coordinate of a symmetric plane is zero.

$$e_M = \begin{pmatrix} v_x + v'_x \\ v_y - v'_y \\ v_z - v'_z \end{pmatrix} \tag{5}$$

We use the length of e_M as an indicator of the asymmetry. When it is small, all its components are also small and no left-right difference in the movement of face landmarks is found. Whereas when it is large, more than one component is also large, and we can say that there is a left-right difference. The length is calculated for each pair of frames. Therefore, the asymmetry for a video image is finally evaluated as the average of the lengths of all e_M.

3 Experimental Result and Discussion

3.1 Experimental Result

We created ten pseudo video images for this experiment and applied our method to them. Five of them are the asym-data, and the others are the sym-data. Each example of the deformation is shown in Fig. 3. Although all the pseudo video images are made from the same point cloud, the amount and direction of the deformation is different.

The average of the matching error is shown in Table 1. The error is the Euclidean distance between the matching point and its true point. True points are obtained by referencing information of the same index in point cloud files because FFD does not alter the order of data, it simply moves the points mathematically. The item "Landmark Detection" means that the result of the face landmark detection is treated as matching points in all frames.

The examples of the symmetry analysis and its asymmetry values are shown in Fig. 4, 5, and 6. In these figures, the lips are enlarged for visibility. The red line is the movement of true points, and the blue line is the movement of matching points. The closer these two lines are, the more accurately the face landmarks are matched. In addition, a blue line is drawn after drawing a red line, and hence if only a blue line is drawn, we can say that the landmark has been correctly matched for all frames.

Finally, the result of the symmetry analysis is shown in Fig. 7. In this figure, the orange points are the sym-data, and the blue points are the asym-data.

Table 1. Matching Error of Each Method.

Method	Matching Error
Landmark Detection [14]	2.36913
Proposed	0.05655

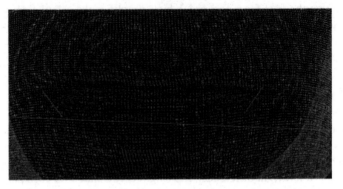

Fig. 4. Analysis of Sym-data (Asymmetry Value: 0.94900).

Fig. 5. Analysis of Asym-data (1) (Asymmetry Value: 1.90769).

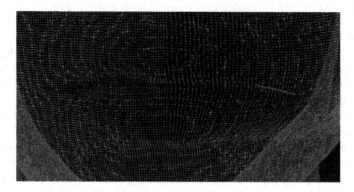

(a) Result of the Analysis.

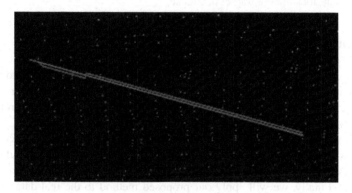

(b) Enlarged Figure of the Line.

Fig. 6. Analysis of Asym-data (2) (Asymmetry Value: 5.57269).

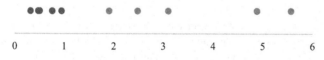

Fig. 7. Asymmetry Value.

3.2 Discussion

From Table 1, we can see that the proposed method has significantly improved to the landmark detection method. Landmark detection is useful for obtaining the positions of key points in the image. However, when it comes to detecting the temporal change of a certain point, the landmark detection method does not have enough power to find point correspondences from different frames of the video image. On the other hand, our matching method based on the FPFH descriptor works with a small error.

Looking at the matching result in more detail, there is no matching error in eight out of ten data. Figure 4 and Fig. 5 are the examples of data without errors: only the blue lines are drawn. For the left corner of the mouth in Fig. 5, the absence of a blue line indicates the correct matching because no deformation is added to this part. On the other hand, an example of data that contains the failure of matching is shown in Fig. 6. We can see from the figure that although the matching is not correct, the movement of the landmark is sufficiently detected. In view of the above, we can say that it is effective to perform the face landmark matching with FPFH.

For Fig. 7, the asymmetry values of the sym-data are distributed approximately 0.60. On the other hand, those of the asym-data are distributed from 1.90 to 5.57. In other words, the asymmetry values of the sym-data are smaller than those of the asym-data, which is a natural result. Furthermore, the validity of the analysis for the asym-data is seen by comparing Fig. 5 with Fig. 6. The data in Fig. 6 has a larger deformation than that in Fig. 5, which is projected to the asymmetry value. This result indicates that the amount of the left-right difference has an influence on the asymmetry value, and hence this assessment does not contradict our sense.

4 Conclusion

We proposed a method for the symmetry analysis of the face based on the movement of face landmarks, and performed an experiment using pseudo video images created from a still 3D point cloud. The experimental result shows that the matching error is small and the movement of the face landmark is sufficiently detected.

In the future, it is necessary to improve the matching algorithm to reduce the error because it is the most important process in our method. Furthermore, we should increase the number of points used for the symmetry analysis in order to achieve more detailed assessments. Finally, we will apply our proposed method to the real data of cleft lip patients and healthy controls and confirm its effectiveness.

References

1. International Clearinghouse for Birth Defects Surveillance and Research. Annual Report 2. http://www.icbdsr.org/wp-content/annual_report/Report2014.pdf. Accessed 14 June 2023
2. Shaw, W.C.: Folklore surrounding facial deformity and the origins of facial prejudice. Br. J. Plast. Surg. **34**, 237–246 (1981)
3. Pausch, N.C., et al.: Nasal appearance after secondary cleft rhinoplasty: comparison of professional rating with patient satisfaction. Oral Maxillofac. Surg. **20**, 195–201 (2016)
4. Trotman, C.A., et al.: Functional outcomes of cleft lip surgery. Part II: quantification of nasolabial movement. Cleft Palate Craniofac. J. **44**, 607–616 (2007)
5. Hosoki, D., et al.: Symmetric plane detection and symmetry analysis from A 3D point cloud data of face. In International Conference on Control, Automation and Systems, pp. 402–406. IEEE (2020)
6. Qi, C.R., et al.: PointNet: deep learning on point sets for 3D classification and segmentation. In IEEE Conference on Computer Vision and Pattern Recognition, pp. 77–85 (2017)
7. Qi, C.R., et al.: PointNet++: deep hierarchical feature learning on point sets in a metric space. In International Conference on Neural Information Processing Systems, pp. 5105–5114 (2017)

8. Lang, A.H., et al.: PointPillars: fast encoders for object detection from point clouds. In: IEEE/CVF Conference on Computer Vision and Pattern Recognition, pp. 12697–12705 (2019)

9. Pham, Q., et al.: JSIS3D: joint semantic-instance segmentation of 3D point clouds with multi-task pointwise networks and multi-value conditional random fields. In: IEEE/CVF Conference on Computer Vision and Pattern Recognition, pp. 8819–8828 (2019)

10. Rusu, R.B., et al.: Fast point feature histograms (FPFH) for 3D registration. In: International Conference on Robotics and Automation, pp. 3212–3217. IEEE (2009)

11. Fischler, M.A., et al.: Random sample consensus: a paradigm for model fitting with applications to image analysis and automated cartography. Commun. ACM **24**(6), 381–395 (1981)

12. Arun, K.S., et al.: Least-squares fitting of two 3-D point sets. IEEE Trans. Pattern Anal. Mach. Intell. **PAMI-9**(5), 698–700 (1987)

13. Besl, P.J., et al.: Method for Registration of 3-D Shapes. IEEE Trans. Pattern Anal. Mach. Intell. **14**(2), 239–256 (1992)

14. Kazemi, V., et al.: one millisecond face alignment with an ensemble of regression trees. In IEEE Conference on Computer Vision and Pattern Recognition, pp. 1867–1874 (2014)

15. Sederberg, T.W., et al.: Free-Form Deformation of Solid Geometric Models. ACM SIGGRAPH Comput. Graph. **20**(4), 151–160 (1986)

A Contrastive Learning-Based Interpretable Prediction Model for Patients with Heart Failure

Jinxiang Zhang, Tianhan Xu, and Bin Li[✉]

YangZhou University, Yangzhou, China
lb_kmis@yzu.edu.cn

Abstract. Heart failure is a group of complex clinical syndromes due to any structural or dysfunctional abnormality of the heart that results in impaired filling or ejection capacity of the ventricles. Using historical Electronic Health Records (EHRs) to forecast the risk of critical events in heart failure (HF) patients is an important area of research in the field of personalized medicine. However, it is difficult for some machine learning models to predict the risk of critical events owing to data imbalance and poor feature performance in the EHR data of HF patients. While time series-based deep neural networks have achieved excellent results, they lack interpretability. To solve these problems, this study focuses on proposing a deep neural network prediction model of critical events in heart failure patients based on Contrastive learning and Attention mechanism (CLANet). We evaluate our model on a real-world medical dataset, and the experimental results demonstrate that CLANet improves by 2–10% over the conventional methods.

Keywords: Heart failure · Contrastive learning · Critical event prediction · Electronic Health Records

1 Introduction

Heart failure is a worldwide disease that has developed into a worldwide healthcare burden [16]. There are currently approximately 26 million Heart failure patients worldwide. The prevalence of HF is estimated to be 1–2%, and the rate in people over 70 years of age in Europe and the United States is more than 10% [13]. Recent epidemiological evidence shows that the prevalence of Heart failure in China has increased by 44% in the last 15 years. More than 9 million people in China have Heart failure. Therefore, early detection of the risk of critical events in HF patients can reduce the cost of medical care and help doctors formulate a more suitable treatment plan based on the prediction results of critical events in HF patients, helping patients prolong their lives [18].

In recent years, some simple and scalable methods inspired by deep learning have been proposed for automatically representing features, such as One-Hot [17] and Skip-Gram [12]. However, these methods often treat each feature as a

H. Lu and J. Cai (Eds.): ISAIR 2023, CCIS 1998, pp. 288–299, 2024.
https://doi.org/10.1007/978-981-99-9109-9_29

discrete and independent word, which introduces the problem of data sparseness, making it difficult for them to capture the latent semantic content between medical variables.

Most previous studies use only a single type of data(e.g., ICD codes or clinical note), or simply concatenate different types of clinical variables into a whole, ignoring the differences between different types of clinical variables [10]. In fact, each type of medical data represents a different health state of patients, so it is necessary to consider the characteristic information contained in each type of medical data separately. However, existing methods largely ignore this phenomenon. Critical event prediction models are primarily designed to help clinicians make clinical decisions. Without interpretability, clinicians cannot determine whether these predictions can be trusted.

To solve the above problems, we have proposed CLANet. When the EHR data of heart failure patients are input, CLANet can mine the semantic information of the same type of medical variables and different types of medical variables through self-attention. Secondly, Bi-LSTM can also be used to capture the temporal dependencies. At the same time, soft-attention is also used to capture variable-level and visit-level attention scores in the patient's EHR. Finally, contrastive learning was used to compute the similarity of patient pairs. At the same time, the patient representation is used to make predictions about the risk of patient critical events.

In summary, our contributions are as follows:

1. We propose CLANet, an interpretable deep learning model for predicting patient risk of critical events using EHR data from patients with heart failure. In particular, CLANet incorporates multi-layered attention mechanisms that can capture the semantic information. It can also track fine-grained effects of each medical variable and each visit in patient's medical records.
2. We introduce contrastive learning by constructing a contrastive loss function. This allows the model to perform well with unbalanced data and effectively improves the predictive performance of the model.
3. We conduct an experimental evaluation on a real EHR dataset, and empirically illustrate that CLANet can achieve state-of-the-art performance.

2   Related Work

In recent years, an increasing number of studies have centred around the use of EHR data to predict patient risk of critical events, including mortality prediction [4], readmission [7], ICU transfer [3], and length of stay prediction [1]. Critical event risk prediction models based on longitudinal EHR data fall into two main categories, namely approaches based on machine learning models and approaches based on deep learning models.

2.1   Machine Learning Predictive Models Using EHR Data

Machine learning [14] methods mainly extract features from EHR datasets manually and then make predictions with machine learning models. For example,

Panahiazar et al. [15] designed a risk prediction model using support vector machines, additional trees, logistic regression, decision trees, and random forests.

Despite the promising results obtained with these methods, the results of these models depend heavily on the quality of the features manually selected by the experimenter. The acquisition of these features requires the introduction of expert knowledge and the use of complex statistics to process the data, which makes it difficult to transfer to other application scenarios. Secondly, the performance of machine learning cannot be guaranteed for datasets with sparse and imbalanced data.

2.2 Deep Learning Predictive Models Using EHR Data

Deep learning is capable to automatically extracting features from patient historical EHR data and is being used by an increasing number of researchers. Two variants of deep learning, CNN and RNN are the most commonly used deep learning models. While CNN [5] can automatically extract features and preserve adjacency relationships between input and neighbouring variables, it treats patient EHR data as chronological records and loses the correlation between parts and wholes.

In comparison, RNN [11] has better temporal modelling capabilities and are therefore more widely used. For example, Le et al. [9] proposed an LSTM-based dual memory neural computer (DMNC) to solve the asynchronous multi-view sequence problem, which allows for view interactions and long-term dependencies to be modelled. The model achieved the best results on the MIMIC-III dataset [8]. Although the RNN performs well in predicting critical events, it lacks interpretability, so the attention mechanism is usually used in EHR-based temporal prediction models. RETAIN [2] is a well-known interpretable prediction model, which consists of two recurrent neural networks and attention mechanism to learn forward and backward representations of patients respectively. Self-attentive and soft-attentive mechanisms are also used in our proposed CLANet.

3 Methodology

The task of predicting critical events in patients with heart failure is mainly divided into two tasks: mortality prediction and ICU transfer prediction. Our proposed model (CLANet) predicts the following four tasks: 48-hour mortality, 7-day mortality, in-hospital mortality and ICU transfer.

3.1 Data Processing

The EHR data used in this paper contain five main types of data. The EHR data of different patients are not the same. Therefore, it is necessary to process the data. If one-hot coding is used to directly represent patients, it will cause data redundancy, because in the MIMIC-III dataset, except for heart failure, there are a total of 3583 diseases in heart failure patients, most of which have

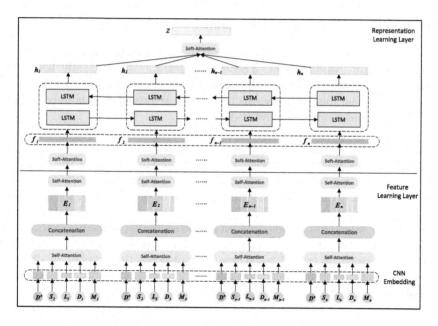

Fig. 1. The architecture of representation learning moudle.

only been diagnosed in a few patients and are easily treatable. Medication and surgery have the same problem (Fig. 1).

To solve the above problems, the method used in this paper is to first extract the heart failure patients in the dataset and divide them into two categories, namely, death and survival. Death is marked as positive and survival is marked as negative. Then the diagnosis, medication and surgery information in the EHR of the patients were extracted, and these variables of each patient were spliced into sentences, each variable was equivalent to a word, and the same type of patients were spliced into an article. Then the importance of each diagnosis, drug and surgery was calculated from the article using the idea of TF-IDF. The formula is as follows:

$$imp_i = \frac{po_i}{\sum_j po_i} \times \log \frac{|POS| + |NEG|}{sn_i} + \frac{pn_i}{\sum_j pn_i} \times \log \frac{|POS|}{sp_i + 1} \quad (1)$$

where po_i represents the number of occurrences of the variable V_i in POS and NEG, $\sum_j po_i$ represents the sum of all variables appearing in POS and NEG, sn_i represents the sentences containing variable V_i in the articles POS and NEG. pn_i represents the number of occurrences of the variable V_i in POS, $\sum_j pn_i$ represents the number of all variables in POS, and sp_i represents the total number of sentences containing variable V_i in POS. In this paper, the basis of the original TF-IDF is improved. Variables that score higher in positive examples are given more weight.

3.2 Representation Learning Moudle

The representation learning module mainly includes a feature learning layer and a representation learning layer. The feature learning layer mainly learns the features in the patient's EHR data through 1D-CNN and self-attention. The representation learning layer obtains the patient representation mainly through the soft-attention mechanism and Bi-LSTM.

Feature Learning Layer. The first layer of the feature learning layer uses the information from each patient visit to obtain the embedding of the variables. There are two main reasons for using 1D-CNN to represent each medical variable: firstly, discrete medical variables cannot be directly used for deep learning networks. Secondly, the direct use of one-hot to represent patient visit information does not well capture the correlation between different medical variables.

We first use 1D-CNN to embed each medical variable, specifically, the input vector $V_i = <v_i^1, v_i^2, \cdots, v_i^m>$, Where m represents the number of different examinations for patients. Then the relevant information embedding R_t of the patient can be obtained by the following formula:

$$R_t = \mathrm{Re}\,LU\left(\sum_{t=1}^{M} W_e v_t + b_e\right) \tag{2}$$

where v_t represents the feature of the tth timestamp, W_e is the convolution kernel, and b_e is the bias parameter.

The second layer of the feature learning layer is the self-attention layer, which performs self-attention on each medical data to obtain the internal relationship of each type of medical variable. A representation of each visit in the EHR of HF patients is then obtained. Firstly, the representation vector R_t obtained by 1D-CNN is used as input, and the self-attention mechanism constructs a key matrix K_i, query matrix Q_i and value matrix V_i according to Eq. (3), where KW_i, QW_i and VW_i are trainable weight parameter matrices. Then, the attention weight matrix A_i is computed according to Eq. (4), where d_k represents the latitude of the input vector. Finally, the output matrix O_i is computed as a weighted sum according to Eq. (5).

$$K_i = KW_i R_i, Q_i = QW_i R_i, V_i = VW_i R_i \tag{3}$$

$$A_i = \mathrm{softmax}\left(\frac{Q_i K_i^T}{\sqrt{d_k}}\right) \tag{4}$$

$$O_i = V_i A_i \tag{5}$$

$$S_i^j = \sum_{k=1}^{m} v_i^k \alpha_i^{jk} \tag{6}$$

where $A_i = <a_i^1, a_i^2, \ldots, a_i^m>$, $a_i^j = <\alpha_i^{j1}, \alpha_i^{j2}, \ldots, \alpha_i^{jm}>$, α_i^{jk} is the influence of variable v_i^k on variable v_i^j. $S_i = <s_i^1, s_i^2, \ldots, s_i^m>$, where s_i^j is the output matrix of r_i^j. It can be calculated by formula (6). We end up with five output vectors.

Then, the obtained output vectors are concatenated to obtain the joint representation Ei of the patient, and then the contextual semantic relationships of different types of data are obtained through the self-attention mechanism. Finally, the output vector Ni is obtained by the following formula:

$$K_i = KW_i E_i, Q_i = QW_i E_i, V_i = VW_i E_i \qquad (7)$$

$$N_i = \text{softmax}\left(\frac{Q_i K_i^T}{\sqrt{d_k}}\right) V_i \qquad (8)$$

Representation Learning Layer. It contains three sub-layers: variable-level attention, Bi-LSTM, visit-level attention. variable-level attention uses the output vector $N_i = <N_i^1, N_i^2, \ldots, N_i^n>$ obtained by the feature learning layer to compute the contribution of medical variable in a visit. Soft-attention is then utilized to obtain the contribution of the medical variables to the visit. The formula is as follows:

$$\alpha_i^j = \text{softmax}\left(g_i^T \tan h\left(CW_i n_i^j\right)\right) \qquad (9)$$

$$f_i = \sum_{j=1}^m \alpha_i^j n_i^j \qquad (10)$$

where CW_i is the trainable weight parameter matrix and g_i is the trainable context vector. According to Eq. (9), the contribution of each medical variable is calculated. Finally, the contribution of all medical variables is aggregated. Obtain the representation vector f_i of patient visits.

Visit-level attention uses the visit vector obtained earlier and computes the importance of each visit. The temporal dependence between visits is first captured by Bi-LSTM, and then the importance of each visit is computed using soft-attention. This is done primarily because patient visits are a sequential process. Specifically, the patient's visit vector f_i is first fed into a Bi-LSTM in chronological order, which is made up of a forward network and a backward network that can make full use of the information from the past and the future. The forward LSTM reads f_1 to f_t and computed the forward hidden state sequence $<\overrightarrow{h_1}, \overrightarrow{h_2}, \ldots, \overrightarrow{h_t}>$, given the input vector $\overrightarrow{f_i}$ and the previous hidden state $\overrightarrow{h_{i-1}}$. The hidden state is computed by the following formula:

$$\overrightarrow{h_i} = \text{LSTM}\left(\overrightarrow{f_i}, \overrightarrow{h_{i-1}}\right) \qquad (11)$$

Similarly, the backward LSTM reads the embedding vector sequence in reverse order, generating the backward hidden state sequence $<\overleftarrow{h_1}, \overleftarrow{h_2}, \ldots, \overleftarrow{h_t}>$. The hidden state h_i is a combination of forward and backward hidden states, calculate by the following formula:

$$h_i = \left[\overrightarrow{h_i}; \overleftarrow{h_i}\right] \qquad (12)$$

Then, soft-attention uses a linear transformation normalized by softmax to calculate attention weights according to Eq. (13). Finally, the representation vector z representing the patient is calculated by summarizing the importance of the medical variables for the heart failure patient according to Eq. (14). where w is a trainable vector, b is a trainable scalar, and β represents the importance of the hospital visit h_i.

$$\beta = \mathrm{softmax}\left(w^T h_i + b\right) \tag{13}$$

$$z = \sum_{i=1}^{n} \beta_i h_i \tag{14}$$

3.3 Contrastive Learning Layer

We introduce contrastive learning [6] to improve the classification ability of the model and solve the sample Sparse data problem in the experimental data. First, we construct the sample pair, if their labels are consistent, the label is set to 0, otherwise the label is set to 1. The representation learning module is used to generate the patient representation, and then the similarity of the patient representation in each sample pair is calculated. The following contrastive loss function is used to bring patients with consistent labels closer together and to pull patients with inconsistent labels apart.

$$\mathcal{L}_{\mathrm{Dist}} = (1 - Y)\frac{1}{2}\left(D_W\right)^2 + (Y)\frac{1}{2}\left\{\max\left(0, m - D_W\right)\right\}^2 \tag{15}$$

where Y is the label. D_w is the Euclidean distance between the patient representations of the model's output. The max function takes 0 or the margin m minus the maximum in the distance. In this experiment, the $m = 1$.

3.4 Loss Function

To obtain appropriate model parameters and predict critical events of heart failure patients, a sigmoid function was used to predict the labels of patients, and the cross-entropy between real visit label y_i and the predicted visit label $\hat{y}_i$ was used as the prediction loss function:

$$\mathcal{L}_{\mathrm{CE}} = -\frac{1}{2N}\sum_{i=1}^{N} y_i^T \log \hat{y}_i + (1 - y_i)^T \log (1 - \hat{y}_i) \tag{16}$$

where y_i is the true label of the ith heart failure patient. $\hat{y}_i$ is the score of the ith patient calculated by CLANet. We use the adma optimizer to optimize the above formulation.

Since the contrastive learning module and the prediction of critical events in heart failure patients can mutually benefit from joint training to obtain the clustered patient representation and the prediction of critical events in heart failure patients, the loss can be expressed as follows:

$$\mathcal{L} = \mathcal{L}_{\mathbf{CE}} + \lambda_{\mathrm{Dist}}\,\mathcal{L}_{\mathrm{Dist}} \tag{17}$$

The contrastive loss function is scaled by a non-negative hyperparameter λ. In this experiment, the hyperparameter $\lambda = 0.5$.

4   Experiments

4.1   Dataset Description

The EHR dataset used in this experiment is the MIMIC-III [8]. Firstly, the data contains demographics, medications, laboratory tests, surgical codes, diagnosis codes. In this study, a variety of information about the patient is used, because whether it is age, laboratory tests, diagnosis, or drug and surgical information, it is essential to predict the health status of the patient. Secondly, because this paper is the critical event prediction of heart failure patients, so 10436 patients diagnosed with heart failure were extracted.

4.2   Implement Details

In this study, machine learning methods are mainly implemented using scikit-learn. All deep learning models in this study were implemented using tensorflow 2.6.0 and all methods used adam optimizer with learning rate set to 0.001. A computer with 90 GB of RAM and a Tesla A40 GPU was used for training. The batch-size was set to 512 for all deep learning models. To avoid overfitting, we introduce dropout strategy and Dropout rate is 0.5. At the same time, the early stopping strategy and L2 regularization are also used. For the proposed CLANet, the embedding size of 1D-CNN for each variable is 256, and the hidden units of LSTM are 30. We randomly split the training, validation and test sets into $0.7 : 0.2 : 0.1$. Three measures were used to evaluate the performance of the model: Accuracy, F1-score, and AUC. For all models, we repeat the experiments 20 times and report the average evaluation metric of the test performance.

4.3   Baselines

LR: It is a generalized linear regression analysis model, which is part of the supervised learning in machine learning.

RF: It is a form of ensemble learning, combining many decision trees into a forest.

XGBOOST: It is a decision tree based ensemble algorithm for classification and regression problems.

Bi-LSTM: It is an important variant of deep learning that can handle sequence problems well.

Diople [11]: It is a Bi-RNN model for diagnostic prediction tasks with an attention mechanism that represents a patient's visit as a series of unordered sets composed of multiple unique medical codes.

Retain: It is a combination of two recurrent neural networks and an attention mechanism to learn forward and backward representations of patients respectively, and visit-level weights and variable-level weights can be obtained.

IoHAN [4]: It is an interpretable outcome prediction model based on hierarchical attention, which obtains variable-level and visit-level attention of patients.

Table 1. Performance of Baselines and CLANet on Four key Event Prediction Tasks.

Model	48 h			7day			in-hosptial			ICU Transfer		
	Acc	F1	AUC	Acc	F1	AUC	Acc	F1	AUC	Acc	F1	AUC
LR	0.727	0.705	0.756	0.725	0.741	0.747	0.731	0.761	0.750	0.798	0.802	0.876
RF	0.756	0.739	0.666	0.763	0.742	0.669	0.779	0.782	0.669	0.819	0.806	0.809
XGBOOST	0.763	0.750	0.671	0.774	0.766	0.694	0.793	0.763	0.702	0.821	0.803	0.842
Bi-LSTM	0.788	0.796	0.726	0.792	0.808	0.752	0.806	0.822	0.758	0.818	0.805	0.879
Diople	0.804	0.821	0.787	0.812	0.822	0.797	0.817	0.826	0.794	0.813	0.806	0.880
Retain	0.813	0.822	0.786	0.806	0.818	0.805	0.819	0.823	0.795	0.814	0.806	0.885
IoHAN	0.817	0.811	0.791	**0.827**	0.834	**0.810**	0.827	0.835	0.796	0.819	0.801	0.886
CLANet	**0.832**	**0.829**	**0.808**	0.826	**0.844**	**0.810**	**0.843**	**0.841**	**0.815**	**0.841**	**0.811**	**0.893**

4.4 Result Analysis

Table 1 presents the average performance of the proposed CLANet and other baseline models on the four tasks. It can be seen that CLANet exhibits stable and excellent performance. And we achieve state-of-the-art performance on most metrics.

We first focus on classical machine learning methods, including LR, RF and XGBOOST. Machine learning methods generally show lower performance compared to deep learning methods. The main reason is that they cannot model a patient's visit as a sequence, but only the patient's visit sequence as a whole. On the mortality prediction task, the machine learning model achieves 5% lower F1-score and AUC scores than deep learning baselines such as Bi-LSTM. However, on the ICU Transfer task, machine learning methods perform no worse or even better than many deep learning-based methods. The reason for this phenomenon may be that individual signals may be more important than timing information for ICU Transfer tasks. In this case, deep learning models such as Bi-LSTM may suffer from overfitting. Through the attention mechanism and contrastive learning, CLANet can extract the medical variables that have a key impact on the outcome, and can distinguish the representations of patients, which can achieve better prediction results.

As an ordinary deep learning model, the performance of Bi-LSTM is stable, and the performance gap between the Bi-LSTM model and any other deep learning models on the ICU Transfer task is not large. This is mainly because heart failure is a chronic disease, and for the ICU Transfer task, simple deep learning models can capture key variables easily. However, it did not perform as well on the mortality prediction task. For the mortality prediction task, the performance of all attention-based models is outstanding, mainly due to the fact that deep learning can capture key variables in time-series information, and then amplify these medical variables through the attention mechanism. Although both RETAIN and IoHAN use hierarchical attention, contrast learning is introduced in our model to better distinguish patient representations and achieve the best classification results. In particular, on the ICU Transfer task, CLANet achieves the optimal performance on each metric.

4.5 Ablation Study

In this section, we focus on the comparison between CLANet and its variants that change parts of the full CLANet model. The setup is the same as the previous experiment, but this time we run it 5 times to get the average performance.

CLANet-TF: It is a variant of CLANet without the critical code extraction module and directly using all medical variables.

CLANet-SEA: It is a variant of CLANet without self-attention. The final representation of the patient is directly obtained through variable-level and visit-level attention and Bi-LSTM.

CLANet-SOA: It is a variant of CLANet without soft-attention. Specifically, it directly uses self-attention and Bi-LSTM to obtain the final representation.

CLANet-ATT: It is a variant of CLANet without attention mechanism. Specifically, it directly uses Bi-LSTM to obtain the final representation.

CLANet-CL: It is a variant of CLANet without contrastive learning, specifically, it does not construct sample pairs and directly uses the cross-entropy loss to predict the critical event risk.

Table 2. Average Performance for CLANet's Variants.

Model	48 h			in-hospital			ICU Transfer		
	Acc	F1	AUC	Acc	F1	AUC	Acc	F1	AUC
CLANet-TF	0.752	0.725	0.729	0.785	0.720	0.796	0.807	0.794	0.825
CLANet-SEA	0.815	0.820	0.804	0.823	0.827	0.789	0.811	0.796	0.889
CLANet-SOA	0.809	0.806	0.795	0.802	0.820	0.785	0.821	0.805	0.882
CLANet-ATT	0.792	0.807	0.759	0.801	0.816	0.796	0.814	0.801	0.877
CLANet-CL	0.819	0.809	0.793	0.820	0.828	0.801	0.809	0.793	0.858
CLANet	**0.832**	**0.819**	**0.808**	**0.843**	**0.841**	**0.825**	**0.841**	**0.811**	**0.893**

The experimental results are presented in Table 2. It can be seen that after the deletion of TF-IDF, the model performance significantly decreases, mainly because the patient visit information is composed of medical variables. The long-tailed distribution of each medical variable may cause redundancy, so this paper uses the keyword extraction method commonly used in NLP to extract key influencing variables and improve the prediction performance of the model. In the mortality prediction task, CLANet-ATT performs the worst and CLANet performs the best. This shows that all sub-layers of CLANet contribute to the final critical event risk prediction.

Secondly, the performance of CLANet-SEA is better than CLANet-SOA, indicating the effectiveness of variable-level and visit-level attention, mainly because the patient information in MIMIC-III is mainly from icu, and the collected information is not rich enough, and the contextual information is relatively fixed, so the contextual information of patient visit information is not obvious enough. However, CLANet-SOA performs better than no attention mechanism, indicating that the self-attention layer improves the predictive ability of the model. Finally, it can be seen that when the contrastive learning module of the model is removed, the predictive ability of the model is significantly decreased, suggesting that contrastive learning has a facilitating effect on critical event prediction. Especially in ICU Transfer task, due to the simple task, the deep learning model has difficulty learning useful knowledge, which is prone to cause overfitting. Therefore, when we remove contrast learning, the model effect will reach the minimum.

5 Conclusions

Predicting the risk of critical events in HF patients using EHR data is one of the key issues in medical event prediction. The existing critical event prediction models cannot solve the problem of multi-data fusion and interpretability well. To solve the aforementioned problems, we propose CLANet, a multi-layer attention mechanism model based on contrastive learning. Experimental results on MIMIC-III show that CLANet outperforms existing models in terms of prediction performance.

References

1. Cai, X., et al.: Real-time prediction of mortality, readmission, and length of stay using electronic health record data. J. Am. Med. Inform. Assoc. **23**(3), 553–561 (2016)
2. Choi, E., Bahadori, M.T., Sun, J., Kulas, J., Schuetz, A., Stewart, W.: Retain: An interpretable predictive model for healthcare using reverse time attention mechanism. In: Advances in Neural Information Processing Systems, vol. 29 (2016)
3. Chou, C.A., Cao, Q., Weng, S.J., Tsai, C.H.: Mixed-integer optimization approach to learning association rules for unplanned ICU transfer. Artif. Intell. Med. **103**, 101806 (2020)
4. Du, J., et al.: An interpretable outcome prediction model based on electronic health records and hierarchical attention. Int. J. Intell. Syst. **37**(6), 3460–3479 (2022)
5. Feng, Y., et al.: Patient outcome prediction via convolutional neural networks based on multi-granularity medical concept embedding. In: 2017 IEEE International Conference on Bioinformatics and Biomedicine (BIBM), pp. 770–777. IEEE (2017)
6. Hadsell, R., Chopra, S., LeCun, Y.: Dimensionality reduction by learning an invariant mapping. In: 2006 IEEE Computer Society Conference on Computer Vision and Pattern Recognition (CVPR 2006), vol. 2, pp. 1735–1742. IEEE (2006)

7. He, D., Mathews, S.C., Kalloo, A.N., Hutfless, S.: Mining high-dimensional administrative claims data to predict early hospital readmissions. J. Am. Med. Inform. Assoc. **21**(2), 272–279 (2014)
8. Johnson, A.E., et al.: MIMIC-III, a freely accessible critical care database. Sci. Data **3**(1), 1–9 (2016)
9. Le, H., Tran, T., Venkatesh, S.: Dual memory neural computer for asynchronous two-view sequential learning. In: Proceedings of the 24th ACM SIGKDD International Conference on Knowledge Discovery & Data Mining, pp. 1637–1645 (2018)
10. Luo, J., Ye, M., Xiao, C., Ma, F.: HiTANet: hierarchical time-aware attention networks for risk prediction on electronic health records. In: Proceedings of the 26th ACM SIGKDD International Conference on Knowledge Discovery & Data Mining, pp. 647–656 (2020)
11. Ma, F., Chitta, R., Zhou, J., You, Q., Sun, T., Gao, J.: Dipole: diagnosis prediction in healthcare via attention-based bidirectional recurrent neural networks. In: Proceedings of the 23rd ACM SIGKDD International Conference on Knowledge Discovery and Data Mining, pp. 1903–1911 (2017)
12. Mikolov, T., Chen, K., Corrado, G., Dean, J.: Efficient estimation of word representations in vector space. arXiv preprint arXiv:1301.3781 (2013)
13. Mosterd, A., Hoes, A.W.: Clinical epidemiology of heart failure. Heart **93**(9), 1137–1146 (2007)
14. Nistal-Nuño, B.: Developing machine learning models for prediction of mortality in the medical intensive care unit. Comput. Methods Programs Biomed. **216**, 106663 (2022)
15. Panahiazar, M., Taslimitehrani, V., Pereira, N., Pathak, J.: Using EHRS and machine learning for heart failure survival analysis. Stud. Health Technol. Inform. **216**, 40 (2015)
16. Ponikowski, P., et al.: Heart failure: preventing disease and death worldwide. ESC Heart Failure **1**(1), 4–25 (2014)
17. Uriarte-Arcia, A.V., López-Yáñez, I., Yáñez-Márquez, C.: One-hot vector hybrid associative classifier for medical data classification. PLoS One **9**(4), e95715 (2014)
18. Wang, Y., et al.: Early detection of heart failure with varying prediction windows by structured and unstructured data in electronic health records. In: 2015 37th Annual International Conference of the IEEE Engineering in Medicine and Biology Society (EMBC), pp. 2530–2533. IEEE (2015)

A Dictionary-Based Concept Extraction Method for Chinese Course Knowledge

Qiang Chen[✉], Bin Li, Liting Wei, Shiqing Yan, and Binbin Wang

YangZhou University, Yangzhou, China
1078216943@qq.com

Abstract. Chinese Course Concept Extraction holds significant importance in the construction process of knowledge graph in the field of education in China. It aims to extract the concept set of corresponding courses from unstructured texts such as textbooks and course outlines. One of the existing methods for course concept extraction is to encode only character information. However, compared with English, Chinese course concept extraction cannot be separated from contextual language. To tackle this issue, we develop a novel approach named Dictionary-based Chinese Concept Extraction Model, which introduces the word information of the course concept and the professional vocabulary of the third-party database to enrich the representation meaning of character vector. Specifically, first, we construct the course concept dictionary through third-party database such as Baidupedia. Second, each character is matched with word information in the dictionary, which is applied the corresponding weight. Third, the input sequences, represented by character vectors that contain word information, are passed through a single layer of bidirectional Long Short-Term Memory (LSTM) for sequence modeling. Finally, we applies a Conditional Random Field (CRF) layer to infer labels for the entire character sequence. Our proposed method was evaluated on a private dataset, and the results demonstrate its superiority over state-of-the-art methods, through extensive experimentation.

Keywords: Concept Extraction · Education · Dictionary

1 Introduction

MOOCs (Massive Open Online Course) the realm of smart education has seen extensive discussions about Massive Open Online Courses (MOOCs) in recent years. When students conduct online education and learning, they will encounter a lot of unstructured text and they cannot accurately find out the corresponding concepts from these unstructured texts for learning. Chinese course concept extraction can extract words or phrases describing a concept from a given Chinese unstructured text and can help students clearly understand the course concepts and knowledge structure, which is helpful to improve learning efficiency

H. Lu and J. Cai (Eds.): ISAIR 2023, CCIS 1998, pp. 300–312, 2024.
https://doi.org/10.1007/978-981-99-9109-9_30

and performance and in recent years, the research on this topic has gained considerable attention from the academic community. One of the existing methods for course concept extraction is to encode only character information. For example, Y Jia et al. [6] proposed a Chinese named entity recognition based on CNN-BiLSTM-CRF. They adopted a character-based method, transforming each character into a vector representation, and introduced CNN and BiLSTM to extract the text feature. These two network structures can effectively model and process text sequences, and can extract part of the semantic information of characters. Therefore, K Wei et al. [10] regard the solution of Chinese course concept extraction as a sequence labeling problem, and proposes a character-based Chinese concept extraction model to improve the overall recognition performance, they input the course text as characters into BERT for encoding and then feed it into the sequence modeling and decoding layer. Meanwhile, Gridach et al. [3] utilized a Bi-LSTM model to perform entity recognition in the biomedical field, by feeding the model with character-level representations. Despite the many workable solutions provided by these studies, there is still an issue with the character-based Chinese concept extraction model is that they only use the feature representation at the character level and do not consider the information at the word level, as a result, certain crucial semantic details may be overlooked or disregarded, leading to a loss of important information.

To tackle this issue, we collect the corresponding set of concepts related to the course through third-party resource libraries such as Baidupedia, and Subsequently, the original text can be segmented using word segmentation tools, which allows for the acquisition of corresponding word vectors through implementation of the Word2vec model. Together, they form the course concept dictionary. And heuristically introduce concept word information into the model, the character vector and the concept word vector are concatenated and sent to a single bidirectional LSTM layer for sequence modeling and prediction. Finally, in order to improve the accuracy of the corresponding character labels, we incorporated a CRF layer, which adds a constraint relationship between the sequences to optimize the labeling results. Since Chinese course concept recognition constitutes a type of domain-specific named entity recognition, the current body of research on domain-specific named entities remains inadequate, and the dataset is not very comprehensive. For this reason, we used a corpus of educational course entities constructed in a manually annotated way, in collaboration with the JingZhi Education Company. This contributions of this work can be summarized as follows:

1. Our proposed method involves creating a Chinese course concept dictionary by utilizing a third-party database, which can effectively use external databases to improve the accuracy of concept extraction.
2. We propose an efficient splicing and fusion method of course concept words based on corresponding character matching, moreover, we validate the efficacy of this fusion approach by conducting ablation experiments.
3. Our model is evaluated on a private dataset and outperforms state-of-the-art methods, demonstrating the effectiveness and feasibility of the proposed

method when utilizing a single-layer bidirectional LSTM for the sequence modeling layer.

2   Related Work

In natural language processing, named entity recognition (NER) [13] is a fundamental task that involves identifying various types of entities, including but not limited to person names, place names, and organization names, within sentences from vast amounts of unstructured text [7]. Named entity recognition plays a crucial role in the field of natural language processing, as it forms the basis for a variety of downstream tasks, such as relation extraction, event extraction, question answering, and text summarization, and it is also the first work to build a knowledge graph.

Over the past few years, with the advancements made in deep learning techniques, due to its model can learn the representation of the distribution characteristics of data and has strong generalization ability, accordingly, the field of named entity recognition has progressively shifted towards the utilization of deep learning models. A system was proposed by Hu et al. [5] which combines RNN model with features, RNN, CRF and rules, and adds a voting mechanism to it. Only when a word is selected by two or more methods, it will be output as an entity. A named entity recognition model that leverages bidirectional gated recurrent units was proposed by Shi Chundan et al. [1]: BGRU-CRF. The bidirectional GRU network is introduced and the semantic information of the text is reused, therefore, it greatly improves the recognition performance. Li Mingyang et al. [9] incorporated the self-attention mechanism to the bidirectional LSTM model, and this approach allows for the utilization of contextual information from the corresponding Weibo named entity recognition dataset, resulting in a substantial improvement in recognition accuracy.

The primary distinction between Chinese and English named entity recognition lies in the fact that there are obvious Spaces between English words to separate each word, while there is no sign of natural segmentation between Chinese sentences. A common approach for Chinese named entity recognition is to utilize pre-existing Chinese word segmentation tools to divide the sentences into meaningful segments. Subsequently, a variety of deep learning models have been employed for the task of Chinese entity recognition [8], but the current Chinese word segmentation system will inevitably produce errors in word segmentation, so it will lead to errors in boundary prediction of named entity recognition. Therefore character-based Chinese named entity recognition alone may not effectively leverage the word-level information, which can potentially lead to lower recognition accuracy. Ding et al. [2] proved through experiments that, adding word information can significantly improve the precision and recall rate of named entity recognition. Therefore, Zhang et al. [12] proposed a Lattice-LSTM model to add lexical information to a character-based named entity recognition model and instead of using a heuristic approach to select a word from the dictionary when a character matches multiple words, the authors suggest retaining all matching words and letting the subsequent named entity recognition model decide which word to use.

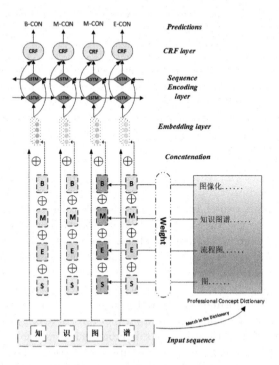

Fig. 1. The overall architecture of the proposed method.

3   Approach

In this work, because the character content of some concept words is hidden in the context of related courses in the field of education, To address the limitations of traditional methods that can not use the information of course concept words, we present a novel approach for extracting course concept. We use a new method on the character representation layer of the concept extraction model, so that the relevant concept vocabulary information can be introduced. We call this approach course lexicon construction. As shown in Fig. 1, to begin with, we represent each character in the input course text sequence as a set of vectors. Then we add the word information from the course dictionary we built to each character vector representation. After the vector representation fused with word information is obtained, it is fed into a Bi-LSTM layer for feature extraction modeling and a CRF layer for sequential relation constraint and inference in a sequential manner, and the prediction results are finally obtained.

3.1   Character Representation Layer

In this layer, for traditional character-based concept extraction, each input character sequence c can be represented by its corresponding vector embedding:

$$x_i^c = e^c(c_i) \tag{1}$$

where e^c represents a two-character sequence embedded in the query table.

Moreover, Zhang et al. have shown that utilizing two-character vector embeddings can be beneficial for character representation, especially for models that do not incorporate word information. As such, it is a conventional approach to enhance the vector representation of a single character sequence by incorporating a two-character embedding:

$$x_i^c = \left[e^c(c_i) ; e^b(c_i \cdot c_{i+1}) \right] \tag{2}$$

where e^b represents a two-character sequence embedded in the query table.

However, due to the broad distribution of knowledge concepts involved in education related courses, there are multiple layers of small knowledge concepts under the main knowledge concept, and a knowledge concept will be associated with many other knowledge concepts. And Bert as the training model of the current natural language processing, can capture the unstructured text input by the context of language information, study the relationship between the continuous text fragment and to calculate the mutual relations between words.

Different from the static bag-of-words model such as word2vector, BERT is used to extract the knowledge concept feature of education-related courses, which not only contains static character information, but also carries the dynamic context information. Therefore, Incorporating pre-trained language models like Bert into the encoding layer can significantly improve the accuracy of concept extraction by taking into account the contextual information of characters. In the following experiments, we also show the effectiveness of using BERT.

Firstly, the educational technology corpus vector passes through three different fully connected layers, and gets three vectors Q (the representation of the current word in the corpus), K (the representation of other words in the corpus) and V (the expression of other words in the Encoder) in the Encoder part. In the Decoder part, three decoded vectors Q (the expression of the current word in the Decoder), K (the expression of all input words after the end of Encoder) and V (all input words after the end of Encoder) are obtained. Then Q and K^T are matrix multiplied to obtain the vector QK^T of the correlation degree between the word and other words. The normalized K^T matrix is fed into the Softmax activation function, resulting in a vector representing the correlation degree between words, and then multiplied by V to obtain the final vector. As the formula shows:

$$\text{Attention}(Q, K, V) = \text{softmax}\left(\frac{QK^T}{\sqrt{d_k}}\right) V \tag{3}$$

And then through the multi-head structure for relative splicing:

$$\text{MultHead}(Q, K, V) = \text{Concat}\left(\text{head}^{1}, \cdots, \text{head}^{h}\right) W \tag{4}$$

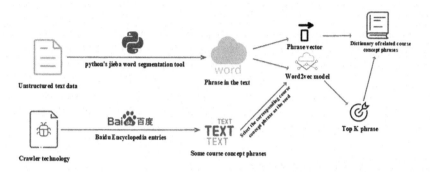

Fig. 2. Flowchart of course concept dictionary construction.

3.2 Construction of Educational Course Dictionary

In this section, we will detail how to construct the dictionary for fusing word information. Figure 2 shows the process of constructing an educational course dictionary. Firstly, for the unstructured text of a course, we first use some word segmentation packages in the python library, such as the general word segmentation tools jieba, Hanlp, and Tsinghua Chinese lexical analysis toolkit THULAC to perform word segmentation operation, get the word set in the unstructured text, and input it into the word2vector model. The model corresponding to the course text and the vector of the word set in the text are trained.

Secondly, through the crawler technology, the concepts of related professional directions are collected from Baidu Baike and other platforms, and some concepts of related courses are manually selected as seeds and input into the above word2vec model. In the professional concept set we collected, the threshold is above the preset value, and the related concept set and its vector representation are similar to the seed set, and they are combined with the word vector in the original text to form our course dictionary.

3.3 Categorizing the Matched Words

We need to classify each character when we input unstructured course text. Firstly, in order to retain relevant concept word information, When a character is inputted from the text, we partition the concept words that match it into four distinct sets: B, M, E, S, and each character is labeled with these four kinds of labels. For each character x_i in the input sequence $L = \{x_1, x_2, \cdots, x_n\}$, the four distinct sets are given by:

$$B(x_i) = \{w_{i,k}, \forall w_{i,k} \in D, i < k \leq n\} \tag{5}$$

$$M(x_i) = \{w_{j,k}, \forall w_{j,k} \in D, 1 \leq j < i < k \leq n\} \tag{6}$$

$$E(x_i) = \{w_{j,i}, \forall w_{j,i} \in D, 1 \leq j < i\} \tag{7}$$

$$S(x_i) = \{x_i, \exists x_i \in D\} \tag{8}$$

Here, D represents the conceptual vocabulary we use in this method. In addition, In case the character in the input text doesn't match any concept word in the corresponding position of the dictionary, we append'NONE' to the type set. Accordingly, when we introduce character embedding, we will not lose the word information of the course concept, because we can accurately recover the word information of the concept through the matching result of the character in the corresponding course concept dictionary.

3.4   Merging the Course Concept Sets

Once the set of course concepts at different positions for each character in the text is obtained, we proceed to fuse them into a fixed-dimensional vector. In contrast to using attention mechanisms or other algorithms, we adopt a simple yet effective approach that utilizes the frequency of occurrence of each concept word in the text as weight coefficients. This not only ensures the efficiency of the algorithm but also makes effective use of course concept word information. This value is a constant, which can be readily computed directly from the educational resources text of the course, and Using word frequency as weights can significantly accelerate the computation of word weights.

Specifically, let $Z(w)$ represent the frequency with which the course concept word w appears in the statistics. Consequently, we get a weighted representation of the word set S, which can be expressed as follows:

$$v^s(S) = \frac{4}{Z} \sum_{w \in S} z(w) e^w(w), \tag{9}$$

$$Z = \sum_{w \in B \cup M \cup E \cup S} z(w). \tag{10}$$

Here w represents the selected course concept dictionary, and all the words in the four course concept word sets are weight normalized. Moreover, if the word w is found to be contained by another subsequence of matching words, the word frequency of w will not increase.

Finally, the four concept word sets are combined into a fixed dimension feature, which was added to the representation of each character in a concatenation manner. Consequently, the each character representation is given by:

$$e^s(B, M, E, S) = [v^s(B); v^s(M); v^s(E); v^s(S)] \tag{11}$$

$$x^c \leftarrow [x^c; e^s(B, M, E, S)] \tag{12}$$

Here, v^s denotes the weighting function above.

3.5   Sequence Encoding Layer

After adding the lexical information of the concept to the characters, The vector representation of the characters is fed into the sequence modeling layer, which is responsible for capturing the dependencies between the characters. In the construction of education-related course entities, the content in the text is implied in the context and reflected in the relationship between the characters. Bi-LSTM can not only save short-term input, but also better capture bidirectional semantic relationships. Therefore, the Bi-LSTM model is used as the word processor to extract the information of single words and the relationship between words in the input sentence. Consequently, We implemented this functionality here using a Bi-LSTM layer, which is defined as follows for a forward LSTM network:

$$\begin{bmatrix} i_t \\ f_t \\ o_t \\ \tilde{c}_t \end{bmatrix} = \begin{bmatrix} \sigma \\ \sigma \\ \sigma \\ \tanh \end{bmatrix} \left(W \begin{bmatrix} x_t^c \\ h_{t-1} \end{bmatrix} + b \right), \tag{13}$$

$$c_t = \tilde{c}_t \odot i_t + c_{t-1} \odot f_t \tag{14}$$

$$h_t = o_t \odot \tanh(c_t) \tag{15}$$

where σ is the sigmoid function after the multiplication of the corresponding matrix elements, and $\odot$ represents the corresponding position elements in the product matrix. The LSTM in the opposite direction, which is defined similarly to the forward LSTM but models sequences in reverse order, is used to capture dependencies between characters in the opposite direction. The hidden states of the forward and backward LSTMs at each step i^{th}, denoted as $h_i = \left[\overrightarrow{h}_i; \overleftarrow{h}_i \right]$, are concatenated to form the context-dependent representation of character c_i.

3.6   Label Inference Layer

Since using the Bi-LSTM layer alone will cause our label classification method to ignore the score corresponding to the character, which will predict some illegal entity types, We utilize a CRF layer, which is a standard layer used on top of the Bi-LSTM layer, to infer the label of the entire character sequence. And the role of CRF layer is the role of CRF is to further modify the recognition results, that is, to extract the dependencies between labels, so that the identified entities meet the labeling rules. The scoring function of Y is computed and used to determine the probability of the predicted sequence Y. In the end, the output is obtained by maximizing the likelihood function of the predicted sequence generation probability and calculating the predicted label sequence. The CRF layer for label inference of character sequences is defined as follows:

$$p(y \mid s; \theta) = \frac{\prod_{t=1}^n \phi_t (y_{t-1}, y_t \mid s)}{\sum_{y' \in \mathcal{Y}_s} \prod_{t=1}^n \phi_t (y'_{t-1}, y'_t \mid s)} \tag{16}$$

$$\phi_t\left(y', y \mid s\right) = \exp\left(\boldsymbol{w}_{y',y}^T \boldsymbol{h}_t + b_{y',y}\right) \tag{17}$$

Here, y_s represents all possible label sequences in s, and where $w_{y',y}$ and $b_{y',y}$ can be optimized during model training. To obtain the final prediction sequence, we utilize the CRF model to search for the most probable sequence y^* based on its conditional probability. The Viterbi algorithm can be utilized to address this issue, which is defined as follows:

$$\boldsymbol{y}^* = \arg\max_{\boldsymbol{y}} p(\boldsymbol{y} \mid s; \boldsymbol{\theta}), \tag{18}$$

where y^* represents the predicted label corresponding to the corresponding unstructured text character.

4 Experiments

We carried out a comprehensive set of experiments to examine the impact of integrating concept word information into characters. Additionally, we aim to compare the character-based concept extraction method with the method that incorporates concept word information, through empirical evaluation. The evaluation metrics used were precision (P), recall (R), and F1-score (F1).

4.1 Dataset

Since there is no open and free educational dataset in the field of educational technology, We cooperate with Jinzhi Education Company to manually annotate some data sets related to computer courses, including Python Language Programming, Computer Vision, Knowledge Graph and other computer-related courses, and review the data to ensure the correctness of annotation. And we label the whole dataset according to the BMES sequence.

There are a total of 4427 designed entities in the dataset, and the total number of labeled entities reaches 444023, which is relatively large. Moreover, to further confirm the efficacy of this model, we further divided the concepts into 14 subdivided knowledge concept types such as function, model and method according to the syllabus, catalog and professional division. Finally, we split the dataset into training set, validation set, and test sets in a 6:2:2 ratio for both types of labeled datasets.

4.2 Results and Analysis

As shown in Table 1, the comparison results of our method with other baselines are presented. In the experiment, we carried out two groups of comparative tests. Firstly, we extracted all the corresponding course professional phrases as course concepts. The P value, R value and F1 value of the concept extraction method with word information in this paper reached 89.79%, 86.78% and 88.26%, which exceeded other baseline methods. Compared with character-based models such as BiLSTM-CRF, The model has demonstrated a notable enhancement in its performance after adding words from external third-party databases and adding relevant course concept word information to character information. Compared with the method of automatically learning concept features such as CNN-BiLSTM-CRF [11], it is often more effective to use the adaptive feature template to extract features from the window. In addition, the model can also learn many constraint rules through the loss function transfer probability matrix of the final CRF layer, which makes the prediction results more accurate. In addition, we compared with Lattice-LSTM and other models with word information. The proposed model outperforms the three models with word information in terms of P, R, and F1 values, demonstrating the efficacy and practicality of integrating concept word information into the model.

Table 1. Performance on the concept extraction dataset of computer science courses.

Only one kind type				Fourteen kind types			
Model	P	R	F1	Model	P	R	F1
BiLSTM-CRF	73.24	74.65	73.94	BiLSTM-CRF	69.52	71.76	70.63
CNN-Bilstm-CRF	73.76	74.87	74.32	CNN-Bilstm-CRF	68.73	70.07	69.40
BiFlaG	83.56	82.45	83.00	BiFlaG	81.64	80.15	80.89
LR-CNN	87.10	85.06	86.45	LR-CNN	83.89	82.09	82.98
LGN	86.53	86.31	86.42	LGN	83.80	80.81	82.28
Lattice-LSTM	88.12	82.87	86.47	Lattice-LSTM	86.57	79.86	83.08
Ours	**89.79**	**86.78**	**88.26**	**Ours**	**88.25**	**81.43**	**84.70**

Secondly, To further validate the efficacy of this model, additional experiments were conducted on a dataset with more kinds of course concepts. We can see that compared with the concept extraction with only one type, the P, R and F1 values of our model are reduced by 1.54%, 5.35% and 3.56% respectively. However, due to the addition of concept word information in the third-party information database, the decrease is smaller than that of CNN-BiLSTM-CRF and LGN [4] models, indicating that the anti-disturbance performance of our model is better. It's robust. In addition, this model is superior to other models in P, R and F1 when extracting multi-type course concepts, and obtains the best performance.

4.3 Ablation Study

In this part, in order to study the effectiveness of external thesaurus and the way of adding word information in our model, ablation experiments are carried out on our own dataset. First of all, as shown in the Table 2, we verified the effectiveness of external third-party dictionary expansion. We tried not to add external dictionaries for specific courses, but only used large general domain dictionaries, and added the marked course concepts to the dictionary as gold segments to varying degrees. The experiments show that with the enrichment of the content of the corresponding domain dictionary, The P, R, and F1 values of the model have been improved, and the external dictionary we collected for the current course also exceeds the effect of adding 40% gold segment word segmentation dictionary. It can also be inferred that the accuracy of our model will increase as we collect more and more external dictionary content. Compared with some previous ways of adding concept word information, the previous way of adding concept word information only considers that each character receives word information from the word at the beginning or end of it, thus ignoring the concept word information containing the character information. However, the group "-M" is added in this model to prevent the loss of intermediate information.

Table 2. Experiments on the effectiveness of adding third-party dictionaries and the way of adding concept word information.

Only one kind type			
Model	P	R	F1
- Without dictionary	88.27	85.01	86.61
- Dictionary+40% concept	89.84	85.21	87.46
- Dictionary+all concept	90.27	90.99	90.63
- Without "M" Information	89.12	85.94	87.50
- Without distinct	87.42	84.61	85.99
- **With external dictionary(Ours)**	**89.79**	**86.78**	**88.26**
Fourteen kind types			
Model	P	R	F1
- Without dictionary	86.28	81.15	83.64
- Dictionary+40% concept	87.342	81.63	84.39
- Dictionary+all concept	88.48	83.54	85.94
- Without "M" Information	87.36	80.73	83.91
- Without distinct	84.14	78.02	80.96
- **With external dictionary(Ours)**	**88.25**	**81.43**	**84.70**

Here, we delete the group of information "-M". In the experiment, P, R and F1 values have different degrees of decline after deleting the intermediate concept word information, which proves the effectiveness of adding the group of information "-M". Secondly, we also modify the way of word information fusion. Here, we do not distinguish the four categories of "BMES" as in the model, but simply add them by weighting. The performance decline in the experiment also proves the importance of making clear distinctions between different matching words.

5   Conclusion

In this study, we studied the technology of concept extraction in the field of education, and designed a method to further improve the performance of concept extraction by collecting an external third-party knowledge base as a corresponding professional course dictionary, To better leverage the word-level information in the course concept dictionary, we integrate it with the character-level information in the concept extraction process. In addition, we label the concepts of computer-related courses by ourselves, and further distinguish the types of concepts. The experimental results obtained on the dataset demonstrate the superior performance of our concept extraction model compared to other existing models.

References

1. Chundan, S., Lin, Q.: Chinese named entity recognition method based on BGRU-CRF. Comput. Sci. **46**(9), 237–242 (2019). (in Chinese)
2. Ding, R., Xie, P., Zhang, X., Lu, W., Li, L., Si, L.: A neural multi-digraph model for Chinese NER with gazetteers. In: Proceedings of the 57th Annual Meeting of the Association for Computational Linguistics, pp. 1462–1467 (2019)
3. Gridach, M.: Character-level neural network for biomedical named entity recognition. J. Biomed. Inform. **70**, 85–91 (2017)
4. Gui, T., et al.: A lexicon-based graph neural network for Chinese NER. In: Proceedings of the 2019 Conference on Empirical Methods in Natural Language Processing and the 9th International Joint Conference on Natural Language Processing (EMNLP-IJCNLP), pp. 1040–1050 (2019)
5. Hu, J., Shi, X., Liu, Z., Wang, X., Chen, Q., Tang, B.: Hitsz_cner: a hybrid system for entity recognition from Chinese clinical text. In: CEUR Workshop Proceedings, vol. 1976, pp. 25–30 (2017)
6. Jia, Y., Xu, X.: Chinese named entity recognition based on CNN-BiLSTM-CRF. In: 2018 IEEE 9th International Conference on Software Engineering and Service Science (ICSESS), pp. 1–4. IEEE (2018)
7. Kainan, J., Xin, L., Rongchen, Z.: Overview of Chinese domain named entity recognition. Comput. Eng. Appl. **57**(16), 1–15 (2021). (in Chinese)
8. Lu, Y., Zhang, Y., Ji, D.: Multi-prototype Chinese character embedding. In: Proceedings of the Tenth International Conference on Language Resources and Evaluation (LREC 2016), pp. 855–859 (2016)
9. Mingyang, L., Fang, K.: Combined self-attention mechanism for named entity recognition in social media (2019). (in Chinese)
10. Wei, K., Wen, B.: Named entity recognition method for educational emergency field based on BERT. In: 2021 IEEE 12th International Conference on Software Engineering and Service Science (ICSESS), pp. 145–149. IEEE (2021)
11. Ya, Q., Guowei, S., Wenbo, Z., Yanping, C.: Research on the method of network security entity recognition based on deep neural network. J. Nanjing Univ. (Nat. Sci.) **55**(1), 29–40 (2019). (in Chinese)

12. Zhang, Y., Yang, J.: Chinese NER using lattice lstm. arXiv preprint arXiv:1805.02023 (2018)
13. Zhao, S., Cai, Z., Chen, H., Wang, Y., Liu, F., Liu, A.: Adversarial training based lattice LSTM for Chinese clinical named entity recognition. J. Biomed. Inform. **99**, 103290 (2019)

Image Recoloring for Color Blindness Considering Naturalness and Harmony

Xin Jin[1], Yiqing Rong[1], Dongqing Zou[2,3(✉)], Wu Zhou[1], and Xiaokun Zhang[1]

[1] Beijing Electronic Science and Technology Institute, Beijing 100070, China
[2] SenseTime Research, Shanghai, China
zoudongqing@sensetime.com
[3] Qing Yuan Research Institute, Shanghai Jiao Tong University, Shanghai 200240, China

Abstract. Despite the existence of numerous methods for recoloring images with diverse effects, challenges such as unnatural and inharmonious colors of the converted objects still persist. To address these issues, we have developed a novel approach to image recoloration. Our method ensures that the resulting images possess three crucial properties: naturalness, harmonization, and distinguishability, making them accessible to individuals with color vision deficiencies. Our approach comprises two main components: recommended palette generation and image recoloring. The former allows us to learn the color distribution of various natural objects, while the latter enables us to recolor the image with the recommended palette. Our results demonstrate that our method outperforms existing approaches to some extent and warrants further exploration.

Keywords: recoloration · colorblind · natural color · color harmonization

1 Introduction

As time progresses, diseases like color blindness (CB) have become more prevalent. Dichromatopsia and achromatopsia are the two most common types of CB. Dichromatic blindness is further categorized into protanopia, deuteranopia, and tritanopia. CB individuals are impacted to varying degrees in their daily lives. For instance, CB can affect a person's ability to perform certain tasks that rely on color recognition, such as reading charts and graphs, identifying traffic lights, and choosing clothing that matches. In some cases, it can also impact a person's ability to perceive depth and contrast, making it more difficult to navigate certain environments. CB can also have social implications, as color is often used as a means of communication and expression in our culture. For example, CB may not be able to appreciate the beauty of a sunset or a colorful painting in the same way as someone with normal color vision. They may also feel left out of certain social activities, such as viewing fireworks or participating in color-coded events.

Despite these challenges, CB individuals can still lead fulfilling lives. With the help of assistive technologies, such as color filters and apps that assist with color recognition, they can overcome many of the obstacles presented by their condition. Additionally, increased awareness and understanding of CB can help to create a more inclusive and

H. Lu and J. Cai (Eds.): ISAIR 2023, CCIS 1998, pp. 313–322, 2024.
https://doi.org/10.1007/978-981-99-9109-9_31

accommodating society for those who live with this condition. The image recoloring technology for people with CB can be used to enhance the readability and aesthetics of images and help people with CB better understand and appreciate images. However, there are some problems with the existing methods, such as color inauthenticity and color disharmony. For this scenario, we have explored a method for recoloring images that ensures the resulting image is natural, harmonious, and distinguishable in color.

In this article, we will explore the technology of image recoloring for people with CB and introduce a method we have developed for achieving this goal. First, we will briefly review the background and current research status of CB, followed by a detailed presentation of our proposed method. We will then conduct experimental validation to demonstrate the effectiveness of our approach. Finally, we will summarize our findings.

2 Related Work

Palette-based color manipulation provides a versatile approach to image editing, utilizing palettes that can be categorized into two main types. The first type [1] involves the utilization of both the original and target palettes. In this method, the key colors of the original image are extracted through clustering techniques, forming the original palette. Simultaneously, the target palette is either predefined or trained in advance. By mapping the colors from the original palette to the corresponding colors in the target palette, effective color manipulation and transformation can be achieved. This approach is commonly employed in tasks such as image recoloration and color theme enhancement. On the other hand, the second type [2] solely relies on the target palette. This approach proves particularly useful for image recoloration and color enhancement, as it eliminates the need for the original palette. By directly mapping the colors in the image to the colors within the target palette, the image's overall color scheme can be effectively modified and transformed.

Colorblindness image recoloring can be categorized into four distinct approaches. The first approach involves grayscale conversion [3, 4], where the image is transformed into grayscale using an objective function that considers the differences in pixel values. However, this method is often considered too simplistic, as it discards the valuable color information embedded within the image. The second approach is based on image segmentation [5, 6], where the image is initially segmented to identify areas that may be indistinguishable from individuals with color vision deficiencies. These identified areas are then replaced with colors that exhibit high contrast, ensuring better visibility for CB individuals. However, this method may be susceptible to external noise and is limited by the accuracy and reliability of the segmentation process. The third approach involves color conversion [7–9], which aims to preserve the color information while adapting it to be more distinguishable for CB individuals. This is achieved by applying linear operations within various color spaces, such as LMS, LAB, or HSV. However, the quality and speed of the results obtained through this approach heavily depend on the specific linear operation algorithms employed. The fourth approach leverages the power of neural networks. X. Zhang [10] proposed the use of generative adversarial networks (GANs) to facilitate image recoloring while incorporating constraints to exert better control over the direction and outcome of the recoloring process. By training the

GAN on a dataset of color-corrected images, the neural network can learn to generate visually appealing recolored versions of input images while considering the constraints imposed during the training process. These various approaches to color manipulation and colorblindness image recoloring provide a range of techniques and methodologies, each with its strengths and limitations. By understanding and leveraging these approaches, we can effectively address the challenges associated with color manipulation and ensure that visual content is accessible and inclusive for individuals with color vision deficiencies.

To simulate CB, researchers have proposed mathematical models for CB simulation. The research progress of simulation models provides robust support in our endeavor to better understand and address CB issues. By simulating the visual perception of CB individuals, we can delve deeper into the impact of CB on daily life and design improved assistive tools and educational training programs. In this paper, we utilized J.-B. Bao's method [11] for CB simulation. By adjusting the weights in the formula, different degrees of CB can be simulated.

The field of CB assistive devices [18] has witnessed significant research advancements, aiming to provide individuals with color vision deficiencies with enhanced color perception and improved visual experiences. Researchers have explored various technological solutions to develop innovative assistive devices. One approach involves the use of augmented reality (AR) and virtual reality (VR) technologies, where wearable devices or headsets are equipped with specialized algorithms to enhance color discrimination. These devices can modify color representations in real-time, allowing users to perceive colors more accurately. Another line of research focuses on developing specialized filters or lenses that can be integrated into eyewear, such as glasses or contact lenses. These filters selectively alter the wavelengths of light to enhance color perception for specific types of CB. Additionally, smartphone applications and digital tools have been developed to assist colorblind individuals in distinguishing colors through real-time image processing and color correction algorithms. These applications provide on-the-go assistance and enable color identification in various contexts. As research progresses, there is a growing emphasis on personalized and customizable approaches, tailoring assistive devices to individual color vision deficiencies. These advancements hold immense potential in improving the quality of life and accessibility for individuals with color vision deficiencies, empowering them to navigate the colorful world more effectively.

3 Approach

Our approach consists of two main parts: recommended palette generation and image recoloring. The color palette generation part is the color palette of different categories of objects produced by statistical data sets of object colors, and the image recoloring part is the use of a series of operations to generate recoloring images for CB. The flowchart of our approach is presented in Fig. 1.

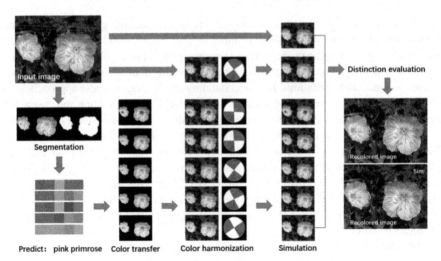

Fig. 1. Flowchart of our method.

3.1 Recommended Palette Generation

We use the clustering method to generate the palette. We choose the Oxford flower dataset [12] as our dataset. According to the size of the dataset, we define the number of object hue clusters as five. We preprocess this dataset and then use tools to batch-remove image backgrounds. We use K-Means to perform two rounds of clustering on the hue distribution of images. The first clustering obtains the hue center value array (hue color palette) of each image arranged in descending order of frequency. The second clustering performs another round of clustering on all the hue color palettes of each image type to obtain five representative hue color palettes.

3.2 Image Recoloring

At present, we have undertaken a comprehensive exploration of the entire process to assess its feasibility. To facilitate the interactive segmentation of the image's foreground and background, we have employed the widely used GrabCut method [13]. This method offers a user-friendly approach, as it requires only the manual drawing of a bounding box around the target object. By leveraging user interaction, the segmentation boundary can be fine-tuned, ensuring precise and accurate results.

In our research, we have placed significant emphasis on achieving accurate and detailed classification through fine-grained training. To accomplish this, we have adopted the transfer learning methodology, a powerful technique that leverages pre-existing knowledge from a pre-trained model. For the fine-grained model training, we have selected ResNet-152 [14], a state-of-the-art deep neural network renowned for its exceptional performance. Our training process begins by utilizing the pre-trained model to train the weights of the fully connected layers. This initial step allows the model to grasp the underlying patterns and features specific to our fine-grained classification task. Subsequently, we proceed to retrain and update the weights of all layers within the network.

This comprehensive training approach ensures that the model becomes well-adapted to our specific dataset, enabling it to accurately recognize and categorize objects at a fine-grained level.

In order to enhance the realism of recolored objects, we implemented a sophisticated approach that involved the utilization of pre-calculated recommended color palettes and conducted color transfer operations in the image foreground. To accomplish this, we employed the method proposed by E. Reinhard [15], which focuses on adjusting the H (hue) channel of the image's HSV (hue, saturation, value) color space while incorporating the information from the recommended palette[19–21]. This meticulous approach enabled us to achieve highly accurate color transfer while ensuring that the natural appearance of the image was preserved. By leveraging pre-calculated recommended color palettes, we were able to tap into a vast collection of carefully curated color combinations that are known to produce visually pleasing and realistic results. These color palettes serve as a valuable resource, providing guidance and inspiration for the recoloring process. The core of our methodology lies in the adjustment of the H channel within the HSV color space. By aligning the hue values of the original image with those recommended in the palette, we ensure that the recolored objects exhibit a harmonious and authentic appearance. This adjustment process takes into account the specific color characteristics of the recommended palette, allowing for seamless integration of the new colors while preserving the overall naturalness and visual coherence of the image.

$$I = \frac{\sigma_t}{\sigma_s}\left(S^H - mean(T^H)\right) + mean(T^H) \qquad (1)$$

It conforms to the color characteristics of the palette and satisfies the naturalness (see examples in Fig. 2).

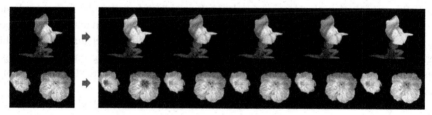

Fig. 2. Several sets of color transfer examples.

In order to solve the problem of disharmony between the image background and adjusted foreground color, we adjust the image background harmoniously. In our image harmonization process, we employed the method proposed by D. Cohen-Or [16], which offers effective techniques for achieving visual harmony in images. To facilitate this harmonization, we carefully selected reference templates provided by D. Cohen-Or, each representing a specific harmonization scheme. These templates consist of color circles, and we considered the shaded area within each circle as the valid region for the template. Furthermore, the templates can be rotated to adapt to different image compositions and requirements. To ensure a harmonious visual composition, we calculated a hue harmony template that best matched the foreground of the image. By analyzing the colors present in the foreground, we determined the optimal hue harmony template that would complement and enhance its visual appeal. Subsequently, we adjusted the hue of the image's background to align with the selected foreground harmony template. This adjustment process aimed to create a coherent and visually pleasing blend between the foreground and background elements. It is worth noting that we introduced an additional judgment criterion in this process. If the optimal palette for the foreground corresponds to a single shadow area template, we adjusted the rotation angle by 180 degrees. This adjustment was made to ensure that the foreground and background elements were sufficiently distinguishable and visually balanced. By rotating the template, we could achieve a better composition and enhance the overall harmony of the image. Several examples of harmonization groups can be seen in Fig. 3.

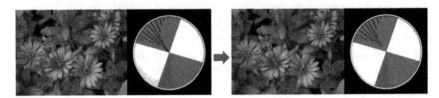

Fig. 3. Color harmonization example.

After recoloring the images, we conducted a CB simulation to ensure their accessibility for individuals. This simulation involved generating a simulation map that represents how the recolored images would appear to individuals with different types of CB. To quantify the hue distinction between the foreground and background in each simulated image, we employed the Bhattacharyya distance metric [17]. This distance measure allowed us to calculate the degree of color differentiation between the foreground and the background. By analyzing the simulated images using the Bhattacharyya distance, we were able to identify the original image from the simulated set that exhibited the highest degree of distinction between the foreground and the background. This image was then selected as the final result, ensuring that it provided the most noticeable and discernible color contrast.

Through the CB simulation and the Bhattacharyya distance calculation, we prioritized the visual clarity and distinguishability of the recolored images for individuals with color vision deficiencies. By selecting the image with the maximum distinction, we aimed to provide an inclusive and accessible viewing experience for individuals with different types of CB. This approach demonstrates our commitment to enhancing the accessibility of visual content, ensuring that individuals with color vision deficiencies can perceive and distinguish important visual elements within the images. By incorporating CB simulation and the Bhattacharyya distance metric, we contribute to creating a more inclusive and accommodating environment for individuals, allowing them to fully engage with and appreciate visual content.

4   Evaluation

Our method belongs to color conversion and is compared to the methods of W. Woods [7], S. Choudhry [8], and Y. Wang [9]. The comparison methods include both objective and subjective evaluations, and the images used for evaluation are all from the Oxford flower dataset [12].

4.1   Objective Evaluation

We utilized four metrics to quantitatively measure the effectiveness of our approach: foreground-background distinction, harmonization, SSIM, and PSNR. Mean measurement results for 15 randomly selected images from the dataset are presented in Tables 1 and 2. Figure 4 presents several sample sets from the objective evaluation.

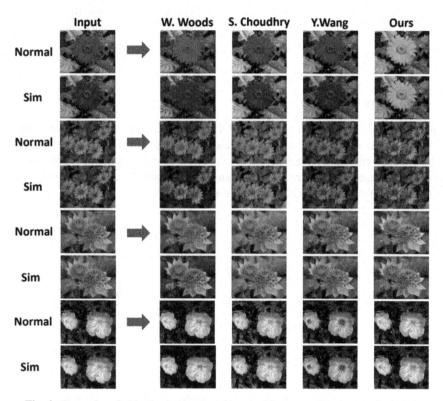

Fig. 4.   Examples of objective evaluation. A total of four sets of images are included.

Table 1 shows that our method has improved compared to others' methods, mainly in the indicators of differentiation and harmony. Table 2 proves that our method is effective in combining various modules after ablation experiments.

Table 1. Statistics of the difference between our method and others.

Methods	Distinction↑	Harmonization↓	SSIM↑	PSNR↑
W. Woods[7]	0.356667	1067.949	0.637333	15.36733
S.Choudhry[8]	0.349333	7593.663	0.883333	18.26267
Y.Wang[9]	0.5078	2247.085	**0.982667**	**31.37333**
Ours	**0.782933**	**328.476**	0.905333	20.25333

Table 2. Ablation experiment.

naturalness constraint	harmonization constraint	Distinction↑	Harmonization↓
√	×	0.717333	3270.105
×	√	0.593533	**103.665**
√	√	**0.782933**	328.476

4.2 Subjective Evaluation

Since there is no accurate way to classify CB in the medical field and it is a non-trivial task to find CB patients, most current related works use simulation programs in this field. We conduct a subjective experiment with 20 participants on multiple groups of CB simulation images that were randomly ordered. The mean scores are shown in Fig. 5. It turns out that our approach has improved to some extent.

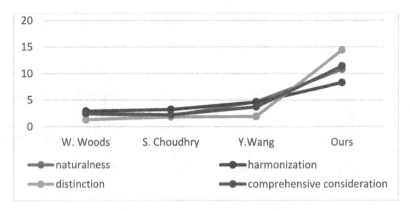

Fig. 5. Mean scores for each method.

5   Conclusion

Given the shortcomings of the existing colorblind recoloration technology, we have explored a set of methods to achieve image recoloration. Good results are obtained through the modules of foreground naturalness adjustment, harmonization adjustment, and distinction evaluation of foreground and background. Our approach focuses on illustrating the workability of the entire process. The advantages and disadvantages of each branching module technique are not the focus. Of course, there are still some shortcomings in our method. Next, we intend to improve the segmentation part first, so that it can automatically recognize multiple objects and adjust the color of each of them. Then, optimize the algorithm to increase the processing speed. Finally, we wanted to create an electronic device (CB aid) that would find a balance between speed and quality to enable real-time recoloring for CB patients.

References

1. Chang, H., Fried, O., Liu, Y., DiVerdi, S., Finkelstein, A.: Palette-based photo recoloring. ACM Trans. Graph. **34**(4), 139–141 (2015)
2. Wang, B., Yizhou, Y., Wong, T.-T., Chen, C., Ying-Qing, X.: Data-driven image color theme enhancement. ACM Trans. Graph. (TOG) **29**(6), 1–10 (2010)
3. Gooch, A.A., Olsen, S.C., Tumblin, J., Gooch, B.: Color2gray: salience-preserving color removal. ACM Trans. Graph. **24**(3), 634–639 (2005)
4. Tirui, W., Toet, A.: Color-to-grayscale conversion through weighted multiresolution channel fusion. J. Electron. Imaging **23**(4), 043004 (2014)
5. Ye, R., Li, C.: Colorblind image correction based on segmentation and similarity judgement. J. Phys. Conf. Ser. **1098**, 012028 (2018)
6. Bruno, A., Gugliuzza, F., Ardizzone, E., Giunta, C.C., Pirrone, R.: Image content enhancement through salient regions segmentation for people with color vision deficiencies. i-Perception **10**(3), 2041669519841073 (2019)
7. William Woods. Modifying images for color blind viewers. Electrical Engineering Department Stanford University Stanford, USA (2005). wwwoods@stanford.edu
8. Choudhry, S.: Live video recoloring. https://github.com/sami14996/Live_video_recoloring (2020)
9. Wang, Y., Li, D., Hu, M., Cai, Li.: Non-local recoloring algorithm for color vision deficiencies with naturalness and detail preserving. In: Zhai, G., Zhou, J., Yang, H., An, P., Yang, X. (eds.) IFTC 2019. CCIS, vol. 1181, pp. 23–34. Springer, Singapore (2020). https://doi.org/10.1007/978-981-15-3341-9_3
10. Zhang, X., Zhang, M., Zhang, L., Shen, P., Zhu, G., Li, P.: Recoloring image for color vision deficiency by gans. In: 2019 IEEE International Conference on Image Processing (ICIP), pp. 3267–3271. IEEE (2019)
11. Bao, J.-B., Wang, Y.-Y., Ma, Y., Gu, X.-D.: Colorblindness correction method based on h-component rotation. Adv. Biomed. Eng. **29**(3), 125–130 (2008)
12. Nilsback, M.-E., Zisserman, A.: Automated flower classification over a large number of classes. In: Proceedings of the Indian Conference on Computer Vision, Graphics and Image Processing (2008)
13. Rother, C., Kolmogorov, V., Blake, A.: "GrabCut": interactive foreground extraction using iterated graph cuts. ACM Trans. Graph. **23**(3), 309–314 (2004)

14. He, K., Zhang, X., Ren, S., Sun, J.: Deep residual learning for image recognition. In: Proceedings of the IEEE conference on computer vision and pattern recognition, pp. 770–778 (2016)

15. Reinhard, E., Adhikhmin, M., Gooch, B., Shirley, P.: Color transfer between images. IEEE Comput. Graph. Appl. **21**(5), 34–41 (2001)

16. Cohen-Or, D., Sorkine, O., Gal, R., Leyvand, T., Xu, Y.-Q.: Color harmonization. ACM Trans. Graph. **25**(3), 624–630 (2006)

17. Bhattacharyya, A.: On a measure of divergence between two multinomial populations. Sankhya: The Indian J. Stat. **7**, 401–406 (1946)

18. Salih, A.E., Elsherif, M., Ali, M., Vahdati, N., Yetisen, A.K., Butt, H.: Ophthalmic wearable devices for color blindness management. Adv. Mater. Technol. **5**, 1901134 (2020). https://doi.org/10.1002/admt.201901134

19. Lu, H., Yang, R., Deng, Z., Zhang, Y., Gao, G., Lan, R.: Chinese image captioning via fuzzy attention-based DenseNet-BiLSTM. ACM Trans. Multimed. Comput. Commun. Appl. **17**(1s), 1–18 (2021)

20. Lu, H., Li, Y., Chen, M., Kim, H., Serikawa, S.: Brain intelligence: go beyond artificial intelligence. Mobile Netw. Appl. **23**(2), 368–375 (2018)

21. Lu, H., Zhang, M., Xu, X., Li, Y., Shen, H.T.: Deep fuzzy hashing network for efficient image retrieval. IEEE Trans. Fuzzy Syst. **29**(1), 166–176 (2021)

Improving PSO-SVM for Fatigue Recognition

Pan Chai[✉], Mei Wang, Xing Chen, and Yangliu Yang

Xi'an University of Science and Technology, Xian 715100, China
2739145066@qq.com

Abstract. Excessive fatigue can cause harm in an individual's life. Therefore, the challenge is how to effectively detect fatigue. To this end, this paper uses an EEG multi-feature fusion method based on Linear Discriminant Analysis (LDA) dimensionality reduction, and uses the dimensionality reduction features as the input of Support Vector Machine (SVM) for classification. In order to improve the classification accuracy of SVM, an improved Particle Swarm Optimization (PSO) algorithm was proposed to optimize the SVM. The improved PSO-SVM algorithm is combined with other classification methods to classify the EEG signals of the subjects in the fatigued and awake states. The experimental results show that the improved PSO-SVM algorithm has achieved the best classification performance, the average accuracy rate reached 84.56%.

Keywords: EEG signal · Feature extraction · Improved particle swarm optimization algorithm · Support Vector Machine

1 Introduction

Fatigue is a common psychological phenomenon. Psychological fatigue can lead to individual anxiety, depression, insomnia, and other negative emotions, which seriously affects the individual's physical and mental health and work efficiency. In order to address the harmful effects of mental fatigue on individuals, an effective and accurate method is needed to measure the degree of individual fatigue. Therefore, this work uses the wavelet packet variation, nonlinear dynamics, combined with automatic door control cycle unit and owe complete encoder neural network (GRU_UAE) characteristics of EEG signals are extracted, then to extract the characteristics of fusion, using LDA for dimension reduction characteristics after the fusion. The improved PSO algorithm combined Chebyshev chaotic map, constructed nonlinear asynchronous learning factor and added Gaussian disturbance to the "cognitive part" of PSO algorithm. Finally using improved PSO algorithm to optimize the SVM to detect fatigue.

The paper is organized as follows. Section 2 is the related works. Section 3 describes the proposed method. Section 4 is the experiment. Section 5 contains the conclusion.

2 Related works

At present, the research on fatigue detection has covered many fields, including but not limited to physiological index monitoring, EEG signal analysis, image analysis, and machine learning algorithm application.

H. Lu and J. Cai (Eds.): ISAIR 2023, CCIS 1998, pp. 323–329, 2024.
https://doi.org/10.1007/978-981-99-9109-9_32

Reference [1] proposed an intelligent algorithm based on neural network and reinforcement learning. The algorithm analyzes multi-dimensional data such as facial expression features, EEG signals, and physiological signals of electron microscopy.

Reference [2] introduced an adaptive multi-scale entropy feature extraction algorithm, including the acquisition method of adaptive scale factor and entropy feature extraction method. The algorithm can effectively detect fatigue driving impairment.

Reference [3], a fatigue detection method based on comprehensive facial features and Door Ring Unit (GRU) judgment neural network was proposed. Reference [4], A two-stage mental state fusion algorithm combining electrocardiogram signals and facial expressions is proposed. Reference [5], to explore human alertness estimation using support vector regression of dynamic spatiotemporal brain network connectivity parameters.

These comprehensive studies contribute to a deeper understanding of fatigue detection methods, covering a variety of methods and demonstrating their potential applications in a variety of situations [8–12].

3 Methods

3.1 EEG Feature Extraction Method Based on Multi-feature Fusion

Wavelet packet variation, nonlinear dynamics, and based on GRU-UAE extraction of EEG signals, the features of three kinds of fusion, the fusion feature after the LDA dimension reduction, by CVM after classifying fusion of EEG signals. The fused features are used as input to the improved PSO-SVM. The structure diagram of feature fusion and dimensionality reduction of EEG signals is shown in Fig. 1.

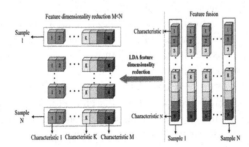

Fig. 1. Structure diagram of EEG signal feature fusion and dimensionality reduction.

3.2 Improved Particle Swarm Optimization

3.2.1 Improved Particle Swarm Algorithm

The PSO algorithm adjusts the position and velocity of each particle in each iteration based on its own past performance and the performance of the best particle in the population.

Particles in the next iteration, its location and speed information for the formula.

$$\begin{cases} v_{id}^{t+1} = wv_{id}^{t} + c_1 r_1 (p_{id}^{t} - x_{id}^{t}) + c_2 r_2 (p_{gd}^{t} - x_{gd}^{t}) \\ x_{id}^{t+1} = x_{id}^{t} + v_{id}^{t+1} \end{cases} \tag{1}$$

where, x_{id}^{t} represents t time the particle, d represents the dimension vector, v_{id}^{t} represents the velocity of the particle at this time, c_1, c_2 is the learning factor, and w is the inertia weight coefficient. The values are in the range (0,1).

The Chebyshev chaotic map method is introduced to initialize the particle population, which is formulated as follows.

$$x_{t+1} = \cos(t \cos^{-1}(x_t)) \tag{2}$$

where, x_{t+1} has the range [0,1], x_t is a random number distributed uniformly in (0,1), and μ is a control parameter in (0,1).

A logarithmic function was introduced to construct a nonlinear asynchronous learning factor to balance the global development ability and local search ability of the algorithm, which is formulated as follows.

$$c_1 = c_{1up} - \ln(1 + (e - 1) \times t/T) \times (c_{1up} - c_{1low})$$
$$c_2 = c_{2low} + \ln(1 + (e - 1) \times t/T) \times (c_{1up} - c_{1low}) \tag{3}$$

In order to avoid the algorithm falling into local optimum, a Gaussian disturbance term is added to the "cognitive learning" part of the velocity formula of the particle, and the formula is as follows.

$$\begin{cases} v_{id}^{t+1} = wv_{id}^{t} + c_1 r_1 (p_{id}^{t} - x_{id}^{t} + r_3 Gaussian_i^k) + c_2 r_2 (p_{gd}^{t} - x_{gd}^{t}) \\ Gaussian_i^k = r_4 Gaussian(\mu, \sigma^2) \end{cases} \tag{4}$$

where, r_3, r_4 is the random number of [0,1], $Gaussian_i^k$ is the Gaussian perturbation generated by the particle i in the second iteration process, σ^2, μ is the mean, and the variance respectively.

3.2.2 The Specific Process of Particle Swarm Optimization Algorithm

Initialization by Chebyshev [6] chaotic mapping group, improve the cognitive learning factor to improve the search range of the algorithm, the convergence speed and convergence precision, and the particle velocity formula of "cognitive learning" to join the gauss perturbation terms, make the algorithm have the ability to jump out of local optimal solution to improve the particle swarm algorithm. The specific improvement steps are as follows.

Step1: initialization population size M, T_{max}, the largest number of iterations random set population initial position $X(0)$ and $V(0)$ speed, the initial position and velocity are as follows:

$$\begin{cases} X(0) = (x_1^0, x_2^0, \cdots, x_M^0)^T \\ V(0) = (v_1^0, v_2^0, \cdots, v_M^0)^T \end{cases} \tag{5}$$

Step2: Initialize the population individuals by chaos, and use Eq. (2) to generate the initial population;

Step3: Calculate particle fitness: For each particle, calculate its fitness, which is the corresponding objective function value.

Step4: Save the fitness value and position information of the best particle in the population and the best particle in the population.

Step5: Update the inertia weight and use Eq. (3) to update the nonlinear asynchronous learning factor.

Step6: Use Eq. (4) to update the particle velocity, and use Eq. (1) to update the particle position.

Step7: Determine whether the termination condition is reached, that is, whether the preset maximum number of iterations is reached. If the maximum number of iterations is reached, the current optimal solution is output and the loop is exited. Otherwise, repeat step Step2 and proceed to the next iteration.

3.3 Improved PSO-SVM Fatigue Recognition Algorithm

The flow of the improved PSO-SVM is as follows.

Step 1: Read the training samples of SVM, use Chebyshev mapping to initialize particle population size N, initial position $x_i = (C_{i1}, g_{i2})^T$ and velocity $v_i = (C_{i1}, g_{i2})^T$ of particles, maximum number of iterations of particles K, c_1 and learning factor c_2.

Step 2: Calculate particle fitness: for each particle, calculate its fitness, that is, the corresponding target function value.

Step 3: Save the fitness value and position information of the best particle in the population and the best particle in the population.

Step 4: Update inertia weight, use Eq. (3) to update nonlinear asynchronous learning factor, then use Eq. (4) to update particle velocity, and the particle position is updated using Eq. (1).

Step 5: Determine whether the termination condition has been met, that is, whether the preset maximum number of iterations has been reached. If the maximum number of iterations is reached, output the current optimal solution and exit the loop. Otherwise, repeat Step 2 and proceed to the next iteration.

Step 6: The optimal parameters C and g are used as the optimal parameters of the SVM model, and SVM pairs of samples are used for training, and the trained SVM pairs of test set are used for classification experiment to achieve the highest classification accuracy.

4 Experiments

4.1 Comparison of Fusion Model Performance

Classification experiments were carried out on the collected fatigue and awake EEG signals. The accuracy of four feature extraction methods for classification was compared to select the best fatigue feature extraction method. Method 1: Wavelet packet variation feature extraction; Method 2: Nonlinear dynamic feature extraction. Method 3: GRU-UAE feature extraction. Method 4: Multi-feature fusion of EEG based on LDA.

Four subjects' binary classification experiments were carried out by four different feature extraction methods. The experimental classification accuracy is shown in Fig. 2. The average classification accuracy of the feature extraction method of Method 4 is 75.76%. It can be seen that the method of extracting EEG signal features using GRE-UAE deep learning is superior to other feature extraction methods.

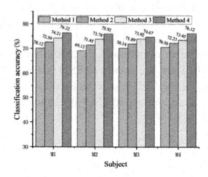

Fig. 2. Average classification accuracy of 4 subjects.

4.2 Performance Testing of Improved PSO Algorithm

In order to ensure scientific this experiment, PSO-LDIW, PSO-TVAC, FOPSO [7], and the improved PSO algorithms were all set with a population size of 50 and a maximum number of iterations of 1000. The parameter settings for the improved PSO algorithm are:$c_{2up} = 2.5c_{1up} = 2.1, c_{1low} = 0.5\infty, c_{2low} = 0.8$, weight coefficient $w_{min} = 0.4, w_{max} = 0.9$. Participate in the experiment of the four algorithms will be

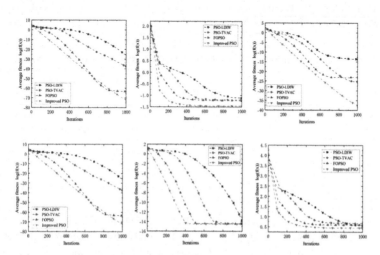

Fig. 3. The change of the average optimal fitness value of the benchmark function in iteration.

used in six benchmark function. Figure 3 shows the change of the average optimal fitness value of the benchmark function in iteration.

4.3 Performance Evaluation of Fatigue Detection Algorithm Based on Improved PSO

This work selection weight coefficient $w_{min} = 0.4, w_{max} = 0.9$. This work selection $c_{2low} = 0.8, c_{1up} = 2.1, c_{1low} = 0.5, c_{2up} = 2.5$. The C search range for the penalty factor is (0, 1000), the g range is (0, 1000), and the maximum number of iterations represents the maximum number of iterations the algorithm runs, selecting a maximum iteration count T_{max} of 200. Then, the improved PSO is used to optimize the SVM, and the classification accuracy of the EEG test set is used as the fitness value of particles. The fitness curve of PSO (a) and improved PSO (b) is shown in Fig. 4.

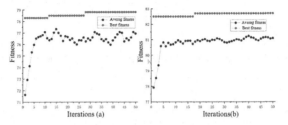

Fig. 4. The fitness curve of PSO (a) and improved PSO (b).

In order to verify the reliability of the algorithm, SVM, PSO-SVM, FOPSO-SVM and other algorithms are used to classify the EEG signals collected in fatigue and awake states, and Gaussian function is selected as the kernel function in SVM. Calculate the corresponding evaluation index values and compare them with the classification algorithm evaluation index proposed in this study. The classification results of several algorithms are shown in Table 1 for each index.

Table 1. Evaluation Indicators for Classification Results of Several Algorithms.

	Accuracy	Recall
SVM	73.12%	75.63%
PSO-SVM	80.00%	82.56%
FOPSO-SVM	82.10%	84.56%
Improving PSO-SVM	84.56%	87.23%

It can be intuitively seen that the improved PSO-SVM classification algorithm in this article has higher performance indicators than other algorithms. Therefore, the improved PSO optimized SVM in this work has better classification performance compared to other algorithms in dealing with mental fatigue state detection problems.

5   Conclusion

In light of challenges such as incomplete signal representation, relying on a single feature for fatigue assessment is suboptimal. To address this limitation, a solution is introduced involving a multi-feature fusion technique rooted in LDA dimensionality reduction. This combined feature set is then employed as input for a SVM to facilitate classification. To enhance the classification accuracy of SVM, an improved PSO algorithm is proposed for SVM parameter optimization. The experimental results demonstrate that the improved PSO-SVM algorithm outperforms other classification methods in the classification of brain EEG signals for fatigue detection, indicating that the enhanced PSO-SVM algorithm exhibits the most favorable classification performance.

References

1. Liang, M., Song, J., Zhao, K., et al.: Optimization of dividing wall columns based on online Kriging model and improved particle swarm optimization algorithm. Comput. Chem. Eng. **166**, 107978 (2022)
2. Xing, Z., Zhu, J., Zhang, Z., et al.: Energy consumption optimization of tramway operation based on improved PSO algorithm. Energy **258**, 124848 (2022)
3. Lu, C., Gao, L., Li, X., et al.: Chaotic-based grey wolf optimizer for numerical and engineering optimization problems. Memetic Comp. **12**(4), 371–398 (2020)
4. Wang, M., Wang, J., Li, Y., et al.: Edge computing with complementary capsule networks for mental state detection in underground mining industry. IEEE Trans. Ind. Inf. **19**(7), 8508–8517 (2023)
5. Wang, M., Ma, C., Li, Z., et al.: Alertness estimation using connection parameters of the brain network. IEEE Trans. Intell. Transp. Syst. **23**(12), 25448–25457 (2021)
6. Chauhan, V.K., Dahiya, K., Sharma, A.: Problem formulations and solvers in linear SVM: a review. Artif. Intell. Rev. **52**(2), 803–855 (2019)
7. Huang, W., Liu, H., Zhang, Y., et al.: Railway dangerous goods transportation system risk identification: comparisons among SVM, PSO-SVM, GA-SVM and GS-SVM. Appl. Soft Comput. **109**, 107541 (2021)
8. Zheng, Y., Li, Y., Yang, S., Lu, H.: Global-pbnet: a novel point cloud registration for autonomous driving. IEEE Trans. Intell. Transp. Syst. **23**(11), 22312–22319 (2022)
9. Li, Y., Yang, S., Zheng, Y., Lu, H.: Improved point-voxel region convolutional neural network: 3D object detectors for autonomous driving. IEEE Trans. Intell. Transport. Syst. **23**(7), 9311–9317 (2022)
10. Lu, H., Yang, R., Deng, Z., Zhang, Y., Gao, G., Lan, R.: Chinese image captioning via fuzzy attention-based DenseNet-BiLSTM. ACM Trans. Multimed. Comput. Commun. Appl. **17**(1s), 1–18 (2021)
11. Lu, H., Li, Y., Chen, M., Kim, H., Serikawa, S.: Brain intelligence: go beyond artificial intelligence. Mobile Netw. Appl. **23**(2), 368–375 (2018)
12. Lu, H., Zhang, M., Xu, X., Li, Y., Shen, H.T.: Deep Fuzzy hashing network for efficient image retrieval. IEEE Trans. Fuzzy Syst. **29**(1), 166–176 (2021)

Parallel Attention Mechanism Based Multi-feature Fusion for Underwater Object Tracking

Jinbiao Sun, Huibin Wang$^{(\boxtimes)}$, Zhe Chen, and Lili Zhang

College of Computer and Information, Hohai University, Nanjing 211100, China
hbwang@hhu.edu.cn

Abstract. Recently, siamese network-based trackers have achieved great success, however underwater object tracking has been rarely studied. In underwater environments, the severe deformation, rapid movement, and complex background interference of objects often lead to low accuracy in underwater object tracking. To address the above challenges, we propose an underwater object tracking method based on siamese networks. The proposed parallel attention module facilitates the aggregation of similar semantic features from different positions and promotes information exchange between the two branches, enhancing the feature expression capability between channels in each branch. Moreover, the multi-scale feature fusion module effectively integrates features from various levels to adapt to changes in the target's appearance. Finally, comprehensive experiments were conducted on the OTB100, VOT2018, and underwater dataset UT40, demonstrating the method has good performance in underwater object tracking.

Keywords: Underwater Object Tracking · Siamese Networks · Attention Mechanism · Feature Fusion

1 Introduction

Underwater object tracking has a wide range of applications in marine resource exploration, underwater biological monitoring, underwater engineering operations and other fields. However, the unique characteristics of the underwater environment often lead to low optical image contrast, low definition, color distortion, etc. Tracking based on optical images faces multiple challenges. The complex and changeable ocean environment brings problems such as occlusion, background interference, and motion blur, making underwater tracking more difficult and complex than terrestrial environments.

In recent years, with the advancement of deep convolutional networks in computer vision, Siamese network-based trackers have demonstrated significant advantages in visual tracking, offering improved speed and accuracy. SiamFC [1] first transformed visual tracking tasks into similarity matching problems between target templates and search regions. Subsequent developments, SiamRPN [2] introduced Region Proposal Networks (RPN) to enhance bounding box prediction, partially overcoming SiamFC's

© The Author(s), under exclusive license to Springer Nature Singapore Pte Ltd. 2024
H. Lu and J. Cai (Eds.): ISAIR 2023, CCIS 1998, pp. 330–341, 2024.
https://doi.org/10.1007/978-981-99-9109-9_33

limitation of insufficient multi-scale feature acquisition with a single-channel correlation. To better fuse features, SiamRPN++ [3] proposed deep cross-correlation and utilized hierarchical and deep aggregation structures to extract superior features. Moreover, anchor-based trackers are highly sensitive to anchor parameter settings, requiring frequent adjustments of predefined anchor positions. In underwater tracking tasks, additional challenges arise due to severe shape variations, abrupt motion changes, variations in illumination caused by shooting angles, and color distortions in underwater targets. Furthermore, underwater scenes may involve multiple similar objects or objects with similar colors to the background, necessitating more accurate feature generation for distinguishing between similar objects and reducing complex background interference. Additionally, the tracker should adapt well to changes in target scale and position.

Based on the above problems, this paper proposes a Siamese network-based underwater object tracking method to improve the accuracy and robustness of the tracker in underwater scenes. It mainly proposes a parallel attention module and a multi-scale feature fusion module to extract and fuse template features and search regions between branches, and uses an anchor-free prediction module for target positioning and state estimation. The main contributions of this work are as follows:

- A parallel attention module has been designed, incorporating two attention mechanisms that are utilized to aggregate similar features from different spatial locations. This module effectively facilitates information exchange between the template and search branches, enhancing the recognition capability of the target.
- The design of a multi-scale feature fusion module that fuses and extracts features from different levels to obtain more discriminative features, while using convolutions of different sizes to capture multi-features and better handle scale changes during tracking.
- Comprehensive experiments on the OTB100, VOT2018, and underwater dataset UT40 were conducted, demonstrating the method's effectiveness in underwater oject tracking.

2 Related Work

In this section, we briefly review siamese network-based object tracking and visual attention mechanisms that are most relevant to our work.

Most siamese network-based trackers are offline trackers that match template features with search features to achieve object localization and tracking. In 2016, Bertinetto et al. [1] proposed the fully-convolutional siamese network (SiamFC), which was the first application of siamese networks in tracking tasks. Following SiamFC, SiamRPN [2] introduced the Region Proposal Network (RPN) into the siamese network, enabling effective handling of multi-scale variations of targets. DaSiamRPN [4] further improved the model's generalization ability through dataset augmentation and enriched negative sample training with semantic information. These methods predominantly used AlexNet as the feature extraction network without employing deeper feature extraction networks.

To address issues caused by deep network boundary padding's impact on translation invariance, SiamRPN++ [3] used ResNet as the feature extraction network and proposed deep correlation for fusing template and search branches' information. SiamDW

[5] introduced internal clipping units into residual networks to eliminate padding effects. Although these anchor-based trackers demonstrated strong tracking capabilities, designing anchor scales, aspect ratios, and quantities required meticulous effort. Therefore, a series of anchor-free tracking methods such as SiamFC++ [6] emerged. SiamCAR [7] added a center branch parallel to the classification branch for object classification. SiamBAN [8] employed multi-layer features for adaptive head prediction and utilized elliptical labels for classification regions.

Due to their simplicity, effectiveness, and plug-and-play nature, attention mechanisms have found widespread applications in computer vision tasks, such as image classification, object detection, and semantic segmentation. SENet [9] adaptively adjusts feature responses between channels to strengthen important features.

SKNet [10] introduced multiple parallel convolutional branches to learn feature map weights at different scales. Non-local [11] models global information to effectively capture long-range dependencies between two positions. Similarly, incorporating attention mechanisms in object tracking tasks has led to performance improvements. RASNet [12] introduced channel attention, residual attention, and general attention in SiamFC to enhance the tracker's discriminative ability, adapting it for both offline learning and online tracking. SiamAttn [13] proposed a deformable siamese attention network that strengthened dependencies between channel features and calculated deep cross-correlation between features using a region refinement module to improve tracking accuracy.

3   Proposed Method

As shown in Fig. 1, the proposed method consists of four main components: feature extraction network, parallel attention module, feature fusion module, and anchor-free prediction network. ResNet-50 is utilized as the backbone network, the parallel attention module is employed to enhance feature representations, distinguishing targets from semantic backgrounds. The feature fusion module aggregates multi-level features to handle scale changes, and finally, the feature maps are fed into the anchor-free prediction network to predict the target's bounding box.

3.1   Feature Extraction Network

Deep neural networks can provide rich semantic information and offer features at different depths for reference [25]. Building upon SiamRPN++, we utilize a pre-trained ResNet-50 as the backbone for the Siamese network. The shallow features of the neural network contain more spatial and detailed information, which facilitates precise target localization. On the other hand, the deep features possess stronger semantic information, enabling us to handle fast target movements and motion blur, and better recognize targets amidst complex backgrounds. Therefore, we extract features from the 3rd, 4th, and 5th convolutional blocks (Conv3_x, Conv4_x, Conv5_x) of ResNet-50 as the foundation for predicting the subsequent target state.

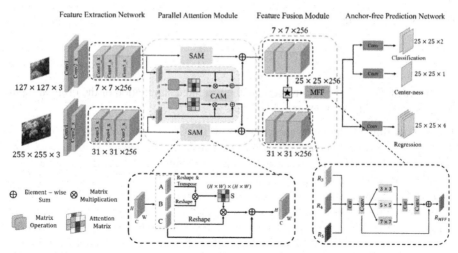

Fig. 1. The overview of the proposed method.

3.2 Parallel Attention Module

The structure of the Parallel Attention Module is illustrated in Fig. 1, which consists of two components: the Spatial Self-Attention Mechanism and the Cross Attention Mechanism. This module aims to extract spatial context relationships in different dimensions and enhance the network's perception ability of the target in both spatial and channel dimensions.

Spatial Attention Module. As shown in Fig. 1, the Spatial Attention Module (SAM) is applied simultaneously to both the template branch and the search branch. The outputs of the last three convolutional blocks from the template branch and the search branch are denoted as $Z \in \mathbb{R}^{C \times H \times W}$ and $X \in \mathbb{R}^{C \times H \times W}$, respectively. Taking the feature Z from the template branch as an example, it is first fed into a 1×1 convolution layer to reduce the channel dimension, obtaining new features $A, B, C \in \mathbb{R}^{K \times H \times W}$, where K represents the reduced channel dimension. The features A, B, and C are then reshaped to $A, B, C \in \mathbb{R}^{K \times N}$, where $N = H \times W$ is the number of pixels. After transposing A to A^T, matrix multiplication is performed between A^T and B, followed by the softmax function to generate the spatial attention map $S \in \mathbb{R}^{N \times N}$:

$$S_{ij} = \frac{\exp(A_i \cdot B_j)}{\sum_{i=1}^{N} \exp(A_i \cdot B_j)} \in \mathbb{R}^{N \times N} \tag{1}$$

Here, S_{ij} represents the influence of the i-th position on the j-th position in Z. The stronger the correlation between the features at two positions, the higher their attention value. The transposed S_{ij} is then matrix-multiplied with the reshaped feature C, and the result is reshaped to $S' \in \mathbb{R}^{C \times H \times W}$. The obtained S' is further scaled with a learnable parameter α, initialized to 0 and gradually learned to allocate appropriate weights. Finally, the original input feature Z is element-wise summed with the scaled attention-enhanced feature S', resulting in:

$$Z_{SA} = \alpha \cdot S' + C \in \mathbb{R}^{C \times H \times W} \tag{2}$$

The final $Z_{SA} \in \mathbb{R}^{C \times H \times W}$ represents the weighted summation of the original input features and the attention-enhanced features.

Cross Attention Module. As shown in Fig. 1, the Cross Attention Module (CAM) is designed based on the channel attention mechanism and is applied simultaneously to both the template branch and the search branch. The outputs of the template branch and the search branch are denoted as $Z \in \mathbb{R}^{C \times H \times W}$ and $X \in \mathbb{R}^{C \times H \times W}$, respectively. Taking the template branch as an example, the feature X from the search branch is fed into a 1×1 convolution layer to obtain new features $X \in \mathbb{R}^{K \times H \times W}$, where K represents the reduced channel dimension. The feature X is then reshaped to $X \in \mathbb{R}^{K \times N}$, , and the transposed feature X^T is matrix-multiplied with X, followed by the softmax function to generate the channel attention map $P_X \in \mathbb{R}^{C \times K}$:

$$P_{X_{ji}} = \frac{\exp(X_i \cdot X_j)}{\sum_{i=1}^{C} \exp(X_i \cdot X_j)} \in \mathbb{R}^{C \times C} \tag{3}$$

After reshaping the feature Z from the template branch, it is matrix-multiplied with the transposed attention map $P_{X_{ji}}$ and reshaped again to obtain $P'_X \in \mathbb{R}^{C \times H \times W}$). A learnable parameter β is then applied to P'_X, initialized to 0 and gradually learned to allocate appropriate weights. Finally, the original template branch feature Z is element-wise summed with the scaled attention-enhanced feature P'_X, resulting in:

$$Z_{CA} = \beta \cdot P'_X + Z \in \mathbb{R}^{C \times H \times W} \tag{4}$$

A similar operation is performed on the search branch as well.

The Cross Attention Module establishes connections between the template branch and the search branch in the channel dimension, allowing them to learn from each other and generate more distinctive feature representations.

3.3 Multi-feature Fusion Module

In underwater tracking tasks, underwater objects vary in size and shape, and the resolution of target features extracted by the neural network also differs. To improve tracking accuracy, a Multi-feature Fusion (MFF) module is designed for feature fusion, as shown in Fig. 1. The features enhanced by the Parallel Attention Module are subjected to depth-wise cross-correlation operations. The depth-wise cross-correlation is similar to depth-wise separable convolution and is used to relate features in the channel dimension, generating multiple semantic similarity maps:

$$R_i = C_i(z) * C_i(x) \tag{5}$$

where $C_i(\cdot)$ represents the output feature of the i-th convolution block, R_i is the generated response map, and * denotes the depth-wise cross-correlation operation.

The cross-correlated features are then concatenated to obtain $R = cat(R_3, R_4, R_5)$, and a 1×1 convolution is applied to reduce the channel dimension of R to 256, resulting in the fused output feature. It is challenging to match features of different sizes or aspect ratios using only one size of convolutional kernel in different scenes. The specific calculation process is represented as follows:

$$R_{MFF} = R + cat(c_3(R), c_5(R), c_7(R)) \tag{6}$$

where c_i represents the convolution operation, and cat denotes the concatenation operation.

4 Experiment

4.1 Implementation Details

During the training phase, we use five datasets for training: ImageNet VID [14], YouTube-BB [15], ImageNet DET [14], and COCO [16]. The size of the target template image is set to 127×127 pixels, and the size of the search region image is set to 255×255 pixels. We adopt an improved ResNet50 as the backbone network and initialize its parameters by pretraining on the ImageNet dataset. We optimize the proposed algorithm using stochastic gradient descent (SGD) with a momentum parameter of 0.9 and weight decay of 1×10^{-4}. The batch size is set to 32. The training process consists of 20 epochs, with a total of 2×10^5 image pairs used per epoch. The learning rate of the optimizer increases from 1×10^{-3} to 5×10^{-3} in the first 5 epochs for warm-up training and then exponentially decays from 5×10^{-3} to 5×10^{-5} in the subsequent 15 epochs. We freeze the weights of the backbone network in the first 10 epochs and then unfreeze the last three convolutional blocks for end-to-end training in the last 10 epochs. The joint loss function defined in this article is as follows:

$$L = \lambda_1 L_{cls} + \lambda_2 L_{cen} + \lambda_3 L_{reg} \tag{7}$$

where, in the present study, we empirically set $\lambda_1 = \lambda_2 = 1, \lambda_3 = 3$. For classification loss, the cross-entropy loss function is used for simple classification; For centrality loss, use the binary cross-entropy loss function. Since the positive samples are all in the truth box and the regression predictions are greater than 0, the IoU loss function is used in the regression loss.

The experiments are conducted using Python 3.7 and the PyTorch. The hardware platform consists of an Intel(R) Xeon(R) CPU E5–2620 v4 @ 2.10 GHz processor and an NVIDIA GTX1080ti GPU.

4.2 Dataset and Evaluation Metrics

To evaluate the performance of the algorithm, we conduct tests on underwater benchmark datasets. Additionally, we select representative land-based benchmark datasets, OTB100 [17], and VOT2018 [18] to comprehensively evaluate the tracker's performance.

OTB100 Benchmark. OTB100 contains sequences with various attributes or categories, including 11 challenge attributes. The OTB benchmark uses the one-pass evaluation (OPE) method with precision and success rate to quantitatively analyze and plot precision and success rate curves. The overlap rate is the evaluation metric for success rate, and the area under the curve (AUC) of the success rate curve is commonly used to evaluate the tracker's success rate performance.

VOT2018 Benchmark. VOT2018 typically includes 60 video sequences with challenging factors. The VOT benchmark uses accuracy (A), robustness (R), and expected average overlap (EAO) as evaluation metrics. Accuracy represents the average overlap between the tracking results and the ground truth labels, robustness measures the tracking failure frequency in video sequences, and EAO is a comprehensive evaluation metric that considers both accuracy and robustness to assess the tracker's performance.

auv   bait1   fish1   fish2   scaleph1

fish3   shark2   seahorse1   person1   turtle2

Fig. 2. Part of the sequence in the UT40.

UT40 Benchmark. To fully evaluate the tracker's performance in underwater scenarios, we collected 40 video clips from the internet to create an underwater dataset UT40, as shown in Fig. 2. Each frame of the videos was extracted, and the ground truth positions of the targets were annotated, resulting in a total of 8519 frames in the underwater dataset. The underwater dataset includes various camera types, observation distances, observation angles, and different water quality conditions, covering a diverse range of underwater environments. The dataset also contains various underwater targets, such as submarines, fish, divers, turtles, jellyfish, seahorses, and sharks. The newly created underwater dataset covers a wide range of challenges, including scale variation, motion blur, occlusion, illumination variation, and low resolution. For evaluation in the underwater dataset, we use OPE from the OTB benchmark to test the tracker's performance and plot precision and success rate curves.

4.3   Results and Discussion

State-of-art Comparison. To evaluate the effectiveness of the proposed method, tests were conducted on the self-constructed underwater target dataset UT40 and two challenging benchmark datasets: OTB100, and VOT2018. The tracking results were analyzed and compared with state-of-the-art tracking algorithms.

On OTB100. In OTB100, the proposed method was compared with eight high-performance tracking methods: SiamFC [1], SiamRPN [2], SiamRPN++ [3], DaSi-amRPN [4], ATOM [19], SiamDW [5], GradNet [20], and Ocean [21]. The success rate and precision curves of these tracking algorithms on the dataset are shown in Fig. 3 from the curves, it can be observed that the proposed algorithm achieved a success rate of 69.7% and a precision of 90.5%. Among all the algorithms, SiamRPN++ achieved the highest precision, while our method achieved the highest success rate. The proposed method ranked second in precision, being 1.0% lower than SiamRPN++, and ranked first in success rate, being 0.2% higher than SiamRPN++.

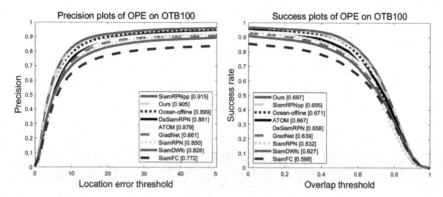

Fig. 3. Precision and success plots on OTB100.

Table 1. Evaluation results of each method on VOT2018.

Tracker	EAO↑	A↑	R↓
SiamMASK [25]	0.381	0.609	0.281
SiamRPN [2]	0.383	0586	0.276
LADCF [23]	0.389	0.503	0.159
ATOM [20]	0.400	0590	0.203
SiamRPN++ [3]	0.414	0.601	0.234
SiamCAR [7]	0.423	0.578	0.197
Ours	0.435	0.598	0.155
DiMP [24]	0.439	0.597	0.152

The top three indicators of each indicator are marked with red, green and blue.

On VOT2018. As shown in Table 1, the proposed method was compared with seven other high-performance tracking algorithms: SiamRPN [2], SiamRPN++ [3], SiamCAR [7], LADCF [22], DiMP [23], SiamMASK [24], and ATOM [19]. Displays the scores of the proposed method in accuracy, robustness, and EAO. Among the algorithms, DiMP achieved the best EAO score. In the comparison of robustness, our method ranked second, with a 0.3% reduction compared to DiMP. In accuracy, our method was 1.1% lower than

SiamMASK. Results show that the proposed method can maintain good robustness while achieving a certain level of accuracy.

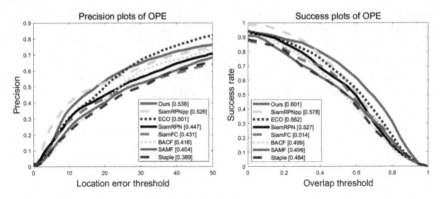

Fig. 4. Precision and success plots on UT40.

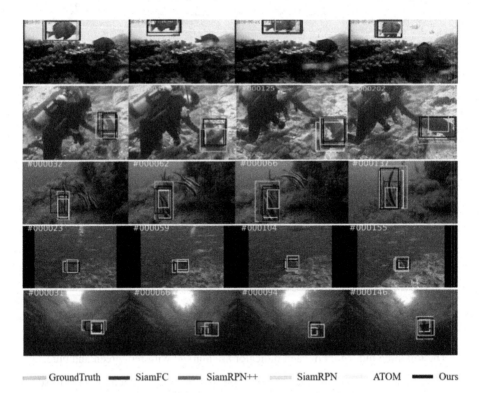

Fig. 5. Visualization Comparison on UT40.

On UT40. The proposed method was compared with other high-performance algorithms, including SiamRPN [2], SiamRPN++ [3], ECO, BACF, SiamFC [1], Staple and

SMAF, and the comparison results are shown in Fig. 4. The best tracking results were achieved on this dataset, and the proposed method achieved the first place in accuracy and success rate, with a success rate of 60.1% and an accuracy of 53.8%. Through experiments, it is found that the proposed method can accurately track the target in the underwater scene.

Visualization Comparison. To further evaluate the effectiveness of the proposed method for underwater object tracking, comparisons were conducted with SiamFC [1], SiamRPN [2], ATOM [19], and SiamRPN++ [3] on UT40. These sequences from top to bottom are fish5, fish9, fish20, person2 and person3. The visualization comparison results are shown in Fig. 5. In the fish5 sequence, where most of the target's body is out of view during movement, also in the person2 sequence, the target experiences significant occlusion due to the movements of the fish, the proposed method can still locate and track the target effectively. In the fish9 and person3 sequence, the target undergoes rotation and shape changes during motion, yet the proposed method maintains robust tracking performance. In the fish20 sequence, the target is affected by lighting variations and deformations, but the proposed method can still achieve effective tracking.

4.4 Ablation Study

In order to validate the effectiveness of the proposed method, ablation experiments were conducted on the VOT2018 and UT40. The experimental results are shown in Table 2. The baseline method also uses a modified ResNet50 as the backbone, including deep cross-correlation and anchor-free modules, with fixed tracking parameters. It can be observed that the tracker's performance significantly improves after the addition of spatial attention and cross attention mechanisms. When only the spatial attention mechanism was added, the EAO score in VOT2018 increased by 1.2%, and the success rate in the underwater dataset improved by 1.1%. When only the cross attention mechanism was added, the tracking performance improved by 1.4% and 1.7%, respectively. Furthermore, it can be seen that the addition of the cross attention mechanism led to better tracking performance. Finally, by combining the attention mechanisms with the feature fusion module, the method achieved the best tracking performance, with improvements of 2.2% and 3.1% in EAO and success rate, respectively, compared to the baseline method.

Table 2. Ablation Study on VOT2018 and UT40.

Method	VOT2018			UT40
	EAO↑	A↑	R↓	AUC↑
Baseline	0.413	0.576	0.198	0.570
Baseline + MFF + SAM	0.425	0.591	0.173	0.584
Baseline + MFF + CAM	0.427	0.595	0.168	0.587
Baseline + MFF + SAM + CAM (Ours)	0.435	0.598	0.155	0.601

5 Conclusion

In this article, we proposed a siamese network-based object tracking method for underwater environments. Our method consists of a feature extraction network, a parallel attention module, a multi-scale feature fusion module, and an anchor-free prediction network. The parallel attention module effectively integrates similar semantic features from different branches and extracting correlated features between branches, enhancing the tracker's feature representation capability. The multi-feature fusion module aggregates features from different layers and extracts multi-scale information, enabling better adaptation to scale changes. Through ablation experiments, we validated the effectiveness of each proposed module. We conducted experiments on OTB100, VOT2018 and UT40, and the results demonstrate that our method performs well, achieving effective tracking in underwater environments.

Acknowledgments. This work was supported by National Natural Science Foundation of China under Grant 62073120, and Natural Science Foundation of Jiangsu Province under Grant BK20201311.

References

1. Bertinetto, L., Valmadre, J., Henriques, J.F., Vedaldi, A., Torr, P.H.S.: Fully-convolutional siamese networks for object tracking. In: Hua, G., Jégou, H. (eds.) ECCV 2016. LNCS, vol. 9914, pp. 850–865. Springer, Cham (2016). https://doi.org/10.1007/978-3-319-48881-3_56
2. Li, B., Yan, J., Wu, W., Zhu, Z., Hu, X.: High performance visual tracking with siamese region proposal network. In: Proceedings of the IEEE Conference on Computer Vision and Pattern Recognition, pp. 8971–8980 (2018)
3. Li, B., Wu, W., Wang, Q., Zhang, F., Xing, J., Yan, J.: SiamRPN++: evolution of siamese visual tracking with very deep networks. In: Proceedings of IEEE Conference on Computer Vision and Pattern Recognition, pp. 4282–4291 (2019)
4. Guo,Q., Feng, W., Zhou, C., Huang, R., Wan, L., Wang, S.: Learning dynamic siamese network for visual object tracking. In: Proceedings of IEEE Conference on Computer Vision, pp. 1763–1771 (2017)
5. Zhang, Z., Peng, H.: Deeper and wider siamese networks for real-time visual tracking. In: Proceedings of the IEEE Conference on Computer Vision and Pattern Recognition, pp. 4591–4600 (2019)
6. Xu, Y., Wang, Z., Li, Z., Yuan, Y., Yu, G.: SiamFC++: Towards robust and accurate visual tracking with target estimation guidelines. In: Proceedings of the Association for the Advancement of Artificial Intelligence, vol. 34, no. 07, pp. 12549–12556 (2020)
7. Guo, D., Wang, J., Cui, Y., Wang, Z., Chen, S.: SiamCAR: siamese fully convolutional classification and regression for visual tracking. In: Proceedings of the IEEE Conference on Computer Vision and Pattern Recognition, pp. 6268–6276 (2020)
8. Chen, Z., Zhong, B., Li, G., Zhang, S., Ji, R.: Siamese box adaptive network for visual tracking. In: Proceedings of the IEEE/CVF Conference on Computer Vision and Pattern Recognition, pp. 6667–6676 (2020)
9. Hu, J., Shen, L., Albanie, S., Sun, G., Wu, E.H.: Squeeze-and-excitation networks. IEEE Trans. Pattern Anal. Mach. Intell. **42**(8), 2011–2023 (2020)

10. Li, X., Wang, W., Hu, X., Yang, J.: Selective kernel networks. In: Proceedings of the IEEE/CVF Conference on Computer Vision and Pattern Recognition, pp. 510–519 (2019)

11. Wang, X., Girshick, R., Gupta, A., He, K.: Non-local neural networks. In: Proceedings of the IEEE Conference on Computer Vision and Pattern Recognition, pp. 7794–7803 (2018)

12. Wang, Q., Teng, Z., Xing, J., Gao, J., Hu, W., Maybank, S.: Learning attentions: Residual attentional siamese network for high performance online visual tracking. In: Proceedings of the IEEE/CVF Conference on Computer Vision and Pattern Recognition, pp. 4854–4863 (2018)

13. Yu, Y., Xiong, Y., Huang, W., Scott, M.R.: Deformable siamese attention networks for visual object tracking. In: Proceedings of the IEEE/CVF Conference on Computer Vision and Pattern Recognition, pp. 6728–6737 (2020)

14. Russakovsky, O., et al.: ImageNet large scale visual recognition challenge. Int. J. Comput. Vis. **115**(3), 211–252 (2015)

15. Real, E., Shlens, J., Mazzocchi, S., Pan, X., Vanhoucke, V.: YouTube-bounding boxes: a large high-precision human-annotated data set for object detection in video. In: Proceedings of the IEEE/CVF Conference on Computer Vision and Pattern Recognition, pp. 5296–5305 (2017)

16. Lin, T.-Y., et al.: Microsoft COCO: common objects in context. In: Fleet, D., Pajdla, T., Schiele, B., Tuytelaars, T. (eds.) ECCV 2014. LNCS, vol. 8693, pp. 740–755. Springer, Cham (2014). https://doi.org/10.1007/978-3-319-10602-1_48

17. Wu, Y., Lim, J., Yang, M.H.: Object tracking benchmark. IEEE Trans. Pattern Anal. Mach. Intell. **37**(9), 1834–1848 (2015)

18. Kristan, M., et al.: The sixth visual object tracking VOT2018 challenge results. In: Leal-Taixé, L., Roth, S. (eds.) ECCV 2018. LNCS, vol. 11129, pp. 3–53. Springer, Cham (2019). https://doi.org/10.1007/978-3-030-11009-3_1

19. Danelljan, M., Bhat, G., Khan, F.S., et al.: Atom: accurate tracking by overlap maximization. In: Proceedings of the IEEE/CVF Conference on Computer Vision and Pattern Recognition, pp. 4660–4669 (2019)

20. Li, P., Chen, B., Ouyang, W., et al.: GradNet: gradient-guided network for visual object tracking. In: Proceedings of the IEEE/CVF International Conference on Computer Vision, pp. 6162–6171 (2019)

21. Zhang, Z., Peng, H., Fu, J., Li, B., Hu, W.: Ocean: object-aware anchor-free tracking. In: Vedaldi, A., Bischof, H., Brox, T., Frahm, J.-M. (eds.) ECCV 2020. LNCS, vol. 12366, pp. 771–787. Springer, Cham (2020). https://doi.org/10.1007/978-3-030-58589-1_46

22. Xu, T., Feng, Z.H., Wu, X.J., et al.: Learning adaptive discriminative correlation filters via temporal consistency preserving spatial feature selection for robust visual object tracking. IEEE Trans. Image Process. **28**(11), 5596–5609 (2019)

23. Bhat, G., Danelljan, M., Gool, L.V., et al.: Learning discriminative model prediction for tracking. In: Proceedings of the IEEE/CVF International Conference on Computer Vision, pp. 6182–6191 (2019)

24. Wang, Q., Zhang, L., Bertinetto, L., et al.: Fast online object tracking and segmentation: a unifying approach. In: Proceedings of the IEEE/CVF Conference on Computer Vision and Pattern Recognition, pp. 1328–1338 (2019)

25. Wang, P., et al.: Numerical and experimental study on the maneuverability of an active propeller control based wave glider. Appl. Ocean Res. (2020). https://doi.org/10.1016/j.apor. 2020.102369,vol104,102369

Cross-Modal Visual Correspondences Learning Without External Semantic Information for Zero-Shot Sketch-Based Image Retrieval

Zhijie Gao[✉] and Kai Wang

University of Electronic Science and Technology of China,
Chengdu 611731, Sichuan, China
wsgaozj@gmail.com

Abstract. In this paper, we study the problem of zero-shot sketch-based image retrieval (ZS-SBIR), which is challenging because of the modal gap between sketch and image and the semantic inconsistency between seen categories and unseen categories. Most of the previous methods in ZS-SBIR, need external semantic information, i.e., texts and class labels, to minimize modal gap or semantic inconsistency. To tackle the challenging ZS-SBIR without external semantic information which is labor intensive, we propose a novel method of learning the visual correspondences between different modalities, i.e., sketch and image, to transfer knowledge from seen data to unseen data. This method is based on a transformer-based dual-pathway structure to learn the visual correspondences. In order to eliminate the modal gap between sketch and image, triplet loss and Gaussian distribution based domain alignment mechanism are introduced and performed on tokens obtained from our proposed structure. In addition, knowledge distillation is introduced to maintain the generalization capability brought by the vision transformer (ViT) used as the backbone to build the model. The comprehensive experiments on three benchmark datasets, i.e., Sketchy, TU-Berlin and QuickDraw, demonstrate that our method achieves superior results compared to baselines on all three datasets without external semantic information.

Keywords: Sketch-based Image Retrieval · Zero-shot Learning · Knowledge Distillation

1 Introduction

Zero-shot sketch-based image retrieval (ZS-SBIR) is from the Sketch-based image retrieval (SBIR) [8,12], that the sketch is used as a query to retrieval relevant images from the gallery. In SBIR, the training and testing data are from the same categories, and the biggest challenge in addressing SBIR is the modal gap between sketch and image. SBIR with zero-shot setting, called as ZS-SBIR,

H. Lu and J. Cai (Eds.): ISAIR 2023, CCIS 1998, pp. 342–353, 2024.
https://doi.org/10.1007/978-981-99-9109-9_34

is proposed due to the data scarcity problem of human sketches and human-annotated samples [7, 23]. The zero-shot setting means that the training categories called as seen categories and the testing categories called as unseen categories are disjoint, and this setting brings up a new issue of semantic inconsistency between seen categories and unseen categories.

In recent years, in order to address the issue of semantic inconsistency, most of the research on ZS-SBIR has focused on incorporating external semantic information to facilitate the transfer of knowledge from seen categories to unseen categories or to alleviate the modal gap between different modalities. At the very beginning, a series of research [4, 7, 15] aims to bridge the seen and unseen classes through semantic embeddings. In general, these semantic embeddings are obtained through annotations. But these annotations require additional human labor costs to obtain. Then, some methods [11, 16, 17] based on pretrained convolutional neural networks (CNN) or pretrained vision transformer (ViT), have utilized knowledge distillation to preserve the powerful representation capability for transferring knowledge from seen categories to unseen categories. Although these methods using knowledge distillation have achieved great success, they still need external semantic information, such as class labels. However, these methods can also result in poorly discriminative features for retrieval due to knowledge distillation. To solve the problem brought by knowledge distillation, they have utilized class labels to make the features more discriminative. Recently, a method called ZSE [9] has been proposed. Compared to previous methods, it has a different perspective on addressing ZS-SBIR: the visual correspondence between sketch and image. It achieves superior performance using a transformer-based model, without relying on any external semantic information such as texts or class labels. However, it designs a kernel-based relation network to learn the relationships between sketches and images at every pair and ignores the relationship at higher levels, such as class-level and modality-level. And it also fails to preserve the generalization capability brought by the ViT used as the backbone to build the model.

Motivated by the above observations, we propose a method that shares the same idea as ZSE to address ZS-SBIR without external semantic information by learning the visual correspondence between sketch and image. Specifically, as shown in Fig. 1, we design a dual-pathway transformer-based structure corresponding to sketches and images, respectively. This structure takes data from the two modalities as input in order to establish local correspondences between them. In addition, a triplet loss is used for preliminary alignment between retrieval tokens from sketch and image. In order to maintain the relationship at various levels, such as instance-level, class-level and modality-level, a distribution alignment loss is employed to prevent the alignment of data only at the instance-level. Besides, a teacher ViT is employed to perform knowledge distillation on the self-attention modules using the instance-level kd loss to maintain the generalization capability brought by the ViT for constructing the self-attention modules. Extensive experiments on three benchmark datasets of ZS-SBIR verify the superiority of our method.

We summarize our contributions in this paper as follows:

1. We propose a novel method based on a transformer-based dual-pathway structure to learn the visual correspondence between sketch and image to address ZS-SBIR. The method achieves superior performance in ZS-SBIR without any external semantic information which requires extra human labor cost.
2. We propose a distribution alignment loss, which aligns the data from sketch and image in a global view and maintains the relationships between sketch and image at various levels, such as instance-level, class-level and modality-level.
3. We introduce knowledge distillation using the instance-level kd loss, which preserve the generalization capability brought by the ViT used as the backbone to build the model.

2 Related Work

2.1 Zero-Shot Sketch-Based Image Retrieval (ZS-SBIR)

ZS-SBIR is a challenging task that must simultaneously address the inherent modal gap and the semantic inconsistency. Pioneering researches [4,7,15] in ZS-SBIR are inspired by the knowledge transfer mechanism in zero-shot learning, has used the semantic embeddings obtained from the labeled category-level texts extracted from the text-based model, to support knowledge transfer from the source domain (seen categories) to the target domain (unseen categories).

Liu et al. [11] used the CNN-based model pretrained in ImageNet as the backbone to map the data from different modalities to the semantic space of the pretrained model, and knowledge distillation was introduced for the first time to preserve the rich semantic information brought by the pretrained model to transfer knowledge. Tian et al. [16] also used knowledge distillation and selected DINO [1] as the backbone, which has a strong ability to detect global structural information. In addition, they proposed the hypersphere learning framework to align the data from different modalities.

Recently, Lin et al. [9] proposed ZSE that differed from previous work in that it thought a cross-modal matching problem such as ZS-SBIR as the comparisons of groups of key local patches, which had the advantage of not requiring external semantic knowledge and achieved superior performances in ZS-SBIR. In this paper, we adopt the same idea of ZSE to address ZS-SBIR by learning a local visual match between sketch and photo, but we perform the match from a global perspective and use knowledge distillation to prevent catastrophic forgetting.

2.2 Vision Transformer(ViT)

Transformer [19] was originally proposed for machine translation and has achieved tremendous success in many fields of artificial intelligence, such as natural language processing and computer vision. ViT [6] comes from the idea of applying Transformer structures to computer vision, and is a transformer-based

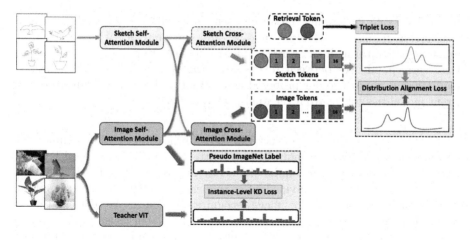

Fig. 1. The overview of our proposed method. A dual-pathway structure is designed to learn visual correspondences between sketches and images. Triplet Loss is applied to retrieval tokens for preliminary alignment. Distribution Alignment Loss eliminates the domain gap between sketch and image by aligning their different latent feature distributions. Instance-level KD Loss is used for the Pseudo ImageNet Label produced by the Self-Attention Module or Teacher ViT, to preserve generalization.

image classification model with excellent representational capabilities and strong transferability that can be applied to other vision tasks such as object detection and semantic segmentation.

Subsequently, several researches [2,5] have found that reasoning based on cross attention was shown effective on image classification, few-shot learning and sketch segment matching, they have tried to learn visual correspondence at different levels between different images by cross-attention mechanism. In this paper, we use the ViT with powerful representation ability to build self-attention module and use it to produce visual tokens that correspond to the most informative local regions, and a cross-attention module followed by self-attention module to learn a local visual match between sketch and photo.

3   Methodology

In this section, following the overall scheme of our proposed framework which is illustrated in Fig. 1, we explain the main modules and learning objectives of our method in detail.

3.1   Cross-Domain ViT

To establish patch-to-patch correspondences between sketches and images, as shown in Fig. 1, we design a dual-pathway structure corresponding to sketches and images, respectively. Specifically, sketches and images are first used to obtain tokens have rich visual information independently within the modality through the corresponding self-attention module, and then interact with tokens from other modality through the corresponding cross-attention module to establish local correspondences between tokens from the two modalities. Furthermore, triplet loss is applied to our proposed method for preliminary alignment of different modalities tokens from the dual-pathway structure.

Self-attention Module. We select ViT to build the self-attention module. ViT is composed of L layers of multi-head self-attention (MSA) and Feed-Forward Network (FFN) blocks. The inputs of ViT are first resized to a fixed resolution. Subsequently, each input is divided into a sequence of patches of fixed resolution. A learnable class token cls for image recognition is added. We replaced the cls with a learnable retrieval token x_{ret} to obtain the global features of an image or sketch for retrieval. All tokens including x_{ret} are $d-$dimensional token and they are $X_0 = (x_{ret}, x_1, \ldots, x_n)$, x_i is the visual token and n is the number of visual tokens. For the $i-$th layer of MSA and FFN, the MSA module has (W_q, W_k, W_v), which project the same token into Queries, Keys and Values, and the whole process of MSA can be formulated as follows:

$$Q = X_{i-1}W_q, \ K = X_{i-1}W_k, \ V = X_{i-1}W_v \tag{1}$$

$$SA(X_{i-1}) = \psi(\frac{QK^T}{\sqrt{d}})V \tag{2}$$

where X_{i-1} is the output of the last layer or X_0 and ψ is softmax operation, the feed-forward process can be formulated as follows:

$$X_i = MSA(LN(X_{i-1})) + X_{i-1} \tag{3}$$

$$X_i = FFN(LN(X_i)) + X_i \tag{4}$$

where LN is layer normalization.

Cross-Attention Module. We use the method proposed by ZSE [9] to build cross-attention module. Each cross-attention module takes visual tokens and x_{ret} from all modalities as inputs to build the pairwise connections between tokens from the two modalities. In detail, the sketch Query Q_s and the image Query Q_p are swapped, and the cross-modal attention of the sketch can be formulated as:

$$CA(X_s) = \psi(\frac{Q_pK_s^T}{\sqrt{d}})V_s \tag{5}$$

Similarly, the cross-modal attention of the image can be formulated as:

$$CA(X_p) = \psi(\frac{Q_sK_p^T}{\sqrt{d}})V_p \tag{6}$$

Triplet Loss. To align retrieval tokens from different modalities, i.e., sketch and image, we use triplet loss to make the sketch retrieval token x_{ret}^{s+} close to the image retrieval token x_{ret}^{p+} that has the same class, and away from the image retrieval token x_{ret}^{p-} that has different class, and the triplet loss for a batch of N can be formulated as:

$$\mathcal{L}_{tri} = \frac{1}{N} \sum_{i=1}^{N} max(\| x_{ret}^{s+} - x_{ret}^{p+} \| - \| x_{ret}^{s+} - x_{ret}^{p-} \| + m, 0) \qquad (7)$$

where m is the margin.

3.2 Gaussian Distribution Based Domain Alignment

Wang et al. [20] propose that different domains datasets with different latent feature distributions can be aligned under the guidance of the Gaussian prior. This alignment can build a common feature space for the datasets from different domains and the common space has the discriminative features to achieve excellent performance in eliminating the domain gap between different domains. So, we adopt a Gaussian prior to guide the alignment between the sketch and image in order to alleviate the domain gap between them, specifically we follow the method proposed by Wu et al. [22] and utilize the Kullback-Leibler divergence to align x_{ret}^s of sketches and x_{ret}^p of images with a common Gaussian distribution. With our proposed dual-pathway structure, a batch of retrieval tokens $X_{ret} = \{x_{ret}^i \in R^d\}^N$ representing the global visual information of sketches or images can be generated from a batch of training samples. We sample a batch of random features $F = \{f_i \in R^d\}^N$ from Gaussian distribution $\mathcal{N}(0,1)$ simultaneously and the distribution alignment loss $\mathcal{L}_{da}$ can be formulated as:

$$\mathcal{L}_{da} = KL(F \| X_{ret}) \qquad (8)$$

where KL is the Kullback-Leibler divergence. By applying $\mathcal{L}_{da}$ to both x_{ret}^s and x_{ret}^p, the distributions of the two modalities can be aligned under the guidance of Gaussian distribution and the domain gap between sketch and image is indirectly mitigated.

3.3 Instance-Level Knowledge Distillation

Since ViT is pretrained on large-scale image dataset, e.g., ImageNet, it has a powerful discrimination capability to provide probability vectors containing fine-grained semantic information for the input images. However, when ViT is used as the backbone to build the self-attention module and finetuned in a much smaller ZS-SBIR dataset, its rich knowledge originally learned from ImageNet is eliminated. Inspired by the method proposed by Tian et al. [17], we introduce instance-level knowledge distillation to our method. More specifically, as the Fig. 1 is illustrated, we use the teacher ViT and self-attention module to produce probability vectors, which are originally used to predict the categories from ImageNet and we dub them as pseudo ImageNet label. Then, we let self-attention module to mimic teacher ViT's response by aligning the pseudo ImageNet label. However, this alignment operation is only applied to images because of the domain gap between the sketches and images from ImageNet.

Given an image p_i, it is fed into the teacher and the self-attention module to obtain pseudo ImageNet label e_i^t and e_i^s, and the instance-level knowledge distillation loss $\mathcal{L}_{ikd}$ can be formulated as:

$$\mathcal{L}_{ikd} = KL(e_i^t \parallel e_i^s) \tag{9}$$

3.4 Overall Objective

Finally, the full objective function of our method can be formulated as:

$$\mathcal{L} = \lambda_1 \cdot \mathcal{L}_{tri} + \lambda_2 \cdot \mathcal{L}_{da} + \lambda_3 \cdot \mathcal{L}_{ikd} \tag{10}$$

where λ_1, λ_2 and λ_3 are weight factors to balance the contributions of $\mathcal{L}_{tri}$, $\mathcal{L}_{da}$ and $\mathcal{L}_{ikd}$, respectively.

4 Experiments

4.1 Datasets and Setup

Datasets. We evaluate our method on three benchmark datasets for ZS-SBIR, i.e., Sketchy [14], TU-Berlin [8] and QuickDraw [4]. Sketchy has 12,500 natural images and 75,471 sketches in 125 categories. Liu et al. [10] extended it by adding another 60,502 natural images to alleviate the data imbalance between two modalities. There are two kinds of seen and unseen class divisions for Sketchy, we refer to them as **Sketchy** and **Sketchy-NO**. The former one [10] randomly selects 25 classes as unseen classes, and the latter one [23] selects 21 classes which do not overlap with the classes in ImageNet. TU-Berlin has 13,419 natural images and 20,000 sketches in 250 categories. Zhang et al. [24] extended it by adding another 204,489 natural images. One seen and unseen class division [15] is widely used for TU-Berlin and it selects 30 categories as unseen classes. QuickDraw has 330,000 sketches and 204,000 images in 110 categories. QuickDraw has a seen and unseen class division [4] and this division also selects 30 classes that do not overlap with the classes in ImageNet.

Implementation Details. We use PyTorch as an implementation framework to implement our method with a Geforce RTX2080ti GPU. The ViT pretrained on ImageNet-1K is used to build the self-attention module, which consists of 12 layers of MSA and FFN blocks and a fully-connected layer to produced 1000 dimensional pseudo ImageNet labels. The cross-attention module only contains one layer. The dimension of retrieval tokens and visual tokens is 768. The input size of the sketch or image is 224×224. AdamW is used as the optimizer and the learning rate is 10^{-5}. The batch size is set as 64 with 2 gradient accumulation steps. To obtain $(x_{ret}^{s+}, x_{ret}^{p+}, x_{ret}^{p-})$ for the triplet loss, each batch consists of 32 sketches from the same category and 32 images from two categories, and half of the images in the batch have the same category as the sketches. Epoch is set to 30 for training the model. λ_1, λ_2 and λ_3 are set to 2.0, 0.1 and 1.0 in all experiments. In the test phase, we use the retrieval tokens for retrieval.

Evaluation Protocol. Following the previous works [11] in ZS-SBIR, we utilize precision (Prec@k) and mean average precision (mAP@k) as the evaluation protocols for fair comparisons. In all experiments, these evaluation protocols are computed using cosine similarity as the distance metric (Table 1).

Table 1. Comparison of our method and compared approaches on Sketchy, Sketchy-NO, TU-Berlin and QuickDraw. "–"means that the results are not reported in the original papers. The best and second-best results are marked in bold and underlined, respectively.

Methods	Semantic	Sketchy		Sketchy-NO		TU-Berlin		QuickDraw	
		mAP@all	Prec@100	mAP@200	Prec@200	mAP@all	Prec@100	mAP@all	Prec@200
ZSIH	✓	0.254	0.340	–	–	0.220	0.291	–	–
SEM-PCYC	✓	0.349	0.463	–	–	0.297	0.426	–	–
DOODLE	✓	0.369	–	–	–	0.109	–	0.075	0.068
SAKE	✓	0.547	0.692	0.497	0.598	0.475	0.599	0.130	0.179
PDFD	✓	0.661	0.781	–	–	0.483	0.600	–	–
DSN	✓	0.583	0.704	0.501	0.597	0.484	0.591	–	–
RPKD	✓	0.613	0.723	0.502	0.598	0.486	0.612	0.143	0.218
SBTKNet	✓	0.553	0.698	0.502	0.596	0.480	0.608	–	–
Sketch3T	✓	0.575	–	–	–	0.507	–	–	–
TVT	✓	0.648	0.796	**0.531**	<u>0.618</u>	0.484	<u>0.662</u>	<u>0.149</u>	**0.293**
ZSE-RN	✗	0.698	0.797	<u>0.525</u>	**0.624**	0.542	0.657	0.145	0.216
ZSE-Ret	✗	<u>0.736</u>	<u>0.808</u>	0.504	0.602	<u>0.569</u>	0.637	0.142	0.202
Ours	✗	**0.757**	**0.827**	0.518	0.605	**0.607**	**0.678**	**0.162**	<u>0.239</u>

4.2 Comparison with the State-of-the-Arts

Comparison Methods. We compared our method with some baselines, including ZSIH [15], SEM-PCYC [7], DOODLE [4], SAKE [11], PDFD [3], DSN [21], RPKD [17], SBTKNet [18], Sketch3T [13], TVT [16], and ZSE [9]. There are two retrieval approaches in which ZSE is used and we compare our method with both approaches for a fair comparation with ZSE. One is using the matching scores of the sketch and image output from the relation network, referred to as ZSE-RN. The other is using retrieval tokens for retrieval, referred to as ZSE-Ret. It is worth noting that all methods, except ours and ZSE, utilize external semantic information, such as text or class labels.

Table 2. Ablation results (mAP@all) for each loss on Sketchy and TU-Berlin datasets. "✓" means that the loss term is used, while "×" does not.

Models	$\mathcal{L}_{tri}$	$\mathcal{L}_{da}$	$\mathcal{L}_{ikd}$	Sketchy	TU-Berlin
Ours-full	✓	✓	✓	0.757	0.607
w/o $\mathcal{L}_{da}$	✓	×	✓	0.673	0.529
w/o $\mathcal{L}_{ikd}$	✓	✓	×	0.746	0.593
w/o $\mathcal{L}_{tri}$	×	✓	✓	0.316	0.301

Overall Results. We evaluate our method on Sketchy, Sketchy-NO, TU-Berlin and QuickDraw, and compare the experimental results with other baselines in the table. Compared to the state-of-the-art ZSE, we surpass it in most of the results, which highlights the superiority of our efficient Gaussian distribution based domain alignment and knowledge distillation for preserving knowledge.

When compared to other methods that use external semantic information, our method significantly outperforms them on Sketchy and TU-Berlin. We also have the best mAP@all result on QuickDraw. The results on Sketchy-NO are slightly worse than some of them, because the unseen categories of Sketchy-NO do not overlap with the classes in ImageNet and it is tough to improve the results without any external semantic information. All of this shows the effectiveness of our method since we do not utilize any external sematic information.

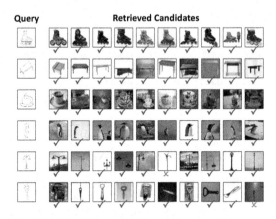

Fig. 2. Retrieval examples of ZS-SBIR results on unseen data of TU-Berlin.

4.3 Further Analysis

Ablation Study. We evaluate the effect of each loss term our method used by ablating one of them in the training phase. The experimental results are shown in

Table 2, where "w/o" means the ablating behavior. From the comparison of each variant and our full model, we can draw the following conclusion: 1) $\mathcal{L}_{tri}$ is the most substantial one among the three losses, which directly aligns the retrieval tokens used for retrieval, since the variant without $\mathcal{L}_{tri}$ drops significantly and preforms worse than other variants. 2) The performance of the variant without $\mathcal{L}_{da}$ indicates that adopting Gaussian prior to guide the alignment between sketch and image can alleviate the domain gap between them. 3) The variant without $\mathcal{L}_{ikd}$ performs slightly worse than the full model. This observation shows that $\mathcal{L}_{ikd}$ can make the backbone retain the extensive knowledge learned from the large-scale ImageNet.

Retrieval Results. As shown in Fig. 2, we visualize the top 10 retrieved results of sketches queries, where correct and incorrect candidates are marked with checkmarks and crosses, respectively. The majority of the top 10 images retrieved using our approach resemble the query sketches in terms of the overall object pose and shape characteristics, even the incorrect retrieved results have a similar shape to the queries. This observation proves the validity of our method.

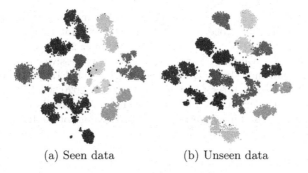

      (a) Seen data   (b) Unseen data

Fig. 3. The t-SNE visualization for seen and unseen data of Sketchy. Colored circles are used to represent images, while upper triangles are used to represent sketches.

Visualization of Embeddings. As shown in Fig. 3, we evaluate the effect of our method in semantic alignments across modalities by utilizing the t-SNE tool. We conduct this visualization on both seen and unseen data from Sketchy. From Fig. 3, we can find that our method successfully clusters seen data from different modalities. To some extent, the unseen data can also cluster together by our method. Furthermore, most of the categories are properly separated regardless of modalities. This observation is a good indication of the effectiveness of our method in aligning different modal data and demonstrates a strong generalization ability to align data from unseen classes.

5   Conclusion

This paper tackled ZS-SBIR by focusing on learning a local visual correspondence between sketch and photo. We proposed a transformer-based dual-pathway model to learn the local visual correspondence between sketch and photo. In this way, the semantic inconsistency is minimized. In order to eliminate the modal gap, triplet loss and distribution alignment loss were introduced to align the data from different modalities. Furthermore, knowledge distillation was introduced to maintain the generalization capability. We conducted extensive experiments on three benchmark datasets, and our method achieves competitive results without external semantic information compared to the baselines. In the future, we will focus on addressing ZS-SBIR by exploring a more effective solution to learn the visual correspondence between sketch and photo.

References

1. Caron, M., et al.: Emerging properties in self-supervised vision transformers. In: Proceedings of the IEEE/CVF International Conference on Computer Vision (ICCV), pp. 9650–9660, October 2021
2. Casey, E., Pérez, V., Li, Z.: The animation transformer: visual correspondence via segment matching. In: Proceedings of the IEEE/CVF International Conference on Computer Vision (ICCV), pp. 11323–11332, October 2021
3. Deng, C., Xu, X., Wang, H., Yang, M., Tao, D.: Progressive cross-modal semantic network for zero-shot sketch-based image retrieval. IEEE Trans. Image Process. **29**, 8892–8902 (2020). https://doi.org/10.1109/TIP.2020.3020383
4. Dey, S., Riba, P., Dutta, A., Llados, J., Song, Y.Z.: Doodle to search: practical zero-shot sketch-based image retrieval. In: Proceedings of the IEEE Conference on Computer Vision and Pattern Recognition, pp. 2179–2188 (2019)
5. Doersch, C., Gupta, A., Zisserman, A.: Crosstransformers: spatially-aware few-shot transfer. In: Proceedings of the 34th International Conference on Neural Information Processing Systems. NIPS'20, Curran Associates Inc., Red Hook, NY, USA (2020)
6. Dosovitskiy, A., et al.: An image is worth 16×16 words: transformers for image recognition at scale (2021)
7. Dutta, A., Akata, Z.: Semantically tied paired cycle consistency for zero-shot sketch-based image retrieval. In: Proceedings of the IEEE/CVF Conference on Computer Vision and Pattern Recognition (CVPR), June 2019
8. Eitz, M., Hildebrand, K., Boubekeur, T., Alexa, M.: An evaluation of descriptors for large-scale image retrieval from sketched feature lines. Comput. Graph. **34**(5), 482–498 (2010)
9. Lin, F., Li, M., Li, D., Hospedales, T., Song, Y.Z., Qi, Y.: Zero-shot everything sketch-based image retrieval, and in explainable style. In: Proceedings of the IEEE/CVF Conference on Computer Vision and Pattern Recognition (CVPR), pp. 23349–23358, June 2023
10. Liu, L., Shen, F., Shen, Y., Liu, X., Shao, L.: Deep sketch hashing: fast free-hand sketch-based image retrieval. In: Proceedings of the IEEE Conference on Computer Vision and Pattern Recognition, pp. 2862–2871 (2017)

11. Liu, Q., Xie, L., Wang, H., Yuille, A.L.: Semantic-aware knowledge preservation for zero-shot sketch-based image retrieval. In: Proceedings of the IEEE/CVF International Conference on Computer Vision (ICCV), October 2019

12. Saavedra, J.M., Barrios, J.M.: Sketch based image retrieval using learned keyshapes (LKS). In: British Machine Vision Conference (2015). https://api.semanticscholar.org/CorpusID:11324587

13. Sain, A., Bhunia, A.K., Potlapalli, V., Chowdhury, P.N., Xiang, T., Song, Y.Z.: Sketch3t: test-time training for zero-shot SBIR. 2022 IEEE/CVF Conference on Computer Vision and Pattern Recognition (CVPR), pp. 7452–7461 (2022). https://api.semanticscholar.org/CorpusID:247762119

14. Sangkloy, P., Burnell, N., Ham, C., Hays, J.: The sketchy database: learning to retrieve badly drawn bunnies. ACM Trans. Graph. (TOG) **35**(4), 1–12 (2016)

15. Shen, Y., Liu, L., Shen, F., Shao, L.: Zero-shot sketch-image hashing. In: Proceedings of the IEEE Conference on Computer Vision and Pattern Recognition, pp. 3598–3607 (2018)

16. Tian, J., Xu, X., Shen, F., Yang, Y., Shen, H.T.: TVT: three-way vision transformer through multi-modal hypersphere learning for zero-shot sketch-based image retrieval. In: Proceedings of the AAAI Conference on Artificial Intelligence, vol. 36, no. 2, pp. 2370–2378, June 2022. https://doi.org/10.1609/aaai.v36i2.20136, https://ojs.aaai.org/index.php/AAAI/article/view/20136

17. Tian, J., Xu, X., Wang, Z., Shen, F., Liu, X.: Relationship-preserving knowledge distillation for zero-shot sketch based image retrieval. In: Proceedings of the 29th ACM International Conference on Multimedia, pp. 5473–5481. MM '21, Association for Computing Machinery, New York, NY, USA (2021). https://doi.org/10.1145/3474085.3475676

18. Tursun, O., Denman, S., Sridharan, S., Goan, E., Fookes, C.: An efficient framework for zero-shot sketch-based image retrieval. Pattern Recognit. **126**, 108528 (2022). https://doi.org/10.1016/j.patcog.2022.108528, https://www.sciencedirect.com/science/article/pii/S0031320322000097

19. Vaswani, A., et al.: Attention is all you need. In: Advances in Neural Information Processing Systems, pp. 5998–6008 (2017)

20. Wang, J., Chen, J., Lin, J., Sigal, L., de Silva, C.W.: Discriminative feature alignment: improving transferability of unsupervised domain adaptation by gaussian-guided latent alignment. Pattern Recognit. **116**, 107943 (2021). https://doi.org/10.1016/j.patcog.2021.107943, https://www.sciencedirect.com/science/article/pii/S0031320321001308

21. Wang, Z., Wang, H., Yan, J., Wu, A., Deng, C.: Domain-smoothing network for zero-shot sketch-based image retrieval. ArXiv abs/2106.11841 (2021). https://api.semanticscholar.org/CorpusID:235593135

22. Wu, Y., Song, K., Zhao, F., Chen, J., Ma, H.: Distribution aligned feature clustering for zero-shot sketch-based image retrieval (2023)

23. Yelamarthi, S.K., Reddy, S.K., Mishra, A., Mittal, A.: A zero-shot framework for sketch based image retrieval. In: Ferrari, V., Hebert, M., Sminchisescu, C., Weiss, Y. (eds.) ECCV 2018. LNCS, vol. 11208, pp. 316–333. Springer, Cham (2018). https://doi.org/10.1007/978-3-030-01225-0_19

24. Zhang, H., Liu, S., Zhang, C., Ren, W., Wang, R., Cao, X.: Sketchnet: sketch classification with web images. In: Proceedings of the IEEE Conference on Computer Vision and Pattern Recognition, pp. 1105–1113 (2016)

Remaining Useful Life prediction of Aircraft Engines Using DCNN-BiLSTM with K-means Feature Selection

Gang Cao[✉]

COMAC Shanghai Aircraft Design and Research Institute, Shanghai, China
caogang@comac.cc

Abstract. Predicting the remaining useful life of aircraft components has emerged as a crucial research focus in the field of aviation maintenance. Traditional methods typically rely on empirical rules and statistical models. However, these methods often face challenges in accurately forecasting the intricate lifespan of components. In recent years, with the rapid advancements in deep learning technology, there has been a growing inclination to apply these techniques to predict the remaining useful life of aircraft components. In this paper, we propose a novel approach to predict the Remaining Useful Life of aircraft engines. Our method integrates the K-means algorithm to reveal meaningful data categories, enhancing data preprocessing efficiency. The processed data is then input to the DCNN model to extract spatial features. Furthermore, we harness the bidirectional time series encoding capability of BiLSTM to capture both long-term and short-term temporal dependencies in the data. Ultimately, regression is utilized to accurately predict the components' remaining useful life. Experimental results using the well-known aircraft remaining useful life C-MAPSS dataset reveal that our approach outperforms several baseline models in terms of predictive performance (the most significant improvement over a single CNN is recorded at 111%). The Root Mean Squared Error (RMSE) values for the four subsets of C-MAPSS are recorded as 13.54, 15.94, 11.56, and 13.77, respectively.

Keywords: DCNN · LSTM · Time Series Prediction · Aircraft Failure Rate Analysis · K-Means

1 Introduction

In recent years, driven by the rapid progress of the aviation industry, there has been an increasing focus on the safety and reliability of airplanes. However, aircraft failure rate prediction [1] is still a challenging problem. Traditional prediction methods often rely on expert experience [2] and statistical models [3], but these methods often fail to fully utilize the large amount of aircraft operation data and failure records. To address this, researchers are turning their attention toward deep learning techniques [4]. Deep learning is a machine learning method based on neural networks [5], which is able to automatically learn and extract key features from data, and make predictions and classifications in a hierarchical way. For the problem of predicting the aircraft failure rate, deep learning can be trained on a large amount of aircraft operation data to discover patterns and rules hidden in the data [19–23]. These patterns and rules can help us predict the probability of aircraft failure and take timely corresponding repair and maintenance measures, thus improving the reliability and safety of the aircraft. Compared with traditional prediction methods, deep learning has the following advantages. First, deep learning can handle large-scale data, including aircraft operating parameters, maintenance records, environmental conditions, etc., thus analyzing the influencing factors of aircraft failures more comprehensively. Second, deep learning can automatically learn and extract features from data without relying on manually selected features, thus improving the accuracy and reliability of predictions. Finally, deep learning can also perform end-to-end learning, i.e., from the raw data to the final prediction result without human intervention, reducing subjectivity and errors in the prediction process. In summary, utilizing deep learning to predict aircraft failure rates carries significant research importance and practical utility. By harnessing the vast repository of aircraft operational data and failure records, deep learning has the potential to enhance aircraft reliability and safety, offering essential technical support for the progress of the aviation industry.

This paper presents a hybrid model designed to predict the Remaining Useful Life (RUL) of aircraft engines. Within this model, we employ the K-means algorithm [6] to uncover potential operational patterns within the dataset, leading to highly efficient data preprocessing. Building upon this, the data undergoes training via the DCNN-BiLSTM network. This network capitalizes on the feature extraction capabilities of Deep Convolutional Neural Network (DCNN) [7] and the bidirectional time-series feature capturing potential of BiLSTM (Bidirectional Long Short-Term Memory) [8]. This powerful combination equips the model to excel in forecasting extended time series, thus showcasing remarkable performance in tackling complex prediction challenges. To validate the effectiveness of our proposed approach, we conduct a series of experiments on the C-MAPSS (Commercial Modular Aero-Propulsion System Simulation) dataset. The results serve to confirm the superiority of our method, surpassing existing techniques and achieving state-of-the-art performance.

The rest of this paper is organized as follows. Section 2 presents the relevant background and related work. Section 3 delineates our algorithmic methodology and framework structure. In Sect. 4, we provide a detailed description of the experimental data and present the experimental results. Finally, Sect. 5 gives conclusion and future work.

2 Related Work

Existing methods for RUL prediction can be categorized into three primary categories: statistically based approaches, machine learning methods and deep learning techniques.

Statistically Based Approaches. These methods rely on historical data and statistical analysis to predict RUL by analyzing equipment operating data and failure records. For instance, literature [9] proposed an ARMA model optimized with genetic algorithms for predicting the remaining service life of solder joints. Additionally, literature [10] used a hybrid model based on empirical pattern decomposition and ARIMA for predicting the

RUL of lithium batteries. These methods are suitable for long-term operating equipment, as they utilize historical data for parameter estimation and prediction.

Machine Learning Methods. Machine learning methods employ algorithms and models to learn the relationship between device operational data and fault information to predict RUL. For example, literature [11] used SVM and hybrid degradation tracking models to predict the RUL of bearings by training SVM classifiers with fitted measurements from a generalized degradation model. In another study, literature [12] proposed a prediction method combining Time Window (TW) and Gradient Boosted Decision Tree (GBDT) to predict the RUL of lithium batteries. These methods can effectively learn device features and patterns from large amounts of data, enabling accurate RUL prediction.

Deep Learning Techniques. These methods harness diverse neural network algorithms to construct models that predict both the operational status and longevity of equipment. By training on extensive device data, they can forecast equipment's remaining life. Literature [13] employed a one-dimensional convolutional neural network (CNN) enhanced with a pooling layer, extracting and amalgamating features from various signals. Moreover, they applied dilated convolution combined with residual connections and an attention mechanism to further refine the features derived from the pooling layer. Another study, literature [14], put forth a recursive neural network-centric method for bearing RUL prediction. It's worth noting that deep learning models typically demand a substantial volume of training data.

Though the aforementioned methods have demonstrated effectiveness in RUL prediction, certain limitations such as suboptimal performance, uniform feature extraction, and inadequate data feature preprocessing can be observed. In order to enhance RUL prediction performance, this paper proposes a deep learning hybrid network model. This model combines K-means feature selection with a hybrid DCNN-BiLSTM approach, facilitating efficient spatial feature extraction while also considering time-series features. Additionally, it provides a mechanism to identify potential data categories during preprocessing, thereby improving the rationality of data preparation for individual samples.

3   Methodology

This section introduces the related technologies utilized in this paper and provides implementation details of the proposed approach.

3.1   K-means Clustering Algorithm

The K-means algorithm is a clustering method aimed at dividing the samples in a dataset into K distinct clusters, ensuring that the distance between each sample and its cluster center is minimized. The C-MAPSS dataset used in this paper contains sub-datasets with six operational conditions determined by the operation setting column. However, the range of these operational settings is unspecified in the dataset. To address this, we employ the K-means algorithm to segregate all data samples into six clusters. Following this, each sample is normalized based on the cluster it belongs to. The specific algorithmic steps for K-means are:

1. A centroid a_1 is randomly selected as the first clustering center in the dataset $\mathcal{X}$.
2. Calculate the farthest distance $D(x)$ from the data distribution to the n cluster centers and select the new centroid a_i with probability $P(x) = \frac{D(x)^2}{\sum_{x \in \mathcal{X}} D(x)^2}$.
3. Repeat the second step until a sufficient number of cluster centers K are chosen.
4. Ultimately, the data of the data set $\mathcal{X}$ is normalized according to the K class, so that the method can be reasonably based on different operational settings to preprocess the corresponding data.

3.2 Deep Convolutional Neural Network

DCNN, a deep learning model based on neural networks, excels in image and video processing tasks. It progressively extracts image features through layered convolutional and pooling stages, culminating in classification or regression through fully connected layers. At its core, DCNN employs Convolutional layers to extract local image features. By stacking multiple convolutional layers, higher-level feature representations are gradually unveiled. Convolutional layers capture spatial features via convolutional operations and nonlinear activations. Simultaneously, pooling layers trim feature map size while retaining essential feature data. The final step involves the fully connected layer, which maps the feature map to the ultimate regression outcome. A schematic depiction of the convolution principle is presented in Fig. 1.

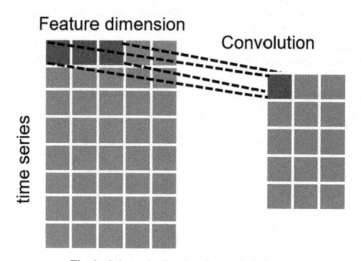

Fig. 1. Schematic diagram of convolution unit.

Convolution is categorized into 1-dimensional convolution, 2-dimensional convolution and 3-dimensional convolution, each of which has its own adaptation range. In this paper, since the C-MPASS dataset can be made up of two dimensions (feature number and time series of each feature), we use a 2-dimensional convolution network to perform convolution on it, due to the fact that the 2-dimensional convolution is in reality 1-dimensional when the input feature map is 2-dimensional, so as to extract the features of the data in it. Suppose the input sequence is $X = [x_1, x_2, \ldots, x_N] \in R^{N \times F}$, where N is the length of the sequence and F is the dimension of the selected features, the multiplication operation between the convolution kernel $w \in R^L$ and the input vector $x_{i:i+L-1}$ in the convolution operation can be defined as:

$$x_{i:i+L-1} = x_i \oplus x_{i+1} \oplus \ldots \oplus x_{i+L-1} \tag{1}$$

In the above equation $x_{i:i+L-1}$ denotes the L-length sequence of signal windows starting from the i_{th} point, and $\oplus$ concatenates each data sample into a longer embedding. The final convolution operation is defined as:

$$z_i = \varphi\left(w^T x_{i:i+L-1} + b\right) \tag{2}$$

where φ is the activation function, b is the bias term, and z_i is the feature obtained from this convolution operation.

3.3 Bidirectional Long Short-Term Memory

BiLSTM is an enhancement of the traditional LSTM [15]. Unlike the standard LSTM, which considers only past contextual information when processing sequence data, BiLSTM incorporates both past and future contexts. This is achieved by adding a reverse LSTM layer, enabling the model to process the input sequence both forwards and backwards in time. The outputs from both directions are then concatenated to form the final output. Additionally, LSTMs address the gradient explosion and vanishing gradient issues often encountered with RNNs in real-world applications. They can discern dependencies in sequences regardless of whether the time intervals are short or long. The BiLSTM unit's schematic representation can be seen in Fig. 2.

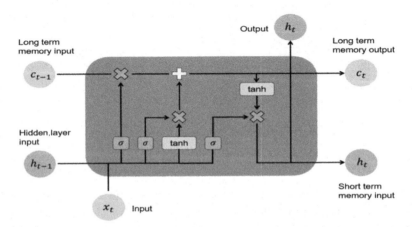

Fig. 2. Schematic diagram of LSTM unit.

This network consists of three structural layers: the input layer, hidden layer, and output layer. The memory unit is intricately designed, with historical information being influenced by the input gate, forget gate, and output gate respectively. The mathematical formulations of BiLSTM are as follows:

1. Input Gate: $i_t = \sigma(W_{xi}x_t + W_{hi}h_{t-1} + b_i)$.
2. Forget Gate: $f_t = \sigma(W_{xf}x_t + W_{hf}h_{t-1} + b_f)$.
3. Formula for Output Gate: $o_t = \sigma(W_{xo}x_t + W_{ho}h_{t-1} + b_o)$
4. Candidate Memory Cell state is calculated by the formula: $\tilde{C}_t = \tanh(W_{xc}x_t + W_{hc}h_{t-1} + b_c)$.
5. The formula for the Memory Cell state: $C_t = f_t \odot C_{t-1} + i_t \odot \tilde{C}_t$.
6. The formula for the Hidden State (Hidden State):$h_t = o_t \odot \tanh(C_t)$.

where x_t denotes the t_{th} element of the input sequence, h_{t-1} denotes the hidden state at the previous time step, W and b refer to the weight matrix and bias vector, σ represents the sigmoid function, and $\odot$ indicates the element-by-element product.

3.4 Architecture of Proposed Approach

The architecture of our proposed hybrid model is illustrated in Fig. 3.

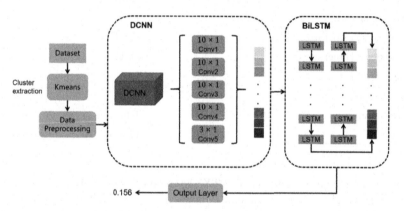

Fig. 3. Model structure diagram

The proposed hybrid model is divided into three main parts:

1. **K-means Component:** This segment is tasked with identifying distinct operating settings within the C-MAPSS dataset. Subsequently, each sample is normalized based on its corresponding operational condition.
2. **DCNN Component:** Let's define the initial input sequence as $X = [x_1, x_2, \ldots, x_N] \in R^{N \times F}$. Firstly, to ensure the dimension of the feature map remains unchanged, we use a complementary zero operation before the convolutional kernel, and then stack 4 convolutional layers for feature extraction with a convolutional kernel size of $L \times 1$, and after these 4 convolutional operations, we get an output with dimension $N \times F$, which is consistent with the original sample. Finally, we use an additional convolutional layer

with a kernel size of 3 × 1 to merge the previous feature maps into a unique feature map, thus obtaining a feature sequence with a high degree of spatial information.

4 Experiment

4.1 Experiment Setup

To ensure consistent experimental outcomes, we set a fixed random seed of 666 for all experiments. To stabilize regression results, we tested the model over 10 runs and took the average value as the final outcome. We set the model's batch size at 2048 and employed the Adam optimizer [16]. To facilitate effective comparison with other models, the maximum remaining lifetime value was set to 125. The specific hyper-parameter settings are provided in Table 1.

Table 1. Hyperparameters.

Hyperparameter	Value
Batch size	2048
Optimizer	Adam
Learning rate	1E-3
Convolutional kernel size (1–4)	(10, 1)
Convolutional kernel size (5)	(3, 1)
Stride	1
Dropout	0.2
Activation function	Tanh
Max life	125

Our training employed NVIDIA's RTX3090 graphics card with 24GB of memory, running on a Windows 10 64-bit system, Python version 3.7, and Pytorch version 1.10.1.

4.2 Evaluation Metric

Given that RUL prediction is a subset of time series forecasting, we adopted the widely-used RMSE (Root Mean Squared Error) to evaluate our model. RMSE, derived from the square root of MSE (Mean Squared Error), measures the mean difference between predicted and actual values. The steps for RMSE calculation are as follows:

1. Compute the difference between predicted and actual values for each sample.
2. Square these differences and then compute the mean difference across all samples.
3. Take the square root of the mean difference to determine the RMSE value.

A smaller RMSE value indicates a diminished disparity between the predicted and actual values, implying a more accurate model prediction. The formula is presented below, wherein d_i signifies the difference between the predicted and actual Remaining Useful Life (RUL) values.

$$\sqrt{\frac{1}{N}\sum_{i=1}^{N}(d_i)^2} \tag{3}$$

4.3 Dataset

This paper utilizes the C-MAPSS dataset, which is widely used in aerospace research related to aero-engine health management and provided by NASA. The dataset contains sensor measurements from four different types of aero-engines operating under various conditions. It serves as a valuable resource for developing and evaluating algorithms and models for engine health management systems.

The C-MAPSS dataset includes multiple sensor measurements for each engine, such as pressure, temperature, vibration, and more. Each engine has a unique history of operation data, including both normal and fault states. The fault states consist of different types and severities, such as worn bearings, damaged turbine blades, etc.

The dataset is divided into four subdatasets, each representing different operating and fault conditions. Within each subdataset, there are separate training and test subsets. The training subset records sampled values of various state parameters of the aero-engine throughout a complete cycle, from normal to fault. On the other hand, the test subset contains the values of state parameters up to a certain point in time before the fault occurred, along with their corresponding remaining lifetimes. In the training set, the magnitude of failures increases until the system fails. In contrast, the test set provides data up to a specific period before the system failure. The objective is to estimate the number of remaining operation cycles before a failure occurs in the test data, as illustrated in Table 2.

Table 2. C-MAPSS Dataset information

Data set	FD001	FD002	FD003	FD004
Train Trajectories	100	260	100	249
Test Trajectories	100	259	100	248
Operating Conditions	1	6	1	6
Fault Conditions	1	1	2	2

4.4 Experimental Results

This paper compares with the most popular traditional methods for predicting RUL, including multilayer perceptron (MLP), support vector regression (SVR), correlation vector regression (RVR), and neural network methods such as CNN [17] and deep LSTM

[18]. As indicated in Table 3, our proposed approach exhibits superior performance on the CMPASS dataset compared to all the traditional machine learning methods and neural network methods being compared. The effectiveness of our model displays discernible enhancement across all four sub-datasets, showcasing performance improvements of up to 104% in comparison to a standalone LSTM method across all four datasets (FD004). Furthermore, the most substantial improvement over a single CNN also registers at 111% (FD004), underscoring the model architecture introduced in this paper's capability to accurately predict the remaining service life for intricate device data.

Table 3. Comparison results of different models with RMSE.

Model	FD001	FD002	FD003	FD004
MLP	37.56	80.03	37.39	77.37
SVR	20.96	42.00	21.05	45.35
RVR	23.80	31.30	22.37	34.34
CNN	18.45	30.29	19.82	29.16
Deep LSTM	16.14	24.49	16.18	28.17
Our proposed approach	**13.54**	**15.94**	**11.56**	**13.77**

Figure 4 depicts the degradation process curves of four randomly chosen engine units within the test set, reflecting genuine variations in the RUL of the turbofan engine. Observing Fig. 4(a), Fig. 4(b), and Fig. 4(c), we note that the predicted RULs slightly undershoot the actual values during the early stages, yet they broadly align with the authentic curves. Notably, Fig. 4(a) and Fig. 4(c) display the closest fit during the initial stages.

This outcome highlights the strengths of DCNN networks in profound feature extraction and the efficiency of BiLSTM in capturing and retaining temporal data insights. DCNN networks excel at abstracting high-level features from raw data through multi-layer convolution and pooling, contributing to improved RUL prediction accuracy. Conversely, BiLSTM excels in adeptly capturing temporal data dependencies, enabling the modeling of historical patterns and future trends, thereby enhancing RUL prediction precision.

In conclusion, the examination of the curves presented in Fig. 4 enables us to ascertain that the DCNN network excels in profound feature extraction, whereas BiLSTM demonstrates proficiency in capturing and retaining temporal data information. The findings from this study bear substantial importance, providing valuable insights for guiding turbofan engine life prediction and fault diagnosis strategies.

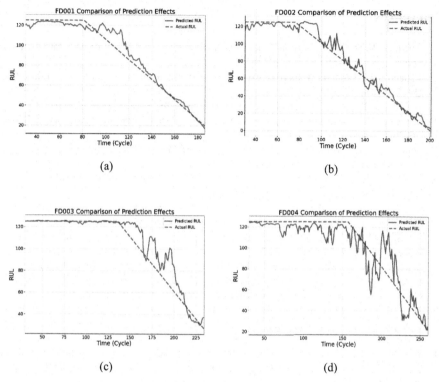

Fig. 4. Engine unit life degradation process curve.

5   Conclusion and Future Work

In this paper, we presented an innovative hybrid deep learning model aimed at enhancing the predictive performance of RUL. The model integrated the K-means algorithm to discern potential categories within the dataset, thus aiding in data initialization including class-based sample normalization. Subsequently, the DCNN processed multi-sensor data and extracted intricate spatial features. To capture temporal relationships, these spatial features were channelled into a BiLSTM layer for comprehensive bi-directional analysis. Ultimately, a linear layer mapped the data to forecast the remaining service life within intricate systems. We also conducted a series of experiments on the well-known aircraft remaining useful life C-MAPSS dataset. When compared to existing models, this approach demonstrated remarkable performance in predicting RUL.

In the future, we strive to refine the hybrid deep learning model by exploring alternative clustering algorithms for heightened accuracy and stability. Furthermore, we intend to explore other deep learning models, such as Transformers, to process multi-sensor data and extract more intricate spatial features, thereby augmenting the predictive prowess of the model.

References

1. Henshaw, M.D.C., et al.: Non-linear aeroelastic prediction for aircraft applications. Prog. Aerosp. Sci. **43**(4–6), 65–137 (2007)
2. Siedentop, D., Eldar, E.: Expertise, experience, and effectiveness. J. Teach. Phys. Educ. **8**(3), 254–260 (1989)
3. McCullagh, P.: What is a statistical model? Ann. Stat. **30**(5), 1225–1310 (2002)
4. Deng, Li.: Deep learning: methods and applications. Found. Trends® Sign. Process. **7**(3–4), 197–387 (2014)
5. Rojas, I., et al.: Soft-computing techniques and ARMA model for time series prediction. Neurocomputing **71**(4–6), 519–537 (2008)
6. Hartigan, J.A., Wong, M.A.: Algorithm AS 136: a k-means clustering algorithm. J. Royal Stat. Soc. Series c (Appl. Stat.), **28**(1), 100–108 (1979)
7. Khan, A., Sohail, A., Zahoora, U., Qureshi, A.S.: A survey of the recent architectures of deep convolutional neural networks. Artif. Intell. Rev. **53**, 5455–5516 (2020)
8. Schuster, M., Paliwal, K.K.: Bidirectional recurrent neural networks. IEEE Trans. Signal Process. **45**(11), 2673–2681 (1997)
9. Long, Y., Luo, H., Zhi, Y., Wang, X.: Remaining useful life estimation of solder joints using an ARMA model optimized by genetic algorithm. In: 2018 19th International Conference on Electronic Packaging Technology (ICEPT), pp. 1108–1111. IEEE (2018)
10. Zhou, Y., Huang, M.: Lithium-ion batteries remaining useful life prediction based on a mixture of empirical mode decomposition and ARIMA model. Microelectron. Reliab. **65**, 265–273 (2016)
11. Yan, M., Wang, X., Wang, B., Chang, M., Muhammad, I.: Bearing remaining useful life prediction using support vector machine and hybrid degradation tracking model. ISA Trans. **98**, 471–482 (2020)
12. Zheng, Z., et al.: A novel method for lithium-ion battery remaining useful life prediction using time window and gradient boosting decision trees. In: 2019 10th International Conference on Power Electronics and ECCE Asia (ICPE 2019-ECCE Asia), pp. 3297–3302. IEEE (2019)
13. Xu, X., Li, X., Ming, W., Chen, M.: A novel multi-scale CNN and attention mechanism method with multi-sensor signal for remaining useful life prediction. Comput. Ind. Eng. **169**, 108204 (2022)
14. Guo, L., Li, N., Jia, F., Lei, Y., Lin, J.: A recurrent neural network based health indicator for remaining useful life prediction of bearings. Neurocomputing **240**, 98–109 (2017)
15. Hochreiter, S., Schmidhuber, J.: Long short-term memory. Neural Comput. **9**(8), 1735–1780 (1997)
16. Kingma, D.P., Ba, J.: Adam: A method for stochastic optimization. arXiv preprint arXiv: 1412.6980 (2014)
17. Sateesh Babu, G., Zhao, P., Li, X.L.: Deep convolutional neural network based regression approach for estimation of remaining useful life. In: Navathe, S.B., Wu, W., Shekhar, S., Du, X., Wang, X.S., Xiong, H. (eds.) DASFAA 2016. LNCS, vol. 9642, pp. 214–228. Springer, Cham (2016). https://doi.org/10.1007/978-3-319-32025-0_14
18. Zheng, S., Ristovski, K., Farahat, A., Gupta, C.:. Long short-term memory network for remaining useful life estimation. In: 2017 IEEE International Conference on Prognostics and Health Management (ICPHM), pp. 88–95. IEEE (2017)
19. Zheng, Y., Li, Y., Yang, S., Lu, H.: Global-pbnet: a novel point cloud registration for autonomous driving. IEEE Trans. Intell. Transp. Syst. **23**(11), 22312–22319 (2022)
20. Li, Y., Yang, S., Zheng, Y., Lu, H.: Improved point-voxel region convolutional neural network: 3D object detectors for autonomous driving. IEEE Trans. Intell. Transport. Syst. **23**(7), 9311–9317 (2022)

21. Lu, H., Yang, R., Deng, Z., Zhang, Y., Gao, G., Lan, R.: Chinese image captioning via fuzzy attention-based DenseNet-BiLSTM. ACM Trans. Multimed. Comput. Commun. Appl. **17**(1s), 1–18 (2021)
22. Lu, H., Li, Y., Chen, M., Kim, H., Serikawa, S.: Brain intelligence: go beyond artificial intelligence. Mobile Netw. Appl. **23**(2), 368–375 (2018)
23. Lu, H., Zhang, M., Xu, X., Li, Y., Shen, H.T.: Deep fuzzy hashing network for efficient image retrieval. IEEE Trans. Fuzzy Syst. **29**(1), 166–176 (2021)

Multiscale Transfer Learning Based Fault Diagnosis of Rolling Bearings

Rong Tang[1], Xinjie Sun[2], Shubiao Wang[2], and Zhe Chen[1]([✉])

[1] College of Computer and Information, Hohai University, Nanjing 211100, China
chenzhe@hhu.edu.cn
[2] State Grid Nanjing Power Supply Company, Nanjing 210000, China

Abstract. This paper aims to address two challenges for fault diagnosis of rolling bearings: full feature representation and feature alignment across working conditions. To tackle these issues, we propose a novel Multiscale Transfer Learning (MSTL) approach. The proposed model is capable of capturing, fusing, and aligning multiscale features across different working conditions. We introduce a novel multi-stream architecture to effectively process multiscale factors of raw signals, and the backend module incorporates a feature aligning and classification unit. Notably, our proposed model provides dynamic weights to optimize the extent of multiscale fusion, thus a task-related fusion mechanism can be adaptively achieved. To measure the difference between feature distributions under changing working conditions, we utilize the Wasserstein distance, which facilitates feature transferring during model learning. Our proposed MSTL method demonstrates superior performance compared to existing methods, resulting in improvements of 12.61% and 17.00% over conventional CNN methods on the CWRU and Paderborn datasets.

Keywords: Fault Diagnosis · Multiscale Learning · Transfer Learning · Rolling Bearings

1 Introduction

Intelligent fault diagnosis of rolling bearings plays a crucial role in ensuring the reliability and safety of machinery during long-term operation. In general, fault diagnosis methods primarily rely on data-driven schemes [1, 2]. In pioneering studies, various signal analysis techniques are leveraged to explore the physical significance of raw signals in both time and frequency domains, which are then recognized by diagnosis models. Some commonly used methods include Principal Component Analysis (PCA) [3], Linear Discriminant Analysis (LDA) [4], Local Preserving Projection [5], and Trace Ratio Linear Discriminant Analysis [6]. However, the primary drawback of these two-stage strategies is that they do not represent error patterns in sufficient detail, which leads to less accurate fault diagnosis. In the past few years, there have been notable advancements in pattern recognition through the utilization of deep learning. Its exceptional ability to represent features has led to significant breakthroughs. Several research studies have

H. Lu and J. Cai (Eds.): ISAIR 2023, CCIS 1998, pp. 366–375, 2024.
https://doi.org/10.1007/978-981-99-9109-9_36

successfully designed various deep learning structures for fault diagnosis and showcased their impressive precision [1–3, 7]. Another advantage of deep learning type lies in that it can learn without hand-crafted features, enabling end-to-end flow. Nevertheless, there are potential drawbacks associated with fault deep learning [2]. However, this task of detecting and recognizing machine errors is somewhat difficult, and these can be explained in two ways. First, current feature representation models of fault patterns are far from complete. In spite of the availability of extensive datasets, it is still difficult to extract invariant models for any fault patterns. It is acknowledged that informative cues can be presented with multiple scales and the importance of different scale factors is distinct. No single scale factor representation can stably model the end-break pattern. Second, the raw signals from the machine have modulated amplitudes and nonstationary properties, due to changing working conditions. In this case, models trained on current working condition can not be generalized to other conditions and the diagnosis performance would be significantly degenerated. Aiming to solve these problems, many studies try to investigate the potential of multi-source fusion, which can increase the available sources for correct fault diagnosis. However, this strategy may significantly enlarge the cost of fault diagnosis in practice. Alternatively, there are many works exploit multiscale factors from any single sources [1, 2]. This seminal research shows that multi-scale feature extraction is very effective for fault diagnosis. However, much previous research has shown that the scale factor of deep learning architectures is difficult to determine, which is closely related to the nature of the input data and the supporting network. Different migration learning architectures for fault diagnosis have been evaluated considering the operating conditions of the machine [18–22]. However, most of the feature transformation methods use single scale features for signals and ignore the reference to multi-scale factors.

This paper delves into practical and methodological issues and proposes a novel multi-scale transfer learning (MSTL) approach for a more comprehensive and flexible representation of fault diagnosis patterns. Overall, this paper constructs a novel multi-stream network as the core framework for handling multi-scale factors. In the feature representation process, Multi-Menu Mixture of Experts (MMoE) [8] is introduced to realize the adaptive fusion of multi-scale factors. In the back-end part, Wasserstein distance-based transfer learning (TL) is established at the backend [9]. Our new architecture is expected to fully utilize the multi-scale factors in the signals and to enable transmission under different operating conditions.

The merits of the proposed architecture are as followings:

- **Overall presentation of fault patterns**: In our approach, fault patterns are represented in a comprehensive manner by effectively utilizing multiscale factors. This enables our model to capture information from different scales, providing abundant clues and insights for fault patterns. By incorporating multiscale features, our model achieves a more robust and accurate representation of fault patterns.
- **Adaptive use of scale-specific representations and inter-scale correlations**: To enhance the fault representation, Mixture-of-Experts (MMoE) modules are inserted in our MSTL architecture. The architecture dynamically adjusts the gating network to allow adaptive utilization of scale-specific representations and inter-scale correlations. This adaptive approach optimally combines information from various scale

factors, allowing our model to leverage the importance of different scales and achieve superior diagnostic accuracy.

- **Robust Solutions for Fault Diagnosis under Varying Working Conditions**: Thanks to the TL mechanism at the backend, our proposed MSTL architecture provides excellent fault diagnosis solutions across working conditions, contributing to enhanced machinery reliability and safety.

Figure 1 presents an overview of the proposed Multiscale Transfer Learning (MSTL) architecture. This architecture is designed to address the challenges of fault diagnosis by effectively leveraging multiscale factors and transfer learning techniques. In the first stage of the MSTL architecture, large-grained operations, involving down-sampling and smoothing calculations, are applied to provide the multiscale factor. This step enables the extraction of essential information at different scales, facilitating a comprehensive representation of fault patterns. Next, the Multi-gate Mixture-of-Experts (MMoE) mechanism is utilized to extract multiscale representations. MMoE dynamically moderates the gating network, allowing for scale-specific representation and inter-scale correlation to be adaptively exploited. The ensemble of experts in MMoE contributes to the dynamic combination of all activations, yielding the best parameters for this dynamic combination during the model training process. This adaptive approach ensures that the model can effectively fuse the extracted multiscale features to achieve enhanced fault diagnosis accuracy. The backend module of the architecture involves Transfer Learning (TL). TL aligns the features extracted from the source domain with those in the target domain. This alignment process is crucial for enabling the model to adapt to different working conditions and improve diagnostic performance across working conditions.

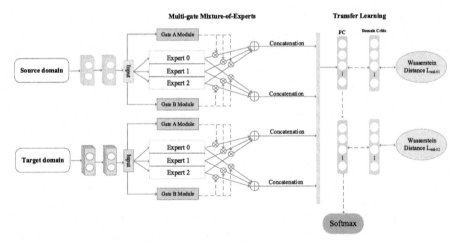

Fig. 1. Multiscale Transfer Learning (MSTL) architecture.

2 Multiscale Transfer Learning

In order to achieve highly accurate troubleshooting under different operating conditions, the proposed model aligns multi-scale features under different operating conditions. In summary, the new MSTL model combined with MMoE provides an end-to-end multi-scale transfer learning architecture for fault diagnosis. The back-end module uses Wasserstein distance to quantify the dissimilarity between the target domain and the source domain.cc To summarize, our model comprises three consecutive stages: feature extraction at multiple scales and transfer learning.

2.1 Multiscale Feature Extraction Stage

In this paper, downsampling and smoothing operations are employed for extracting multi-scale factors [10]. Specifically, the size of the time scale is determined by the size of the downsampling window.

For a one-dimensional signal vector $\mathbf{y} = \{y_1, y_2, \cdots, y_N\}$, a large-particle signal sample is given:

$$\mathbf{y}_i^c = \frac{1}{c} \sum_{j=(\varepsilon(i-\eta/c-1)c-\eta)(i-1)+1}^{ic-\varepsilon(i-\eta/c-1)(i-1)\eta} x_j, \quad 1 \leq i \leq \frac{L}{c-\eta} - 1 \tag{1}$$

where $\mathbf{y}_i^c$ is given by the large-grained reconstruction; c defines the scale size; $\varepsilon(t)$ is the step; η is the coverage; and L is the length of the original signal. Varying the parameter c can produce the multiscale factors. This paper takes advantage of two factors, i.e., $c = 1$ and $c = 3$.

MMoE is employed to process the multi-stream [10]. Formally, the output of the stream with the scale factor c is

$$R_c = h^c(f^c(\mathbf{y})) \tag{2}$$

where h^c is the tower network with the scale factor c,

$$f^c(\mathbf{y}) = \sum_{\tau=0}^{2} g_\tau^c(\mathbf{y}) f_\tau(\mathbf{y}) \tag{3}$$

where $\sum_{\tau=1}^{n} g_\tau^c(\mathbf{y}) = 1$ for any scale factor c, $g_\tau^c(\mathbf{y})$ is the τ th logit of the output of gating network $g_\tau^c(\mathbf{y})$ which indicates the probability for expert f_τ. In this study, $\tau = 0, 1, 2$ denote three expert networks. More specifically, the gating network $g_\tau^c(\mathbf{y})$ fits a distribution over three experts, and the output $f^c(\mathbf{y})$ can be deem a weighted fusion of all experts.

To illustrate this architecture effectively, we employ a dynamic multi-scale typical module depicted in Fig. 1. A and Gate B modules are implemented using layered perceptrons with ReLU activation. Consequently, our gated network applies a linear transformation to input data via its 'softmax' layer:

$$g_\tau^c(\mathbf{y}) = \text{softmax}(W_\tau^c \mathbf{y}) \tag{4}$$

where $W_\tau^c \in \Re^{\tau \times d}$ is the weight matrix, d is the dimension of the feature.

The gating networks in the Multi-gate Mixture-of-Experts (MMoE) architecture operate similarly to the attention mechanism. It allows for the optimal fusion of a subset of experts based on the input example. This adaptive process enables MMoE to achieve an optimal balance between scale-specific representation and inter-scale correlation, which is dynamically determined by the characteristics of the input data. As a result, MMoE can effectively capture the essential features of fault patterns across different scales and adapt to various working conditions.

2.2 Wasserstein Distance-Based Transfer Learning

The transfer learning module in Fig. 1 plays a crucial role in aligning features from varying working conditions. Once MMoEs architecture extracts the features, the next step is to align these features. In specific, Wasserstein-1 distance-based Transfer Learning (TL) is employed, aiming to obtain invariant feature representations in a same hyperspace.

For the instances $\{y^s\}_{i=1}^n$ and $\{y^t\}_{i=1}^n$ from $\mathbf{y}^s$ and $\mathbf{y}^t$ for $n < N^s$ and N^t. These instances are passed through a parameter function for DMR, and directly generate the source feature R^s and target feature R^t, where $R^s = \{R_c^s\}_{c=1}^3$, $R^t = \{R_c^t\}_{c=1}^3$. Let P^s and P^t be the distribution in the source domain R^s and target feature R^t. To measure the diversity across domains, we introduce a domain critic that maps features to real numbers. By Kantorovich-Rubinstein duality, we employ Wasserstein-1 distance:

$$W(P^s, P^t) = \sup_{||\Gamma|| \leq 1} E_{R^z \sim P^z}[\Gamma(R^s)] - E_{R^t \sim P^t}[\Gamma(R^t)] \tag{5}$$

where Γ represents the solution obtained from the domain critic. The empirical Wasserstein-1 distance can be formally computed:

$$L = \frac{1}{N^s} \sum_{y^t \in y^t} \Gamma(R^s) - \frac{1}{N^t} \sum_{y^t \in y^t} \Gamma(R^t) \tag{6}$$

where L denotes the domain critic loss.

The optimization of the $E_{R^t \sim P^t}[\nabla_R \Gamma(R^t)]$ can be achieved by gradient update, but this process is time-consuming. In order to efficiently minimize the Wasserstein distance, a gradient penalty $L_g = (||\nabla_\mathbf{R} \Gamma(\mathbf{R})||_2 - 1)^2$ is used to learn the domain critic.

We can transform optimization of our critic into following problem:

$$\max\{L - \sigma L_g\} \tag{7}$$

where σ is the moderation parameter.

3   Experimental Evaluations

3.1   Dataset

To evaluate the performance of our proposed model, we conducted experiments on datasets from Case Western Reserve University (CWRU) [11] and Paderborn University [12]. The experiments on these two data sets can fully prove the correctness of the diagnosis under cross-operating conditions. The testbed for the CWRU and Paderborn datasets is shown in Fig. 2. In the first experiment, a comprehensive evaluation of our proposed approach was conducted using CWRU fault data. Acceleration data at the end of SKF bearing DE (drive end accelerometer data), the speed is 1730r/min, and the sample frequency is 12 kHz. The single point diameter damage of bearings selected in the experiment was 0.007 mm, 0.014 mm and 0.021 mm respectively. Each fault diameter contained three fault types: rolling element fault, inner ring fault and outer ring fault. At motor loads from 1730 to 1797 rpm, 120,000 samples were recorded per failure. Table 1 shows the transfer experiment setup on the CWRU dataset.

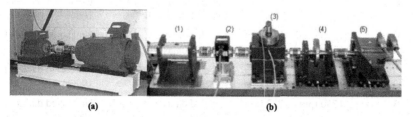

Fig. 2. Experimental test-bed in (a) CWRU [11] and (b) Paderborn datasets [12].

The University of Paderborn's Bearing System Platform comprises a motor and a bearing housing. The test rig is composed of various modules, including the motor, torque measuring shaft, rolling bearing test module, flywheel, and load motor as depicted in the provided image. By installing ball bearings with different types of damage in the bearing test module, we generated experimental data. Specifically, there were 12 artificially damaged bearings (7 outer rings and 5 inner rings), 14 accelerated life test damaged bearings (5 outer rings, 6 inner rings, and 2 composites of inner and outer rings), 6 healthy bearings. Table 2 presents the transmission experimental setup for the Paderborn dataset.

Table 1. Transferring experiment setup on the CWRU dataset.

Transfer cases	Source domain	Training dataset cases	Test dataset
A → B	1797 rpm - 1772 rpm	Labeled dataset A: 100% Labeled dataset B: 0%	Unlabeled dataset B: 100%
A → C	1797 rpm - 1750 rpm	Labeled dataset A: 100% Labeled dataset C: 0%	Unlabeled dataset C: 100%
A → D	1797 rpm - 1730 rpm	Labeled dataset A: 100% Labeled dataset D: 0%	Unlabeled dataset D: 100%
B → A	1772 rpm - 1797 rpm	Labeled dataset B: 100% Labeled dataset A: 0%	Unlabeled dataset A: 100%

(continued)

Table 1. (*continued*)

Transfer cases	Source domain	Training dataset cases	Test dataset
B → C	1772 rpm - 1750 rpm	Labeled dataset B: 100% Labeled dataset C: 0%	Unlabeled dataset C: 100%
B → D	1772 rpm - 1730 rpm	Labeled dataset B: 100% Labeled dataset D: 0%	Unlabeled dataset D: 100%
C → A	1750 rpm - 1797 rpm	Labeled dataset C: 100% Labeled dataset A: 0%	Unlabeled dataset A: 100%
C → B	1750 rpm - 1772 rpm	Labeled dataset C: 100% Labeled dataset B: 0%	Unlabeled dataset B: 100%
C → D	1750 rpm - 1730 rpm	Labeled dataset C: 100% Labeled dataset D: 0%	Unlabeled dataset D: 100%
D → A	1730 rpm - 1797 rpm	Labeled dataset D: 100% Labeled dataset A: 0%	Unlabeled dataset A: 100%
D → B	1730 rpm - 1772 rpm	Labeled dataset D: 100% Labeled dataset B: 0%	Unlabeled dataset B: 100%
D → C	1730 rpm - 1750 rpm	Labeled dataset D: 100% Labeled dataset C: 0%	Unlabeled dataset C: 100%

Table 2. Transferring experiment setup on the Paderborn dataset

Loads [HP]	Rotational speed [rpm]	Load torque [Nm]	Radial force [N]	Setting name
0	1500	0.7	1000	N15_M07_F10
1	900	0.7	1000	N09_M07_F10
2	1500	0.1	1000	N15_M01_F10
3	1500	0.7	400	N15_M07_F04

3.2 Compared Methods and Implementation Details

In this section, we compare our proposed method with several state-of-the-art models. In multi-class support vector machines (SVMs) [13] and transfer component analysis (TCA) [14], utilize labeled samples from the source domain to train classifiers for the target domain. We employ convolutional neural networks (CNNs) as the foundation for deep learning on faults. For experimental comparisons, we selected deep adaptive networks (DAN) [15], CNNs with training interference (TICNN) [16], deep CNNs with wide first-layer cores (WDCNN) [17], AlexNet, and the multiscale shared learning network (MSSLN) [10] are selected for experimental comparisons. Additionally, experiments were conducted on both single loads and across loads to demonstrate the accuracy and generalization capabilities for fault diagnosis. All deep models w ere trained using the Adam method with hyperparameters: batch size m = 64, learning rate $a = 10^{-3}$, and

1000 generator iterations for our MSTL model. The pre-train iterations nc $= 10^3$ and adversarial iterations nt $= 10^3$.

3.3 Diagnosis Across Domains

As illustrated in Fig. 3, SVMs and TCA exhibit satisfactory performance under low load shifts conditions. Figure 3 showcases results obtained by MSSLN, AlexNet, TICNN and other conventional methods. In terms of TL, MSTL achieves an average accuracy of 99.84%, which significantly outperforms CNN, DAN, and WDCNN, TICNN, AlexNet, MSSLN, and our proposed model show similar results, while our proposed model wins the best result, which demonstrates the robustness of our multiscale transmission strategy.

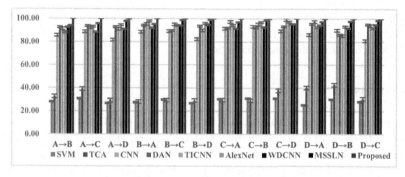

Fig. 3. Comparison results of the CWRU dataset (%).

To provide additional evidence of the effectiveness and versatility of our approach, we performed fault detection on the Paderborn dataset and compared our proposed method with it. The comparison results are detailed in Fig. 4. Our MSTL method exhibits the best and most reliable diagnostic results in the transfer learning task. The method achieves an average diagnostic accuracy of 99.73% under various working conditions, we achieved a notably superior performance compared to the CNN model. Furthermore, our suggested method exhibits commendable results when compared to alternative deep learning models.

In conclusion, the experimental results clearly indicate that our new model has superior performance in all conditions compared to other methods. This is mainly due to two factors. First, since our model is multiscale representable, it is able to adequately represent various failure modes. First, since our model is multiscale representable, it is able to adequately characterize various fault modes. By comprehensively capturing and incorporating multiscale factors, our model achieves a more comprehensive and accurate representation of fault patterns. This improved feature representation enables our model to generate more precise and reliable diagnosis results. Secondly, the Transfer Learning (TL) component in our method plays a pivotal role in achieving feature-aligning performance. Through TL, our model learns to align the features extracted from different working conditions into a common hyperspace. This alignment process ensures that the model can effectively generalize well to new working conditions, reducing the impact

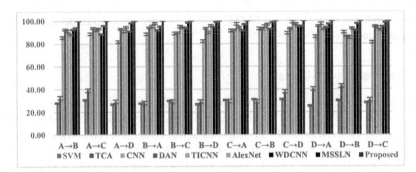

Fig. 4. Comparison results of the Paderborn dataset (%).

of variations in fault patterns due to changes in operating scenarios. As a result, our model demonstrates excellent generalizability, outperforming compared methods that may lack such feature-aligning capabilities.

4 Conclusion

This paper presents a novel Multiscale Transfer Learning (MSTL) model for fault diagnosis of rolling bearings. The proposed model effectively addresses the challenges of full feature representation and feature alignment across working conditions. By incorporating dynamic fusion and Wasserstein distance-based feature transferring, our MSTL model demonstrates superior performance on both CWRU and Paderborn datasets. The contributions of this study offer valuable insights into improving fault diagnosis of rolling bearings, with potential applications in various industrial domains. However, the proposed MSTL model is acknowledged to fall within the domain of large models. The MSTL model necessitates a comprehensive dataset for effective training. Future research endeavors will be directed towards developing fault diagnosis models that strike an optimal balance between efficiency and accuracy.

Acknowledgments. This work was supported in part by National Natural Science Foundation of China under Grant 62073120, Natural Science Foundation of Jiangsu Province under Grant BK20201311 and Science and Technology Project of State Grid Jiangsu Elect Power Co Ltd under Grant J2022103.

References

1. Hoang, D.T., Kang, H.J.: An motor current signal-based bearing fault diagnosis using deep learning and information fusion. IEEE Trans. Instrum. Meas. **69**(6), 3325–3333 (2020)
2. Chen, Z., et al.: Construction of a hierarchical feature enhancement network and its application in fault recognition. IEEE Trans Industr Inform. **17**(7), 4827–4836 (2021)
3. Wang, T., Xu, H., Han, J., Elbouchikhi, E., Benbouzid, M.E.H.: Cascaded h-bridge multilevel inverter system fault diagnosis using a PCA and multiclass relevance vector machine approach. IEEE Trans. Power Electron. **30**(12), 7006–7018 (2015)

4. Bazdar, A., Kazemzadeh, R.B., Aniaki, S.T.: Fault diagnosis within multistage machining processes using linear discriminant analysis: a case study in automotive industry. Qual. Technol. Quant M. **14**(2), 129–141 (2017)
5. Rong, G., Liu, S.Y., Shao, J.D.: Fault diagnosis by Locality Preserving Discriminant Analysis and its kernel variation. Comput. Chem. Eng. **49**, 105–113 (2013)
6. Mbo'o, C.P., Hameyer, K.: Fault diagnosis of bearing damage by means of the linear discriminant analysis of stator current features from the frequency selection. IEEE Trans. Ind. Appl. **52**(5), 3861–4386 (2016)
7. Li, J., Ding, D., Tsung, F.: Directional PCA for fast detection and accurate diagnosis: a unified framework. IEEE Trans. Cybern. **52**(11), 11362–11372 (2022)
8. Ma, J. Q., Zhao, Z., Yi, X.Y., Chen, J.L., Hong, L.C., Chi, E.H.: Modeling task relationships in multi-task learning with multi-gate mixture-of-experts. In Proceedings of the 24th ACM SIGKDD International Conference on Knowledge Discovery and Data Mining (KDD'18), pp. 1930–1939 (2018)
9. Hasan, M.N., Jan, S.U., Koo, I.: Wasserstein GAN-based digital twin-inspired model for early drift fault detection in wireless sensor networks. IEEE Sens. J. **23**(12), 13327–13339 (2023)
10. Chen, Z., Tian, S., Shi, X., Lu, H.: Multiscale shared learning for fault diagnosis of rotating machinery in transportation infrastructures. IEEE Trans. Industr. Inform. **19**(1), 447–458 (2023)
11. Case Western Reserve University Bearing Data Center Website. http://csegroups.case.edu/bearingdatacenter/home
12. Paderborn University Website. https://mb.uni-paderborn.de/en/kat/main-research/datacenter/bearing-datacenter/data-sets-and-download
13. Zheng, J., Pan, H., Cheng, J.: Rolling bearing fault detection and diagnosis based on composite multiscale fuzzy entropy and ensemble support vector machines. Mech. Syst. Signal Process. **85**, 746–759 (2017)
14. Ma, P., Zhang, H., Wang, C.: Improved transfer component analysis and it application for bearing fault diagnosis across diverse domains. In: 2019 CAA Symposium on Fault Detection, Supervision and Safety for Technical Processes (SAFEPROCESS), pp. 501–506 (2019)
15. Xia, B., Wang, K., Xu, A., Zeng, P., Yang, N., Li, B.: Intelligent fault diagnosis for bearings of industrial robot joints under varying working conditions based on deep adversarial domain adaptation. IEEE Trans. Instrum. Meas. **71**, 1–13 (2022)
16. Zhang, W., Li, C.H., Peng, G.L., et al.: A deep convolutional neural network with new training methods for bearing fault diagnosis under noisy environment and different working load. Mech. Syst. Signal Process. **100**, 439–453 (2018)
17. Zhang, W., Peng, G.L., Li, C.H., Chen, Y.H., Zhang, Z.J.: A new deep learning model for fault diagnosis with good anti-noise and domain adaptation ability on raw vibration signals. Sensors **17**(2), 425–446 (2017)
18. Zheng, Y., Li, Y., Yang, S., Lu, H.: Global-pbnet: a novel point cloud registration for autonomous driving. IEEE Trans. Intell. Transp. Syst. **23**(11), 22312–22319 (2022)
19. Li, Y., Yang, S., Zheng, Y., Lu, H.: Improved point-voxel region convolutional neural network: 3D object detectors for autonomous driving. IEEE Trans. Intell. Transport. Syst. **23**(7), 9311–9317 (2022)
20. Lu, H., Yang, R., Deng, Z., Zhang, Y., Gao, G., Lan, R.: Chinese image captioning via fuzzy attention-based DenseNet-BiLSTM. ACM Trans. Multimed. Comput. Commun. Appl. **17**(1s), 1–18 (2021)
21. Lu, H., Li, Y., Chen, M., Kim, H., Serikawa, S.: Brain intelligence: go beyond artificial intelligence. Mobile Netw. Appl. **23**(2), 368–375 (2018)
22. Lu, H., Zhang, M., Xu, X., Li, Y., Shen, H.T.: Deep fuzzy hashing network for efficient image retrieval. IEEE Trans. Fuzzy Syst. **29**(1), 166–176 (2021)

Experimental Comparison of Three Topic Modeling Methods with LDA, Top2Vec and BERTopic

Lin Gan[1], Tao Yang[1(✉)], Yifan Huang[1], Boxiong Yang[1], Yami Yanwen Luo[2], Lui Wing Cheung Richard[3], and Dabo Guo[1]

[1] Department of Information and Intelligence Engineering, University of Sanya, Sanya 572022, China
missmissganlin@qq.com
[2] Department of Computer Science, The University of Hong Kong, Pokfulam, Hong Kong
[3] Department of Computing, The Hong Kong Polytechnic University, Hung Hom, Hong Kong

Abstract. Text clustering can automatically analyze hot events from large-scale data and provide key feature descriptions of event topics. This paper selected #ChatGPT as the text training object, and conducted a comparative analysis of topic clustering on domestic Weibo and overseas Twitter social platforms. Weibo and Twitter are characterized by a large number of active users, high discussion heat, and wide public attention. Therefore, we chose the text in the #ChatGPT topic of these two platforms as the main data for data analysis in the experimental part.

This study aims to evaluate the independence (separateness) between topic clusters. Finally, through the 3-D scatterplot of cosine similarity and Pearson's correlation coefficient, we conclude that BERTopic has better topic separation, more independence between the eight topics, relatively clear semantics, and better understanding of text data structure and content. Compared with the other two methods (LDA and Top2Vec), the BERTopic model in the experiment is at least 34.2% better than the other algorithm models in Chinese and English clustering, and a better topic clustering effect is obtained.

Keywords: Clustering Algorithms · LDA · Top2Vec · BERTopic · ChatGPT · Weibo · Twitter

1 Introduction

Many social media platforms currently collect topics supported by product strategies and related technologies, such as allowing users to customize topics and identify them with specific symbols, such as #ChatGPT#. ChatGPT is a popular pre-training language generation model, and the number of relevant user discussions has certain research significance and value. This paper attempts to evaluate the topic separateness and consistency of different clustering models in ChatGPT by comparing and analyzing three clustering algorithms.

© The Author(s), under exclusive license to Springer Nature Singapore Pte Ltd. 2024
H. Lu and J. Cai (Eds.): ISAIR 2023, CCIS 1998, pp. 376–391, 2024.
https://doi.org/10.1007/978-981-99-9109-9_37

Text topic modeling is an important task in the field of natural language processing, which aims to discover the underlying topic structure from large-scale text data and help people better understand the relationship between text content and text. Over the past few decades, researchers have proposed a number of text topic modeling algorithms. In the experimental part of this paper, we apply three common algorithms to the clustering and comparative analysis of Weibo and Twitter # ChatGPT# topics. It includes traditional LDA (Latent Dirichlet Allocation), Top2Vec combined with Doc2Vec and Bert-based BERTopic calculation model. In previous topic modeling applications, researchers have tended to experiment with different thematic modeling methods, and few studies have used multi-thematic modeling methods on specific data sets and conducted comparative analyses of these methods.

LDA is a classic probabilistic topic model for text topic modeling and topic clustering. It is a form of unsupervised learning that treats a document as a bag of words. LDA works by first making a key assumption: The way to generate a document is to select a set of topics and select a set of words for each topic. (Alghamdi & Alfalqi, 2015)[1]. The other two algorithms in the paper are BERTopic and Top2Vec, which use raw text and rely on embedding methods. BERTopic is a text topic modeling algorithm based on the pre-trained BERT model, which can better capture the semantic information of the document. The performance of different text datasets and tasks may vary. Kuzma Kukushkin et al. used BERTopic and LDA models in 2022 to conduct topic modeling analysis of the literature related to digital twins, and through the topic modeling and analysis of 8693 publications published between January 1993 and September 2022, it was finally confirmed that the research on digital twins is still in the early stage of development. Out of more than 100 topics identified, the most popular and fastest-growing topic was: "Digital twins of industrial robots, production lines and objects."[2] BERTopic and Top2Vec are relatively new technologies, and there are some similarities between the two algorithms, such as finding potential topics in documents that neither requires the use of human-labeled training data, and both algorithms use embeddings to represent documents as continuous vector spaces to capture similarities between words and documents. There are also some similarities between the two algorithms, which are compared in detail in the second part. For the comparative study of BERTopic, Top2Vec and LDA traditional methods, in 2022, Eagger&Yu took Twitter as a reference object to analyze the advantages and disadvantages of different algorithms of LDA, Top2Vec and BERTopic from a sociological perspective, and summarized the details and quality problems of different algorithms in the article.[3]

For this purpose, the paper structure is as follows. In the second section, we summarize the traditional literature of LDA, Top2vec and BERTopic algorithms. In third section, we provide the detailed about methodology which includes data process and

---

[1] Alghamdi, R., & Alfalqi, K. (2015). A Survey of Topic Modeling in Text Mining. International Journal of Advanced Computer Science and Applications, 6.

[2] Kukushkin, K., Ryabov, Y.F., & Borovkov, A. (2022). Digital Twins: A Systematic Literature Review Based on Data Analysis and Topic Modeling. Data, 7, 173.

[3] Egger, R. and Yu, J. (2022)"A topic modeling comparison between LDA, NMF, Top2Vec, and Bertopic to demystify twitter posts", Frontiers in Sociology, 7. https://doi.org/10.3389/fsoc. 2022.886498.

three clustering models. In the fourth part, we evaluate the effect of topic clustering in this paper through cosine similarity calculation, Pearson's coefficient and Silhouette Coefficient to verify our conclusions. The last section, we summarize this paper.

2 Related Works

The topic model is modeled to dig out potential topics between texts and find connections between related words.

2.1 LDA

At present, LDA is effective in exploring potential topics, so it is widely used in topic clustering and other fields. LDA is a classic algorithm in the field of text topic modeling, proposed in 2003 by David Blei, Andrew Ng, and Michael I. Jordan. LDA is a probabilistic approach to topic modelling (Guo, C., Lu, M., & Wei, W. 2019)[4] that represents each document as a mixture of multiple topics by inferring the underlying variables of the model, including the topic distribution of the document and the word distribution of the subject.

The advantage of LDA is its simplicity and interpretability. Because LDA is based on the bag-of-word model, LDA can be applied to large-scale text datasets, and it is relatively good for modeling long text. However, LDA also has some limitations, mainly reflected in the insufficient capture of semantic information and the difficulty of processing new topics. Because the bag-of-words model ignores the order and semantic relationships between words, LDA's understanding of text content is limited. In addition, LDA requires manually specifying the number of topics K (Islam, 2019), which is too large or too small to affect the results, and it is difficult to handle the addition of new topics.[5]

2.2 Top2Vec

Top2Vec is a topic modeling algorithm proposed in 2020 by Malte Pietsch and Tim Rocktäschel in 2020. Top2Vec combines traditional LDA and Doc2Vec and aims to overcome some of the limitations of LDA, especially the lack of semantic information (Angelov, 2020).[6]

Top2Vec's workflow consists of two key steps: document embedding and clustering. First, each document is converted into a vector representation by Doc2Vec, and the document is embedded in the vector space. Then, apply a clustering algorithm, such as DBSCAN or HDBSCAN, to cluster document vectors into topics. For each topic,

---

[4] Guo, C., Lu, M., & Wei, W. (2019). An Improved LDA Topic Modeling Method Based on Partition for Medium and Long Texts. Annals of Data Science, 8, 331–344.

[5] Islam, T. (2019b). Yoga-veganism: Correlation Mining of Twitter Health Data. Retrieved from https://arxiv.org/abs/1906.07668.

[6] Angelov, D. (2020). Top2Vec: Distributed Representations of Topics. ArXiv, abs/2008.09470.

important words can be extracted from it to form a topic representation (Ma, P., Zeng-Treitler, Q., & Nelson, S.J. 2021).[7]

The advantage of Top2Vec is its better capture of semantic information and automatic determination of the number of topics. Thanks to the use of Doc2Vec for document embedding, Top2Vec can better reflect the complex relationships of document content (Ma, P., Zeng-Treitler, Q., & Nelson, S.J. 2021). In addition, the number of topics is automatically determined by the clustering algorithm, which avoids the trouble of manually specifying the number of topics. However, Top2Vec also has some challenges, especially in the document embedding stage, which is computationally expensive, especially for large-scale text datasets.

2.3 BERTopic

BERTopic is another popular text topic modeling algorithm in recent years, proposed by Rodrigo Nogueira and Kyunghyun Cho in 2019. BERTopic uses a pre-trained BERT (Bidirectional Encoder Representations from Transformers) model to obtain vector representations of documents and topics (Lande, J., Pillay, A., & Chandra, R. 2023).[8]

BERTopic's workflow consists of two key steps: document encoding and topic modeling. First, each document is encoded using a pre-trained BERT model to obtain a vector representation of the document. Then, the HDBSCAN algorithm is applied to cluster the document vectors to form a topic. For each topic, important words can be extracted from it to form a topic representation.

The advantage of BERTopic lies in its powerful ability to capture semantic information and its ability to process large-scale text data (Grootendorst, M.R, 2022)[9]. Thanks to the use of pre-trained BERT models, BERTopic can better capture the semantic information of documents, especially for complex text data. In addition, BERTopic does not need to manually specify the number of topics, and the number of topics is automatically determined by the clustering algorithm. However, the document encoding stage of BERTopic requires significant computational overhead, especially for large collections of text.

LDA, Top2Vec, and BERTopic are all techniques used for text topic modeling and clustering, but they have different methods and characteristics.

---

[7] Ma, P., Zeng-Treitler, Q., & Nelson, S.J. (2021). USE OF TWO TOPIC MODELING METHODS TO INVESTIGATE COVID VACCINE HESITANCY. Proceedings 14th International Conference on ICT, Society and Human Beings (ICT 2021), the 18th International Conference Web Based Communities and Social Media (WBC 2021).

[8] Lande, J., Pillay, A., & Chandra, R. (2023). Deep learning for COVID-19 topic modelling via Twitter: Alpha, Delta and Omicron. PloS one, 18(8), e0288681. https://doi.org/10.1371/journal.pone.0288681.

[9] Grootendorst, M.R. (2022). BERTopic: Neural topic modeling with a class-based TF-IDF procedure. ArXiv, abs/2203.05794.

3   Proposed Methodolgy

3.1   Data Collection

We aim to target streaming data on social media platforms, and the dataset used in this article is derived from text posts in Sina and Twitter #ChatGPT (topics), the dataset time range is from November 2022 to May 2023, Chinese Weibo dataset n = 42177 and English Twitter dataset n = 49815.

3.2   LDA Topic Model

$$p(\text{w|d}) = \sum_{k=1}^{K} p(w|z_k) \times p(z_k|d) \tag{1}$$

In the formula, w represents a word, d represents an article, Z_k is the kth topic, K is the number of preset topics, p(w|d) is the probability of the word w appearing in article d, $p(z_k|d)$ and the probability that document d belongs to the topic z_k.

3.3   Data Cleaning and Preprocessing

In the data cleaning process, since our dataset is divided into two versions, Chinese (WeiBo) and English (Twitter), I will introduce the cleaning and word segmentation of Chinese (Weibo) and English (Twitter) datasets respectively.

Chinese Data Cleaning and Preprocessing. We removed punctuation marks and other types of characters in the text, such as: URL, username (@. + ?), Weibo reply username, topic (#), and non-user writing [. + ?], leaving only the three parts of the text: Chinese characters, numbers, and English letters. The word segmentation uses the jieba library, first remove the stop word and then perform word segmentation, but the effect of the previous rounds of the stop word list is not ideal, there are some numbers and word interference, so we repeatedly filter the dictionary obtained after word segmentation, add new stop words to the stop word list, and finally, the words in the stop word list in this article are 375, including conjunctions, modal words, transfer symbols, etc., according to the new part of speech text to filter out more redundant words.

In the text: #artificial intelligence# Will artificial intelligence replace humans and evolve into silicon-based organisms??? For example, the content after word segmentation and de-stop words is: (artificial intelligence replaces humans to evolve into silicon-based organisms).

Since the first round of multiple data cleaning did not achieve the expected results, in the second round of data cleaning process, we added the text less than 30 characters in the original dataset before the above (URL, username (@. + ?), remove Weibo reply username, topic (#), non-user writing content [. + ?],), and finally obtained 7221 Weibo text data.

English Data Cleaning and Preprocessing. Before processing the English dataset, we first use SPILT to separate a sentence with spaces, store each word in a list, calculate the length of the list, and count the total number of words in each entry, which can filter out text below 25 words. The subsequent English dataset cleaning and word segmentation process is roughly similar to Chinese processing, only the stop thesaurus is replaced, the English stop thesaurus is 390 words, and finally, the English Twitter text retention data is 7262.

3.4 Build LDA Model

The following needs to determine the number of topics, and we chose to measure the optimal number of topics in terms of perplexity and coherence in our experiments. Topic consistency and perplexity are two commonly used indicators to assess the quality of LDA models.

Perplexity. The degree of perplexity focuses on the generalization ability of the model, and the degree of perplexity comes from the concept of entropy in information theory and measures the discrete probability distribution, and the formula of entropy is as follows:

$$2^{H(p)} = 2^{-\sum_x p(x) \log_2 p(x)} \tag{2}$$

The perplexity is established in the discrete probability model. The higher the probability value of the text in the data set, the better the model effect is, and the smaller the confusion degree of the corresponding topic is. The calculation formula is as follows:

$$perplexity(D_{test}) = \exp\{\frac{-\sum_{d=1}^{M} \log(p(w_d))}{\sum_{d=1}^{M} N_d}\} \tag{3}$$

In the formula, M represents the number of documents, N_d refers to the number of words in d documents, and $p(w_d)$ the probability of documents. This is the simplest perplexity calculation.

Topic perplexity refers to the degree of uncertainty when the user model divides the topic of the document, and for the model trained on different topics, the minimum perplexity response topic is the optimal number of topics. The lower the topic perplexity, the better the effect of the model; As the number of topics increases, the perplexity generally presents one or several obvious inflection points.

Topic Consistency. Topic coherence focuses on the degree of connection between words within a topic, also known as topic coherence. In articles on topic modeling, topic coherence or topic coherence metrics are commonly used to represent the interpretability of the overall topic and used to evaluate the quality of the topic. Generally, the higher the topic coherence, the better the coherence of the topic and the higher the interpretability of the topic.

In the experiment, we use topic coherence and perplexity to evaluate the performance of the model. In this paper, the bag-of-words model is used for modeling, and the "topic-coherence" curve is drawn through matplotlib to determine the optimal number of topics. Specifically, first construct the LDA model under different number of topics, then calculate the consistency score of each topic, and finally average the scores as the consistency score of the whole model. By continuously changing the number of topics and calculating the consistency score, a series of topic-coherence data points are obtained, and the optimal number of topics is selected according to the trend of the curve. Finally, 8 topics are selected in this paper.

Parameter Optimization. In the experiment, the text vector was obtained by using gensim. In gensim, each vector transformation operation corresponds to a topic model, and each model is a standard Python object.

In the experiment, the bag-of-words model is used to convert each text content into a bag-of-words vector for model training. Because LDA needs to specify the number of topics, the optimal number of topics has passed coherence in the previous step, so in this step we set 8 topics. Print out the first 30 feature words.

Visualization. In this experiment, the bag-of-words model is selected as the method of constructing word vectors, and the most likely topics are output.

pyLDAvis library is a Python library for visualizing the results of the LDA model, rendering the results of the topic model interactively. pyLDAvis produces LDA visualizations that visually understand the similarities between topics and the importance of each topic. Each bubble represents a topic, the area of the circle represents the size of the topic in the whole collection, and the distance between the circles represents the distance between the topics, and the closer the distance indicates the higher degree of correlation between them. From the center of each circle can be seen the specific word frequency ranking of the topic, these words are the characteristic words that distinguish the topic from other topics.

In this experiment, the results of the LDA model are visualized based on the lexicon. Use the training LDA model for visualization, and analyze the visualization results and feature words under each topic. The results of the LDA model trained by TF-IDF have good differences in different topic feature words. To a certain extent, it can explain that the topic classification effect is better, but the results are mainly concentrated. On a particular subject, the other subject circles are very small, making it difficult to distinguish between different subjects. In addition, we also have overlaps in the previous rounds of experiments, indicating that the topics have a containment relationship, and the correlation and similarity between them are too high, which to a certain extent shows that the topic differentiation is not very clear.

3.5 Top2Vec

Data Cleaning. According to Top2Vec's own calculation principle, Top2Vec can automatically find the number of topics without stop word list, stemming or lemmatization, while other topic modeling methods need to know in advance how many topics are in the corpus. Because a data set is uniformly used in this article, the steps and processes of data preprocessing will not be described repeatedly.

We use Python's Top2Vec model to analyze the data set. After importing the data set, we adjusted two parameters. Min_count indicates the minimum number of occurrences of words, which can prevent words lower than min_count in the text from being added to the model. Speed refers to the training Speed, the parameter is "learn" by default, there are three parameters "fast-learn", "learn" and "deep-learn" in the speed parameter, fast-learn means that the model training speed is the fastest, but the training effect is the worst; learn Refers to the standard speed, the training effect is medium, deep-learn refers to the slowest speed, but the training effect is the best. Worker refers to the number of parallel operations, and the maximum value is the number of cores of the computer CPU (Fig. 1).

```
Top2Vec(documents=df['notice'].to_list(),
        min_count=45,
        speed="deep-learn",
        workers=16,
        topic_merge_delta=0.7)
```

Fig. 1. Chinese Model Training Parameters.

In the Top2Vec experiment, we also conducted two versions of the experiment in Chinese and English. Among the Chinese Weibo topic clustering parameters, the default value of min_count is 50. After many experiments, we changed it to 45, and adjusted the speed to 'deep-learn', workers are adjusted to 16, the last topic_merge_delta is adjusted to 0.7, and finally 8 Chinese topics are obtained.

In the clustering process of English Twitter text, the parameters have been modified compared with Chinese, min_count is changed to 46, speed remains unchanged ('deep-learn'), works setting remains unchanged, and the last topic_merge_delta is adjusted to 0.367, and finally we get 8 English topics. In the final running result, 'Topic _sizes' and 'topic-ids' represent the number of each topic and the corresponding topic respectively.

Get Topics. In the experiment part, we choose pycharts word cloud to display topic information. In order to simplify the code, we encapsulate this function as a function: get Topic_words, word_socores and topic_id and display the final word cloud.

It is worth noting that the dimensionality reduction algorithm UMAP and the clustering algorithm HDBSCAN used in Top2Vec have their own parameters, and all parameters in these two classes are optimized for topic modeling. In order to compare the results of Top2Vec with those of the previous LDA, we decided to limit the number of topics to 8 for both models. Under normal circumstances, Top2Vec automatically finds the optimal number of topics. When we introduced 8 topics, we noticed that Cosine similarity changes with topic reduction.

3.6 BERTopic

An advantage of using BERTopic is that each major step in the algorithm can be clearly defined, making the process transparent and intuitive.

Training Model. In Chinese Weibo topic training, an open source Weibo word vector pre-training model is introduced. For English Twitter topic training, we introduce BERT's default embedding model (embedding model). In BERTopic, any sentence-transformers can be selected models, but two models are set as default: all-MiniLM-L6-v2 and paraphrase- multilingual- MiniLM- L12-v2, the former is an English language model trained specifically for semantic similarity tasks, which is useful for most use cases All very effective. The second model is very similar to the first, with the main difference being that the multilingual model works for more than 50 languages. This model is much larger than the first model and will only be selected if a language other than English is selected.

After a document has been represented digitally, the dimensionality of the representation must be reduced. There are many methods for dimensionality reduction, but BERTopic chooses UMAP by default. This is a technique that can preserve the local and global structure of data while reducing dimensionality.

After completing the dimensionality reduction step, we can cluster the data. The density-based clustering technique HDBSCAN can find clusters of different shapes and can identify outliers under certain circumstances. Therefore, we do not force documents into clusters that they may not belong to.

Topic Representation. This step requires modifying TF-IDF so that all documents in a single cluster are treated as a single document, and the more important a word is in the clustering process, the more representative the word is of the topic. The expression formula of TF-IDF is as follows:

$$W_{x,c} = ||tf_{x,c}|| \times \log(1 + \frac{A}{f_x}) \tag{4}$$

where $tf_{x,c}$ represents the frequency of word x in cluster c, f_x represents the frequency of word x in all clusters, and A represents the average number of words contained in each cluster.

Because the number of topics output by the model cannot be modified through parameters or assignments during the training process, we used the reduce_topics() method to compress the number of topics in this round of experiments, and finally compressed both Chinese and English texts into 8 topics.

4   Result

We use LDA, Top2Vec and BERTopic three clustering methods to get the relevant topics discussed by domestic and foreign users on ChatGPT on Weibo and Twitter platforms. For comparison of clustering performance, samples of the same cluster should be as similar as possible, and samples of different clusters should be as different as possible, that is, the Intra-Cluster Similarity is high and between the Inter-Cluster similarity is low.

When choosing the method to evaluate the optimality of the three clustering methods in the experiment, finally it is decided to choose the separability of the topic model and compare it to determine the degree of distinction between different topics, that is, to ensure that each topic is relatively independent in semantics, which helps to ensure that the topic model can extract a certain representative topic.

In this experiment, we use three algorithms to calculate the topic similarity, including cosine similarity calulations, Pearson's correaltion and Sihouette coefficient.

4.1 Cosine Similarity Calculation

Cosine similarity is a commonly used vector similarity measurement method, which is used to measure the angle between two vectors. The value of cosine similarity is between $[-1, 1]$, 1 means completely similar, 0 means irrelevant, and -1 means completely opposite. Larger distances between topics indicate that they have larger semantic differences, which enhances model separation. Then perform vectorization calculations, take several feature words for each topic, and then represent each word with a word vector (Word2Vec pre-trained word vector). After that, the word vectors of each subject word are weighted and averaged.

The inter-topic distance reflects the difference and separation between different topics in the topic model. When the inter-topic distance is large, it means that different topics are more dissimilar in word distribution, that is, they have large differences in semantics, which indicates that the topic model can better decompose text data into relatively independent and non-overlapping topics. Conversely, when the distance between topics is small, it means that different topics have a high similarity in word distribution, and they may overlap some specific words, which may indicate that the effect of the topic model is not good, and the extracted topics are too vague or not independent enough.

In the experiment, we use gensim to train word vectors. Word2vec and other models are packaged in gensim. During model training, sg uses the default value of 0, and size (int) is the dimension of the output word vector. The default value is 100. If the corpus text is less than 100M in training, it is recommended to use the default value. Window(int) indicates the maximum distance between the current and predicted words in a sentence. In this experiment, window uses the default value of 5, and min_count also selects the default value parameter.

LDA Cosine Similarity Complement Calculation. After calculating the complement of cosine value between topics and topics, we get the minimum and maximum values between topics, and the average value of topics. Then analyze Weibo text and Twitter text.

Suppose we define the complement of cosine similarity as 1 minus cosine similarity, i.e.:

$$Supplementary = 1 - Cosine\_Sunularity \tag{5}$$

We list the top 5 topic calculations with large topic spacing. As shown in the following Table 1:

Table 1. LDA topic distance caculation table.

LDA Chinese	Distance	LDA English	Distance
Topic 1 v.s. Topic 7	0.411	Topic 3 v.s. Topic 8	0.155
Topic 2 v.s. Topic 7	0.367	Topic 1 v.s. Topic 8	0.129
Topic 5 v.s. Topic 7	0358	Topic 5 v.s. Topic 8	0.128

(*continued*)

Table 1. (*continued*)

LDA Chinese	Distance	LDA English	Distance
Topic 1 v.s. Topic 3	0.333	Topic 1 v.s. Topic 7	0.114
Topic 3 v.s. Topic 7	0.326	Topic 1 v.s. Topic 3	0.112

The LDA Chinese minimum distance between topics is 0.118; the maximum distance between topics is 0.411; the average distance between topics is 0.265.

The LDA English minimum distance between topics is 0.040; the maximum distance between topics is 0.155; the distance between topics: 0.088.

From the LDA cosine complement calculation results, it can be seen that the maximum inter-topic value of Weibo #ChatGPT = 0.411, and the maximum inter-topic value of Twitter = 0.155. The 8 topics in Chinese are more dispersed and independent, and the semantics are more clear, which can better understand the text data structure and content. The topic clustering distance of Twitter is smaller than that of Weibo, so the separation effect of LDA model on Twitter topic clustering is not good.

Top2Vec Cosine Calculation. Analyze Top2Vec Weibo text and Twitter text. We list the top 5 topic calculations with large topic spacing. As shown in the following Table 2:

Table 2. Top2Vec topic distance caculation table.

Top2vec Chinese	Distance	Top2vec English	Distance
Topic 4 v.s. Topic 6	0.423	Topic 4 v.s. Topic 5	0.107
Topic 1 v.s. Topic 4	0.411	Topic 4 v.s. Topic 7	0.103
Topic 1 v.s. Topic 5	0.408	Topic 4 v.s. Topic 6	0.099
Topic 2 v.s. Topic 5	0.399	Topic 4 v.s. Topic 8	0.088
Topic 5 v.s. Topic 7	0.385	Topic 2 v.s. Topic 4	0.088

The Top2vec Chinese minimum distance between Top2Vec Weibo topics is 0.113; the maximum distance between topics is 0.423, and the average distance between topics is 0.298.

The Top2vec Chinese minimum distance between Top2Vec Twitter topics is 0.039; the maximum distance between topics is 0.107, and the average distance between topics is 0.071.

From the calculation results of Top2Vec cosine complement, we can see that the maximum inter-topic value of Weibo #ChatGPT = 0.423, and the maximum inter-topic value of Twitter = 0.107. The 8 topics in Chinese are more dispersed and independent, and the semantics are more clear. The topic clustering distance of Twitter is smaller than that of Weibo, so the Top2Vec model is not good at separating the topic clustering effect of Twitter. The result of Top2Vec is similar to the cosine value result of the LDA model, and the clustering effect of the model is also relatively close.

BERTopic Cosine Value Calculation. Analyze BERTopic Weibo text and Twitter text. We list the top 5 topic calculations with large topic spacing. As shown in the following Table 3:

Table 3. BERTopic topic distance calculation table.

BERTopic Chinese	Distance	BERTopic English	Distance
Topic 2 v.s. Topic 3	0.688	Topic 3 v.s. Topic 7	0.375
Topic 3 v.s. Topic 6	0.589	Topic 6 v.s. Topic 7	0.364
Topic 3 v.s. Topic 8	0.570	Topic 4 v.s. Topic 7	0.332
Topic 3 v.s. Topic 4	0.570	Topic 7 v.s. Topic 8	0.325
Topic 2 v.s. Topic 3	0.688	Topic 3 v.s. Topic 7	0.375

The BERTopic Chinese minimum distance between topics on BERTopic Weibo is 0.148, the maximum distance between topics is 0.688, and the average distance between topics is 0.400.

The BERTopic Chinese minimum distance between topics in BERTopic Twitter is 0.113, the maximum distance between topics is 0.375, and the average distance between topics is: 0.214.

From the BERTopic cosine complement calculation results, it can be seen that the maximum value between topics of Weibo #ChatGPT = 0.688, and the maximum value between topics of Twitter = 0.375. The separation of the 8 topics on Weibo is higher than that of Twitter. From the perspective of the three model clustering methods, BERTopic topic clustering has the best effect, and the topic classification is more independent and clear.

In this experiment for two topics, if their cosine similarity complement is greater, then the content of the two topics is more different and more independent. In the context of topic clustering, we usually expect more similar topics to be grouped into the same category, so by measuring in this way, the larger the complement, the more independent the topics are and the topics cannot be merged into one topic. Comparing the three topic clustering methods, it is found that BERTopic has a more clustering effect, its topic dispersion is more independent, and the semantics are more clear, because BERTopic needs to import and train the model, it has stronger representation ability.

4.2 Pearson's Correlation

To verify the cosine distance results between topics, we use the Pearson's correlation coefficient to calculate the degree of linear correlation between variables. The Pearson's correlation coefficient is a statistical method used to measure the strength of the linear relationship between two variables, and its value ranges from -1 to 1. In general, a coefficient close to 1 means that the two variables are positively correlated, close to -1 means that the two variables are negatively correlated, and close to 0 means that there is no linear relationship between the two variables.

In topic clustering, we can use the Pearson's correlation coefficient to evaluate the similarity between topics. Specifically, each topic can be represented as a vector where each dimension of the vector corresponds to the weight or TF-IDF value of each term in the topic. We can calculate the Pearson's correlation coefficients between each pair of topics and form these correlation coefficients into a similarity matrix.

In our experiment, the best way to determine the topic independence of the three clustering methods (LDA, TOP2Vech, and BERTopic) is by using the similarity matrix to evaluate the similarity between the grouped topics, and by taking the mean or median of the non-diagonal elements (close to zero).

In our experiment, each document in the three computational models can be represented in these three dimensions, forming a set of points. Pearson's three-dimensional scatter plot can be used to represent the distribution of points in 3-D space.

When evaluating the effectiveness of the clustering model, there are clear differences between the different clusters in each cluster (that is, the documents of the different clusters should be significantly different). In the following Pearson 3D scatterplots, we can see that the points close to each other form independent intervals (Figs. 2, 3 and 4).

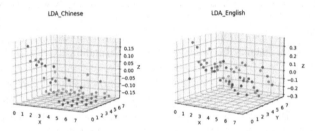

Fig. 2. LDA-Weibo Model Training Parameters(left)&LDA-Twitter Model Training Parameters(right).

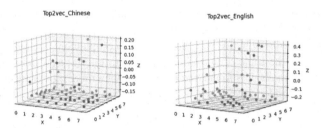

Fig. 3. Top2vec-Weibo Model Training Parameters(left)&Top2vec-Twitter Model Training Parameters(right).

Through the 3-D scatter plots of the three algorithms, it can be concluded that the Z-axis dependent variable of BERTopic is closer to 0, that is, the value of Bertopic-Chinese is −0.14, and the value of BERT-English is −0.15. Moreover, BERTopic generates a relatively small matrix of the correlation coefficient model. In our independent evaluation of #ChatGPT# topic clustering, it is consistent with the results of cosine similarity calculation.

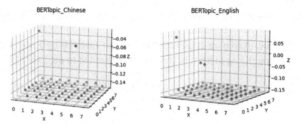

Fig. 4. BERTopic-Weibo Model Training Parameters(left)&BERTopic-Twitter Model Training Parameters(right).

4.3 Sihouette Coefficient

In related experiments, the results obtained by the Sihouette Coefficient differed from the cosine similarity, because the Sihouette Coeeicient evaluation may not be applicable to the results of testing the cosine similarity. The main reason is that the profile coefficients may not correctly reflect the cluster quality when the cluster has a non-spherical structure or is a high-dimensional data.

Top2Vec and BERTopic are two models for working with text data. Since they are all based on word embedding models (e.g., Word2Vec, Doc2Vec, BERT), their internal structure is not intended to describe the distribution of data points in a high-dimensional space in a traditional way (e.g., waveform, sphere, or other centroid shape).

Therefore, different clustering algorithms may require different evaluation methods, and require multiple evaluation indicators, or even custom evaluation indicators, to more accurately evaluate the performance of clustering.

5 Conclusion

In this paper, we propose a framework for modeling the topic #ChatGPT# in Twitter and Twitter. Topic modeling based on Top2Vec and BERTopic is compared with traditional method, In cluster separation, we found that BERTopic has better performance and better independence in topic clustering by calculating cosine similarity and Pearson's coefficient, which is better than LDA and Top2Vec clustering methods. For other common methods for evaluating internal indicators of clusters, we use the sihouette coefficient as one of the supporting methods in this experiment, but for models whose internal structure is not traditionally distributed in a high-dimensional space, using the sihouette coefficient to evaluate the model may not be the best choice.

Therefore, we will further expand the correlation work for other indicators of intra-cluster assessment and external evaluation indicators (Purity, Normalized Mutual Information, etc.); In addition, we will further explore related methods such as mix-modeling and deep learning to find the best topic modeling methods.

Data Availability and Access
The datasets used and/or analyzed during the current study are available from the corresponding author on reasonable request.

Acknowledgment. I would like to express my gratitude to all those who helped the writing of this paper.

I would like to thank Assistant Professor.Yingqi Guo from Hong Kong Baptist University, when we first met in HongKong in March, she patiently listened to the idea of my paper and gave me some support.

Last my thanks would go to my beloved mom for her loving considerations and great confidence.

References

Alghamdi, R., Alfalqi, K.: A survey of topic modeling in text mining. Int. J. Adv. Comput. Sci. Appl. **6**(1), 147–153 (2015)

Kukushkin, K., Ryabov, Y.F., Borovkov, A.: Digital twins: a systematic literature review based on data analysis and topic modeling. Data **7**, 173 (2022)

Egger, R., Yu, J.: A topic modeling comparison between LDA, NMF, Top2Vec, and Bertopic to demystify twitter posts. Front. Sociol. **7**, 886498 (2022). https://doi.org/10.3389/fsoc.2022.886498

Guo, C., Lu, M., Wei, W.: An improved LDA topic modeling method based on partition for medium and long texts. Ann. Data Sci. **8**, 331–344 (2019)

Islam, T.: Yoga-veganism: Correlation Mining of Twitter Health Data (2019b). https://arxiv.org/abs/1906.07668

Angelov, D.: Top2Vec: Distributed Representations of Topics. ArXiv, abs/2008.09470 (2020)

Ma, P., Zeng-Treitler, Q., Nelson, S.J.: Use of two topic modeling methods to investigate covid vaccine hesitancy. In: Proceedings 14th International Conference on ICT, Society and Human Beings (ICT 2021), the 18th International Conference Web Based Communities and Social Media (WBC 2021) (2021)

Lande, J., Pillay, A., Chandra, R.: Deep learning for COVID-19 topic modelling via Twitter: Alpha Delta and Omicron. PloS one **18**(8), e0288681 (2023). https://doi.org/10.1371/journal.pone.0288681

Grootendorst, M.R.: BERTopic: Neural topic modeling with a class-based TF-IDF procedure. ArXiv, abs/2203.05794 (2022)

Li, C.-H., Kuo, B.-C., Lin, C.-T.: LDA-based clustering algorithm and its application to an unsupervised feature extraction. IEEE Trans. Fuzzy Syst. **19**(1), 152–163 (2011). https://doi.org/10.1109/TFUZZ.2010.2089631

Graves, K.E., Nagarajah, R.: Uncertainty estimation using fuzzy measures for multiclass classification. IEEE Trans. Neural Netw. **18**(1), 128–140 (2007). https://doi.org/10.1109/TNN.2006.883012

Albalawi, R., Yeap, T.H., Benyoucef, M.: Using topic modeling methods for short-text data: a comparative analysis. Front. Artif. Intell. **3**, 42 (2020)

Mifrah, S.: Topic modeling coherence: a comparativestudy between LDA and NMF models using COVID'19 corpus. Int. J. Adv. Trends Comput. Sci. Eng. **9**(4), 5756–5761 (2020). https://doi.org/10.30534/ijatcse/2020/231942020

Bignell, J.T., Chantziplakis, G., Daneshkhah, A.: Comparing the behaviour of two topic-modelling algorithms in COVID-19 vaccination tweets. Int. J. Strateg. Eng. **5**(1), 1–20 (2022). https://doi.org/10.4018/ijose.292445

Karas, B., Qu, S., Xu, Y., Zhu, Q.: Experiments with LDA and Top2Vec for embedded topic discovery on social media data-A case study of cystic fibrosis. Front. Artif. Intell. **18**(5), 948313 (2022). https://doi.org/10.3389/frai.2022.948313.PMID:36062265;PMCID:PMC9433987

Kalepalli, Y., Tasneem, S., Phani Teja, P.D., Manne, S.: Effective comparison of LDA with LSA for topic modelling. In: 2020 4th International Conference on Intelligent Computing and Control Systems (ICICCS), pp. 1245–1250. Madurai, India (2020). https://doi.org/10.1109/ICICCS 48265.2020.9120888

Williams, T., Betak, J.: A comparison of LSA and LDA for the analysis of railroad accident text. J. Ubiquitous Syst. Pervasive Netw. 11(1), 11–15 (2019). https://doi.org/10.5383/juspn. 11.01.002

Bergamaschi, S., Po, L.: Comparing LDA and LSA topic models for content-based movie recommendation systems. In: Monfort, V., Krempels, K.-H. (eds.) Web Information Systems and Technologies: 10th International Conference, WEBIST 2014, Barcelona, Spain, 3–5 Apr 2014, Revised Selected Papers, pp. 247–263. Springer International Publishing, Cham (2015). https://doi.org/10.1007/978-3-319-27030-2_16

Ponay, C.S.: Topic modeling on customer feedback from an online ticketing system using latent dirichlet allocation and BERTopic. In: 2022 2nd International Conference in Information and Computing Research (iCORE, pp. 1-6). Cebu, Philippines (2022).https://doi.org/10.1109/iCO RE58172.2022.00020

Zheng, Y., Li, Y., Yang, S., Lu, H.: Global-pbnet: a novel point cloud registration for autonomous driving. IEEE Trans. Intell. Transp. Syst. 23(11), 22312–22319 (2022)

Li, Y., Yang, S., Zheng, Y., Lu, H.: Improved point-voxel region convolutional neural network: 3d object detectors for autonomous driving. IEEE Trans. Intell. Transport. Syst. 23(7), 9311–9317 (2022)

Lu, H., Yang, R., Deng, Z., Zhang, Y., Gao, G., Lan, R.: Chinese image captioning via fuzzy attention-based DenseNet-BiLSTM. ACM Trans. Multimed. Comput. Commun. Appl. 17(1s), 1–18 (2021)

Lu, H., Li, Y., Chen, M., Kim, H., Serikawa, S.: Brain intelligence: go beyond artificial intelligence. Mobile Netw. Appl. 23(2), 368–375 (2018)

Lu, H., Zhang, M., Xu, X., Li, Y., Shen, H.T.: Deep fuzzy hashing network for efficient image retrieval. IEEE Trans. Fuzzy Syst. 29(1), 166–176 (2021)

Unsupervised Person Re-identification via Differentiated Color Perception Learning

Feng Chen[1], Heng Liu[1], Jun Tang[2(✉)], and Yulin Zhang[3]

[1] School of Computer Science and Technology, Anhui University of Technology,
Ma'anshan, China
{chenfeng,hengliu}@ahut.edu.cn

[2] School of Electronics and Information Engineering, Anhui University, Hefei, China
tangjunahu@163.com

[3] School of Computer Science and Technology, Beijing Institute of Technology,
Beijing, China
zhangyulin@bit.edu.cn

Abstract. Unsupervised person re-identification (re-ID) encounters two key problems. One is the lack of label annotation in the target domain, and the other is the domain gap between different cameras. They are addressed in this paper based on the framework of pseudo label estimation-based re-ID. For the former issue, we firstly take advantage of HSV color space to design a novel data augmentation strategy, with which generated samples with controllable color components can be obtained. We then construct self-contained feature-level supervision on the augmented samples. For the latter issue, we design an explicit camera-related correction term to relieve the negative effects of camera differences, rather than suppressing the sensibility of the model to views through adversarial learning. Therefore, our model can better hold the perception to pedestrian appearance. Comprehensive experiments on three benchmark datasets have verified the superiority of our approach. Specifically, our method achieved over 1.0% performance improvement in terms of mAP compared to state-of-the-art methods. Code is available at https://github.com/flychen321/DCPL.

Keywords: Person re-identification · Unsupervised learning · Data augmentation · Camera domain adaptation · Pseudo label estimation

1 Introduction

Person re-identification (re-ID) refers to the issue of retrieving images that contain the individual of interest across disjoint camera views, which can be regarded as a specific case of image retrieval tasks [1,2]. It plays an important role in areas such as intelligent security and autonomous driving [3]. Recent deep learning-based methods have obtained remarkable progress, but their success depends

H. Lu and J. Cai (Eds.): ISAIR 2023, CCIS 1998, pp. 392–414, 2024.
https://doi.org/10.1007/978-981-99-9109-9_38

heavily on massive annotated data that requires expensive labeling cost. It is well-known that the re-ID model is sensitive to domain gap and performance degradation is unavoidable when it is deployed to a new scene [4]. On the other hand, it is not that difficult to collect a large amount of unlabeled pedestrian data. Accordingly, it is of great importance to investigate the effective approach to unsupervised domain adaptive re-ID.

Recently, plentiful unsupervised person re-ID approaches have been presented. Among them, the approaches based on pseudo label estimation achieve the state-of-the-art performance since they fully exploit the correlation among samples of the target domain [5]. These methods generally consist of two stages: (1) acquiring a pre-trained model by supervised learning in the labeled source domain; (2) making the pre-trained model as adaptable as possible to the unlabeled target domain by conducting pseudo label generation and model fine-tuning iteratively. Despite their effectiveness, there are still two unresolved issues. Firstly, in the process of pseudo label estimation, existing methods cluster samples according to their similarity and the noisy pseudo labels will mislead the model to converge along an undesirable direction [6]. Secondly, person re-ID is a cross-camera matching task as pedestrian images are taken from different views [5]. The differences of camera parameters and deployment location cause data style discrepancy across different cameras, resulting in the distance between intra-camera negative samples may be less than that between cross-camera positive samples. Existing methods usually address this problem by improving the robustness of the model to camera change [5,7]. Specifically, camera tags are employed to train a model via adversarial learning to achieve domain confusion between samples from different cameras. Such approaches will inevitably reduce the perception of the model to some appearance imaging factors caused by camera variation, which plays a positive role in distinguishing different pedestrians. Therefore, how to eliminate the negative impact of camera difference without reducing the perception of the re-ID model is a direction worthy of exploration.

To address the aforesaid issues, we present a Differentiated Color Perception Learning (DCPL) method based on self-supervised learning, which integrates the construction of exact supervision and the elimination of camera domain discrepancy into a unified framework. Person re-ID retrieval results depend heavily on the appearance of samples, and the richness of color diversity in the dataset should lead to an improvement in the model's generalization ability. Existing works [8,9] implemented data augmentation by changing the order of RGB channels to enrich the diversity of appearance. Motivated by these works, as illustrated in Fig. 1, we achieve data augmentation via the operation on HSV color space. New samples with color changes can be generated by rotating the Hue component of the original image in HSV space. Intuitively, only the color information of each group of images is different, and other information has not changed (e.g., pose, body size). Therefore, we can construct the exact self-contained supervision according to above correlation. Compared with RGB-based methods [8,9], our approach is able to manipulate specific color components quantitatively, making it more flexible and interpretable. Moreover, there

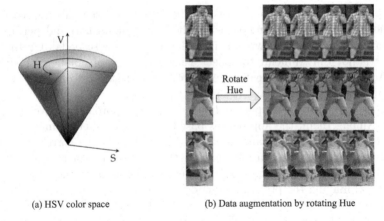

(a) HSV color space   (b) Data augmentation by rotating Hue

Fig. 1. The motivation of our data augmentation. Multiple new images can be produced by rotating the Hue component of an original image at different angles. Each row is regarded as a group, in which the color of samples is different from each other, but the structural information such as contour and edge are the same.

are two differences that need to be emphasized between the color change in our method and the color jitter in other computer vision tasks. Firstly, in the process of using color jitter to enrich data diversity, object detection and classification tasks [10,11] almost always assume that color jitter dose not change the category of samples, thereby enhancing the robustness of the model. Secondly, the current individual person re-identification task [12] utilizes additional color annotation to enrich sample color diversity through adversarial learning and considers that the category of generated data is different from that of the original counterpart, thereby constructing weakly supervised information (indicating whether the generated data and original counterpart belong to the same category). Unlike above two methods, our approach can effectively enhance the sensitivity of the model to appearance without requiring additional color annotations. Meanwhile, strong supervised information can be constructed by mining the characteristics of the data itself (indicating which category the generated data and original counterpart belong to), and the specific feature-level label assignment strategy is discussed in Sect. 3.1. The aforementioned two differences make our approach fundamentally different from other methods. To our knowledge, this is the first work in person re-ID to enhance sample diversity and mine latent self-supervised information by exploiting the characteristic of HSV color space.

Furthermore, to mitigate the side effect of camera gap on distance measurement between samples in clustering without reducing the discrimination of the model, we propose an Explicit Adaptive Camera-related distance correction strategy (EACam), in which a camera-related correction term is applied to pull images from different cameras closer. With the aid of the camera-related correction item, the measurement of cross-camera distance and intra-camera distance is more consistent. As shown in Fig. 2, samples taken from different cameras

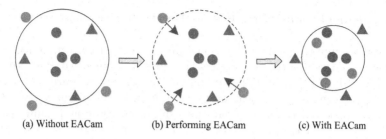

(a) Without EACam   (b) Performing EACam   (c) With EACam

Fig. 2. Illustration of our explicit adaptive camera-related distance correction strategy (EACam). Different shapes denote different pedestrian IDs and different colors indicate different cameras, and circles represent cluster boundaries.

suffer from appearance variations in the clustering procedure, which may lead to some positive samples from different cameras farther than negative samples from the same camera and group samples into an incorrect cluster. In contrast, a better clustering result can be obtained with our EACam. Compared with the widely used methods of reducing the camera gap based on adversarial learning [7,25], our proposed EACam is designed as a metric and embedded into clustering for generating pseudo labels, which works in a light-weight way and do not need extra training cost. Therefore, EACam provides a different perspective for exploiting camera tags.

Our main contributions can be summarized as follows:

1. We present a differentiated color perception learning method, which embeds supervision mining and camera gap elimination into a unified framework.
2. As far as we know, we make the first attempt to enrich data diversity with the aid of HSV color space in the re-ID task. Meanwhile, we utilize the correlation of augmented samples to mine exact self-supervision and design a feature-level label assignment strategy.
3. We introduce an explicit correction scheme to eliminate the distance measurement inconsistency between intra-camera and cross-camera settings
4. Comprehensive experiments demonstrate that our approach is competitive with the state-of-the-art methods on the benchmark datasets.

The rest of this paper is organized as follows: Sect. 2 reviews some related works from three aspects. Section 3 describes our proposed Differentiated Color Perception Learning method in detail. The experimental evaluation is carried out in Sect. 4. Finally, we conclude our work and present some future research lines in Sect. 5.

2 Related Work

This work is connected to data augmentation-based person re-ID, pseudo label estimation-based person re-ID, and camera gap reduction. We briefly retrospect relevant literatures from these three aspects.

Data Augmentation-Based Person Re-ID. In accordance with the data-driven characteristic of deep learning, enriching the diversity of training datasets is pivotal in improving the re-ID model performance. However, collecting and labeling a good deal of training data is laborious and expensive. Recently, many GAN-based data augmentation methods have been put forward to tackle this issue. Some methods concentrate on the overall migration of image style. Chong et al. [13] converted the source data into the target style and maintained the ID information unchanged, and then exploited both source images and style transferred samples to obtain a style-independent person re-ID model. Other approaches pay attention to narrowing the domain differences in a specific aspect. Considering the prominent difference of image background in different domains, Wei et al. [14] alleviated the domain discrepancy from the background by separating the foreground and background and synthesizing new images. In order to address the issue of illumination change, Bak et al. [15] trained an illumination inference model to judge the lighting of the target domain with the aid of a synthetic person dataset rendered with multiple lighting conditions, so as to narrow the illumination bias between different domains. To solve the impact of pose variation on performance, [16] utilized the original image and pose skeleton to produce enough quantity of pose-rich data for subsequent model training. Chen et al. [17] utilized both cross-view generation and contrastive learning to extract view-invariant semantic features. There are also a few efforts that combine specific factors with overall transferring. Liu et al. [18] considered that the domain shift is caused by a variety of factors, including resolution, illumination, and camera views. Therefore, this method introduced an adaptive ensemble framework to fuse factor-wise transfers by perceiving the affects of different factors. Different from these GAN-based methods, our proposed data augmentation strategy does not require any additional annotation, including illumination or pose. Moreover, compared with the time-consuming training process for GANs, it is time efficient to obtain new data by rotating the Hue component of images.

Pseudo Label Estimation-Based Person Re-ID. Clustering-based pseudo label estimation is another effective means to tackle the unsupervised re-ID task. Lin et al. [19] designed a bottom-up clustering approach, which takes diversity across different pedestrians and similarity within the same pedestrian into account and employs repelled loss to optimize the network. To alleviate the incorrect guidance come from clustering error. Zhu et al. [20] embed pseudo label correction via neighbor consistency into an easy-to-hard model collaborative training to eliminate noise in the training stage. In order to acquire a better clustering result, some methods attempted to cluster based on multiple semantic features. Xuan et al. [21] decomposed the identity similarity calculation into two phases to progressively obtain more reliable pseudo labels, including intra- and inter-camera similarity computations. Yin et al. [22] extracted holistic and patch-level features simultaneously, and then clustered them by using weighted summation results. Yang et al. [23] proposed a part-aware progressive adaptation model based on human part detection, which explicitly performs cross-domain feature alignment in a progressive manner. Zhang et al. [5] extracted multi-scale feature representations, and then obtained pseudo labels based on multiple clustering results. Li et al. [24] adopted various clustering strategies adaptively and alternately to make full use of their complementary information and restrain noisy pseudo labels. The above methods usually utilize a single feature or different-scale spatial features for clustering, without fully considering the complementarity between different semantic information. In contrast, we obtain more diverse and complementary features through feature decoupling to improve the clustering result.

Camera Gap Domain Adaptation. Due to the camera characteristics and deployments of different domains are usually with a certain gap, intra-identity images from different cameras may suffer from the variation of views. To address this issue, Zhong et al. [7] took advantage of GANs to generate camera style-transferred samples, and then exploited the constraints of camera invariance to narrow cross-camera variation between samples. Zhang et al. [5] applied a gradient reverse layer to obtain view-invariant features for samples of the same identity captured by different cameras. Li et al. [25] integrated a cross-adversarial consistency module and a consistency self-prediction module into an end-to-end framework to achieve domain-invariant feature extraction. Bertocco et al. [26] proposed a triplet construction strategy in compliance with the diversity of cameras within a cluster to enhance the model's robustness. Zheng et al. [27] disentangled camera and identity features in the latent space based on Camstyle Shuffling and Retraining (CSR) scheme, and hence obtained more ID-preserved and camera-invariant feature representation. The aforementioned methods rely on model training to discover camera-invariant features. In contrast, we adopt a more explicit strategy to tackle this problem, directly exploiting the statistical distance change caused by the variation of views to correct the distance calculation and ensure the consistency of distance measurement without impairing the discrimination of the re-ID model.

3   Method

The framework of our proposed DCPL is presented in Fig. 3. For conciseness, it only shows the process of fine-tuning for the target domain. Meanwhile, this section only introduces the mechanism of the fine-tuning stage. The pre-training phase for the source domain is similar to fine-tuning, which only omits pseudo label estimation. Next, we introduce our method from three aspects: data augmentation, network structure and loss functions.

3.1   Data Augmentation and Feature-Level Self-supervision Construction

Color information acts a dominant role in the person re-ID task. Therefore, enriching the color diversity of the training dataset is an effective manner to improve performance and enhance generalization ability.

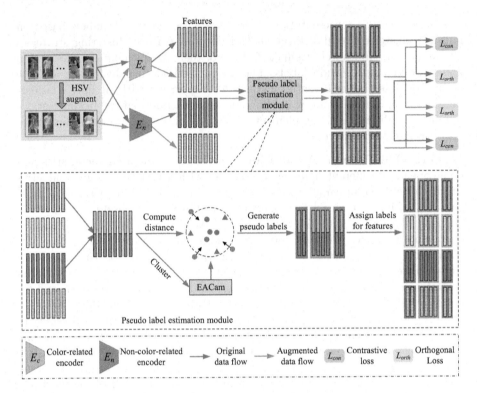

Fig. 3. The overview of our approach. For target domain, we first achieve data augmentation and feed the original samples and generated counterparts into both E_c and E_n simultaneously to extract features. Afterwards, two semantic features of the original data are concatenated together to compute distance between samples with taking EACam into account. Then, we obtain pseudo labels and further assign reasonable labels to different features. Finally, loss functions are elaborated to train the re-ID model with the aid of pseudo labels (For brevity, the ID loss and triplet loss are not depicted).

A given image I_o can be decomposed into three components in HSV space, including hue (H), saturation (S), and value (V). As a result, we design a data augmentation strategy by manipulating HSV components. It is assumed that each pixel's H range is between $0°$ and $360°$, and the scope of S and V is between 0 and 255. We adopt applicable processing schemes for different components. Specifically, for each pixel of I_o, we rotate the H component at equal intervals within $360°$. In order to effectively simulate the variation of illumination and the difference of camera parameters, we jitter the S and V components respectively. The illustration of our data augmentation is shown in Fig. 4, and it can be seen that the diversity of data has indeed been effectively enriched. Compared with other GAN-based methods, this strategy has higher time efficiency as it does not need to train a generator and can produce sufficient new samples.

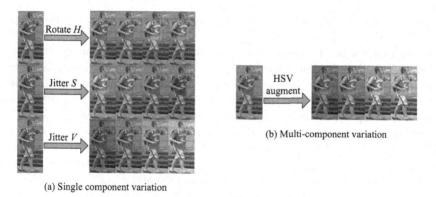

(a) Single component variation

(b) Multi-component variation

Fig. 4. Illustration of data augmentation via HSV color space.

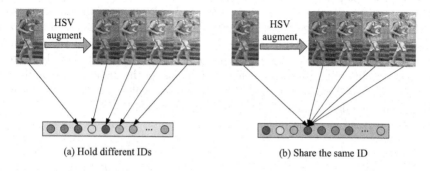

(a) Hold different IDs

(b) Share the same ID

Fig. 5. Diagram of label assignment. (a) deems that ID is related to color, and concentrates on color-related component; (b) considers that ID is unrelated to color, and pays attention to non-color-related aspect.

As illustrated in Fig. 4(b), if we regard the original image and generated samples as a group, only color-related information changes between samples in a group. In contrast, other non-color-related information (i.e. contour, texture, and geometric structure) remains unchanged. This observation inspires us to construct two different constraints to focus on various semantic information within the image. As depicted in Fig. 5, for the sake of emphasizing color-related and non-color-related components, respectively, two feature-level label assignment strategies are elaborated to achieve feature decoupling. It is worth emphasizing that the supervision contained in the two label schemes is constructed from the augmented data itself. Accordingly, the self-contained supervised information is exact, regardless of whether the original sample has manual annotation or not.

3.2   Network Structure

As illustrated in Fig. 3, our network is made up of two branches with identical structure but different parameters, in which E_c is used to extract color-related features and E_n is applied to obtain non-color-related features. For the simplicity of description, we assume that only one augmented sample is generated for one original image. The extension to multiple generated counterparts can be easily achieved. Subscript is used to denote data indices, and superscript is used to indicate whether the data is original or augmented. For the target domain, let $\mathcal{X}^o = \{x_i^o\}_{i=1}^{N^o}$, $\mathcal{Y}^o = \{y_i^o\}_{i=1}^{N^o}$ represent the original images and corresponding labels, respectively, where N^o is the number of original samples and $\mathcal{Y}^o$ is unknown. We employ similar notations to indicate the augmented samples, i.e., $\mathcal{X}^a = \{x_i^a\}_{i=1}^{N^a}$, $\mathcal{Y}^a = \{y_i^a\}_{i=1}^{N^a}$, and $N^a = N^o$, $\mathcal{Y}^a$ is also unknown.

For each input original image x^o, we first generate one augmented counterpart x^a. When x^o is fed into the encoders, $E_c(x^o)$ and $E_n(x^o)$ can be obtained respectively. Similarly, we acquire $E_c(x^a)$ and $E_n(x^a)$ for x^a. Then, the concatenated features $[E_c(x^o), E_n(x^o)]$ are used to estimate pseudo labels.

DBSCAN [28] is a commonly used strategy for clustering as it can filter outliers to some extent as samples are not forced to be grouped into valid clusters. In this work, we achieve clustering by DBSCAN based on original samples and clusters are generated relying on the distance threshold (δ) and the minimum quantity of samples (λ) within the range of δ. The pivotal factor in obtaining a satisfactory clustering result is to effectively measure the distance (or similarity) between samples. Existing methods usually simply exploit Euclidean (or Cosine) distance to calculate similarity, and the original camera-related distance matrix D can be defined as follows.

$$D_{i,j} = \left\| [E_c(x_i^o), E_n(x_i^o)] - [E_c(x_j^o), E_n(x_j^o)] \right\|_2, \tag{1}$$

where $[E_c(x_i^o), E_n(x_i^o)]$ denotes concatenating $E_c(x_i^o)$ and $E_n(x_i^o)$ into a whole, $D_{i,j}$ indicates the Euclidean distance between x_i^o and x_j^o in feature space, and $i, j \in \{1, 2, ..., N^o\}$. As a cross-view retrieval task, re-ID inevitably has significant adverse effects on distance measuring due to camera differences. To tackle this problem, we design the explicit adaptive camera-related distance correction approach (EACam). In order to obtain a better correction effect, we need to ensure the consistency of other information as much as possible when determining the camera-related bias, i.e., maintaining the identity unchanged. Therefore, it is necessary to obtain the preliminary clustering result, and then respectively calculate the intra-camera and cross-camera distance within samples of the same pedestrian, so as to obtain the average distance of all persons, i.e., the view-related correction term. As a result, EACam takes the original camera-related distance matrix $D(\mathcal{X}^o)$, the corresponding camera matrix $C(\mathcal{X}^o)$, and the preliminary clustering result $C^p(\mathcal{X}^o)$ based on $D(\mathcal{X}^o)$ as the input, and takes the corrected camera-unrelated distance matrix $D'(\mathcal{X}^o)$ as the output. The camera matrix is used to indicate whether the pairwise samples come from the same view, which can be formulated as:

$$C_{i,j}(\mathcal{X}^o) = \begin{cases} 0, & cam_i \neq cam_j \\ 1, & cam_i = cam_j, \end{cases} \tag{2}$$

where cam_i and cam_j represent which camera x_i^o and x_j^o are collected from, and $i, j \in \{1, 2, ..., N^o\}$. The preliminary clustering result $C^p(\mathcal{X}^o)$ is obtained by DBSCAN and described as follows:

Algorithm 1: Workflow of EACam

Input: Original camera-related distance matrix $D(\mathcal{X}^o)$, camera matrix $C(\mathcal{X}^o)$ and preliminary clustering result $\mathcal{C}^p(\mathcal{X}^o)$.

Output: Corrected camera-unrelated distance matrix $D'(\mathcal{X}^o)$.

1   $\kappa_{correction} \leftarrow 0,\ cnt \leftarrow 0$;
2   **for** $i{=}1$ **to** η **do**
3     $n_{diff} \leftarrow 0,\ n_{same} \leftarrow 0,\ \epsilon_{diff} \leftarrow 0,\ \epsilon_{same} \leftarrow 0$;
4   **for** $j{=}1$ **to** N^o **do**
5   **for** $k{=}1$ **to** N^o **do**
6   **if** $x_j \in c_i^p$ and $x_k \in c_i^p$ and $j \neq k$ **then**
7   **if** $C_{j,k}(\mathcal{X}^o) = 0$ **then**
8             $\epsilon_{diff} \leftarrow \epsilon_{diff} + D_{j,k}(\mathcal{X}^o)$;
9             $n_{diff} \leftarrow n_{diff} + 1$;
10   **else**
11             $\epsilon_{same} \leftarrow \epsilon_{same} + D_{j,k}(\mathcal{X}^o)$;
12             $n_{same} \leftarrow n_{same} + 1$;
13   **end**
14   **end**
15   **end**
16   **end**
17   **if** $n_{diff} > 0$ and $n_{same} > 0$ **then**
18       $\kappa_{correction} \leftarrow \kappa_{correction} + (\epsilon_{diff}/n_{diff} - \epsilon_{same}/n_{same})$;
19       $cnt \leftarrow cnt + 1$;
20   **end**
21 **end**
22 $\kappa_{correction} \leftarrow \kappa_{correction}/cnt$;
23 $D'(\mathcal{X}^o) \leftarrow D(\mathcal{X}^o) + \kappa_{correct} * C(\mathcal{X}^o)$;
24 **return** $D'(\mathcal{X}^o)$.

$$\mathcal{C}^p(\mathcal{X}^o) = \{c_i^p\}_{i=1}^{\eta}, \tag{3}$$

where c_i^p denotes a specific cluster and η indicates the number of clusters.

Intuitively, the compensation term should be subtracted from the cross-view distances to unify all items into the intra-view pattern. Unfortunately, this maybe lead to some negative values, and interference the subsequent clustering. Therefore, we exploit the manner of adding a correction to intra-view items for unifying all distances into the cross-view style. The detailed workflow of EACam is shown in Algorithm 1.

After obtaining the corrected distance matrix $D'(\mathcal{X}^o)$, we conduct clustering via DBSCAN and acquire $\mathcal{Y}^o = \{y_i^o\}_{i=1}^{N^o}, y_i^o \in \{1, 2, ..., C^o\}$ for original data, where C^o denotes the number of valid clusters. For augmented data $\mathcal{X}^a$, as shown in Fig. 6, in order to focus on different semantic aspects, we assign distinguished labels to corresponding features that come from various encoders. Specifically, $E_n(\mathcal{X}^a)$ produced by E_n branch are assigned the same labels as the counterparts in original data, i.e., $\mathcal{Y}_n^a = \mathcal{Y}^o$. $E_c(\mathcal{X}^a)$ generated by E_c branch are allocated

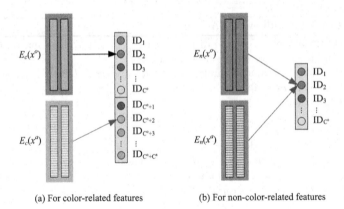

(a) For color-related features   (b) For non-color-related features

Fig. 6. Illustration of feature-level label assignment. We assign feature-level labels to different semantic features of original samples (x^o) within a specific cluster and their corresponding augmented counterparts (x^a). (a) For color-related features produced by E_c, we assign a pseudo label to $E_c(x^o)$ according to the clustering result and dispense a different label to $E_c(x^a)$. (b) For non-color-related features generated by E_n, we allocate the same pseudo label to $E_n(x^o)$ and $E_n(x^a)$ according to the clustering result.

different labels from corresponding original samples, i.e., $\mathcal{Y}^a_c = \{y^a_i\}^{N^a}_{i=1}$, $y^a_i \in \{C^o + 1, C^o + 2, ..., C^o + C^a\}$, where $C^a = C^o$ as we consider that each original only generate one augmented counterpart for simplicity of expression.

3.3   Loss Functions

In this part, we elaborate the objective functions for our model. First of all, we introduce the softmax cross-entropy loss (ID loss) to boost the discrimination ability among identities. For the sake of computing the ID loss, two classifiers FC_c and FC_n are respectively stacked to the top of E_c and E_n, and applied to map the feature to a score vector, in the form of $p(x_i) = softmax(FC(E(x_i)))$, where $FC \in \{FC_c, FC_n\}$, $E \in \{E_c, E_n\}$, and $x_i \in \{x^o_i, x^a_i\}$. We compute the ID loss for classification predicted results of four features (i.e., $E_c(x^o)$, $E_c(x^a)$, $E_n(x^o)$, and $E_n(x^a)$) based on the feature-level label assignment strategy illustrated in Fig. 6, and the ID loss can be described as:

$$L_{ID} = \frac{1}{n_{bz}} \sum_{i=1}^{n_{bz}} -log(p_{y_i}(x_i)), \qquad (4)$$

where n_{bz} represents batch size, y_i denotes the ground truth label and $p_{y_i}(x_i)$ indicates the predicted probability of the input x_i at the y_i-th bit produced by the softmax output.

Furthermore, the triplet loss with hard samples mining is adopted to learn such a feature space, in which the negative pair is farther than the positive pair. P identities and K instances within every identity are randomly sampled to constitute a batch. For each anchor feature $E(x_a)$, the corresponding hardest positive feature $E(x_p)$ and the hardest negative feature $E(x_n)$ within a batch are chosen to constitute a triplet. The triplet loss is also respectively calculated on four features similar to the ID loss, which can be defined as follows:

$$
L_{trip} = \frac{1}{PK} \sum_{i=1}^{P} \sum_{a=1}^{K} max(0, \; \mu + \overbrace{\max_{p=1...K} \|E(x_{i,a}) - E(x_{i,p})\|_2}^{hardest\ positive}
$$
$$
- \underbrace{\min_{\substack{n=1...K \\ j=1...P \\ j \neq i}} \|E(x_{i,a}) - E(x_{j,n})\|_2),}_{hardest\ negative} \tag{5}
$$

where $E \in \{E_c, E_n\}$, $x \in \{x^o, x^a\}$, μ denotes the expected margin between positive and negative images and it is set to 0.5.

Moreover, we exploit the contrastive loss to promote the decoupling ability. Specifically, this term is used to push the color-related features (i.e., $E_c(x^o)$ and $E_c(x^a)$) extracted from the original sample and generated counterpart away, and pull non-color-related features (i.e., $E_n(x^o)$ and $E_n(x^a)$) closer. The contrastive loss function is expressed as:

$$
L_{con} = \frac{1}{n_{bz}} \sum_{i=1}^{n_{bz}} (max(0, \; \tau - \|E_c(x_i^o) - E_c(x_i^a)\|_2) + \|E_n(x_i^o) - E_n(x_i^a)\|_2), \tag{6}
$$

where τ represents the desired gap between color-related features of the original and produced sample, and it is specified as 0.5.

In addition, in order to promote different semantic features as irrelevant as possible, we introduce the orthogonal loss, which reduces their relevance in feature space by minimizing the cosine similarity of various semantic features and it can be formulated as follows:

$$
L_{orth} = \frac{1}{n_{bz}} \sum_{i=1}^{n_{bz}} (\frac{E_c(x_i^o)^T E_n(x_i^o)}{\|E_c(x_i^o)\|_2 \|E_n(x_i^o)\|_2} + \frac{E_c(x_i^a)^T E_n(x_i^a)}{\|E_c(x_i^a)\|_2 \|E_n(x_i^a)\|_2}). \tag{7}
$$

Finally, the weighted total of all the loss components listed above becomes our ultimate goal, and it has the form,

$$
L_{total} = \alpha * L_{ID} + \beta * L_{trip} + \gamma * L_{con} + \xi * L_{orth}, \tag{8}
$$

where α, β, γ, and ξ are hyper-parameters to balance the importance of the corresponding part and we set them to 0.8, 0.2, 0.3, and 0.2, respectively.

4   Experiments

4.1   Datasets and Evaluation Metrics

In this section, we evaluate our proposed DCPL on three canonical datasets, including Market-1501 (Market), DukeMTMC-reID (Duke) and MSMT17 (MSMT) [14]. The details of aforementioned datasets are described in Table 1.

Table 1. Description of three datasets in our experiments.

Dataset	Market	Duke	MSMT
train images	12,936	16,522	32,621
train IDs	751	702	1,041
query images	3,368	2,228	11,659
gallery images	19,732	17,661	82,161
test IDs	750	702	3,060
cameras	6	8	15

During the training phase, we adopt a labeled training dataset as the source domain for pre-training and an unlabeled training dataset as the target domain for fine-tuning. In the test phase, two popular metrics, including Rank-k accuracy and mean Average Precision (mAP) are utilized to evaluate the performance of our method. All evaluation experiments are implemented under the single query setting.

4.2   Implementation Details

In this section, we firstly introduce network structure design. E_c and E_n take ResNet-50 pre-trained on ImageNet as backbones. Furthermore, two classifiers (FC_c and FC_n) based on the fully-connected layer are added to the top of E_c and E_n, respectively, where he number of neurons is set to the quantity of identities in line with our feature-level label assignment scheme. They are applied to predict the classification probability distribution.

Then, we present the training and test configuration in detail. In the training phase, for each batch, we produce a group of augmented samples with the same rotation angle of the H component corresponding to their counterparts, and resize all input images to 256×128. $P = 16$ identities and $K = 4$ images for per identity (cluster) are randomly selected to constitute a batch with size 64. The SGD optimizer is applied to optimize our network. Specifically, during the pre-training subphase, the learning rate initialized with 0.01 for the original ResNet-50 layers and 0.1 for the newly added classification layers. The learning rate decays to 10% of the initial value in the 7-th and 12-th epoch, respectively, and the model has been trained for a total of 16 epochs. In the fine-tuning subphase, the learning rates of all layers are kept at 5% of their corresponding initial learning rates in the pre-training subphase. We conduct 10 rounds of iteration for clustering and fine-tuning, and the model is trained for 8 epochs in each iteration. In the test phase, we extract the color-related and non-color-related features for each image and concatenate them into a whole to present the pedestrian and estimate the similarity between samples based on the Euclidean distance.

Table 2. Comparison of our method with the state-of-the-art ones (Market → Duke).

Method	Market → Duke			
	Rank-1	Rank-5	Rank-10	mAP
STReID [13] (NC'2021)	52.3	65.9	71.1	29.2
IPES-GAN [29] (TMM'2023)	55.7	71.4	75.5	33.3
TAL-MIRN [30] (TCSVT'2022)	63.5	76.6	-	41.3
ADFL [31] (TIFS'2021)	64.1	77.2	81.4	43.1
DTDN+IN [32] (TIP'2022)	70.0	78.9	82.0	47.7
SDAAL [33] (KBS'2022)	72.8	82.5	86.1	52.3
DSAF [34] (PR'2023)	73.8	83.9	87.5	55.7
PREST [5] (TIP'2021)	74.4	83.7	85.9	56.1
DCCL [39] (TCSVT'2023)	75.9	-	-	60.0
MDJL [9] (PR'2023)	78.6	86.6	88.7	62.8
CTFRN [35] (PR'2022)	79.1	88.9	92.7	65.4
MPC [36] (CVIU'2023)	79.2	87.4	90.3	63.6
EQGAN [37] (MM'2021)	79.4	88.6	91.0	64.4
MetaCam+DSCE [6] (CVPR'2021)	79.5	-	-	65.0
GCL [17] (CVPR'2021)	81.9	88.9	90.6	67.6
LAADD [4] (TPAMI'2023)	82.3	90.8	93.2	69.0
RSS [38] (TIP'2023)	82.7	91.1	93.5	69.1
Our Approach	**83.2**	**92.4**	**94.4**	**70.9**

4.3 Comparison with State-of-the-Art Methods

It can be seen from Tables 2, 3, 4 and 5 that our method has acquired competitive performance compared with other state-of-the-art methods. We consider that effectively enriching the diversity of data via our HSV data augmentation strategy is the key factor in inhibiting over-fitting and promoting the re-ID model's performance. Specifically, as described in Tables 4 and 5, our approach can also achieve commendable experimental results on MSMT, demonstrating the effectiveness of our approach on the large-scale dataset. Furthermore, comparing Table 4 with Table 5, it is evident that taking Duke as the source domain can obtain better performance than Market. We consider the reason is that Duke holds richer color diversity compared to Market. Moreover, ameliorating the distribution of samples in the feature space through EACam to acquire more reliable pseudo labels is also a vital ingredient in fine-tuning.

Table 3. Comparison of our method with the state-of-the-art ones (Duke → Market).

Method	Duke → Market			
	Rank-1	Rank-5	Rank-10	mAP
STReID [13] (NC'2021)	62.3	79.1	84.4	31.6
IPES-GAN [29] (TMM'2023)	66.8	81.2	85.4	34.4
ADFL [31] (TIFS'2021)	71.8	85.9	90.1	39.6
TAL-MIRN [30] (TCSVT'2022)	73.1	86.3	-	40.0
MDJL [9] (PR'2023)	80.3	87.4	89.9	59.8
PREST [5] (TIP'2021)	82.5	92.1	94.4	62.4
SDAAL [33] (KBS'2022)	82.6	91.7	94.7	56.7
DTDN+IN [32] (TIP'2022)	84.0	91.5	93.8	52.4
DCCL [39] (TCSVT'2023)	85.3	-	-	63.2
DSAF [34] (PR'2023)	88.7	95.0	96.5	69.9
CTFRN [35] (PR'2022)	90.0	96.8	97.9	76.1
MetaCam+DSCE [6] (CVPR'2021)	90.1	-	-	76.5
GCL [17] (CVPR'2021)	90.5	96.2	97.1	75.4
LAADD [4] (TPAMI'2023)	90.7	96.3	97.5	77.1
MPC [36] (CVIU'2023)	90.9	96.4	97.6	77.4
RSS [38] (TIP'2023)	92.3	96.6	97.8	79.2
Our Approach	**92.5**	**96.9**	**98.0**	**80.3**

4.4 Ablation Studies

This section investigates the contribution of each part in our method, including HSV data augmentation (DA), feature-level label assignment (FLS), and explicit adaptive camera-related distance correction (EACam). For fair comparison, we change one of the components in each experiment and keep the others unchanged.

Baseline. We simultaneously disable DA, FLS, and EACam in the proposed method. As a result, the model degrades to a single-branch structure built upon ResNet-50, and the triplet loss and ID loss are utilized to train the model. In the fine-tuning stage, we cluster directly according to the distribution of original samples in the feature space and obtain pseudo labels. In this case, feature decoupling cannot be realized as only a single branch exists. Therefore, we use a single 512-dim feature for testing in the test phase.

Baseline+DA. We add DA to "Baseline", and regard the generated sample hold the same ID with its original counterpart.

Baseline+DA+FLS. We further introduce FLS to "Baseline+DA" and the model upgrades into a two-branch network for feature disentangling. Specifically, the features extracted from different semantic branches are assigned different labels for the same input image according to our FLS. Meanwhile, the contrastive

Table 4. Comparison of our method with the state-of-the-art ones (Market → MSMT).

Method	Market → MSMT			
	Rank-1	Rank-5	Rank-10	mAP
IPES-GAN [29] (TMM'2023)	20.2	31.2	37.2	6.9
ADFL [31] (TIFS'2021)	30.5	42.6	48.8	11.4
TAL-MIRN [30] (TCSVT'2022)	30.9	43.5	-	11.2
UTAL [40] (TPAMI'2020)	31.4	-	-	13.1
DTDN+IN [32] (TIP'2022)	33.5	44.1	49.3	11.6
MDJL [9] (PR'2023)	34.3	44.5	50.6	13.4
MetaCam+DSCE [6] (CVPR'2021)	35.2	48.3	-	15.5
SDAAL [33] (KBS'2022)	40.1	51.5	**56.8**	17.4
Our Approach	**43.7**	**52.9**	53.1	**19.4**

Table 5. Comparison of our method with the state-of-the-art ones (Duke → MSMT).

Method	Duke → MSMT			
	Rank-1	Rank-5	Rank-10	mAP
IPES-GAN [29] (TMM'2023)	23.1	32.6	39.1	7.4
UTAL [40] (TPAMI'2020)	31.4	-	-	13.1
MetaCam+DSCE [6] (CVPR'2021)	35.2	48.3	-	15.5
DTDN+IN [32] (TIP'2022)	37.7	49.3	54.3	13.4
ADFL [31] (TIFS'2021)	38.6	50.8	56.1	14.0
TAL-MIRN [30] (TCSVT'2022)	39.0	51.5	-	14.2
MDJL [9] (PR'2023)	40.3	51.2	56.3	17.1
SDAAL [33] (KBS'2022)	47.0	58.1	63.7	20.4
Our Approach	**47.3**	**58.5**	**64.0**	**21.5**

loss and orthogonal loss are also applied to train the model. Moreover, in the test stage, two different semantic features are concatenated into a 1024-dim feature for retrieving.

Baseline+DA+FLS+EACam. Our method can be regarded as "Baseline+DA+FLS" equipped with EACam. During pseudo label estimation, we first cluster based on the original distribution of features, and then calculate the average camera-related bias for each pedestrian under intra-view and cross-view settings. Afterwards, the view-related correction term is obtained and the distances of all sample pairs can be unified to the cross-view style. Finally, the corrected sample similarity is used for secondary clustering, and the pseudo labels are obtained.

The ablation studies are illustrated in Tables 6 and 7. Comparing "Baseline" with "Baseline+DA", we can see that our proposed HSV data augmen-

Table 6. Results of ablation studies (Market → Duke).

Method	Market → Duke			
	Rank-1	Rank-5	Rank-10	mAP
Baseline	72.1	83.7	87.2	48.7
Baseline+DA	76.5	84.9	88.1	57.5
Baseline+DA+FLS	81.3	89.3	92.4	66.9
Baseline+DA+FLS+EACam (Our Approach)	**83.2**	**92.4**	**94.4**	**70.9**

Table 7. Results of ablation studies (Duke → Market).

Method	Duke → Market			
	Rank-1	Rank-5	Rank-10	mAP
Baseline	81.2	90.2	93.6	59.3
Baseline+DA	86.7	93.9	96.0	63.7
Baseline+DA+FLS	89.4	94.9	97.1	75.1
Baseline+DA+FLS+EACam (Our Approach)	**92.5**	**96.9**	**98.0**	**80.3**

tation method is capable of enriching data diversity and promoting feature discrimination effectively. Furthermore, from the results of "Baseline+DA" and "Baseline+DA+FLS", it shows that FLS can adapt well to our data augmentation and two-branch network structure, and effectively decouple various semantic features. Combining two complementary semantic features for retrieval can further enhance the performance of the model. Moreover, The performance of "Baseline+DA+FLS+EACam" is further improved compared with that of "Baseline+DA+FLS". We consider the reason is that EACam can improve the similarity distribution of samples in feature space by eliminating the view-related gap and bring the accuracy of pseudo labels to a better level. By gradually applying DA, FLS and EACam, it also demonstrates that these three components are compatible and can cooperate with each other.

4.5   Hyper-parameter Evaluation

Next, we conduct quantitative analysis on the most important hyper-parameter in our approach. Experiments are evaluated in the cases of "Market → Duke" and "Duke → Market", respectively.

The Number of Augmented Samples. Let the number of augmented samples obtained from each original image be N_H, which determines the rotation angle of the H component in HSV space. We investigate the performance with the variation of this parameter. As depicted in Fig. 7, the performance promotes with the increase of N_H until it reaches saturation at 8, and then slowly decreases. The phenomenon demonstrates the effectiveness and stability of our proposed

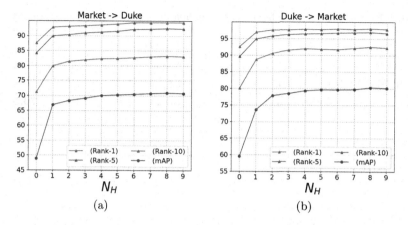

Fig. 7. The influence of the number of augmented samples for each original image (N_H) on performance.

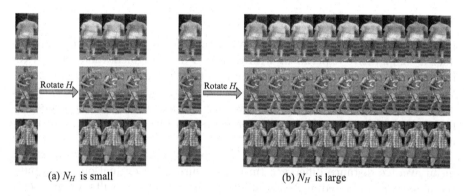

(a) N_H is small   (b) N_H is large

Fig. 8. Illustration of data augmentation when N_H takes different values. (a) N_H is 3, it means that H component rotates every 90° to generate a new image. (b) N_H equals to 9, it signifies that H component rotates every 36° to produce a new sample. Intuitively, the diversity of samples generated in (a) is relatively limited, while the differentiation between adjacent images in (b) is relatively insufficient. Therefore, the former perhaps brings about limited discrimination of the model, while the latter maybe give rise to insufficient robustness of the model.

data augmentation. As for the reasons behind this change trend, we believe that when N_H is too small, the diversity of samples is relatively limited, resulting in insufficient generalization ability of the model. On the contrary, when N_H is too large, the difference between augmented samples is inconspicuous, leading to the model being too sensitive and declining robustness. In order to better support this assertion, as shown in Fig. 8, some augmented images are illustrated.

Table 8. Comparison of different data augmentation methods (Market → Duke).

Method	Market → Duke			
	Rank-1	Rank-5	Rank-10	mAP
RGB data augmentation	81.4	89.7	92.3	67.5
HSV data augmentation (Our Approach)	**83.2**	**92.4**	**94.4**	**70.9**

Table 9. Comparison of different data augmentation methods (Duke → Market).

Method	Duke → Market			
	Rank-1	Rank-5	Rank-10	mAP
RGB data augmentation	90.4	95.2	97.3	76.7
HSV data augmentation (Our Approach)	**92.5**	**96.9**	**98.0**	**80.3**

4.6 More Discussions

In order to demonstrate the superiority of our HSV data augmentation, we conduct a comparative experiment with the RGB data augmentation [9], and the results are shown in Tables 8 and 9. Our method achieved better performance. We believe the reason is that the data generated through RGB channel exchange has limitations in both quantity and diversity. On the contrary, our data augmentation method based on HSV color space has more flexibility and can generate more diverse data.

To verify the effectiveness of EACam, we introduce an evaluation metric, mean average distance difference (mADD). During the evaluation, the ground truth labels are adopted. For each sample in the clustering results, we first separately calculate the difference of the average distance between the sample and all positive and negative samples in its own cluster. Afterwards, we further compute the mean value of all sample distance differences. The calculation process can be expressed as follows:

$$
mADD = \frac{1}{\eta}\sum_{i=1}^{\eta}\frac{1}{n_{c_i}}\sum_{j=1}^{n_{c_i}}\left(\frac{1}{n_{neg}}\sum_{\substack{x_j,x_{neg}\in c_i \\ y_j\neq y_{neg}}}\|E(x_j)-E(x_{neg})\|_2\right.
$$
$$
\left.-\frac{1}{n_{pos}}\sum_{\substack{x_j,x_{pos}\in c_i \\ y_j=y_{pos}}}\|E(x_j)-E(x_{pos})\|_2\right),
$$

(9)

where η and n_{c_i} represent the number of clusters and the number of samples in a specific cluster c_i. x_j is sequentially sampled from c_i. x_{neg} and x_{pos} denote negative samples and positive samples of x_j come from c_i, respectively. n_{neg} and n_{pos} refer to the number of negative samples and positive samples, respectively. As shown in Fig. 9, We can get two aspects of information. Firstly, no matter whether EACam is applied or not, the distance between positive and negative

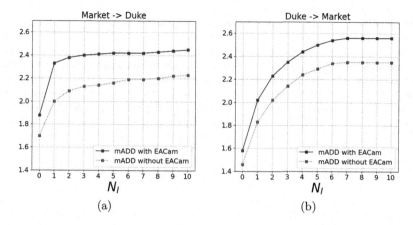

Fig. 9. The influence of EACam on mADD. N_I denotes the number of iterations of clustering and fine-tuning.

samples is increasing with the updating of the model, which indicates that the fine-tuning operation based on pseudo label estimation can promote the model to converge in the direction we expect. Secondly, after using EACam, the distance between positive and negative samples is further enlarged, which means that our EACam can effectively improve the distribution of samples in the feature space.

5 Conclusions

In this paper, we have proposed a two-stage method for unsupervised person re-ID. In particular, we first presented a delicate data augmentation strategy, which can effectively enrich the diversity of data and provide perceivable data correlation by exploiting the characteristic of HSV color space. We applied this correlation to construct feature-level supervised information, and utilized them to decouple various semantic features. Furthermore, we designed a novel plug-and-play module named explicit adaptive camera-related distance correction strategy (EACam), which can effectively ensure the consistency of the sample distance under the conditions of cross-view and intra-view measurement. And then, we integrated it into clustering-based pseudo label generation to group images come from disjoint cameras into proper clusters and produce high-quality pseudo labels. Comprehensive experiments have validated the effectiveness of each component and the superiority of the overall method.

Acknowledgements. This work is supported by the Natural Science Foundation of China under grants No. 62206006, 61971004 and 61772032, Natural Science Foundation of Anhui Provincial Education Department under grant No. KJ2021A0375, and Anhui Provincial Key Research and Development Project under grant No. 202004a07020050.

References

1. Chen, H., Wang, Y., Lagadec, B., Dantcheva, A., Bremond, F.: Learning invariance from generated variance for unsupervised person re-identification. IEEE Trans. Pattern Anal. Mach. Intell. **45**(6), 7494–7508 (2023)
2. Lu, H., Zhang, M., Xu, X., Li, Y., Shen, H.T.: Deep fuzzy hashing network for efficient image retrieval. IEEE Trans. Fuzzy Syst. **29**(1), 166–176 (2020)
3. Zheng, Y., Li, Y., Yang, S., Lu, H.: Global-PBNet: a novel point cloud registration for autonomous driving. IEEE Trans. Intell. Transp. Syst. **23**(11), 22312–22319 (2022)
4. Luo, C., Song, C., Zhang, Z.: Learning to adapt across dual discrepancy for cross-domain person re-identification. IEEE Trans. Pattern Anal. Mach. Intell. **45**(02), 1963–1980 (2023)
5. Zhang, H., Cao, H., Yang, X., Deng, C., Tao, D.: Self-training with progressive representation enhancement for unsupervised cross-domain person re-identification. IEEE Trans. Image Process. **30**, 5287–5298 (2021)
6. Yang, F., et al.: Joint noise-tolerant learning and meta camera shift adaptation for unsupervised person re-identification. In: CVPR, pp. 4855–4864 (2021)
7. Zhong, Z., Zheng, L., Luo, Z., Li, S., Yang, Y.: Learning to adapt invariance in memory for person re-identification. IEEE Trans. Pattern Anal. Mach. Intell. **43**(8), 2723–2738 (2020)
8. Wang, J., Yuan, L., Xu, H., Xie, G., Wen, X.: Channel-exchanged feature representations for person re-identification. Inf. Sci. **562**, 370–384 (2021)
9. Chen, F., Wang, N., Tang, J., Yan, P., Yu, J.: Unsupervised person re-identification via multi-domain joint learning. Pattern Recogn. **138**, 109369 (2023)
10. Li, G., Li, X., Wang, Y., Wu, Y., Liang, D., Zhang, S.: PseCo: pseudo labeling and consistency training for semi-supervised object detection. In: Avidan, S., Brostow, G., Cissé, M., Farinella, G.M., Hassner, T. (eds.) ECCV 2022. LNCS, vol. 13669, pp. 457–472. Springer, Cham (2022). https://doi.org/10.1007/978-3-031-20077-9_27
11. Zhu, X., Lyu, S., Wang, X., Zhao, Q.: TPH-YOLOv5: improved YOLOv5 based on transformer prediction head for object detection on drone-captured scenarios. In: ICCV, pp. 2778–2788 (2021)
12. Wang, G., Yang, Y., Cheng, J., Wang, J., Hou, Z.: Color-sensitive person re-identification. In: IJCAI, pp. 933–939. AAAI Press (2019)
13. Chong, Y., Peng, C., Zhang, J., Pan, S.: Style transfer for unsupervised domain-adaptive person re-identification. Neurocomputing **422**, 314–321 (2021)
14. Wei, L., Zhang, S., Gao, W., Tian, Q.: Person transfer GAN to bridge domain gap for person re-identification. In: CVPR, pp. 79–88 (2018)
15. Bak, S., Carr, P., Lalonde, J.-F.: Domain adaptation through synthesis for unsupervised person re-identification. In: ECCV, pp. 189–205 (2018)
16. Zhang, C., Zhu, L., Zhang, S., Yu, W.: PAC-GAN: an effective pose augmentation scheme for unsupervised cross-view person re-identification. Neurocomputing **387**, 22–39 (2020)
17. Chen, H., Wang, Y., Lagadec, B., Dantcheva, A., Bremond, F.: Joint generative and contrastive learning for unsupervised person re-identification. In: CVPR, pp. 2004–2013 (2021)
18. Liu, J., Zha, Z. J., Chen, D., Hong, R., Wang, M.: Adaptive transfer network for cross-domain person re-identification. In: CVPR, pp. 7202–7211 (2019)

19. Lin, Y., Dong, X., Zheng, L., Yan, Y., Yang, Y.: A bottom-up clustering approach to unsupervised person re-identification. In: AAAI, vol. 33, pp. 8738–8745 (2019)

20. Zhu, X., Li, Y., Sun, J., Chen, H., Zhu, J.: Learning with noisy labels method for unsupervised domain adaptive person re-identification. Neurocomputing **452**, 78–88 (2021)

21. Xuan, S., Zhang, S.: Intra-inter camera similarity for unsupervised person re-identification. In: CVPR, pp. 11 926–11 935 (2021)

22. Yin, Q., Ding, G., Gong, S., Tang, Z., et al.: Multi-view label prediction for unsupervised learning person re-identification. IEEE Signal Process. Lett. **28**, 1390–1394 (2021)

23. Yang, F., et al.: Part-aware progressive unsupervised domain adaptation for person re-identification. IEEE Trans. Multimedia **23**, 1681–1695 (2020)

24. Li, S., Yuan, M., Chen, J., Hu, Z.: AdaDC: adaptive deep clustering for unsupervised domain adaptation in person re-identification. IEEE Trans. Circuits Syst. Video Technol. **32**(6), 3825–3838 (2021)

25. Li, H., Pang, J., Tao, D., Yu, Z.: Cross adversarial consistency self-prediction learning for unsupervised domain adaptation person re-identification. Inf. Sci. **559**, 46–60 (2021)

26. Bertocco, G.C., Andaló, F., Rocha, A.: Unsupervised and self-adaptative techniques for cross-domain person re-identification. IEEE Trans. Inf. Forensics Secur. **16**, 4419–4434 (2021)

27. Zheng, R., Li, L., Han, C., Gao, C., Sang, N.: Camera style and identity disentangling network for person re-identification. In: BMVC, p. 66 (2019)

28. Ester, M., Kriegel, H. P., Sander, J., Xu, X., et al.: A density-based algorithm for discovering clusters in large spatial databases with noise. In: KDD, vol. 96, pp. 226–231 (1996)

29. Verma, A., Subramanyam, A., Wang, Z., Satoh, S., Shah, R.R.: Unsupervised domain adaptation for person re-identification via individual-preserving and environmental-switching cyclic generation. IEEE Trans. Multimedia **25**, 364–377 (2023)

30. Li, H., Dong, N., Yu, Z., Tao, D., Qi, G.: Triple adversarial learning and multi-view imaginative reasoning for unsupervised domain adaptation person re-identification. IEEE Trans. Circuits Syst. Video Technol. **32**(5), 2814–2830 (2022)

31. Li, H., Chen, Y., Tao, D., Yu, Z., Qi, G.: Attribute-aligned domain-invariant feature learning for unsupervised domain adaptation person re-identification. IEEE Trans. Inf. Forensics Secur. **16**, 1480–1494 (2021)

32. Dai, P., et al.: Disentangling task-oriented representations for unsupervised domain adaptation. IEEE Trans. Image Process. **31**, 1012–1026 (2022)

33. Xu, S., Luo, L., Hu, J., Yang, B., Hu, S.: Semantic driven attention network with attribute learning for unsupervised person re-identification. Knowl.-Based Syst. **252**, 109354 (2022)

34. Qi, L., Liu, J., Wang, L., Shi, Y., Geng, X.: Unsupervised generalizable multi-source person re-identification: a domain-specific adaptive framework. Pattern Recogn. **140**, 109546 (2023)

35. Zheng, D., Xiao, J., Chen, K., Huang, X., Chen, L., Zhao, Y.: Soft pseudo-label shrinkage for unsupervised domain adaptive person re-identification. Pattern Recogn. **127**, 108615 (2022)

36. Li, X., Li, Q., Liang, F., Wang, W.: Multi-granularity pseudo-label collaboration for unsupervised person re-identification. Comput. Vis. Image Underst. **227**, 103616 (2023)

37. Jiang, Y., Chen, W., Sun, X., Shi, X., Wang, F., Li, H.: Exploring the quality of GAN generated images for person re-identification. In: ACM MM, pp. 4146–4155 (2021)
38. Han, X., et al.: Rethinking sampling strategies for unsupervised person re-identification. IEEE Trans. Image Process. **32**, 29–42 (2023)
39. Gong, T., Chen, K., Zhang, L., Wang, J.: Debiased contrastive curriculum learning for progressive generalizable person re-identification. IEEE Trans. Circuits Syst. Video Technol. (2023)
40. Li, M., Zhu, X., Gong, S.: Unsupervised tracklet person re-identification. IEEE Trans. Pattern Anal. Mach. Intell. **42**(7), 1770–1782 (2020)

A Quantitative Evaluation Method
for Parkinson's Disease

Xue Ding[1], Ping Liang[2], and Hao Gao[1(✉)]

[1] College of Automation and the College of Artificial Intelligence, Nanjing University of Posts and Communications, Nanjing, China
tsgaohao@gmail.com
[2] Department of Neurology, Southeast University Zhongda Hospital, Nanjing, China

Abstract. Objective, quantifiable, and easy to operate evaluation methods are crucial for assisting in the diagnosis of Parkinson's disease. In the widely used Unified Parkinson's Disease Rating Scale (UPDRS) III, item 3.12 (postural stability) is used to evaluate the patient's body balance. But in actual clinical scenarios, doctors' judgments are subjective and have high internal variability. We propose a method based on monocular vision to objectively evaluate patients' body balance. Firstly, we use a combination of deep algorithms to obtain joint point sequences of patients and doctors in the video. Then, we use these sequences to further extract three features to evaluate the patient's balance, which are the patient's backward steps, the patient's body tilt, and the patient doctor's body distance. We collected and tested 23 Parkinson's disease patients. The experimental results indicate that our proposed method provides valuable and quantifiable patient posture and motion data in clinical settings, and to some extent reduces the subjective judgment of doctors and increases the accuracy of diagnosis.

1 Introduction

Parkinson's disease can cause motor disorders and even disabilities in patients, seriously affecting their quality of life and self-care ability. It is the second most common neurological disease in the world, second only to Alzheimer's disease [1, 2].

In clinical practice, doctors directly observe patients based on MDS-UPDRS III [3] and subjectively score various movements. This diagnostic method is highly subjective and relies on the experience of doctors. The accuracy and stability of the diagnosis are not high, and misjudgment and misjudgment often occur. According to a meta-analysis study, the error rate of expert physicians varies from 16.1% (initial diagnosis) to 20.4% (follow-up diagnosis) [4]. Meanwhile, traditional diagnostic methods require the use of expensive medical equipment, such as head CT and magnetic resonance imaging (MRI), which brings a certain economic burden and many inconveniences to patients. Although precise information on patient movement can currently be obtained through wearable motion sensors such as surface electromyography (EMG), accelerometer (ACC), gyroscope (GYRO), inertial measurement unit (IMU), etc. [5, 6], However, compared to non-contact collection schemes, wearable sensors have the disadvantages of heavy load, incomplete information extraction (a single device lacks comprehensive observation,

H. Lu and J. Cai (Eds.): ISAIR 2023, CCIS 1998, pp. 415–421, 2024.
https://doi.org/10.1007/978-981-99-9109-9_39

and the simultaneous use of multiple devices increases the difficulty for doctors and patients to use the product), and high difficulty in multimodal information fusion.

Compared with sensor-based methods, vision-based methods do not require additional equipment to wear and only require a mobile phone for shooting, which reduces the difficulty of doctors' operations and avoids additional inconvenience for patients. Currently, many scholars have utilized computer vision for Parkinson's auxiliary diagnosis. [7, 8] used graph convolutional networks to analyze the grading of patient conditions, [9, 10] and other articles proposed a visual based MDS-UPDRS gait score to evaluate the severity of Parkinson's disease movement, with a rating accuracy of around 80–85%. [11] used the 2D and 3D coordinates of key points obtained by DeepLabCut and HandGraphCNN networks, motion parameters can be accurately analyzed, Thus, the MDS-UPDRS method can provide a reliable score for motor delay in Parkinson's disease patients. We can see that video-based Parkinson's rating assisted diagnosis has great potential, and it can also be applied to the assessment and diagnosis of MDS-UPDRS body balance, which is also our ongoing work. We propose a new method based on computer vision to estimate the score of item 3.12 "Posture Stability" in MDS-UPDRS III for PD patients, which only requires one monocular video. In a standard clinical environment, doctors or patients only need to use the camera of their smartphone or tablet to record the patient's process of standing up from the chair. Our method can be used for remote home assessment or routine clinical follow-up of PD patients in clinical trials.

2 Method

2.1 2D Human Pose Estimation Algorithm

Compared with common human skeleton detection datasets (such as human3.6 M [14], MPII Human Pose Dataset [15], COCO [16]), Parkinson's patient data itself has the inescapable attribute of "tremor", which is determined by the mandatory characteristics of Parkinson's syndrome [12, 22]. The current mainstream human body detection algorithm will also have jitter when detecting key Video-Based Automated Assessment of Movement Parameters Consistent with MDS-UPDRS III in Parkinson's Disease points of the human body in the video (Even if the human body pose is estimated for a completely still person, the output skeleton will still have varying degrees of jitter, and the degree of jitter is determined by the robustness of the algorithm), this jitter is caused by pose estimation errors [13].

When algorithmic analysis is performed on motion videos of Parkinson's patients, the patient's own tremors and algorithmic jitters are often confused and cannot be distinguished. To solve this problem, we use two deep learning algorithms to analyze the video and obtain the patient's key points coordinates: HRNet [17, 23] and SmoothNet [13]. At the same time, we have changed the target detection module of HRNet to yolov7 [18] to improve the accuracy of multi person detection and ensure accurate acquisition of patient key point information in multi person scenarios with doctors or family members (see 3.1 for this experimental section). The 2d key points of the human body are shown in Fig. 1.

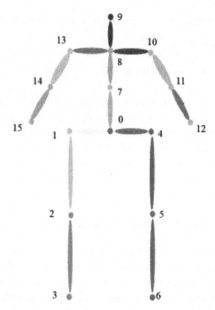

Fig. 1. The 16 body keypoints from HRNet. For each frame of a video the data consisted of the positional coordinates of 16 keypoints of the body.

2.2 Indicator

In order to obtain the key actions of the patient during " Arising from the chair", we take the estimated key points coordinates of each frame to construct two time-series indicators for each video, and the definitions of these three indicators are as follows:

$$P_{step} = P_{1,3} - P_{1,6} \tag{1}$$

Among them, $P_{1,3}$ represents the two-dimensional coordinate position of the patient's right ankle key point in each frame, $P_{1,6}$ represents the two-dimensional coordinate position of the patient's right ankle key point in each frame, P_{step} represents the Euclidean distance between the patient's ankles in each frame, which can effectively represent the patient's number of backward steps.

$$P_{ankle} = 90° - arccos\frac{\left|\overrightarrow{P_{1,10} - P_{1,6}}\right|}{\vec{\eta}} \tag{2}$$

where, $P_{1,10}$ represents the two-dimensional coordinate position of the patient's right shoulder key point in each frame, $P_{1,6}$ represents the two-dimensional coordinate position of the patient's right ankle key point in each frame, where $\vec{\eta}$ is the unit vector in the horizontal direction, P_{ankle} represents the angle between the patient's torso and the ground in each frame, which can effectively represent the degree of tilt of the patient's body.

$$P_{distance} = P_{1,3} - P_{2,3} \tag{3}$$

Among them, $P_{1,3}$ represents the two-dimensional coordinate position of the patient's right shoulder key point in each frame, $P_{2,3}$ represents the two-dimensional coordinate positions of the patient's right shoulder key points in each frame, $P_{distance}$ represents the distance between the patient and the doctor in each frame, indicating whether the patient needs the help of a doctor.

The above three indicators aim to provide more objective and accurate quantitative or qualitative analysis values that are closer to the description in the item 3.12 of the MDS-UPDRS III. Combining these three indicators can to some extent reduce the subjectivity of doctors and improve the objectivity of scoring.

3　Experiment

3.1　Performance Comparison of Object Detection Algorithms

We extracte 6 videos from the 23 videos we collected. We extracte 7% - 8% of the video frames from these 6 videos, with a total of 289 video images. The positions of patients, family members, and doctors in the images are annotated with real boxes, and labeled as "person". The real boxes and labels together form the ground truth of the dataset. After completing the above work, we feed these 289 images into different object detection algorithms to obtain object detection results. These results are compared and calculated with the ground truth of the dataset, and the most suitable object detection algorithm for the application scenario of item 3.12 of the MDS-UPDRS III is selected.

We conduct comparative experiments on current mainstream object detection algorithms (Faster-Rcnn-Resnet [20], Faster-Rcnn-Vgg [20], Yolov3 [19], Yolov5, Yolov7 [18]) on our dataset. The experimental results are shown in Table 1.

Table 1. Performance of Five Object Detection Algorithms on Parkinson's Datasets.

	P			R		
Algorithm	All	Single-person scene	Multi-person scene	All	Single-person scene	Multi-person scene
Yolov7 [18]	**0.9990**	1	1	**0.9990**	1	**0.9980**
Yolov5	0.9970	0.9980	0.9960	0.9640	1	0.9490
Yolov3 [19]	0.9931	1	0.9886	0.9810	0.9684	0.9894
Faster-rcnn-resnet [20]	0.7622	0.7171	0.7960	0.9916	0.9987	0.9868
Faster-rcnn-vgg [20]	0.6191	0.5614	0.6657	0.9905	1	0.9841
	$AP^{IoU=.50}$			F1		
Algorithm	All	Single-person scene	Multi-person scene	All	Single-person scene	Multi-person scene
Yolov7 [18]	1	1	1	**0.9990**	1	**0.9989**
Yolov5	0.9940	0.9950	0.9930	0.9800	0.9989	0.9720

(continued)

Table 1. (*continued*)

Algorithm	P			R		
	All	Single-person scene	Multi-person scene	All	Single-person scene	Multi-person scene
Yolov3 [19]	0.9888	0.9762	0.9973	0.9900	0.9800	0.9900
Faster-rcnn-resnet [20]	0.9903	0.9818	0.9918	0.8600	0.8300	0.8800
Faster-rcnn-vgg [20]	0.9886	0.9982	0.9838	0.7600	0.7200	0.7900

Subsequently, we considered that when the coincidence degree between a prediction box and the real box is greater than IoU, the prediction box is considered a positive sample, otherwise it is a negative sample. Therefore, the larger the value of IoU, the more accurate the prediction box needs to be in order to be considered a positive sample, and the lower the calculated AP value. So we tested the performance of five algorithms at IoU = 0.75, 0.85, and 0.90 (As shown in Table 2).

Table 2. Top2Vec topic distance caculation table

Algorithm	AP75	AP85	AP90
Yolov7 [18]	**0.9670**	**0.5760**	**0.2205**
Yolov5	0.9590	0.5180	0.1990
Yolov3 [19]	0.9034	0.2984	0.0650
Faster-rcnn-resnet [20]	0.7605	0.2034	0.0210
Faster-rcnn-vgg [20]	0.8356	0.3059	0.0597

3.2 Indicator Correlation

We calculated the correlation between three indicators and the rating results, as shown in Table 3.

Table 3. The correlation between P_{step}, P_{ankle}, $P_{distance}$ and scoring results

{UPDRS = 0, 1, 2, 3, 4}	
Feature	ICC
P_{step}	correlation = 0.782722919095314, pvalue = 3.4448053960751466e-35
P_{ankle}	correlation = 0.54385690264932015, pvalue = 2.634123103278836e-09
$P_{distance}$	correlation = 0.7665482903739859, pvalue = 5.639775561309672e-33

From the comparison of the results shown in Table 3, it can be found that the three objective indicators we propose have a high correlation with the scoring results, and can indeed provide valuable and quantifiable data in clinical practice, reducing to some extent the data bias and drift caused by subjective experience [21].

4 Conclusion

We collect some clinical data, extract features with stronger robustness and greater correlation, and can more comprehensively reflect the true clinical state.

We use HRNet + YOLOv7 + SmoothNet to detect the 2D coordinates of 16 pre-defined human key points, extract three time series indicators, and these indicators aim to provide more objective and accurate quantitative or qualitative analysis values that are closer to the description in the item 3.12 of the MDS-UPDRS III. Meanwhile, due to the convenience and operability of the hardware equipment required by our method, this advantage is conducive to remote home assessment or routine clinical follow-up of PD patients in clinical trials.

References

1. Tolosa, E., Garrido, A., Scholz, S.W., et al.: Challenges in the diagnosis of Parkinson's disease. The Lancet Neurology. **20**(5), 385–397 (2021)
2. Armstrong, M.J., Okun, M.S.: Diagnosis and treatment of Parkinson disease: a review. Jama **323**(6), 548–560 (2020)
3. Goetz, C.G., Tilley, B.C., Shaftman, S.R., et al.: Movement disorder society-sponsored revision of the unified parkinson's disease rating scale (MDS-UPDRS): scale presentation and clinimetric testing results. Move. Disor. Offi. J. Move. Disor. Soc. **23**(15), 2129–2170 (2008)
4. Rizzo, G., et al.: Accuracy of clinical diagnosis of Parkinson disease: a systematic
5. Poewe, W., Seppi, K., Tanner, C.M., et al.: Parkinson Disease. Nature Reviews Disease Primers 17013 (2017)
6. Lonini, L., Dai, A., Shawen, N., et al.: Wearable sensors for Parkinson's disease: which data are worth collecting for training symptom detection models. NPJ Digital Medicine 64 (2018)
7. Talitckii, A., Kovalenko, E., Shcherbak, A., et al.: Comparative study of wearable sensors video, and handwriting to detect Parkinson's disease. IEEE Trans. On Instrumen. Measure. **71**(2509910) (2022)
8. Guo, R., Shao, X.X., Zhang, C.C., et. al.: Sparse adaptive graph convolutional network for leg agility assessment in Parkinson's disease. IEEE Trans. on Neural Sys. Rehabilit. Eng. **28**(12), 2837–2848 (2020)
9. Guo, R., Shao, X.X., Zhang, C.C., et al.: Multi-scale sparse graph convolutional network for the assessment of parkinsonian gait. IEEE Trans. on Multimedia **24**, 1583–1594 (2021)
10. Lu, M., Poston, K., Pfefferbaum, A., et al.: Vision-based estimation of MDS-UPDRS gait scores for assessing Parkinson's disease motor severity. In: MICCAI (2020)
11. Abe, K., Tabei, K.I., Matsuura, K., et al.: OpenPose-based gait analysis system for Parkinson's disease patients from arm swing data. In: 2021 In Conference on Advanced Mechatronic Systems (ICAMechS). In IEEE (2021)
12. Vignoud, G., et al.: Video-based automated assessment of movement parameters consistent with MDS-UPDRS III in parkinson's disease. Journal of Parkinson's Disease **12**(7), 2211–2222 (2022)

13. Zeng, A., Yang, L., Ju, X., et al.: Smoothnet: a plug-and-play network for refining human poses in videos. In: ECCV (2022)
14. Ionescu, A., Papava, D., Olaru, V., Sminchisescu, C.: Human3.6M: large scale datasets and predictive methods for 3d human sensing in natural environments. IEEE Trans. Pattern Analy. Machi. Intell. **36**(7), 1325–1339 (2014)
15. Andriluka, M., Pishchulin, L., Gehler, P., et al.: 2d human pose estimation: new benchmark and state of the art analysis. In: CVPR (2014)
16. Lin, T.Y., Maire, M., Belongie, S., et al.: Microsoft coco: common objects in context. In: ECCV (2014)
17. Sun, K., Xiao, B., Liu, D., et al.: Deep high-resolution representation learning for human pose estimation. In: CVPR (2019)
18. Wang, C.Y., Bochkovskiy, A., Liao, H.Y.M.: Yolov7: trainable bag-of-freebies sets new state-of-the-art for real-time object detectors. In: arxiv.2207.02696 (2022)
19. Redmon, J., Farhadi, A.: Yolov3: An incremental improvement. In: arXiv:1804.02767 (2018)
20. Ren, S., He, K., Girshick, R., et al.: Faster r-cnn: Towards real-time object detection with region proposal networks. Advances in neural information processing systems 28 (2015)
21. Lumley, T., McNamara, T.F.: Rater characteristics and rater bias: implications for training. Lang Test **12**(1), 54–71 (1995)
22. Lu, H., et al.: Brain intelligence: go beyond artificial intelligence. Mobile Networks and Applications **23**, 368–375 (2018)
23. Zheng, Q., et al.: Generalized label enhancement with sample correlations. IEEE Trans. Knowl. Data Eng. **35**(1), 482–495 (2021)

Mobile Robot Path Planning Based on Improved Ant Colony Optimization

Song Chunfeng and Wang Fengqi[✉]

School of Electrical and Control Engineering, Xi'an University of Science and Technology,
Xi'an 710699, China
15136692861@163.com

Abstract. Aiming at the traditional Ant Colony Optimization in planning the path of mobile robot, which has the problems of more iterations, long time consuming, low search efficiency, low convergence speed and easy to fall into the local optimal situation, an improved Ant Colony Optimization is put forward: firstly, the concave obstacles in the raster environment are dealt with, which improves the search efficiency of the ant colony in the early stage; secondly, the pheromone negative feedback strategy is introduced into the node transfer formula to further improve the convergence speed and accuracy; finally, the pseudo-random proportional state transfer strategy is added to increase the possibility of selecting the optimal path prematurely while having high global search capability. The simulation results show that the algorithm performs better than the traditional Ant Colony Optimization in terms of the optimal path length and the number of iterations.

Keywords: Ant Colony Optimization · Path Planning · Pheromone · Raster Environment

1 Introduction

With the progress of science and technology and industrial changes, the level of mobile robot intelligence has been gradually improved, and has gradually penetrated into various fields of daily production and life. Due to the uncertainty and complexity of the robot's working environment, how to quickly and accurately search a collision-free path from the initial state to the target state has become the current technical difficulty of robot obstacle avoidance [1]. The selection of the optimal path is generally evaluated on the basis of indicators such as the shortest path, the shortest time, the smallest energy consumption and the highest safety. Superior path planning algorithms are not only able to plan efficient paths suitable for robot movement in roads with complex environmental information, but also able to improve the efficiency of the robot and reduce the wear and tear. Due to the important application value of path planning for mobile robots, it has become a hot research topic at home and abroad [2].

Path planning for mobile robots means that the robot plans the optimal or better safe path in its workspace by itself. The path planning algorithms that are often used can be divided into three categories: search algorithms such as A* algorithm, DFS algorithm,

H. Lu and J. Cai (Eds.): ISAIR 2023, CCIS 1998, pp. 422–432, 2024.
https://doi.org/10.1007/978-981-99-9109-9_40

BFS algorithm; intelligent optimisation algorithms such as ACO algorithm, BP algorithm, RRT algorithm; and autonomous learning algorithms such as DQN algorithm, DDPG algorithm, and so on [3]. Each algorithm possesses its own advantages and disadvantages. Compared with other traditional algorithms, the Ant Colony Optimization is more robust, and each search has the characteristics of relative independence and positive feedback, but the Ant Colony Optimization also has the problems of poor ability to find the optimal path in complex environments, and is easy to fall into the problem of local optimality [4]. In order to improve the performance of ACO algorithm, scholars at home and abroad have carried out a lot of research to improve these problems. Hou Wenbin et al. expanded the roulette algorithm to accelerate the convergence, and designed the adaptive S-shaped decay curve to optimise the heuristic function [5]. Xue Tian et al. used the multi-step search strategy instead of the single-step search strategy, and re-designed pheromone updating mechanism and configured the path smoothing to improve the algorithm performance [6]. Jiang Ming et al. went to improve the performance and convergence speed of the algorithm by adjusting the initial pheromone concentration [7]. Xu Xing et al. investigated an improved ACO algorithm that extends the original 2D planar search route space to 3D space, and carried out a path optimisation study of the improved ACO algorithm for warehousing in 3D space [8]. Xu Xiaofei et al. on the other hand, proposed an ant colony reinforcement learning algorithm based on knowledge migration to solve the rectangular sampling problem [9]. Liao B et al. proposed a feedback mechanism based on the order of convergence, replacing the positive feedback mechanism of the Ant Colony Optimization with a negative feedback mechanism, which improves the convergence speed to a certain extent, but reduces the robustness of the algorithm [10].

In this paper, an optimized Ant Colony Optimization is proposed to address the problems of traditional Ant Colony Optimization's insufficient ability to find the optimum, easy to fall into local optimum, and slow convergence. Firstly, the concave obstacles in the grid environment are processed to improve the search efficiency of the ant colony in the early stage; secondly, the pheromone negative feedback strategy is introduced into the node transfer formula to further improve the convergence speed and accuracy of the Ant Colony Optimization; finally, the pseudo-random proportional state transfer strategy is added to increase the possibility of selecting the optimal path, preventing the algorithm from converging prematurely while having a high global search capability.

2 Environmental Modelling

In the path planning of mobile robots, the environment modelling methods that are often used are the visual map method, the grid method and the topology method. In this paper, the raster method is used for environment modelling, where the motion environment is abstracted as a two-dimensional planar environment map consisting of $m \times n$ grid cells, whereby the motion process of a mobile robot in this environment can be regarded as the motion of a prime point [11, 13]. Figure 1 shows a 5×5 grid environment, the lower left corner as the coordinate origin O, to the right for the positive direction of the X-axis up for the positive direction of the Y-axis, the establishment of a planar Cartesian coordinate system, the length of the grid cells is selected as 1 cm. the shaded grid indicates the obstacles in the environment, the feasible grid is indicated by the white grid, and less than one grid is calculated according to one grid.

Label the raster environments in the order shown, from left to right and from top to bottom, with the serial number of each raster. In an $m \times n$ raster environment, the serial number S corresponds one-to-one with the coordinates (x, y):

$$\begin{cases} x = \mathrm{mod}(S - 1, \, m) + 0.5 \\ y = m + 0.5 - \mathrm{ceil}\left(\frac{S}{m}\right) \end{cases} \tag{1}$$

where: mod is the remainder operation, ceil is the upward rounding operation. Thus, the travelling route of a mobile robot can be represented as a series of sequential numbered arrays [12, 14].

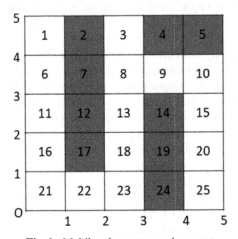

Fig. 1. Mobile robot raster environment.

The direction of motion of the mobile robot is shown in Fig. 2, except for the grids at the edges, each grid has eight directions of motion: up, down, left, right, top left, top right, bottom left, bottom right, and each direction is numbered with the numbers 1–8, respectively.

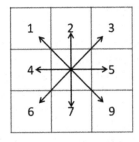

Fig. 2. Direction of motion diagram of mobile robot.

3 Ant Colony Optimization

3.1 Basic Principles

The Ant Colony Optimization by was first proposed by was first proposed by Italian scholars Dorigo, Maniezzo and others in the 1990s and is an algorithm inspired by the behaviour of ants that discover paths in their search for food and is used to find optimal paths. Ants release a pheromone on the paths they pass while searching for a food source and are able to perceive the pheromone released by other ants. The magnitude of the pheromone concentration characterises the proximity of the path, with a higher pheromone concentration indicating a shorter corresponding path distance. The pheromone concentration decreases with time. Normally, ants will prefer the path with higher pheromone concentration with a higher probability and release a certain amount of pheromone to enhance the pheromone concentration on that path, thus, a positive feedback is formed. Eventually, the ant is able to find an optimal path from the nest to the food source, i.e., the shortest distance. The algorithm that evolved from the above model of ants finding food is the Ant Colony Optimization. This algorithm has the characteristics of distributed computing, positive feedback of information and heuristic search, which is essentially a heuristic global optimisation algorithm in evolutionary algorithms.

3.2 State Transfer Probabilities

Let the number of ants in the whole ant colony be m, the number of nodes be n, the mutual distance between node i and node j be $d_{ij} (i, j = 1, 2, \ldots, n)$, and the pheromone concentration on the path connecting node i and node j at the moment t be $\tau_{ij}(t)$. At the initial moment, the pheromone concentration on the connection path between each node is the same, and it is useful to set $\tau_{ij}(0) = \tau_0$.

Ant $k(k = 1, 2, \ldots, m)$ decides its next visited node based on the pheromone concentration on the connection path between each node, and let $P_{ij}^k(t)$ denote the probability that ant k transfers from node i to node j at the moment t, which is calculated as follows:

$$P_{ij}^k(t) = \begin{cases} \dfrac{[\tau_{ij}(t)]^\alpha \cdot [\eta_{ij}(t)]^\beta}{\sum_{=allowed_k} [\tau_{ij}(t)]^\alpha \cdot [\eta_{ij}(t)]^\beta} & , j \in allowed_k \\ 0 & , otherwise \end{cases} \tag{2}$$

where: α is the pheromone importance factor, which indicates the relative importance of the pheromone concentration in the ant's selection of the next node; β is the expected heuristic factor, which indicates the importance of the distance between the current node and the next node; $\eta_{ij}(t)$ is the heuristic function, $\eta_{ij}(t) = \frac{1}{d_{ij}}$, which represents the inverse of the Euclidean distance of the ant's movement from node i to node j; and allowed k is the set of the ant k the next feasible node.

In the basic Ant Colony Optimization, the ants search for paths using pheromones released by other ants while releasing pheromones on the paths themselves, when the first batch of so ants searching for the paths complete the path search, the global pheromone is updated in the following way:

$$\tau_{ij}(t+1) = (1-\rho)\tau_{ij}(t) + \Delta\tau_{ij} \tag{3}$$

$$\Delta\tau_{ij} = \sum_{k=1}^{m} \Delta\tau_{ij}^{k} \tag{4}$$

$$\Delta\tau_{ij}^{k} = \begin{cases} \frac{Q}{L_k}, & \text{Ant } k \text{ passes through the path in that generation}(i,j) \\ 0, & otherwise \end{cases} \tag{5}$$

where: ρ is the pheromone volatilization coefficient, the larger ρ is, the faster the pheromone volatilization on the path and $\rho \in (0,1)$; $\Delta\tau_{ij}^{k}$ is the pheromone increment of the first k ant on the path (i,j); Q is the pheromone enhancement coefficient.

4 Mobile Robot Path Planning Based on Improved Ant Colony Optimization

4.1 Raster Environment Processing

In the grid environment, when a feasible grid of the upper, lower, left, right three of the four directions of the obstacle grid obstruction, it constitutes a concave obstacle, concave obstacles will make the Ant Colony Optimization deadlock phenomenon, that is, lead to the ants in the process of searching for the path of the road to go to the end of the road, so this kind of grid not only increases the unnecessary paths, but also reduces the quality of the ants' search for the path. In this paper, we optimise for this kind of situation, and the raster environment before and after processing is shown in Fig. 3. From Fig. 3(a), it can be seen that from grid 5 to grid 19, the length of the path through grid 13 is longer than that of grid 12; from grid 35 to grid 33, the length of the path through grid 41 is longer than that of grid 34; from grid 15 to grid 17, the length of the path through grid 23 is longer than that of grid 16, and if the ants move to grid 30, 37 at grid 23, then it will cause deadlock. Move, then it will cause deadlock. In this paper, the algorithm will detect the feasible status of the grids in the four directions of the feasible grids: up, down, left, and right, and if there are three or more grids that are not feasible, then this grid will be marked as an obstacle grid, and the whole grid continues to repeat the detection of the marking until the number of obstacles is no longer increasing, and the effect of the implementation is shown in Fig. 3(b).

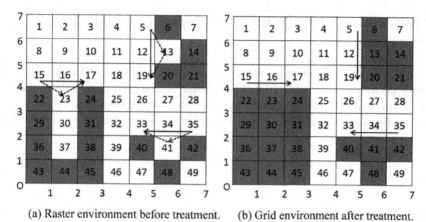

(a) Raster environment before treatment.   (b) Grid environment after treatment.

Fig. 3. Before and after raster environment processing.

4.2 Introduction of Negative Pheromone Feedback

The traditional Ant Colony Optimization adopts a uniform allocation to initialise the pheromone, and this allocation method cannot make use of the map information, so the initial exploration is more blinders. In this paper, the pheromone negative feedback strategy is introduced by combining the map information:

$$I = C + E \tag{6}$$

$$E = 1/U \tag{7}$$

where: I denotes the initial pheromone concentration from node i to node j at moment t; C denotes a constant; E is the obstacle avoidance function; and U denotes the number of neighbouring obstacle grids at the current location.

From Eq. (6), it can be seen that the higher the number of neighbouring obstacle grids to the current position, the lower the number of feedback messages allocated towards this path, which consequently makes it easier for the ants to avoid obstacle-dense regions, i.e., improves the algorithm's ability to explore and converge on high-quality paths [13].

5 Introducing a Pseudo-Random Proportional State Transfer Strategy

A pseudo-random proportional state transfer strategy is proposed for the basic Ant Colony Optimization in which the state transfer of ants from one node to the next node is a separate roulette wheel selection method, which is likely to result in the ants concentrating on a certain path faster and resulting in the optimal path searched is not globally optimal:

$$j = \begin{cases} j_1, q \le q_0 \\ j_2, q > q_0 \end{cases} \tag{8}$$

where: j_1 is the next node randomly selected at node i; j_2 is the next node selected using Eq. (2); q is a random number between 0 and 1; $q0$ is the switching value selected by the pseudo-random proportional state-transfer strategy, $q_0 = \frac{1}{N+1}$, is an adaptive dynamic variable, which is decreasing as the number of iterations increases; and N is the number of iterations of the optimized ACO algorithm. Under this strategy, q_0 can take a larger value in the early stage, which will increase the diversity of search paths; q_0 is smaller in the later stage, which will make the ants concentrate on pheromone-rich paths and accelerate the convergence of the algorithm.

6 Simulation Results and Analysis

To verify the performance of the improved ACO algorithm, simulation experiments were conducted using MATLAB software. The simulation experiments are carried out on a *20 × 20* size raster environment, and the starting point is set to be *(0.5,19.5)* and the target point is set to be *(19.5,0.5)*. The simulation experiments on the paths are carried out by the traditional Ant Colony Optimization and the improved Ant Colony Optimization, and each parameter of the improved Ant Colony Optimization is set as follows: $m = 50$, $\alpha = 1$, $\beta = 7$, $\rho = 0.3$, and $Q = 100$.50 independent experiments are carried out on both algorithms, and the path planning of the two algorithms as well as the comparison of convergence curves are shown in Figs. 4 and 5:

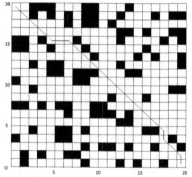

(a)   Conventional Ant Colony Optimization Path Planning before Raster Environment Processing.

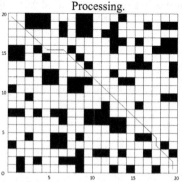

(b)   Improved Ant Colony Optimization Path Planning after Raster Environment Processing.

Fig. 4. Comparison of path planning in raster environment before and after improvement.

From Fig. 4, it can be seen that the optimal paths planned by the two algorithms are the same, but through Fig. 5, it can be seen that the improved ACO algorithm has better convergence. From the data in Table 1, it can be learnt that the optimal paths of the improved ACO algorithm in this paper in 50 simulation experiments are all global optimal paths, while the probability of searching the optimal paths of the traditional ACO algorithm is lower compared to the traditional ACO algorithm, and at the same time, there is a significant reduction in the average number of iterations for reaching the optimal paths of the improved ACO algorithm.

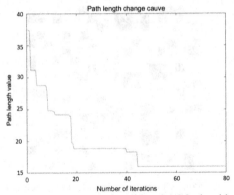

(a) Convergence curve of traditional ACO algorithm.

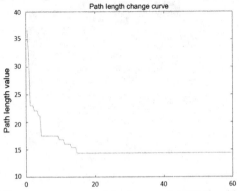

(b) Convergence curve of the improved ACO algorithm.

Fig. 5. Comparison of convergence curves before and after improvement.

Table 1. Data statistics of the running results of the 2 algorithms.

Performances	Traditional Ant Colony Optimization	Improved Ant Colony Optimization
Optimal path length/cm	28.0416	28.0416
Worst path length /cm	28.7153	28.0416
optimal path rate /%	93	100
Average number of iterations	44.39	15.49

7   Conclusions

Based on the traditional Ant Colony Optimization, this paper proposes an optimized Ant Colony Optimization, which optimizes the grid environment, reduces the blindness of the main ant colony searching paths in the early stage, introduces the pheromone negative feedback, improves the searching efficiency and searching quality of the Ant Colony

Optimization, and introduces the pseudo-random proportional state transfer strategy based on the traditional Ant Colony Optimization, which increases the possibility of selecting the optimal path, and prevents the algorithm from converging too early. MAT-LAB simulation experimental results show that the optimized ACO algorithm proposed in this paper is more efficient in searching the optimal path and faster in convergence compared with the traditional ACO algorithm, which effectively improves the performance of the algorithm.

Acknowledgements. This work is supported by Science and Technology Innovation 2023 "New Generation of Artificial Intelligence" Major project (2022ZD0119000).

References

1. Li, X., Ma, X., Wang, X.: A review of path planning algorithms for mobile robots. Comp. Measure. Cont. **30**(07), 9–19 (2022). https://doi.org/10.16526/j.cnki.11-4762/tp.2022.07.002
2. Ye, H.Z., Ming, W.L., Xia, A.C.: Path planning for the mobile robot: a review. Symmetry **10**(10) (2018)
3. Zhao, T.: Research on intelligent vehicle path planning and trajectory tracking control method. Hebei University of Technology (2022). https://doi.org/10.27105/d.cnki.ghbgu.2022.000794
4. Yang, S., Dong, X.: Application of improved ant colony optimization in mobile robot path planning. Info. Record Mat. **24**(08), 186–188+191 (2023). https://doi.org/10.16009/j.cnki.cn13-1295/tq.2023.08.046
5. Wenbin, H., Zhihua, X., Changsheng, W., et al.: Enhanced ant colony optimization with communication mechanism for mobile robot path planning. Robo. Autono. Sys. (2021). (prepublish).
6. Tian, X., Liu, L., Liu, S., et al.: Path planning of mobile robot based on improved ant colony optimization for logistics. Mathema. Biosci. Eng. MBE **18**(4) (2021)
7. Jiang, M., Wang, F., Ge, W. et al.: Research on mobile robot path planning based on improved Ant Colony Optimization. J. Instrument. **40**(02), 113–121 (2019). https://doi.org/10.19650/j.cnki.cjsi.J1804429
8. Xu, X., Qian, Y., Zhao, Y., et al.: Three-dimensional spatial path optimisation for three-dimensional warehouse based on improved Ant Colony Optimization. Comp. Integ. Manuf. Sys. **27**(01), 206–213 (2021). https://doi.org/10.13196/j.cims.2021.01.019
9. Xu, X., Chen, J., Rao, Y., et al.: Reinforcement learning algorithm for migrating ant colony and its application to rectangular nesting. Comp. Integr. Manuf. Sys. **26**(12), 3236–3247 (2020). https://doi.org/10.13196/j.cims.2020.12.006
10. Liao, B., Li, X., Zhu, W., et al.: Multiple ant colony optimization method for selecting tag SNPs. J. Biomed. Info. **45**(5) (2012)
11. Wu, D.: Research on the application of AGV control system based on Ant Colony Optimization. Harbin Institute of Technology (2020). https://doi.org/10.27061/d.cnki.ghgdu.2018.001311
12. Zhang, S.-C.: Research on mobile robot path planning based on Ant Colony Optimization. Henan Uni. Sci. Technol. (2023). https://doi.org/10.27115/d.cnki.glygc.2021.000089
13. Ruijun, H., Yulin, Z.: Fast path planning for long-range planetary roving based on a hierarchical framework and deep reinforcement learning. Aerospace **9**(2) (2022)

14. Wang, T., Ji, X., Song, A., et al.: Output-bounded and RBFNN-based position tracking and adaptive force control for security tele-surgery. ACM Trans. Multi. Comp. Commu. Appl. **17**(2s), 1–15 (2021)
15. Zhu, J., Hu, J., Lu, H., et al.: Robust motion averaging under maximum correntropy criterion. In: 2021 IEEE International Conference on Robotics and Automation (ICRA). IEEE, pp. 5283–5288 (2021)

Learning Communication with Limited Range in Multi-agent Cooperative Tasks

Chengyu Ning and Guoming Lu[✉]

University of Electronic Science and Technology of China, No. 2006, Xiyuan Avenue,
High-Tech Zone (West District), Chengdu 611731, Sichuan, China
lugm@uestc.edu.cn

Abstract. In a multi-agent system, communication is an effective way for multi-agents to cooperate. However, when the number of agents in the environment is large, receiving large amounts of messages requires high bandwidth and results in long latency and high computational complexity. Predefined communication architectures, such as master-slave communication architectures, may help, but they limit communication between specific agents, inhibiting potential cooperation. Therefore, we propose a model, which enables the agent to effectively select communication agents and aggregate communication messages, so as to carry out effective communication. Finally, we demonstrate the advantages of our model in multi-agent cooperative navigation scenarios where agents are able to develop more coordinated and complex policies than existing Methods.

Keywords: Multi-agent System · Communication · Cooperative Navigation · Reinforcement Learning

1 Introduction

In real world, there are many scenarios that involve multiple agents cooperating with each other in order to perform tasks together, such as autonomous driving [1], environmental monitoring and exploration [2], disaster relief/search and rescue [3]. These problems can be solved by Multi-Agent Reinforcement Learning (MARL).

One of the key methods to solve partial observability and non-stationary problems in multi-agent systems is communication. Agents can communicate their information, such as observation, action intention or historical experience, to stabilize learning. However, when there are a large number of agents in the environment, receiving a large amount of information requires high bandwidth, which leads to long delay and high computational complexity. Predefined communication architectures, such as master-slave [4] communication architectures, may be helpful, but they restrict communication among specific agents, thus restrain potential cooperation.

Therefore, we propose a model to enable agents to learn effective and efficient communication in the partially observable distributed environment of MARL. In our model, each agent generates messages with its own local observation, and a communication object selection module selects some agents within the communication range to communicate with. This way, each agent receives and aggregates the messages in its communication group, and finally the policy network chooses actions according to the messages and observations. We carried out experiments in multi-agent particle environment and compared with the baseline, which showed better performance and proved the effectiveness of communication.

2   Related Work

Seminal works such as CommNet [5], DIAL [6] and RIAL [6] allow learning to communicate among deep reinforcement learning agents in cooperative games. CommNet learns a shared neural network for agents to process local observations. DIAL aggregates the learning of communication and environmental policy into a unit, and enables the gradient to flow across agents. This training paradigm is called end-to-end training and has been followed by many works [7–11]. If the communicated message are discrete values and thus the gradient cannot be calculated, RIAL uses another RL algorithm to learn the content of the message, as we can see in recent works [12–16, 20]. CommNet, DIAL and RIAL are evaluated on fully-cooperative environments with a low number of agents. They use the structure of complete connection among agents, and leave the problem of how to communicate more effectively as an open question.

ATOC [12] is proposed to communicate with certain agents in an observation filed. IC3Net [13] extended from CommNet, and also uses the gate mechanism, and deterministically decides to send messages to all agents or not to any agents at all. SchedNet [14] learned to choose a certain number of agents to broadcast their messages. GA-Comm [11], MAGIC [7, 21] and FlowComm [8] learn a sharing graph for agents to decide whether and with whom to communicate. Some jobs use predefined relations among agents to decide when and with whom to communicate, while learning the content of messages. Agent-Entity Graph [17, 22] uses a pre-trained graph to maintain relations among agents.

3   Background

3.1   Multi-agent Reinforcement Learning

MARL is a Markov game process and can be described by a tuple $(N, S, A, R, T, O, Z, \rho, \gamma)$. Where N is the number of agents, S is the state space, and A is the joint action space, defined as $A = A_1 \times A_2 \times ... \times A_N$. R is a reward function, defined as $R: S \times A \times S \rightarrow R^N$, and the rewards $[r_1, r_2, ..., r_N]$ are computed for each agent in each time step. T is a transfer function, defined as $T: S \times A \times S \rightarrow [0, 1]$, which defines the probability of reaching the state s' after taking a joint action $a = [a_1, a_2, ..., a_N]$ in the state s. $O = [O_1, O_2, ..., O_N]$ are a set of observation functions, and the observation $O_i(s)$ of each agent is sampled at each time step: $S \times A \rightarrow Z_i$, where $Z = [Z_1, Z_2, ..., Z_N]$ are the observation spaces of the agents. Finally, $\rho(s_0)$ and γ are initial state distribution and discount factor respectively.

3.2 Centralized Training and Decentralized Execution (CTDE)

Centralized training models a multi-agent system as a single agent, and aims to learn a joint action from the joint observation of all agents. Centralized learners are convenient to model and enjoy centralized access to all available environmental information, but fully centralized learners are severely limited in scalability and difficult to optimize.

The CTDE paradigm aims to get the best of both centralized and independent learning paradigms, by allowing agents to learn in a centralized setting while executing policies in a decentralized setting. This enables agents to benefit from the additional information available during centralized training and enjoy the scalability benefits of decentralized execution.

4 Method

In this section, we will introduce our model framework, focusing on learning who to communicate with and how to communicate in a multi-agent cooperative environment.

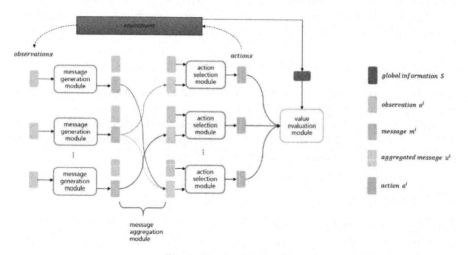

Fig. 1. Frame of the Model.

4.1 Model Frame

We propose a MARL model with communication, which is an extension of Actor-Critic model.

As shown in Fig. 1, the model consists of a message generation network, a message aggregation module, a policy network and a Q network.

We consider the environment with partial observability for MARL, and represent the total number of agents by n, in which each agent i receives the local observation o_t^i related to the state s_t at every time step t. The message generation network takes observation as input and generates a message code corresponding to each agent i, that is, a communication vector m_t^i.

$$m_t^i = f_{Message\_generator}(o_t^i) \tag{1}$$

where $f_{Message\_generator}$ represents the message encoding function, and the communication vector is fixed in length, and its length depends on a hyperparameter l.

In the message transmission aggregation module, the agents are selected to communicate with and the received communication vectors are aggregated.

$$u_t^i = f_{Message\_aggregation}(o_t^j, m_t^j), j = 1, 2, ..., N \tag{2}$$

As shown in Eq. 2, $f_{Message\_aggregation}$ is the message aggregation module, which receives the observation and communication vectors of all agents as input, selects the agents with the maximum number of k as communication agents through certain rules, and aggregates the messages of these agents, where k is a hyperparameter. u_t^i is the communication vector aggregated by each agent with the received messages.

The policy network chooses actions for agents according to the aggregated communication vector and observation vector of each agent, which is shown in Eq. 3.

$$a_t^i = f_{Action\_selector}(o_t^i, u_t^i) \tag{3}$$

where $f_{Action\_selector}$ represents the policy network and a_t^i represents the action output by the i-th agent at time step t.

After the agent takes action, the value evaluation network evaluates the action value according to the reward from environment, and updates each network in the back propagation, so as to obtain better results in future decisions.

4.2   Communication

Establish Communication Groups. When each agent chooses other agents to communicate, it only considers the agents within its observable range and ignores the agents outside the observable range, and we call the agent who is selected to communicate as the communicator. The reasons are as follows: first, one of the purposes of communication is to share their partial observations, so that adjacent agents can understand each other's messages more easily; Secondly, the policy made by an agent in the environment has a greater impact on the surrounding agents to choose their policies. Neighboring agents can cooperate better, which makes decision-making more efficient.

The communicator selection module is as Fig. 2.

In Fig. 2. (a), the function of f_i network is to encode observation. Because each agent's observation vector contains its own position information, this step will first extract the position information and generate a weight for each message:

$$h_t^i = (w_t^i, p_t^i) \tag{4}$$

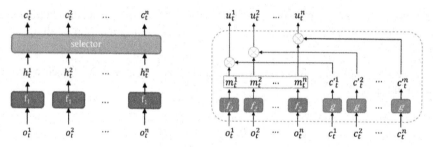

Fig. 2. (a) Communicator selection module (left) and (b). Message aggregation module (right).

In Eq. 4, w_t^i is the weight of agent i and p_t^i represents the position vector of agent i. The weight vector and position vector provide the basis for the selection of communicator in the future, and the weight vector will also be used in the process of message aggregation.

The selector is used to select communicators that needs to communicate for each agent.

Firstly, the distance is calculated according to the location information p_t^i, and the radius r of communication range is set to filter out the agents outside the communication range.

$$w_t^{ij} = \begin{cases} w_t^j, & \text{dist}(p_t^i, p_t^j) \leq r \\ 0, & \text{dist}(p_t^i, p_t^j) > r \end{cases} \tag{5}$$

where w_t^{ij} is the weight of agent j's communication message to agent i, and dist(x_1, x_2) function is used to calculate the Euclidean distance of two vectors x_1, x_2. Thus, for agent i, the agent with a distance greater than r are ignored and only the messages of neighboring agents are concerned.

Secondly, the communicators are further screened according to the weights. Each agent maintains a communication group for its communicators. For each agent, the weight w_t^{ij} of neighboring agents is sorted, and the k agents with non-zero weight and the largest weight are selected to join the communication group S. If the number of agents in the communication range is n_1 and $n_1 < k$, all n_1 agents are selected to join the communication group S.

Finally, a communication receiving weight vector c is generated for each agent.

$$c_t^{ij} = \begin{cases} w_t^{ij}, & j \in S \\ 0, & j \notin S \end{cases} \tag{6}$$

In Eq. 6, c_t^i represents the communicator selection result of agent i at the t time step, the message weight of agents in the communication group is not 0, and the message weight of other agents is 0. In particular, an agent's communication group does not include itself, because its own observations will be directly used as an input in the policy network.

Message Generation and Aggregation. Figure 2. (b) shows the process of message generation and aggregation. Where f_2 is the message coding function, and the agent uses the existing information, that is, the observation o_t^i obtained from the environment, to code the communication message m_t^i. The message coding function of all agents is shared.

G is a normalization function, which standardizes the c vector of each agent, as shown in Eq. 7.

$$c'^{ij} = g(c_t^{ij}) = \frac{c_t^{ij}}{\sum_{k=1}^{n} c_t^{ik}} \tag{7}$$

where c' is the normalized vector.

Let $m_t = (m_t^1, m_t^2, ..., m_t^n)$. Agents need to aggregate one or more received messages into a whole. We consider the importance of the message, that is, the value of the message has an impact on the agent who receives the message. The combination of messages can be modeled as a neural network, which implicitly imposes preferences on messages, but here we use the c vector calculated in the previous step to weight and aggregate messages.

The operation of each agent as the receiver is to aggregate the communication messages in the communication group according to the receiving weight vector, the communication message aggregation process is shown in Eq. 8.

$$u_t^i = m_t \cdot c_t^i = \sum_{j=1}^{n} m_t^j \times c_t^{ij} \tag{8}$$

where u_t^i is a fixed-length vector, which is equal to the length of m_t^i and is not affected by the number of agents in the communication group. Especially, if the communication group S of agent A is empty, its aggregated communication vector u_t^a is 0 vector, that is, the agent has not received any messages.

4.3 Execution and Training

This paper adopts the framework of centralized training and decentralized execution.

Specifically, in the training process, consider a system with n agents, and the Critic network, Actor network, weight generation network and message generation network are parameterized by θ_q, θ_μ, θ_w and θ_c respectively. Considering that all agents are isomorphic, these networks share parameters among agents. For the sake of simplicity, we drop time t in the following notations. In order to speed up the convergence, the global information S is used in the training process.

The records in the experience replay buffer are tuples (S, O, A, R, S', O', C') containing all the experiences of agents, where $O = (o_1, o_2, ..., o_n)$, $A = (a_1, a_2, ..., a_n)$, $R = (r_1, r_2..., r_n)$, $O\prime = (o_1\prime, o_2\prime, ..., o_n\prime)$, and C' is an n × n matrix, which records the communication groups and the importance of the messages. We choose the experience that the agent determine the action independently (that is, there is no communication) and the experience with communication, respectively, to update the action value function Q_μ as Eq. 9.

$$\mathcal{L}(\theta^Q) = E_{s,o,a,r,o}[(Q^\mu(o, a) - y)^2], \ y = r + \gamma Q^{\mu\prime}(o\prime, a\prime)|_{a\prime=\mu\prime(o\prime)} \tag{9}$$

The policy gradient can be written as:

$$\nabla_{\theta^\mu} J(\theta^\mu) = E_{o,a \sim \mathbb{R}}[\nabla_{\theta^\mu}(a|o) \nabla_a Q^\mu(o,a)]_{a=\mu(o)} \quad (10)$$

5 Results

Experiments are performed based on the multi-agent particle environment [18, 19], which is a two-dimensional world with continuous action space and discrete time, and is composed of agents and some landmarks. Each agent has only local observation, can acts independently or cooperate with each other and collect its own local reward or a shared global reward. We tested the model performance in different scales for multi-agent cooperative navigation tasks, and compared it with some baseline models.

5.1 Task

In the multi-agent cooperative navigation task, we set N agents and L landmarks. In this scenario, N agents need to reach L landmarks cooperatively and avoid the collisions among agents. Each agent has a certain communication range, and will be rewarded according to its proximity to the nearest landmark, but will be penalized when it collides with other agents. Ideally, each agent predicts the actions of nearby agents based on its own observation and information received from other agents, and determines his own action to occupy a landmark without colliding with other agents.

5.2 Configure

In a 2×2 two-dimensional continuous space, we set $N = 30$ and $L = 30$ environments to train our model and baselines, in which each agent can observe the relative positions of agents and landmarks within the communication range of 0.5. At each time step, the agent's reward is $-d$, where d is the distance between the agent and its nearest landmark. In addition, we stipulate that if the distance between two agents is less than the diameter of the agents at a certain moment, it is considered that a collision has occurred. If there is a collision, the reward is $-d$-1.

We compare our model with MADDPG, CommNet and SchedNet. MADDPG trains an independent policy network for each agent, and there is no communication between them; CommNet learns the policy and content of continuous communication, and does not distinguish the importance of communication agents and messages; SchedNet selects the communication agents according to the specially generated weight vector, but this selection is indistinguishable for each agent.

5.3 Result and Analysis

Compare with Baselines. We stipulate that each episode contains 80 steps. Figure 3 (a) shows the learning curve of 5000 episodes in the training process, and the mean reward that averaged over all agents and timesteps. It can be seen that our model converges to a higher mean reward than baselines.

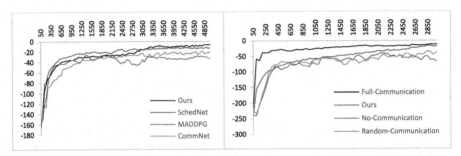

Fig. 3. (a). The learning curve of 5000 episodes in the training process (left) and (b). Mean return under different communication policies during 3000 training episodes (right).

We evaluate our model and baselines by running 30 test environments, and measure the mean reward, the number of collisions and the percentage of occupied landmarks. The results are as Table 1.

Table 1. Cooperative navigation results under different scales.

		ours	maddpg	commnet	schednet
N = 5 L = 5	mean reward	-0.09	-0.22	-0.41	-0.12
	collisions	2	6	4	3
	% occupied landmarks	96.00%	91.30%	88.00%	96.40%
N = 10 L = 10	mean reward	-0.13	-0.38	-0.62	-0.21
	collisions	19	34	57	26
	% occupied landmarks	92.70%	77.00%	64.30%	85.60%
N = 30 L = 30	mean reward	-0.21	-1.25	-0.73	-0.44
	collisions	35	67	91	48
	% occupied landmarks	87.00%	33.70%	27.60%	76.00%

It can be seen in Table 1 that our model performs better than MADDPG without communication because of learning communication policy. Compared with CommNet and SchedNet, considering the different importance of messages of different agents to other agents, the communication efficiency is improved by our model, and the mean reward of our model is higher.

Self-comparison. We changed the communication policy in the model to no communication, random communication and full communication respectively, and compared them with the current policy to prove the efficiency of our communication policy. In the absence of communication, we only use local observation as the input of the action policy network, regardless of communication messages; in random communication, we randomly select agents to join the communication groups for each agent, and use random weights to aggregate messages; in full communication, we assume that the communication range of agents is unlimited, and all agents' messages are received.

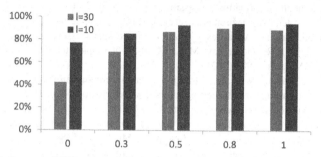

Fig. 4. Influence of different communication ranges on cooperative navigation tasks.

Figure 3. (b) shows the learning curve in the training process under four communication policies. It can be seen that the mean return of our model is higher than that of no communication and random communication policies, and only slightly lower than that of all communication policies, but the training cost is much lower than that of all communication policies.

We also discussed the influence of different communication range on cooperative navigation tasks. As shown in Fig. 4, with the expansion of communication range, the coverage rate of landmarks increases. After reaching a certain value, this growth becomes slow, because the importance of non-adjacent agent information decreases, so the gain brought by the communication of distant agents is not obvious, and even noise will be introduced.

6 Conclusion

We propose a communication model based on Actor-Critic extension for multi-agent environment, in which agents learn a selection module that dynamically decides who to communicate with. According to the experiment, our model can effectively use communication to make cooperative decisions, and it is superior to the existing methods in the multi-agent environment of cooperative navigation.

References

1. Shalev-Shwartz, S., Shammah, S., Shashua, A.: Safe, multi-agent, reinforcement learning for autonomous driving. arXiv preprint arXiv:1610.03295 (2016)
2. Ma, K.C., Ma, Z., Liu, L., et al.: Multi-robot informative and adaptive planning for persistent environmental monitoring. Distributed Autonomous Robotic Systems: The 13th International Symposium. Springer International Publishing, pp. 285–298 (2018)
3. Wang, H., Zhang, C., Song, Y., et al.: Master-followed multiple robots cooperation SLAM adapted to search and rescue environment. Int. J. Control Autom. Syst. **16**(6), 2593–2608 (2018)

4. Kong, X., Xin, B., Liu, F., et al.: Revisiting the master-slave architecture in multi-agent deep reinforcement learning. arXiv preprint arXiv:1712.07305 (2017)

5. Sukhbaatar, S., Fergus, R.: Learning multiagent communication with backpropagation. Advances in neural information processing systems, p. 29 (2016)

6. Foerster, J., Assael, I.A., De Freitas, N., et al.: Learning to communicate with deep multi-agent reinforcement learning. Advances in neural information processing systems, 29 (2016)

7. Niu, Y., Paleja, R.R., Gombolay, M.C.: Multi-agent graph-attention communication and teaming. AAMAS 964–973 (2021)

8. Du, Y., Liu, B., Moens, V., et al.: Learning correlated communication topology in multi-agent reinforcement learning. In: Proceedings of the 20th International Conference on Autonomous Agents and MultiAgent Systems. Pp. 456–464 (2021)

9. Das, A., Gervet, T., Romoff, J., et al.: Tarmac: targeted multi-agent communication. In: International Conference on Machine Learning. PMLR, pp. 1538–1546 (2019)

10. Wang, R., He, X., Yu, R., et al.: Learning efficient multi-agent communication: an information bottleneck approach. In: International Conference on Machine Learning. PMLR, pp. 9908–9918 (2020)

11. Liu, Y., Wang, W., Hu, Y., et al.: Multi-agent game abstraction via graph attention neural network. In: Proceedings of the AAAI Conference on Artificial Intelligence **34**(05), 7211–7218 (2020)

12. Jiang, J., Lu, Z.: Learning attentional communication for multi-agent cooperation. Adv. neural Info. Proc. Sys. 31 (2018)

13. Singh, A., Jain, T., Sukhbaatar, S.: Learning when to communicate at scale in multiagent cooperative and competitive tasks. arXiv preprint arXiv:1812.09755 (2018)

14. Kim, D., Moon, S., Hostallero, D., et al.: Learning to schedule communication in multi-agent reinforcement learning. arXiv preprint arXiv:1902.01554 (2019)

15. Mao, H., Zhang, Z., Xiao, Z., et al.: Learning agent communication under limited bandwidth by message pruning. In: Proceedings of the AAAI Conference on Artificial Intelligence **34**(04), 5142–5149 (2020)

16. Hu, G., Zhu, Y., Zhao, D., et al.: Event-triggered multi-agent reinforcement learning with communication under limited-bandwidth constraint. arXiv preprint arXiv:2010.04978 (2020)

17. Agarwal, A., Kumar, S., Sycara, K.: Learning transferable cooperative behavior in multi-agent teams. arXiv preprint arXiv:1906.01202 (2019)

18. Lowe, R., Wu, Y.I., Tamar, A., et al.: Multi-agent actor-critic for mixed cooperative-competitive environments. Adv. neural Info. Proc. Sys. 30 (2017)

19. Mordatch, I., Abbeel, P.: Emergence of grounded compositional language in multi-agent populations. In: Proceedings of the AAAI conference on artificial intelligence **32**(1) (2018)

20. Zheng, Y., Li, Y., Yang, S., et al.: Global-PBNet: A novel point cloud registration for autonomous driving. IEEE Trans. Intell. Transp. Syst. **23**(11), 22312–22319 (2022)

21. Yang, S., Lu, H., Li, J.: Multifeature fusion-based object detection for intelligent transportation systems. IEEE Trans. Intell. Transp. Syst. **24**(1), 1126–1133 (2022)

22. Teng, Y., Lu, H., Li, Y., et al.: Multidimensional deformable object manipulation based on DN-transporter networks. IEEE Trans. Intell. Transp. Syst. **24**(4), 4532–4540 (2022)

Intelligent Pet House Environment Control System Based on Decoupling Fuzzy Neural Network

Chun-feng Song[(✉)] and Xin-xue Wang

Xi'an University of Science and Technology, Xi'an 710054, Shaanxi, China
18092319878@163.com

Abstract. In recent years, the number of pets in China has increased, and intelligent pet houses have developed rapidly. However, most intelligent pet houses use traditional PID control methods to control environmental parameters. However, the air conditioning process often has strong coupling and time-varying characteristics. The traditional control method is too rough, and there are problems such as high energy consumption and poor anti-interference ability. In this paper, a design scheme of intelligent pet house environment control system based on decoupled fuzzy neural network is proposed. The scheme combines multivariable decoupling model, fuzzy control and neural network control algorithm to solve the difficulty of system control. The experimental data show that the temperature and humidity control overshoot of the algorithm is reduced by 66.9% and 56.6% respectively compared with the conventional PID control, and the control time is shortened by 38.44% and 35.39% respectively compared with the original PID control, which improves the problems existing in the traditional control.

Keywords: Smart Pet House · Multivariable Decoupling Model · Fuzzy Neural Network · Environmental Parameter Control

1 Introduction

In recent years, more and more people like to keep cats, dogs and other pets. Therefore, smart pet houses are becoming more and more popular [1]. For the intelligent pet house environment control system, the control difficulty lies in the fact that there are many factors affecting the temperature and humidity parameters, and there are characteristics such as nonlinearity, time-varying, large delay and strong coupling [2], which are difficult to accurately and effectively control. Aiming at this difficulty, this paper proposes a design scheme of intelligent pet housekeeper system based on multivariable decoupling fuzzy neural network control algorithm.

In this paper, based on the law of conservation of energy and mass, the mathematical model of temperature and humidity control of intelligent pet house is established. Considering the coupling effect between temperature and humidity control loops, the mathematical model after decoupling is obtained by using multivariable decoupling method. The fuzzy neural network controller is designed for the obtained mathematical

© The Author(s), under exclusive license to Springer Nature Singapore Pte Ltd. 2024
H. Lu and J. Cai (Eds.): ISAIR 2023, CCIS 1998, pp. 443–453, 2024.
https://doi.org/10.1007/978-981-99-9109-9_42

model, and the system control model is finally obtained. Through simulation experiments, the advantages and disadvantages of the strategy compared with the traditional control method are analyzed.

2 System Analysis and Modeling

2.1 Overall Overview of the System

The background environment of this paper is a family of cats. Now a smart pet house with a length, width and height of 1.2 m is designed. The system has several sensors to collect environmental data, and controls environmental temperature and humidity through air conditioning air supply volume and air conditioning chilled water flow. The data of system environment control parameters are given in Table 1 according to Reference [3].

Table 1. System parameters in stable operation.

Parameter	Numerical Value
Ambient Temperature T_o	30 °C
Ambient Humidity H_i	18.8 g/kg
Preset Temperature T_i	26 °C
Preset Humidity H_c	9.8 g/kg

According to the working principle of temperature and humidity regulation of the whole intelligent pet housekeeper system, this paper chooses air supply volume of air conditioning and chilled water flow of air conditioning as control variables, and indoor temperature and indoor humidity as controlled variables. The system transfer function matrix can be expressed as:

$$G(s) = \begin{bmatrix} g_{11} & g_{12} \\ g_{21} & g_{22} \end{bmatrix} \tag{1}$$

In the above formula: g_{ij} ($i = 1,2; j = 1,2$) represents the transfer function between the controlled quantity: indoor temperature ($i = 1$), indoor humidity($i = 2$) and the control quantity: air supply volume ($j = 1$), chilled water flow ($j = 1$).

2.2 Mathematical Model Analysis of the System

In this paper, the heat conduction of windows and walls, the heat dissipation of indoor pet activities and the cooling capacity provided by the central air conditioning system are considered [4]. The heat balance equation of the room can be expressed as follows:

$$MC\frac{dT_i}{dt} = Q_i + A(T_o - T_i) + mC(T_c - T_i) \tag{2}$$

M is the indoor air quality (kg), C is the air specific heat capacity [$J/(kg \cdot {}^\circ C)$, T_i is the indoor temperature (${}^\circ C$), Q_i is the heat gain in the room (W), A is the wall thermal conductivity ($W/{}^\circ C$); T_o is the outdoor temperature; m is the inlet air volume kg/s, and T_c is the supply air temperature (${}^\circ C$).

Considering the moisture content of indoor pet activities, outdoor air moisture content and air conditioning supply air moisture content [5], the moisture balance equation of the room can be expressed as follows:

$$M\frac{dH_i}{dt} = A_i + m(H_c - H_i) \tag{3}$$

In the formula: H_c is the moisture content of the air supply (g/kg); H_i is indoor moisture content (g/kg); A_i is the amount of pet moisture [$g/(kg \cdot s)$].

3 Decoupling Fuzzy Neural Control Strategy Design

3.1 Decoupling Design Method of Multivariable System

The traditional temperature and humidity control process generally regards temperature and humidity as two unrelated loops to control. However, in the actual operation process, there is a coupling relationship between the two control loops. Taking the summer system control situation as an example, when the temperature in the system is high, the system usually increases the opening of the chilled water valve, so that the air supply temperature of the air conditioner is reduced to reduce the ambient temperature in the system. However, the increase of the opening of the chilled water valve will increase the air humidity in the system, which will easily make the humidity in the system exceed the comfort range. The existence of this coupling effect often deteriorates the control performance of the individually tuned control loop under actual operating conditions. Therefore, this paper first deals with the coupling between variables.

The decoupling system structure is shown in Fig. 1. Among them: the input signal [u_1, u_2] = [temperature setting value, humidity setting value]; output signal [y_1, y_2] = [indoor temperature, indoor humidity]; C_1 and C_2 are temperature and humidity loop controllers, respectively. The decoupler $W_F = [w_{ij}]$ ($i = 1,2; j = 1,2$).

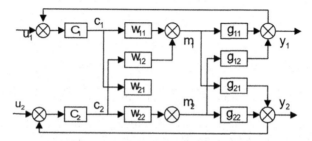

Fig. 1. Decoupling system structure diagram [6].

In this paper, the output of controllers C_1. nd C_2 is assumed to be c_1 and c_2, then the system output can be expressed as:

$$\begin{cases} y_1 = (g_{11}w_{11} + g_{12}w_{21})c_1 + (g_{11}w_{12} + g_{12}w_{22})c_2 \\ y_2 = (g_{21}w_{11} + g_{22}w_{21})c_1 + (g_{21}w_{12} + g_{22}w_{22})c_2 \end{cases} \tag{4}$$

In order to achieve decoupling, formula (4) must satisfy the formula:

$$w_{11} = w_{22} = 1 \tag{5}$$

and

$$\begin{cases} g_{11}w_{12} + g_{12}w_{22} = 0 \\ g_{21}w_{11} + g_{22}w_{21} = 0 \end{cases} \tag{6}$$

Then the initial static decoupling matrix of the air conditioning system can be obtained:

$$W_F = \begin{bmatrix} 1 & \frac{-g_{12}}{g_{11}} \\ \frac{-g_{21}}{g_{22}} & 1 \end{bmatrix} = \begin{bmatrix} 1 & \lambda_1 \\ \lambda_2 & 1 \end{bmatrix} \tag{7}$$

Since the decoupling matrix is derived from the steady-state gain, the coupling can be completely eliminated in the static state, but the temperature and humidity control exists [7]. Therefore, in order to minimize the impact of coupling, this paper uses fuzzy control technology to adjust the decoupling matrix coefficients online.

From the above figure:

$$\begin{bmatrix} m_1 \\ m_2 \end{bmatrix} = \begin{bmatrix} w_{11} & w_{12} \\ w_{21} & w_{22} \end{bmatrix} \begin{bmatrix} c_1 \\ c_2 \end{bmatrix} \tag{8}$$

In the formula, c and m represent the output of the controller and the decoupled output of the system respectively.

From Fig. 1, the output increments at n − 1 and n are:

$$m_1(n - 1) = w_{11}c_1(n - 2) + w_{12}c_2(n - 2) \tag{9}$$

$$m_1(n) = w_{11}c_1(n - 1) + w_{12}c_2(n - 1) \tag{10}$$

Then we can get

$$w_{12} = \frac{m_1(n - 1)c_1(n - 1) - m_1(n)c_1(n - 2)}{c_2(n - 2)c_1(n - 1) - c_2(n - 1)c_1(n - 2)} \tag{11}$$

It can be known from the purpose of decoupling that to eliminate the influence of loop 2 on 1, $w_{12} = 0$ must be made. The unit matrix synthesis method is:

$$\begin{bmatrix} g_{11} & g_{12} \\ g_{21} & g_{22} \end{bmatrix} \begin{bmatrix} 1 & \lambda_1 \\ \lambda_2 & 1 \end{bmatrix} = \begin{bmatrix} 1 & 0 \\ 0 & 1 \end{bmatrix} \tag{12}$$

Then there can be

$$g_{11} \cdot \lambda_1 + g_{12} = w_{12} \tag{13}$$

$$g_{22} \cdot \lambda_2 + g_{21} = w_{21} \tag{14}$$

From the above reasoning, it can be concluded that λ_1 and λ_2 are negative. When w_{12} deviates from 0 and changes in the direction greater than zero, λ_1 should change in a negative direction to make w_{12} return to 0. When w_{12} changes in the negative direction, λ_1 should be greater than the direction of zero. Therefore, a table of correction rules for λ_1 as shown in Table 2 can be obtained. λ_2 is the same logic, not repeated here.

Table 2. .

w_{12}	NB	NS	O	PS	PB
λ_1	PB	PS	O	NS	NB

3.2 The Design Method of Fuzzy Controller

According to the decoupled system obtained above, a fuzzy controller is designed. Firstly, the variables are determined. The fuzzy controller input of loop 1 is mainly the deviation e_1 and its change rate ec_1 between the measured value of the system ambient temperature and the given temperature, and the output is the system air supply volume m. Similarly, the system ambient humidity constitutes the decoupled control loop 2, and the humidity content deviation, change rate and its control quantity are $e_1 \setminus ec_1$ and m_w respectively.

The universe of discourse of fuzzy control must be finite and discrete, and the elements should not be too many. Usually, the universe of discourse of error and error change is $[-6,6]$ [8]. The fuzzy subset is divided into seven grades, namely { PB, PM, PS, ZE, NS, NM, NB} = { 'positive big', 'positive middle', 'positive small', 'zero', 'negative small', 'negative middle', 'negative big'}. The membership function takes the Gaussian function, that is,

$$f(x_i) = \frac{-(x_i - a_{ik})^2}{b_{ik}^2} \tag{15}$$

where x_i is the input variable, i is the serial number of the number of inputs, a_{ik} and b_{ik} are the center position and width of the function, respectively. The initial membership function of the system is shown in the Fig. 2.

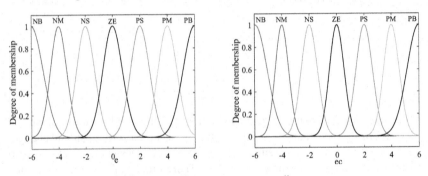

Fig. 2. Decoupling system structure diagram.

According to the above structure, each fuzzy subsystem is a two-input single-output system. According to the grid method of fuzzy subsets, the fuzzy rules are a combination of fuzzy subsets. Then each subsystem has 49 rules, and the fuzzy control rules are shown in Table 3.

Table 3. Fuzzy control rules

E	EC						
	NB	NM	NS	ZE	PS	PM	PB
NB	PB	PB	PM	PM	PS	ZE	ZE
NM	PB	PB	PM	PS	PS	ZE	NS
NS	PM	PM	PM	PS	ZE	NS	NS
ZS	PM	PM	PS	ZE	NS	NM	NM
PS	PS	PS	ZE	NS	NS	NM	NM
PM	PS	ZE	NS	NM	NM	NM	NB
PB	ZE	ZE	NM	NM	NM	NB	NB

After the fuzzy control rules are established, the fuzzy output can be obtained. The approximate reasoning synthesis rules proposed by L.A.Zaden can obtain the fuzzy output, and the defuzzification form is obtained by using the weighted average method:

$$u^* = \frac{\sum_{i=1}^{m}\left[\mu_{A_1^i}(x_1) \wedge \mu_{A_2^i}(x_2) \wedge \ldots \wedge \mu_{A_n^i}(x_n)\right]w^i}{\sum_{i=1}^{m}\left[\mu_{A_1^i}(x_1) \wedge \mu_{A_2^i}(x_2) \wedge \ldots \wedge \mu_{A_n^i}(x_n)\right]} \tag{16}$$

where m is the number of fuzzy rules, $m = 49$, n is the number of inputs of the controller, $n = 2$, w is the center value of the membership function of the output fuzzy quantity, and μ is the membership function of each input fuzzy set.

3.3 Learning Algorithm of Neural Network

Based on the fuzzy control rules and the form of defuzzification established above, this paper combines the fuzzy controller with the neural network learning algorithm to obtain the following fuzzy neural network controller as shown in the Fig. 3.

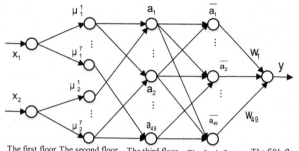

The first floor The second floor The third floor The forth floor The fifth floor

Fig. 3. Decoupling system structure diagram.

The center value of each rule conclusion in the fuzzy controller is used as the weight of the neural network, which can be adjusted online. The layers of the neural network correspond to each part of the fuzzy control rules. The initial values of the center values of the membership functions of each fuzzy variable are $\{-6, -4, -2, 0, 2, 4, 6\}$, and the quantization factors $k_1 = \frac{x_m}{x}$, $k_2 = \frac{y_n}{y}$. $[-x, x]$ and $[-y, y]$ are the actual ranges of error and error change, respectively.

The node function of each layer is given below.

The first floor:

$$\text{Input} \quad f_i^{(1)} = x_j^0 = x_i \tag{17}$$

$$\text{Output} \quad x_j^{(1)} = g_j^{(1)} = f_i^{(1)} i = 1, 2 \tag{18}$$

The second floor:

$$\text{Input} \quad f_{ij}^{(2)} = \frac{-\left(x_j^{(1)} - a_{ij}\right)^2}{b_{ij}^2} \tag{19}$$

$$\text{Output} \quad x_{ij}^{(2)} = \mu_i^j = g_{ij}^2 = e^{f_{ij}^{(2)}} \, i = 1, 2 j = 1 \ldots 7 \tag{20}$$

The third floor:

$$\text{Input} \quad f_j^{(3)} = x_{1i_1}^{(2)} x_{2i_2}^{(2)} \cdots x_{ni_n}^{(2)} = \mu_1^{i_1} \mu_2^{i_2} \cdots \mu_n^{i_n} \tag{21}$$

$$\text{Output} \quad x_j^{(3)} = g_j^{(3)} = f_j^3 = a_j, n = 2, m = \prod_{i=1}^n m_i j = 1, 2 \cdots m \tag{22}$$

The forth floor:

$$\text{Input } f_j^{(4)} = x_j^3 / \sum_{i=1}^{m} x_i^{(3)} = a_j / \sum_{i=1}^{m} a_i \qquad (23)$$

$$\text{Output } x_j^{(4)} = g_j^{(4)} = f_j^{(4)} = \overline{a_j} \qquad (24)$$

The fifth floor:

$$\text{Input } f_j^{(5)} = \sum_{j=1}^{m} w_j x_j^{(4)} = \sum_{j=1}^{m} w_j \overline{a_j} \qquad (25)$$

$$\text{Output } x_i^{(5)} = y_i = f_i^{(5)} \qquad (26)$$

Among them, x_i represents the input of the network, a_i and b_i represent the center and width value parameters of the Gaussian membership function, w_j represents the connection weight of the network, and y_i represents the output value of the network, that is, the actual control quantity.

The learning algorithm of parameter adjustment is:

$$w_j(k+1) = w_j(k) - \beta \frac{\partial E}{\partial w_j} \quad i = 1 \quad j = 1, 2 \cdots 49 \qquad (27)$$

$$a_{ij}(k+1) = a_{ij}(k) - \beta \frac{\partial E}{\partial a_{ij}} \quad i = 1 \quad j = 1, 2 \cdots 7 \qquad (28)$$

$$b_{ij}(k+1) = b_{ij}(k) - \beta \frac{\partial E}{\partial b_{ij}} \quad i = 1 \quad j = 1, 2 \cdots 7 \qquad (29)$$

a_{ij} and b_{ij} are the center value and width of membership function, respectively.
β is the learning rate.

4 Simulation and Analysis

4.1 Comparative Analysis of Simulation

Based on the system data modeling, the step response simulation diagram:Fig. 4 and step response simulation data table of the system: Table 4 are obtained.

It can be seen from Fig. 4 and Table 4 that when the traditional PID control algorithm controls the temperature, the overshoot of the step function is less than 1% after 382.6 s, and the overshoot of the step function is less than 0.1% after 608.9 s. The maximum overshoot of the system regulation is 22.41%; when controlling the humidity, the overshoot of the system is less than 1% after 323.4 s, and the overshoot is less than 0.1% after 548.7 s. The maximum overshoot of the system is 19.96%.

The decoupling fuzzy neural network control algorithm has a maximum overshoot of 7.41% when controlling the temperature. After the initial state is adjusted by 230.9S, the system output overshoot difference is less than 1%, and the output overshoot is less than 0.1% after 374.8S. The maximum overshoot is 8.66% when the humidity is controlled.

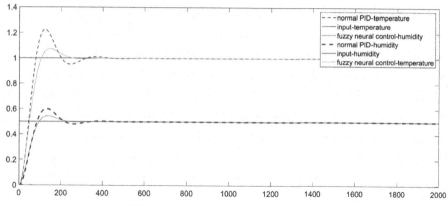

Fig. 4. Simulation comparison diagram.

Table 4. Simulation performance comparison table

Algorithm		Control-time (s)(<1%)	Control-time (s)(<0.1%)	Maximum overshoot (%)
Tradition PID	Temperature	382.6	608.9	22.41
	Humidity	323.4	548.7	19.96
Fuzzy neural control	Temperature	230.9	374.8	7.41
	Humidity	265.4	355.1	8.66

After 265.4S adjustment from the initial state, the system output overshoot difference is less than 1%, and the output overshoot is less than 0.1% after 355.1S.

It can be seen that the overshoot of the system under the traditional PID control is too large and the regulation time is too long, whether it is temperature or humidity. And the decoupling fuzzy neural network control algorithm can maintain a fast response speed and a small overshoot in the step response of the system temperature and humidity control.

4.2 Anti-interference Performance Analysis

Because the environment is susceptible to external and human factors, in the simulation model, 20% interference signal is continuously added in 10 s between 1000 s and 1010 s. The simulation of the two intelligent control algorithms after adding interference is shown in Fig. 5. And the data comparison table is shown in Table 5.

It can be seen that the stability of the decoupled fuzzy neural network control algorithm in the face of system interference is much better than that of the traditional PID control.

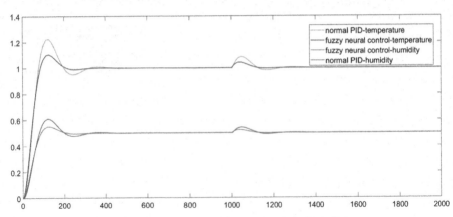

Fig. 5. Anti-interference performance comparison diagram.

Table 5. Anti-interference performance comparison table.

Algorithm		Control-time (<1%) (s)	Control-time(<0.1%) (s)	Maximum overshoot (%)
Tradition PID	Temperature	281.2	420.5	8.52
	Humidity	301.7	412.9	8.22
Fuzzy neural control	Temperature	113.4	228.9	4.26
	Humidity	117.7	237.2	4.61

5 Conclusion

The multivariable decoupling fuzzy neural network control strategy proposed in this paper is based on a mathematical model with clear physical meaning, decoupling the mutual influence of temperature and humidity, and designing a fuzzy neural network controller. The simulation results show that compared with the traditional PID control strategy, the control strategy has obvious advantages in control time, control accuracy and anti-interference ability, and has higher energy saving rate while maintaining indoor air quality. It solves the control difficulties in the pet intelligent housekeeper system well and has the promotion value.

Fund Project. Science and technology innovation 2030- 'new generation of artificial intelligence' major project (2022ZD0119005).

References

1. Wang, B.: Development status and trend analysis of China 's pet market. Guizhou Animal Husbandry and Veterinary **47**(02), 6–8 (2023)

2. Liu, M., Zhang, L., Gou, J., et al.: Design and simulation analysis of a temperature and humidity control box. Tropical Agricultural Engineering **45**(06), 5–8 (2021)
3. Li, J., Tan, Y.: Foster space design based on cat behavior needs. Guangdong Animal Husbandry and Veterinary Science and Technology **47**(03), 122–125 (2022). https://doi.org/10.19978/j.cnki.xmsy.2022.03.24
4. Feng, L.: Research on decoupling internal model control strategy of air conditioning in railway passenger station. Railway Construction Technology (12), 20–25 (2022)
5. Li, F., Zhang, G., Liang, H.: Design of temperature and humidity control system based on neural network PID. Computer and Digital Engineering **49**(06), 1097–1101 + 1106 (2021)
6. Ren, L., Song, C., Han, J., et al.: Bidirectional DC/DC converter based on fuzzy neural network PID control. Journal of Beihua University (Natural Science Edition) **24**(05), 671–677 (2023)
7. Luo, Z., Wang, X., Xu, G., et al.: Classification of precipitation particles based on convolutional neural network combined with SVM. Radar Science and Technology **21**(04), 391–399 + 404 (2023)
8. Li, H.: Research on temperature and humidity control of plant factory based on fuzzy neural network. Tianjin Polytechnic Normal University (2019). Wang Bing, F.: Development status and trend analysis of China's pet market. Guizhou Animal Husbandry and Veterinary **47**(02), 6–8 (2023)

Research on Automatic Medicine Box System for Community with Extreme Learning Machine Based on Sparrow Search Algorithm Improvement

Chunfeng Song and Xin Zhang[✉]

School of Electrical and Control Engineering, Xi'an University of Science and Technology, Xi'an 710699, China
15661537131@163.com

Abstract. Intelligent healthcare is an important industry and the automatic pill box project combines fingerprint recognition and embedded control. This project mainly researches the fingerprint recognition algorithm of extreme learning machine improved based on sparrow search algorithm and embedded technology to realize the automatic control of medicine box. STM32 is used as the main controller, and the state is obtained through the fingerprint module, and then the fingerprint image processing technology determines the feature information, which is matched by the fingerprint recognition algorithm. The accuracy of fingerprint image recognition judgment is improved. The embedded control part receives the processing signals through the 32-bit microcontroller and drives the servo to realize the opening and closing of the medicine box. The infrared temperature measurement module carries out non-contact body temperature detection and voice broadcasting to realize unmanned self-service medicine collection. After debugging and testing, the expected goals are successfully realized. This research has reference significance in the field of fingerprint image processing technology and embedded control technology.

Keywords: SSA-ELM · STM32 · Embedded single chip microcomputer · Fingerprint identification · Healthcare

1 Introduction

In the era of Industry 4.0 and the rapid development of science and technology, the new Crown Pneumonia epidemic has had a major impact on the world. The Chinese government has adopted a number of response strategies, including strengthening medical prevention and control. However, the outbreak also exposed the inadequacy of the traditional healthcare service model and strained healthcare resources, putting tremendous pressure on healthcare organizations. In the post-epidemic era, utilizing IoT and automation technologies to enhance medical and healthcare services is an important means of coping with epidemics and other types of infectious diseases.

And the use of fingerprint image recognition technology to realize unmanned automatic medicine collection has become one of the means to solve this problem. And fingerprint image recognition faces the traditional algorithm recognition accuracy is not high, can not be effectively used in the future of fingerprint recognition requirements are higher in the future. Based on the above problems, this paper proposes an extreme learning machine algorithm based on the improvement of sparrow algorithm and deployed in the unmanned medicine box end by embedded technology. The research of this project is of great significance for the construction of community service healthcare and the service of people's daily life through the convergence of Internet of Things (IoT).

In summary, this paper proposes an improved Extreme Learning Machine algorithm based on Sparrow's algorithm that improves the fingerprint image recognition rate by 0.1 on a self-constructed dataset and deploys it at the automated medicine box end. In this paper, Sect. 2 describes the traditional ELM algorithm and the sparrow search algorithm and the improvement of them, Subsect. 3 describes the hardware design of the automated pillbox system, and Subsect. 4 describes the embedded program control method of the automated pillbox. In Subsect. 5 simulation tests are done on the improved algorithm to verify the experimental results with improved accuracy. Subsection 6 makes a conclusion of the whole paper.

2 Improving Extreme Learning Machine Based on Sparrow Search Algorithm

2.1 Traditional Extreme Learning Machine Algorithm

Extreme Learning Machine (ELM) is a fast learning algorithm for solving single hidden layer neural networks with good generalization performance as well as extremely fast learning capability.

Given N arbitrarily different training samples $\{(x_i, y_i)\}_{i=1}^{N}$, where $x_i = [x_{i1}, x_{i2}, \cdots x_{i3}]^T \in R^n$ is the input vector and $t_i = [t_{i1}, t_{i2}, \cdots t_{i3}]^T \in R^m$ is the corresponding desired output vector. The standard ELM network with n input neurons, L hidden layer neurons and m output neurons and activation function g(x) is represented by the following mathematical model.

$$H\beta = T \tag{1}$$

included among these,

$$H = \left[h(x_i)^T, \cdots h(x_N)^T \right]^T$$
$$= \begin{bmatrix} g(w_1 \cdot x_1 + b_1) & \cdots & g(w_L \cdot x_1 + b_L) \\ \vdots & \ddots & \vdots \\ g(w_1 \cdot x_N + b_1) & \cdots & g(w_L \cdot x_N + b_L) \end{bmatrix}_{N \times L} \tag{2}$$

In ELM, H is also known as the stochastic feature mapping matrix, $w_i =$ $[x_{i1}, x_{i2}, \cdots x_{i3}]^T$ denotes the input weights connecting the ith hidden layer neuron to the neuron in the input layer, b_i denotes the bias of the ith hidden layer neuron, $\beta_i = [\beta_1, \beta_2, \cdots \beta_L]^T$ denotes the weight matrix between the output layer and the hidden layer, $T = [t_1, t_2, \cdots t_N]^T$ denotes the expected output matrix of the training samples.After the parameters of the hidden layer neurons (w_i, b_i) are randomly generated according to the probability of any continuous sampling distribution and given the training samples, the hidden layer output moments Chen H are practically known and remain unchanged. In this way, Eq. (1) is transformed into solving the least-paradigm least-squares solution of the linear system $H\beta = T \hat{\beta}$.

$$\hat{\beta} = H^+T \tag{3}$$

where, H^+ denotes the Moore-Penrose generalized inverse of the hidden layer output matrix H. where, H^+ denotes the Moore-Penrose generalized inverse of the hidden layer output matrix H.

2.2 Sparrow Algorithm Improved Extreme Learning Machine Algorithm for Fingerprint Recognition

From the previous analysis, it can be seen that ELM can randomly generate w and b before training, which can be calculated by simply determining the number of neurons in the hidden layer and the activation functions (infinitely differentiable) of the hidden layer and neurons.

So it can be seen that the initial weights and thresholds of ELM are generated randomly. The initial weights and thresholds generated each time have fullness. In this paper, the initial weights and thresholds are optimized using the sparrow search algorithm. The fitness function is designed as the MSE of the error of the training set:

$$\text{fitness} = \text{argmin}\left(\text{MSE}_{pridect}\right) \tag{4}$$

The fitness function is selected as the MSE error after training. The smaller MSE error indicates that the predicted data overlap with the original data. The final optimized output is the best initial weights and thresholds. The network trained with the best initial weights threshold is then utilized to test the fingerprint image test dataset (Figs. 1 and 2).

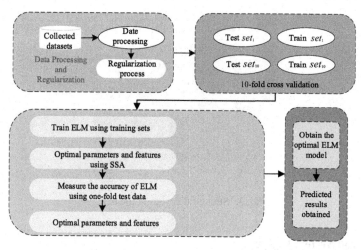

Fig. 1. The Flowchart of the SSA-ELM.

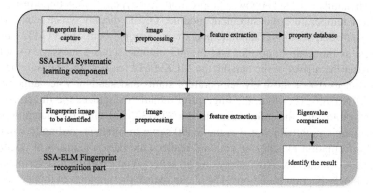

Fig. 2. Fingerprint Recognition Implementation for SSA-ELM.

3   System Hardware Design

3.1   Box Structure Design

The medicine box is made of acrylic boards spliced together and reserved a certain area, the use of servo connected to the loose-leaf driven box-type revolving door, the battery is placed in the right side of the medicine box on the reserved position. Infrared temperature measurement part, key and OLED display operation part integrated in the left end of the reserved area, the servo through the loose-leaf to drive the two sides of the revolving door rotation, the overall level of separation, the box structure diagram shown in Fig. 3.

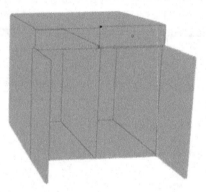

Fig. 3. Structural design of the box.

3.2 Overall System Design

Figure 4 shows the block diagram of the hardware design of the automatic pill box system, which mainly consists of power supply module, keypad, AS608 fingerprint module, MLX90614 temperature measurement module, OLED display, voice announcement, STM32 controller, servo, 4G module, and so on. Among them, the STM32 microcontroller acts as the main controller and the 4G module sends a message to notify the pickup. After the arrival of the person, the MLX90614 temperature measurement module is driven to detect the body temperature status and sends a voice announcement through SYN6288. After that, the fingerprint module recognizes the fingerprint of the person, and transmits the information to the STM32 controller for matching through serial communication, which drives the SG90 servo to rotate according to whether the acquired information matches or not, and realizes the basic operation of opening and closing the medicine box. After analyzing all aspects and experimental verification, the hardware block diagram based on STM32 can realize the function of this project.

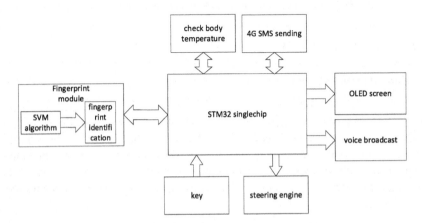

Fig. 4. Block diagram of STM32 based automatic pill box system.

In this project, the main control unit adopts STM32 series microcontroller, in which STM32 as the main controller is responsible for driving and communicating with each hardware module and controlling the servo, recognizing and controlling the information of each module, and sending the step data to the STM32 controller through the serial port. The serial port of STM32 microcontroller receives the step information from the hardware, and sends the PWM pulse signals to the corresponding position to control the servo rotation. to control the rotation of the servo.

3.3 Main Controller

The STM32F103C8T6 from ST is used as the main controller chip for this project design. Its hardware platform is a 32-bit microcontroller based on ARM Cortex-M3 core. Its own design has high computing power and processing speed, which can meet the requirements of most application scenarios. In addition, the chip has 64K bytes of FLASH and 20K bytes of SRAM storage space, and supports floating point FPU.

4 System Programming

4.1 General Design Flow of the Program

The general flow of the program design of the whole automatic medicine box system is that the system is powered on and notified to the personnel by sending SMS through the 4G module, several basic function options are shown on the OLED display, the fingerprint matching option is selected, the STM32 drives the AS608 and makes fingerprint identification judgment and stores the fingerprint information in the constructed fingerprint saving array, and then the feature is performed by the fingerprint identification algorithm based on the SVM point matching. Finally, the steps are transmitted to STM32 through UART, and STM32 outputs pulses to control the precise rotation of the servo through the timer PWM mode. The overall design flowchart of the pillbox software system is shown in Fig. 5. The overall design flowchart of the pillbox software system is shown in Fig. 5.

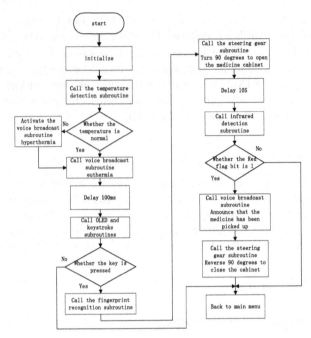

Fig. 5. Main flow chart of the pillbox system.

5   Test of Fingerprint Recognition Algorithm Based on Sparrow Algorithm Improved Extreme Learning Machine Improvement

Sparrow Algorithm Improved Extreme Learning Machine Simulation Test is implemented through MATLAB software to classify a self-constructed dataset for prediction and get the output in the form of images. A randomized method is used to generate the training and test sets, where the training set contains 1,900 fingerprint image samples and the test set contains 100 fingerprint image samples. In order to reduce the impact of large differences in variables on the model performance, the data is normalized before building the model (Figs. 6 and 7).

After simulation test, the accuracy of fingerprint image classification prediction of Extreme Learning Machine improved based on Sparrow Algorithm reaches more than 92%, which is an average improvement of 0.1 meets the expected standard than the traditional ELM algorithm. The algorithm can be used to realize the classification and matching of the features of fingerprints to effectively solve the problems of noise, deformation and displacement in fingerprint identification. The matching accuracy of fingerprint image is improved.

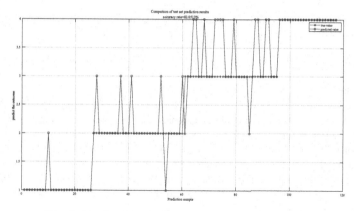

Fig. 6. Predicted results for the traditional ELM test set.

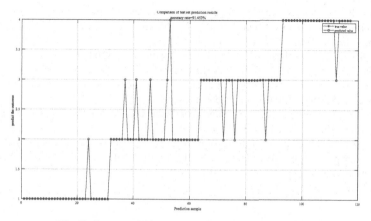

Fig. 7. Improved SSA-ELM test set prediction results.

6   Conclusion

In this paper, an automatic medicine box for the community of extreme learning machine based on the improvement of sparrow algorithm is proposed and the box structure of the medicine box is designed. Hardware design and program design were carried out. The simulation of the adopted algorithm was carried out based on MATLAB software, and the results show that SSA-ELM improves 0.1 compared with traditional ELM, which improves the accuracy of the recognition of fingerprint images. It has been tested to realize unmanned drug access and has the advantages of reasonable structure and simple control. It is expected to solve the problem of providing emergency medicines to residents in emergency situations without waiting for the pharmacy to open. It can also reduce manual operation when infectious diseases or epidemics occur, improve personnel safety and the efficiency of drug distribution to meet the needs of residents.

Acknowledgments. This work is supported by Science and Technology Innovation 2023- "New Generation of Artificial Intelligence" Major project (2022ZD0119000).

References

1. Liu, B., Peng, M.: Reflections on China's national public health emergency management system in the post epidemic era. China Public Health **36**(12), 1697–1699 (2020)
2. Mohammad, S., Bhowmick, T., Siddique, M.S.U.Z., et al.: Research and development of a artificial intelligence based smart medicine box. In: 2022 6th International Conference on Computing Methodologies and Communication (ICCMC), pp. 407–412. IEEE (2022)
3. Divakar, D., Singh, S.K., Dkhar, F.: Smart medicine box using IoT with alarm and SMS notification. Telecom Bus. Rev. **15**(1), 30 (2022)
4. Author, F.: Contribution title. In: 9th International Proceedings on Proceedings, pp. 1–2. Publisher, Location (2010)
5. Hammi, B., Zeadally, S., Khatoun, R., et al.: Survey on smart homes: vulnerabilities, risks, and countermeasures. Comput. Secur. **117**, 102677 (2022)
6. Wang, J., Lu, S., Wang, S.H., et al.: A review on extreme learning machine. Multimed. Tools Appl. **81**(29), 41611–41660 (2022). https://doi.org/10.1007/s11042-021-11007-7
7. Oleiwi, B.K., Abood, L.H., Farhan, A.K.: Integrated different fingerprint identification and classification systems based deep learning. In: 2022 International Conference on Computer Science and Software Engineering (CSASE), pp. 188–193. IEEE (2022)
8. Zheng, Q., Zhu, J., Tang, H., et al.: Generalized label enhancement with sample correlations. IEEE Trans. Knowl. Data Eng. **35**(1), 482–495 (2021)
9. Fu, Y., Zhang, M., Xu, X., et al.: Partial feature selection and alignment for multi-source domain adaptation. In: Proceedings of the IEEE/CVF Conference on Computer Vision and Pattern Recognition, pp. 16654–16663 (2021)

Multimodal Depression Detection Network Based on Emotional and Behavioral Features in Conversations

Peng Wang[1], Biao Yang[1], Suhong Wang[2], Xianlin Zhu[2], Rongrong Ni[1], and Changchun Yang[1(✉)] (iD)

[1] School of Microelectronics and Control Engineering, Changzhou University, Changzhou 213000, China
00000312@cczu.edu.cn

[2] Department of Clinical Psychology, The Third Affiliated Hospital of Soochow University, Changzhou 213000, China

Abstract. Early detection of depression has always been a challenge. Currently, research on automatic depression detection mainly focuses on using low-level features such as audio, text, or video from interview dialogue as input data, ignoring some high-level features contained in the dialogue. We proposes a multimodal depression detection method for extracting emotional and behavioral features from dialogue and detecting early depression. Specifically, we design an emotional feature extraction module and a behavioral feature extraction module, which input the extracted emotional and behavioral features as high-level features into the depression detection network. In this process, a weighted attention fusion module is used to guide the learning of text and audio modalities and predict the final result. Experimental results on the public dataset DAIC-WOZ show that the extracted emotional and behavioral features effectively complement the high-level semantics missing in the network. Our proposed method improves the F1-score by 6% compared to traditional approaches. The experimental data also indicate the importance of the model's detection results in early depression detection. This technology has certain application value in professional fields such as caregiving, emotional interaction, psychological diagnosis, and treatment.

Keywords: Deep learning · High-level features · Depression detection · Multimodal learning · Interview dialogue · Feature fusion

---

P. Wang and B. Yang—contribute equally to this work.

H. Lu and J. Cai (Eds.): ISAIR 2023, CCIS 1998, pp. 463–474, 2024.
https://doi.org/10.1007/978-981-99-9109-9_44

Table 1. Keyword-containing interrogative sentences

Question	Key words
What advice would you give yourself ten of twenty years ago?	advice, yourself
Is there anything you regret?	anything, regret
When was the last time you argued with someone and what was it about	argued, someone
How are you at controlling your temper?	controlling, temper
What's your dream job?	dream, job
How easy is it for you to get a good night's sleep?	easy, sleep
How are you been feeling lately?	feeling, lately
How would your best friend describe you?	friend, describe
When was the last time you felt really happy?	last, happy
What are you most proud of in your life?	proud, life

1   Introduction

Depression is one of the common mental disorders and has become a significant factor affecting human mental health [1]. Clinical practitioners rely on interview conversations to observe the external behaviors of subjects and determine the presence of depressive symptoms [2]. However, in real-world situations, individuals with genuine depression often struggle to capture the attention of professional mental health practitioners. Several underlying factors contribute to this, such as limited medical resources, high costs, and individual characteristics of the subjects [3]. With the rapid advancement of deep neural networks [4,5] and multimodal learning [6], researchers have shown considerable interest in computer technology for automated depression detection. Traditional depression detection methods suffer from various issues, including lengthy detection times, complex procedures, and the involvement of specialized mental health professionals. Conversely, automated depression detection emphasizes speed, convenience, and the absence of supervision. Depending on the data source, automated depression detection can be categorized into two approaches: content-based on social media and behavior-based on external indicators. Among them, the behavior-based approach has garnered more attention from scholars due to its simplicity in acquiring multimodal data and the greater diversity of the data.

Several behavior-based automated depression detection methods have been developed. Existing methods primarily focus on neural network models and multimodal fusion techniques, yielding some achievements [7,8]. However, these methods often rely on low-level features such as audio, text, or video as model input data, overlooking the higher-level features present in interview conversations. Influenced by the field of affective computing [9,10], two crucial feature attributes, namely emotional information and behavioral information, are recognized within interview conversations. Figure 1 showcases a dialogue instance from the Distress Analysis Interview Corpus-Wizard of Oz (DAIC-WOZ) dataset [11], where an agent simulates a psychologist conducting an interview with a subject. The audio contains the subject's emotional features, while the transcribed text includes the subject's behavioral features, with the red font representing behavioral tendencies corresponding to the green font in the agent's questions. These features can serve as high-level semantic features to aid in more accurate depression detection. Table 1 presents key words and questions [12] extracted from critical dialogues in the dataset that can influence the subject's behavioral tendencies. Therefore, this study proposes a multimodal depression detection approach that extracts emotional and behavioral features from conversations. By leveraging audio and text modalities, emotional and behavioral features are extracted and complemented as high-level features in the model to enhance depression detection.

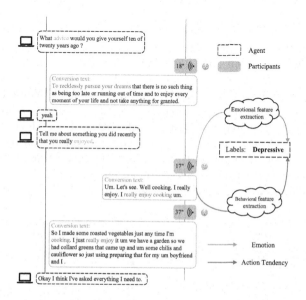

Fig. 1. An example of a subject from the DAIC-WOZ dataset.

We will present the related work on automated depression detection in Sect. 2 and provide a detailed description of our proposed method in Sect. 3. The effectiveness and performance of this method will be demonstrated through experiments in Sect. 4. Finally, Sect. 5 will summarize the research conducted in this work and discuss the potential applications of automated depression detection technology in everyday life.

2   Related Work

Automated depression detection tasks can be categorized into two types based on different modal sources. One type is detection methods based on social media content, while the other is detection methods based on clinical interview conversations.

The first type of method utilizes personal information shared by users on social media platforms such as text, images, and videos to reflect their current state, mood, or thoughts. With the popularity of social media platforms like Twitter, Facebook, and Weibo, an increasing number of people prefer to share personal content on these platforms. These social platforms can store various forms of personal content over a long period, making it possible to track users' historical content and predict their depression. For instance, An et al. [13] achieved depression prediction by performing topic modeling on the textual content posted by Twitter users. Gui et al. [14] created a Twitter depression dataset and used a multimodal neural network to predict users' depression. Yang et al. [15] designed a neural model to predict the severity and causes of depression among Weibo users.

The second type of method involves conducting interview conversations with subjects to observe their external behavioral characteristics, such as facial expressions, movements, tone of voice, and linguistic information. Inspired by these methods, Wei et al. [16] utilized bidirectional long short-term memory (BiLSTM) for depression prediction modeling during thematic interviews and performed weighted fusion of multimodal features from videos, audios, and texts. Chen et al. [17] considered the structural features of speech in conversations and designed the SpeechFormer framework for speech emotion recognition and depression detection. Zhao et al. [18] proposed the KBCIN model, which leveraged commonsense knowledge (CSK) to build semantic, affective, and behavioral interaction modules for emotion recognition in dialogues.

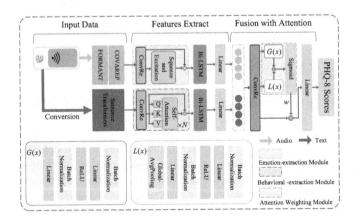

Fig. 2. The overall framework of the proposed method.

3   Method

Figure 2 illustrates the overall framework of a multimodal depression detection method based on dialogues, which achieves depression detection through the extraction of emotional and behavioral features. The entire framework includes input data preprocessing, emotional and behavioral feature extraction, and a high-level feature weighted attention fusion module. Initially, the model takes audio and text data as input and learns depression-related features during the feature extraction stage. Subsequently, through the weighted attention fusion stage, the model effectively outputs features and performs classification on the detection results. In the following sections, we will provide a detailed description of the proposed framework.

3.1 Data Preprocessing

In the audio modality, this study first preprocesses the participants' speech signals using COVAREP and formant extraction and converts them into Mel spectrograms to obtain input-ready audio data. Compared to the audio modality, text content typically contains underlying information such as behavioral tendencies. Hence, text data utilizes a pre-trained model of Google's Universal Sentence Encoder [19,20] to generate sentence embeddings for the extracted responses.

3.2 Feature Extraction Stage

The audio and text data are input into the emotional feature extraction module and the behavioral feature extraction module, respectively, to extract corresponding high-level features. The designed high-order feature extraction module is illustrated in (a) and (b) of Fig. 3. The computation process of the designed emotional feature extraction module is as follows:

$$\tilde{X}_{audio} = F_{scale}(x, h) = X \odot h \tag{1}$$

$$h = F_{att}(s, W) = \sigma_{sigmoid}(W_2(f_{\text{ReLU}}(W_1 s))) \tag{2}$$

$$s_j = \frac{1}{T}\sum_{i=0}^{T-1}(X_{audio})_{i,j} \tag{3}$$

Among them, $(X_{audio})_{i,j}$ represents the unit at the i-th time step and the j-th feature dimension of X_{audio}. W_1 and W_2 are the weight matrices of the linear layer, and h indicates the importance of feature channels. The designed behavioral feature extraction module is based on the Transformer structure, where a convolution and ReLU are used instead of the FFN (Feed-Forward Network) layer, enabling better focus on action trends in the text. For the input text sequence, the features are first projected to obtain the query Q, key K, and value V. QKV is then divided into h parts, generating features of d_h dimensions, where $d_h = \frac{d_m}{h}$, h is the number of heads, and d_m is the dimension of the input features. The calculation of self-attention (SA) in this work is as follows, with a stacking quantity of $N = 3$:

$$SA(Q, K, V) = Soft\max(\frac{QK^T}{d_h})V \tag{4}$$

Finally, the obtained high-order features from different modalities are separately input into a bidirectional LSTM [21]. The feature X is fed into the forward propagation layer to learn future time step feature information $\boldsymbol{A} = \{A_{P1}, A_{P2}, ..., A_{Pn}\}$, while is fed into the backward propagation layer to learn past time step feature information $\overleftarrow{A} = \{A_{R1}, A_{R2}, ..., A_{Rn}\}$. The feature vectors at the corresponding time steps from the forward and backward directions are concatenated to obtain the output vector $y = \{\boldsymbol{A}, \overleftarrow{A}\} = \{y_1, y_2, ..., y_n\}$, where $y_i = [A_{Pi}, A_{Ri}](i = 1, 2, ..., n)$, and n represents the total number of feature vectors. Next, the model autonomously trains and learns a set of weight coefficients $\alpha_t (t = 1, 2, 3, ..., n)$ and assigns them to y,to highlight key text features, resulting in the depression features Y corresponding to the respective modality.

$$Y_{\mathrm{mod}\ al} = \sum_{i=1}^{n} \alpha_i y_i, \mathrm{modal} = [audio, text] \tag{5}$$

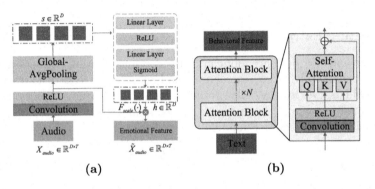

Fig. 3. (a) Structural diagram of emotion feature extraction module. (b) Behavioral feature extraction module.

3.3   Weighted Fusion Module

The fusion module adopts a weighted self-attention fusion method. The obtained depression features are concatenated and separately input into the global feature attention function $G(Y)$ and the local feature attention function $L(Y)$. The resulting global attention and local attention are then added together and passed through the *Sigmoid* function to obtain the attention weights w. The calculation process is as follows:

$$w = \sigma_{sigmoid}(G(Y) \oplus L(Y)) \tag{6}$$

After the feature extraction of each modality through the weighted fusion module, the features will be subjected to decision fusion, and finally mapped to the specified output dimension through a fully connected layer.

4   Experimental Analysis

4.1   Dataset

The DAIC-WOZ dataset [11] is a dataset proposed by researchers at the University of Southern California for detecting depression. The dataset consists of a virtual host and 189 participants numbered from 300 to 492. Due to technical reasons, the information of participants with numbers 342, 394, 398, and 460 is incomplete and has been removed. The collected data mainly include approximately 50 h of video-audio recordings and audio transcriptions during the interviews between Ellie and the participants. The dataset provides the PHQ-8 scores and labels for each participant, serving as the standard to assess the severity of depression in the participants.

Table 2. Ablation Experiments on Emotion Feature Extraction Module and Behavior Feature Extraction Module.

Advanced Feature Extraction Module	F1-Score	Recall	Precision
✕	0.85	0.81	0.83
✓	0.91	0.85	0.96

4.2   Experimental Setup

The experiment was conducted on a single GPU equipped with 8 GB of VRAM (NVIDIA GeForce RTX 3070). The neural network was built using PyTorch 1.11.0. In the experiment, the number of modules for behavioral feature extraction was set to N = 3, and the number of multi-head attentions was set to 8. The batch size was set to 32, and the Adam optimizer was used with a base learning rate of 0.00001. To compare with similar methods, the following experiments were conducted on the validation set of DAIC-WOZ and F1 scores were calculated.

4.3   Ablation Study

To demonstrate the effectiveness of the proposed innovative components, namely the emotional feature extraction and behavioral feature extraction modules, Table 2 presents a performance comparison before and after adding these feature extraction modules. In the absence of the feature extraction modules, convolutional layers were used as substitutes. The experimental results indicate that the model incorporating emotional and behavioral features outperforms the original model, with significantly improved performance across all metrics. This suggests that the model can effectively utilize high-level features such as emotions and behaviors as cues, guiding other modalities to pay more attention to detailed changes in the participants' emotions. As a result, the model becomes more capable of perceiving potential depressive symptoms and providing more flexible predictions.

Table 3. Results of Different Fusion Methods

Fusion method	F1-Score	Recall	Precision
Concatenation	0.72	0.80	0.89
Mean	0.80	0.79	0.91
Attention	0.85	0.83	0.93
Attention with weight	**0.91**	**0.85**	**0.96**

In this work, we compared three fusion methods for text and audio features: concatenation fusion, average fusion, attention fusion, and the proposed weighted attention fusion. Table 3 summarizes the results of these different fusion methods. The experimental findings demonstrate that the weighted attention fusion module effectively guides the model's learning of text and audio modalities. By learning the weights, the model can adaptively focus on the most relevant information in the input. This capability is particularly beneficial for complex structured data, such as input sequences or images, as it helps the model better understand and process key components, thereby enhancing its performance.

4.4   Comparative Method

Table 4 presents the performance comparison with baseline methods. It can be observed that the approach used in this study outperforms other single-modal or multi-modal methods and achieves a level similar to state-of-the-art (SOTA) methods in terms of F1 score and Precision. However, it is worth noting that the Recall score of the model is affected. This could be due to the addition of emotional and behavioral features, which makes the model more sensitive in its predictions, leading to some erroneous predictions caused by noise.

5   Visualisation

For further analysis, we present the results of selected participants from the test set in Fig. 4. Since the interview content of each participant varies, the number of dialogue segments containing the keywords from Table 1 is not equal. However, this does not affect the final prediction results. In the DAIC dataset, the diagnosis of depression for participants is not based on a single dialogue segment but on the entire interview. Therefore, the analysis of participants is conducted by recombining the segments and their corresponding prediction results to reconstruct the original dialogue for each participant. The scores of all segments are averaged to obtain the final PHQ-8 score for each participant.

Table 4. Comparison with other baseline methods

Modality	Method	F1-score	Recall	Precision
Audio	VL-Forments [22]	0.89	–	–
	Gaussian Staircase Model [23]	0.57	–	–
	DepAudioNet [24]	0.52	1.00	0.35
	Multi-modal LSTM [3]	0.63	0.56	0.71
	GRU model [25]	0.77	1.00	0.63
Text	Multi-modal LSTM [3]	0.67	0.80	0.57
	Cascade Random Forest [26]	0.55	0.89	0.40
	BiLSTM model [25]	0.83	0.83	0.83
Multimodal	Multi-modal LSTM [3]	0.77	0.83	0.71
	GRU/BiLSTM-based model [25]	0.85	0.92	0.79
	Our	**0.91**	0.85	**0.96**

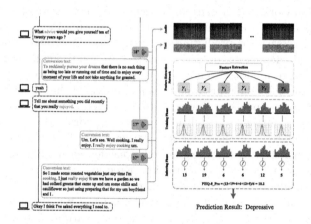

Fig. 4. Framework diagram of the designed method. In the training phase, a subject's interview dialogue is segmented into multiple segments according to keywords, and each segment is labelled with the subject label. In the inference phase, the final evaluation result is obtained by averaging the prediction scores of all segments after adding them together.

Figure 5 shows a selection of the first eight segments extracted from the dialogues of some participants. Overall, the predicted results of the proposed method align well with the true labels. For instance, in the case of participant 323, the predicted PHQ-8 scores for each dialogue segment closely match the actual scores. As for participant 311, the segmentation of segments is fewer due to the limited presence of keywords in the overall dialogue. In other words, despite having fewer behavioral features in this participant's sample, the emotional features in their voice still enable the prediction of depression labels. The overall results indicate that the proposed method effectively leverages higher-order features and flexibly adjusts the learning weights of modalities through the fusion module.

ID	PHQ-8 GT		PHQ-8 Prediction		chat_01	chat_02	chat_03	chat_04	chat_05	chat_06	chat_07	chat_08
	Binary	Score	Binary	Score								
323	0	1	0	2	1	1	8	2	0	2	0	2
334	0	5	0	4.7	3	3	3	7	1	14	2	9
311	1	21	1	12.5	14	9	17	10				
332	1	18	1	10.2	13	19	6	6	12	5		
407	0	3	0	7.1	6	11	8	7	6	6	4	10
450	0	9	0	7	4	10	1	1	11	15	11	0

Fig. 5. Selected subject-level visual analyses. PHQ-8 scores and binarised labels for each segment were replaced with colour blocks, with a white background representing a normal prediction and a grey background representing a depressed prediction.

6   Conclusion

We presents a multimodal approach for detecting depression by extracting emotional and behavioral features from dialogues. We have developed modules for extracting emotional and behavioral features to capture more advanced semantic features necessary for predicting depression. By integrating these semantic features into the depression detection process, we guide the processing of other modalities. This technique also holds therapeutic value and can assist in psychological diagnosis and follow-up appointments, provided that informed consent is obtained from participants or diagnosed individuals.

In the future, further research is required to address these limitations and explore more effective methods for integrating multiple modalities. Enhancing attention mechanisms to comprehensively consider all modalities can improve the overall performance of the depression detection model. Additionally, careful ethical considerations should be taken into account when deploying such technology in clinical settings to ensure patient privacy and obtain appropriate consent. Overall, the advancements in multimodal learning and artificial intelligence offer promising avenues for enhancing depression detection and supporting mental healthcare.

Acknowledgements. This work has been supported by The Jiangsu Province Graduate Research and Practice Innovation Program No. KYH21020530.

References

1. Hao, F., Pang, G., Wu, Y., Pi, Z., Xia, L., Min, G.: Providing appropriate social support to prevention of depression for highly anxious sufferers. IEEE Trans. Comput. Soc. Syst. **6**(5), 879–887 (2019)
2. Haque, A., Guo, M., Miner, A.S., Fei-Fei, L.: Measuring depression symptom severity from spoken language and 3d facial expressions. arXiv preprint arXiv:1811.08592 (2018)
3. Al Hanai, T., Ghassemi, M.M., Glass, J.R.: Detecting depression with audio/text sequence modeling of interviews. In: Interspeech, pp. 1716–1720 (2018)

4. Lu, H., Zhang, M., Xu, X., Li, Y., Shen, H.T.: Deep fuzzy hashing network for efficient image retrieval. IEEE Trans. Fuzzy Syst. **29**(1), 166–176 (2020)

5. Ma, C., et al.: Visual information processing for deep-sea visual monitoring system. Cogn. Robot. **1**, 3–11 (2021)

6. Lu, H., Teng, Y., Li, Y.: Learning latent dynamics for autonomous shape control of deformable object. IEEE Trans. Intell. Transp. Syst. (2022)

7. Niu, M., Chen, K., Chen, Q., Yang, L.: HCAG: a hierarchical context-aware graph attention model for depression detection. In: ICASSP 2021–2021 IEEE International Conference on Acoustics, Speech and Signal Processing (ICASSP), pp. 4235–4239. IEEE (2021)

8. Solieman, H., Pustozerov, E.A.: The detection of depression using multimodal models based on text and voice quality features. In: 2021 IEEE Conference of Russian Young Researchers in Electrical and Electronic Engineering (ElConRus), pp. 1843–1848. IEEE (2021)

9. Hazarika, D., Poria, S., Mihalcea, R., Cambria, E., Zimmermann, R.: Icon: interactive conversational memory network for multimodal emotion detection. In: Proceedings of the 2018 Conference on Empirical Methods in Natural Language Processing, pp. 2594–2604 (2018)

10. Liu, S., et al.: Towards emotional support dialog systems. arXiv preprint arXiv:2106.01144 (2021)

11. Gratch, J., et al.: The distress analysis interview corpus of human and computer interviews. In: LREC, pp. 3123–3128. Reykjavik (2014)

12. Flores, R., Tlachac, M., Shrestha, A., Rundensteiner, E.: Temporal facial features for depression screening. In: Adjunct Proceedings of the 2022 ACM International Joint Conference on Pervasive and Ubiquitous Computing and the 2022 ACM International Symposium on Wearable Computers, pp. 488–493 (2022)

13. An, M., Wang, J., Li, S., Zhou, G.: Multimodal topic-enriched auxiliary learning for depression detection. In: Proceedings of the 28th International Conference on Computational Linguistics, pp. 1078–1089 (2020)

14. Gui, T., et al.: Cooperative multimodal approach to depression detection in twitter. In: Proceedings of the AAAI Conference on Artificial Intelligence, vol. 33, pp. 110–117 (2019)

15. Yang, T., et al.: Fine-grained depression analysis based on Chinese micro-blog reviews. Inf. Process. Manag. **58**(6), 102681 (2021)

16. Wei, P.C., Peng, K., Roitberg, A., Yang, K., Zhang, J., Stiefelhagen, R.: Multimodal depression estimation based on sub-attentional fusion. In: Karlinsky, L., Michaeli, T., Nishino, K. (eds.) Computer Vision – ECCV 2022 Workshops. ECCV 2022. LNCS, vol. 13806, pp. 623–639. Springer, Cham (2023). https://doi.org/10.1007/978-3-031-25075-0_42

17. Chen, W., Xing, X., Xu, X., Pang, J., Du, L.: Speechformer: a hierarchical efficient framework incorporating the characteristics of speech. arXiv preprint arXiv:2203.03812 (2022)

18. Zhao, W., Zhao, Y., Li, Z., Qin, B.: Knowledge-bridged causal interaction network for causal emotion entailment. In: Proceedings of the AAAI Conference on Artificial Intelligence, vol. 37, pp. 14020–14028 (2023)

19. Cer, D., Yang, Y., Kong, S.V., Hua, N., Limtiaco, N.: Rhomni st john, noah constant, mario guajardo-cespedes, steve yuan, chris tar, and others. 2018. universal sentence encoder. arXiv preprint arXiv:1803.11175 (2018)

20. Cer, D., et al.: Universal sentence encoder. arXiv preprint arXiv:1803.11175 (2018)

21. Liu, G., Guo, J.: Bidirectional LSTM with attention mechanism and convolutional layer for text classification. Neurocomputing **337**, 325–338 (2019)

22. Cummins, N., Vlasenko, B., Sagha, H., Schuller, B.: Enhancing speech-based depression detection through gender dependent vowel-level formant features. In: ten Teije, A., Popow, C., Holmes, J.H., Sacchi, L. (eds.) AIME 2017. LNCS (LNAI), vol. 10259, pp. 209–214. Springer, Cham (2017). https://doi.org/10.1007/978-3-319-59758-4_23

23. Williamson, J.R., et al.: Detecting depression using vocal, facial and semantic communication cues. In: Proceedings of the 6th International Workshop on Audio/Visual Emotion Challenge, pp. 11–18 (2016)

24. Ma, X., Yang, H., Chen, Q., Huang, D., Wang, Y.: Depaudionet: an efficient deep model for audio based depression classification. In: Proceedings of the 6th International Workshop on Audio/Visual Emotion Challenge, pp. 35–42 (2016)

25. Shen, Y., Yang, H., Lin, L.: Automatic depression detection: an emotional audio-textual corpus and a GRU/BiLSTM-based model. In: ICASSP 2022–2022 IEEE International Conference on Acoustics, Speech and Signal Processing (ICASSP), pp. 6247–6251. IEEE (2022)

26. Sun, B., Zhang, Y., He, J., Yu, L., Xu, Q., Li, D., Wang, Z.: A random forest regression method with selected-text feature for depression assessment. In: Proceedings of the 7th Annual Workshop on Audio/Visual Emotion Challenge, pp. 61–68 (2017)

Enhancing Nighttime Vehicle Segmentation for Autonomous Driving Based on YOLOv5

Jiayi Huang$^{(\boxtimes)}$

Department of Artificial Intelligence, School of Science and Technology, Beijing Normal
University - Hong Kong Baptist University United International College, Zhuhai, China
1605862735@qq.com

Abstract. Recognizing vehicles in low-light conditions during nighttime poses
significant challenges in autonomous driving scenarios due to unclear contours.
While instance segmentation models have been extensively studied, their application in autonomous driving night scenes remains relatively unexplored. This paper
proposes a method to enhance nighttime vehicle segmentation using instance segmentation models. The BDD100K dataset is leveraged to label autonomous driving
daytime scenes and simulate nighttime driving scenarios through data augmentation using gamma correction during the training phase. During the prediction
phase, an improved gradient increasment low light enhancement algorithm based
on RetinexNet is employed to enhance night driving scene images. Additionally, the proposed method is evaluated using the YOLOv5 model. Experimental results demonstrate that the enhanced YOLOv5 model exhibits significantly
improved nighttime segmentation capability, leading to more accurate and robust
vehicle segmentation during nighttime. This method shows promise for real-world
application in nighttime autonomous driving scenarios.

Keywords: Nighttime Vehicle Segmentation · Instance segmentation ·
Autonomous driving · YOLOV5 · Low light enhancement retinex

1 Introduction

With the development of technology, autonomous driving is becoming increasingly popular, and autonomous driving is gradually entering our lives for future safe, efficient,
and low-carbon transportation [1]. This type of car that does not require human operation can be driven independently through various perception technologies and artificial intelligence systems, thereby reducing traffic accidents, alleviating traffic conges-
tion, and improving travel efficiency and safety. In particular, in autonomous driving,
recent research proposes formal languages such as temporal logics to specify driving
behaviors ranging from safety [2]. Therefore, unmanned visual perception systems are
particularly valuable, as their recognition is mainly based on methods such as object
detection, semantic segmentation, and instance segmentation. Target detection is particularly important for unmanned driving. Detection is divided into road detection, vehicle
detection, indicator signal detection, obstacle detection, and object detection.

H. Lu and J. Cai (Eds.): ISAIR 2023, CCIS 1998, pp. 475–482, 2024.
https://doi.org/10.1007/978-981-99-9109-9_45

During the day, cameras can be used for classification, and in Apollo, cameras are mainly used for traffic signal classification and lane detection. However, at night or with unsignalized intersections [3], due to reduced visibility, brightness, and field of view, many cameras are unable to recognize and detect road targets, resulting in traffic accidents. Efficient understanding of the environment is a crucial prerequisite for autonomous driving [4, 11].

The DMV accident report reflects a nightmare scenario for unmanned vehicles - a crossroads [5]. By organizing the data in the report, it can be found that nearly half of the accidents occurred at intersections. At intersections, the most common problem for unmanned vehicles is rear end collision. Due to complex road conditions and poor visibility, unmanned vehicles often face a formidable enemy at intersections, and their driving actions are often cautious - pedestrians crossing the road, slowing down, and braking; When turning right, there is traffic in the same direction, slowing down and braking to a stop; Slight wind and grass movement, slowing down and braking [6, 12].

This article provides four methods of image enhancement to enhance the brightness and visibility of nighttime images, and uses the YOLOv5 algorithm to detect images. Firstly, daytime image training is conducted, followed by nighttime image detection to obtain data and generate a PR curve.

2   Related Work

2.1   Yolo5

The YOLOv5 algorithm is improved on the basis of YOLOv4, and the YOLOv5 series has a total of 4 different networks, namely YOLOv5s, YOLOv5m, YOLOv5l, and YOLOv5x.Considering the need to accurately identify various information in images in unmanned target detection, this project adopts the Yolov5 algorithm. YOLOv5 is mainly composed of four parts: input, Backone, Neck and Prediction. Thereinto:

- Backbone: A convolutional neural network that aggregates and forms image features at different image fine-grains.
- Neck: A series of network layers that blend and combine image features and pass image features to the prediction layer.

At this point, a new term appeared is Adaptive anchor box calculation. In Yolo's algorithm, there will be an anchor box with an initial length and width for different data sets. In network training, the network outputs the prediction box on the basis of the initial anchor box, and then compares it with the real box ground truth, calculates the gap between the two, and then updates it in reverse to iterate the network parameters [7]. However, Yolov5 embeds this functionality into the code, and adaptively calculates the best anchor box values in different training sets each time it is trained.

The following promotion points are mainly used: Focus structure, CSP structure [8, 13]. The focus structure is actually the equivalent of the ReOrg+Conv operation of the YOLOV2 passthrough layer. Cross Stage Partial Network (CSPNet) is to solve the problem of large calculation in the inference process of previous work from the perspective of network structure design (Fig. 1).

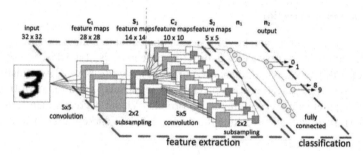

Fig. 1. Predicts image features, generates bounding boxes and predicts categories.

2.2 Retinex

Retinex, is one effective theory aiming at simulating Human Visual System (HVS) to achieve color constancy and dynamic range compression. Retinex can be applicable to nighttime images even under extreme conditions [7]. It helps improve dark details and contrast to enhance the visualization of nighttime images. Under nighttime conditions, images often face problems such as insufficient lighting and color distortion, making them blurry, dim, or lacking in detail. In 1986, Edwin Land [9] proposed the last version of his retinex theory as a model for human color constancy.Retinex enhancement technology can effectively overcome these problems and enhance the quality of nighttime images by simulating human eye perception and visual processing processes. The application of Retinex theory covers various models and algorithms: Single scale Retinex (SSR), Multi scale Retinex (MSR), Adaptive Retinex (AR), Multi scale Retinex with Color Recovery (MSRCR) [10].

MSR (Multi-Scale Retinex) is a color image enhancement algorithm based on human perception, which can reliably provide color constancy and Dynamic range compression (DRC). In mathematics, MSR is represented as

$$R(x, y) = K \sum kwk\{\log S(x, y) - \log Fk(x, y) * S(x, y)\} \tag{1}$$

MSRCR (Multi-Scale Retinex with Color Restoration) and MSR algorithms have better color reproduction, brightness constancy and Dynamic range compression characteristics. It has better image enhancement effect and more realistic colors than SSR, but the enhancement effect is limited. The local contrast of the image processed by the MSRCR algorithm is improved, and its brightness is similar to that of a real scene, making the image appear more realistic under visual perception.

3 Method

In order to enhance the ability of autonomous vehicles to detect road information at night, this study will mainly use two image enhancement methods and conduct data comparison.

- Data augmentation based on brightness. Simulate nighttime driving visual imaging through daytime autonomous driving visual data.
- Improvement of illumination enhancement algorithm based on Retinex

3.1 1: Gamma Correction

There are various lighting and brightness situations in autonomous driving application scenarios, and the brightness varies at different time periods of the day. To simulate the gradient effect of night autonomous driving scenes, we use power law transformation for gamma correction, scaling each pixel of the input image to a range of 0 to 1, and adjusting the pixel values according to the formula. When r is greater than 1, the overall histogram shifts to the left a, causing the output image to darken (Fig. 2).

$$O = I\,\gamma \qquad\qquad (2)$$

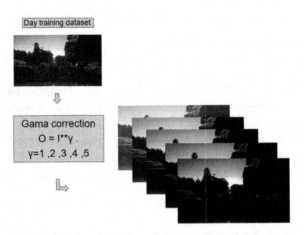

Fig. 2. Five Effects of Gamma Correction

On the contrary, when r is less than 1, the overall histogram moves to the right, and the output image is brighter than the input image. We use five levels to simulate various brightness conditions at night in driving scenes at different time periods. With the normal daytime scene picture as the input, use the r values of 1, 2, 3, 4, and 5 to process respectively, and get five pictures with different brightness. The output pictures gradually darken, corresponding to 1 to 5. This data augmentation algorithm can not only increase the number of nighttime features in the dataset, but also increase the number of datasets.

3.2 Evolution

Retinex multi-scale image enhancement is different in different weather and different brightness, and then we evaluate it through different images. The MSR algorithm has good robustness to problems such as lighting changes, background clutter and target boundary blur, and is suitable for target detection. The MSRCR algorithm has an advantage in image enhancement. It combines the multi-scale Retinex algorithm and color restoration technology to improve contrast and brightness without losing image detail.

It can effectively restore the color and details of the image and improve the image quality for problems such as uneven illumination or overexposure of the image. The SSR algorithm is mainly used to enhance the detail and contrast of the image. It adjusts the brightness of pixels by analyzing the light distribution in the image, which highlights details in the image and improves the contrast of the image, so it is more suitable for pictures in low-light conditions (Fig. 3).

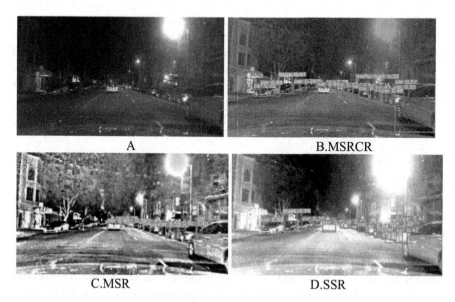

Fig. 3. Retinex image enhancement rendering.

From the above images, we can see that MSRCR and SSR work better in low light, compared to MSR.

4 Experiment

4.1 Data

The experiment will train the model using daytime driving photos from the BDD100K dataset released by the University of California, Berkeley in 2018 [11]. To test the model's performance in nighttime autonomous driving scenarios, a separate test dataset consisting of nighttime driving images will be used. This evaluation aims to determine if our improved algorithm allows the model to handle nighttime scenarios even in the absence of dedicated nighttime scene data in the training set.

4.2 Labeling Tool

Use the labelme tool to finish labeling the cars in day and night scenes' images. The labelme tool used to polygonal label and classify objects.

4.3 Evolution Set up

- Experimental equipment (the experimental environment)
- Operating system: windows11
- Python version: 3.9. 13
- PyTorch version: 1.12.0+cu116
- GPU model: RTX3060Ti

This article evaluates the performance of the model using precision recall (PR) curves and average precision (AP) curves. Compare the predictions with ground truth boxes and masks, and calculate their IoU. This article takes IoU = 0.5 as the critical value. If the predicted value is greater than or equal to 0.5, we call the predicted value a positive sample, otherwise it is a negative sample. The formula for calculating accuracy and recall is as follows:

$$\text{Prediction: } P = TP/(TP + FP)P = TP/(TP + FP) \tag{3}$$

$$\text{Recall: } R = TP/(TP + FN)R = TP/(TP + FN) \tag{4}$$

In the formula, the number of true positive samples is represented by TP, the number of false positive samples is represented by FP, and FN is the number of false negative samples. We can draw the PR inverse curve on the Cartesian coordinate system. The PR inverse curve needs to be drawn based on some points, which are obtained by changing the confidence level to obtain a set of (pre recall, pre recall) points. The horizontal axis of the PR inverse curve is related to recall, while the vertical axis is related to accuracy. AP is the integral of the PR curve, which is the area surrounded by the curve, horizontal axis, and vertical axis. The specific calculation method is as follows: The AP under each category is obtained by calculation, and the mean of AP of each category is mAP.

4.4 Experimental Comparison Model

We compared the improvement of YOLOv5 with that of YOLOv5 after using Retinex enhancement. In the experiment, we used models such as MSR, MSRCR, AR, etc.

5 Result

Compared with the original image, the experimental results show that retinex further improves the ability of object detection in autonomous driving nighttime scenes (the mAP of the box increased from 29.03% to 32.49%, and the mAP95 increased from 17.40% to 19.30%). We can also observe that multi-scale images have different enhancement effects, and under different images, some have higher accuracy while others are even worse than before enhancement. Therefore, before image enhancement, it is necessary to select the corresponding model based on the environment (Table 1).

Table 1. Comparison of MAP-50 and MAP50-95 of seven models

	MAP-50	MAP50-95
YOLOV5	0.291	0.17
SSR	0.30	0.19
MSR	0.294	0.201
MSRCR	0.390	0.210
AR	0.324	0.192

6 Conclusion

In this paper, through the application of unmanned night driving, a detection model YOLAV5 is proposed to detect road information. And both algorithms are enhanced using gamma correction and Retinex images. Algorithm 1, Gamma correction is a nonlinear storage/reduction algorithm for brightness in the dynamic range, that is, a nonlinear operation of the input value, so that the output value has an exponential relationship with the input value; In terms of effect, Gamma correction adjusts the overall brightness of the image, and the image without correction may look too bright or too dark, so if you want the image display effect to be more perfect, Gamma correction is very important. The second method is to make the model (Retinex) have the ability to gradient the brightness of the night scene by improving the lighting enhancement algorithm. We compared the ground truth box and mask with the model predictions to verify the effect of the model. This model further improves the recognition ability of autonomous driving night scenes. We conducted comparative experiments using four enhancement algorithms: SSR, MSR, MSRCR, and AR, and found that the overall effect of MSRCR is the best. Of course, under different road conditions and lighting conditions, these four algorithms also have their own advantages. This work solved the problem of enhancing unmanned target detection under insufficient lighting conditions and found the optimal algorithm. But the accuracy of target detection still needs to be improved, and the training volume of the dataset is relatively low. These shortcomings should be improved.

References

1. Ruan, J., Cui, H., Huang, Y., Li, T., Wu, C., Zhang, K.: A review of occluded objects detection in real complex scenarios for autonomous driving. Green Energy Intell. Transp. 2(3), 100092 (2023)
2. Mehdipour, N., Althoff, M., Tebbens, R.D., Belta, C.: Formal methods to comply with rules of the road in autonomous driving: state of the art and grand challenges. Automatica **152**, 110692 (2023)
3. Spatharis, C., Blekas, K.: Multiagent reinforcement learning for autonomous driving in traffic zones with unsignalized intersections. J. Intell. Transp. Syst. 1–17 (2022)
4. Hu, J., Kong, H., Zhang, Q., Liu, R.: Enhancing scene understanding based on deep learning for end-to-end autonomous driving. Eng. Appl. Artif. Intell. **116**, 105474 (2022)

5. Kortmann, F., Fassmeyer, P., Funk, B., Drews, P.: Watch out, pothole! Featuring road damage detection in an end-to-end system for autonomous driving. Data Knowl. Eng. **142**, 102091 (2022)

6. Yang, L., Lu, C., Xiong, G., Xing, Y., Gong, J.: A hybrid motion planning framework for autonomous driving in mixed traffic flow. Green Energy Intell. Transp. **1**(3), 100022 (2022)

7. Land, E.H.: Recent advances in retinex theory. In: Central and Peripheral Mechanisms of Colour Vision: Proceedings of An International Symposium Held at The Wenner-Gren Center Stockholm, 14–15 June 1984, pp. 5–17. Palgrave Macmillan, London (1985)

8. Lin, H., Shi, Z.: Multi-scale retinex improvement for nighttime image enhancement. Optik **125**(24), 7143–7148 (2022)

9. Liu, S., Han, Y., Xu, L.: Recognition of road cracks based on multi-scale Retinex fused with wavelet transform. Array **15**, 100193 (2022)

10. Veluchamy, S., Mahesh, K., Pon Bharathi, A., Sheeba, P.: BerkeleyDeepDrive (2022). https://bdddata.berkeley.edu/index.html

11. Chen, Z., Lu, H., Tian, S., et al.: Construction of a hierarchical feature enhancement network and its application in fault recognition. IEEE Trans. Ind. Inform. **17**(7), 4827–4836 (2020)

12. Xu, X., Tian, J., Lin, K., et al.: Zero-shot cross-modal retrieval by assembling autoencoder and generative adversarial network. ACM Trans. Multimedia Comput. Commun. Appl. (TOMM) **17**(1s), 1–17 (2021)

13. Wang, G., Xu, X., Shen, F., et al.: Cross-modal dynamic networks for video moment retrieval with text query. IEEE Trans. Multimedia **24**, 1221–1232 (2022)

Improved YOLOv7 Small Object Detection Algorithm for Seaside Aerial Images

Miao Yu(✉) and YinShan Jia(✉)

Liaoning Petrochemical University, Fushun 113001, Liaoning, China
15542425860@163.com, yinshanjia@163.com

Abstract. Seaside aerial images due to the high number of small object instances, interference from the background, and occlusion caused by crowded personnel. These issues result in low accuracy of this scenario in the field of object detection. By improving the YOLOv7 algorithm, we proposed a YOLOv7-B model. We reconstructed the detection layer to reduce the miss rate of small objects. The Improved Bi-directional Feature Pyramid Network (IBi-FPN) replaced the Pyramid Attention Network (PANet) of YOLOv7, better integrating deep feature information with shallow feature information. Finally, we added Convolutional Block Attention Module (CBAM) to improve the utilization of effective features. Experiments show that the YOLOv7-B model can improve the detection accuracy of small objects at the seaside while reducing the number of parameters.

Keywords: YOLOv7 · Convolutional Block Attention Module · small object detection · Improved Bi-directional Feature Pyramid Network

1 Introduction

The coastal tourism industry is one of the most vibrant and fastest-growing areas in modern international tourism. However, the safety issues of beach tourists have not been perfectly solved [1]. There are dangers such as drowning, rip currents, and toxic marine life near the beach. In order to reduce safety hazards, coastal areas have taken measures such as controlling the entry and exit of tourists, equipping with water safeguards, and installing a monitoring system. Due to environmental restrictions, coastal areas cannot be fully covered by surveillance, and the proportion of tourist targets in the images obtained by drone aerial photography is very small. Therefore, proposing a detection algorithm for small targets on the seaside to ensure the safety of people near the seaside has important practical significance.

Beach tourists in aerial images have problems such as low resolution, easy occlusion due to dense targets, and less feature information [1]. The existing object detection algorithm is not accurate enough for small object detection in such complex scenes. For example, Yim [2] and others proposed a new cutting method, clipping the target with the largest proportion and the smallest size of the dataset. Gong [1] and others proposed to introduce fusion factors into FPN to control the information from deep layers to shallow layers to improve the detection effect of small targets, but the feature extraction ability is

H. Lu and J. Cai (Eds.): ISAIR 2023, CCIS 1998, pp. 483–491, 2024.
https://doi.org/10.1007/978-981-99-9109-9_46

poor in the case of dense people on the beach. This paper proposes a YOLOv7-B model by improving YOLOv7 [1].

We reconstructed the detection layer, the original 20 × 20 large object detection layer is deleted, and the 160 × 160 small object detection layer is added. By reducing the number of convolutions, the purpose of retaining more shallow information is achieved.

An IBi-FPN multi-scale feature fusion network structure is designed, we added skip connections between feature maps of the same scale to retain detail information.

The CBAM module is added to the feature fusion network part, giving small targets higher weight and suppressing useless information to improve the detection accuracy of the model for small targets.

The rest of the paper is constructed as follows. In Sect. 2, we introduce related works. In Sect. 3, we present the proposed methodology. Section 4 presents the results, Sect. 5 is the conclusion.

2   Related Works

2.1   Object Detection Algorithm

The object detection algorithm can be divided into two-stage detection algorithm and one-stage detection algorithm [1]. The main idea of the two-stage detection algorithm is to extract candidate regions firstly, and then classify and regress based on the generated bounding boxes. The first model is R-CNN [2] which was created in 2015. Then Fast R-CNN [1] and Faster R-CNN [1] were released with improvements. The benefit of this type of algorithm is high accuracy, but they are also more complicated and have a slow speed. The one stage detection algorithm is to directly regress and predict the feature map, and the input image only needs to pass through a convolutional neural network to predict the categories and positions of different targets. YOLO [1, 2, 22] series algorithm and SSD [1] series algorithm is undoubtedly representative of the one-stage detection algorithm.

2.2   Multi-scale Feature Fusion

The fusion of feature information at different levels is a useful method to enhance precision in the field of object detection [1]. Lin proposed the Feature Pyramid Networks (FPN) [2] algorithm, which constructs a top-down path in the network to generate feature maps of different sizes. The Pyramid Attention Network (PANet) [3] proposed by Shu Liu and others adds a bottom-up path to the FPN, fusing the features extracted by the main network with the features after upsampling to enrich the feature detail information. Tan and others proposed an Bi-directional Feature Pyramid Network (Bi-FPN) [4]. Different from the PANet, a skip connection will be added between these two nodes which on the same layer.

2.3   Attention Mechanism

The attention mechanism originates from human vision [5, 23]. Due to the limited information received by humans, we will concentrate on useful information and overlook useless information [6]. In recently years, common used attention mechanisms include representative models of channel attention mechanisms such as Squeeze-and-Excitation Networks (SE-NET) [7], the more flexible Coordinate Attention (CA) [8] and Convolutional Block Attention Module (CBAM) [9, 24], a model combining spatial attention and channel attention.

3 Methodology

3.1 Overall Architecture

Figure 1 shows the overall structure of the YOLOv7-B algorithm.

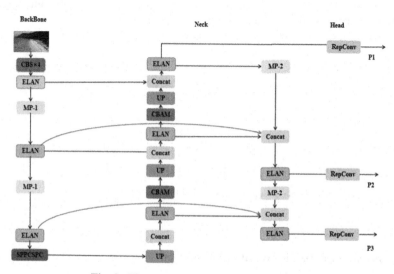

Fig. 1. The structure of YOLOv7-B network.

3.2 Restructuring the Detection Layer

The YOLOv7 algorithm uses feature maps of sizes 20×20, 40×40, and 80×80. We modify the YOLOv7 algorithm based on this, achieving the extraction of 160×160 size feature maps, and removing the 20×20 scale receptive field, thereby increasing the small receptive field and enhancing its weight. Compared to the original output layer, by adjusting the number of subsampling operations and the layout of the fusion connection positions, the current output layer retains more position information from shallow feature maps in the feature fusion network part due to fewer convolutions on the input image, making it more suitable for seaside small target detection and reducing the parameter volume of the model.

3.3 Multi-scale Feature Fusion Network

Figure 2 shows the Comparison of PANet, Bi-FPN and IBi-FPN structures. We used the core idea of the Bi-FPN network structure to design a new network IBi-FPN, as shown in Fig. 2(c).

After the images are entered into the network, it forms feature maps of sizes 160 × 160, 80 × 80, and 40 × 40 through three ELAN modules. These feature maps are input into the neck network for continuous upsampling and concatenation with the feature maps formed in the backbone network. Finally, these maps with stacked channel numbers are subsampled to form the final feature maps, which enter the detection layer and output. The IBi-FPN network structure combines the feature maps subsampled from the backbone network part with the same scale maps from the bottom-up path of the original PANet. That is, when the input node and output node are on the same level and the feature map sizes are consistent, a skip connection is added.

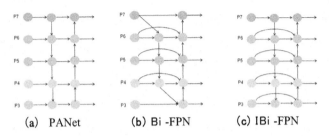

(a) PANet   (b) Bi -FPN   (c) IBi -FPN

Fig. 2. Comparison of PANet, Bi-FPN and IBi-FPN structures.

3.4 Convolutional Block Attention Mechanism

The feature fusion brings not only useful information but also a large part of useless information. The model needs to suppress useless information while retaining useful information. In the IBi-FPN network structure, we add the CBAM behind each ELAN module and before the upsampling module, that is, a CBAM module is added between the feature fusion of two scale feature maps to enhance the ability to focus on small target information. The flow of the CBAM is shown in Fig. 3.

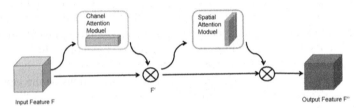

Fig. 3. The structure of CBAM network

4 Results

4.1 Dataset Introduction

We use TinyPerson as the experimental dataset. The TinyPerson dataset includes aerial images of tiny objects by the sea, containing a large number of dense human images under seaside scenes, which can be used for application scenarios such as sea rescue.

4.2 Experiment Results of Reconstructing the Detection Layer

Table 1 shows the consequences of comparing the detection layers. Experiment A is the detection layer of yolov7. In experiment B we added a small object detection layer directly. Finally, we deleted the large layer and added a small one in experiment C. Experimental C method can greatly reduce parameter quantity while taking into account the accuracy.

Table 1. The results of comparing the detection layers.

	mAP@0.5 (%)	mAP@.5:.95(%)	P (%)	R (%)	Parameter (M)
Exp A	25.2	7.56	45	30	36.8
Exp B	27.0	8.11	47.1	33.2	38.9
Exp C	26.6	8.04	46.2	32.6	25.4

4.3 Experiment Results of IBi-FPN

The IBi-FPN network structure adds skip connection without removing nodes with only one input edge to keep more information on small seaside targets. This structure can combine shallow and deep feature map information of the same scale. We can see from Table 2, IBi-FPN network structure improves algorithm mAP 1.1% more than Bi-FPN structure and 1.1% more than PANet. Precision and recall rates have also improved significantly.

Table 2. The results of changing the feature fusion network.

	mAP@0.5 (%)	mAP@.5:.95 (%)	P (%)	R (%)
YOLOv7	25.2	7.56	45	30
YOLOv7+Bi-FPN	25.8	7.78	45.3	31.2
YOLOV7+IBi-FPN	26.9	8.05	45.7	32.7

4.4 Experiment Results of Attention Mechanism

We use channel attention mechanism SE-NET, more flexible attention mechanism CA and CBAM to conduct a comparative experiment. The experimental results show that, CBAM with both spatial attention model and channel attention model has better performance in the detection of small seaside targets (Table 3).

Table 3. The results of different attention mechanism.

	mAP@0.5(%)	mAP@.5:.95(%)	P (%)	R (%)
YOLOv7	25.2	7.56	45	30
YOLOv7+SE	26.0	7.92	45.3	31.2
YOLOv7+CA	25.8	7.71	45.1	30.8
YOLOV7+CBAM	26.9	8.05	45.7	32.7

4.5 Ablation Experiment

To prove the validity of the improvements made in this paper for seaside small object detection, an ablation experiment will be conducted on the results under the same conditions. The consequences are shown in Table 4. Experiment B proves that reconstructing the detection layer and removing some deep feature map information can significantly decrease the model parameters and simplify the model while improving the accuracy of seaside small target detection. Experiment C proves that the IBi-FPN multi-scale feature fusion network has the most significant effect on improving seaside small target detection, with a single module mAP increase of 1.7%. Experiment D proves that adding attention mechanism in the IBi-FPN network structure can increase map by 1.3%. It can also be seen from the various combination experiments of the three improved modules that there is no repulsion effect between the improved modules. From Experiment F, the mAP of the YOLOv7-B model increased by 4.1% compared to the YOLOv7 model, the accuracy rate increased by 4.6%, and the model parameters decreased by 11.2M. It can be proven that the improvements made by each module to the model are effective.

4.6 Visualization Analysis

So as to vividly demonstrate the detection effect of YOLOv7-B on tiny targets at the seaside, a comparison of the inference results on the TinyPerson dataset between YOLOv7-B and the baseline model YOLOv7 is presented below. As shown in Fig. 4, for seaside small targets, the detection effect of the YOLOv7 model is poor, especially for the tiny targets at a distance in the image, where there is a serious case of missed detection. The improved YOLOv7-B model has significantly better detection results. The number of detections for densely populated crowds with severe occlusion, targets that are difficult to distinguish from the background, and extremely small targets in the distance has increased noticeably, with a significant improvement in detection accuracy.

Table 4. Ablation experiment.

		mAP@0.5(%)	mAP@.5:.95(%)	P(%)	R(%)	P(M)
A	YOLOv7	25.2	7.56	45	30	36.8
B	YOLOv7+p2	26.6	8.04	46.2	32.6	25.4
C	YOLOv7+IBi	26.9	8.05	45.7	32.7	36.2
D	YOLOv7+CBAM	26.3	8.04	45.9	32	35.4
E	YOLOv7+p2+IBi	28.1	8.45	48.5	33	26.0
F	YOLOv7+p2+CBAM	27.9	8.39	47.8	32.8	25.8
G	YOLOv7+Bi+CBAM	28.2	8.46	48.8	33.5	36.5
H	YOLOv7+p2+IBi+CBAM	29.3	9.05	49.6	34.2	25.6

Fig. 4. Experiment results comparison.

5 Conclusion

We propose an improved multi-scale feature fusion detection algorithm, YOLOv7-B, effectively addresses the problem of current detection algorithms not being able to satisfy the detection task of small targets in such complex coastal scenarios. The method reconstructs the detection layer, inserts an IBi-FPN multi-scale feature fusion network structure and adds CBAM module between the feature fusion layers of the IBi-FPN structure. The improvements we made to the model can concentrate on small objects by seaside, improve the utilization rate of effective information and reduce the waste of computational resources on invalid information. But we only improve the network structure, the subsequent consideration is to improve the resolution of seaside aerial images in terms of data enhancement.

References

1. Balena, P., Bonifazi, A., Torre, C.M.: Social value of nature amenities: WTP for the use of public seasides. In: Misra, S. (ed.) Computational Science and Its Applications – ICCSA 2019. ICCSA 2019, vol. 11622, pp. 132–144. Springer, Cham (2019). https://doi.org/10.1007/978-3-030-24305-0_11

2. Simonyan, K., Zisserman, A.: Very deep convolutional networks for large-scale image recognition. In: ICLR (2015)

3. Yim, S., Cho, M., Lee, S.: Object-oriented cutout data augmentation for tiny object detection. In: 2023 International Technical Conference on Circuits/Systems, Computers, and Communications, Jeju, Korea, pp. 1–4 (2023)

4. Gong, Y.Q., Yu, X.H., Ding, Y., et al.: Effective fusion factor in FPN for tiny object detection. In: IEEE Winter Conference on Applications of Computer Vision (WACV), pp. 1159–1167 (2020)

5. Wang, C.Y., Bochkovskiy, A., et al.: YOLOv7: trainable bag-of-freebies sets new state-of-the-art for real-time object detectors. arXiv:2207.02696v1 (2022)

6. Li, D.J., Yu, L., Jin, W., et al.: An improved detection method of human target at sea based on Yolov3. In: 2021 IEEE International Conference on Consumer Electronics and Computer Engineering (ICCECE), Guangzhou, China, pp. 100–103 (2021)

7. Girshick, R., Donahue, J., Darrell, T., Malik, J.: Rich feature hierarchies for accurate object detection and semantic segmentation. In: IEEE Conference on Computer Vision and Pattern Recognition, Columbus, OH, USA, pp. 580–587 (2014)

8. Girshick, R.: Fast R-CNN. arXiv:1504.08083v2 (2015)

9. Ren, S., He, K., Girshick, R., et al.: Faster R-CNN: towards real-time object detection with region proposal networks. In: Advances in Neural Information Processing Systems, Waikoloa, pp. 91–99. IEEE (2015)

10. Redmon, J., Divvala, S., Girshick, R., et al.: You only look once: unified, real-time object detection. In: Computer Vision & Pattern Recognition. IEEE (2016)

11. Redmon, J., Farhadi, A.: YOLOv3: an incremental improvement. In: 2018 IEEE Conference on Computer Vision and Pattern Recognition, Washington, DC, pp. 89–95. IEEE Computer Society Press (2018)

12. Liu, W., et al.: SSD: single shot multibox detector. In: Leibe, B., Matas, J., Sebe, N., Welling, M. (eds.) ECCV 2016. LNCS, vol. 9905, pp. 21–37. Springer, Cham (2016). https://doi.org/10.1007/978-3-319-46448-0_2

13. Szegedy, C., et al.: Going deeper with convolutions. In: CVPR (2015)

14. Lin, T.Y., Dollar, P., Girshick, R., et al.: Feature pyramid networks for object detection. arXiv:1612.03144v2 (2017)

15. Liu, S., Qi, L., Qin, H.F., et al.: Path aggregation network for instance segmentation. In: Computer Vision and Pattern Recognition, Piscataway, pp. 8759−8768. IEEE (2018)

16. Tan, M., Pang, R., Le, Q.V.: EfficientDet: scalable and efficient object detection. In: 2020 IEEE/CVF Conference on Computer Vision and Pattern Recognition (CVPR). IEEE (2020)

17. Szegedy, C., Vanhoucke, V., Ioffe, S., Shlens, J., Wojna, Z.: Rethinking the inception architecture for computer vision. In: CVPR (2016)

18. Jawahar, C.V., Li, H., Mori, G., Schindler, K. (eds.): ACCV 2018. LNCS, vol. 11365. Springer, Cham (2019). https://doi.org/10.1007/978-3-030-20873-8

19. Hu, J., Shen, L., Sun, G.: Squeeze-and-excitation networks. In: 2018 IEEE/CVF Conference on Computer Vision and Pattern Recognition, pp. 7132–7141 (2018)

20. Hou, Q.B., Zhou, D.Q., Feng, J.S.: Coordinate attention for efficient mobile network design. In: 2021 IEEE/CVF Conference on Computer Vision and Pattern Recognition (CVPR), Nashville, TN, USA, pp. 13708–13717 (2021)

21. Woo, S., Park, J., Lee, J.Y., et al.: CBAM: convolutional block attention module. arXiv:1807.06521v2 (2018)
22. Chen, Z., Lu, H., Tian, S., et al.: Construction of a hierarchical feature enhancement network and its application in fault recognition. IEEE Trans. Ind. Inform. **17**(7), 4827–4836 (2020)
23. Xu, X., Tian, J., Lin, K., et al.: Zero-shot cross-modal retrieval by assembling autoencoder and generative adversarial network. ACM Trans. Multimedia Comput. Commun. Appl. (TOMM) **17**(1s), 1–17 (2021)
24. Wang, G., Xu, X., Shen, F., et al.: Cross-modal dynamic networks for video moment retrieval with text query. IEEE Trans. Multimedia **24**, 1221–1232 (2022)

Research on Lightweight Road Semantic Segmentation Algorithm Based on DeepLabv3+

Jian Song and Yinshan Jia(✉)

Liaoning Petrochemical University, Fushun 113001, Liaoning, China
yinshanjia@163.com

Abstract. A lightweight image semantic segmentation model called MCDF is proposed based on the DeepLabv3+ to balance accuracy in light of the issues such as unclear boundary segmentation and misjudgments in road segmentation for mobile terminals like wheeled robots during autonomous driving, as well as the requirement of lightweight in practical application scenarios. The improvements mainly focus on two aspects: lightweight and accuracy. In terms of lightweight, the backbone network is replaced with the lightweight MobileNetV2 network, and the regular convolutions in the ASPP module are replaced with Depthwise Separable Convolutions, reducing the number of computations. In terms of accuracy, the Coordinate Attention is introduced after the backbone network, and then a feature enhancement extraction structure is concatenated at the decoder end to enrich boundary information. Finally, the mIoU obtained on the Cityscapes dataset is 72.68%, with only a 2.86% decrease. The model size is approximately 1/14 of the original, measuring only 14.84 MB. This achieves a balance between lightweight design and accuracy, effectively meeting the requirements for outdoor road scene segmentation.

Keywords: Road segmentation · DeepLabv3+ · MobileNetV2 · Attention mechanisms · Enhanced structure

1 Introduction

Semantic segmentation, as an important application field in computer vision, has received widespread attention [1]. It is widely used in scenarios like autonomous driving and emergency rescue [2]. In autonomous driving, there are high requirements for the accuracy and real-time performance of the model to ensure stable driving on the road. In traditional image semantic segmentation methods, shallow learning algorithms are often used [3], and the deep semantic information of the image is not fully utilized. As a result, the segmentation results are not satisfactory. Compared with traditional methods, methods based on deep neural networks have made qualitative leaps in both speed and accuracy. Shelhamer et al. [4] proposed an end-to-end fully convolutional semantic segmentation network. CHEN et al. [5, 21] proposed the DeepLab series of semantic segmentation networks, which gradually improved the segmentation effect. However, in the field of autonomous driving, the model needs to run on resource-limited terminals, which

H. Lu and J. Cai (Eds.): ISAIR 2023, CCIS 1998, pp. 492–500, 2024.
https://doi.org/10.1007/978-981-99-9109-9_47

imposes strict requirements on indicators such as model size and segmentation accuracy. This paper makes the following improvements based on the DeepLabv3+ [6]. On the one hand, the backbone network is replaced with the MobileNetV2 [7], and the regular convolution in the ASPP module is replaced with Depthwise Separable Convolution (DSC), greatly reducing the computation. On the other hand, the Coordinate Attention (CA) [8] is introduced after the backbone network, and then the Feature Enhancement Structure (FES) for multi-scale feature fusion is implemented in the decoder. These improvements effectively balance the requirements of lightweight and accuracy in road segmentation. Section 1 is the introduction, Sects. 2 and 3 introduce the related work and experiments, and Sect. 4 concludes the paper.

2   Related Work

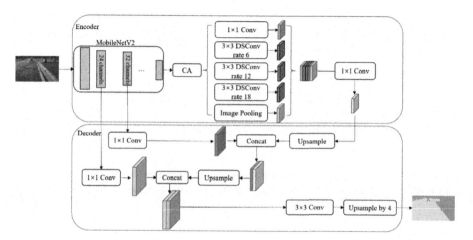

Fig. 1. Overall architecture of the model.

In the encoder, two shallow feature maps and one deep feature map are obtained through the MobileNetV2. The deep feature map extracts richer information through CA and uses the result as the input for the next module. In the ASPP module, dilated convolutions [9] are used to extract multi-scale features, resulting in five feature maps. Finally, a convolution is used to reduce the channel dimension, achieving multi-scale feature fusion of the five feature maps.

In the decoder, the FES structure is used to perform two upsampling [10, 23] operations on the feature maps, achieving the fusion of shallow feature maps. Finally, convolution is applied to reduce the channel dimension to the number of categories for image segmentation (see Fig. 1).

2.1 Lightweight Backbone Feature Extraction Network - MobileNetV2

The proposal of MobileNetV2 aims to address the issue of limited hardware resources during model training. Model lightweighting is one of the important ways to deploy models on mobile devices. The network structure takes a 3 × 3 convolution as input to increase the number of channels and extract features through 17 bottleneck blocks. In the bottleneck block, this structure first uses 1 × 1 point convolution to increase the number of channels, followed by 3 × 3 depthwise convolution. With the increase in channel numbers, more semantic information can be obtained. Finally, 1 × 1 point convolution is applied to reduce dimensionality and avoid loss of semantic information. The core of the bottleneck block is DSC, while the residual block prevents gradient disappearance. The figure below shows the bottleneck block (see Fig. 2).

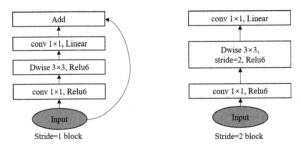

Fig. 2. Bottleneck block.

The essence of DSC is to convert the continuous multiplication during computation into continuous addition. Compared to regular convolution, using DSC significantly improves computational efficiency without significant loss in accuracy (see Fig. 3).

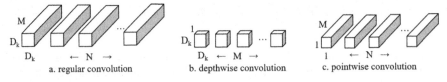

Fig. 3. Different convolution methods.

Let the size of the input feature map be $D_f \times D_f \times M$ and the size of the convolution kernel be $D_k \times D_k \times M$. For regular convolution, the required computation is $D_f \times D_f \times D_k \times D_k \times M \times N$. For DSC, the calculations required for depthwise convolution and pointwise convolution are $D_f \times D_f \times D_k \times D_k \times 1 \times N$ and $D_f \times D_f \times 1 \times 1 \times M \times N$, respectively. From the above calculations, it can be seen that the computation is reduced. The following Table 1 shows the results obtained using different convolution methods under DeepLabv3+ with MobileNetV2 as the backbone network. The obtained results can confirm the above conclusion.

Table 1. Comparison of experimental results of different convolutional methods

Convolution method in ASPP	mIoU/%	Params/MB
Regular convolution	71.35	19.73
DSC	71.02	13.48

2.2 Coordinate Attention Mechanism

Previous researchers have employed various attention mechanisms to optimize semantic segmentation networks. For instance, SENet [11] extracts semantic information through two steps: Squeeze and Excitation. However, it only considers channel information at the local level.

The CA decomposes channel attention into two 1D feature encoding processes, each capable of capturing long-range dependencies in a separate direction. When combined, it provides regional positional information, effectively considering both spatial and channel information. Additionally, this attention module exhibits strong portability. It is also compact and hardly incurs any additional resource overhead, making it highly beneficial for lightweight model designs. Compared to SENet and CBAM [12], the effect is better (see Fig. 4).

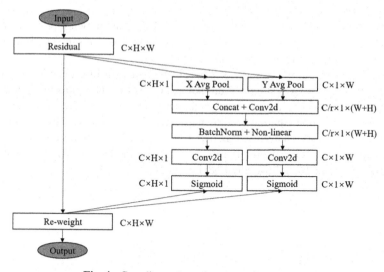

Fig. 4. Coordinate Attention network structure.

It decomposes a 2D input into a vector X as input and outputs an enhanced and equally sized vector Y with increased expressive power. Firstly, Coordinate information embedding. Secondly, Coordinate attention generation.

To verify the effectiveness of the CA module, different mechanisms were compared. The following Table 2 shows the comparison of experiments using different attention mechanisms.

Table 2. Comparison of experimental using different attention mechanisms

Module adopted	mIoU/%	Params/MB
CA	71.96	20.23
SENet	71.72	20.13
CBAM	71.73	20.13

2.3 FES Module

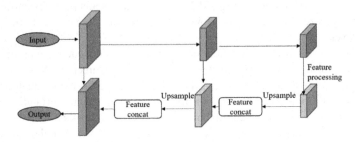

Fig. 5. FES module.

Feature Pyramid Networks [13] (FPN) is a pyramid structure network proposed by Lin et al. in 2017. This structure effectively addresses the problem of semantic information loss while minimizing the increase in parameter count.

The original model only used a shallow feature map to fuse deep-level features. Although this structure was simple, it did not achieve sufficient segmentation accuracy. Deep feature maps can make accurate semantic predictions, but they lack clear pixel localization information. Shallow feature maps have clear boundaries but contain a large amount of label noise. Therefore, this paper proposes the following improvements to the original structure: introducing the FES module in the decoder part to enhance the accuracy loss caused by lightweight model design (see Fig. 5).

3 Experimental Results and Analysis

3.1 Introduction to Experimental Environment

The experimental environment is PyTorch 1.12.0. Due to hardware performance and data constraints, transfer learning was employed by using ImageNet weights as the initial weights for the backbone network. The initial learning rate is 7e-3. The batch size is 16, and the input images were uniformly cropped to a size of 512×512.

The Cityscapes dataset [14] was used, which consists of 19 classes for semantic segmentation. These classes include road, sidewalk, building, wall, fence, pole, traffic light, traffic sign, vegetation, terrain, sky, person, rider, car, truck, bus, train, motorcycle, and bicycle. There are a total of 5000 images in the dataset, with 2975 images in the training set, 500 images in the validation set, and 1525 images in the test set.

In order to evaluate the performance of the improved model, three commonly used semantic segmentation evaluation metrics were employed as references. These metrics are mIoU, mPA and Params [15, 22].

3.2 Experimental Details

From Table 3, it can be observed that the module described in this paper achieves a good balance between lightweight design and accuracy. In terms of the number of parameters, Method 2 has a parameter size of 19.73 MB, which is approximately 1/10 of Method 1. As for mIoU, Method 1 achieves the highest value among the nine methods, reaching 75.54%. Although Method 1 has a 4.19% higher mIoU than Method 2, it has significantly fewer parameters. Method 3, after adding the DSC module to the model, reduces the parameter size by 6.05 MB without significant loss in accuracy. Method 4 and 5, which respectively incorporate the CA and FES modules into the model, both show an improvement in accuracy, demonstrating the effectiveness of these modules.

Table 3. Ablation experiment.

NO.	Methods	Backbone	mPA/%	mIoU/%	Params/MB
1	DeepLabv3+	Xception	85.93	75.54	206.23
2	DeepLabv3+	MobileNetV2	81.22	71.35	19.73
3	DeepLabv3++ DSC	MobileNetV2	80.44	71.02	13.48
4	DeepLabv3++ CA	MobileNetV2	81.97	71.96	20.23
5	DeepLabv3++ FES	MobileNetV2	82.24	72.14	20.55
6	DeepLabv3++ DSC+ CA+ FES	MobileNetV2	82.52	72.68	14.84

The model proposed in this paper is named MCDF. According to Table 4, although the traditional DeepLabv3+ model has a segmentation accuracy 2.86% higher than the model proposed in this paper measured by mIoU, its huge parameter size makes it difficult to deploy on mobile devices and does not meet the requirements of lightweight design.

Compared with BFS [16], the proposed model improves the segmentation accuracy by 0.42%. Compared with A-LinkNet [17], the two models have similar parameter sizes, but the proposed model improves the segmentation accuracy by 7.81%.

Table 4. Comparison experiment of different model.

Model	mPA/%	mIoU/%	Params × 10^6	Params/MB
DeepLabv3 +	85.93	75.54	54.06	206.23
U-Net	83.54	73.36	–	167.59
A-LinkNet	–	64.87	–	15.91
BFS	–	72.26	4.15	–
SwiftNetRN-18 [18]	–	75.50	11.80	–
DFANet A [19]	–	71.30	7.80	–
MCDF (ours)	82.52	72.68	3.89	14.84

The comparison results of the proposed model and other models obtained from the above experiments are shown in Fig. 6. It can be seen that compared with networks such as U-Net [20], the proposed method can capture more edge and detail information. In addition, it has lower computational cost and better segmentation performance compared to DeepLabv3+ using different backbone networks. Therefore, it can be concluded that the optimization of model lightweight design achieved by DSC and the effective improvement of model accuracy by CA and FES modules have been demonstrated.

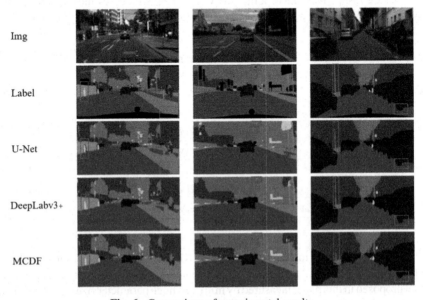

Fig. 6. Comparison of experimental results.

4 Conclusion

This paper proposes a semantic segmentation model based on DeepLabv3+, which to some extent balances efficiency and accuracy, and has strong practical significance in the field of autonomous driving. To make the model lightweight, the heavyweight Xception network in the backbone was replaced with the lightweight MobileNetV2 network. The design of depthwise separable convolutions greatly improves computational efficiency and reduces inference time, making it possible to apply the model to mobile devices. To ensure that the model's accuracy would not be significantly reduced while being lightweight, a channel attention (CA) mechanism was introduced after the backbone network to better capture long-range dependencies, reduce complex noise interference, and make the semantic information more comprehensive and accurate. In addition, the FES structure was used in the decoder to integrate multi-scale semantic information. FES enriches the position information by extracting multiple shallow features, thereby enhancing the semantic expression capability of the feature map.

However, there is still room for improvement in this model, such as its inability to accurately segment very small objects. Therefore, further research can be conducted in the future to address this issue.

References

1. Liu, X., et al.: Recent progress in semantic image segmentation. Artif. Intell. Rev. **52**, 1089–1106 (2019). https://doi.org/10.1007/s10462-018-9641-3
2. Shinde, S.S., Tarchi, D.: Joint air-ground distributed federated learning for intelligent transportation systems. IEEE Trans. Intell. Transp. Syst. **24**(9), 9996–10011 (2023)
3. Chaibou, M.S., et al.: Adaptive strategy for superpixel-based region-growing image segmentation. J. Electron. Imaging **26**(6), 061605 (2017)
4. Shelhamer, E., et al.: Fully convolutional networks for semantic segmentation. IEEE Trans. Pattern Anal. Mach. Intell. **39**(4), 640–651 (2017)
5. Chen, L.C., et al.: DeepLab: semantic image segmentation with deep convolutional nets, atrous convolution, and fully connected CRFs. IEEE Trans. Pattern Anal. Mach. Intell. **40**(4), 834–848 (2017)
6. Chen, L.C., et al.: Encoder-decoder with atrous separable convolution for semantic image segmentation. In: Proceeding of the European Conference on Computer Vision, pp. 801–818 (2018)
7. Sandler, M., et al.: MobileNetV2: inverted residuals and linear bottlenecks. IEEE Access **5**, 1–12 (2018)
8. Hou, Q., et al.: Coordinate attention for efficient mobile network design. In: Proceedings of the IEEE/CVF Conference on Computer Vision and Pattern Recognition, pp. 13713–13722 (2021)
9. Li, D., Chen, H., Jin, G., et al.: A multiscale dilated residual network for image denoising. Multimed. Tools Appl. **79**, 34443–34458 (2020). https://doi.org/10.1007/s11042-020-09113-z
10. Wang, Z., et al.: Deep learning for image super-resolution: a survey. IEEE Trans. Pattern Anal. Mach. Intell. **43**(10), 3365–3387 (2020)
11. Hu, J., et al.: Squeeze-and-excitation networks. IEEE Trans. Pattern Anal. Mach. Intell. **42**(8), 2011–2023 (2020)

12. Woo, S., et al.: CBAM: convolutional block attention module. arXiv e-prints (2018)

13. Lin, P., et al.: Feature pyramid networks for object detection. In: 2017 IEEE Conference on Computer Vision and Pattern Recognition (CVPR), Honolulu, HI, USA, 21–26 July 2017, pp. 936–944. IEEE Press, New York (2017)

14. Cordts, M., et al.: The cityscapes dataset for semantic urban scene understanding. In: 2016 IEEE Conference on Computer Vision and Pattern Recognition (CVPR), Las Vegas, NV, USA, 27–30 June 2016, pp. 3213–3223. IEEE Press, New York (2016)

15. Ulku, I., et al.: A survey on deep learning-based architectures for semantic segmentation on 2D images. Appl. Artif. Intell. **36**(1), 2157 (2022)

16. Ma, D., et al.: Image semantic segmentation based on feature fusion and attention mechanism. Comput. Eng. Sci. **45**(03), 495–503 (2023)

17. Du, M., et al.: A-LinkNet: semantic segmentation network with attention and spatial information fusion. Liq. Cryst. Displays **37**(09), 1199–1208 (2022)

18. Orsic, M., Kreso, I., Bevandic, P., et al.: In defense of pre-trained imagenet architectures for real-time semantic segmentation of road-driving images. In: Proceedings of the IEEE/CVF Conference on Computer Vision and Pattern Recognition, pp. 12607–12616 (2019)

19. Chen, Q., et al.: Multi-path semantic segmentation based on edge optimization and global modeling. Comput. Sci. **50**(S1), 431–437 (2023)

20. Ronneberger, O., Fischer, P., Brox, T.: U-Net: convolutional networks for biomedical image segmentation. In: Navab, N., Hornegger, J., Wells, W.M., Frangi, A.F. (eds.) MICCAI 2015. LNCS, vol. 9351, pp. 234–241. Springer, Cham (2015). https://doi.org/10.1007/978-3-319-24574-4_28

21. Chen, Z., Lu, H., Tian, S., et al.: Construction of a hierarchical feature enhancement network and its application in fault recognition. IEEE Trans. Ind. Informat. **17**(7), 4827–4836 (2020)

22. Xu, X., Tian, J., Lin, K., et al.: Zero-shot cross-modal retrieval by assembling autoencoder and generative adversarial network. ACM Trans. Multimedia Comput. Commun. Appl. (TOMM) **17**(1s), 1–17 (2021)

23. Wang, G., Xu, X., Shen, F., et al.: Cross-modal dynamic networks for video moment retrieval with text query. IEEE Trans. Multimedia **24**, 1221–1232 (2022)

What is a Proper Face Registration for Face Recognition?

Yaotang Lv$^{(\boxtimes)}$, Zhantao Fan, Kun Zhang, Zhizhong Li, and Kun Sun

China Southern Power Grid Company Limited, Guangzhou, China
traccce_tam@163.com

Abstract. Face recognition systems have now made significant progress. In practice, we may face the important question of what is a better face registration for a typical face recognition algorithm, but this problem has often been overlooked in the past. In this paper, we aim to answer this question by investigating the relationship between different face registration methods and the performance of different face recognition algorithms. Both the global and the local affine transform based face registration methods are investigated. Our conclusions are that a more accurate face registration is not necessarily for different face recognition algorithms. In most cases, a face registration based on the global rigid transformation with three landmarks works well enough. On the contrary, an excessive registration based on the non-rigid transformation with a large number of landmarks can lead to a distortion of the face structure and then weaken the recognition performance. Furthermore, the face contour is important for distinguishing different faces and should be preserved in the cropping stage of face registration.

Keywords: Face registration · Face alignment · Face recognition · Landmark

1 Introduction

A complete face recognition system generally includes the following four parts: 1) face image acquisition and registration, 2) optional preprocessing (illumination normalization, pose correction, et al., 3) feature extraction, and 4) face matching. A face registration step consists of the face alignment and the face cropping. The face alignment is to casts a face image into a reference coordinate system through transferring the original image. The face cropping is to extract the interest face region and to ensure the same size of pixels for images.

With the dramatic increase in the amount of face recognition systems, a wide variety of face registration methods have been proposed. Beyond the accuracy of landmark localization [1], various numbers of landmarks are used, like two landmarks [26, 28], three landmarks [9], 17 landmarks [22], 21 landmarks [2], 29 landmarks [16], 31 landmarks [6], 33 landmarks [17], 68 landmarks [18, 19], 83 landmarks [20], and 98 landmarks [21]. The 3D dense face alignment algorithms [23, 24, 37] developed in recent years consider thousands of landmarks, but this technique is generally applied to 3D face reconstruction rather than 2D face recognition. There also exist various manners of face cropping, for examples, some ones extract only the interest region included internal structures such as the brow, eyes, nose, mouth, and chin but did not extend to the occluding contour by using different masks [2, 9, 26]. Some other ones keep the region included the full face [5–7, 28]. For the face recognition systems using multiple facial features, the mixed cropping manners are employed [27]. The combination of different face transformation (alignment) and cropping methods has resulted in a variety of face registration approaches.

Many researchers have pointed out that the accurate registration[1] of the faces is of vital importance to obtain acceptable performance of the face recognition [4], however, we may still face with the following questions:

1) Is a more accurate face registration necessary a more proper face registration for different face recognition system?
2) Which kind of face registration is more suitable for a typical face recognition algorithm?

In this paper we seek to answer these two questions. We investigate these questions in two ways. First, we study the distribution of registered faces under different registration methods in the linear subspaces learned by PCA [7] and LLE [3], respectively. Secondly, the effect of face registration approaches on the performance of different face recognition algorithms is investigated. Here, the face recognition algorithms investigated differ mainly in their feature extraction, since face recognition depends strongly on the particular choice of features used by the classifier [8, 37].

Our conclusion is that more accurate face registration is not necessary for achieving more accurate face recognition. In most cases, a face registration based on the global affine transformation with three landmarks works well enough. On the contrary, an excessive registration based on a non-rigid transformation with a large number of landmarks can lead to a distortion of the face structure and then weaken the recognition performance. Furthermore, the face contour is important for face discrimination and should be preserved in the registered image.

1.1 Related Work

The investigation of relationship between face registration and face recognition performance can be found in previous literatures [10–13]. These existing works focus mainly on the impact of registration accuracy especially the landmark error on face recognition. The authors in [11] analyze quantitatively the impact of face registration errors on different face recognition algorithms by distorting the landmark co-ordinates with Gaussian noise. In [13], Shan et al. evaluate the Fisherface's sensitivity to mis-alignment by perturbing the eye coordinates, which reveals that the imprecise localization of the facial landmarks abruptly degrades the Fisherface system. Araujo et al. [12] study the importance of face registration on the PCA-based recognition algorithms by rotating and shifting the face images. In the issue [10], the authors point out that using more landmarks results in better face verification performance, even when the landmarking

---

[1] Here, the accurate face registration relates to two items: 1) correct location of landmarks, and 2) employing more landmarks.

is not so accurate. On the same landmarks, the most accurate landmarking method will give the best verification performance.

Fig. 1. Examples of face registration. From left to right are the input face image and the results of face registration by global affine transformation based on 2, 3, 5, 21, and 33 landmarks, respectively.

In this works, we don't go on studying the effect of landmark accuracy on face recognition, but focus on the effect of various face alignment method, including landmark-based and landmark-free alignment, as well as the face cropping on face recognition performance. Contrarily, to ignore the effect of landmark accuracy on our investigation, all landmarks will be manually located in the experiment.

2 Face Registration Methods

A face registration generally consists of the face alignment and the face cropping. The face alignment is to casts a face image into a reference coordinate system. The face cropping is to extract the interest face region and to guarantee the same size of pixel of images. In this section, we introduce the common face registration methods.

2.1 Face Alignment

The face registration is to fit the facial landmarks to the pre-defined landmark locations by deforming the input image. A global rigid affine transformation including rotation, scaling, and translation with few (generally less than 5) landmark is always employed for such a registration. When using many (such as 68) landmarks, a triangulation-based affine transformation is employed.

Global Rigid Affine Transformation
Let $X^0 = \{x_1^0, \cdots, x_N^0\}$ and $P = \{x_1, \cdots, x_N\}$ denote the corresponding landmark sets from input face and template images, respectively, where $x_i \in R^{2 \times 1}$ denotes the 2D coordinate of a landmark. The affine registration problem seeks for an affine transformation $T = (A, t)$ that minimizes the following least-square error function:

$$E(A, t) = \sum_{i=1}^{N} \left\| A x_i^0 + t - x_i \right\|^2 \qquad (1)$$

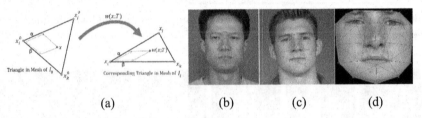

(a)   (b)   (c)   (d)

Fig. 2. Demonstration of the triangulation-based affine transformation for face alignment. (a) illustrates the affine warp $W(x;T)$ for a triangle pair, (b) is the reference template with Delaunay triangulation based on 33 landmarks, (c) is the input target face with Delaunay triangulation, (d) is the wrapped target face aligned to the reference template.

where $A \in R^{2 \times 2}$ is a non-singular matrix and $t \in R^{2 \times 1}$ is the translational component of the affine transformation. For the rigid case, A is an orthogonal matrix. The above optimization problem can be easily solved by solving a system of linear equations. Since there are total six variables in (1), using three non-collinear landmarks ensures an unique solution for T. Employing more than three landmarks, however, may leave out strict alignment[2]. In piratical, the centers of the eyes, the tip of nose, and the center of the mouth are always used as landmarks for attaining a suitable affine registration. When getting the affine transformation $T = (A, t)$, the deformed face image I from input image I_0 can be produced by

$$I(x) = I_0(A^{-1}x - t) \tag{2}$$

The global affine transform essentially inducts a rigid deformation for the face image. Figure 1 shows the examples of face alignment based on the global affine transform with various landmarks.

Local Non-rigid Affine Transformation

To achieve an accurate registration, many landmarks should be considered. Employing more than three landmarks, however, generally won't cause a strict alignment by the global affine deformation. To address this problem, the affine alignment based on a triangulation is always used [29]. Given the input image I_0 and target image I_t, they are both triangulated based on their landmarks. Then, the face deformation is achieved by applying the affine transformation (piecewise linear mapping functions) $w(x; T)$ that is unique to each triangle pair between the meshes from I_0 and I_t. For each triangle region, there are three landmarks (vertexes of the triangle) resulting in an exact solution for T, thus a strict alignment can be achieved for the whole face image. The example of such face alignment is shown in Fig. 2. Some more details could be referred in [18]. The triangulation-based affine alignment is good for extracting the face texture, hence always bundled to the Active Appearance Models (AAM) [15] with lots of landmarks.

2.2 Face Cropping

Besides the face alignment, the face cropping also plays an important role in face recognition. There exist various manners of face cropping. In this paper, we investigate two

---

[2] The strict alignment means casting the landmarks to the destinations exactly.

kind of cropping for face image, with one extracting only the interest region inside the occluding contour, with another one preserving the full face. The examples of these two face cropping manners are illustrated in Fig. 3.

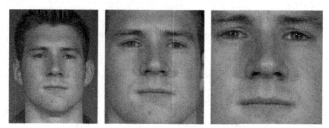

Fig. 3. Examples of face cropping. From left to right are the aligned face image, the cropped result containing facial contour, and the cropped result inside the facial contour.

3   Impact of Face Registration on Sample Distribution

This section investigates the distribution of face samples corresponding to different kinds of face alignment on various feature spaces. In particular, the samples are discussed in terms of their level of within-class scatter and between-class scatter. The features considered include the original grey values as well as the reduced-dimensional map by PCA and LLE, respectively. To eliminate the impact of positioning error on landmarks, we locate all the landmarks manually.

3.1   Within-Class Scatter

The within-class scatter is defined as follows.

$$S_i = \frac{1}{n_i} \sum_{x \in D_i} \frac{\|x - m_i\|_2}{d} \tag{3}$$

where x is the vector of a face image, D_i are the image set of the i-th person. The $m_i = \frac{1}{n_i} \sum_{x \in D_i} x$ is the sample mean of the i-th person. The n_i is the number of images of the i-th person, and d is the number of pixels in an image. Obviously, the smaller S_i is, the more clustered the distribution of samples in class i is, and the more favorable it is for sample classification. On the contrary, the larger S_i is, the more dispersed the distribution of samples in class i is.

Table 1 displays the mean values of S_i computed with multiple face feature from the CMU-PIE face database [33]. In this case, PCA reduces the samples to 25 dimensions and LLE to 7 dimensions. From Table 1, it can be seen that face alignment by global affine transformation with 2 or 3 landmarks does not change much in the intra-class distribution of the samples. However, strict alignment by triangulation-based affine transformation with 30 or 68 landmarks does not result in a significantly greater aggregation of samples from the same class; on the contrary, the distribution of within-class samples corresponding to this alignment is much more dispersed in the subspace by PCA and LLE. This is mainly due to the fact that the triangle warping processing leads to severe distortion of the image texture. In addition, the case of preserving contours performed better than the case of not preserving contours.

Table 1. Average within-class scatter on CMU-PIE.

#land-mark	2	2	3	3	30	68
Preservation of contours	No	Yes	No	Yes	Yes	Yes
Original	0.418	0.364	0.417	0.362	0.325	0.322
PCA	161.6	159.2	161.5	158.1	172.2	171.8
LLE	0.179	0.084	0.200	0.134	0.264	0.256

Table 2. Between-class scatter on CMU-PIE.

#land-mark	2	2	3	3	30	68
Preservation of contours	No	Yes	No	Yes	Yes	Yes
Original	0.226	0.241	0.223	0.246	0.165	0.154
PCA	83.10	101.1	82.15	103.2	82.65	81.37
LLE	0.119	0.188	0.131	0.185	0.126	0.118

3.2 Between-Class Distribution

The between-class scatter is defined as follows.

$$S_b = \frac{1}{n} \sum_{i=1}^{c} n_i \frac{\|m_i - m\|_2}{d} \tag{4}$$

where m is the mean of all samples, n is the total number of samples, and the significance of n_i, m_i, and d is the same as (1). Obviously, the larger Sb is, the greater the distinguishability of different classes of samples is, and vice versa, the smaller the distinguishability is. Table 2 displays the Sb computed with multiple face features on the CMU-PIE face database. From Table 2, in general, the between-class gap of the samples based on the alignment of 3 landmarks is larger than that of the samples based on the alignment using 2 landmarks. In addition, the between-class gap obtained by the cropping method that preserves the contours of the face is larger compared to the one by cropping method that preserves only part of the face region. It is particularly noteworthy that the between-class gap becomes rather smaller using a strict alignment with 30 or 68 landmarks, which is not conducive to sample classification.

Table 3. Face recognition rates (rank-1, %)

Dataset	CMU-PIE					
#landmark	2	2	3	3	30	68
Keep Contours	No	Yes	No	Yes	Yes	Yes
LBP	70.5	85.3	73.2	87.7	60.3	61.0
HGPP	68.1	83.2	70.4	85.8	58.3	58.4
Eigenfaces	48.7	66.7	66.7	67.6	47.8	47.2
Fisherfaces	50.1	68.6	66.3	70.3	45.3	45.6
ArcFace	90.7	99.9	95.4	99.9	81.9	81.7
CosFace	89.4	99.6	94.7	99.7	81.4	81.3
SphereFace	88.9	99.0	94.1	99.2	80.3	80.2
Dataset	LFW					
LBP	59.4	76.6	65.9	73.8	49.9	51.5
HGPP	55.2	75.9	63.1	74.2	48.3	48.2
Eigenfaces	48.7	66.7	64.7	67.6	47.8	47.2
Fisherfaces	50.1	68.6	66.3	70.3	45.3	45.6
ArcFace	84.5	99.7	90.6	99.8	75.8	73.2
CosFace	83.7	98.2	90.4	99.1	73.9	72.9
SphereFace	82.6	98.1	89.8	99.0	72.3	71.8
Dataset	YTF					
LBP	60.1	73.5	63.8	71.9	46.6	45.9
HGPP	54.7	72.4	61.7	70.2	45.0	44.2
Eigenfaces	46.1	64.3	63.2	65.8	44.6	44.4
Fisherfaces	48.0	66.2	64.0	69.8	43.1	42.7
ArcFace	80.3	96.1	88.2	96.2	73.2	71.8
CosFace	79.4	95.4	87.9	95.8	72.7	70.7
SphereFace	78.3	95.2	85.4	95.3	71.9	70.3

4   Effect of Face Registration on Face Recognition

The impact of face registration on face recognition is also investigated. For face recognition algorithm, we consider the local descriptors including LBP [26] and Gabor feature HGPP [28], the holistic facial descriptors including Eigenfaces [5] and Fisherfaces [7], and the deep learning models including ArcFace [30], CosFace [31], and SphereFace [32]. The Nearest Neighbor is used for the final face classification. The experiments are conducted on the CMU-PIE [33], LFW [34] and YTF [35] datasets which are the most widely used benchmark for unconstrained face verification. For each person, one image is randomly selected as a query and the rest of the images are used as gallery.

The face recognition results in Table 3 show that 1) in most cases, the recognition effect of face alignment based on 3 landmarks is better than that based on 2 landmarks; 2) retaining the face contour when cropping is more favorable to face recognition than retaining only part of the internal region of the face; and 3) strict face alignment with 30 or 68 landmarks, on the contrary, leads to a significant decrease in the recognition rate of the face. Swapping more landmarks leads more similar shapes for the registered faces, but also changes the personal facial structures and even the facial texture. The above three experimental conclusions are basically consistent with the results of the previous analysis of the sample distribution, and the different face alignment methods mainly lead to different gaps between classes thus affecting the recognition results.

5   Conclusion

This paper presents an experimental study on the effect of face alignment on face recognition. The study shows that it is not necessary to perform a very strict alignment of faces for face recognition, and an alignment based on three landmarks (two eyes and the center of the mouth) is basically sufficient. On the contrary, strict face alignment with too many landmarks can lead to distortion of face information and narrowing of the inter-class gap, which is not conducive to between-class differentiation. In addition, face contours are important information to distinguish different faces and should be preserved as much as possible when performing face cropping. This paper gives several guiding suggestions for the implementation of face recognition systems, and will later be combined with theoretical in-depth studies for more general cases.

References

1. Li, H., Guo, Z., Rhee, S.M., Han, S., Han, J.J.: Towards accurate facial landmark detection via cascaded transformers. In: Proceedings of the IEEE/CVF Conference on Computer Vision and Pattern Recognition (2022)
2. Xie, X.D., Lam, K.M.: Face recognition under varying illumination based on a 2D face shape model. Pattern Recognit. **38**(2), 221–230 (2005)
3. Roweis, S.T., Saul, L.K.: Nonlinear dimensionality reduction by locally linear embedding. Science **290**(5000), 2323–2326 (2000)
4. Beumer, G.M., Spreeuwers, L.J., Veldhuis, R.N.J.: The effect of image resolution on the performance of a face recognition system. In: The 9th International Conference on Control, Automation, Robotics and Vision, ICARCV 2006 (2006)
5. Turk, M., Pentland, A.: Eigenfaces for recognition. J. Cogn. Neurosci. **3**(1), 71–86 (1999)
6. Wiskott, L., Fellous, J.-M., Krüger, N., von der Malsburg, C.: Face recognition by elastic bunch graph matching. IEEE Trans. Pattern Anal. Mach. Intell. **19**(7), 775–779 (1997)
7. Belhumeur, P.N., Hespanha, J.P., Kriegman, D.J.: Eigenfaces vs. fisherfaces: recognition using class specific linear projection. IEEE Trans. Pattern Anal. Mach. Intell. **19**(7), 711–720 (1997)
8. Liu, C., Wechsler, H.: Evolutionary pursuit and its application to face recognition. IEEE Trans. Pattern Anal. Mach. Intell. **22**(6), 570–582 (2000)
9. Xie, X., Zheng, W.-S., Lai, J., Yuan, P.C.: Face illumination normalization on large and small scale features. In: IEEE Conference on Computer Vision and Pattern Recognition (CVPR), Alaska (2008)

10. Beumer, G., Tao, Q., Bazen, A., Veldhuis, R.: A landmark paper in face recognition. In: Proceedings of the 7th International Conference on Automatic Face and Gesture Recognition, Southampton, UK (2006)
11. Rentzeperis, E., Stergiou, A., Pnevmatikakis, A., Polymenakos, L.: Impact of face registration errors on recognition. IFIP Int. Fed. Inf. Process. **204**, 187–194 (2006)
12. Araujo, B.S., Machado, AM.C.. Towards a better comprehension of the role of image registration in face recognition algorithms. In: IEEE Workshop on Biometric Measurements and Systems for Security and Medical Applications (BIOMS) (2011)
13. Shan, S.-G., Gao, W., Chang, Y.-Z., Cao, B., Chen, X.-L.: "Curse of mis-alignment" problem in face recognition. Chin. J. Comput. (Chin.) **28**(5) (2005)
14. Cootes, T.F., Taylor, C.J., Cooper, D.H., Graham, J.: Active shape models-their training and application. Comput. Vision Image Underst. **61**(1), 38–59 (1995)
15. Cootes, T.F., Edwards, G.J., Taylor, C.J.: Active appearance models. IEEE Trans. Pattern Anal. Mach. Intell. **23**(6), 681–685 (2001)
16. Burgos-Artizzu, X.P., Perona, P., Dollár, P.: Robust face landmark estimation under occlusion. In: ICCV, pp. 1513–1520 (2013)
17. Liu, M.: Discriminative face alignment. IEEE TPAMI **31**(11), 1941–1954 (2009)
18. Matthews, I., Baker, S.: Active appearance models revisited. Int. J. Comput. Vision **60**(2), 135–164 (2004)
19. Jin, H., Liao, S., Shao, L.: Pixel-in-pixel net: towards efficient facial landmark detection in the wild. IJCV **129**, 1–21 (2021)
20. Yan, S., Liu, C., Li, S.Z., Zhang, H., Shum, H.-Y., Cheng, Q.: Face alignment using texture-constrained active shape models. Image Vision Comput. **21**(1), 69–75 (2003)
21. Wu, W., Qian, C., Yang, S., Wang, Q., Cai, Y., Zhou, Q.: Look at boundary: a boundary-aware face alignment algorithm. In: CVPR, pp. 2129–2138 (2018)
22. Beumer, G., Tao, Q., Bazen, A., Veldhuis, R.: A landmark paper in face recognition. In: Automatic Face and Gesture Recognition, FG 2006. IEEE (2006)
23. Zhu, X., Lei, Z., Liu, X., Shi, H., Li, S.Z.: Face alignment across large poses: a 3D solution. In: Proceedings of the IEEE Conference on Computer Vision and Pattern Recognition (2016)
24. Guo, J., Zhu, X., Yang, Y., Yang, F., Lei, Z., Li, S.Z.: Towards fast, accurate and stable 3D dense face alignment. In: Vedaldi, A., Bischof, H., Brox, T., Frahm, J.-M. (eds.) ECCV 2020. LNCS, vol. 12364, pp. 152–168. Springer, Cham (2020). https://doi.org/10.1007/978-3-030-58529-7_10
25. Spreeuwers, L.J., Boom, B.J., Veldhuis, R.N.J.: Better than best: matching score based face registration. In: Proceedings of the 28th Symposium on Information Theory in the Benelux, 24–25 May 2007, Enschede, The Netherlands (2007)
26. Ahonen, T., Hadid, A., Pietikainen, M.: Face Description with local binary patterns: application to face recognition. IEEE Trans. Pattern Anal. Mach. Intell. **28**(12), 2037–2041 (2006)
27. Su, Y., Shan, S., Chen, X., Gao, W.: Hierarchical ensemble of global and local classifiers for face recognition. IEEE Trans. Image Process. **18**(8), 1885–1896 (2009)
28. Zhang, B., Shan, S., Chen, X., Gao, W.: Histogram of gabor phase patterns (HGPP): a novel object representation approach for face recognition. IEEE Trans. Image Process. **16**(1), 57–68 (2007)
29. Goshtasby, A.: Piecewise linear mapping functions for image registration. Pattern Recognit **19**(6), 459–466 (1986)
30. Deng, J., Guo, J., Xue, N., Zafeiriou, S.: ArcFace: additive angular margin loss for deep face recognition. In: Proceedings of the IEEE/CVF Conference on Computer Vision and Pattern Recognition, pp. 4690–4699 (2019)
31. Wang, H., et al.: CosFace: large margin cosine loss for deep face recognition. In: Proceedings of the IEEE Conference on Computer Vision and Pattern Recognition, pp. 5265–5274 (2018)

32. Liu, W., Wen, Y., Yu, Z., Li, M., Raj, B., Song, L.: SphereFace: deep hypersphere embedding for face recognition. In: Proceedings of the IEEE Conference on Computer Vision and Pattern Recognition, pp. 212–220 (2017)

33. Sim, T., Baker, S., Bsat, M.: The CMU pose, illumination, and expression (PIE) database. In Proceedings of Fifth IEEE International Conference on Automatic Face Gesture Recognition, pp. 53–58. IEEE (2002)

34. Huang, G.B., Ramesh, M., Berg, T., Learned-Miller, E.: Labeled faces in the wild: a database for studying face recognition in unconstrained environments. Technical report (2007)

35. Wolf, L., Hassner, T., Maoz, I.: Face recognition in unconstrained videos with matched background similarity. In: CVPR (2011)

36. Zhao, W., Lu, H., Wang, D.: Multisensor image fusion and enhancement in spectral total variation domain. IEEE Trans. Multimed. **20**(4), 866–879 (2017)

37. Chen, Z., et al.: Construction of a hierarchical feature enhancement network and its application in fault recognition. IEEE Trans. Industr. Inform. **17**(7), 4827–4836 (2020)

An Effective Hand Pose Estimation Based Evaluation Method in Assessing Parkinson's Finger Tap Movements

Qingyun He and Hao Gao[✉]

Nanjing University of Posts and Communications, Nanjing, China
tsgaohao@gmail.com

Abstract. Parkinson's disease (PD) a neurodegenerative disorder that affects motor function and significantly impacts the quality of life. Accurate and objective assessment of motor impairments, such as finger tapping movements, is crucial for diagnosis and monitoring disease progression. Traditional methods for assessing finger tapping movements in PD have limitations in terms of subjectivity, limited metrics, invasiveness, and limited monitoring scope. In this study, we propose an effective assessment method that combines hand pose estimation, feature extraction, and score generation to evaluate finger tapping movements in PD patients. The method utilizes non-contact hand pose estimation techniques to accurately capture hand movements. Relevant motion parameters, such as finger opening amplitude and tapping speed, are extracted using feature extraction algorithms. Then, the extracted parameters are used as features and input into a trained TCN classification network to generate an assessment score reflecting finger tapping performance. Experimental results demonstrate that the proposed method achieves an accuracy of 84.75% in evaluating finger tapping actions in PD patients, can effectively assessing finger tapping movements.

Keywords: Parkinson's disease (PD) · Finger tapping movement · Hand pose estimation · Non-contact technology

1 Introduction

Parkinson's disease is the second most common neurodegenerative disease characterized by motor symptoms such as tremors, rigidity, bradykinesia, and postural instability [1–3]. Accurate and objective assessment of motor impairments is crucial for diagnosis and monitoring disease progression. The finger tapping test is a commonly used assessment to evaluate motor dysfunction in Parkinson's disease (PD) [4]. It is also utilized in neurophysiological examinations [5]. This test is particularly relevant as the motor characteristics observed during finger tapping, such as speed and coordination, are closely associated with bradykinesia [6, 7]. However, manual observation and subjective scoring introduce variability and subjectivity.

Smith et al. [4] developed a wearable sensor system using inertial sensors like accelerometers and gyroscopes to monitor hand motion during tapping tests. Lones et al. [8] utilized lightweight sensors equipped with gyroscopes and accelerometers to evaluate the efficacy of levodopa therapy. St. Louis et al. [9] conducted research involving electromyography (EMG) to investigate the rapid eye movement (REM) sleep behavior disorder (RBD) associated with Parkinson's disease (PD). Li et al. [5] utilized deep learning algorithms for pose estimation in video-based evaluations of parkinsonism and Levodopa-Induced Dyskinesia (LID).

This study presents a method for evaluating finger tapping movements in Parkinson's disease patients. It combines hand pose estimation, feature extraction, and scoring to accurately assess finger tapping performance. The method utilizes non-contact hand pose estimation, extracts relevant features, and generates evaluation scores reflecting tapping performance, demonstrating high objectivity and accuracy in experiments.

2   The Proposed Method

Figure 1 illustrates an overview of our method, which comprises three main components: pose estimation, feature extraction, and score generation.

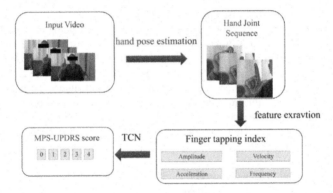

Fig. 1. Pipeline of our method.

In the pose estimation phase, advanced algorithms track hand joint movements for insights into hand motion. During feature extraction, we compute four key parameters capturing relevant hand movement traits. These parameters serve as input features for a trained classifier, generating a 5-point assessment score. This objective score informs clinicians about bradykinesia severity based on quantifiable data. We aim to enhance the accuracy and reliability of bradykinesia assessment, ultimately advancing the diagnosis and treatment of Parkinson's disease.

2.1   Data Preparation

We collected data from Parkinson's disease (PD) patients at Southeast University Zhongda Hospital from December 2021 to March 2023. The dataset includes videos of patients performing the finger tapping test (item 3.4 of the MDS-UPDRS III assessment) and corresponding neurologist scores.

Recordings were made with a smartphone at 30 frames per second and 1920x1080-pixel resolution. Patients were positioned 1.5 m from the smartphone on a tripod, focusing on their upper body. They performed 10-s finger tapping sequences for both hands.

The conventional clinical assessment for bradykinesia relies on visual evaluation by experienced clinicians using Item 3.4 of the UPDRS. It considers factors like tapping speed, finger opening extent, hesitations, and finger opening decline, with scores ranging from 0 (normal) to 4 (severe). For detailed score distributions, please refer to Table 1.

Table 1. Score distribution of data set.

Score	0	1	2	3	4	Total
Quantity	18	14	14	30	4	80
Proportion (%)	22.5	17.5	17.5	37.5	5	100

2.2 Hand Pose Estimation

We employ the robust Mediapipe [7] pose estimation algorithm to extract hand skeleton sequences from finger-tapping test videos of PD patients. This widely-used framework predicts key point coordinates such as wrist, finger joints, and fingertips, even when the hand is partially visible or occluded. Mediapipe Hands utilizes a two-model approach, with the Palm Detection Model predicting the hand's bounding box and the Hand Landmark Model operating within this region, accurately identifying hand landmarks and providing precise coordinates for 21 knuckles, as illustrated in Fig. 2, along with their respective positions and labels.

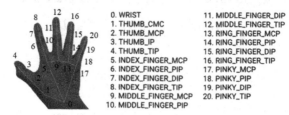

Fig. 2. The location and name of the 21 coordinates returned by MediaPipe Hands.

In Fig. 2, we utilize the coordinate to denote the joint i. Assume that each hand skeleton comprises i joint points, and each video consists of T frames. The hand feature M_t of frame t can be represented as (Fig. 3):

$$M_t = \left\{ J_1^t, J_2^t, ..., J_i^t \right\} \tag{1}$$

Fig. 3. The effect of extracting hand key points in patients' finger tapping by Mediapipe Hands.

2.3 Feature Extraction

In UPDRS item 3.4, we assess the severity of motor impairment in Parkinson's disease by examining factors such as the speed and amplitude of finger opening, the presence of hesitation or pauses, and the trend of decreasing amplitude in finger tapping. To establish action rules for this assessment, our study introduces a novel feature extraction method. This method involves using the index fingertip coordinates (x_4, y_4) and the thumb fingertip coordinates (x_8, y_8) as reference points. We calculate the Euclidean distance between these two points to generate fingertip distance data for frame t. This data helps us analyze changes in range and velocity during finger tapping, as depicted below:

$$D_t = \sqrt[2]{\left(x_4^t - x_8^t\right)^2 + \left(y_4^t - y_8^t\right)^2} \tag{2}$$

D_t values, originally based on pixel distances in images, can be influenced by shooting distance and camera jitter variations, leading to data scale differences. To rectify this, we employ Z-score standardization. We first calculate the μ and σ values for D_t.

$$\mu = \frac{D_1 + D_2 + ... + D_T}{T} = \frac{\sum_{t=1}^{T} D_t}{T} \tag{3}$$

$$\sigma = \sqrt{\frac{\sum_{t=1}^{T} (D_t - \mu)^2}{T}} \tag{4}$$

Then the standardized data of frame t can be expressed as:

$$S_t = \frac{D_t - \mu}{\sigma} \tag{5}$$

Due to camera movement and inaccuracies in hand pose estimation, the distance curve often contains noise and false local extrema. To address this issue, we follow the approach of Li et al. [10] and apply a Savitzky-Golay filter with a polynomial order of 3 and a window length of 7. This filtering helps reduce noise and results in a smoother curve. Additionally, we use the following formulas for speed and acceleration:

$$V_t = D_{t+1} - D_t \tag{6}$$

$$A_t = V_{t+1} - V_t \tag{7}$$

At the same time, we define one finger tap as a period T, and the frequency F is defined as:

$$F = \frac{1}{T} \tag{8}$$

2.4 Feature Extraction

Our study's feature data, when processed with TCN (Temporal Convolutional Networks) [11], shows promise for time series analysis. TCN is a deep learning model employing one-dimensional CNN structures to effectively capture data patterns. It uses convolutional kernels with different dilation factors to handle various time scales. To combat deep network degradation, TCN employs residual connections, merging convolutional layer outputs with inputs to enhance feature extraction. See Fig. 4 for the flowchart.

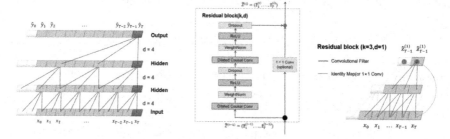

Fig. 4. Illustrates TCN architectural elements: (a) Dilated causal convolution with various dilation factors and filter size. (b) TCN residual block with optional 1x1 convolution. (c) An example of a residual connection in TCN, showing filters in the residual function (purple lines) and identity mappings (blue lines).(Color figure online)

3 Experiment and Results

Due to our small dataset, we applied 5-fold cross-validation for dependable model accuracy assessment, dividing the dataset into five subsets for iterative training and evaluation, resulting in a robust performance estimate. The final results in Table 2 average all five rounds, achieving an 84.75% classification accuracy.

The results in Table 2 were obtained through 5-fold cross-validation, which demonstrates the reliable and stable performance of our proposed algorithm. The overall performance indicators reflect the excellent performance of the model. This paper employs four metrics, namely Accuracy, Precision, Recall, and F1-Score, to evaluate the effectiveness of classification and recognition. The calculation methods of the four indicators are listed as follows:

$$\text{Accuracy} = \frac{TP + TN}{TP + TN + FP + FN} \tag{9}$$

Table 2. Results of five-fold cross validation results.

5-fold	1	2	3	4	5	Average
Accuracy (%)	82.35	84.90	87.10	83.20	86.20	84.75

$$Pricision = \frac{TP}{TP + FP} \tag{10}$$

$$Recall = \frac{TP}{TP + FN} \tag{11}$$

$$F1 - Score = \frac{2 \times Precision \times Recall}{Precision + Recal} \tag{12}$$

TP is correct positives, FP is misclassified negatives as positives, FN is misclassified positives as negatives, and TN is correct negatives. Table 3 shows the results of four indicators, which are also obtained by the 5-fold cross validated.

Table 3. Results of five-fold cross validation results.

Score	Accuracy (%)	Precision (%)	Recall (%)	F1 (%)
0	78.75	62.5	55.56	58.82
1	88.75	87.5	50.0	63.64
2	88.75	90.0	64.29	75.0
3	75.0	78.95	50.0	61.45
4	92.5	66.67	50.0	57.14

Figure 5's confusion matrix, based on classification results, reveals that the model demonstrates strong robustness, with error rates for each score being acceptable and mainly occurring in adjacent scores.

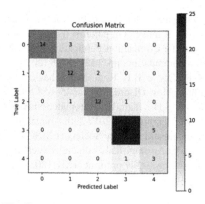

Fig. 5. The confusion matrix of the model.

4 Conclusion

We used hand pose estimation to assess Parkinson's motor impairments in the Tapping Test. Our approach employed the Mediapipe algorithm to analyze finger-tapping videos for features like speed and amplitude. Through 5-fold cross-validation on a limited dataset, our model achieved an 84.75% average accuracy. Our method offers objective, real-time, non-intrusive, and remote assessment without extra sensors. It was validated through expert rating comparisons. Future work aims to improve accuracy and generalizability by refining the classification model and adding more features.

References

1. Arias, P., Robles-García, V., Espinosa, N., Corral, Y., Cudeiro, J.: Validity of the finger tapping test in Parkinson's disease, elderly and young healthy subjects: is there a role for central fatigue? Clin. Neurophysiol. **123**(10), 2034–2041 (2012)
2. Cao, Z., Hidalgo, G., Simon, T., Wei, S.E., Sheikh, Y.: Openpose: realtime multiperson 2D pose estimation using part affinity fields. IEEE Trans. Pattern Anal. Mach. Intell. **43**(1), 172–186 (2021)
3. Fang, C., Lv, L., Mao, S., et al.: Cognition deficits in Parkinson's disease: mechanisms and treatment. Parkinson's Dis. (2020)
4. Foki, T., et al.: Finger dexterity deficits in Parkinson's disease and somatosensory cortical dysfunction. Parkinsonism Relat. Disord. **21**(3), 259–265 (2015)
5. Goetz, C.G., et al.: Movement disorder society-sponsored revision of the unified Parkinson's disease rating scale (MDS-UPDRS): scale presentation and clinimetric testing results. Move. Disord.: Off. J. Move. Disord. Soc. 2129–2170 (2008)
6. Leijnse, J.N., Campbell-Kyureghyan, N.H., Spektor, D., Quesada, P.M.: Assessment of individual finger muscle activity in the extensor digitorum communis by surface EMG. J. Neurophysiol. **100**(6), 3225–3235 (2008)
7. Li, M.H., Mestre, T.A., Fox, S.H., Taati, B.: Automated vision-based analysis of levodopa-induced dyskinesia with deep learning. In: 2017 39th Annual International Conference of the IEEE Engineering in Medicine and Biology Society (EMBC), pp. 3377–3380. IEEE (2017)

8. Lones, M.A., Alty, J.E., Duggan-Carter, P., Turner, A.J., Jamieson, D.S., Smith, S.L.: Classification and characterisation of movement patterns during levodopa therapy for Parkinson's disease. In: Proceedings of the Companion Publication of the 2014 Annual Conference on Genetic and Evolutionary Computation, pp. 1321–1328 (2014)
9. St Louis, E.K., Boeve, A.R., Boeve, B.F.: Rem sleep behavior disorder in Parkinson's disease and others ynucleinopathies. Mov. Disord. **32**(5), 645–658 (2017)
10. Li, M.H., Mestre, T.A., Fox, S.H., Taati, B.: Automated vision-based analysis of levodopa-induced dyskinesia with deep learning. In: 2017 39th Annual International Conference of the IEEE Engineering in Medicine and Biology Society (EMBC), pp. 3377–3380. IEEE (2017)
11. Bai, S., Kolter, J.Z., Koltun, V.: An empirical evaluation of generic convolutional and recurrent networks for sequence modeling. arXiv preprint arXiv:1803.01271 (2018)

3D Segmentation of Bin Picking by Domain Randomization

Zijiang Zhang$^{(\boxtimes)}$, Shinya Tsuchida, and Humin Lu

Kyushu Institution of Technology, Kitakyushu, Japan
zhang.zijiang971@mail.kyutech.jp

Abstract. Bin picking is a fundamental task in robotic manipulation and widely used in industrial manufacturing. Despite the significant progress in applying 3D visual guidance to bin picking, accurate segmentation of one object from a large number of parts in the presence of occlusion and stacking remains challenging. To tackle this problem, recent research has proposed general deep learning-based approaches. However, manual annotation requires significant effort, which we aim to address in this paper by implementing automatic annotation via domain randomization. Domain randomization is one of Sim2Real's approaches to validate real data through annotation in a simulated environment.In this paper, we propose a bin-picking segmentation method by combining 2D object detection and a deep learning based 3D semantic segmentation model. We also propose a novel domain randomization method for both object detection and semantic segmentation. In addition, we train the bin-picking deep learning model with proposed method and validate it on test data obtained from real RGB-D camera. The experimental results presented in this paper demonstrate the advanced capabilities of our hybrid method. We have achieved high-precision segmentation,even in challenging scenarios characterized by substantial stacking, disorder, and the presence of noise, which validate the effectiveness of our approach.

Keywords: Domain Randomization · point cloud segmentation · Bin Picking

1 Introduction

Bin picking, a task in which objects are randomly placed in a bin and need to be grasped by a robot, has been studied in the field of robotics for many years [5]. The reason that bin picking is more challenging than grasping individual objects is that a segmentation task needs to be implemented to distinguish individual objects from the scene under stacking and occlusion conditions. There are two main approaches for segmentation: rule-based and deep learning-based methods. For example, a rule-base method extracts the desired data from parameters such as point cloud position, normal vector, and curvature using k-means method, nearby point search with Octree, and RANSAC [6]. This approach has been studied for many years and several effective methods have been proposed so far. Deep learning-based methods can discriminate complex features and have the potential to build versatile models that can be applied to shape-free objects. Furthermore, since deep learning starts from an image task, various methods are used to process an image in bin-picking and reflect the results in a point cloud or Depth image. For instance, some methods calculate the pixel region of an object through semantic segmentation of an image and extract only the point cloud data corresponding to the pixel [7]. The improvement of [7] is to reduce the noise components which are not reflected from a point cloud to an image, such as noise from nearby parts of the target part. In recent years, there has been a growing emphasis on the PointNet [8] model in 3D research. This model enables the utilization of deep learning techniques to extract object point clouds, even in scenarios where sparse noise is present. In this paper, we propose a method that uses a 2D object detection model to obtain a point cloud of a rectangular region surrounding a target object and a 3D semantic segmentation model to extract the object point cloud.

In contrast, deep learning-based algorithms typically entail a substantial need for training data, a process that can incur significant expenses related to date collection and annotation. To develop highly accurate deep learning models, it is typically necessary to prepare high-quality training data over hundreds to thousands of units. While one approach is to use pre-trained models or annotated datasets, self-annotation becomes inevitable in more specific contexts such as bin-picking. Consequently, when multiple deep learning models, such as the one presented in this paper, are utilized, the time required for annotation is multiplied.

Therefore, to address the challenge of collecting and annotating large amounts of training data for deep learning-based bin-picking models, we propose a method that use the simulation environment to automatically generate and annotate data. Specifically, we utilize the Sim2Real research tool, which includes various approaches such as system identification, domain application, and domain randomization. While system identification attempts to replicate real-world scenarios in a simulated environment, it is limited by the inability to accurately model the non-rigid, worn, fluid, and noisy properties of physical objects present in real sensors. On the other hand, domain application aims to learn feature representations that enable the distribution of features in the training and test data to be similar. However, domain application requires access to real-world data. In contrast, domain randomization addresses these limitations by introducing stochastic variation to the environmental features of the training data, which enhances the robustness of the model and enables accurate estimation even on unknown data. To ensure key features are not lost, careful implementation of the simulation environment is necessary.

In this paper, our objective is to tackle the challenge of automated annotations through the application of domain randomization techniques. We develop domain randomization methods for 2D object detection and 3D semantic segmentation models for bin-picking application. The annotation was done in the simulation environment in both models. Domain randomization has mainly focused on image randomization, and there is a lack of research on point cloud data. Our proposed approach in this paper provides a novel deep learning-based strategy to solve bin-picking by combining 2D object detection and 3D semantic segmentation.

In summary, our main contributions are as follows:

- We proposed a novel domain randomization based point cloud segmentation method for bin-picking by combining 2D object detection and 3D semantic segmentation.

- We decrease the efforts from manual annotation by implementing automatic annotation via domain randomization.
- 3D Segmentation of Bin Picking through domain randomization demonstrate promising performance on real data.

2 Related Works

2.1 Domain Randomization

Domain randomization is a machine learning method that generates training data by introducing random variations to non-critical environmental properties, thus creating robust models against large fluctuations in the environment. Inspired by evolutionary robotics, this approach adds random noise to every aspect of the non-real part of the simulated environment, while only a small amount of randomization is performed in the real part, resulting in a more robust model [1]. In computer vision, domain randomization was first proposed in [3], where training data is collected and annotated through randomization in a simulator (MuJoKo), leading to a 95% success rate for a robot with a pose error of within 1.5 [cm]. Since then, domain randomization has been widely applied in computer vision research. In [2], for instance, randomization was applied to object detection by introducing only two items, camera viewpoint, and texture, as opposed to the extra items in [3]. Different textures, such as flat, gradient, checkerboard, and noise, were added to the object's surface, and the effect of each texture was verified. The results showed great performance on real-world data. In [10], a Domain Randomization approach is presented for transferring experience in entanglement detection and separation from simulation to a real-world bin-picking application. Researchers, in [11, 36], have presented a framework for object detection that leverages synthetic images to train deep neural networks. The network's performance is improved through additional fine-tuning on real data compared to using real data alone. Reference [12, 27] presents a method for 3D orientation estimation. This method utilized Denoising Autoencoder trained on simulated views of a 3D model, employing Domain Randomization as a key training strategy. Moreover, Domain Randomization is also utilized in the application of semantic segmentation [13].

2.2 Object Detection and Semantic Segmentation for Robotics

Our research is connected to previous studies in the domain of object detection and semantic segmentation within the context of robotic grasping. The problem of object detection and pose estimation for robots have been well-studied in several years. Traditional grasp detection approaches rely on information regarding geometry, physics models, and force analysis [14, 38]. In recent times, data-driven techniques based on deep learning have gained prominence. Initial methods, exemplified by [15] and [16], harnessed deep neural networks and supervised learning to predict multiple grasp candidates for a single object. Two-stage object detectors, featuring a region proposal network and a detector, extract features from proposals and subsequently detect objects in the second stage, as demonstrated in methods [17–25]. In contrast, single-stage detectors, as detailed in [2, 26, 27, 29–31], partition the input image into a grid and perform detection at each pixel. While this approach reduces computation time, it may lead to decreased prediction accuracy. Deep learning-based point cloud semantic segmentation is currently one of the dominant approaches used for this task. This method involves the use of deep learning models, such as convolutional neural networks (CNN) and fully convolutional networks (FCN), to perform direct semantic segmentation of point cloud data. The pioneering deep learning model for point cloud classification and segmentation, PointNet [1], is capable of processing entire point cloud data. PointNet++ [32] represents an evolution of PointNet and introduces the use of Recurrent Neural Networks (RNN) to hierarchically process point cloud data and extract both local and global features more effectively. Another method for point cloud segmentation, PointCNN [33–35], utilizes CNN to perform convolution operations on point cloud data in a manner that is similar to traditional convolutional neural networks.

3   Method

In this study, we employed the Single Shot Multibox Detector (SSD) as a representative model for the 2D object detection approach, and the PointNet model for point cloud semantic segmentation [1, 2]. The proposed method for segmenting the point cloud of the grasped object through bin-picking combines SSD and PointNet. PointNet is a pioneering deep learning method with a simple structure that is specifically designed to process entire point clouds as inputs, making it an ideal choice for this study. We considered several representative methods for 2D object detection, but ultimately adopted SSD due to its effectiveness in detecting small and dense objects, which is particularly relevant for bin-picking. An overview of the entire process is presented in Fig. 1.

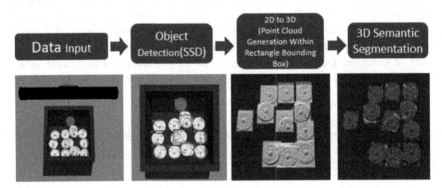

Fig. 1. Overview of proposed 3D segmentation method of bin-picking.

3.1   Randomization of 2D Object Detection

The propose of domain randomization of 2D object detection is to provide enough simulated variability when training a deep learning model. We randomization the following aspects of the domain for each sample used during training:

- Position and orientation of the camera.
- The direction and brightness of the light source.
- Texture of background (Fig. 2).

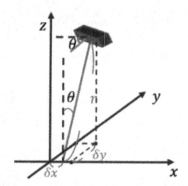

Fig. 2. Relationship diagram of sensor position

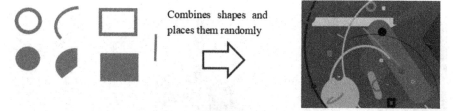

Fig. 3. Texture generation method

Randomizing the position, brightness, and direction of the light source in the simulated environment, as well as changing the color and brightness of the box for the target object, enables robust detection of real data taken in any brightness environment, as depicted in Fig. 5. The randomized texture, which is the texture of a background part other than the object and the box, is automatically generated in the environment. In previous studies [2, 3], plane, gradient, and chess graphics were used as added elements, but this paper utilizes graphic elements of circle, ellipse, arc, rectangle, and line with quantity variations for dimension, position, and texture, as shown in Fig. 3. The reason for this is that the wires and cables of the robot are often reflected in the actual image, and the goal is to construct a model that is resistant to these disturbance elements. Although different texture patterns were added to the object itself in [2, 3], this paper adds the object to the background area as it is. This is because one of the objects used in this paper is a rotary valve. An example of annotated data obtained by texture randomization is shown in Fig. 6 (Fig. 4).

Fig. 4. Randomization annotation data of camera viewpoint

Fig. 5. Randomization annotation data of light direction and brightness

Fig. 6. Randomized texture annotation data

3.2 Randomization in 3D Semantic Segmentation

When performing 3D semantic segmentation annotation on point cloud data that is limited to a single rectangular region, several items are randomized to increase the robustness and effectiveness of the segmentation:

- Position and orientation of RGB-D camera.
- Size of rectangle, position of part on rectangle.
- Generation of random noise.

The LiDAR viewpoint randomization is performed in a similar fashion to that of camera viewpoint randomization. The sensors employed in the simulated environment have both camera and LiDAR capabilities embedded. An example of point cloud annotation data obtained with LiDAR viewpoint randomization is shown in Fig. 8.

To ensure that the segmentation model is not biased towards the region in the middle of the rectangle, the size of the rectangle and object position on the rectangle were randomized through the variation of the length of the rectangle edges and the shift of

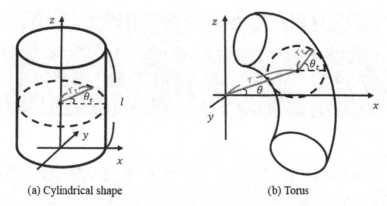

(a) Cylindrical shape   (b) Torus

Fig. 7. Relationship diagram of cylinder and torus, the unit of noise point cloud

object position from the rectangle center during the geometric transformation process that reflects the single rectangle information surrounding the object in 2D object detection onto the point cloud. As shown in Fig. 9, the rectangle randomization approach has led to a diverse set of annotated data for training and evaluation purposes.

The noisy point clouds are generated by generating the point clouds as cylindrical or torus-shaped units as shown in Fig. 7 and permuting these noisy point clouds by randomizing their size, number, and position. In general, Gaussian or Gomacio noise is considered to be added to the entire point cloud. However, the noise seen in actual LiDAR is more like a collection of tiny objects near an object than noise in the entire space (Fig. 10). Therefore, in order to be closer to the noise component that is unique to the actual sensor, we set the in Fig. 16 to a relatively small value to make the point cloud smaller and to localize the noisy point cloud close to the object. From (a) in Fig. 7, the cylindrical point cloud $p(x_p, y_{p,} z_p)$ is determined as follows:

$$
\begin{aligned}
x_p &= r_t cos\theta [m] \\
y_p &= r_t sin\theta_t \\
z_p &= N_z
\end{aligned}
\tag{1}
$$

Here N_z takes a random value in $N_Z \in [-l/2, l/2]$. . From (b) in Fig. 7, the torus-type point cloud $p(x_p, y_p, z_p)$ is determined as follows.

$$
\begin{aligned}
x_p &= (r + r_t cos\theta_t) cos\theta \\
y_p &= (r + r_t cos\theta_t) sin\theta \\
z_p &= r_t sin\theta_t
\end{aligned}
\tag{2}
$$

Finally, for both 2D object detection and 3D semantic segmentation, the annotations in this paper obtain correct labels only for occluders. The reason is that occluded parts lose key features of the surface and thus cannot be used as proper correct data, and the purpose of this study is to achieve segmentation of objects that are easier to grasp.

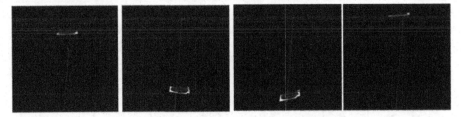

Fig. 8. Point cloud annotation data obtained by LiDAR viewpoint randomization

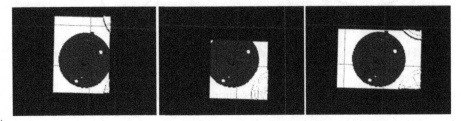

Fig. 9. Point cloud annotation data obtained by random rectangle

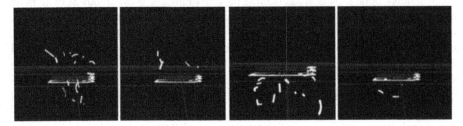

Fig. 10. Annotation data of point cloud generated by noise point cloud generation

4   Experiments

4.1   Experimental Setup

The RGB-D camera used in this paper has a built-in camera capable of simultaneously capturing both point cloud data and RGB images (Fig. 11).

The real RGB-D camera sensor is used to obtain images and point clouds, and the segmentation accuracy is compared using the procedure described in Fig. 1. To perform 3D semantic segmentation, the model weights are trained on the annotated data under the experimental conditions of experiments 1 and 2. The setup details of experiments 1 and 2 are described below.

Fig. 11. Experimental environment.

Experiment 1:

In the proposed method, the accuracy was evaluated on datasets containing 1000 to 5000 data points per 1000 points. The model was trained for 200 epochs.IoU can be calculated by Eq. (3)

$$IoU = \frac{N_{A \cap B}}{N_{A \cup B}} \tag{3}$$

If the instance label of the segmentation is 1, then A is the point cloud with the correct instance label = 1, and B is the point cloud with the estimated instance label = 1. Also, NA is the number of point clouds with label = 1 for the correct instance. The validation 3D segmentation test data for Experiments 1 and 2 were conducted following a procedure that involved establishing a reference coordinate point, generating a mesh point cloud from the coordinate points, changing the color of the points where the sensor point group and the mesh point group overlapped, and finally minutely adjusting the reference coordinate points until the colors matched perfectly with the object.

Experiment 2:

The randomization parameters of the proposed method have been integrated and annotated. In this evaluation, we assess the impact of each domain randomization parameter on the enhancement of accuracy. The training dataset size is fixed at 2000 samples.

4.2 Experimental Results

The results of experiment 1 are shown in Table 1. Among the proposed domain randomization methods, the highest accuracy was attained in the case of 4000 datasets.

Table 1. Results of experiment 1.

Number of training data sets	1000	2000	3000	4000	5000
Accuracy	0.740	0.864	0.875	0.914	0.847

The results of experiment 2 are given in Table 2. However, the row term is compared to the accuracy of the test data type, and the column term is compared to the accuracy when the randomization condition is changed. In addition, the visualization results of the segmentation are shown in Figs. 12, 13 and 14. The proposed method achieves the highest accuracy among all test data items.

Table 2. Results of experiment 2.

Test data	Random item			
	Fixed sensor	Fixed rectangle	Noise free	Proposed method
Single object	0.548	0.705	0.879	0.944
occlusions	0.766	0.719	0.874	0.932
Lots of noise	0.578	0.597	0.645	0.822
All test data	0.588	0.682	0.824	0.914

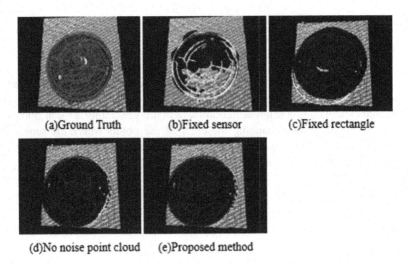

(a)Ground Truth　　　(b)Fixed sensor　　　(c)Fixed rectangle

(d)No noise point cloud　　(e)Proposed method

Fig. 12. Segmentation results of experiment 2 (single part).

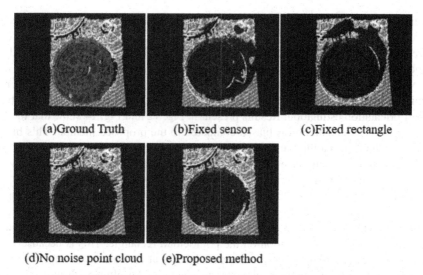

(a)Ground Truth   (b)Fixed sensor   (c)Fixed rectangle

(d)No noise point cloud   (e)Proposed method

Fig. 13. Segmentation results of experiment 2 (occlusion exist).

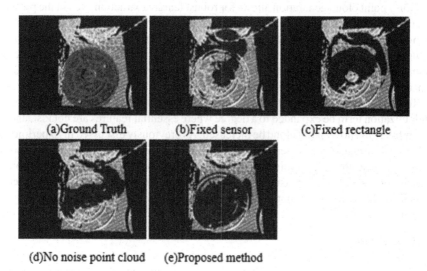

(a)Ground Truth   (b)Fixed sensor   (c)Fixed rectangle

(d)No noise point cloud   (e)Proposed method

Fig. 14. Segmentation results of experiment 2 (large amount of noise).

4.3 Comparison

In Experiment 1, the proposed method exhibited an increase in accuracy from 1000 to 4000 appropriately annotated data. One possible reason for this improvement is that an increase in the amount of data results in a more diverse range of items for randomization, which in turn enhances the ability to differentiate important features from non-important ones. Additionally, by approximating the maximum variance in the data set caused by the assumption of randomization in the range between 4000 and 5000 for the reduced accuracy, we can reduce the variance of the datasets. As a result, high accuracy can still be maintained even if the number of datasets exceeds a certain threshold. Therefore, to increase the upper bound on the number of datasets, it is more efficient to expand the range of randomization while ensuring that key features are retained.

Next, we consider the impact of domain randomization in Experiment 2. By randomizing the sensor's position and pose, the system becomes more resilient to variations in part orientation estimation. Results present in Fig. 12 and Fig. 14 show that the orientation of the segmentation is biased compared to the proposed method. This bias is caused by the fact that the training datasets mostly consists of object instances in specific orientations, which makes the model more sensitive to point cloud features in the direction of the annotation during pose estimation, compared to other features.

Randomizing the size and center position of the bounding box is believed to maintain accuracy regardless of the object's position on the rectangle. When fixed rectangles are used, as shown in Figs. 12, 13 and 14, most results exhibit a blue circle from the center, regardless of the object's position on the point cloud rectangle. This is because when fixed rectangles are used, the correct instance label is always assigned to the data from the center of the rectangular point cloud in the annotation, resulting in the central region of the rectangle responding more strongly than other features during estimation.

Noisy point cloud generation allows for robust feature extraction even in the presence of strong noise in the test data. As shown in Fig. 14, the blue region of the proposed method is smaller than that of the noiseless point cloud. Furthermore, the proposed method achieves an IoU of 0.822, compared to 0.644 for the noise-free point cloud method. These results confirm that noisy point cloud generation has a significant positive impact on the performance of the proposed method.

To enhance the proposed method, it is suggested that the parameter range of the randomization term be expanded to a degree where essential features are not lost, and the variability of the noisy point cloud be increased. As previously discussed in Experiment 1, widening the range of non-essential items' variability enables the learning to concentrate on essential features. Concerning the latter, the proposed method's accuracy is prone to decrease on test data with considerable noise compared to single objects. Consequently, we believe that there is still potential to advance in noisy point cloud learning.

5   Conclusion

In this paper, we propose a domain randomization approach for 3D segmentation to attain highly accurate object extraction and segmentation in bin picking. By introducing random sensor positions and orientations, as well as random rectangle size and center position for point cloud data within a rectangular region, along with the generation of noisy point clouds, we achieve high-precision object extraction even in real-world data that contains a significant amount of occlusion and noise. As a result, we obtain a maximum accuracy of 0.914 for 4000 datasets. In our future work, it will be necessary to verify whether this approach is valid for parts with small shapes and less occlusion.Additionally, we will explore the addition of a variation of the noisy point cloud and the expansion of the randomization range to further improve the accuracy of our method.

Acknowledgement. This work is partially supported by NSFC No.62206237, JSPS No.22K12093, and JSPS No. 22K12094. This research is supported by JST START University Ecosystem Promotion Type (Supporting Creation of Startup Ecosystem in Startup Cities), Grant Number JPMJST2281, Japan.

References

1. Qi, C.R., Su, H., Mo, K., Guibas, L.J.: PointNet: deep learning on point sets for 3D classification and segmentation. arXiv preprint arXiv:1612.00593 (2016)
2. Liu, W., et al.: SSD: single shot multibox detector. In: Leibe, B., Matas, J., Sebe, N., Welling, M. (eds.) ECCV 2016. LNCS, vol. 9905, pp. 21–37. Springer, Cham (2016). https://doi.org/10.1007/978-3-319-46448-0_2
3. Tobin, J., Fong, R., Ray, A., Schneider, J., Zaremba, W., Abbeel, P.: Domain randomization for transferring deep neural networks from simulation to the real world. In: IROS, pp. 23–30 (2017)
4. Dehban, A., Borrego, J., Figueiredo, R., Moreno, P., Bernardino, A., Santos-Victor, J.: The impact of domain randomization on object detection: a case study on parametric shapes and synthetic textures. In: IROS, pp. 2593–2600 (2019)
5. Borrego, J., Figueiredo, R., Dehban, A., Moreno, P., Bernardino, A., Santos-Victor, J.: A generic visual perception domain randomisation framework for gazebo. In: ICARSC, pp.273–242. IEEE (2018)
6. Tremblay, J., et al.: Training deep networks with synthetic data: bridging the reality gap by domain randomization. In: IEEE/CVF CVPRW, pp. 1082–10828 (2018)
7. Guo, J., Fu, L., Jia, M., Wang, K., Liu, S.: Fast and robust bin-picking system for densely piled industrial objects. In: 2020 Chinese Automation Congress (CAC), pp. 2845–2850 (2020)
8. Wang, M., Deng, W.: Deep visual domain adaptation: a survey. ISSN, pp. 135–153 (2018)
9. Quigley, M., Conley, K., Gerkey, B., et al.: ROS: an open-source robot operating system. In: ICRA Workshop on Open Source Software, vol. 3, no. 3.2, p. 5 (2009)
10. Moosmann, M., Spenrath, F., Rosport, J., et al.: Transfer learning for machine learning-based detection and separation of entanglements in bin-picking applications. 2022 IEEE/RSJ International Conference on Intelligent Robots and Systems (IROS) , pp. 1123–1130. IEEE (2022)
11. Tremblay, J., Prakash, A., Acuna, D., et al.: Training deep networks with synthetic data: Bridging the reality gap by domain randomization. In: Proceedings of the IEEE Conference on Computer Vision and Pattern Recognition Workshops, pp. 969–977 (2018)
12. Sundermeyer, M., Marton, Z.C., Durner, M., et al.: Augmented autoencoders: implicit 3D orientation learning for 6d object detection. Int. J. Comput. Vision **128**, 714–729 (2020)
13. Yue, X., Zhang, Y., Zhao, S., et al.: Domain randomization and pyramid consistency: simulation-to-real generalization without accessing target domain data. In: Proceedings of the IEEE/CVF International Conference on Computer Vision, pp. 2100–2110 (2019)
14. Bicchi, A., Kumar, V.: Robotic grasping and contact: a review. In: IEEE International Conference on Robotics and Automation (ICRA), vol. 1, pp. 348–353 (2000)
15. Redmon, J., Angelova, A.: Real-time grasp detection using convolutional neural networks. In: IEEE International Conference on Robotics and Automation (ICRA), pp. 1316–1322 (2015)
16. Lenz, I., Lee, H., Saxena, A.: Deep learning for detecting robotic grasps. Int. J. Robot. Res. **34**(4–5), 705–724 (2015)
17. Girshick, R., Donahue, J., Darrell, T., et al.: Rich feature hierarchies for accurate object detection and semantic segmentation. In: Proceedings of the IEEE Conference on Computer Vision and Pattern Recognition (2014)

18. He, K., Zhang, X., Ren, S., et al.: Spatial pyramid pooling in deep convolutional networks for visual recognition. IEEE Trans. Pattern Anal. Mach. Intell. **37**(9), 1904–1916 (2015)

19. Girshick, R.: Fast R-CNN. In: Proceedings of the IEEE International Conference on Computer Vision, pp. 1440–1448 (2015)

20. Kong, T., Yao, A., Chen, Y., et al.: HyperNet: towards accurate region proposal generation and joint object detection. In: Proceedings of the IEEE Conference on Computer Vision and Pattern Recognition, pp. 845–853 (2016)

21. Dai, J., Li, Y., He, K., et al.: R-FCN: object detection via region-based fully convolutional networks. In: Advances in Neural Information Processing Systems, vol. 29 (2016)

22. Kim, K.H., Hong, S., Roh, B., et al.: PVANet: deep but lightweight neural networks for real-time object detection. arXiv preprint arXiv:1608.08021 (2016)

23. He, K., Gkioxari, G., Dollár, P., et al.: Mask R-CNN. In: Proceedings of the IEEE International Conference on Computer Vision, pp. 2961–2969 (2017)

24. Zhu, Y., Zhao, C., Wang, J., et al.: CoupleNet: coupling global structure with local parts for object detection. In: Proceedings of the IEEE International Conference on Computer Vision, pp. 4126–4134 (2017)

25. Li, Z., Peng, C., Yu, G., et al.: Light-head R-CNN: in defense of two-stage object detector. arXiv preprint arXiv:1711.07264 (2017)

26. Sermanet, P., Eigen, D., Zhang, X., et al.: OverFeat: integrated recognition, localization and detection using convolutional networks. arXiv preprint arXiv:1312.6229 (2013)

27. Redmon, J., Divvala, S., Girshick, R., et al.: You only look once: unified, real-time object detection. In: Proceedings of the IEEE Conference on Computer Vision and Pattern Recognition, pp. 779–788 (2016)

28. Jeong, J., Park, H., Kwak, N.: Enhancement of SSD by concatenating feature maps for object detection. arXiv preprint arXiv:1705.09587 (2017)

29. Fu, C.Y., Liu, W., Ranga, A., et al.: DSSD: deconvolutional single shot detector. arXiv preprint arXiv:1701.06659 (2017)

30. Shen, Z., Liu, Z., Li, J., et al.: DSOD: learning deeply supervised object detectors from scratch. In: Proceedings of the IEEE International Conference on Computer Vision, pp. 1919–1927 (2017)

31. Kong, T., Sun, F., Yao, A., et al.: RON: reverse connection with objectness prior networks for object detection. In: Proceedings of the IEEE Conference on Computer Vision and Pattern Recognition, pp. 5936–5944 (2017)

32. Qi, C.R., Yi, L., Su, H., et al.: PointNet++: deep hierarchical feature learning on point sets in a metric space. In: Advances in Neural Information Processing Systems, vol. 30 (2017)

33. Li, Y., Bu, R., Sun, M., et al.: PointCNN: convolution on x-transformed points. In: Advances in Neural Information Processing Systems, vol. 31 (2018)

34. Li, Y., Cai, J., Zhou, Q., et al.: Joint semantic-instance segmentation method for intelligent transportation system. IEEE Trans. Intell. Transp. Syst. (2022)

35. Zheng, Y., Li, Y., Yang, S., et al.: Global-PBNet: a novel point cloud registration for autonomous driving. IEEE Trans. Intell. Transp. Syst. **23**(11), 22312–22319 (2022)

36. Lu, H., Liu, Q., Tian, D., et al.: The cognitive internet of vehicles for autonomous driving. IEEE Netw. **33**(3), 65–73 (2019)

37. Lu, H., Li, Y., Mu, S., et al.: Motor anomaly detection for unmanned aerial vehicles using reinforcement learning. IEEE Internet Things J. **5**(4), 2315–2322 (2017)

38. Teng, Y., Lu, H., Li, Y., et al.: Multidimensional deformable object manipulation based on DN-transporter networks. IEEE Trans. Intell. Transp. Syst. **24**(4), 4532–4540 (2022)

Author Index

H. Lu and J. Cai (Eds.): ISAIR 2023, CCIS 1998, pp. 533–535, 2024.
https://doi.org/10.1007/978-981-99-9109-9

Printed in the United States
by Baker & Taylor Publisher Services